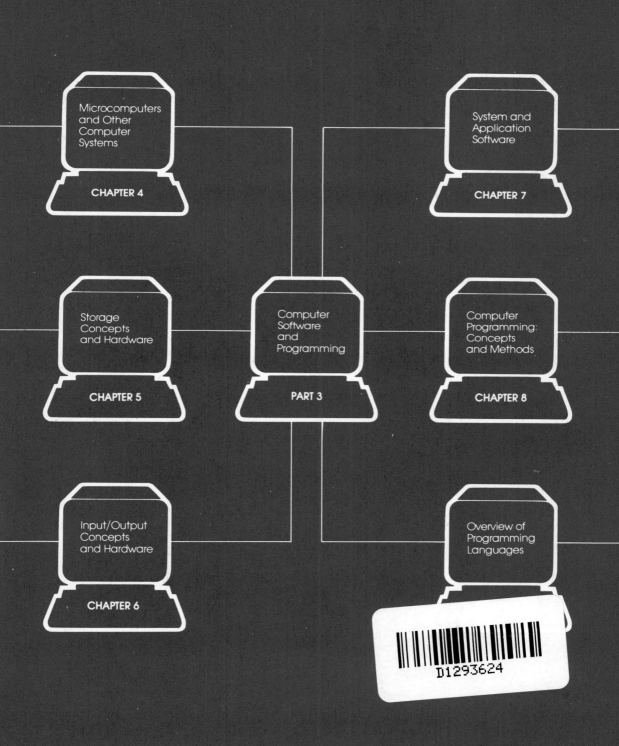

Microcomputers and Other Computer Systems

CHAPTER 4

System and Application Software

CHAPTER 7

Storage Concepts and Hardware

CHAPTER 5

Computer Software and Programming

PART 3

Computer Programming: Concepts and Methods

CHAPTER 8

Input/Output Concepts and Hardware

CHAPTER 6

Overview of Programming Languages

DATE DUE

Computers in Business Management

The Irwin Series in Information and Decision Sciences

Consulting Editors

Robert B. Fetter
Yale University

Claude McMillan
University of Colorado

Computers in Business Management

An Introduction

James A. O'Brien

College of Business
Administration

Northern Arizona
University

Fourth Edition 1985

RICHARD D. IRWIN, INC.
Homewood, Illinois 60430

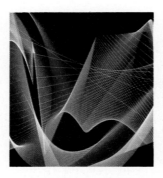

Images for all part openers by
Melvin L. Prueitt
Los Alamos National Laboratory, author of
Art and the Computer, McGraw-Hill, 1984.

Cover photography by
Guy Powers
Equipment Exxon Office Systems
520 Word Processor & 935 Printer

Dow Jones-Irwin, a division of Richard D. Irwin, Inc.,
has developed Personal Learning Aids (PLAIDS)
to accompany texts in this subject area. Copies can
be purchased through your bookstore or by writing
PLAIDS, 1820 Ridge Road, Homewood, IL 60430.

ISBN 0-256-03211-4

Library of Congress Catalog Card No. 84–82008
Printed in the United States of America
1 2 3 4 5 6 7 8 9 0 K 2 1 0 9 8 7 6 5

With love and gratitude to

Eileen McCann O'Brien

newspaper reporter, magazine editor, author . . .
and my mother.

Preface

It's been a wild 10 years. Since the first edition of this text was published in 1975, a multitude of changes have taken place, not only in computer and information processing technology but also in the conceptual foundations and pedagogical approaches to the study of computer-based information systems in organizations. These changes have caused each succeeding edition of this text to be a major revision of its predecessor. This fourth edition continues this trend. I only wish that the several hundred thousand students and hundreds of instructors who used previous editions of this text could have used the text that you are reading now. That's how confident I am that it represents a significant improvement over both its predecessors and competitors.

However, several basic characteristics and principles on which this book is based have not changed. Its content is still business oriented, user oriented, and application oriented. Its organization and style is still straightforward, concise, and comprehensive. This text is still based on the following fundamental positions:

- Computers are essential tools and resources in the operation and management of modern business firms and other organizations.
- Most students in collegiate business programs will be future **computer users,** not *computer specialists*. As future managers or staff specialists in computer-using organizations, students need a basic understanding of computers and how they can be applied to the information processing needs of business firms. This is the type of **computer literacy** that should be demonstrated by educated people in business.
- The primary goal of introductory computer courses in business curriculums should be to help students become knowledgeable business users of computer resources, as opposed to knowledgeable technicians in electronic data processing and computer programming. Specifically, students should be able to demonstrate:
  (1) A basic understanding of computers and how they can be used to meet the information processing needs of business firms.
  (2) A basic understanding of information processing concepts, terminology, and techniques in business.

Thus, this text introduces students to:

- The fundamentals of computers and information processing.
- The wide range of hardware and software available to computer users.
- The microcomputer and its impact on computer users.

- The process of computer programming and several widely used programming languages.
- Modern information processing technology and methods.
- Computer-based information systems in business.
- Management information and decision support systems.
- The process of information systems development.
- The management of information system resources.
- The impact of computers on management and society.
- How to use popular software packages.

FEATURES OF THE FOURTH EDITION

Of course this edition had to be updated to reflect major developments in both computer and information processing technology and in the use of computer-based information systems for business operations and management. For example, material on microcomputers and data communications had to be updated, as well as material on database systems and decision support systems. But this edition represents more than an updating of factual material. It reflects the following changes in emphasis and coverage:

- Expanded coverage of **microcomputers** and their hardware, software, acquisition, and uses, throughout the text but especially in Chapter 4.
- Expanded coverage of **software packages** such as electronic spreadsheet, word processing, database management and integrated packages in Chapter 7 and other chapters of the text, as well as in the Appendix to the text.
- The Appendix, **Using Popular Software Packages: A Tutorial Introduction,** is a major addition to the text. This appendix provides students with a step-by-step introduction to the use of the most popular types of software packages for microcomputers and many larger computers. They are: (1) simple business programs, (2) word processing programs, (3) electronic spreadsheet programs, (4) database management programs, and (5) integrated packages. These tutorials can be used anytime during the course to give students hands-on experience with the use of computers and software packages.

The goal of this appendix is to teach students how to use packages such as WordStar, VisiCalc, dBASE II, and Lotus 1-2-3 so that they will understand:

- How to load and use simple application packages on a microcomputer.
- How to create, edit, store, and print a document using word processing functions.

■ How to build, modify, store, print, and use an electronic spread-sheet.

■ How to create and use a database and retrieve, display, and report information.

■ How to use graphics displays to analyze data and communicate information.

Thus, the Appendix is written to stress the basic operations and use of such packages, not the details of the particular packages used as examples. Therefore, the Appendix should be useful even for courses that use different word processing, spreadsheet, database management, and integrated packages.

■ An **information processing system model** is emphasized throughout the text as a conceptual framework to tie together the many facts, concepts, and developments that are part of the dynamic field of computers and information processing. This model stresses the concept that:

Information processing is a system of input, processing, output, storage, and control functions that transform data resources into information products using hardware, software, and people as resources.

This simple yet comprehensive model is illustrated in many figures in the text (see Figure 1–2, for example). These figures and the related text material help students realize that there is a simple yet powerful concept that they can use to help them understand, analyze, evaluate, and develop computer-based information systems.

■ A major effort has been made to make the text more attractive and easy-to-read. This ranges from the use of color photographs and improved illustrations throughout the text to a shift toward a more personal and direct writing style.

■ The applications orientation and "real-world" emphasis of the text has been strengthened by supplementing the three **Real World Applications** in each chapter with five **Application Problems** at the end of each chapter. The chapters on computer-based information systems in business (Chapters 15 and 16) have also been revised and strengthened.

■ Many other changes have been made. This includes splitting the third edition's chapter on computer hardware into two chapters, which stress both the concepts and hardware of the storage and input/output functions of modern information processing systems. Another major change involves an emphasis on the changes taking place in user involvement in computer programming and systems development through developments such as fourth generation languages (4GL) and information centers.

Other features of the text and its supporting materials have been retained from the third edition. However, in all cases a major effort has been made to improve the material involved. Let's take a quick look at some of these features:

■ This edition continues to be a language-independent text. However, Chapter 8, Computer Programming: Concepts and Methods, introduces students to the programming process, and Chapter 9, Overview of Programming Languages, provides students with a survey of popular computer programming languages. Thus the fourth edition can be used:

(1) As the only textbook needed for courses that do not require instruction in computer programming.

(2) As the main text but supplemented with the improved appendixes on BASIC or Pascal in the **Student Study Guide.** This provides sufficient text material for courses that require a brief introduction to programming in one of these languages.

(3) As the core text used in conjunction with a supplementary programming language text in courses that require significant instruction and assignments in computer programming. Many excellent paperback texts are available for this purpose.

■ Each chapter begins with a **Chapter Outline** and **Learning Objectives** and ends with a **Summary,** a listing of **Key Terms and Concepts, Review and Application Questions,** and **Application Problems.** Each chapter also contains three **Real World Applications,** which apply chapter material to actual business situations. The text also contains an extensive **Glossary** of information processing terms.

■ The **Student Study Guide** that supplements the text has been improved for this edition. It contains detailed chapter outlines, chapter learning objectives, chapter overviews, definitions of key terms and concepts, chapter test-yourself questions (true-false, multiple choice, fill-in the blanks, matching), answers to test-yourself questions, and short chapter assignments. It also contains four major **integrative cases** and **introductory appendixes** on BASIC and Pascal. The study guide should thus be a valuable supplement to the main text.

■ An **Instructor's Guide** is available to instructors upon adoption of the text. It contains instructional aids and suggestions, answers to chapter questions and problems, solutions to Appendix assignments, and answers and solutions to the questions and programming assignments in the Student Study Guide. Transparency masters of important figures in the text are also provided.

■ The **Test Bank** has been extensively revised and improved and contains over 1,500 true-false and multiple choice questions. The Test Bank is available as a separate test manual and in computerized form on tape or floppy disk for use with the Irwin Test Generator Program.

ᴵᴵ ACKNOWLEDGMENTS

The author wishes to acknowledge the assistance of consulting editors Robert Fetter of Yale University and Claude McMillan of the University of Colorado; reviewers Gloria J. Fabrey of Kutztown State College, (who authored some of the end-of-chapter application problems) J. Joseph Harrington of Boston College, Robert E. Miller of the University of Notre Dame, Bernard Sheehan of the University of Calgary, Gary A. Wicklund of the University of Iowa, and Ronald B. Wilkes of the University of Minnesota—Minneapolis. In particular, I wish to acknowledge the contributions of my former Eastern Washington University colleagues, Ray Hamel, who wrote the sections on the Pascal language in the text and the Study Guide, and Susan Solomon, who wrote the Integrative Cases in the Study Guide. A special acknowledgment is owed to Craig Van Lengen of Northern Arizona University, who coauthored the Student Study Guide and revised its BASIC appendix and the test bank. My thanks also goes to Jackie Begay, who used WordStar and a succession of IBM PCs to complete the manuscript. The contributions of computer manufacturers and others who provided photographs and illustrations used in the text are gratefully acknowledged. I also wish to express my gratitude to the dean and faculty of the College of Business Administration at Northern Arizona University, whose assistance and support helped make this edition possible. Finally, but most importantly, I wish to thank my wife Sandi, and children, David, Susan, and Michael, for their gifts of time and patience, which allowed me to complete this revision.

A Special Acknowledgment

A special acknowledgment is due the many business firms and other computer-using organizations that are the subjects of the **Real World Applications** in each chapter. In order of appearance in the text they are:

General Motors Corporation; Treasury Department–Commonwealth of Pennsylvania; Cabarrus Urology Clinic; the Atlantic City

Press; the Kula Onion; Connecticut Mutual Life Insurance Company; Mellon Bank; Hubert Distributors; Federal Express; Physician's Microcomputer, Inc.; Spectra Physics, Inc.; PPG Industries; Analysts International Corporation; Monsanto Corporation; Automobile Club of Michigan; U.S. Department of Defense; the Reserve Fund; Commercial Office Products Co.; the Veterans Administration; Bearings, Inc.; Best Western International; Aetna Life and Casualty Company; First Interstate Bank Corporation; Hyatt Hotels Corporation; Hewlett-Packard Company; Eastman Kodak; Sunset Magazine; TRW Incorporated; Thermo Electron Corporation; Westinghouse Electric Corporation; Schwinn Bicycle Company; Anheuser-Busch Companies, Inc.; Hayden Publishing Company; the Bullard Company; Western Engine Company; W. H. Shurtleff & Co.; Borg-Warner Corporation; RCA Corporation; IBM Corporation; Apple Computer, Inc.; Bechtel Group, Inc.; Guardian Life Insurance Company; Martin Marietta Corporation; and Bergen Brunswig Corporation.

The real-life situations faced by these firms provide a valuable demonstration of the benefits and limitations of using computers in modern organizations.

James A. O'Brien

Contents

Micrographics Hardware: *Advantages and Disadvantages.* I/O Interface Hardware: *Buffers. Channels. Input/Output Control Units.*

PART 3

Computer Software and Programming   234

CHAPTER 7

System and Application Software   236

Introduction. System Software: *Operating Systems. Control Programs in an Operating System. Database Management Systems. Communications Monitors. Language Translator Programs. Service Programs. Other System Software Packages.* Application Software: *Popular Application Packages.* Spotlight on Electronic Spreadsheet Packages: *Spreadsheet Format and Use. Advances in Electronic Spreadsheets. Advantages of Spreadsheet Packages.*

CHAPTER 8

Computer Programming: Concepts and Methods   268

Why Learn Computer Programming? Changes in Computer Programming: *Structured Programming. Computer-Assisted Programming. User Programming.* The Programming Process: *The Systems Development Cycle. The Stages of the Programming Process.* Program Analysis. Program Design: *Top-Down Design. Structure and Hierarchy Charts. HIPO Charts. Layout Forms. Flowcharts. System Flowcharts. Program Flowcharts. Structured Flowcharts. Pseudocode. Decision Tables.* Program Coding: *Structured Coding. Types of Instructions.* Program Verification: *Programming Errors. Checking. Structured Walkthroughs. Testing.* Program Documentation. Program Maintenance.

CHAPTER 9

Overview of Programming Languages   312

Types of Programming Languages: *Machine Languages. Assembler Languages. High-Level Languages. Fourth-Generation Languages.* Popular Programming Languages. BASIC: *BASIC Statements. Sample BASIC Program.* COBOL: *The COBOL Divisions. COBOL Procedure Division Statements. Sample COBOL Program.* FORTRAN: *FORTRAN Statements. Sample FORTRAN Program.* PL/1: *PL/1 Statements. Sample PL/1 Program.* Pascal: *Pascal Statements. Sample*

CHAPTER 13

Word Processing and Automated Office Systems   460

Introduction to Automated Office Systems. A Word Processing System Model: *Advanced System Functions. Office Word Processing Example.* Word Processing Hardware. Word Processing Software: *Features of Word Processing Packages. Benefits of Word Processing Packages. Developments in Word Processing Packages.* Automated Office Systems: *Electronic Office Communications Systems. Electronic Mail. Teleconferencing.* Advantages and Disadvantages.

PART 5

Computer-Based Information Systems   490

CHAPTER 14

Management Information and Decision Support Systems   492

Computer-Based Information Systems. The Business Firm as a System. Types of Information Systems: *Operational Information Systems. Programmed Decision Systems.* Information Requirements of Management: *The Functions of Management. Management as a System. Management Information Requirements.* Management Information Systems: *The Management Information System Concept.* Decision Support Systems: *The Decision Support System Concept. Artificial Intelligence and Expert Systems.* Integrated Information Systems: *Business Information Systems. Advanced Integrated Systems.*

CHAPTER 15

Computer-Based Information Systems: Marketing, Production/Operations, and Personnel   524

How Are Computers Used in Business? Trends in Computer Use in Business. Section I: Computer-Based Information Systems in Marketing: *Marketing Information Systems. Computer Applications in Retailing. The Point-of-Sale Revolution.* Section II: Computer-Based Information Systems in Production/Operations: *Manufacturing Information Systems. Process Control. Numerical Control and Robotics. Physical Distribution Information Systems.* Section III: Other Computer-Based Information Systems: *Personnel Information Systems. Operations Research Applications. Other Business Applications.*

CHAPTER 19

Managing Information
System Resources   668

Organizing for Information Services: *Systems Development. User Services. Data Administration. Operations. Administration. Organizational Location.* Careers in Information Services: *Careers in Systems Development. Careers in User Services. Careers in Data Administration. Careers in Programming. Careers in Computer Operations. Careers in Administration of Information Services.* Information Resource Management: *Information Services Planning. Managing Systems Development. Managing Computer Operations. Managing Information Services Personnel.* Computer Security and Control: *Information Processing Controls. Organizational Controls. Facility Controls. Auditing Electronic Information Processing.*

CHAPTER 20

Computers, Management,
and Society   706

The Challenge of Computer Performance: *Poor Computer Performance. Management Involvement. The User Generation. User Resistance. User Involvement.* The Challenge to Management Performance: *The Impact of Computers on Management. The Systems Approach to Management. Enlarging the Job of Management.* The Social Challenge of the Computer: *The Impact of Computers on Society. Impact on Employment and Productivity. Impact on Competition. Impact on Individuality. Impact on the Quality of Life. Impact on Privacy. Other Effects. Social Applications. Systems Design and Social Responsibility.*

Appendix

Using Popular Software
Packages: A Tutorial
Introduction   A

Glossary for Computer Users   G–1

Illustration Credits   C–1

Index   I–1

Computers in Business Management

PART

1

Introduction to Computers and Information Processing

CHAPTER 1

The Computer Revolution

CHAPTER OUTLINE

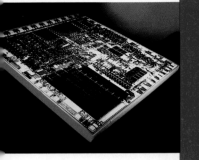

LEARNING OBJECTIVES

The purpose of this chapter is to develop a basic
appreciation for the electronic computer by analyzing
the development and revolutionary impact of
computers on information processing. After reading
and studying this chapter, you should be able to:

1. Explain the importance of computers and
   information processing in today's society, and to
   your present and future activities.
2. Define the terms: *computer, hardware, software,
   computer specialist, and computer user*.
3. Explain why the development and use of computers
   is called a computer revolution.
4. Identify the major changes that have occurred in
   each generation of computers; the trends that will
   continue into the future, and their effect on
   computer users.
5. Explain the impact of the microcomputer revolution
   in terms of (*a*) microcomputer technology, (*b*)
   distributed processing, (*c*) personal computing, and
   (*d*) smart products.
6. Use a personal computer or computer terminal and
   a prewritten program to solve a short problem
   similar to the example in the section called Getting
   Started with Software Packages in the appendix
   at the end of this book.

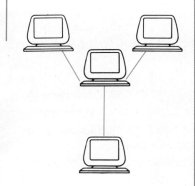

Terms such as *data processing systems, computer systems,* and *information systems* can easily evoke images of mysterious, complicated, and technically sophisticated activities. Understanding the concepts behind such activities would seem to be a difficult task. Nothing could be further from the truth. For as you begin to read these opening lines of the first chapter, you are engaged in data processing! In fact, several observations could be made concerning your present book-reading activity.

- You are gathering **data**.
- You are storing **information**.
- You are engaged in **data processing**.
- You are an **information processing system**.
- You are being affected by **computer systems**.
- You are part of an educational **information system**.

The purpose of this text is to explain the fundamental concepts that underlie such observations. These concepts are essential to an understanding of the present and future uses of the computer. Such an understanding can be acquired without an extensive technical background. Computers, data processing, and information systems will be revealed as important but understandable tools in today's society.

WHY LEARN ABOUT COMPUTERS AND INFORMATION PROCESSING?

Why is a basic understanding of computers, data processing, and information systems so important? Volumes could be written to answer this question. However, at this point in your reading, three major points should be made:

- **Information**, along with energy and materials, is a basic resource in today's world. We are living in an *information society* whose economy is heavily dependent on the creation and distribution of information by *knowledge workers*. We must learn to harness our information resources to benefit society, including finding ways to use information to make better use of our limited supplies of material and energy resources.
- A major, even revolutionary, tool in the production and use of information is the **electronic computer**. The use of computers is widespread and vital to business, government, and society. It has become even more so due to the rapidly growing use of the *microcomputer*. We must learn to use this tool in order to properly harness the information resources in today's dynamic society.

- The proper flow of information is vital to the success of any organization. Thus, **information processing** activities which transform data into information for users represent:
  - A major cost of doing business.
  - A major job responsibility for many employees of a business.
  - A major factor in employee morale and customer satisfaction.
  - A major source of information needed for effective decision-making by the managers of an organization.
  - A vital, dynamic, and expanding career choice for millions of men and women.

Computers, data processing systems, and information systems have become essential tools in the operation and management of modern business firms and other organizations. As a present and future **computer user**, you should learn how to use these tools in order to minimize their detrimental effects and to maximize the benefits to be derived from their proper use.

THE COMPUTER REVOLUTION

The development of computers has been acclaimed as the most important technological development of the 20th century, a development that has caused a *computer revolution* that rivals the Industrial Revolution of the 19th century. This sweeping claim is supported by evidence that the computer has significantly magnified our ability to analyze, compute, and communicate, thereby greatly accelerating human technological progress. Thus the development of the computer is also called the information revolution, the electronic revolution, or the second industrial revolution. It has succeeded in vastly multiplying human brainpower with the same impact that the first industrial revolution had in multiplying human musclepower. Thus the term *computer revolution* reflects the rapid and enormous changes brought about by the widespread use and dependence on computers in modern society. See Figure 1–1.

WHAT IS A COMPUTER?

Before we briefly review the origins and development of modern computers, let us define what we mean by the term **computer**. There are several varieties of computers and each has a variety of characteristics. However, in information processing, in the computer industry, and in the popular literature the term *computer* refers primarily to a particular type of computer: the *electronic, digital, stored-program, general-purpose computer*. Such computers are used for almost all business applications and are the subject of this book. We can therefore use this definition:

A computer is an electronic device that has the ability to accept data, internally store and automatically execute a program of instructions, perform mathematical, logical, and manipulative operations on data, and report the results.

FIGURE 1–1 Computers in action. Computers large and small are being used in the office, the factory, and at home.

REAL WORLD APPLICATION 1–1

Computers in the Real World

For a society that once banished science fiction writers to the pulp paperback kingdom, it's remarkable how easily the computer has slipped into the vernacular. Housewives know of chips, carpenters speak of microprocessors, mechanics replace bad boards along with cracked bearings, and working people hook computers to TVs so their kids can play Dungeons and Dragons with machines.

In just 25 years a citizenry that once chafed at the implicit scolding of a punched card's "Do not fold, spindle, or mutilate" had made of the computer and its electronic progeny the latest fad.

Products undreamed of a few decades ago now talk to schoolchildren, translate foreign languages for tourists, and run warehouses without human intervention. Others play blackjack and Space Invaders with white-collar professionals in their offices.

In fact, though, the awakening in everyone to the excitement of computer technology is but icing on a cake baked over the last decade by business and industry. For if the populace now views the computer as fashionable, business and industry consider it heavy armament in a war against paper, inefficiency, and falling productivity. For example:

■ Manufacturing designers routinely use computers and computer graphics to design parts and to generate the tapes for running numerically controlled machine tools. Now they are starting to use computers to tie design, manufacture, inventory control, and other functions into whole systems. The result: drastic drops in inventory-in-progress, quicker machine setup times, more commonality of parts.

■ As the nursing force dwindles, health care industries use computers in patient monitoring and drug dosage calculation; doctors are discovering the potential for computerized diagnosis assistance.

■ Retailers reap benefits by capturing stock data electronically—for reorder, pricing, and merchandising, using electronic point-of-sale terminals.

■ Automated teller machines allow banks to stay open around the clock. Competing banks even share machines in cases where one bank's business alone won't generate enough traffic.

■ Publishers shove deadlines hours closer to print runs by computerization from original typing—through editing, revision, layout, and pasteup—to automated phototypesetting.

■ Robots are used widely by auto makers in spray painting and other nasty applications; in Japan, whole automated factories are on stream.

■ Energy management is suddenly worth computerizing. Computers track the sun in solar installations, cycle thermostats in office buildings, and even heat buildings as a by-product of operation.

■ Artists play with computer imaging technology; animators use computers to make the repetitive drawings needed to produce cartoons.

■ Offices everywhere are bursting with new automated typing equipment—word processors, microprocessor-based typewriters, small computers with text editing software—presaging an era where integrated word and data processing are commonplace, where voice, video, and data traffic all run on the same communications network.

The litany is endless. In every nook and cranny of the factory and the office, the computer—or some chip-based relative—is finding employment.

■ Can you think of other uses of computers than those mentioned above?
■ Which is the most important or appealing to you? Why?
■ Do any computer uses upset you? Explain.

Source: International Data Corporation.

As the photographs in this text indicate, there are many types and uses of computers. In Chapter Four we will see that there are digital and analog computers, special-purpose and general-purpose computers, microcomputers, minicomputers, and many large types of computer systems, including *supercomputers*! In the remaining chapters of this text, we will explore fundamental concepts of the hardware, software, people, and uses of computerized information processing systems.

COMPUTERS AND INFORMATION PROCESSING: AN OVERVIEW

It is important for you to understand computers in the context of their use in **information processing**, which is also called **data processing**. Computers are now the primary tool in the production of information for users. But it is more important to understand information processing in the following context:

> Information processing is a system of input, processing, output, storage, and control functions that transform data resources into information products using hardware, software, and people as resources.

Figure 1–2 illustrates this fundamental conceptual framework or *model*. We will discuss this model briefly now, and in more detail beginning in the next chapter. This concept is so important that it will be emphasized in every chapter of this text. It will help you tie together the many facts and concepts involved in the study of computers and information processing.

Hardware Resources

Figure 1–3 illustrates the difference between hardware and software. Computing equipment and devices of many kinds are known as **hardware**. This includes a class of devices known as *data media*, which consist of any tangible objects on which data can be recorded. Examples of *hardware* include equipment and media, such as:

- The *central processing unit* (CPU) of a computer system.
- *Computer terminals,* which use a keyboard for input of data and a video screen or printer for output of information.
- *Magnetic disk media,* which can store millions of items of data as magnetic spots on circular metal or plastic disks.

Software Resources

Sets of operating instructions (called *programs*) that direct and control computer processing are called **software**. Software includes all types of operating instructions which direct and control computer hardware in the performance of information processing assignments. (See Figure 1–4.) This might include:

- *System software,* such as an *operating system* program, which controls and supports the operations of a computer system.
- *Application software,* which are programs that direct processing for a particular use of the computer, such as an *inventory* program, or a *payroll* program.

FIGURE 1–2 The information processing system model

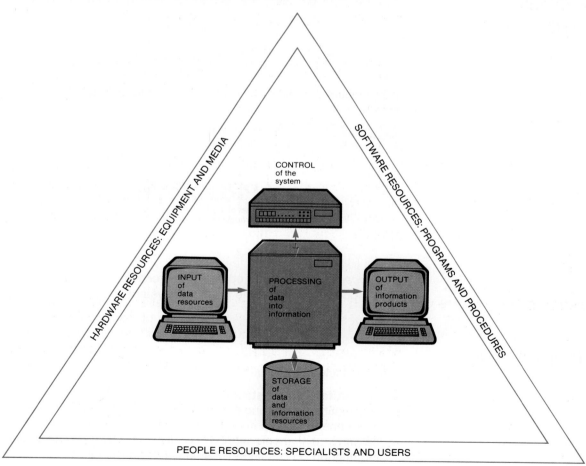

FIGURE

1–3 Computer hardware and software

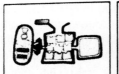

the devices themselves, the electronics and mechanics are referred to as hardware, but...

the directions that make the hardware perform operations are known as

SOFTWARE

A computer's programs, plus the procedure for their use.

(**PROGRAM**)
A set of instructions for performing computer operations.

■ *Procedures,* which are operating instructions for the people who will operate and use the computer system.

People Resources

The people required for the operation of information processing systems include *computer specialists* and *computer users*.

■ **Computer specialists** are the people who develop and operate information processing systems. They include systems analysts, programmers, computer operators, and other managerial, technical, and clerical personnel. Basically, *systems analysts* design information processing systems based on the information requirements of users; *programmers* prepare computer programs

FIGURE 1–4 Computer software in action

```
The IBM Personal Computer DOS
Version 1.10 {C}Copyright IBM Corp 1981, 1982

A>BASIC

The IBM Personal Computer Basic
Version D1.10 Copyright IBM Corp. 1981, 1982
61371 Bytes free
Ok
10 REM PROGRAM TO ADD ANY TWO NUMBERS
20 INPUT "PLEASE ENTER ANY TWO NUMBERS"; A,B
30 LET SUM = A+B
40 PRINT "THE SUM IS";SUM
50 END

RUN
PLEASE ENTER ANY TWO NUMBERS? 200, 300
THE SUM IS 500
Ok
```

The operating system being used: DOS.

The language translator program being used: BASIC.

The application program being used: A program to add any two numbers. It consists of only five instructions in the BASIC language.

Using the program. Note the procedure which asks the user to enter any two numbers. This user entered 200 and 300, which results in a sum of 500.

based on the specifications of systems analysts; and *computer operators* operate the computer.

- A **computer user** or *end user* is anyone who uses a computer system or the information it produces, whether he or she be an accountant, salesperson, engineer, clerk, or manager. Most of us are computer users.

The characteristics and functions of computer hardware, software, and people—and their use in processing data resources into information products—will be covered in subsequent chapters. Let us now take a brief look at how electronic computers developed into the vital and revolutionary tools they are today.

THE DEVELOPMENT OF COMPUTERS

Origin of Computing Machines

The electronic computer sprang from many origins, some well known, some lost in antiquity. Early manual computing devices and the use of machinery to perform arithmetic operations were important advancements. However, these and other devices were not computers, though they were important contributions to the development of machine computation.

The earliest data processing devices included the use of fingers, stones, and sticks for counting, and knots on a string, scratches on a rock, or notches in a stick as record-keeping devices. The Babylonians wrote on clay tablets with a sharp stick, while the ancient Egyptians developed written records on papyrus using a sharp-

14

FIGURE

1–5 An abacus

FIGURE

1–6 Blaise Pascal

pointed reed as a pen and organic dyes for ink. The earliest form of manual calculating device was the abacus. The use of pebbles or rods laid out on a lined or grooved board were early forms of the abacus and were used for thousands of years in many civilizations. The abacus in its present form originated in China and is still used as a calculator. See Figure 1–5.

The use of machinery to perform arithmetic operations is frequently attributed to Blaise Pascal of France and Gottfried von Leibnitz of Germany for their development of the adding machine and the calculating machine, respectively, in the 17th century. (The programming language **Pascal** is named in honor of Blaise Pascal.) However, the inventions of Pascal and Leibnitz incorporated some ideas similar to those used in the clockwork mechanism and the odometer, both of which had been developed as far back as the Greek and Roman civilizations. It must also be recognized that the calculators of Pascal and Leibnitz—and other early mechanical data processing devices—were not reliable machines. The contributions of many persons were necessary during the next two centuries before practical, working data processing machines were developed. See Figure 1–6.

Electromechanical Punched Card Machines

The use of electromechanical machines for the automatic processing of data recorded by holes punched in paper cards was another major development in machine computation. Punched cards were developed in France by Joseph Jacquard during the 18th century to automatically control textile weaving equipment. However, their use in data processing originated with the work of the statistician Dr. Herman Hollerith during the 1880s. Dr. Hollerith was hired by the U.S. Bureau of the Census to develop new ways to process census data. The 1880 census report had not been completed until 1887, and it became evident that the processing of the 1890 census might not be completed before the 1900 census would get under way. Dr. Hollerith responded by developing a punched paper card for the recording of data, a hand-operated card punch, a sorting box, and a tabulator that allowed the 1890 census to be completed in less than three years. Dr. Hollerith's work at the Census Bureau was supplemented by the work of James Powers, who developed punched card machines that were used in the 1910 census. Both men left the Census Bureau to start business firms to produce their machines. The International Business Machines Corporation (IBM) is a descendant of Dr. Hollerith's Tabulating Machine Company, while the UNIVAC Division of the Sperry Corporation is descended from the Powers Accounting Machine Company founded by James Powers.

Mechanical and electrical improvements in punched card machines led to their widespread use for business and government applications in the late 1930s. These machines could "read" the data from punched cards when electrical impulses were generated by the action of metal brushes making electrical contact through the holes punched in a card. Data processing operations were "programmed" by an externally wired removable control panel. Electromechanical punched card machines continued to be the major method for large-scale "automatic data processing" (ADP) in business and government until the late 1950s, when they were made obsolete by the development of electronic computers. See Figure 1–7.

Computer Pioneers

■ Charles Babbage is generally recognized as the first person to propose the concept of the modern computer. He designed and partially built a steam-driven mechanical calculator called the "Difference Engine" with the help of a grant from the British government. In 1833, this English mathematician outlined in detail his plans for an "Analytical Engine," a mechanical steam-driven computing machine that would accept punched card input, automatically perform any arithmetic operation in any sequence under the direction of a mechanically stored program of instructions, and produce either punched card or printed output. He produced thousands of detailed drawings before his death in 1871, but the machine was never built.

FIGURE 1–7 Electromechanical punched card accounting machine

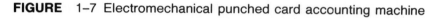

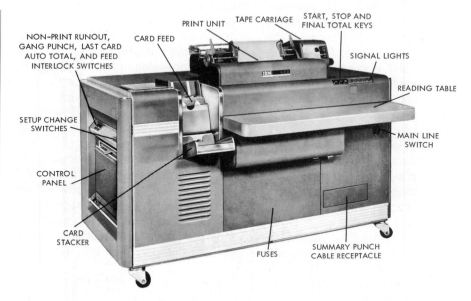

Babbage had designed the world's first general-purpose, stored-program, digital computer, but his ideas were too advanced for the technology of his time. See Figure 1–8.

■ Many of Babbage's ideas were recorded and analyzed by Lady Augusta Ada Byron, Countess of Lovelace, the daughter of Lord Byron, the famous English poet. She is considered by some to be the world's first computer programmer. The programming language **Ada** is named in her honor. See Figure 1–9.

Almost a hundred years passed before the ideas outlined by Babbage began to be developed. Highlights of this pioneering period include:

■ Vannevar Bush of the Massachusetts Institute of Technology (MIT) built a large-scale electromechanical analog computer in 1925.

■ Konrad Zuse of Germany built an electromechanical digital computer in 1941. Called the Z3, it used electrical switches (relays) to perform its computations.

■ The first large-scale electromechanical digital computer was developed by Howard Aiken of Harvard University with the support of IBM in 1944. Aiken's Automatic Sequence Controlled Calculator, nicknamed MARK I, embodied many of the concepts of Charles Babbage, but used electrical relays instead of mechanical gears.

FIGURE

1–8 The difference engine

FIGURE

1–9 Augusta Ada Byron

It relied heavily on the concepts of IBM's punched card calculator developed in the 1930s.

■ The first working model of an electronic digital computer was built by John Atanasoff of Iowa State University in 1942. The ABC (Atanasoff-Berry Computer) used vacuum tubes instead of electrical relays to carry out its computations.

■ The first operational electronic digital computer, the ENIAC (Electronic Numerical Integrator and Calculator), was developed by John Mauchly and J. P. Eckert of the University of Pennsylvania in 1946. The ENIAC weighed over 30 tons and utilized over 18,000 vacuum tubes instead of the electromechanical relays of the Mark I. The ENIAC was built to compute artillery ballistic tables for the U.S.

Army; it could complete in 15 seconds a trajectory computation that would take a skilled person with a desk calculator about 10 hours to complete. However, the ENIAC was not a "stored program" computer and utilized the decimal system. Its processing was controlled externally by switches and control panels that had to be changed for each new series of computations. See Figure 1–10.

■ The first stored-program electronic computer was EDSAC (Electronic Delayed Storage Automatic Computer) developed under the direction of M. V. Wilkes at Cambridge University, England, in 1949.

■ The EDSAC and the first American stored-program computer, the EDVAC (Electronic Discrete Variable Automatic Computer), which was completed in 1952, were based on concepts advanced in 1945 by Dr. John von Neumann of the Institute for Advanced Study in Princeton, New Jersey. He proposed that the operating instructions, or *program*, of the computer be stored in a high-speed internal storage unit, or *memory*, and that both data and instructions be represented internally by the *binary* number system rather than the decimal system. These and other computer design concepts form the basis for much of the design of present-day computers.

Several other early computers and many individuals could be mentioned in a discussion of the pioneering period of computer development. However, the high points discussed should illustrate that many persons and many ideas were responsible for the birth of the electronic digital computer.

FIGURE

1–10 The ENIAC computer

The First Generation

The UNIVAC I (Universal Automatic Computer), the first general-purpose electronic digital computer to be commercially available, marks the beginning of the first generation of electronic computers. Highlights of this generation included:

- The first UNIVAC was installed at the Bureau of Census in 1951. The UNIVAC I became the first computer to process business applications when it was installed at a General Electric manufacturing plant in Louisville, Kentucky, in 1954. An innovation of the UNIVAC I was the use of *magnetic tape* as an input and output medium.
- Another first-generation computer, the IBM 650, was an intermediate-size computer designed for both business and scientific applications. It had a *magnetic drum* memory and used punched cards for input and output.
- Computers developed before the first generation were special-purpose one-of-a-kind machines, whereas 48 UNIVAC Is and almost 2,000 IBM 650s were built.
- The first generation of computers were quite large and produced enormous amounts of heat because of their use of **vacuum tubes**. They had large electrical power, air conditioning, maintenance, and space requirements. See Figure 1–11.

The Second Generation

The second generation of computers was introduced in 1959. Highlights of this generation included:

- Vacuum tubes were replaced by **transistors** and other *solid state, semiconductor* devices. Transistorized circuits were a lot

FIGURE

1–11 The UNIVAC I

smaller, generated little heat, were less expensive, and required less power than vacuum tube circuits.

- Second-generation computers were significantly smaller and faster and more reliable than first-generation machines.
- The number of computers in use grew rapidly, with the IBM 1400 series computers accounting for over 17,000 installations.
- The use of *magnetic cores* as the primary internal storage medium, and the introduction of removable *magnetic disk packs* were other major hardware developments of the second generation. Magnetic tape emerged as the major input/output and *secondary* storage medium for large computer installations, with punched cards continuing to be widely used.

The Third Generation

The introduction of the IBM System/360 series of computers in 1964 signaled the arrival of the third generation of computers. Highlights of this generation included:

- Transistorized circuitry was replaced by **integrated circuits** in which all the elements of an electronic circuit were contained on a small silicon wafer or *chip*. These microelectronic circuits were smaller and more reliable than transistorized circuits and significantly increased the speed and reduced the size of third-generation computers.
- Significant improvements were made in the speed, capacity, and types of computer storage, and magnetic disk units came into widespread use.
- The *family* or *series* concept, which provides standardization and compatibility between different models in a computer series, was developed. Manufacturers claimed to have developed computers that could handle both business and scientific applications and process programs written for other models without major modifications.
- The emergence of *time sharing* (where many users at different terminals can share the same computer at the same time), *data communications* applications, and the ability to process several programs simultaneously through *multiprogramming* were other features of the third generation.
- The third generation marked the growth in importance of software as a means of efficiently using computers. **Operating systems** of control programs were developed to supervise computer processing. High-level programming languages, such as FORTRAN and COBOL, greatly simplified computer programming,

since they allowed program instructions to be expressed in a form that resembles human language or the standard notation of mathematics. **Application software packages** (prewritten programs for users) proliferated as the number of independent software companies grew rapidly. This was the result of the *unbundling* of software and hardware in 1969 by IBM and other manufacturers. They began to charge separately for software and other services instead of including them in the price of the hardware.

- The first **minicomputer** was marketed by the Digital Equipment Corporation in 1965. These desk-top minicomputers and other small computers had greater computing power than larger second-generation systems and came into widespread use. This so swelled the number of computers installed that by the early 1970s over 100,000 larger "mainframe" computers were being used. The number of minicomputers and other specialized computers also exceeded 100,000.

The Fourth Generation

Changes of sufficient significance to merit the fourth-generation designation were displayed by several computer systems beginning in the 1970s and continuing to the present time. Highlights of the present fourth generation include:

- The use of LSI **(large-scale integration)** semiconductor circuits for both the *logic* and *memory* circuitry of the computer is a major technological development of the fourth generation. The use of LSI semiconductor technology enables thousands of electronic components to be placed on a tiny *chip* of silicon. For example, a chip less than a quarter of an inch square may contain between 10,000 to 500,000 transistors and other electronic circuit elements! See Figure 1–12.

- In 1972, several models of the IBM System/370 computer series became the first electronic computers with their main memories composed entirely of LSI semiconductor circuits. The use of such microelectronic **semiconductor memories** was a dramatic change from the *magnetic core memories* used in second- and third-generation computers.

- Main memory capacity of fourth-generation computers increased dramatically. For example, a medium-size second-generation business computer like the IBM 1401 had a memory of 4K to 16K—4,000 to 16,000 character positions of storage. In comparison, the fourth-generation IBM 4341 medium-size computer has a main memory capacity of 4M to 16M—4 to 16 *million* charac-

FIGURE

1–12 Four generations of computer circuitry

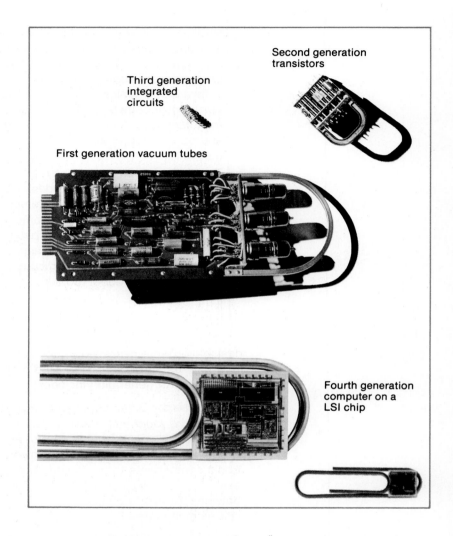

Second generation transistors

Third generation integrated circuits

First generation vacuum tubes

Fourth generation computer on a LSI chip

ters of storage. The cost of such memory capacity dropped in the same period from about $2 per character to only a fraction of a cent per character of storage.

■ The trend toward increased microminiaturization significantly reduced the cost, size, and power requirements of fourth-generation computers, and greatly increased their processing speeds, compared to third-generation computers. Processing speeds in the nanosecond range and in millions of instructions per second are common. The decrease in computer hardware costs is reflected in the fact that the computing power of a $100,000 third-generation business computer of 1970 can be purchased with a fourth-generation **small business computer** costing less than $10,000 in the mid-1980s.

■ Another trend was the increased use of *direct input/output* devices. Data and instructions were increasingly entered into a computer system directly through the keyboard of a small computer or terminal. Other similar input devices include *light pens*, *touch screens*, *data tablets*, *optical scanning wands*, and even the *electronic mouse*! Direct output of information through video displays and audio (voice) response devices also became commonplace.

■ The trend toward programming languages that were easy to use and more like human languages continued. *Database management systems (DBMS)* and *natural* or *fourth-generation* languages (4GL) not only make programming computers easier for programmers but eliminate the need for traditional programming. Users do not have to tell the computer *how* to do a task (using *procedural* languages), but only *what* task (using *nonprocedural* languages) they want accomplished. The development of easy-to-use software packages for microcomputer users, such as *electronic spreadsheet* and *word processing* programs, accelerated this trend.

■ LSI technology led to the development of a **microprocessor** in 1971 by M. E. Hoff of the Intel Corporation and Victor Poor of the Datapoint Corporation. All of the circuitry for the main processing unit of a computer was placed on a single chip! This was followed by the development of the Intel 8080 microprocessor in 1974, which was used in the first commercially available **microcomputer** system, the Altair 8800 in 1975.

Other impressive fourth-generation advancements, though first developed in some earlier computers, are being used extensively by fourth-generation computer systems. They are summarized in Figure 1–13 and explained in detail later in this text. (Refer to the Glossary and Index at the back of this text if you want to look up some of these terms now.)

These developments have greatly increased the usability, versatility, and capacity of fourth-generation computers. Computers have come into such widespread use that by the mid-1980s millions of computer systems were in use. Most of these computers were not large "mainframes" systems, but were smaller microcomputer and minicomputer systems purchased for scientific, educational, industrial, business, and personal use. These estimates do not include the millions of microprocessors used in a wide variety of industrial and consumer products. Figures 1–13 and 1–14 summarize major characteristics and trends of the four computer generations. Let

FIGURE 1–13 Characteristics of the computer generation

Major Characteristics	First Generation	Second Generation	Third Generation	Fourth Generation
ELECTRONIC CIRCUITRY	Vacuum tubes	Transistors	Integrated semiconductor circuits	Large-scale integrated (LSI) semiconductor circuits
MAIN MEMORY	Magnetic drum	Magnetic core	Magnetic core	LSI semiconductor circuits
SECONDARY MEMORY	Magnetic tape Magnetic drum	Magnetic tape Magnetic disk	Magnetic disk Magnetic tape	Magnetic disk Floppy disk Magnetic bubble
INPUT MEDIA/ METHOD	Punched cards Paper tape	Punched cards	Key to tape/disk	Keyboard data entry direct input devices Optical recognition
OUTPUT MEDIA/ METHOD	Punched cards Printed reports	Punched cards Printed reports	Printed reports Video display	Video display Audio response Printed reports
SOFTWARE	User-written programs Machine language	Packaged programs Symbolic languages	Operating systems High-level languages	Database management systems Fourth generation languages Microcomputer packages
OTHER CHARACTERISTICS	Batch processing	Overlapped processing Real time processing Data communications	Time sharing Multiprogramming Multiprocessing Minicomputers	Microprogramming Virtual memory Distributed processing Word processing Microcomputers

us now examine more closely the fourth-generation phenomenon that we call the "microcomputer revolution."

THE MICROCOMPUTER REVOLUTION

The development of the *microcomputer*, or "computer on a chip," is being heralded not only as a major development of the fourth computer generation, but as a major technological breakthrough that has started a "second computer revolution."

Are such claims justified? It appears that they are. The microcomputer revolution can be described as a technological break-

FIGURE

1–14 Trends in computer size, speed, and cost

Trend in Size of Computers

ENIAC computer	House size (1,500 square feet!)
First-generation computer	Room size
Second-generation computer	Closet size
Third-generation minicomputer	Desk size
Fourth-generation microcomputer	From "chip" to typewriter size

Trend in Computation Speed of Computers

First generation	300 multiplications per second
Second generation	200,000 multiplications per second
Third generation	2 million multiplications per second
Fourth generation	20 million multiplications per second

Trend in Computation Cost of Computers

Average cost of doing 100,000 multiplications:

1952 = $1.26   1958 = 26¢   1964 = 12¢   1974 = 1¢

Today, the cost is only a fraction of a cent!

through that is bringing *computer power* to both *people and products*. The four major dimensions of this revolution are (1) microcomputer technology, (2) "distributed processing," (3) "personal computing," and (4) "smart products."

Microcomputer Technology

The development of microcomputers represents a major revolution in computer science and technology due to accelerating trends in microelectronics. See Figure 1–15. The microcomputer is a very small computer, ranging in size from a "computer on a chip" to a small typewriter-size unit. Thus, computers of extremely small size and cost—but of great speed, capacity, and reliability—are now a reality. Microprocessors and microcomputers are changing the design and capabilities of computer hardware and software. They are even being "embedded" into large computers to increase their speed and power!

Microcomputer technology requires a complex and delicate process for the production of microelectronic circuit chips. Crystals of pure silicon are grown in the laboratory and sliced into paper-thin *wafers*. Microscopic circuits are etched on the silicon wafer in a series of layers in a complex photolithographic process. This process involves repeatedly bathing the wafer in chemicals and exposing it to ultraviolet light through circuit patterns called *masks*. Gradually, the process results in a complex grid of circuits composed of transistors, resistors, capacitors, and other circuit elements. (It should be noted that several firms have begun to produce microelectronic circuits by drawing them directly on a wafer with a computer-

REAL WORLD APPLICATION 1-2

The Boeing 767, ENIAC, and the Microcomputer

If the aircraft industry had evolved as spectacularly as the computer industry over the past 25 years, a Boeing 767 would cost $500 today, and it would circle the globe in 20 minutes on five gallons of fuel. Such performance would represent a rough analog of the reduction in cost, the increase in speed of operation, and the decrease in energy consumption of computers. The cost of computer logic devices is falling at the rate of 25 percent per year, and the cost of computer memory at the rate of 40 percent per year. Computational speed has increased by a factor of 200 in 25 years. In the same period the cost, the energy consumption, and the size of computers of comparable power have decreased by a factor of 10,000.

The result is the advent of the personal computer, which for less than $500 can put at the disposal of an individual about the same basic computing power as a mainframe computer did in the early 1960s and as a minicomputer did in the early 1970s. Today's home microcomputer, at a cost of a few hundred dollars, has more computing capacity than the first large electronic computer, ENIAC. It is 50 times faster, has at least four times as much memory, is thousands of times more reliable, consumes the power of a light bulb, rather than that of a locomotive, occupies 1/30,000th the volume, and costs 1/10,000th as much.

Twenty years ago the cost of a computer could be justified only if the machine met the needs of a large organization. The minicomputers introduced in the 1970s are appropriate for a department or a working group within such an organization. Today the personal computer can serve as a workstation for the individual. Moreover, just as it has become financially feasible to provide a computer for the individual worker, so also technical developments have made the interface between man and machine increasingly "friendly," so that a wide array of computer functions are now accessible to people with no technical background.

The first personal computer was put on the market in 1975. Ten years later, more than 20 million personal computers were in service in the United States alone. There has been talk of a "computer revolution" ever since the electronics industry learned in the late 1950s to inscribe miniature electronic circuits on a chip of silicon. What has been witnessed so far has been a steady, albeit remarkably speedy, evolution. With the proliferation of person computers, however, the way may indeed be open for a true revolution in how business is conducted, in how people organize their personal affairs, and perhaps even in how people think.

- Why has the rate of progress in the computer industry been so great? Do you expect it to continue?
- What has been the impact of such progress on computers and their uses?

Source: Adapted from Hoo-Min D. Tong and Amar Gupta, "The Personal Computer," *Scientific American*, September 1982, p. 87. Copyright © 1982 by Scientific American, Inc. All rights reserved.

FIGURE

1–15 Trends in microelectronics

Trend in Density
Maximum number of components per electronic circuit:
1959 = 1   1969 = 1,024   1979 = 1 million
mid-1980s = over 50 million
Maximum number of binary digits (bits) per memory chip:
1970 = 1,024   1980 = 65,536   mid-1980s = over 1 million

Trend in Speed
Speed of an electronic logic circuit:
Mid-1950s (vacuum tube circuit) = one microsecond
Early 1960s (transistorized printed circuit) = 100 nanoseconds
Late 1970s (integrated circuit chip) = 5 nanoseconds
Mid-1980s (integrated circuit chip) = 0.2 nanoseconds

Trend in Cost
Cost per integrated logic circuit:
1964 = $16   1972 = 75¢   1977 = 15¢
mid-1980s = 1¢
Cost per bit of integrated circuit memory:
1973 = 0.5¢   1977 = 0.1¢   mid-1980s = .01¢

Trend in Reliability
Reliability of electronic circuits:
Vacuum tube = one failure every few hours
Transistor = 1,000 times more reliable than vacuum tube
Integrated circuit = 1,000 times more reliable than transistor

controlled electron beam!) After testing the circuits on the wafer it is sectioned into several hundred chips. Defective chips are discarded and good chips are sealed with external wiring in individual packages. Since only a single speck of dust can ruin a chip, this entire process is done in "clean rooms," where workers are dressed in surgical-type clothing and the air is constantly filtered. See Figures 1–16, 1–17, and 1–18.

FIGURE

1–16 Microcomputer Technology

A This microprocessor chip has as much processing power as some large-scale computers.

B A wafer containing 64 microelectronic chips.

A

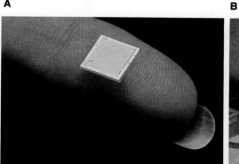

B

FIGURE

1–17 How microelectronic chips are made

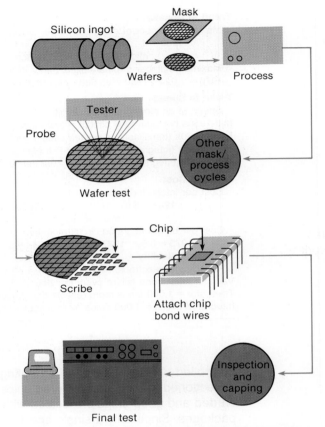

Source: Adapted from Monte, Phister, Jr., *Data Processing Technology and Electronics,* 2d ed. (Bedford, Mass.: Digital Press, 1980).

FIGURE

1–18 The layers of a microelectronic chip

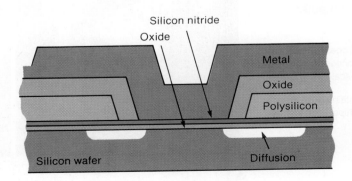

Distributed Processing

Distributed processing is a new type of information processing made possible by a network of computers "dispersed" throughout an organization. Microprocessors and microcomputers now allow many data input, output, storage, and communication devices to become powerful "intelligent" processors or terminals with their own computer capability. Though started by the minicomputer, the microcomputer thus makes truly possible the "dispersion" of computer processing away from a central computer and out to the users in an organization. Distributed processing in branch offices, retail stores, factories, office buildings, remote locations, and other worksites is the result of this development. See Figure 1–19.

FIGURE

1–19 A distributed processing network of computers

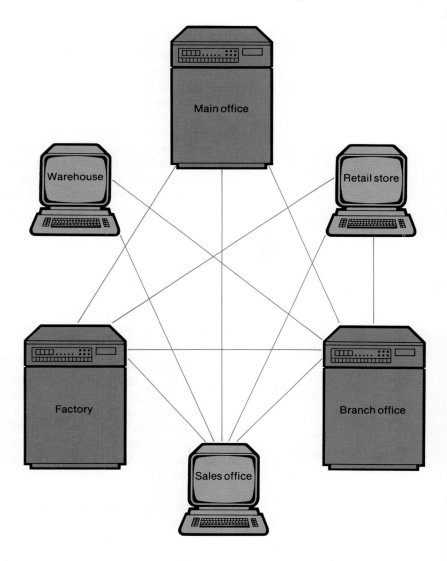

Personal Computing

Personal computing involves the use of microcomputers as "personal computers" by individuals for business, professional, educational, recreational, home management, and other personal applications. Thus, the power of computerized data processing is now finally available to everyone. Microcomputers are small, affordable, powerful, and easy to use. Millions of these computer systems are currently in use. Personal computing at home, at work, or at play is the result of this development. Much of this text and its photographs emphasize the role played by microcomputers for personal computing.

Smart Products

It is now economically and technologically feasible to use microcomputers to improve and enhance a host of present industrial and consumer products and to create many new ones. *Smart products* with "intelligence" provided by built-in microcomputers or microprocessors that significantly improve their performance and capabilities are the result of this development. Smart consumer products range from electronic games and toys (some with "talking" microprocessor chips) to microwave ovens and automobiles with microprocessor intelligence, and even "smart cards"—credit cards with microelectronic memory chips embedded in them! Smart commercial and industrial products range from talking calculators and smart copying machines to industrial robots. See Real Word Application 1–3.

A CONTINUING REVOLUTION

The developments of the fourth computer generation and the microcomputer revolution indicate the continued revolutionary impact of the computer on business and the rest of society. It is apparent that several major trends will continue into the foreseeable future:

- A **fifth generation** of "intelligent" computers with the ability to see, listen, talk, and think will emerge! Japan is at the forefront of this development. The Japanese have committed themselves to an ambitious government and industry project which hopes to produce an intelligent computer by 1990. Both the United States and Japan hope to produce such computers with a new *parallel processing* computer architecture that is different from the traditional *von Neumann design* of current computers. Fifth-generation computers will process data and instructions in *parallel* (many at a time), instead of *sequentially* (one at a time) as done by today's computers. Such intelligent computers would

REAL WORLD APPLICATION 1–3

General Motors Corvette

Zero to 300,000 in one second? The new Corvette's two on-board computers and their microchips transmit 300,000 instructions every second. That's every second! Science fiction? No, science fact. The new Corvette is equipped with two on-board computers armed with a combined 14-K memory and more than 6,600 individual instructions that monitor, control, and compute at precise split-second intervals. Yet these computers perform real world functions that make your Corvette unlike any other automobile on the road.

A brain in your engine

The primary computer system, the Electronic Control Module (ECM), literally works like a brain in your engine, controlling such functions as spark timing, idle speed, fuel mixture, and the automatic transmission converter clutch. ECM acts to give you optimal engine performance under a wide range of atmospheric and climatic conditions.

Driver data center

Corvette's second computer, the driver data center, functions as a monitor, calculator, and transmitter of vital data to you, the driver. And it does all this with astounding speed and precision. For example, the speedometer and tachometer bar graphs on the instrument panel are updated every 65 milliseconds. Digital readouts for both are also provided. And the tachometer bar graph displays at what rpm the engine is delivering its peak horsepower. Want to know how many miles per gallon you're getting or what your mileage range is? The Corvette's computer can tell you in less than three milliseconds, while it would take you 10–15 seconds with a handheld calculator. Want to know your speed in kilometers? Flick a switch and the entire system changes into metric readouts.

Comprehensive instrumentation

Corvette's computer instrumentation also provides you with readouts for oil pressure, oil temperature, coolant temperature, voltage, fuel level, and so on, in addition to a complete bank of warning lights. This is one of the most comprehensive instrument panels ever offered in a sports car—a total of 14 instrument readouts in nine display areas.

Space technology today

Just a few short years ago, such electronic wizardry was impossible in an automobile. Size, weight, and cost of required hardware were insurmountable barriers. But advanced cybernetic technology and by-products of U.S. space programs have given dramatically broader dimensions to what is possible and practical. Space-age technology is no longer relegated to the distant future. It's here now, harnessed for real world applications in Corvette.

- Would you call the new Corvette a smart product? Why?
- List the tasks done by the Corvette's twin microcomputers.
- What are the advantages and disadvantages of having these tasks done by computers?

Source: Courtesy General Motors Corporation.

make possible one of the main goals of the science of *artificial intelligence* (AI), the creation of *computers that think*! The fifth generation will also accelerate the trend toward direct input/output of data and instructions. Voice and visual input will be coupled with voice and visual output to make obsolete most present methods of communicating with a computer.

■ Computer hardware costs and sizes will continue to decrease steadily. This will be a major effect of the increased use of VLSI (very large-scale integration) technology where hundreds of thousands and even millions of circuit elements are placed on a microelectronic chip. This will result in the development of extremely small *nanocomputers*, where the power and memory of a large computer of today is packed onto a single chip! Also on the horizon are computers with *optical processors*, which use *photonic* rather than electronic circuits. They process data using laser beams, instead of electronic pulses, and operate near the speed of light.

■ Computer software will continue to grow in its ease of use and versatility. Users will converse with computers in natural human languages. Application software packages will become integrated general-purpose programs that can easily handle a variety of tasks for nontechnical users.

■ Use of microcomputers and microprocessors will continue to increase dramatically. Smart products—especially industrial *robots*—will multiply as microcomputer intelligence is built into more and more consumer, commercial, and industrial products. Information processing devices of all kinds, as well as minicomputers and larger computers, will use microprocessors to increase their speed, power, and flexibility.

■ The *office of the future* will become a reality by blending computerized word processing, electronic data processing, and telecommunications. Distributed networks of intelligent terminals and other computerized office devices will create *automated office* typing, dictation, copying, and filing systems, as well as *electronic mail* and message systems.

■ Advanced information processing systems will merge the transmission and processing of data, images, and voices. This will involve extensive use of earth satellites, *fiber optics*, and *laser/video disk* technology in advanced telecommunication systems.

■ Computers and computerized *workstations* will become integrated into everyday business operations in offices, small business firms, wholesale and retail outlets, warehouses, and factories. Managers will rely heavily on computer-based management information systems (MIS), decision support systems

(DSS), and *expert systems* based on artificial intelligence to help them make better business decisions.

■ Society as a whole will become increasingly reliant on computers in many areas. Everyday use of computer-based systems—such as *electronic funds transfer* (EFT) systems in banking, *point-of-sale* (POS) systems in retailing, *computer-assisted instruction* (CAI) systems in education, and *videotex* systems for electronic shopping, banking, and information services in the home—will increase dramatically.

All of these trends indicate that the computer revolution will be a continuing phenomenon in the future. (See Figure 1–20.)

FIGURE 1–20 The continuing computer revolution

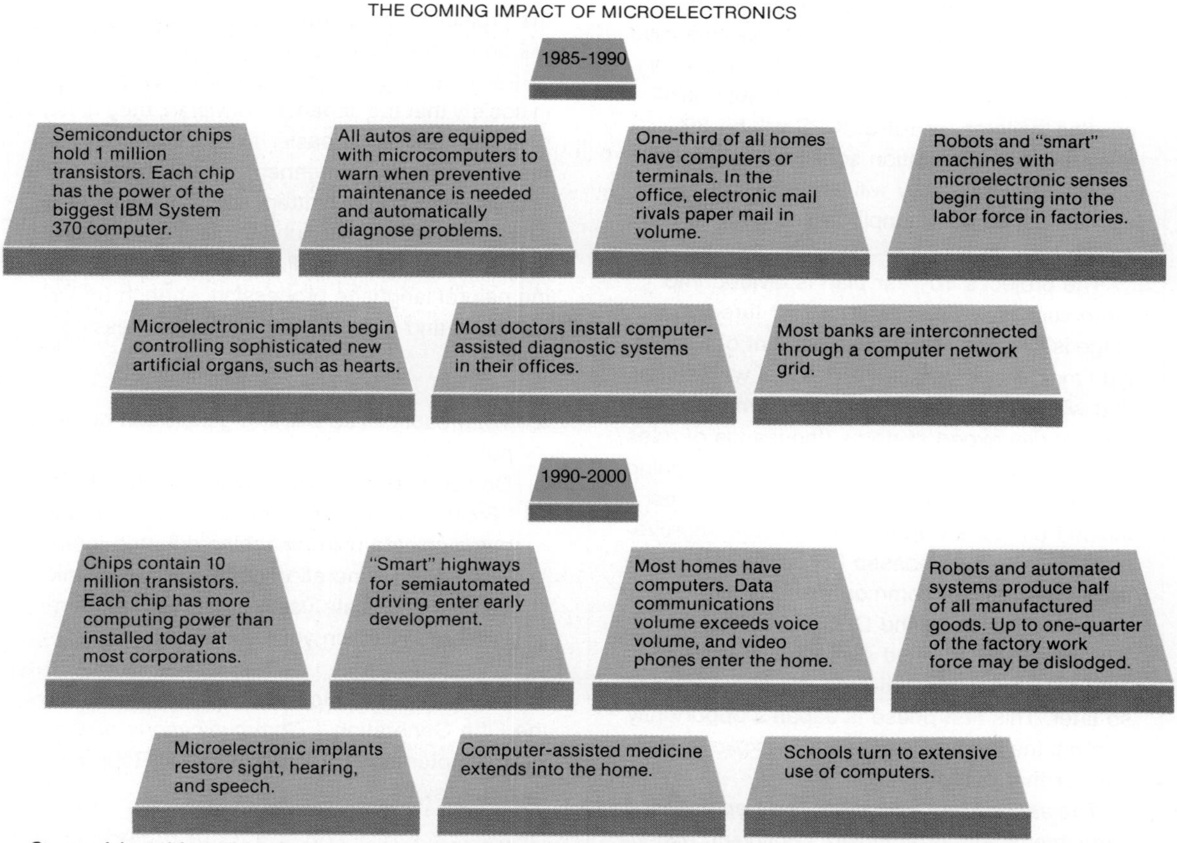

THE COMING IMPACT OF MICROELECTRONICS

1985-1990

Semiconductor chips hold 1 million transistors. Each chip has the power of the biggest IBM System 370 computer.

All autos are equipped with microcomputers to warn when preventive maintenance is needed and automatically diagnose problems.

One-third of all homes have computers or terminals. In the office, electronic mail rivals paper mail in volume.

Robots and "smart" machines with microelectronic senses begin cutting into the labor force in factories.

Microelectronic implants begin controlling sophisticated new artificial organs, such as hearts.

Most doctors install computer-assisted diagnostic systems in their offices.

Most banks are interconnected through a computer network grid.

1990-2000

Chips contain 10 million transistors. Each chip has more computing power than installed today at most corporations.

"Smart" highways for semiautomated driving enter early development.

Most homes have computers. Data communications volume exceeds voice volume, and video phones enter the home.

Robots and automated systems produce half of all manufactured goods. Up to one-quarter of the factory work force may be dislodged.

Microelectronic implants restore sight, hearing, and speech.

Computer-assisted medicine extends into the home.

Schools turn to extensive use of computers.

Source: Adapted from "High Technology," *Business Week.* Reprinted from the November 10, 1980, issue of *Business Week* (p. 96) by special permission. © 1980 by McGraw-Hill, Inc., New York, N.Y. 10020. All rights reserved.

REAL WORLD APPLICATION 1–4

Japan and the Fifth Computer Generation

In October 1981, Japan's Ministry of International Trade and Industry (MITI) sponsored a conference to announce a new national project. Alongside national projects in supercomputing and robotics, there would be an effort to develop a new generation (the fifth, by their reckoning) of computers.

The fifth generation will not be traditional computers; instead, they'll be symbolic inference machines, capable of reasoning their way swiftly through massive amounts of knowledge and data. They'll be computers that can learn, associate, make inferences, make decisions, and otherwise behave in ways considered the exclusive province of human reason. Even their name signals the change: knowledge information processing systems, or KIPS. KIPS will be the engine of the information society; small, robust, and inexpensive. They will appear as universal appliances, as commonplace and easy to use as the telephone.

The project's 10-year plan is divided into three successive stages. The *first* three-year stage is devoted to the development of a prototype machine, a personal PROLOG workstation that will have a knowledge base comparable to present-day expert systems (thousands of rules and thousands of objects) but whose reasoning powers will be a million logical inferences per second (LIPS), an order of magnitude improvement over software-based PROLOG implementations on today's common mainframe computers, such as the DEC 2060. The prototype should be finished sometime in the mid-1980s, with commercial products due a year or so later. This first phase is Japan's opportunity to climb the learning curve, and is explicitly planned for that purpose.

The *second* four-year stage is for engineering experimentation, prototyping, continuing experiments at significant applications, and the initial experiments at systems integration. The first thrust at the major problems of parallel processing will be done in those years.

The *final* three-year phase will concentrate on advanced engineering, building the final major engineering prototypes, and further systems integration work. The ultimate goal, scheduled for the early 1990s, is nothing less than an inference supercomputer capable of a million to a billion LIPS, with a knowledge base that can handle tens of thousands of inference rules and hundreds of millions of objects—about the right size to encompass the Encyclopaedia Britannica. The Japanese will rely heavily on bootstrapping: the project's earlier work on CAD, for example, will be used in later hardware design.

For these machines to play the central role in society that the Japanese envision, they must, of course, be much easier to use than today's machines. Thus, fifth-generation machines will understand spoken, written, and graphical input. The Japanese are launching intense research and development in intelligent interfaces, including natural language processing, speech understanding, and graphics and image processing.

- What capabilities will fifth-generation computers have?
- Do you agree with the following statement? "Fourth-generation computers compute and communicate using machine-oriented interfaces. Fifth-generation computers will think and communicate using human-oriented interfaces." Explain your answer.

Source: Pamela McCorduck, "Introduction to the Fifth Generation," *Communications of the ACM*, September 1983, pp. 629–30. Reprinted by permission.

FIGURE

1–21 Levels of computer use

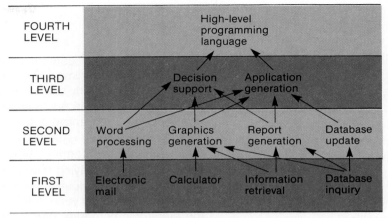

FOURTH LEVEL	High-level programming language		
THIRD LEVEL	Decision support	Application generation	
SECOND LEVEL	Word processing	Graphics generation	Report generation	Database update
FIRST LEVEL	Electronic mail	Calculator	Information retrieval	Database inquiry

Source: Adapted from James Martin, *Application Development without Programming* (Englewood Cliffs, N.J.: Prentice-Hall, 1982), p. 109. Reprinted with permission.

GETTING STARTED IN COMPUTERS

Today's computers and many of the programs that operate them are so easy to use that anybody, including a beginner like yourself, can quickly learn to use them. Right now is a perfect time to start! You should move from a simple level of computer use to more complicated levels as you gain skills and experience. Figure 1–21 illustrates four levels of increasing sophistication in the use of computers. You should start at the first level and work your way up as far as you care to go. This text, its appendix on using software packages, and the BASIC and Pascal appendices of the Student Study Guide should help you accomplish most of the activities in each level of computer use.

The end of this book contains an appendix entitled **Using Popular Software Packages: A Tutorial Introduction**. You should read the first section, which is called Getting Started with Software Packages. Then use a personal computer or computer terminal and a prewritten program available to you to solve a short problem similar to the example illustrated in this section of the appendix. It should only take a few minutes to get accustomed to the peculiarities of your computer and to learn how to use a simple application program to solve a short problem in business, statistics, or personal finance. Try it, you'll like it!

SUMMARY

- An understanding of computers, data processing, and information systems is very important today. They are major tools by which we can properly use information resources for the benefit of society and for the operation and management of business firms and other organizations.

- The development of computers is a revolutionary technological development of the 20th century. The computer revolution has succeeded in multiplying human brainpower with the same impact that the first industrial revolution multiplied human musclepower. Less than 20 years after it was commercially introduced, the electronic computer had revolutionized data processing in science, engineering, industry, business, and many other fields.

- The computer is an electronic device that has the ability to accept data, internally store and automatically execute a program of instructions, perform mathematical, logical, and manipulative operations on data, and report the results.

- Computer equipment and devices are known as "hardware," while the various sets of operating instructions, or programs that direct and control computer processing, are called "software." Information processing should be understood as a system of input, processing, output, storage, and control functions that transform data into information using hardware, software, and people as resources.

- The ideas and inventions of many persons were responsible for the development of the electronic digital computer. *First-generation* computers were first produced in 1951 and were large devices that used vacuum tubes in their circuitries. Transistors and other solid-state devices were used in the *second generation* of computers, which were introduced in 1959 and were smaller, faster, and cheaper than first-generation machines. Magnetic cores were the primary internal storage medium, while magnetic tapes were widely used for input/output and secondary storage. *Third-generation* computers were introduced in 1964 and replaced transistorized circuitry with integrated circuits. The third generation also featured improvements in the speed, capacity, and types of computer input/output and storage devices, including the widespread use of magnetic disk units. Time sharing, data communications, operating systems, high-level programming languages, and minicomputers were other developments of the third generation. *The fourth generation* began in the early 1970s with the introduction of computers that utilize such developments as large-scale integrated circuits, microprogramming, virtual memory, and the replacement of magnetic cores with integrated circuitry for main memory. Distributed processing, data base management systems, natural languages, and the microcomputer are other fourth-generation developments.

■ The development of microcomputers in the fourth computer generation has been acclaimed as a second computer revolution because it is bringing computer power to both people and products. The microcomputer represents a major technological breakthrough in computer science and technology. Computer processing capability is being brought to the users in an organization through distributed processing and to everyone in society through personal computing and smart products.

■ The computer revolution will continue into the future. Major trends expected are the development of a fifth generation of intelligent computers, continued decreases in the size and cost of computer hardware, and the growth of general-purpose, easy-to-use software. Smart products will multiply, the automated office will become a reality, managers will use computer-assisted decision systems, and the everyday use of computers in society will accelerate.

KEY TERMS AND CONCEPTS

Computer
Hardware
Software
Program
Computer revolution
Computer specialist

Computer user
Computer generations
Microcomputer
Distributed processing
Personal computing
Smart products

REVIEW AND APPLICATION QUESTIONS

1. Why is a basic understanding of computers, data processing, and information systems so important?
2. Why is the development and use of computers called a "computer revolution"? How has this computer revolution affected you?
3. What is a computer? What are hardware and software?
4. What is the difference between a computer specialist and a computer user?

5. What roles are played by hardware, software, and people in information processing?
6. How are early computing devices related to the development of the electronic computer?
7. Who were some of the pioneers in the development of the computer? Explain the major contribution of each person.
8. What are some of the major characteristics of each of the four generations of computers?
9. What is the microcomputer revolution? How has it affected you?
10. The microcomputer revolution represents a major technological breakthrough that is bringing computer power to both people and products through distributed processing, personal computing, and "smart" products. Explain.
11. What have been some of the trends in size, speed, cost, and reliability due to the developments of microelectronics?
12. What are "smart" products? Provide examples of smart commercial and consumer products to illustrate your answer.
13. What will be the major capabilities of the fifth generation of computers?
14. What are some of the major trends of the continuing computer revolution that are expected to continue into the future? Do these trends seem realistic? How will they affect your use of the computer?

APPLICATION PROBLEMS

1. If you have not already done so, read and answer the questions after each Real World Application in this chapter.
2. Get started in the use of computers! Complete the assignment suggested in the last section of this chapter entitled Getting Started in Computers.

CHAPTER 2

Introduction to Information Processing

CHAPTER OUTLINE

LEARNING OBJECTIVES

The purpose of this chapter is to promote a basic
understanding of information processing by analyzing
(1) the concepts of data, information, and systems;
(2) the fundamental conceptual framework of
information processing as a system of resources,
functions, and products; and (3) the benefits and
limitations of manual and electronic information
processing. After reading and studying this chapter,
you should be able to:

1. Give an example to illustrate the difference between
   data and information.
2. Explain and give examples of the concept of
   information processing as a system of input,
   processing, output, storage, and control functions
   that transform data resources into information
   products using hardware, software, and people as
   resources.
3. Give examples that illustrate the processing of data
   by each of the basic functions of information
   processing.
4. Identify several benefits and limitations of manual
   and electronic information processing.
5. Identify the four basic advantages of using
   computers for information processing.

INTRODUCTORY CONCEPTS

Data versus Information

The word *data* is the plural of *datum*, though data is commonly used to represent both singular and plural forms. *Data* can be defined as *any representation of facts, observations, or occurrences*. Data usually takes the form of numbers, words, or codes composed of numerical or alphabetical characters or special symbols. However, data can also take such forms as lines on a graph or other types of graphic representation.

The terms *data* and *information* are often used interchangeably. However, a distinction should be made. Data should be viewed as raw material *resources* that are *processed* into finished information *products*. *Information* can then be defined as *data that has been transformed into a meaningful and useful form for specific human beings*.

Example.   Names, quantities, and dollar amounts recorded on sales invoices represent data, not information, to a sales manager. Only when such facts are properly organized and manipulated can meaningful sales information be provided, such as the amount of sales by product type, sales territory, or salesperson.

In some cases, data may not require processing before constituting information for a human user. However, data is usually not useful until subjected to a process where its form is manipulated and organized and its content is analyzed and evaluated. Then data becomes information. See Figure 2–1.

Data and Information Processing

Data processing has traditionally been defined as the processing of data to transform it into information. Thus, **data processing** consists of any actions that make data usable and meaningful (i.e., transforms data into information). However, the term **information processing** is gradually replacing the term *data processing*. Why? For two major reasons:

- *Information processing* is a more generic concept that covers both the traditional concept of processing numeric and alphabetic data and the concept of **word processing**, in which *text data* (words, phrases, sentences, paragraphs) are processed into letters, memos, reports, and other *documents*.
- *Information processing* is a concept emphasizing that the production of *information products* for users should be the focus of processing activities. It also emphasizes that the raw material resources being processed no longer consist only of numeric and alphabetic data but of such newer forms as text, images, and voices.

FIGURE 2–1 Data versus information

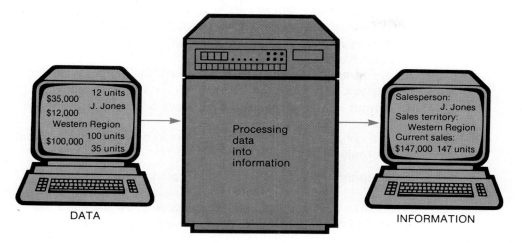

Example. Your reading of this text is one type of data or information processing. Your eyes are transmitting the *text data* of letters and words to your brain, which transforms these images into *information* by organizing and evaluating them and storing them for later use.

The Systems Concept

The activity of data processing can be viewed as a "system." What is a system? A **system** can be very simply and broadly defined as *a group of interrelated or interacting elements*. Many examples of systems can be found in the physical and biological sciences, in modern technology, and in human society. Thus, we can talk of the physical system of the sun and its planets, the biological system of the human body, the technological system of an oil refinery, and the socioeconomic system of a business organization. However, a more specific and appropriate concept of a system is used in information processing and computer technology.

A **system** can be defined as a group of interrelated components that work toward the attainment of a common goal by accepting inputs and producing outputs in an organized transformation process.

Such a system (sometimes called a "dynamic system") has three basic components:

- **Input** consists of elements that enter the system so they can be processed.

  Examples: Raw materials, energy, data, human effort, etc.

- **Processing** involves "transformation" processes that convert input into output.

  Examples: A manufacturing process, the human breathing process, data calculations, etc.

- **Output** represents elements that have been produced by the transformation process.

  Examples: Finished products, human services, management information, etc.

These three basic components interact to form a "system."

Examples. A manufacturing system accepts raw materials as inputs and produces finished goods as output. An **information**

FIGURE

2–2 Three systems

A FUNDAMENTAL SYSTEM CONCEPT

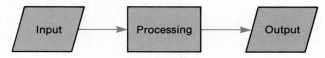

A MANUFACTURING SYSTEM

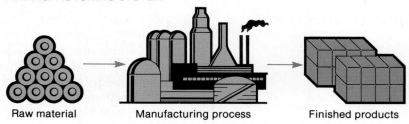

AN INFORMATION PROCESSING SYSTEM

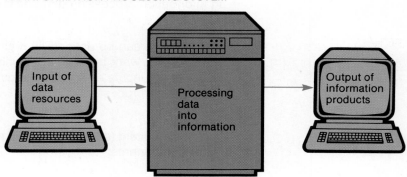

processing system can be viewed as *a system which accepts data resources as input and processes them into information products as output*. In this context, you as a reader of this book are an information processing system. See Figure 2–2.

The systems concept can be made even more useful by including two additional components: *feedback* and *control*. Figure 2–3 illustrates a system with feedback and control components. Such a system is sometimes called a "cybernetic" system, that is, *a self-monitoring and self-regulating system*.

- **Feedback** is information concerning the components and operations of a system.

- **Control** is a systems component that monitors and evaluates feedback to determine whether the system is moving toward the achievement of its goal, and then it makes any necessary adjustments to the input and processing components of the system to ensure that proper output is produced. *Note:* The feedback function is frequently included as part of the control function of a system. The responsibility of the control function then is to *develop* as well as monitor and evaluate feedback and make necessary adjustments to a system. We will use this concept of the control function in this text.

Examples. A familiar example of a self-monitoring and self-regulating system is the thermostatically controlled heating system found in many homes, which automatically monitors and regulates itself to produce a desired temperature. Another familiar example is the human body, which can be considered an adaptive cybernetic system that automatically monitors and adjusts many of its functions, such as temperature, heartbeat, and breathing.

The feedback-control concept can also be applied to information processing systems. *Feedback* would consist of information describing the input, processing, and output activities of the system. *Control* would involve monitoring and evaluating feedback to determine if the system is operating according to the established information

FIGURE

2–3 System concept with feedback and control

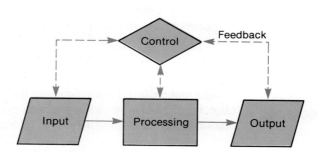

processing procedures and is producing the proper output. If not, the control function would make necessary adjustments to input and processing activities so proper information output would be produced.

Example. If *subtotals* of sales amounts in a sales report do not add up to *total sales*, then input or processing procedures may have to be changed to correctly accumulate all sales transactions.

A final basic component found in information processing systems is the *storage* function.

- **Storage** is the system function in which data and information are stored in an organized manner for further processing or until needed by users of the system.

Example. Sales data is accumulated and stored for subsequent processing, which produces daily, weekly, and monthly sales analysis reports for management.

We have now explained and given examples of the fundamental components (the input, processing, output, storage, and control functions) of a system. This concept is a vital foundation for the development and use of computers in information processing. In the next section, you will see how this system concept fits into the framework of information processing as a system of resources, functions, and products. However, let's first look at an example of the use of computers for information processing in the real world. Read Real World Application 2–1.

THE INFORMATION PROCESSING SYSTEM CONCEPT

In Chapter One, we introduced the concept that **information processing is a system of input, processing, output, storage, and control functions that transform data resources into information products using hardware, software, and people as resources.** This concept or *model* should serve as a framework or structure that ties together the many facts, concepts, and developments of the exciting and dynamic field of computers and information processing. Let's examine this model in more detail, and see how it applies to the real world of information processing. See Figure 2–4.

Information Processing Resources

Information processing requires the use of the organizational resources of hardware, software, and people to transform the data resources of an organization into information products. This is true

REAL WORLD APPLICATION 2–1

ABC Department Stores

ABC Department Stores is a regional chain of small department stores in the Southwest. It uses computers for various information processing jobs, such as processing sales transactions, analysis of sales performance, employee payroll processing, and preparation of monthly customer statements. Here's what happened on a typical day in an ABC Department Store.

Marsha Johnson walked up to the customer service counter and presented an automatic toaster she wanted to buy, along with her plastic credit card to the salesclerk, Dave Kent. Dave used a point-of-sale (POS) terminal (an electronic cash register terminal) to record the sale. He entered the details of the transaction (product, department, and store codes) into the store's computer system using a hand-held optical scanning *wand* to scan the special coding on the toaster's merchandise tag. The correct recording of this data was signaled by an audible "beep" from the POS terminal.

Information about the sale was immediately shown on the terminal's display screen. Dave inserted Marsha's credit card into a slot in the POS terminal. The terminal read her customer account number from the magnetic stripe on the back of the card. This data was transmitted to the store's computer along with information about her purchase. The computer checked her customer record, which was stored on its magnetic disk units. Then it completed the rest of the tasks required by the instructions in the *sales transaction* program it was following. This included changing Marsha's customer record to reflect the details of the sale and causing a sales receipt to be printed by Dave's POS terminal. Dave then taped the receipt to the boxed toaster and handed it to Marsha. "Thank you, have a nice day," he said.

Meanwhile Jennifer Baker, the store buyer, was using her video display terminal to find out which types of small appliances were the most popular with the store's customers. "DISPLAY ALL SALES OF APPLIANCES FOR TYPE = SMALL AND YEAR = 1985" she typed, using the keyboard of her terminal. Instantly, the information was displayed on her video screen. The computer had translated and acted on her request by following the instructions in a *database management* program which extracted sales data from the company's computerized files.

While this was going on, Joan Alvarez, the store manager, was talking to the Jim Klugman, vice president for information systems of the company. "I need more information about sales than I am getting from these reports that the computer keeps printing," she was saying. "When will the systems analyst and programmer be done with the new sales analysis program and procedures they're developing? It's taking me too long to interpret our sales analysis reports." Jim Klugman responded: "We will be done soon. We lost some time yesterday when one of our computer operators erased the wrong magnetic disk. Luckily, our backup and recovery procedures and our operating system control program got us running again quickly." Joan replied, "I hope the new sales analysis system is operational by the end of this month. If not, I'm going to have to consider buying an electronic spreadsheet program for my personal computer and try to get the information I want from our sales data that way."

- Identify the basic system components (the input, processing, output, storage, and control *functions*) of the information processing system for ABC Department Stores.
- Can you identify the hardware, software, people, and data *resources*, and the information *products* of this information processing system? Try it. Then read the next two sections of this chapter.

FIGURE 2–4 The information processing system model: Resources, functions, and products

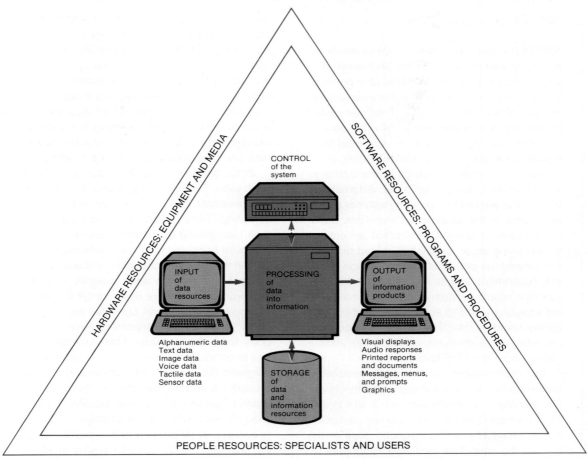

whether we use manual methods or electronic computers for information processing. Let's briefly review how the concepts we introduced in Chapter One apply to all types of information processing.

■ Hardware Resources.   We should include in our concept of hardware resources *all physical devices and materials* used in information processing. Specifically, this should include not only **equipment**, such as computers or calculators, but also all data **media**— that is, *all tangible objects on which data is recorded*, whether a sheet of paper or a magnetic disk.

■ Software Resources.   We should have a concept of software resources that includes *all sets of information processing instructions*. Specifically, this includes not only the sets of computer instructions called **programs** but also the sets of information processing instructions needed by people, called **procedures**.

■ People Resources.   As we said in Chapter One, the people resources needed for information processing include both the **specialists** who develop and operate information processing systems and the **users** who use an information processing system or the information it produces. The job activities of computer specialists (systems analysts, programmers, computer operators, etc.) are discussed in the *Careers in Information Services* section of Chapter Nineteen. Five basic categories of computer users are shown and explained in Figure 2–5.

FIGURE   2–5 Five categories of computer users

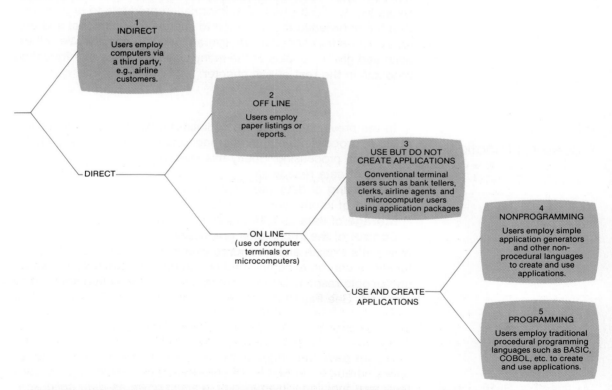

Source: Adapted from James Martin, *Application Development without Programmers,* p. 103. © 1982. Reprinted with permission of Prentice-Hall Inc., Englewood Cliffs, N.J.

■ Data Resources. In the opening pages of this chapter, we defined and gave examples of the concept of data. Data is a very important resource to individuals and organizations. Figure 2–4 lists six major types of data: (1) traditional alphanumeric data composed of numbers and alphabetical and special characters; (2) text data consisting of sentences and paragraphs used in written communications; (3) image data, such as graphic shapes and figures; (4) voice data—the human voice; (5) tactile data—generated by touch-sensitive materials; and (6) sensor data provided by a variety of sensors used in the control of physical processes in manufacturing, military systems, space travel, etc.

Information Products

The production of **information products** for users is the only reason for the existence of all information processing resources and functions. Information is provided to users in a variety of forms. Such information products include *video displays, audio responses, messages, prompts, menus, forms, documents, reports, and listings*. Users like you and I use such information products to provide us with the knowledge that we need to improve our personal and professional performances as we live and work in society. We will explain and give examples of the many types and uses of information products in the rest of this chapter.

Information Processing Functions

In the previous section, we outlined the basic system functions of input, processing, output, storage, and control as they apply to information processing. Briefly this involves:

Input of data resources.
Processing of data into information.
Output of information products.
Storage of data and information resources.
Control of the information processing system.

Now, let's explain and give more examples of how these system functions can be accomplished by the use of hardware, software, and people resources to transform data resources into information products. See Figure 2–6.

Input

Before data can be processed into information, it first must be collected and entered into the information processing system by the **input** function. This function is also known as *data collection*, *data capture*, or *data entry*.

FIGURE 2–6 Information processing system functions and activities

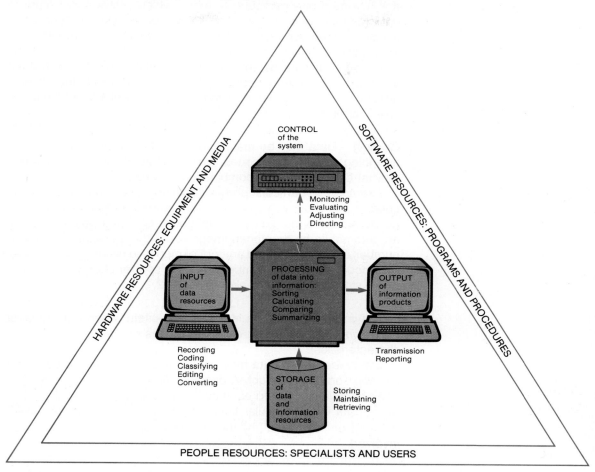

Recording. Data must be recorded while events, transactions, and other phenomena occur and are observed. The recorded observations may take the form of a measurement, or take some other numerical or verbal description of the observed activity. The data may then be recorded in tangible form on various types of **data media**, which are the tangible objects or devices where data is recorded. For example, data may be recorded on paper **source documents**, which are the original written records of an activity, such as purchase orders, checks, or sales invoices. Other more machine-usable types of data media may be used, such as magnetic disks or punched cards. However, it should be noted that data may be captured without the use of data media by such devices as the keyboard of a computer terminal, which allows direct entry of data (as electronic impulses) into a computer system. Touch-sensitive video screens and voice input are other direct input methods.

Example: A salesperson records the type of product and the amount of a sale on a written sales invoice or enters this data directly into the computer system by using an electronic "point-of-sale" terminal.

Coding.   Data may be made more suitable for processing by assigning identification codes, which consist of numbers, letters, special characters, or a combination of these.

Examples: A particular person could be represented by a *numeric* code, a social security number, such as 578-34-8473; his or her academic performance by an alphabetic code, the letter grade A; an automobile by an alphanumeric code, the automobile license number *CJD-682;* and the amount of money in his or her possession by a code using both numbers and the special characters of the dollar sign and the decimal point—$1.42.

Classifying.   Coding data is particularly useful when data requires *classifying* (i.e., arranging data into groups or classes with like characteristics).

Examples: Sales data may be classified according to customer, salesperson, and product. A business firm could assign numerical or alphabetical codes to each customer, salesperson, and product. Sales data for a particular time period could then be more easily grouped or "classified" by the customer, salesperson, or product involved.

Editing.   The editing activity consists of checking the data for completeness and correctness. The objective of editing is to ensure that the collection and conversion of data is done correctly.

Example: Visually *verifying* that the codes and amounts on a sales invoice are correct.

Converting.   The final activity of the input function may be the conversion of the data from one data medium to another.

Example: The data may be transformed from written notations on a sales invoice into holes in a punched card, then transformed into magnetic spots on magnetic tape, and then transformed again into electronic impulses in the circuitry of a computer.

Processing

After data is collected and converted, it is then ready for the **processing** function, in which data is processed into information.

Sorting. First of all, data may be "put in order" in the *sorting* activity. This may involve arranging the data in a predetermined sequence or order, and grouping the data into several classifications. Sorting may also involve *merging* data, from several classifications into a larger classification, or involve *extraction*, where a particular group of data is selected from a larger data classification.
   Examples: Sales data could first be segregated by product classification; within each product classification, sales data could be grouped by customer; the customer groupings of sales data could then be sorted into an alphabetical order.

Calculating. The processing activity of calculating refers to the *manipulation* of data by mathematical processes and the creation of new data.
   Example: Multiplying the dollar amount of a sale by a discount percentage would produce a sales discount amount.

Comparing. The comparing activity performs comparisons on data to discover meaningful facts and relationships.
   Example: Sales data may be analyzed to discover whether any of the sales made during a period exceed a certain dollar amount and, thus, qualify for a volume discount, or whether any salesperson has failed to make the required minimum amount of sales during a period.

Summarizing. The summarizing activity condenses data by counting or accumulating totals of the data in a classification or by selecting strategic data from the mass of data being processed.
   Example: The summarizing activity may be designed to provide a general manager with the sales totals by major product line; the sales manager with sales totals by individual salesperson, as well as by product line; and a salesperson, with sales data by customer, as well as by product line.

Control

All information processing systems require a **control** component. This component includes the **feedback** concept, which provides information on how the system is operating. The control function consists of the following activities:

Monitoring.   This consists of developing and receiving feedback from the system describing its input, processing, output, and storage activities.

Example: Feedback methods could be so built into a sales analysis program that the computer could check automatically to see if it is correctly accumulating all sales transactions.

Evaluating.   Analyzing feedback to determine if the system is operating according to established procedures and producing the proper output.

Example: Control procedures could be so instituted that sales employees would do spot checks to determine if sales are being correctly charged to the proper customer accounts.

Adjusting.   Making necessary adjustments to input, processing, and storage activities so proper information output is produced.

Example: Procedures for manual input of sales transactions could be used whenever it was determined that there was a malfunction in the automated capture of sales data by computer devices.

Directing.   Directing the information processing activities of the system according to specific instructions and procedures.

Example: The processing of sales data may be directed by a series of manual **procedures** or by a **program** of computer instructions for processing sales transactions.

Storage

The **storage** function is a major component of an information processing system. Stored data and information can be considered as an important foundation or base **(database)**, which supports every information processing system. The storage function includes the concept of storing data and information in an organized manner to facilitate its use in information processing. See Figure 2–7.

Storing.   Data and information collected and produced by the information processing system are frequently stored for further use. Data and information can be stored temporarily between processing cycles or for longer periods and be retrieved as needed by the users of the system.

Example: Sales transaction data captured by the system is stored in a sales transaction *file* for later processing.

Maintaining.   The quality of the data and information stored in the system must be maintained by a continual process of adding, deleting, correcting, and updating activities.

Example: The sales *records* of a business are updated to reflect the latest sales made by the firm.

Retrieving. The retrieving activity involves the recovery of stored data and information for subsequent processing or output.
Example: Retrieving a copy of a sales invoice from a filing cabinet, or retrieving customer records from a magnetic disk unit prior to processing or displaying the records.

Output

The final information processing function is **output.** It involves the transfer of data and information produced by the system to the prospective users of such information or to another information processing system.

FIGURE 2–7 The common data elements

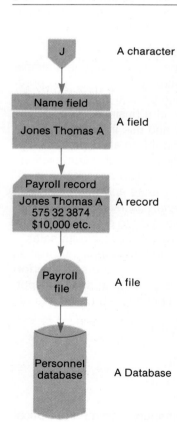

J — A character

Name field
Jones Thomas A — A field

Payroll record
Jones Thomas A
575 32 3874
$10,000 etc. — A record

Payroll file — A file

Personnel database — A Database

Data and information must be organized in some systematic way for proper information processing, whether manual or computerized methods are used. We will discuss the topic of *data organization* in detail in Chapter Eleven, but you need to be introduced to some basic concepts now. Just as written text material is typically organized into letters, words, sentences, and paragraphs, data is commonly organized in the following *hierarchy* of **common data elements** in modern information processing systems:

- A **character** consists of a single alphabetic, numeric, or other symbol. Examples are the letters of the alphabet, numbers, and special symbols, such as dollar signs and decimal points.
- A **field** is a grouping of characters that represent a characteristic of a person, place, thing, or event. That is, your *name field* would consist of the alphabetic characters of your name, while your social security number, annual salary, and home address *fields* would each consist of a combination of numbers, letters, and special characters.
- A **record** is a collection of interrelated fields. For example, an employee's *payroll record* might consist of a name field, a social security number field, a department field, and a salary field.
- A **file** is a collection of interrelated records. For example, a *payroll file* might consist of the payroll *records* of all employees of a firm.
- A **database** is a collection of interrelated files and records. For example, the *personnel database* of a business might contain payroll, personnel action, and employee skills files.

Transmission. The transmission activity involves the movement of data or information from one location to another so it may be conveyed to its ultimate user or be introduced as input into another information processing system.

Example: Information is frequently transmitted by telephone circuits between computers and computer terminals installed at distant locations.

Reporting. The reporting activity involves furnishing information produced by the information processing system to the ultimate users of this information.

Examples: Information may be reported in the form of *printed* documents, such as invoices, statements, and printed reports of all kinds. Information can also be reported in *graphic* form on charts, maps, and pictures. The reporting activity can also be accomplished by displaying information in *visual* form on *video display terminals* or in *audible* form by word of mouth or by computer *audio responses* units.

ANALYSIS OF AN INFORMATION PROCESSING SYSTEM

Real World Application 2–1: ABC Department Stores is a simple business example that shows how resources, functions, and products are used in an information processing system in the real world. It illustrates these components in action in a business firm (ABC Department Stores) that needs to know and use information about one of its important activities (sales). The information processing jobs that need to be done are frequently called sales transaction processing and sales analysis. *Sales transaction processing* involves collecting, processing, and storing facts and figures about each sale made by the company. *Sales analysis* involves the manipulation and organization of such data resources to produce a variety of reports to the managers of the company concerning its sales activity. Managers use the knowledge gained from such information products to help them make decisions to improve the sales performance of the company. Figure 2–8 and the following analysis spotlight many examples of the resources, functions, and products of the information processing system described in Real World Application 2–1. How many of them did you identify?

Information Processing Resources at ABC Department Stores

- **Hardware Resources.**
  Equipment: Point of sale (POS) terminals. Computers. Optical scanning wand. Magnetic disk drives. Video display terminals. Printers.

FIGURE 2–8 Analysis of the sales information processing system at ABC Department Stores

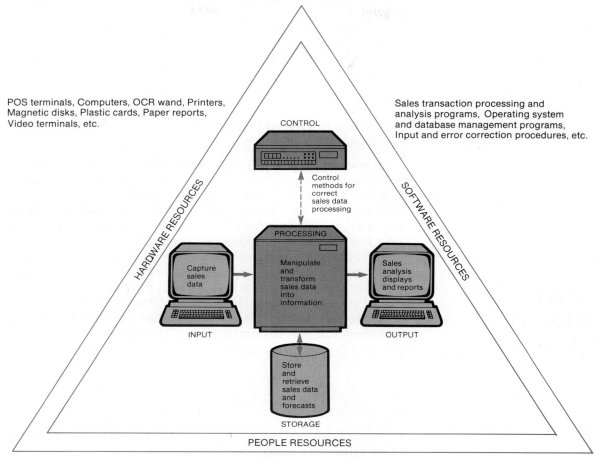

POS terminals, Computers, OCR wand, Printers, Magnetic disks, Plastic cards, Paper reports, Video terminals, etc.

Sales transaction processing and analysis programs, Operating system and database management programs, Input and error correction procedures, etc.

Computer operator, Systems analyst, Programmer, Customer, Salesperson, Buyer, Store manager, etc.

Media: Magnetic disks. Paper merchandise tags. Plastic credit card with magnetic stripe. Paper sales receipts. Paper reports.

■ **Software Resources.**

Programs: Sales transaction processing program. Sales analysis program. Operating system control program. Database management program.

Procedures: POS terminal input procedures. Error correction procedures. Credit authorization procedures. Computer backup and recovery procedures. Sales analysis interpretation procedures.

- **People Resources.**
  Specialists: Computer operators. Systems analysts. Programmers. VP for Information Services.
  Users: Customers. Salesclerks. Buyers. Store manager.
- **Data Resources.**
  Customer data. Product data. Salesperson data. Department data. Store data. Company data.

Information Processing Products at ABC
Department Stores

Information products produced by the ABC Department Stores information processing system include video displays and paper reports for managers and buyers. Video displays include menus and prompts to help managers and buyers obtain the information they want, as well as several that display report formats. Both displays and reports can provide a variety of sales analysis information. For example, information can be presented by customer, product, salesperson, department, or store categories. Or information about sales can be obtained on a daily, weekly, monthly, or yearly basis and be compared to both historical and forecasted sales. Salesclerks are provided audible signals and video displays of input control information, and customers are provided with information in the form of a printed sales receipt.

Information Processing Functions at ABC
Department Stores

- **Input.** Data describing individual sales transactions is collected by salesclerks using POS terminals, and other devices and entered into the information processing system according to established procedures.
- **Processing.** The sales data is manipulated and organized by a computer according to instructions contained in sales transaction processing and analysis programs and in other programs. The company's customer and sales data in storage is updated, and information products are prepared for output.
- **Output.** Sales analysis displays and reports are produced for managers and buyers. These information products reveal important trends in sales activity, organized according to such categories as customer, product, salesperson, and department. Audible signals and visual displays of data entry are provided to salesclerks. Sales receipts are produced for customers.

- **Storage.** Sales data is stored in a variety of formats (by customer, product, salesperson, department, and so on) on magnetic disk units. This data, along with historical sales data and sales forecasts, are updated and retrieved by the processing function.

- **Control.** Various methods are used to control this information processing system so it correctly performs its sales transaction processing and sales analysis tasks. For example, the computer hardware contains circuitry that can detect errors during processing, the computer programs contain instructions that can detect errors during input and storage activities, and procedures have been developed to help the salesclerks detect and correct errors during data input.

MANUAL VERSUS ELECTRONIC INFORMATION PROCESSING

There are many kinds of information processing systems. They range from a solitary human data processing system to large sophisticated systems using electronic computers. Materials as simple as a paper and pencil or equipment as advanced as the latest electronic computers can be used to process data into information. However, most information processing can be placed into two major categories: *manual* and *electronic*. Figure 2–9 contrasts methods and devices that may be used to perform basic system functions in manual and electronic systems.

FIGURE 2–9 Manual versus electronic information processing: Selected methods and devices

	Input	Processing	Output	Storage	Control
Manual information processing	Human observation Written records Typewriter Cash register Calculator keyboard	Human brain Written calculations and analysis Calculators	Human voice Written reports Telephone Typewritten documents Calculator display	Human brain Written records Filing cabinets Microfilm Duplicating machines	Human brain Written procedures Calculator control circuitry
Electronic information processing	Data entry terminals Punched cards Magnetic diskettes Optical character readers	Computer processing units	Visual display, audio response, and printing terminals High-speed printers	Semiconductor storage circuitry Magnetic disks and tape	Computer control unit Computer programs

Manual information processing involves human use of such simple tools as paper, pencils, and filing cabinets to process raw data into information. Manual processing may also use mechanical, electrical, and electronic devices—such as electric typewriters and electronic calculators—as data processing tools. Use of such devices requires a combination of manual procedures and electromechanical equipment to carry out the basic functions of information processing. Data and instructions must be manually entered through a keyboard (such as a calculator or typewriter keyboard), and human intervention during the data processing cycle is required. Therefore, all nonautomatic processing, even if it includes **machine-assisted manual** methods, can be classified as manual information processing.

Figure 2–10 illustrates the components of a manual information processing system. Data is received as **input** by telephone or mail. An electronic calculator is used for **processing** by a clerk who **controls** the process according to written operating instructions. Data and information **storage** are provided by a filing cabinet. Typewritten reports are the **output** of this manual system.

Electronic information processing (also widely known as **electronic data processing,** or EDP) is the use of electronic computers

FIGURE

2–10 A manual information processing system

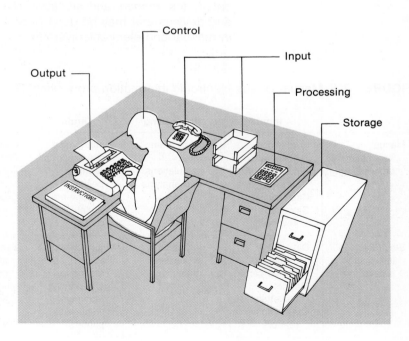

to process data automatically. Human intervention in the processing cycle is not necessary, since an electronic computer can automatically execute a stored program of processing instructions. The term *automatic data processing* (ADP) is sometimes used (especially by government agencies) because of the automation of data processing functions and activities caused by electronic computers. The term **computer application** is also used to describe such use of a computer to solve a specific problem or accomplish a data processing job for a computer user.

Benefits and Limitations

Manual information processing systems are beneficial to individuals or organizations if their information requirements are simple and if the amount of data to be processed is limited. In manual processing, transactions can be recorded easily in a human-readable form, and changes and corrections to such systems can easily be made. Manual processing is also quite inexpensive at low volumes. As information requirements become more complex and the volume of data increases, the limitations of manual information processing begin to exceed its benefits. Then automated processing systems become more efficient and economical. The major limitations of manual information processing include its inability to handle large volumes of work and its reliance on many cumbersome and tedious methods. It is also more susceptible to error and is slower than other information processing methods because it requires human effort in most processing activities. Therefore, electronic information processing systems are typically used by all organizations with complex or high-volume data processing requirements.

Why Use Computers for Information Processing?

Today's business firms are faced with information requirements of increased complexity and ever-increasing volumes of data to be processed. This is why so many firms, both large and small, have turned to the use of computers for information processing. What has caused this growth in complexity and volume of processing requirements? Three reasons stand out.

- Most business firms are faced with growth in the size, complexity, and scope of their operations. They are providing more products and services to more customers at more locations with more employees. Thus their need for information has increased.

REAL WORLD APPLICATION 2–2

Treasury Department—Commonwealth of Pennsylvania

The Treasury Department of Pennsylvania has a complete appropriation control and financial reporting system called TABS (Treasury Automated Bookkeeping System). It processes all daily Commonwealth revenues and general disbursements.

The Treasury uses a computer with over 20 terminals and a full range of peripherals. Treasury computer operations have progressed from the mere automation of check writing to the initial phases of a comprehensive database-oriented information processing facility supporting critical management systems. Information retrieval impossible before TABS is now an everyday occurrence.

Check production capability has increased from a maximum daily capacity of 20,000 to 30,000 checks to over 150,000 checks. In addition, normal processing time for vendors' bills was reduced from eight days to three days. This is from the time of submission of a bill to the issuance of a check.

TABS replaced an antiquated manual ledger-card operation and increased processing capability by approximately 75 percent. At the same time, financial controls were strengthened over the processed transactions and the results of operations.

■ Identify the benefits of the computerized information processing system described above compared to the manual system it replaced.

Source: "Automated Bookkeeping System Saves State Treasury Time and Money," *Infosystems*, December 1980, p. 72. Copyright 1980, Hitchcock Publishing Co. Reprinted with permission.

■ Business firms must respond to increased requirements for information from local, state, and federal governmental agencies. Such demands have become a major political issue as well as a major information processing problem.

■ Managers and other users of information in the organization are demanding more kinds of information to support the management and operations of the business firm. The information demanded must be accurate, timely, and "tailored" to the needs of the manager or user.

Thus, for many firms, using computers for information processing is an absolute necessity. *For example,* banks, stock exchanges, and airlines would not be able to process the millions of checks, stock trades, and travel requests made each day. Thousands of business firms in many other industries could not operate without the basic information concerning their customers, suppliers, inventories, and finances provided by their computerized information processing systems. Why can computers meet the present and future information processing requirements of such business firms? The answer lies in four basic advantages of computerized systems compared to manual processing methods.

Speed

We have previously mentioned the impressive speed of computers that are capable of executing millions of instructions per second. Thus, it takes a computer only seconds to perform millions of data processing functions that human beings would take years to complete. This processing speed of the computer allows electronic information processing systems to provide information in a **timely** manner to the managers and other users of information within a business firm. This is a major benefit of such systems. If a computerized information processing system is not providing timely information, corrective measures must be taken by management to ensure that the speed capability of the computer is properly used.

Accuracy

Computers can accurately process large volumes of data according to complex and repetitive processing procedures. This contrasts with manual processing systems, where the constant repetition of the same processing tasks by human beings becomes a cumbersome and tedious chore, one extremely susceptible to errors. This is not to say that computers always produce accurate information. However, computer errors are minimal compared to the volume of data being processed and are frequently the result of human error. For example, errors in management reports or customer statements are usually the result of incorrect data input supplied by humans, or errors in a computer program developed by a human programmer. Thus the term *garbage in, garbage out* (GIGO) is used by computer professionals to emphasize that incorrect input data or programs will result in incorrect output from the computer. It also emphasizes the importance of **control** procedures to ensure accuracy of such systems.

Reliability

The accuracy of electronic information processing is directly related to the exceptional reliability of computers and their electronic circuitry. Modern computers consistently and accurately operate for long time periods without failure. Their electronic circuitry is inherently reliable and includes self-checking features that ensure accuracy and automatically diagnose failure conditions. Such built-in "diagnostics" and regular preventive maintenance checks help ensure consistent reliability. Computers do "go down" or "crash" (stop working), but such *downtime* is only a fraction of a percent of the operating time of most systems.

Economy

The speed, accuracy, and reliability of computers would be available to only a few large organizations if it were not for the very real economy of computer usage. Except for very simple and low-volume tasks, electronic information processing is more economically justifiable than manual data processing for most firms. This cost advantage continues to increase as new developments in computer technology continue to drive down the historical cost of computer processing. (See Figure 2–11.) Of course, as in other areas of business activity, the cost of information processing for a business firm can go out of control unless proper procedures are developed by management to control such costs.

FIGURE

2–11 Decline in cost of computer processing

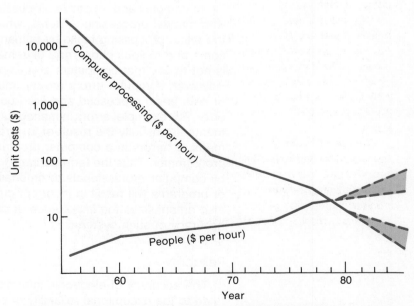

Source: Adapted from James Martin, *Application Development without Programmers*, p. 3. © 1982. Reprinted with permission of Prentice-Hall Inc., Englewood Cliffs, N.J.

REAL WORLD APPLICATION 2-3

Cabarrus Urology Clinic

The morning rush is on at the Cabarrus Urology Clinic in Concord, North Carolina. Patients line the waiting room while nurses scurry about with charts and syringes and little vials. One doctor is busy with X rays, another with a consultation, a third is in surgery. The only person who doesn't have anything to do for the moment is the general secretary and computer operator.

Sherry Aldridge sits at her desk with a cup of coffee. Behind her, the clinic's IBM microcomputer is hard at work, keeping up with the enormous amount of paperwork generated by this busy three-doctor clinic. And while Ms. Aldridge isn't complaining about the time she now has available for other, routine tasks, she is still somewhat amazed at the difference the microcomputer has made at the clinic.

"We billed almost $100,000 in insurance claims in just two days last month," she says. "It used to take one person—me—three or four weeks to file that many claims manually."

Going online with insurance claims has not only eased the load on the bookkeeper but also has improved both cash flow and patient services.

"We use the computer's magnetic diskettes to store all the information on insurance claims," Ms. Aldridge explains, "and we also use its printer to print statements for both the insurance companies and our patients. The computer includes the correct procedure code for each item on a statement, which means we no longer get a lot of phone calls from the insurance companies asking us to explain the charges on a claim. Our turnaround time on insurance claims has gone from 90 days in some cases to about 30. The insurance companies are even paying more on some claims because the information is more specific.

"At the end of the month the computer prints a total register of all charges, all payments received, and all insurance claims filed. The computer has even stopped us from having to pull patient charts when people call up to see if their insurance has been filed. We used to spend several hours a day on this—now we know at a glance. We just key in the patient's account code and the information is displayed instantly on the video screen."

- What are some of the information processing system resources, products, and functions that you can identify in the example above?
- How does this example demonstrate the speed, accuracy, reliability, and economy of using computers for information processing versus manual processing?

Source: Adapted from "Results for Aircraft Consultant, Medical Clinic," *Viewpoint Magazine*, January–February 1979, p. 14. © 1979. Used with permission.

66

SUMMARY

- A system is a group of interrelated components that seeks the attainment of a common goal by accepting inputs and producing outputs in an organized transformation process. Feedback is information concerning the components and operations of a system. Control is the component that monitors and evaluates feedback to determine whether the system is moving toward the achievement of its goal, and then makes necessary adjustments to the input and processing components to ensure that proper output is produced.

- An information processing system (or data processing system) accepts raw data resources as input and processes it into finished information products as output. All information processing systems perform common system functions and activities using hardware, software, and people as resources. Data is first collected and converted to a form that is suitable for processing (input). Then the data is manipulated or converted into information (processing), stored for future use (storage), or communicated to its ultimate user (output) according to correct processing procedures (control).

- The concept of hardware resources includes both equipment and media used in information processing. Software resources include both computerized instructions (programs) and instructions for people (procedures). People resources include both information processing specialists and users. Data resources include both traditional numeric and alphabetic data, and text, image, and voice data. Information products produced by an information processing system can take a variety of forms, including paper reports, visual displays, documents, messages, menus, graphics, and audio responses.

- The two major types of information processing are manual and electronic processing. Manual information processing systems are simple and inexpensive if an organization's information requirements are simple and if the amount of data to be processed is limited. As information requirements become more complex and the volume of data increases, the speed, accuracy, reliability, and economy of using computers for information processing becomes a necessity.

KEY TERMS AND CONCEPTS

Data
Information
Data processing
Information processing
System
Information processing system
Information processing
  functions:
  Input
  Processing
  Output
  Storage
  Control

Information processing
  resources:
  Hardware
  Software
  People
  Data
Information products
Procedures
Data media
Source documents
Manual and electronic
  information processing
Benefits of computer use

REVIEW AND APPLICATION QUESTIONS

1. Why are you an information processing system? Explain.
2. What is the difference between data and information? Use an example to illustrate this difference.
3. What is data or information processing? How is it similar to a manufacturing process?
4. What is a system? What are its basic components? Give examples to illustrate your answer.
5. What are the basic resources, products, and functions of an information processing system? What role does each component play in the operation of the system? Use an information processing system from your experience to illustrate your answer.
6. What are the two major types of information processing systems? Which type do you use most frequently?
7. Does all information processing require the performance of the basic system functions and activities described in the chapter? Explain.
8. Use an example to illustrate the processing of data by each of the five basic functions of information processing for both manual and electronic processing systems.
9. Explain the relationship between feedback and control. Are they both necessary? Why or why not?
10. What are several benefits and limitations of manual information processing?
11. How do the four basic advantages of using computers for information processing help managers of business firms cope with

the increased volume and complexity of information processing requirements? Use examples to illustrate your answer.

APPLICATION PROBLEMS

1. If you have not already done so, read and answer the questions after each Real World Application in this chapter.
2. Have you read and done one of the assignments of the Getting Started with Software Packages section of the appendix at the end of this text? Its purpose it to give you a "hands-on" experience with using a computer to solve a simple problem in personal finance, business, or statistics. Now you should apply the *information processing system concept* explained in this chapter to your experience. What are the hardware, software, people, and data resources you used? Identify the input, processing, output, storage, and control functions involved. What information products did you produce?
3. Each statement below gives an example of information processing resources, products, functions, or activities. Identify them.
   a. A fire occurs in the data center, and all data stored on magnetic tapes or disks in the data center are lost. However, copies of these files have been stored in the vault at a local bank.
   b. Sales reports are not only printed on paper but are also written on magnetic tape.
   c. In the general ledger accounting system, each account (i.e., payroll expense) is given a number.
   d. The sales order processing system will not allow anyone to enter an order unless the quantity is present.
   e. A special report is printed listing customers in order of greatest sales volume to least sales volume.
4. In Real World Application 2–3 Cabarrus Urology Clinic, you were asked to identify the five basic information processing system functions. Now try to give an example of each activity (i.e., recording) within each function (i.e., input). Since not all the details of the system are given, you must think about how the system might work.
5. Each major function of an information processing system (input, processing, output, storage, and control) appears in the flowchart of a computerized payroll system shown in Figure 2–12. Each letter represents a different function. Match the letter with the function.
   1. Input.
   2. Processing.

3. Output.
4. Storage.
5. Control (procedure).
6. Control (feedback).
6. The Holiday Cheer Company, a manufacturer of Christmas orna-
   ments and artificial Christmas trees, has been having problems
   with sales order processing. Currently the system is totally manual. The company has a competitive edge in the marketplace
   because of its outstanding designs and efficiency in production.
   The growth in sales has been 20 percent per year. The problems
   in sales order processing stem from a high volume of sales transactions and a lack of time to respond. Customers order 70 percent
   of their merchandise in the spring. Once they see what is selling
   during the fall, they order the remaining 30 percent of their merchandise. Most problems occur in processing these fall orders.
   Several days are required to process an order through the accounting department. Also the inventory records often indicate
   sufficient stock is on hand to fill an order when it really isn't.
   Once production receives an order it can take up to 10 days
   to fill. Should this company convert from manual processing to
   electronic information processing? Justify your answer.

FIGURE 2–12 Payroll information processing system

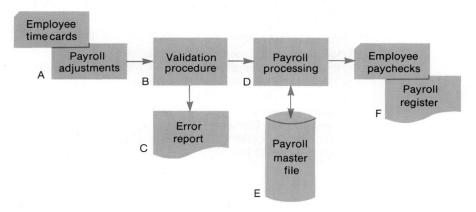

CHAPTER 3

Introduction to Computers

CHAPTER OUTLINE

THE COMPUTER AS A SYSTEM
 Input
 Processing
 Arithmetic-Logic
 Storage
 Control
 Output
HOW COMPUTERS WORK
 CPU Components
 Computer Instructions
 How Computers Execute Instructions
 How Fast Are Computers?
HOW COMPUTERS REPRESENT DATA
 Computer Number Systems
 Computer Codes
 Computer Data Elements
OVERVIEW OF COMPUTER HARDWARE
OVERVIEW OF COMPUTER SOFTWARE

LEARNING OBJECTIVES

The purpose of this chapter is to promote a basic understanding of modern computers by analyzing (1) the components and functions of a computer system, (2) how a computer works, (3) how a computer represents data, and (4) basic types of hardware and software. After reading and studying this chapter, you should be able to:

1. Identify the components and functions of a computer system.
2. Describe how a computer executes an instruction.
3. Explain how a computer represents data and why it is based on the binary number system.
4. Differentiate between a bit, byte, and word.
5. Describe the basic types of computer hardware and software.

THE COMPUTER AS A SYSTEM

What is your first impression when you see a computer? Does a microcomputer look like a combination typewriter/TV set? Does a large computer seem like a strange grouping of metal cabinets and flashing lights? Such impressions are understandable, but miss a very important concept. It is absolutely vital to your effective use of computers to understand that the computer is not a solitary electronic data processing "black box," nor is it an unrelated grouping of electronic devices performing a variety of information processing activities. You should learn to understand the computer as a **system**, that is, as an interrelated grouping of components which perform the basic system functions of **input, processing, output, storage, and control**. Your understanding of the computer as a **computer system** is one of the most important basic objectives of this text. For example, you should be able to visualize any computer (from a microcomputer to a supercomputer!) as a system of hardware devices organized according to the following system functions:

■ Input. The input devices of a computer system include the keyboard of computer terminals, punched card readers, optical scanners, and so on. They convert data into electronic form for input into the computer system.

■ Processing. The *central processing unit* (CPU) is the main processing component of a computer system. In particular, the *arithmetic-logic unit*, one of the major components of a CPU, performs the arithmetic and logic functions required in computer processing.

■ Storage. The storage function of a computer system takes place in the *primary storage unit* of the CPU and in *secondary storage* devices such as magnetic disk and tape units. These devices store data and program instructions needed for computer processing.

■ Control. The *control unit* of the CPU is the control component of a computer system. It interprets computer program instructions and transmits directions to the other components of the computer system.

■ Output. The output devices of a computer system include video display units, printers, card punch units, and so on. They convert electronic information produced by the computer system into a *human-intelligible* or machine-readable form.

Figure 3–1 illustrates this concept of the functions and hardware components of a computer system. Figure 3–2 identifies some of the actual devices used in several types of computer systems. You should now be able to see that a **computer system** is the single most important **hardware resource** of the computerized **information processing systems** introduced in Chapter Two. Let's take a closer look at how each of the system functions are implemented in the hardware components of a computer system.

Input

Data and *program instructions* are entered into the computer in the *input* function. Data and instructions may be entered directly into the computer system (through the keyboard of a computer termi-

FIGURE

3–1 The computer system concept

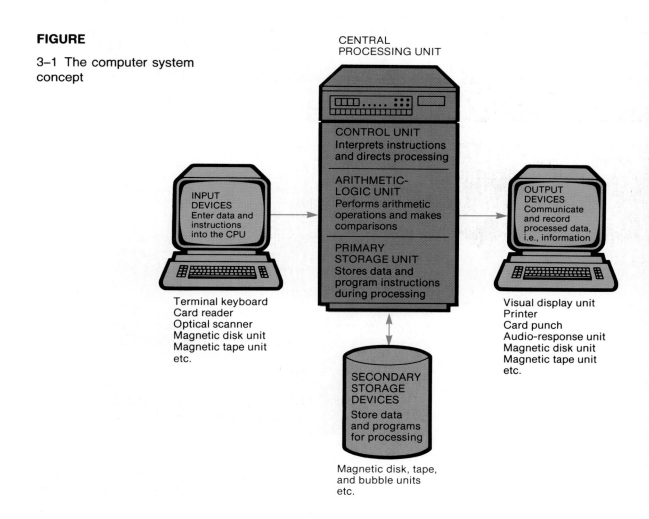

CENTRAL PROCESSING UNIT

CONTROL UNIT
Interprets instructions and directs processing

ARITHMETIC-LOGIC UNIT
Performs arithmetic operations and makes comparisons

PRIMARY STORAGE UNIT
Stores data and program instructions during processing

INPUT DEVICES
Enter data and instructions into the CPU

Terminal keyboard
Card reader
Optical scanner
Magnetic disk unit
Magnetic tape unit
etc.

OUTPUT DEVICES
Communicate and record processed data, i.e., information

Visual display unit
Printer
Card punch
Audio-response unit
Magnetic disk unit
Magnetic tape unit
etc.

SECONDARY STORAGE DEVICES
Store data and programs for processing

Magnetic disk, tape, and bubble units etc.

FIGURE

3–2 Computer systems and their input, processing, output, storage, and control devices

A A large-scale computer system.

B A microcomputer system.

A

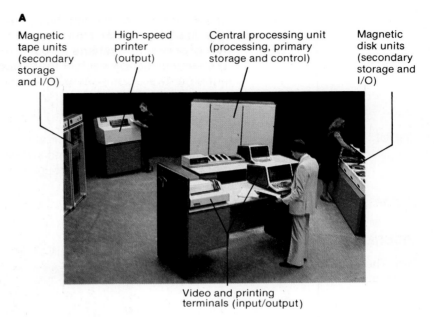

Magnetic tape units (secondary storage and I/O)

High-speed printer (output)

Central processing unit (processing, primary storage and control)

Magnetic disk units (secondary storage and I/O)

Video and printing terminals (input/output)

B

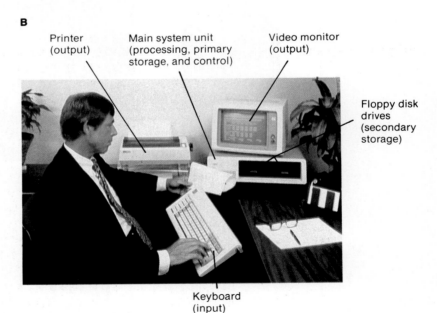

Printer (output)

Main system unit (processing, primary storage, and control)

Video monitor (output)

Floppy disk drives (secondary storage)

Keyboard (input)

nal, for example) or may first be converted into a machine-readable input medium, such as magnetic disks or tape. For example, data from source documents could be recorded on magnetic disks and then be entered into the computer system through a magnetic disk unit. Most computer systems automatically control the flow of data and instructions into the computer from many types of input devices. These input devices convert program instructions and data into electrical impulses that are then routed to the primary storage unit where they are held until needed.

Processing

The processing function of a computer system is performed by the **central processing unit**, the most important hardware component of any computer system. This unit is also known as the CPU, the *central processor*, or the *mainframe* in large computers, and as the **microprocessor** or MPU in a microcomputer. This is the unit that accomplishes the processing of data and controls the other parts of the system. The CPU consists of three subunits known as the *arithmetic-logic unit*, the *control unit*, and the *primary storage unit*. Let's take a brief look at how they perform their system functions.

Arithmetic-Logic

Arithmetic and comparison operations occur in the **arithmetic-logic unit** (or ALU). Depending on the application being processed, data may be transferred from storage to the arithmetic-logic unit and then returned to storage several times before processing is completed. The arithmetic-logic unit also performs such operations as shifting and moving data. Through its ability to make comparisons, it can test for various conditions during processing and then perform appropriate operations.

The arithmetic-logic unit allows a computer to perform the arithmetic operations of addition, subtraction, multiplication, and division, and identify whether a number is positive, negative, or equal to zero. It can thus compare two numbers to determine which is higher than, equal to, or lower than the other. This ability of the computer to make comparisons gives it a **logic** capability, for it can make logical changes from one set of operating instructions to another based on the results of comparisons made during processing. This ability of a computer to change the sequence of its use of instructions in a program is called *program modification*. For example, in a payroll program the computer can test if the hours worked by employees exceed 40 hours per week. Payments for such "overtime" would be computed using a different sequence of instructions than that used for employees without such overtime. We will explain this process in more detail in the next section.

Storage

The computer can store both data and instructions internally in its "memory." This internal storage enables the computer to "remember" the details of many assignments and to proceed from one assignment to another automatically, since it can retain data and instructions until needed. The ability of the computer to store its operating instructions internally (the *computer program*) allows the computer to process data *automatically*, that is, without continual human intervention. This *stored program* concept is a major capability of computers that allows them to easily do a variety of tasks automatically.

The storage function takes place in the *primary storage unit* of the CPU and in *secondary storage* devices. All data and programs must be placed in the **primary storage unit** (also called "main memory" or "main storage") before they can be used in processing. The primary storage unit is also used to hold data and program instructions between processing steps, and after processing is completed, but before release as output. In modern computers, the primary storage unit consists of microelectronic semiconductor storage circuitry in the form of integrated circuit memory "chips." This storage technology is explained in Chapter Five.

Primary storage is subdivided into many small sections called *storage positions* or *storage locations*. Primary storage is frequently compared to a group of mailboxes, where each mailbox has an address and is capable of storing one item of data. Similarly, each position of storage has a specific numerical location called an *address* so that data stored in its contents can be readily located by the computer. In most modern computers, each position of storage can usually hold one alphabetic or special character or two numeric digits.

Data and programs can also be stored in **secondary storage** devices, such as magnetic disk and tape units, and thus greatly enlarge the storage capacity of the computer system. However, the contents of such secondary storage devices cannot be processed without first being brought into the primary storage unit. Thus, external secondary storage devices play a supporting role to the primary storage unit of a computer system. Typically, programs and files of data are stored until needed on "floppy" magnetic diskettes in microcomputer systems and large magnetic tape and disk units on larger computer systems.

It should be emphasized that magnetic disk and tape devices perform both an *input/output* function and a *secondary storage* function. For example, data can be recorded on a magnetic diskette and entered into a computer system (input), then stored on magnetic disk units until needed (secondary storage). After processing, information can be recorded by the computer on magnetic disks (output).

Control

Every other component of the computer system is controlled and directed by the **control unit**. The control unit obtains instructions from the primary storage unit. After interpreting the instructions, the control unit transmits directions to the appropriate components of the computer system, ordering them to perform the required data processing operations. The control unit tells the input and secondary storage devices what data and instructions to read into memory, tells the arithmetic-logic unit where the data to be processed is located in memory, what operations to perform, where in memory the results are to be stored; and, finally, it directs the appropriate output devices to convert processed data into machine or human-readable output media.

Output

The function of *output* devices is to convert processed data (information) from electronic impulses into a form that is intelligible to human beings or into a machine-readable form. For example, output devices such as high-speed printers produce printed reports; card-punch units produce punched cards; video terminals produce visual displays; and *audio response* units produce audible sounds and speech as output. Most computers can automatically control several types of output devices.

HOW COMPUTERS WORK

Every computer user should have a basic understanding of how a computer executes instructions to carry out an information processing assignment. Such an understanding helps you to appreciate why a CPU or microprocessor consists of the special-purpose circuitry and devices described in this chapter. It should also help you to appreciate modern *high-level programming languages* that have simplified the task of developing computer programs. It is no longer necessary to write computer instructions that use complex *machine language* coding, which tells the computer in detail each step it must take to carry out (execute) an information processing task.

CPU Components

The internal "architecture" of a CPU or microprocessor can be quite complex. A detailed knowledge of the circuitry and scientific

REAL WORLD APPLICATION 3-1

The *Atlantic City Press*

Like many other newspapers, the *Atlantic City Press,* of Atlantic City, New Jersey, relies on computers. Dual computer systems support many editing terminals for local editors and re-porters, plus portable terminals and microcom-puters by which remote news correspondents can transmit news stories to the newspaper's main office.

When a story breaks, reporters gather the facts and enter their reports through individual keyboard terminals. Rewrite personnel go to work on the basic story via their own terminals. Last-minute details and additional facts are molded into the story, and it begins to take its final form. Copy entered by the rewrite desk is recorded electronically and filed for retrieval on magnetic disk units. These units are located in the newspaper's computer center, along with the CPUs and other devices of both computer systems.

Each story file can then be called forth by the managing editor on a video terminal. While the managing editor reviews the story, high-speed line printers furnish printed copies for proofreading and editing; type corrections and changes can be entered through any terminal. Once this process is complete, the story file is automatically justified and hyphenated. Typeset-ting instructions are specified, and the file is sent to production for printing on computer-controlled printing presses.

- What computer system components and functions can you identify in the example above?

Source: Digital Equipment Corporation.

principles involved is beyond the scope of this book. However, you should understand the basic functions of the arithmetic-logic, control, and primary storage units of the CPU as they were described in the previous section. In addition, you should realize that a CPU or microprocessor includes several types of special-purpose circuitry, such as *registers, counters, adders, decoders*, and the like. These electronic circuitry elements serve as temporary work areas, analyze instructions, or perform required arithmetic and logical operations. The number, function, and capacity of such circuits in a CPU depends on the internal architecture of each particular computer. Figure 3–3 summarizes some of these CPU components. We will briefly mention the functions of these components as we explain how a computer works.

Computer Instructions

The specific form of a computer instruction depends on the type of programming language and computer being used. However, a computer instruction usually consists of:

- An **operation code** which specifies what is to be done (add, compare, read, etc.).

- **Registers.** These are small high-speed storage circuitry areas used for temporary storage of an individual instruction or data element during the operation of the control and arithmetic-logic units.
- **Counters.** Devices whose contents can be automatically increased or decreased by a specific amount, thus enabling them to "count" the number of particular computer operations.
- **Adders.** Circuits that perform the arithmetic operations of the arithmetic-logic unit.
- **Decoders.** Circuits that analyze the instruction code of the computer program and start the execution of instructions.
- **Internal clock.** Circuits that emit regular pulses at frequencies ranging from several million to billions per second. The clock generates the electrical pulses that are used to energize the circuitry of the CPU and insure the exact timing necessary for its proper operation.
- **Buffer.** A high-speed temporary storage area for storing parts of a program or data during processing (also called a *cache* memory).
- **I/O interface or port.** Circuitry for the interconnection ("interface") required for access to input/output devices.
- **Bus.** A set of conducting paths (for movement of data and instructions) that interconnects the various components of a CPU or microprocessor. It may take the form of a cable containing many wires or of microscopic conducting lines on microprocessor chips.
- **Channels.** Special-purpose processors that control the movement of data between the CPU and input/output devices.

- One or more **operands**, which specify the primary storage addresses of data or instructions, and/or indicate which input/output and secondary storage devices will be used. See Figure 3–4.

How Computers Execute Instructions

The operation code and operands of the instruction being executed, as well as data elements affected by the instruction, are moved through the special-purpose circuitry of the CPU or microprocessor during the execution of an instruction. A fixed number of

Operation Codes	Operand(s)
Start I/O	Channel 1, Device 191
Read	One Record into Storage Positions 1000–1050
Add	Quantity in Storage Location 1004 into Storage Location 2000
Subtract	Quantity in Storage Location 1005 from Contents of Register 10
Branch	To Instruction in Storage Location 5004

electrical pulses emitted by the CPU's timing circuitry or *internal clock* determines the timing of each basic CPU operation. This time period is called a **machine cycle**. The number of machine cycles required to execute an instruction varies with the complexity of the instruction. During each machine cycle, electrical pulses generated by the internal clock energize special-purpose circuitry elements, which sense and interpret specific instructions and data and move them (in the form of electrical pulses) between the various specialized circuitry components of the CPU summarized in Figure 3–3. One of the most important of these are **registers**, which are small high-speed storage circuit areas used for the temporary storage of an individual instruction or data element during the operation of the control and arithmetic-logic units.

The execution of an instruction can be divided into two segments, the *instruction cycle* and the *execution cycle*. Simply stated, the **instruction cycle** consists of processes in which an instruction is *fetched* from primary storage and *interpreted* by the control unit. The **execution cycle** consists of *performing* the operations specified by the instruction that was interpreted during the instruction cycle. Figure 3–5 is a simplified illustration and explanation of what happens in a CPU during the instruction and execution cycles.

Let's look at the execution of a typical instruction by a computer. First we will state the instruction in conversational English, then in a form more like the instructions used by computers. Then we will follow the steps used by the computer to execute this instruction.

■ English Instruction:
  Add the amount of hours worked today by an employee to his or her total hours worked this week.
■ Computer Instruction:
  Add the amount stored in primary storage at address 006 to the amount contained in the *accumulator register* and store the result in primary storage location 008.

The Instruction Cycle

1. First, an instruction is *fetched* from its location in primary storage and temporarily stored in the registers of the control unit. In this example, the instruction had been stored in primary storage location 001. The operation code part of the instruction (ADD) is moved to an **instruction register**, and its operand portion (006) is moved to an **address register**.
2. Next, the instruction is *interpreted* by the circuitry of the control unit. This involves decoding the operation code and operands of the instruction. Specialized **decoder** circuits interpret the operation code and operand of the instruction.

3. Finally, the control unit prepares electronic circuitry "paths" within the CPU to carry out the required operations. For example, this may involve activating the circuits that will "read" the data stored in the memory location (006) described in the operand of the instruction.

The Execution Cycle

4. First, the data to be processed is fetched from its locations in primary storage and temporarily stored in a **storage register** of the arithmetic-logic unit. In this example, storage location 006 contained a value of 0012 (12 hours).

FIGURE

3–5 How computers execute an instruction

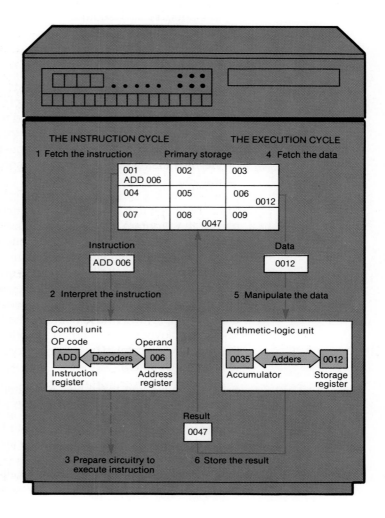

THE INSTRUCTION CYCLE		THE EXECUTION CYCLE
1 Fetch the instruction	Primary storage	4 Fetch the data

001 ADD 006	002	003
004	005	006 0012
007	008 0047	009

Instruction   Data

ADD 006   0012

2 Interpret the instruction   5 Manipulate the data

Control unit
OP code   Operand
ADD ← Decoders → 006
Instruction   Address
register   register

Arithmetic-logic unit
0035 ← Adders → 0012
Accumulator   Storage register

Result
0047

3 Prepare circuitry to execute instruction   6 Store the result

5. Next, the operations specified by the operation code of the instruction are performed (addition, subtraction, comparisons, and so on). In this example, the contents of the storage register (0012) are added to the contents of an important register known as the **accumulator** by the use of specialized circuitry called **adders**. For this example, let's assume that the amount of hours worked this week (0035) was stored in the accumulator by a previous instruction.

6. Finally, the result arising from the manipulation of the data is stored in primary storage. In this example, the contents of the accumulator after the addition of today's hours to the weekly hours worked will be 0047. This amount will be transferred to primary storage at address 008 when the operand specifying this address is executed.

The Order of Execution

The computer automatically repeats instruction and execution cycles until the final instruction of a program is executed. Usually, instructions are sequentially executed in the order in which they are stored in primary storage. An **instruction counter**, which automatically advances or "steps" in sequential order to the address of the next instruction stored in memory, is used to indicate what instruction is to be executed next.

Sometimes, a **branch instruction** is brought from storage. It tells the control unit that it may have to execute an instruction in another part of the program, instead of the next sequential instruction. This change in the sequence of instructions can be *unconditional or conditional*. A *conditional branch* is usually the result of a **test** or **comparison instruction**, which can cause a change in the sequential order of processing if a specified condition occurs. For example, in a payroll program, a different sequence of instructions is typically used for employees whose hours worked exceed 40 hours per week. These employees have earned "overtime" pay (usually 1 ½ times the regular pay rate). Thus, the payroll program could contain the following instruction:

- **If** hours worked this week is greater than 40, **then** execute the instruction at storage address 020 next.

Since the employee in our example has worked 47 hours this week, the control unit would reset the instruction counter to address 020. The CPU would then "branch" or "jump" to that part of the program and begin executing the instructions for computing overtime pay, rather than the instructions for computing regular pay.

How Fast Are Computers?

Do you know how fast a computer works? Computer operating speeds that were formerly measured in **milliseconds** (thousandths of a second) are now being measured in the **microsecond** (millionth of a second) and **nanosecond** (billionth of a second) range, with **picosecond** (trillionth of a second) speed being attained by some computers. Such speeds seem almost incomprehensible. For example, an average person taking one step each nanosecond would circle the earth about 20 times in one second! Computers operating at such speeds can process several **million instructions per sec-**

FIGURE

3–6 Speed and power of the computer

In the computer, the basic operations can be done within the order of a

NANOSECOND

One thousandth of a millionth of a second.

Within the half second it takes this spilled coffee to reach the floor, a medium-size computer could—

(given the information in magnetic form)

Debit 2000 checks to 300 different bank accounts,

and *examine the electro-cardiograms of 100 patients and alert a physician to possible trouble,*

and *score 150,000 answers on 3000 examinations and evaluate the effectiveness of the questions,*

and *figure the payroll for a company with a thousand employees.*

and a few other chores.

ond (MIPS). For example, the large-scale IBM 3083 executes instructions at a rate of 4 MIPS. However the CRAY 1 supercomputer is rated up to 80 MIPS!

Other measures of the internal operating speed of electronic computers are *machine cycle time* and *memory cycle time*. **Machine cycle** time is the time necessary to complete one machine cycle, while **memory cycle** time is the time necessary for a computer to recall data from one primary storage position. Machine cycle times are now *below 100 nanoseconds* for many large computers, while memory cycle times of *several hundred nanoseconds* are common. One final measure of speed that is applied primarily to microprocessors is the frequency of machine cycles as generated by microprocessor timing circuits. For example, the Intel 8088 microprocessor used in the IBM Personal Computer is rated at 4.7 **megahertz** (MHz), or 4.7 *million cycles per second*. In contrast, the Intel 80186 Microprocessor used in the Tandy Model 2000 microcomputer and the Motorola MC 68000 used in the Apple Macintosh microcomputer are both rated at 8 megahertz.

What do these speeds mean in terms of a computer's information processing capabilities? If you have a microcomputer, you can do your personal and professional information processing chores much faster than you ever could. In fact, you can type, file, analyze, and display information in ways that were not even possible before the development of personal computers! Users who rely on larger computer systems for business information processing also depend on the processing speed of their systems. See Figure 3–6.

HOW COMPUTERS REPRESENT DATA

The letters of the alphabet in this book are symbols that when properly organized or "coded" into the English language will "represent" data that you, the reader, can process into information. Thus, we can say that words, numbers, and punctuation are the human-sensible code by which data is represented in this book. Similarly, data must be represented in a machine-sensible code before it can be processed by a computer system.

Data is represented in a computer system by either the presence or absence of electronic or magnetic "signals" in its circuitry or in the media it uses. This is called **binary** or "two state" representation of data, since the computer is indicating only two possible states or conditions. For example, transistors and other semiconductor circuits are either in a conducting or nonconducting state. Media such as magnetic disks and tapes indicate these two states by the presence or absence of magnetized spots on their surfaces. These binary characteristics of computer circuitry and media are the primary reason why the binary number system is the basis for data representation in computers. Thus, for electronic circuits, the conducting *(ON)* state represents a *one* and the nonconducting *(OFF)* state represents a *zero*. For magnetic media, the presence of a magnetized spot represents a *one* and its absence represents a *zero*.

Computer Number Systems

The binary number system has only two symbols, 0 and 1, and is, therefore, said to have a *base* of two. The familiar decimal system has a base of 10, since it uses 10 symbols (0 through 9). The binary symbols 0 and 1 are commonly called **bits**, which is a contraction of the term *binary digits*. In the binary number system, all numbers are expressed as groups of binary digits (bits), that is, as groups of zeros and ones.

Just as in any other number system, the value of a binary number depends on the position or place of each digit in a grouping of binary digits. Values are based on the right-to-left position of digits in a binary number, using powers of 2 (2^0, 2^1, 2^2, 2^3, and so on) as position values. Therefore, the rightmost position has a value of *one* (2^0), the next position to the left has a value of *two* (2^1), the next position a value of *four* (2^2), the next, *eight* (2^3), the next *sixteen* (2^4), and so forth. Thus the value of any binary number consists of adding together the values of each position in which there is a binary *one* digit, and ignoring those positions that contain a binary *zero* digit. Figure 3–7 gives a simple illustration of how the binary number system can represent decimal values.

The **octal** (base 8) and the **hexadecimal** (base 16) number systems are used as a shorthand method of expressing the binary data representation within many modern computers. The binary number system has the disadvantage of requiring a large number of digits to express a given number value. The use of octal and hexadecimal number systems, which are proportionately related to the binary number system, provides a shorthand method of reducing the long "string" of ones and zeros that make up a binary number. This simplifies the jobs of programmers and computer operators who frequently have to determine the data or instruction contents of the computer.

Figure 3–8 shows the binary, octal, and hexadecimal equivalents of the decimal numbers 0 through 16. Using the relationships in Figure 3–8, you should be able to determine that the decimal number 17 would be expressed by the binary number 10001, the octal number 21, and the hexadecimal number 11, and so on. Several methods

FIGURE

3-7 How the binary
number system represents
decimal values

BINARY POSITION VALUES							
	2^6	2^5	2^4	2^3	2^2	2^1	2^0
	64	32	16	8	4	2	1

BINARY NUMBERS							EQUIVALENT DECIMAL NUMBERS
0	0	0	0	0	0	1	1
0	0	0	0	0	1	0	2
0	0	0	0	0	1	1	3
0	0	0	0	1	0	0	4
0	0	0	0	1	0	1	5
0	0	0	0	1	1	0	6
0	0	0	0	1	1	1	7
0	0	0	1	0	0	0	8
0	0	0	1	0	0	1	9
0	0	0	1	0	1	0	10 ··· 15
0	0	0	1	1	1	1	
0	0	1	0	0	0	0	16
0	0	1	0	0	0	1	17 ··· 31
0	0	1	1	1	1	1	
0	1	0	0	0	0	0	32
0	1	0	0	0	0	1	33 ··· 63
0	1	1	1	1	1	1	
1	0	0	0	0	0	0	64
1	0	0	0	0	0	1	65 ···

FIGURE

3-8 Equivalents of
decimal numbers

Decimal	Binary	Octal	Hexadecimal
0	0	0	0
1	1	1	1
2	10	2	2
3	11	3	3
4	100	4	4
5	101	5	5
6	110	6	6
7	111	7	7
8	1000	10	8
9	1001	11	9
10	1010	12	A
11	1011	13	B
12	1100	14	C
13	1101	15	D
14	1110	16	E
15	1111	17	F
16	10000	20	10

can be used to convert decimal numbers to a binary, octal, or hexa-decimal form, or vice versa, or to use them in arithmetic operations, but they are beyond the scope of this text.

Computer Codes

The internal circuitry of the computer uses only binary ones and zeros in its operations. However, several coding systems have been devised to express the *machine language* instruction codes executed by the CPU, and to represent the characters of *data* processed by the computer. These codes make the job of communicating with a computer easier and more efficient. They should be considered as shorthand methods of expressing the binary patterns within a computer. These computer codes can also be thought of as methods of organizing the binary patterns within a computer to more efficiently use its arithmetic, logic, and storage capabilities.

The most basic computer code would be the use of the "pure" binary number system to represent data for all computer operations. Some scientific and special-purpose computers do use the pure binary code as their only method of internal data representation. However, most modern computers, though they may use a pure binary code for some operations, use special codes based on the binary, octal, or hexadecimal number systems.

Most common computer codes are versions of the **binary coded decimal** (BCD) coding system. In this system, decimal digits are expressed in a binary form using only the first four binary positions. Referring back to Figure 3–8, we see that the decimal digits 0 through 9 can be expressed by four binary positions. Therefore, any decimal number can be expressed by stringing together groups of four binary digits. For example, the decimal number 1987 would be expressed in BCD form as shown below.

Decimal Form	1	9	8	7
BCD Form	0001	1001	1000	0111

The **Extended BCD Interchange Code** (EBCDIC) (pronounced eb′-si-dick) is used by most current computers and can provide 256 (2^8) different coding arrangements. The middle column of Figure 3–9 shows that this eight-bit code consists of four *numeric* bits (on the right) and four *zone* bits (on the left). The letters of the alphabet or special characters can be represented when combinations of zone and numeric bits are used.

Another popular code is the **American Standard Code for Information Interchange** (ASCII) (pronounced as'-key). This seven-bit code can represent 128 (2^7) different characters. It is a standardized code first developed for data communications between computers and input/output devices. However, it is used by many microcomputers as well as several larger computers. Because of the differences between EBCIDIC and ASCII codes, computers must be able to convert from one code to the other. ASCII has been adopted as a standard code by national and international standards organizations. Its use is expected to continue to grow in the future.

Most computer codes include an additional bit called the **check bit**. The check bit is also known as a "parity" bit and is used for

FIGURE

3–9 Common computer codes

Character	EBCDIC	ASCII
0	1111 0000	011 0000
1	1111 0001	011 0001
2	1111 0010	011 0010
3	1111 0011	011 0011
4	1111 0100	011 0100
5	1111 0101	011 0101
6	1111 0110	011 0110
7	1111 0111	011 0111
8	1111 1000	011 1000
9	1111 1001	011 1001
A	1100 0001	100 0001
B	1100 0010	100 0010
C	1100 0011	100 0011
D	1100 0100	100 0100
E	1100 0101	100 0101
F	1100 0110	100 0110
G	1100 0111	100 0111
H	1100 1000	100 1000
I	1100 1001	100 1001
J	1101 0001	100 1010
K	1101 0010	100 1011
L	1101 0011	100 1100
M	1101 0100	100 1101
N	1101 0101	100 1110
O	1101 0110	100 1111
P	1101 0111	101 0000
Q	1101 1000	101 0001
R	1101 1001	101 0010
S	1110 0010	101 0011
T	1110 0011	101 0100
U	1110 0100	101 0101
V	1110 0101	101 0110
W	1110 0110	101 0111
X	1110 0111	101 1000
Y	1110 1000	101 1001
Z	1110 1001	101 1010

FIGURE

3–10 Data representation: EBCDIC code

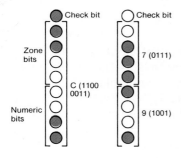

verifying the accuracy or validity of the coded data. Many computers have a built-in checking capacity to detect the loss or addition of bits during the transfer of data between components of a computer system. For example, the computer may be designed to continuously check for an *odd parity*; that is, an odd number of *binary one* (electronically *ON* bit positions) in each character of data that is transferred. In such cases, a check bit is turned on automatically to ensure that an odd number of electronically *ON* bit positions is present in each character of data in storage. Thus the check bit allows the computer to automatically determine whether the correct number of bit positions representing a character of data has been transferred.

Figure 3–10 concludes this section on data representation with an illustration of how data is physically represented in many modern computers. Assuming the use of the eight-bit EBCDIC code, Figure 3–10 reveals that one alphabetic or special character or two decimal numbers can be represented by an eight-bit code. The circles represent semiconductor circuit elements or other forms of storage media. The shaded circles represent an electronic or magnetic *ON* state, while the nonshaded circles represent the *OFF* state of binary devices. Thus, the first column of circles represents the letter C while the second column of circles is called the *packed decimal* format, since two decimal numbers, in this case a seven and a nine, are represented by only eight bits.

You should now realize that each storage location of computers using the EBCDIC code consists of electronic circuit elements or magnetic media positions that can represent at least eight binary digits. Thus each storage location can hold one alphabetic or special character or can be *packed* with two decimal digits. This grouping of eight binary digits in EBCDIC (seven in ASCII) is known as a **byte**. Also notice that in the case of the letter C in Figure 3–10, the ninth or check bit is *ON* to indicate *even parity*; that is, an even number of bits (four) are turned on. In the case of the packed decimal byte containing a seven and a nine, the check bit is *OFF,* indicating *odd parity*; that is, an odd number of bits (five) are turned on.

Computer Data Elements

The organization of data within a computer is a function of the internal design of the computer circuitry and of the coding system used. Since most current computers are designed to use the EBCDIC coding system, we will confine our discussion to data organization based on that system. Computers that use other schemes of data organization differ in the size and names of the data elements used, rather than in the basic concepts required.

Bits

Figure 3–11 illustrates the hierarchy of data elements used by many computers. The smallest element of data is the **bit**, or binary digit, which can have a binary value of either zero or one.

Bytes

The grouping of bits required to represent a character by such coding systems as EBCDIC and ASCII is called a **byte**. Remember that in the eight bit EBCDIC code, a byte can contain either one alphabetical or special character, or can be *packed* with two decimal digits. The byte is the basic unit of data in most modern computer systems.

The storage capacity of most computers and storage devices is usually expressed in terms of bytes. Storage capacity is typically measured in **kilobytes** (abbreviated as KB or K) or **megabytes** (abbreviated as MB or M). Although "kilo" means one thousand in the metric system, the computer industry uses K to represent 1,024 (2^{10}) storage positions. Therefore, a memory size of 256K, for example, is really 262,144 storage positions, rather than 256,000 positions; but such differences are frequently disregarded in order to simplify descriptions of storage capacity. Thus a **megabyte** is roughly one million bytes, while a **gigabyte** is roughly one billion bytes of storage, and a **terabyte** represents one trillion bytes of storage! Typically, computer primary storage capacities might range from 64K bytes (65,536 bytes) for some microcomputer memories to 40M bytes (40 megabytes or 40 million bytes) of memory for a large computer system.

Words

The next major computer data element is the **word**. The word is a basic grouping of binary digits or bytes, that is transferred on electronic circuitry "data paths" between primary storage and the registers of the arithmetic-logic unit and control unit. Thus a computer with a 32-bit word length might have registers with a capacity of 32 bits, and transfer data and instructions within the CPU in groupings of 32 bits. It should process data faster than computers with a 16-bit or 8-bit word length. However, word size does not depend only on the capacity of the registers in the CPU or microprocessor. It also depends on the capacity or "width" of the **data path** or *data bus* on which data and instructions are moved through the circuitry of the CPU or microprocessor.

Thus, some large computers that typically have 32-bit registers may move data in *half words* of 16 bits or *double words* of 64

FIGURE

3–11 Typical computer data elements

Name	Size
BIT	One binary digit.
BYTE	Eight bits (EBCDIC).
WORD	Fixed word-length format:
	8, 16, or 32 bits.
	Variable word-length format:
	1 to 256 bytes.
PAGE	2K or 4K bytes.

bits. Also, some microprocessors use a *bit slice* design, in which data is moved in "slices" of 2 bits or 4 bits (called a **nibble**) within the circuits of the microprocessor.

Many current microcomputers have microprocessors with 16-bit registers but have data paths that are only 8-bits wide. Thus their "true" word size is said to be 8 bits, since they must make two 8 bit transfers of data from memory to fill a 16-bit register. Obviously, this reduces the processing speed of the microcomputer.

Thus word size is important in determining the processing speed of a computer. However, it is also related to three other important computer capabilities. Computer word size helps determine:

- The number of basic types of instructions which can be executed by a CPU or microprocessor. For example, a 32-bit word-size computer typically has a larger *instruction set* of basic machine instructions than a 16-bit computer.
- The precision of arithmetic computations. For example, a 32-bit machine can manipulate numbers equivalent to 32 binary positions, whereas a 16-bit computer might be limited to manipulating numbers containing 16 binary positions. In both cases, hardware and software can be added to increase arithmetic precision.
- The amount of primary storage capacity. For example, several popular 8-bit microprocessors can directly access only about 64K bytes of memory. On the other hand, many popular 16-bit microcomputers can have up to one million bytes of directly addressable memory.

The size of a word also depends on whether the computer is operating in a *fixed word-length* or a *variable word-length* format. Computers operate in a fixed word-length mode when each word consists of a fixed number of bits or bytes. In the variable word-length format, the size of a word depends on the instruction being executed and the size of the data elements that are being processed. For many computers, a word consists of four bytes (32 bits) in a fixed word-length format and can vary from one byte to 256 bytes in a variable word-length format. All of these variations in word-length, register capacity, and the width of data paths are designed to either lower the cost and complexity or enhance the speed and efficiency of computer processing devices. See Figure 3–12.

Pages

Finally, an important computer data element of modern computer systems is the **page**. The page is a computer data element that

FIGURE

3–12 The new
generation of
microprocessors

A Intel 80286. An advanced 16-
bit microprocessor with a 16-
bit data path and a 24-bit address register. Used in the IBM
PC AT. Note the functions performed by major parts of the
chip.

B Motorola MC68020. A 32-bit
microprocessor "mainframe on
a chip" with a 32-bit data path.

A

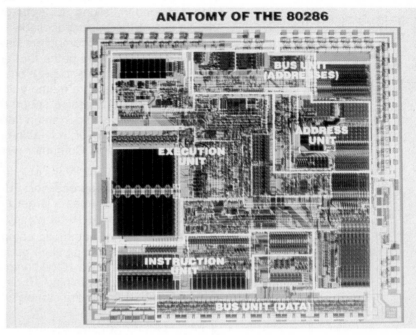

B

REAL WORLD APPLICATION 3-2

IBM-Apple-Tandy: Bits, Bytes, and Words

In the old days, a typical microcomputer had an 8-bit word length, a minicomputer had a 16-bit word length, and a mainframe computer had at least a 32-bit word length. How times have changed! Now we hear talk of a 16-bit word length as the *standard* for personal computers and watch the growth of *super-micro* and *super-mini* computers with 32-bit word lengths. Even more confusing is talk that some microcomputers are not "real" 16-bit computers, whereas others are.

Here are a few examples. The IBM Personal Computer uses the 16-bit Intel 8088 microprocessor, which has registers with a 16- bit capacity. However, it moves only one byte of data or instructions at a time along a data path only eight bits wide. This means that it takes two transfers of data from memory to fill a register, thus slowing the processing speed of the PC. In contrast, the Tandy Model 2000 uses the Intel 80186 microprocessor, which has 16-bit registers and a 16-bit data path. It claims to be more than twice as fast as the IBM PC, since it can stuff two bytes of data at a time into its registers. The Apple Macintosh microcomputer is another example of a difference between register and data path capacity. It uses a Motorola MC 68000 microprocessor with 32-bit registers (thus it is called a 32-bit microprocessor) but has a data path only 16 bits wide.

Get the idea? Word size depends not only on the capacity of the registers in a microprocessor but also on the size of its data paths. It is obvious that microcomputer manufacturers have had to balance the speed and efficiency of using registers and data paths of equal capacity with the reduction in complexity and cost of using smaller data paths. As technology continues to improve, such a balancing act should becomes unnecessary.

- What is the difference between the word size of current microcomputers? Why is there such a difference?
- Do current microprocessors move bits, bytes, or words along their data paths into their registers? Explain.

has been created due to the development of *virtual memory*, in which secondary storage is treated as an extension of a computer's primary storage. Pages are transferred between primary and secondary storage in the virtual memory process known as *paging*. Pages of programs or data are continually transferred between primary and secondary storage in such virtual memory systems. For many computers, the page consists of 2K or 4K bytes.

OVERVIEW OF COMPUTER HARDWARE

Computer hardware consists of **equipment** that makes up a computer system, plus input/output and storage **media** (such as magnetic tapes or disks) which are the tangible materials on which data is recorded. Computer hardware can be subdivided into three major categories:

■ Computer Processors

The primary hardware unit of a computer system is the *central processing unit* (CPU), which is called a *microprocessor* in microcomputer systems. We have seen that the CPU includes the arithmetic-logic unit, the control unit, and the primary storage unit. It also includes other specialized devices (such as *registers* and *adders*) and **input/output interface devices** (such as *buffers* and *ports*). In addition, many computer systems now include additional **specialized processors** (such as arithmetic and input/output processors), which assist the CPU in its processing tasks.

■ Peripheral Equipment and Media

This hardware category includes all devices that are separate from, but are (or can be) **online**, that is, electronically connected to and controlled by the central processing unit. **Peripherals** include a wide variety of **input/output** (I/O) equipment (such as video display terminals) and **secondary storage** devices (such as magnetic disk drives),which depend on a direct connection or communication link to the CPU. The media used by peripheral equipment consists primarily of magnetic disks and tape, and paper documents.

■ Auxiliary Equipment and Media

This category includes equipment that is **offline**, that is, equipment separate from and *not* under the control of a central processing unit. Auxiliary equipment assists the input, output, and storage functions of the computer system, and include: (1) **offline data entry** (input preparation) equipment, such as key-to-tape or disk machines which convert data from *source documents* into magnetic input media for later entry into a computer system; (2) **offline output** and **storage** equipment, such as copiers and filing devices; and (3) **data processing supplies**, such as paper forms which are used in operating a computer system.

Figure 3–13 is an overview of the major types of hardware found in many computer systems. These devices will be explained in the three chapters of Part 2: Computer Systems and Hardware. Besides illustrating the variety of hardware devices available, Figure 3–13 makes two additional points about computer hardware:

■ Many types of computer peripherals and media can be used for both input and output or for all three functions of **input, output**, and **secondary storage**. For example, magnetic disk equipment uses magnetic disks as a data medium and performs all three functions of input, output, and secondary storage.

■ Some peripheral devices do not need to use *data media* for input or output. For example, many computer terminals consist of a keyboard to enter data directly into the computer system and a CRT video screen to directly display visual output. Since such peripherals do not use data media, they are called **direct input/output** devices.

FIGURE 3–13 Overview of hardware in a computer system

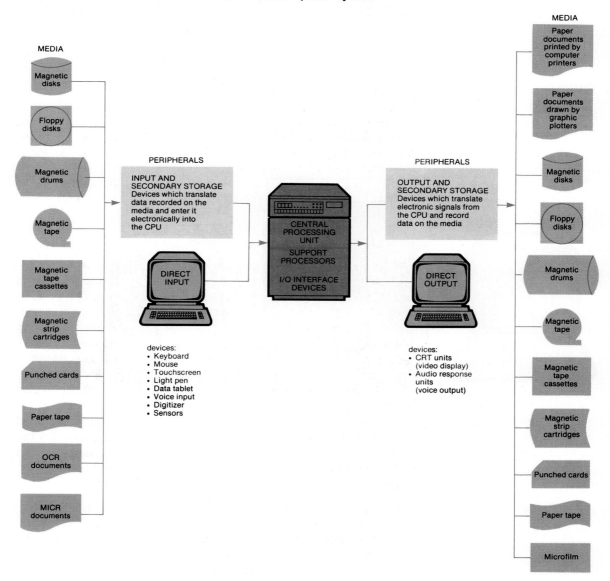

OVERVIEW OF COMPUTER SOFTWARE

Computer software includes all types of programs which direct and control *computer hardware* in the performance of information processing functions. It is often said that software "gives life" to hardware. Computer software can be subdivided into two major categories: *system software* and *application software*.

■ **System software**—programs that control and support operations of a computer system. System software includes a variety of programs, such as operating systems, data base management systems, communications control programs, service and utility programs, and programming language translators. Each of these

FIGURE 3–14 Overview of software in a computer system

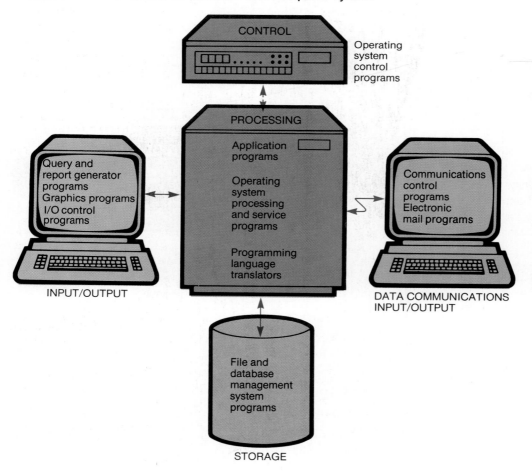

programs perform an important function in modern computer systems and should be understood by knowledgeable computer users.

■ **Application software**—programs that direct the processing of a particular use or *application* of computers. Application software or *application programs* specify the information processing activities required for the completion of specific tasks of computer users. Thus application software is sometimes called *user programs* and is frequently subdivided into *business* application programs, *scientific* applications programs, and a variety of other applications program categories. Examples would be inventory control or payroll processing programs in business, chemical process control or structural stress analysis programs in science and engineering, and computer-assisted instruction or video game programs in education and entertainment.

Figure 3–14 is an overview of the major types of software used in many computer systems. These programs will be explained in Chapter Seven: System and Application Software and other chapters of the text. Besides illustrating the variety of programs available, Figure 3–14 emphasizes how software supports the functions of *input, processing, output, storage*, and *control* of a computer system.

There has been a tremendous growth recently in the sales of **software packages**, which are prewritten system and application

FIGURE

3–15 Examples of system and application software packages

SYSTEM SOFTWARE

■ **Operating System**—an integrated group of programs that supervise and support the operations of a computer system as it executes the application programs of users.

■ **Database Management System (DBMS)**—a group of programs that control the creation, maintenance, and use of a *database* of stored data and information that can be accessed for several different user applications.

■ **Programming Language Translator**—a program that converts the instructions of programs written in a programming language like BASIC or COBOL into binary-based *machine language* instruction codes that the CPU can execute. It also allows users and programmers to write their own programs.

APPLICATION SOFTWARE

■ **Electronic Spreadsheet Package**—a program that displays a worksheet of rows and columns into which a user can insert data and formulas that represents a *model* of the user's problem. The program then automatically manipulates the data in the spreadsheet in response to commands of the user, thus providing an excellent tool for analysis and planning.

■ **Word Processing Package**—a program that automates the creation, editing, and printing of *documents* (letters, reports, etc.) by electronically processing *text data* (words, phrases, sentences, and the like) for a user.

■ **Common Business Packages**—programs that perform the information processing activities required by common accounting and other business functions. Examples are sales analysis, billing, accounts receivable and payable, inventory control, general ledger accounting, and payroll processing.

REAL WORLD APPLICATION 3-3

Anatomy of a Computer System

The following computer system is a composite of features found in many current medium-size computers.

■ A central processing unit using advanced LSI semiconductor logic and memory circuits, and a 32-bit word-length architecture.

■ Four megabytes of main memory, with over four gigabytes of auxiliary memory available on disk.

■ High-speed buffer (cache) storage of 128 kilobytes and 16 32-bit general purpose registers.

■ Machine cycle time = 200 nanoseconds. Memory cycle time = 500 nanoseconds.

■ Six I/0 channels that can support up to 96 terminals, 16 magnetic disk drives, 4 line printers, 8 magnetic tape drives, and 6 communications lines.

■ Multiuser operating system, which supports BASIC, Pascal, FORTRAN, and COBOL. DBMS with online user query capability. Application software available includes spreadsheet, word processing, and common business packages.

■ Can you identify the functions and explain the capabilities of the computer system components outlined above? Give it a try!

programs available for purchase by computer users, especially for microcomputer systems. The most important and widely used types of system software packages are *operating systems*, *programming language translators*, and *data base management systems*. The most popular types of application software include two *general-purpose application programs*: *electronic spreadsheet packages* and *word processing packages*, as well as several common business application programs. Figure 3–15 summarizes these popular types of software. They will be explained in more detail in Chapter Seven and in other chapters. In addition, a hands-on introduction to the use of several of these packages is contained in the appendix at the back of the book entitled: Using Popular Software Packages: A Tutorial Introduction.

SUMMARY

- A computer is a system that performs input, storage, arithmetic-logic, control, and output functions. The hardware components of a computer system include input devices, a central processing unit, storage devices, and output devices.

- The execution of a computer instruction can be subdivided into an instruction cycle (when the computer prepares to execute an instruction) and an execution cycle (when it actually executes the instruction).

- Data is represented in a computer in a binary form because of the two-state nature of the electronic and magnetic components of the computer. Most computers use special codes based on the binary number system, including the EBCDIC and ASCII codes.

- Within the computer, data is usually organized into bits, bytes, words, and pages. In most modern computers, each position of storage can store one byte, and has a specific numerical location so the data stored in its contents can be readily located.

- The major categories of computer hardware and software are summarized in Figures 3–13 and 3–14.

KEY TERMS AND CONCEPTS

Computer system
Input devices
Central processing unit
Primary storage unit
Secondary storage devices
Arithmetic-logic unit
Control unit
Output devices
Registers
Executing computer
  instructions
Binary representation
Binary number system

Computer codes: EBCDIC and
  ASCII
Computer data elements: bit,
  byte, word, page
Computer processors
Peripheral equipment and
  media
Auxiliary equipment and media
Online
Offline
System software
Application software

REVIEW AND APPLICATION QUESTIONS

1. Why is it important to think of a computer as a system?
2. What are the basic components and functions of a computer system?

3. What three major subunits make up the central processing unit of a computer? What are the functions of each of these units?
4. What is the difference in the functions of primary and secondary storage?
5. Do computers have a memory and logic capability? Explain.
6. Explain how a computer executes an instruction.
7. How fast do computers execute instructions?
8. Why do computers use binary number systems as the basis for data representation?
9. Explain how data is physically represented in the memory of a computer using the EBCDIC code.
10. Differentiate between the bit, byte, word, and page computer data elements.
11. How much data can a typical computer hold in each position of storage? How can the computer readily locate the data in a specific location?
12. What are the three major categories of computer hardware? What types of devices are included in each category?
13. What is the basic distinction between online and offline devices? Give examples of each.
14. Which computer peripheral devices do not need to use data media for input or output? Explain.
15. What is the difference between system software and application software? Give an example of each.

APPLICATION PROBLEMS

1. If you have not already done so, read and answer the questions after each Real World Application in this chapter.
2. Have you had an opportunity for a hands-on experience with a computer yet? Did you use a microcomputer or larger computer system? Indicate the hardware (equipment and media) you used to perform the system functions listed below. Also indicate the system and application software packages you used:
   a. *Input*   a. *System software*
   b. *Processing*
   c. *Output*   b. *Application software*
   d. *Storage*
   e. *Control*
3. Natalie Dreste, an enterprising young college student, has just started a mail order catalog business selling silk blouses. She processes all orders manually but plans to purchase an IBM PC to handle order processing as soon as possible. Natalie places all orders to be processed in a special in-box. On her

desk she has a copy of the catalog to look up prices, colors, etc., and a calculator to calculate the total of the order. When finished with the order, she places it in a special out-box and also places a copy of the order in the customer's file. Natalie has all the customer files alphabetically stored in a file cabinet. When a customer calls with a question, she can retrieve the file from the file cabinet and answer the question. When Natalie buys her IBM PC, all the components of her manual system will exist in the hardware components of the computer system. Match each component of the manual system with the corresponding component of the computer hardware system.

1. Natalie.   *a.* Input device.
2. Calculator. *b.* Control unit.
3. Catalog.   *c.* Arithmetic-logic unit.
4. File cabinet. *d.* Primary storage unit.
5. In-box.   *e.* Secondary storage devices.
6. Out-box.   *f.* Output devices.

4. For the following computer instructions, identify the (1) operation code and (2) the operands:
   a. Read data from cards to addresses 01,02,03,04.
   b. Read contents of address 01 into arithmetic-logic unit.
   c. Multiply contents of arithmetic-logic by contents of address 04, store result in address 18.
   d. Write contents of address 18 on printer.
5. If the EBCDIC character M, which equals 1101 0100, is transfered from a CRT to the CPU using odd parity, what value will the parity bit have? In even parity, what value will the parity bit have? If the ASCII character 8, which equals 001 1000, is transfered from a CRT to the CPU using odd parity, what value will the parity bit have? In even parity, what value will the parity bit have?
6. Learn more about the capabilities of the computer available for your use. For example, determine the speed, memory capacity, and word-size of its central processing unit, the capacity of its secondary storage devices; and the speed of its printer.

PART
2

Computer Systems and Hardware

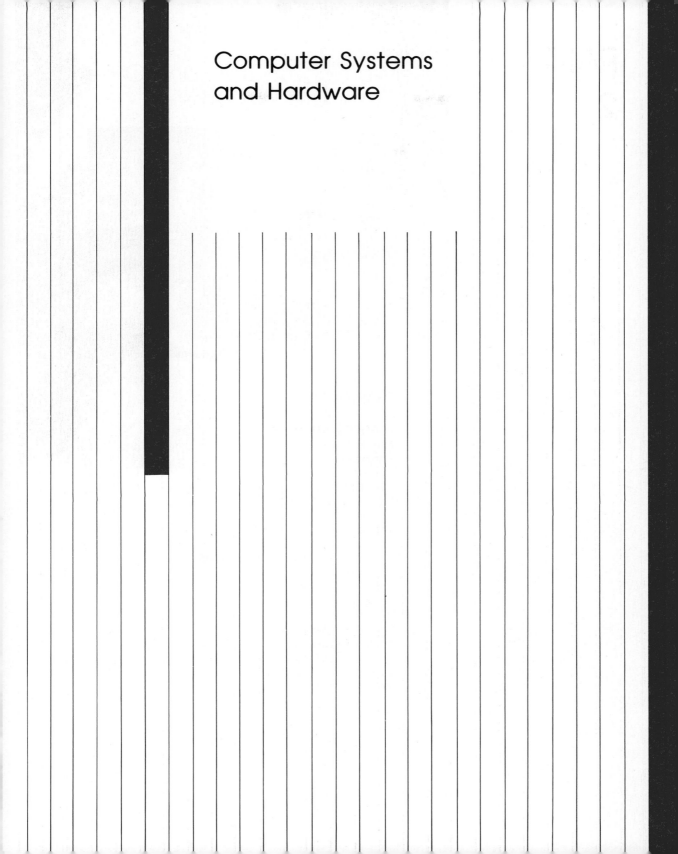

CHAPTER 4

Microcomputers and Other Computer Systems

CHAPTER OUTLINE

LEARNING OBJECTIVES

The purpose of this chapter is to promote a basic understanding of microcomputers and other types of computer systems in use today. After reading and studying this chapter, you should be able to:

1. Explain the use of microcomputers for home, personal, professional, and business applications.
2. Discuss some of the hardware, software, and other factors that need to be considered in the purchase and use of microcomputer systems.
3. Outline the major differences and uses of microcomputers, minicomputers, and mainframe computers.
4. Identify the major characteristics and uses of supercomputers, analog computers, special-purpose computers, and scientific computers.
5. Discuss the trend toward multiprocessor computer systems.

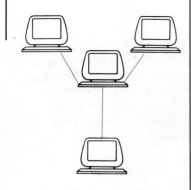

Now that you have been introduced to computers and their hardware and software, you are ready to analyze the important characteristics of modern computer systems. Today's computer systems display striking differences as well as basic similarities. Differences in computer characteristics and capabilities have resulted in the development of several major categories of computer systems. Computer systems are frequently classified by:

- **Size**—micro-, mini-, mainframe, and supercomputers.
- **Type**—digital and analog computers.
- **Purpose**—general-purpose and special-purpose computers.

All computers fall into these three categories, even though other names are frequently given to computers, such as *personal computer, small business computer, scientific computer,* and *multiprocessor computer.* In this chapter, we will analyze all of these types of computer systems, concentrating on **microcomputers** and their hardware, software, applications, cost, and sources.

MICROCOMPUTER SYSTEMS

Introduction

Microcomputers have arrived. What started out as a $395 kit for electronic hobbyists in 1975 blossomed into a commonplace personal and professional appliance less than 10 years later. They come in all shapes and sizes, from devices that are as small as chips, pockets, and notebooks, to models that are as big as briefcases, typewriters, and TV sets. With over 10 million of these computing appliances in use in the United States by 1985, there is no question that the computer revolution is in full force. People are using microcomputers in their homes and schools, in businesses and factories, and in laboratories and the great outdoors. They are using them to play video games, type letters, keep records, learn their lessons, compose music, do accounting, perform financial analysis and modeling, draw pictures, send electronic mail, and yes, even crunch a few numbers. Obviously, we had better take a hard look at the device responsible for all of this activity, the microcomputer.

To be an informed microcomputer user, you should have a basic understanding of microcomputer hardware, software, and applications. Also, you should have a basic idea of how to evaluate the costs, capabilities, and sources of microcomputer hardware and software. This chapter will give you a good start toward attaining those goals. The rest of this text should complete the job.

REAL WORLD APPLICATION 4–1

The Kula Onion

Bernie Eiting owns a delicatessen and specialty grocery store, the Kula Onion, in the Kula district of Maui, Hawaii, and a marketing company in Chicago. After looking at various machines, he bought a Z80-based Vector Graphic system, including a keyboard, dual floppy disk drives, video monitor, and printer.

"We use it in the managing of the little store," says Eiting. "We have the Peachtree accounting package. We're in the process of putting out a quarterly newsletter for the store. I use the word processing program for that and for general business correspondence. I also have a mailing-list program that merges with my word processing. Through our database management system, we can do some independent programming in English, without having to call in a programmer. I produce management indexes, such things as

the kind of return I get on my investment and so forth." Eiting also does direct-mail advertising for himself and for clients of his Chicago company, Marketing Dynamics. Eventually he intends to upgrade his system with a hard-disk setup for mass storage.

■ Can you identify the hardware and software of this microcomputer system?
■ List the ways Bernie Eiting uses his microcomputer.
■ Is such versatility unusual for a microcomputer system? Explain.

Source: "The Data Game: Business and the Microcomputer," *Passages*, May 1981, p. 21. Copyright 1981 by The Webb Company. Reprinted with permission.

HARDWARE

What is a **microcomputer**? A microcomputer is the smallest current type of computer. It usually consists of a **microprocessor** or MPU (a central processing unit on a chip) and associated control, primary storage, and input/output circuitry on one or more circuit boards, plus a variety of input/output and secondary storage devices. Microcomputers are given a lot of other names, however, because they come in a variety of sizes and shapes, and are used for a variety of purposes. For example, microcomputers categorized by *size* may be called: **single chip, pocket, hand-held, lap-size, portable, transportable**, and **desktop-size** microcomputers. Or based on their *use*, they may be called **special-purpose, home, personal, professional, small business**, and **workstation** microcomputers. However, the most popular alternative name for microcomputers right now is **personal computer**, because they are so widely owned and used by individual persons for use at home, at school, and at work. See Figure 4–1.

What hardware does a microcomputer system have? That depends on its size and use. However, the typical hardware components of a personal computer are shown in Figure 4–2. Remember

FIGURE 4–1 Microcomputer systems

A The IBM Personal Computer AT.

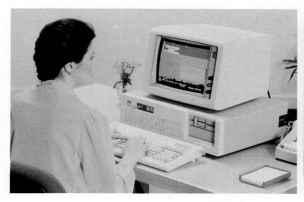

B The Apple Macintosh.

C The Portable by Hewlett-Packard.

D The AT&T Personal Computer.

that a microcomputer is a **computer system** and uses a variety of devices to perform the system functions of *input, processing, output, storage,* and *control.* Typical personal computer components are summarized below and discussed in more detail in the next few sections.

- **Input**—keyboard (plus *electronic mouse* and other devices).
- **Processing** and **control**—main system unit containing the main microprocessor and other devices on circuit boards.

FIGURE 4–2 Hardware diagram of a microcomputer system

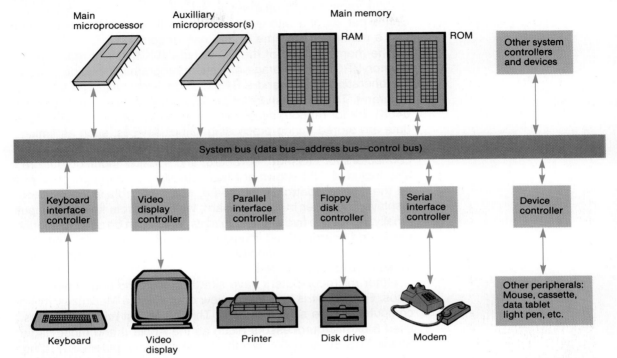

- **Storage**—*primary storage*: RAM and ROM chips on the circuit boards in the main system unit. *Secondary storage*: floppy disk drives (plus hard disk drives and other devices), which can be part of the main system unit or be externally connected.
- **Output**—video display monitor and printer (plus audio speaker and other devices).

Processing and Control Hardware

Let's look at what's inside a popular microcomputer to get a better idea of what makes a microcomputer tick. Figure 4–3 is a picture of the insides of the IBM Personal Computer (PC) with its main circuit board and other devices identified. The integrated circuit chips are enclosed in rectangular plastic packages fitted with electrodes. They are interconnected with other circuit elements, such as resistors and capacitors, by a pattern of conductors printed on the circuit board, which measures approximately 8 ½ by 11 inches. The main chip is the Intel 8088 microprocessor, containing eight general-purpose 16-bit registers, an 8-bit data path (*bus*), and over 20,000 transistors. It operates at a frequency of almost 5 million cycles per second with a machine cycle time of 210 nanoseconds and a memory cycle time of 840 nanoseconds.

The memory chips of the PC include 40K bytes of read only memory (ROM) for storage of system programs, including parts of the operating system and a BASIC *interpreter* (language translator program). The major share of primary storage chips (from 64K to 640K) are for random access memory (RAM) where programs and data are stored during processing. Other devices, such as timing and clock circuits, input/output *ports*, memory access circuits, and connectors for cassette, keyboard, and speaker input/output are also included. Not shown are two subsidiary microprocessors: one on the display control circuit board, which controls video monitor displays, the other in the keyboard, which controls keyboard input. Finally, notice the five *expansion slots*, which can be used to support expansion boards for additional memory and input/output devices, such as a printer, color monitor, data communications *modem*, electronic mouse, and the like.

Other microcomputers have similar processing and control devices. Figure 4–4 is a cutaway view of the Apple Macintosh microcomputer. As we said in Chapter Three, the first microcomputers used 8-bit microprocessors (such as the Apple II and most Radio Shack TRS 80 models), and the latest microcomputers are using 32-bit microprocessors (such as Apple's Lisa and Macintosh models). Popular 8-bit microprocessors are the Intel 8080, and the Zilog Z80, while the Intel 8088 has become a 16-bit standard used in

FIGURE

4–3 Inside the IBM PC

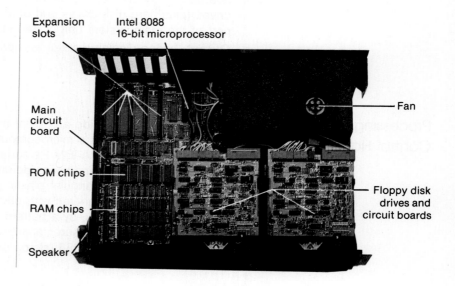

Expansion slots

Intel 8088 16-bit microprocessor

Main circuit board

ROM chips

RAM chips

Speaker

Fan

Floppy disk drives and circuit boards

many microcomputers. The Motorola MC68000, used in the newer Apple models, is a popular 32-bit microprocessor.

As we mentioned in Chapter Three, the word size of a microprocessor is dependent on the size of its registers and data path. We also mentioned the effect this has on the speed, accuracy, and memory capacity of the computer in which it is used. The type of microprocessor used also has a major bearing on the software available for a microcomputer. System and application software are written with specific microprocessors in mind. So microcomputers using the more popular microprocessors will have a greater number and variety of software for you to choose from.

Storage Hardware

Microcomputers use integrated circuit memory chips plugged into their circuit boards for **primary storage** or memory. Capacity typically ranges from 64K to one megabyte. As we will discuss further in Chapter Five, this takes the form of either RAM or ROM storage chips. Most of the memory capacity of a microcomputer consists of **random access memory** (RAM), in which data and instructions are stored during processing. The rest of memory is composed of **read only memory** (ROM) chips, in which software, such as parts of the operating system program or a language translator program (typically a BASIC interpreter), are permanently stored so they are

FIGURE

4–4 Inside the Apple Macintosh

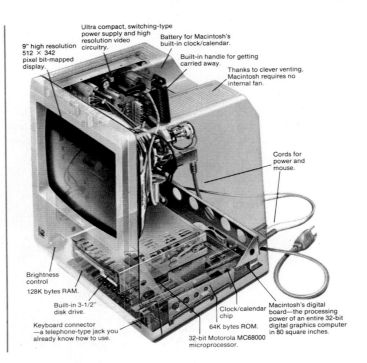

Ultra compact, switching-type power supply and high resolution video circuitry.

9" high resolution 512 × 342 pixel bit-mapped display.

Battery for Macintosh's built-in clock/calendar.

Built-in handle for getting carried away.

Thanks to clever venting, Macintosh requires no internal fan.

Cords for power and mouse.

Brightness control 128K bytes RAM.

Built-in 3-1/2" disk drive.

Keyboard connector —a telephone-type jack you already know how to use.

Clock/calendar chip

64K bytes ROM.

32-bit Motorola MC68000 microprocessor.

Macintosh's digital board—the processing power of an entire 32-bit digital graphics computer in 80 square inches.

FIGURE

4–5 Microcomputer storage devices

A Floppy disks are the most popular secondary storage media.

B The unit atop this Apple Lisa microcomputer provides five million bytes of hard disk storage.

A

B

ready as soon as the computer is turned on. Unlike RAM, the programs in ROM cannot be erased. Also, they are not *volatile* like RAM, which loses its contents when electrical power is interrupted.

The most popular **secondary storage** devices for microcomputers are magnetic disk drives using flexible magnetic diskettes or **floppy disks**. The 5 ¼-inch (diameter) *minifloppy* size is the most popular, with storage capacities of 16OK to over three megabytes available on each disk. However, the 8-inch size and the 3¼ or 3½-inch *microfloppy* are also used. Lower-priced microcomputers frequently use **magnetic tape cassette** and **cartridge** devices for secondary storage. **Magnetic hard disk** devices have become popular for business users of more expensive microcomputers. Though they cost over a thousand dollars, such devices offer up to 20 megabytes of storage and are much faster than floppy disks. Other devices include **magnetic bubble** plug-in cartridges and plug-in **RAM cards** (circuit boards) that provide additional storage capability much faster than other media. We will discuss these types of storage media further in Chapter Five. See Figure 4–5.

Input Hardware

The most popular input device for microcomputers is the familiar **keyboard**, which can be part of the main system unit or be a separate device. It comes in a variety of styles, including inexpensive models that use only a touch-sensitive *membrane keyboard*. Some keyboards have 10-key *numeric pad*, (for numeric input) *cursor control* keys (to move the cursor on the screen), and special *function keys*, which reduce the number of keystrokes needed to enter selected commands into the computer.

Other input devices are available that are easier to use than a keyboard when you are moving a *cursor*, making selections from a *menu* display, entering commands or doing specialized tasks. (The **cursor** is a point of light that indicates the position on the screen where the next entry will appear.) The Apple Lisa and Macintosh microcomputers emphasize use of the **electronic mouse**. It is a small device connected to the computer that you move by hand on a flat surface (a desktop). This moves the cursor on the screen in the same direction. The buttons on the mouse allow you to make a selection or issue a command. Hewlett-Packard microcomputers emphasize use of a **touch-sensitive screen** to accomplish similar functions. Other specialized hardware include *optical scanning wands, light pens, graphic tablets, joysticks, game paddles, digitizers*, and *voice recognition units*. We will discuss the functions of these and other input devices in Chapter Six. See Figure 4–6.

114

Output Hardware

The two most common microcomputer output devices are the video display monitor and the printer. The **video display monitor** allows you to see the output of the computer, as well as your input, while you are entering instructions or data. Inexpensive microcomputers include a device called an RF modulator, which allows you to use a TV set as a monitor. Better microcomputers assume you will use a specially designed monochrome or color monitor that allows a sharper image to be displayed. Video monitors come in various types and costs, depending on the clarity and number of colors displayed. For example, a full-color monitor for graphics displays will cost several times as much as a monochrome monitor for viewing text and numeric output.

If you are a serious microcomputer user, you will want a *hard copy* of some of your output printed on paper. That's where **printers** come in. An inexpensive (and quiet) *thermal* (heat transfer) printer can be purchased at low cost for portable computers. The most popular types of printers print one character a time using a *dot matrix* or *daisy wheel* print head. Speeds range from 15 to 300 characters per second, though 100 characters a second is common. The speed, quality and cost of printers varies widely. For example, *draft* quality printers are cheaper than *correspondence quality* printers.

Other output devices include **audio speakers, voice synthesizers,** and **graphic plotters**. An important input/output interface device that should also be mentioned is the **modem**. It converts the computer's digital output into analog signals (and vice versa) for

FIGURE

4–6 Microcomputer input devices

This personal computer uses a keyboard, light pen, mouse, and joystick as input devices.

data communications over telephone lines with other computers. This capability can be built into one of a microcomputer's circuit boards, or it can be an external device. We will discuss these and other input/output devices in more detail in Chapter Six. See Figure 4–7.

SOFTWARE AND APPLICATIONS

The hardware of a microcomputer system is lifeless without **software** (programs) to direct it to accomplish specific *applications* (tasks) for users. It takes a combination of both **system software** and **application software** to bring hardware to life.

We presented an overview of the major types of software at the end of Chapter Three. We also summarized the most popular types of system and application software in use today. (Refer back to Figures 3–14 and 3–15.) All of these types of software are available for microcomputers! We will go into more detail on the functions and characteristics of these and other types of computer software in Chapter Seven. Major business applications of the computer will be discussed in later chapters. Also, a hands-on introduction to the use of several types of popular software packages for microcomputers is provided in the Appendix at the back of the book. But for now, let's look briefly at what types of software and applications are most popular with today's microcomputer users. See Figure 4–8.

FIGURE

4–7 Microcomputer output devices

A video monitor and printer are the most widely used output devices.

FIGURE 4–8 Popular microcomputer software

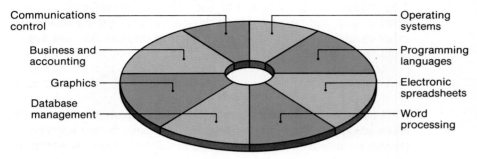

Communications control — Operating systems

Business and accounting — Programming languages

Graphics — Electronic spreadsheets

Database management — Word processing

System Software

The most important system software package is an **operating system** program, which supervises and supports the operations of the microcomputer as it executes the application programs of a user. Popular microcomputer operating systems are CP/M and CP/M-86 by Digital Research, MS-DOS and XENIX by Microsoft, and APPLE-DOS and TRS-DOS by Apple and Radio Shack respectively. CP/M was the most widely used operating system for 8-bit microcomputers, while MS-DOS is the most popular operating system for 16-bit micros, especially the IBM PC and similar computers. The Xenix operating system and IBM's PCIX are microcomputer versions of the AT&T UNIX system for larger computers. Other versions of this popular operating system are being developed for microcomputers, especially the newer 32-bit *supermicros*.

Another important system software category for microcomputers is **language translator** programs. They translate programs written in a variety of programming languages into machine language codes the computer can execute. They also allow you (and programmers) to write your own programs. The most popular microcomputer language translators are those for the BASIC programming language (called BASIC *interpreters*). Many microcomputers come with BASIC interpreters already built into their ROM storage circuits. Other popular language translators are those for the Assembler, C, FORTRAN, COBOL, LOGO and Pascal programming languages.

One of the most important types of system software packages available for microcomputers are **database management systems** (DBMS). They control the creation, maintenance, and use of a database of stored data or information that can be accessed by several different user applications. They allow you to build files of data and information in your database on any subject you wish, whether it's a homemaker's recipe file or the inventory and customer files of a business. Then you can use your database to get quick answers to questions about your data, and even produce formal reports.

Some of the popular DBMS packages are dBASE II and III by Ashton-Tate, R:base 4000 by Microrim, and Condor 3 by Condor.

Other types of system software used on microcomputers include communications control programs, application development systems, and various service and utility programs. Communications control programs help you use your microcomputer as an *intelligent terminal* to communicate with other computers tied into a *data communications network*. Application development systems are programs that help you develop your own application programs. Numerous service and utility programs are available to augment similar programs provided in many operating systems. A *sort* program, which sorts data, or an *editor* program, which creates and edits data and program files, are examples.

Application Software

What can you do with a microcomputer? The answer to the question of what **applications** (uses) can be accomplished by a microcomputer is tied directly to the **application software packages** available. Fortunately, a wide variety of application packages are available for purchase at reasonable prices for many microcomputers. Of course, you could always write your own programs, but this is not necessary for most microcomputer users. Thus microcomputers can do most of the things that larger computers can do, only they do it just for you!

There are literally thousands of application software packages available for you to use with a microcomputer system. They allow you to use a microcomputer to accomplish thousands of specific tasks. We introduced several of types of application programs in the last chapter, all of which are very popular with microcomputer users. Examples of some of the most widely used application packages for both personal and professional applications are summarized below.

■ **Word processing packages**—programs that automate the creation, editing, and printing of *documents* (letters, reports, etc.) by electronically processing *text data* (words, phrases, sentences, etc.) for a user. Thus the microcomputer, with the help of word processing packages (like WordStar, Volkswriter, and Multimate), has made traditional typing and typewriters obsolete, and has become an excellent **office computer**.

■ **Electronic spreadsheet packages**—programs that display a worksheet of rows and columns where a user can insert data and formulas that represent a *model* of the user's problem. The programs then automatically manipulate the data in the spreadsheet in response to commands of the user, thus providing an excellent tool for analysis and planning. Thus the microcomputer, with the help of electronic spreadsheet packages (like VisiCalc, Multiplan, and SuperCalc), has outmoded the use of calculators and paper worksheets and has become the premier **professional computer**.

■ **Graphics packages**—programs that transform numeric data into graphics displays (such as line charts, bar charts, and pie charts) on a video monitor, or make paper copies on a printer or plotter. Examples of some popular packages are Graphplan, Business Graphics, and Graphpak. Thus the microcomputer and graphics packages have outmoded the laborious hand drawing of graphics media especially for business presentations and home use.

■ **Integrated packages**—programs that combine the ability to do several applications with your microcomputer without having to change between separate programs. Electronic spreadsheets, database management, graphics, data communications, word processing, and other functions may be integrated into one package. Examples are Lotus 1-2-3, Symphony, Corporate MBA, and various **operating environment** packages, such as VisiOn, Topview, and DESQ. Thus the microcomputer, with the help of these integrated packages, has become a versatile **intelligent workstation**.

■ **Common business packages**—programs that accomplish the information processing tasks required by common accounting and other business functions. Examples are sales analysis, billing, accounts receivable and payable, inventory control, general ledger accounting, and payroll processing. Thus the microcomputer has outmoded manual methods for such functions with the help of these programs and has become a versatile **small business computer**.

Personal and Home Applications

One of the great attractions of microcomputers is their use for personal and home applications. The comparative simplicity and low entrance cost, as well as the many possible personal uses of the microcomputer, have caused a tremendous boom in personal computing. Of course, additional increments of hardware and software can escalate the cost of personal and home computers as users become more proficient and want additional computing power to expand and improve their systems' capabilities. The cost of such high-priced personal computer systems may be hard to cost-justify on the basis of personal pleasure and home applications. This is why many personal computer systems are being used for business and professional applications, which can more easily justify their expense. In any event, there are a large number of personal and home uses for microcomputers that we can group into *five major categories*.

■ Entertainment and Hobbies

The availability of "video game" programs is a strong attraction for many personal computer users. Many users moved up to microcomputers after first trying their hand at "dumb" electronic TV game devices. Microcomputers can provide more challenging games like electronic chess or backgammon or complex "fantasy" games like Dungeons and Dragons. Computer games can provide many hours of stimulating and creative individual and family entertainment. Personal computers can themselves become a personal hobby. Some hobbyists enjoy developing new and unique uses for their microcomputers, and in continually testing and modifying such applications. Other people may use their personal computers to support their own hobbies. For example, ham radio operators may use their personal computers to calculate and keep track of the locations of their overseas contacts; amateur musicians might use a "music synthesizer" attachment to generate new musical scores; while amateur artists can use the graphics capability of their computers to draw electronic designs, pictures, and other visual art.

■ Personal Finance

Personal computer systems can be used for financial recordkeeping, analysis, and planning. Financial data, such as family budgets, taxes, mortgage and other installment payments, transportation and other expenses, and investments, can be organized and stored for later retrieval and analysis. The personal computer, therefore, can help with personal and family budgets, income tax preparation, bank checking and savings account balancing, medical and other insurance claims processing, tracking the stock market, evaluating various investment opportunities, and other forms of financial analysis and planning.

■ Home Management

Personal computers are versatile home management tools. They can help control home heating systems to conserve energy, run security alarm systems, control household appliances, maintain fire alarm systems, control home lighting, and automate lawn and garden sprinkler systems. They can also help with household recordkeeping, such as maintaining an inventory of all major items in a home, a file of recipes and menus, or a file of names, addresses, and phone numbers. Personal word processing applications can use the microcomputer to automate letter writing and other correspondence, produce mailing lists, keep dairies, and prepare other forms of typewritten material.

- Education and Personal Development

Microcomputers are already being used for computer-assisted instruction (CAI) in grade schools, high schools, and colleges. This trend has extended into the home as educational "programmed learning" software is used in microcomputer systems. The computer can tutor students (both children and adults) in almost any subject, because many educational program packages are available on magnetic tape cassettes, cartridges, and floppy disks. Thus, personal computers can tutor students in everything from mathematics to music, from English and French to BASIC and Pascal. Program packages are also available for such "personal development" applications as relaxation therapy, self-hypnosis, assertiveness training, positive thinking, and other forms of development. Software is even available that can direct the microcomputer to chart biorhythms and give astrological advice!

- Information and Communication

Personal computers have become intelligent terminals that are tied into public computer-based **information networks**, such as *The Source* and *CompuServe*. These networks offer access to commercial **data banks** and software packages and support limited *electronic mail* services between users. Figure 4–9 illustrates the wide variety of services offered. Costs are presently about $6 per hour for evening, nighttime, and weekend use of regular telephone lines. Of course, your microcomputer needs to have a **modem** and communications control software, too. Still being tried out on a limited basis is the provision of **videotex** services that allow two-way transmission of pictures and sound between a computerized home TV set and computerized national data bank services.

SELECTING A MICROCOMPUTER SYSTEM

Which microcomputer system should you buy? That's a question you will be faced with sooner than you think. It's a difficult question to answer quickly, but it can be answered after a reasonable amount of research and analysis. That should include reading Chapter Eighteen, Acquiring Information System Resources, which discusses the subject of evaluating computer hardware and software in greater detail. But let's briefly hit the high points of what you should consider.

FIGURE 4–9 Home computer network services

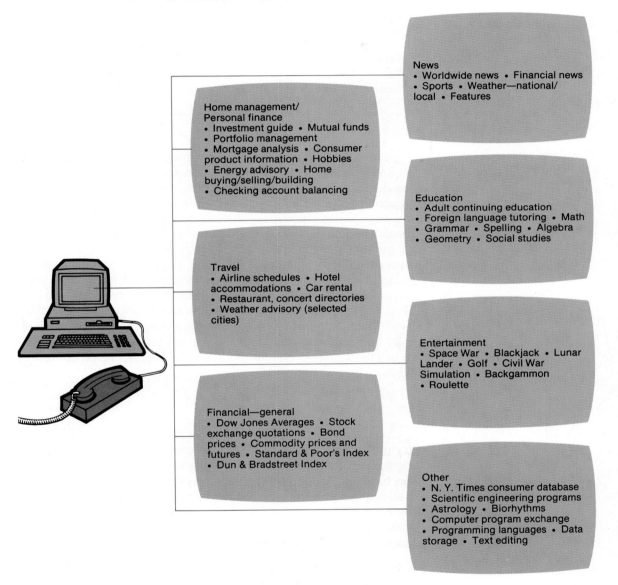

We have just covered the hardware, software, and applications of microcomputer systems. Those are exactly the topics you should evaluate, only in reverse order! Then you should evaluate three other important factors: capabilities, costs, and sources. See Figure 4–10.

FIGURE

4–10 Six basic microcomputer selection questions

- **Applications.**   What do I want to do with my microcomputer?
- **Software.**   What system and application software packages will I need?
- **Hardware.**   What microprocessor, memory capacity, and peripheral devices are needed?
- **Capabilities.**   What specific software and hardware capabilities will I need?
- **Costs.**   How much can I afford to pay?
- **Sources.**   Where should I purchase the hardware, software, and other services I need?

Applications

What do you want to do with your microcomputer? Since there are so many things that microcomputers can do, you have to answer this question first. How you answer will then determine the microcomputer software and hardware you should buy. For example, do you want to use it primarily for word processing? Games? Financial spreadsheet analysis? Common business applications? Home management? Graphics? Database management? Or a combination of these uses? For example, if you want a computer to play video games, plus do a few simple home management tasks, then you can get by with the lower-priced microcomputer systems (about $200 to $1,000) generally called **home computers**. If, on the other hand, you want to do word processing, spreadsheet analysis, database management, and graphics, you will probably have to move up to a medium-priced (about $1,800 to $3,000) **personal computer** system.

Software

Once you have narrowed the applications you are interested in doing, you can then investigate the software that will allow your microcomputer to accomplish these tasks. You should ask yourself two basic questions: What types of **system software** (operating systems, programming languages translators, database management systems, communications control programs, etc.) are needed? What types of **application software** (word processing package, electronic spreadsheet package, game programs, home management package, graphics package, common business applications packages, and so on) will I need? How you answer these questions will play a major role in determining the hardware you will need.

Hardware

Once you have narrowed your applications and software alternatives, you can determine your basic hardware requirements. You have to answer two basic hardware questions:

- What **microprocessor** and **primary memory** capacity is needed?
- What **peripheral devices** are required?

For example, the software needed for some applications will only work with specific microprocessors, a minimum memory capacity, and minimum peripheral requirements. Here's a more specific example. Many business application packages for microcomputers will only work with the Microsoft DOS operating system, the Intell 8088 microprocessor, at least 64K of main memory, one floppy disk drive, a video monitor, and a printer if you want printed output. Why? Because those are the minimum specifications for the popular IBM Personal Computer and its many "compatible" cousins. By the way, be sure to demand proof that a microcomputer is **compatible** with another microcomputer's software (i.e., that programs written for one microcomputer can run without modification on another). For example, there are many supposed IBM PC *compatibles* or *clones* that cannot run the same software without significant modifications.

Capabilities

Once you have listed the *types* of hardware and software you will probably need, you must determine the specific hardware and software *capabilities* that are required for your applications. Some examples: Should you settle for a microcomputer model that just meets your needs or one that can expand its capabilities as your needs grow? Will you need a *graphic high-resolution color* video monitor or will a *low-resolution monochrome* monitor work well enough? Will you need a *correspondence*-quality printer, or will a *draft*-quality printer be OK? Should you buy a powerful *command driven* word processing software package, or settle for a less-powerful but more *user-friendly menu-driven* package? Will you need a simple file management package or a more powerful DBMS package that can handle your business records as your needs grow? Note that these hardware and software questions deal with specific capabilities (power, clarity, print quality, ease-of-use, expandability, and so on) that may vary among different hardware and software products.

Costs

Before you finally select the types and capabilities of hardware and software you will need, you had better look at the costs involved. You will quickly see that every hardware of software capability has its price, and that the price of a computer system that does all that you want can escalate out of sight! At this point, you will probably have to lower your expectations, tighten your belt, and settle for less than you originally wanted.

One of the first things you will discover is that the microprocessor is one of the cheapest parts of a microcomputer system. By itself, it may cost less than $20! Even the cost of the main system unit with all of its circuitry can be surpassed by the cost of peripheral devices, such as some high resolution color graphics video monitors ($900) or some correspondence quality printers ($2,000). And don't forget software. List prices for some popular software packages are: word processing ($375), electronic spreadsheet ($275), database management system ($695), graphics package ($150), integrated applications package ($700), and more! Of course, some computers systems come with specific hardware and software *bundled* together in one package. For example, you can get a system with a built-in video monitor and disk drive, plus spreadsheet and word processing software packages included in one price. Only you can determine whether this combination of products and features meets your needs.

Sources

Microcomputer hardware and software are available from many sources. You can deal direct with some hardware manufacturers and software suppliers, though you will probably do most of your shopping at one of the thousands of retail computer stores (like Computerland and The Computer Store.) They sell many different brands of microcomputers, peripheral devices, and software packages, and also may provide educational and maintenance services. IBM and some other manufacturers have retail outlets in major cities, and Radio Shack has a chain of thousands of stores selling its computers. Sears and other department stores, as well as discount stores, also carry microcomputer products. Many hardware and software products are available by mail order, usually at lower prices than at computer retail stores.

Of course, the saying "you get what you pay for," has a lot of truth to it. Buying a less-expensive off-brand microcomputer, peripheral device, or software package will likely lead to performance, reliability, and maintenance problems. Also, though *full-service* computer retail outlets may have higher prices, they sell products from the more reputable hardware and software suppliers, have on-site education and repair services, and thus provide you with more reliable service and support. However, once you become an experienced and knowledgeable microcomputer user, you can probably deal safely with reputable mail order, discount, and specialized hardware and software suppliers.

REAL WORLD APPLICATION 4-2

Connecticut Mutual Life Insurance Company

The corporate headquarters of the Connecticut Mutual Life Insurance Company is located in Hartford. So is its central computer, an IBM 3081 mainframe. Connecticut Mutual's agents (working in offices all across the country) need to communicate with the 3081 to access the data stored there. To serve their clients better, the agents also need their own individual computers for jobs like financial planning and sales proposals. The problem was finding a tool that could both *communicate and compute*. Working with one of IBM's national account marketing teams, Connecticut Mutual found the solution: 1,000 IBM Personal Computers.

With all the other personal computers out there, why did Connecticut Mutual choose the IBM Personal Computer? The company's own data processing experts recommended it. After extensive comparison, they concluded that the IBM Personal Computer was the superior performer overall. Its BASIC language for communication support was better. Its keyboard, with 10 programmable function keys, was more responsive and made the computer easier to use. Its display was crisper and easier to read. The modular design was more flexible. The price was more competitive. And they believed that the

IBM Personal Computer would ultimately be the most widely supported—in terms of both hardware and software. The differences were substantial and the choice was clear.

Today, Connecticut Mutual's agents take advantage of their IBM Personal Computers in many ways. For a more efficient approach to financial analyses and planning, they use the program called VisiCalc. To correspond with current customers and future prospects, they use word processing programs. To communicate with headquarters and field offices, they use the IBM Personal Computer for "electronic mail." And they use custom applications (developed using IBMs Advanced BASIC) for sales charts and graphs. All told, they use their IBM Personal Computers to be more productive. But Connecticut Mutual expected more from IBM than years in computer experience and a superior product. They expected IBM support and got it.

- Why did Connecticut Mutual need so many microcomputers?
- Why did they select the IBM Personal Computer?
- How are they using their PCs?

Source: Courtesy of IBM.

You can become a more knowledgeable microcomputer user by more education and hands-on experience, and by reading books about computers and various computer industry and consumer periodicals. A flood of computer books and periodicals are being published, some of them of questionable value. However, among the many excellent periodicals are *Personal Computing, Popular Computing, Creative Computing, Infoworld, Byte,* and magazines for specific types of computers, like *PC Magazine* for owners of the IBM PC and compatible computers, and *A+* for Apple Computer users.

FIGURE 4–11 Comparative guide to selected microcomputer systems

System	Base Price	Processor	Memory (Bytes) RAM Standard Maximum	ROM Standard Maximum	Secondary Storage	Operating System	Programming Languages Included	Available from Manufacturer	Software Availability	Service and Support	Notes
Commodore 64	Under $200	6510 8-bit Z-80 optional	64K 64K	20K 20K	Includes cassette interface Optional floppy disks Accepts ROM cartridges	Included in ROM	BASIC, Assembler	None	Growing; a great deal is expected	Good through dealers	Very popular home computer system
Atari 800XL	Under $200	6502C 8-bit	64K 64K	24K 24K	Includes cassette interface Optional floppy disks Accepts ROM cartridges	Included in ROM	Atari BASIC in ROM	LOGO, Pilot, Microsoft BASIC Assembler	Good through Atari; excellent elsewhere	Good through dealers and service centers	Popular, but uncertain prospects
Radio Shack TRS-80 Model 100 Portable	Under $1,000	8085 8-bit	8K 32K	32K 32K	Includes cassette interface	Included in ROM	BASIC in ROM	None	Scheduler, address book, WP, and communications included in ROM	Excellent from Radio Shack	An excellent portable work-station. Small LCD screen
Apple IIe	Under $1,000	6502A 8-bit	64K 128K	6K 16K	Includes cassette interface Optional floppy disks	Included in ROM and on disk	Extended BASIC in ROM	Pascal, Pilot, FORTRAN, LOGO, Assembler	Good through Apple, very good elsewhere	Good through dealers	Most popular 8-bit microcomputer
IBM PC Junior (Enhanced Version)	Under $1,000	8088 16-bit	128K 512K	64K 64K	Includes Cassette interface 5¼" floppy disk included (360K) Accepts ROM cartridges	PC-DOS in ROM	BASIC in ROM	LOGO	Good from IBM; excellent where compatible with PC software	Good through dealers	IBM's entry into the home market.
Kaypro II	Under $1,500	Z-80 8-bit	64K 64K	2K 2K	Dual 5¼" floppy disk drives included (190K each)	CP/M on disk	S-BASIC, M-BASIC	Assembler, C, COBOL, FORTH, FORTRAN, LISP, Pascal	Word processing, spreadsheet, and file management included; more through CP/M sources	Good through dealers	A good deal for the money. Portable and popular.

Computer	Price	Processor	Memory	Display	Disk	DOS	BASIC	Languages	Software availability	Service	Comments
IBM Personal Computer	Under $2,000	8088 16-bit	64K 640K	40K 40K	Includes cassette interface Optional dual 5¼" floppy and hard disk drives	PC-DOS in ROM and on Disk	Extended BASIC in ROM and on disk	Assembler, C, BASIC, Pascal, FORTRAN, COBOL	Excellent through outside sources, some from IBM	Good through dealers	Most popular 16-bit professional microcomputer
Radio Shack TRS-80 Model 4	Under $2,000	Z-80A 8-bit	16K 128K	14K 14K	Includes cassette interface dual 5¼" floppy disks included Optional hard disk	Included in ROM	Extended BASIC in ROM	C-BASIC, COBOL, FORTRAN, Assembler, LOGO, Pascal, Pilot	Good through Radio Shack, excellent elsewhere	Good through dealers and Computer Centers	Very popular. Can use Model III software.
Texas Instruments Professional	Under $2,000	8080 16-bit	64K 256K	8K 16K	Optional dual floppy disk drives	MS-DOS on disk	M-BASIC	Assembler, C-BASIC, C, COBOL, FORTRAN, Pascal	Excellent from TI and MS-DOS sources	Good through TI and dealers	An excellent alternative to the IBM PC.
Apple Macintosh	Under $2,500	MC 68000 32-bit	128K 512K	64K	3½" floppy disk drive built-in	Included in ROM	None	BASIC, Pascal, LOGO, Assembler	Some in ROM. Limited but growing availability	Good through dealers	Popular 32-bit microcomputer.
Compaq Portable	Under $3,000	8088 16-bit	128K 640K	N/A	Dual 5¼" floppy disk drives included (320K each)	MS-DOS on disk	BASIC	COBOL, FORTRAN, Pascal	IBM PC-compatible; excellent from PC sources	Good through dealers	Portable, rugged, and PC-compatible. An excellent value.
Hewlett-Packard HP-150	Under $4,000	8088 16-bit	256K 640K	160K 160K	Dual 3½" disk drives included (256K each)	MS-DOS on disk	Microsoft BASIC	Pascal	Good through HP; excellent from MS-DOS sources	Good through HP and dealers	A unique, touch-screen system that could become popular.

Source: Adapted from Carlton Shrum, *How to Buy a Personal Computer* (Sherman Oaks, Calif.: Alfred Publishing, 1984), pp. 54–61.

In addition, there are many hardware and software catalogs and *buyers guides* that are good sources of comparative product information. Last, visiting computer stores, joining computer clubs and users groups, and attending national and regional computer shows are good ways to get "inside information," product literature, and see equipment demonstrations. Figure 4–11 closes our discussion of microcomputers with a brief comparative guide to some of the more popular microcomputer systems.

MINICOMPUTER SYSTEMS

Minicomputers are small general-purpose computers that are larger and more powerful than most microcomputers but are smaller and less powerful than most of the models of mainframe computer systems. However, this is not a precise distinction, since high-end models of microcomputer systems are more powerful than some minicomputers, and high-end models of minicomputers are more powerful than some small and medium-size mainframe computers. Minicomputers thus have a wide range of processing capabilities and hardware characteristics.

In Chapter One we reported that the minicomputer was a development of the third generation of computers, which began in the mid-1960s. Sales of minicomputers accelerated during the late 60s and 70s when minicomputers became the fastest-growing segment of the computer market. The reasons for their great popularity are obvious. At one time, most computer manufacturers and DP managers believed that all of the data processing needs of an organization could be handled by conventional larger-scale computer systems. However, many *end users* in scientific laboratories, engineering departments, manufacturing and industrial process plants, and many smaller organizations could not afford larger computer systems, or they were dissatisfied with the level of service provided by large central computer installations. These users needed a smaller, less-costly computer system that was still large enough to handle their information processing requirements.

Minicomputers were designed to handle a limited set of jobs and peripheral devices. Thus they could be physically smaller and less costly than larger computers. Most minicomputers can also function in ordinary operating environments, do not need special air conditioning or electrical wiring, and can be placed in most offices and work areas. In addition, since they are comparatively easy to operate, the smaller models of minicomputers do not need a staff of DP professionals but can rely on properly trained regular employees. Therefore, large numbers of users purchased and continue to acquire minicomputer systems. See Figure 4–12.

FIGURE

4–12 Minicomputer systems

A VAX 11/730.

B Prime 850 Super-Minicomputer.

A

B

Hardware

Minicomputers can perform all of the functions of larger computers but are typically smaller, low-cost machines, which usually have fewer registers, smaller word length, slower processing speeds, smaller memories, and less input/output and data communication capabilities. Standard minicomputers typically have a 16-bit word length, but there has been a major shift to 32-bit **super-minicomputers**. Primary storage capacity might range from 256K to several megabytes of semiconductor memory. A wide variety of *miniperipherals* are available for minicomputer systems. Smaller minicomputers might be limited to a CRT terminal, slow-speed character printer, and floppy disk secondary storage, while larger minicomputers use more peripherals, such as multiple CRT terminals, larger capacity hard magnetic disk units, faster line printers, and punched card and magnetic tape devices. Typically, CRT terminals are used for keyboard input and video displays, and printing terminals or small line printers are used for hard copy paper output. Magnetic floppy disks and removable disk packs are used to provide several megabytes of secondary storage. Smaller versions of standard magnetic tape and disk units, faster printing devices, and many other peripheral devices are available. Many minicomputers also have a data communications capability since they are widely used in distributed processing networks.

Software and Applications

Software is an important component of minicomputer systems. A full range of software packages is available, including operating systems, major programming languages, and application software packages developed for a large number of specific industries and types of businesses. FORTRAN, COBOL, BASIC, and RPG and several other languages are available on minicomputers, as are database management systems (DBMS) and communications control programs. Many prewritten application software packages are available, which make it unnecessary for minicomputer users to develop many of their own programs.

Minicomputers are quite versatile. They are being used for a large number of business data processing and scientific applications. Minicomputers first became popular for use in scientific research, instrumentation systems, engineering analysis, and industrial process monitoring and control. Minicomputers can easily handle such uses because these applications are narrow in scope and do not demand the processing power of large systems. Minicomputers are now being used as *intelligent terminals* and *end-user* computer systems in *distributed processing networks*. They serve as industrial process-control and manufacturing plant computers, where they play a major role in computer-assisted manufacturing (CAM) and computer-assisted design (CAD) applications. They are also being used as **front-end computers** to control data communications networks and large numbers of data-entry terminals. Also, many current **office computers**, or **word processing computers**, are either special-purpose or dedicated minicomputers supporting several word processing terminals. In addition, a large number of minicomputers are used as **small business computers**. They provide more processing power and online storage and can support more users at the same time than microcomputers used for business applications.

Cost and Sources

The wide variation of minicomputer capabilities is reflected in a wide range of prices for minicomputer systems. The majority of minicomputers cost between $10,000 and $50,000, though prices between $50,000 and $100,000 and even higher must be paid for some *super-mini* systems. Like microcomputer systems, the cost of input/output and secondary storage peripheral devices frequently exceed the cost of the minicomputer CPU. Each unit of software needed must also be purchased unless it is "packaged" along with the computer hardware.

The leading manufacturers of minicomputers include Digital Equipment Corporation (DEC), IBM, Honeywell, Hewlett-Packard, Data General, Wang Laboratories, Prime Computer, Datapoint, Perkin-Elmer, and Texas Instruments. Examples of some popular minicomputers include the DEC VAX-11/730, The Wang 2200 systems, the Data General Eclipse C/150, the IBM System/36 and 38, the Hewlett-Packard HP1000 series, the Texas Instruments DS 990, and the Honeywell DP/S 6 series. Minicomputers can be purchased directly from a local or regional office of the larger computer manufacturers or through independent distributors who represent one or more minicomputer manufacturers who do not sell directly to end users.

MAINFRAME COMPUTER SYSTEMS

What is a **mainframe** computer? That's the name given to computers that are larger and more powerful than microcomputers and minicomputers. *Larger* is understandable, but what does *more powerful* mean? Let's just say that mainframe computer systems frequently have:

- One or more processors with larger word lengths (32 bits or more) and greater processing speed (up to several million instructions per second-MIPS)

FIGURE

4–13 Mainframe computer systems

A Sperry UNIVAC 1100/AVP multiprocessor computer system.

B IBM 4341 medium-size computer system.

A

B

- Larger primary storage capacities (several megabytes) and greater secondary storage capacities (several gigabytes of online magnetic disk and tape storage).
- The ability to service many users at once, because they can process several programs at the same time (*multiprogramming*) and can handle more peripheral devices (many terminals, disk and tape drives, printers, etc.).

We have already indicated that the development of microcomputers and minicomputers has erased many of the traditional distinctions between various sizes of computers. For example, many *supermini* computers are frequently less expensive and more powerful than some medium-size mainframe computers. Though these developments have weakened the traditional size distinctions between full-scale computer systems, the concept of mainframe computers is still used in the computer industry.

Hardware

Several large computer manufacturers produce *families* or *product lines* of mainframe computers that have models ranging in size from *small* to *medium* to *large*. This allows them to provide a range of choices to their customers, depending on their information processing needs. Most models in a family are compatible (i.e., programs written for one model can usually be run on other models of the same family with little or no changes). This allows customers to move up to larger models of the same mainframe family, as their needs grow. A classic example is IBM's System/370 family (though it is being phased out by newer models), which has small (Model 115), medium (Models 138 and 148), and large (Models 158 and 168) sizes of mainframe computers.

Mainframe computers may combine several CPUs in a *multiprocessor* arrangement, have memories ranging from 1 to 50 megabytes, have operating speeds in the low nanosecond range, and processing speeds from one to several MIPS. Depending on their size, they can use many high-capacity magnetic disk drives to provide several gigabytes of online secondary storage. They can also handle a variety of magnetic tape drives, printers, and other specialized input/output devices, and can support many (up to several hundred) remote terminals.

Software and Applications

A complete line of system and application software is provided by manufacturers and other software suppliers for mainframe computers. This includes advanced operating systems, database management systems, communications control programs, and language translator programs for many different programming languages. A wide selection of sophisticated and specialized application packages are also available to handle the information processing needs of specific industries, such as manufacturing, banking, airlines, and retailing. Such software uses the advanced hardware features of mainframe computers to process many different jobs for many different users at the same time.

Whereas microcomputers and minicomputers may be used by one individual or a few people, mainframe computers are designed to handle the information processing needs of organizations in business, government, and education with many employees and customers or complex computational problems. Small and medium sizes of mainframe computers can handle the processing chores of smaller organizations or the regional divisions of larger organizations. They can handle the processing of thousands of customer inquiries, employee paychecks, student registrations, sales transactions, and inventory changes, to name a few. You can't beat such computers when it comes to processing large volumes of data. They can also handle large numbers of users needing access at the same time to the centralized databases and libraries of application programs of *timesharing* networks.

Large mainframe computer systems are used by major corporations and government agencies, which have enormous and complex data processing assignments. For example, large computers are necessary for organizations processing millions of transactions each day, such as major national banks or the national stock exchanges. Large mainframes can also handle the great volume of complex calculations involved in scientific and engineering analysis and simulation of complex design projects, such as the design of aircraft and spacecraft. A large computer can also act as a *host computer* for *distributed processing networks* that include many smaller computers. Thus, large mainframe computers are used in the national and international computing networks of such major corporations as airlines, banks, and oil companies.

Cost and Sources

The cost of a mainframe computer can range up into the millions of dollars! Therefore, many mainframes are leased instead of purchased outright. Of course, costs will vary greatly depending on such features as the amount of primary memory, input/output *channels*, and data communications *ports*, as well as the number and types of input, output, and secondary storage devices included in the system. Purchase prices for small mainframes may vary from

REAL WORLD APPLICATION 4–3

Mellon Bank

Everything about Mellon Bank is big, especially its computers. The bank, headquartered in Pittsburgh, is the 15th largest financial institution in the United States, with assets of over $16 billion. Its the biggest bank outside the money centers of New York, Chicago, and Los Angeles. The bank's computers are large, partly because of the views held by George P. DiNardo, senior vice president and director of the bank's Information Management and Research Department. "We believe entirely in the economies of scale, and, therefore, I am a devotee of the big iron," DiNardo says, adding that he has long resisted the widespread trend to implement minicomputers and other methods to distribute processing. "I stood alone for 10 years while the rest of the world went into distributed data processing. But now they're coming back into my camp," he says. "We eschewed the medium-sized hardware when it came out. And the bigger the machine, the better we like it."

Mellon Bank currently has one IBM 3081 processor—with plans to add two more—along with two 3033s and two 370/168s. But it is more than simply a preference with DiNardo. The "big iron" he wholeheartedly embraces is there for a purpose: to support the more than 160 highly integrated systems that drive Mellon's array of banking services. To Mellon, integration means the ability of one system to feed data to the next, without human intervention. "If you are offering integrated systems, you'll need a big piece of machinery to drive them, " DiNardo says. "Our goal is to reduce the cost of computing per unit of work by 10 percent per year, a goal we have achieved for the last five years. Big computers help us do it."

DiNardo's Information Management and Research Department serves all of Mellon Bank, which has 120 branches in contiguous counties in Pennsylvania, and services the other subsidiaries of Mellon National Corporation, Mellon Bank's holding company, as well. It is also responsible for servicing almost 300 correspondent banks in 12 states. That makes Mellon Bank "perhaps the largest bank-owned DP service bureau in the United States. We are also, we believe, the most automated financial institution in the country," DiNardo says.

DiNardo admits that Mellon has experienced some problems with big iron, and says there were times when he and his staff were "sweating bullets." "However, on the whole," he says, "large centralized processors are increasingly attractive as the state of the art improves. Each iteration of big hardware has higher levels of reliability and price performance," DiNardo believes. "For example, IBM has really outdone itself with the 3081, and we are very, very pleased with it," he says. "The point is, with competition, you're getting a better product no matter whom you get it from, and these improvements have done away with most of the reasons why people were afraid of going big iron." Sticking to his guns in regard to large processors has paid off in another dimension, DiNardo says. "We got a head start in integrated systems, as well as in tying the big iron together," while others were concerned with spreading it out.

- Why does the Mellon Bank need large mainframe computer systems?
- Why doesn't Mellon Bank use more small computers distributed throughout the organization in a distributed processing network?

Source: William P. Martorelli, "Mellon Bank Holds Down Costs with Big Iron,'" *Information Systems News,* June 16, 1982. Copyright 1982 by CMP Publications, Inc. Reprinted by permission.

$50,00 to $250,000, with monthly rentals from $1,000 to $5,000 per month. Medium-size mainframes may cost between $200,000 and $1 million, and rent for between $5,000 and $20,000 per month. Large mainframes have purchase prices that may vary from about $1 million to $5 million, and rent for between $20,000 to $200,000 per month.

Mainframe computers are manufactured by several large firms, including IBM, Control Data, Sperry, Burroughs, NCR, Honeywell, DEC, Hewlett-Packard, Tandem, and Amdahl. They produce a variety of small, medium, and large mainframe computers. Examples of some current small mainframes are the IBM 4331, most of Hewlett-Packard's 3000 series, DEC's VAX 11/780, and NCR's V-8535 II. Medium-size mainframes include the IBM 4341, the Burroughs 4700, and Honeywell's DPS 7 series. Examples of large mainframes include the IBM 3033 and 3083, the Honeywell 66/80, the Amdahl 5860 and 5880, and the Univac 1100/60.

OTHER TYPES OF COMPUTERS

Though most computers fit into the micro, mini, and mainframe categories, several other classifications of computers exist. They include *supercomputers, analog* computers, *special purpose* computers, *scientific* computers, and *multiprocessor* computer systems. Let's take a brief look at these computers to round out our coverage of the major types of computer systems in use today.

Supercomputers

The term **supercomputer** has been coined to describe a category of extremely large computer systems. A small number of supercomputers are built each year for large government research agencies, military defense systems, national weather forecasting agencies, and very large time-sharing networks. The leading maker of supercomputers is Cray Research, which produces the Cray-I, CRAY Is, and the CRAY X-MP, the most widely used supercomputers. They have a 64-bit word length, an effective machine and memory cycle time of 9.5 to 12.5 nanoseconds, and are rated at 20 to over 80 MIPS. Control Data is the other major manufacturer of supercomputers. The CDC Cyber 205 supercomputer is capable of 800-million arithmetic floating-point operations per second and is rated at 50 MIPS. Purchase prices for supercomputers are in the $5 million to $15 million range. These massive computer systems are extremely large and fast and advance the state of the art for the entire computer industry.

Analog Computers

Most computers in use today are **digital computers**, which *count* discrete units (digits) as they perform their arithmetic and logical operations. However, there also are electronic **analog computers**, which perform arithmetic operations and comparisons by *measuring* changes in magnitudes of a continuous physical phenomenon, such as electronic voltage, which represents, or is "analogous" to, the numerical values of the data being processed. Analog computers are used on a limited basis to process the data arising from scientific or engineering experiments, manufacturing processes, and military weapons systems. *For example*, the temperature changes of a chemical process can be converted by the analog computer into variations in electronic voltage and mathematically analyzed. The results of the processing could be displayed on dials, graphs, or TV screens or be used to initiate changes in the chemical process.

Special-Purpose Computers

Computers used for information processing are typically **general-purpose computers**, which are designed to process a wide variety of applications. For example, applications ranging from scientific and engineering analysis to business data processing are possible merely by changing the program of instructions stored in the machine. A **special-purpose computer** is specifically designed to process one or more specific applications. Some of these computers are so specialized that part or all of their operating instructions are built into their electronic circuitry. However, the use of built-in microprocessors and microelectronic memories makes it possible to easily customize computers for specific uses.

FIGURE

4–14 The Cray-I supercomputer

Special-purpose computers have been built for both military and civilian applications (such as aircraft and submarine navigation, and for aircraft, missile, and satellite tracking), airline reservation systems, and industrial process control. Special-purpose computers are widely used as **front-end processors** for control of data communication networks and are beginning to be used as **back-end processors** for management of database systems. Many computerized **word processors** for automatic typing and text editing are special-purpose computers found in modern offices. Other examples are electronic video game computers, computerized robots, computers used for computer assisted design and manufacturing (CAD/CAM), and computers used in a multitude of **smart products**, from digital watches and automatic cameras to microwave ovens and automobiles.

You should also realize that a general-purpose computer can be "dedicated" or committed to a particular data processing task or application, even though it is capable of performing a wide variety of other tasks and applications. Such **dedicated computers** are frequently used to perform such jobs as data communications network control, database management, input/output control for larger computer systems, online banking, and automated manufacturing. The development of minicomputers and microcomputers has accelerated the trend toward the use of dedicated computers. It has become economically feasible to dedicate these small yet powerful general-purpose computers to more specific data processing tasks, such as word processing or small business accounting applications.

Scientific Computers

Previously, computers were designed as fixed word-length machines for scientific data processing, or as variable word-length computers for business data processing. Present general-purpose computers can be programmed to operate for either scientific data processing (using fixed-length words) or business data processing (using variable-length words). However, **scientific computers** are still being built for the high-speed processing of numerical data involving complex mathematical calculations. Some scientific computers are large *supercomputers*, while others are powerful special-purpose processing units called *array processors*, which can be attached to a CPU to vastly increase the arithmetic processing power of a computer system. Scientific computers are typically designed with limited input, output, and storage capabilities. But they have advanced "number crunching" computational power in order to handle the large amount of computations that are typical of scientific applications.

MULTIPROCESSOR COMPUTER SYSTEMS

Many fourth-generation computers, from microcomputers to mainframes, can be classified as **multiprocessor computer systems** since they use multiple processors for their processing functions. Instead of having one CPU with a single control unit, arithmetic-logic unit, and primary storage unit (called a **uniprocessor design**), the CPUs of these computers contain several types of processing units. The two major types of multiprocessor architecture involve:

- **Support processor systems**. The key to this new multiprocessor design is the use of *microprocessors* to control the operations of several major processing functions, such as input/output, primary storage management, arithmetic operations, and data communications, thus freeing the main **central processor** (sometimes called the *instruction processor*) to do the major job of executing program instructions.
- **Coupled processor systems**. This multiprocessor design uses multiple CPUs, or CPU configurations consisting of multiple arithmetic-logic and control units that share the same primary storage unit.

In addition, there are two types of multiprocessor systems that involve the control and coordination of several separate computer systems.

- **Subsidiary processing systems**. One or more separate computer systems handle specific functions (such as input/output) for and under the complete control of a larger computer system. For example, a large *master* computer may utilize smaller *slave* computers to handle "housekeeping chores," such as input/output operations. In other cases, several computers may be interconnected in order to handle large processing assignments and to provide a *backup* capability that would not be present if only one large computer was used. This *fault-tolerant* capability is a major benefit of multiprocessor systems.
- **Distributed processing systems**. A network of cooperating but *independent* computer systems are physically and organizationally dispersed throughout a computer-using organization. (We will discuss such distributed processing systems in Chapter 10.)

Support Processor Systems

Figure 4–15 illustrates the *support processor* design of the IBM 4341, presently the most widely used midsize mainframe computer system. Notice how there are four separate processors: (1) the instruction processing unit, (2) the storage control unit, (3) the channel execution unit, and (4) the service processor unit. The *instruction processing unit* includes the computer's control unit and arithmetic logic unit. It controls and directs the processing of the other processing units. Thus the other processing units are *support processors*

FIGURE

4–15 Support processor design of the IBM 4341 computer system

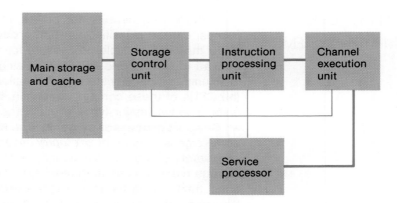

for the instruction processing unit. The *storage control unit* manages the transfer of data and instructions from the primary storage and cache units to the instruction processing unit and the channel execution unit. The channel execution unit manages the input/output control functions of the *channels* of the computer system. The *service processor* handles a variety of functions, including the operator console, a magnetic diskette drive for loading microprograms, and the circuitry for the computer's automatic and remote maintenance service functions.

Many other variations of the support processor design are used by modern computer systems. Take microcomputers, for instance. The IBM Personal Computer (and several others) now offer an optional **coprocessor**. This **arithmetic processor**, the Intel 8087, supports the main Intel 8088 microprocessor. The 8087 is a special-purpose arithmetic microprocessor to which the 8088 transfers arithmetic instructions for processing. This speeds up the processing of applications with a lot of mathematical computations. For example, Intel estimates that the 8087 executes floating-point arithmetic operations up to 200 times faster than the 8088. The IBM PC also contains two additional special-purpose support microprocessors: the Intel 8048, which handles keyboard input, and the Motorola 648Z, which controls the video monitor displays. Several other microcomputers include both an 8-bit microprocessor (like the Z80) and a 16-bit microprocessor (like the Intel 8088) to allow the use of software written for both types of microprocessors. So you see, even microcomputers take advantage of the benefits of multiprocessor design!

Coupled Processor Systems

The **coupled processor** design is illustrated by Figure 4–16, which shows two multiprocessor designs in the IBM 3000 large computer series. IBM calls this a *tightly coupled* processor design. In this configuration, two or more central processing units are interconnected so they can execute two or more instructions *simultaneously*, one in each processor. This ability of a multiprocessor computer system to execute several instructions simultaneously is known as **multiprocessing**.

It should not be confused with **multiprogramming**, which is the ability of a computer to process more than one *program* in the same time period. In multiprogramming, the CPU only executes one instruction at a time. However, it switches from the execution of an instruction from one program to the execution of an instruction from another so quickly that it gives users the appearance of simultaneous execution. We will discuss multiprogramming and other types of computer processing capabilities in Chapter Ten.

Notice that in the 3033 multiprocessor design two CPUs share the same primary storage and are coordinated by a *multiprocessing* control unit. The 3081 *processor complex* is a large computer system that IBM calls a *dyadic processor*. In this configuration, two separate CPUs and a channel processing unit are coordinated by a system control unit and share the same primary storage. The *tightly coupled* processor design allows CPUs to share access to all available primary storage, and all CPUs are under the control of a single operating system. However, there are many other coupled processor configurations. In a loosely coupled design, processors are connected by channel-to-channel adapters or system busses. For example, Figure 4–17 shows a multiprocessor design of Tandem Computers, in which multiple CPUs are interconnected by two independent busses. Notice that each *processor module* has its own primary storage and I/O processor.

Reasons for Multiprocessor Systems

Computer manufacturers are now moving toward multiprocessor architectures primarily because of the availability of powerful, low-cost microprocessors, which can be dedicated to handle specific CPU functions. Therefore, attaining the advantages of multiprocess-

FIGURE

4–16 Tightly coupled multiprocessor designs

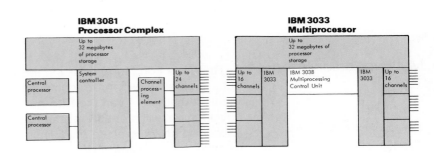

FIGURE 4–17 A loosely coupled multiprocessor design

DYNABUS™ (dual independent interprocessor busses)

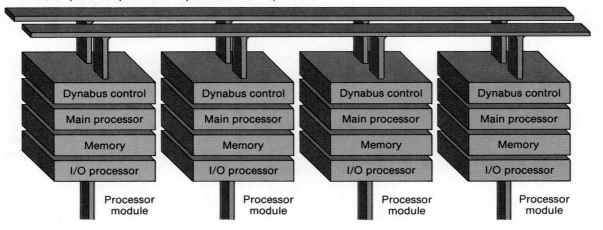

Processor module   Processor module   Processor module   Processor module

ing has become technologically and economically feasible. Multiprocessor computer systems do cost more than uniprocessor systems and may require more expensive and advanced operating systems. However, they have the following benefits:

- Significantly greater and faster processing capability.
- Better use of primary storage, since processors share primary storage units.
- More efficient use of input/output and secondary storage peripheral devices.
- Increased reliability, since multiple processors provide a backup (*fault-tolerant*) capability as well as help to meet peak load processing.
- Reduced software problems, since processors may share the same system control and service programs.
- A more economical arrangement than having several independent computer systems share processing responsibilities.

Multiprocessor Trends

There is a trend toward the increased use of multiprocessor computer architectures in microcomputers, minicomputers, and mainframe computers. Even the **fifth-generation computers** still under development will probably rely heavily on clusters of *instruction processors* that will execute many instructions at the same time in **parallel**, as opposed to present one-at-a-time (*serial*), execution.

Computers are using and will increase their use of multiprocessor designs, which might include components like the following:

- A **front-end processor** for data communications control.
- A **back-end processor** or *database machine* for management of large integrated databases.
- One or more **input/output processors** or *channel management processors* to manage the I/O channels and control units for input/output functions.
- An **arithmetic processor** or *array processor* to handle complex and large-volume arithmetic "number crunching."
- **Language processors**, which would allow direct execution of programs written in high-level programming languages (for example, a FORTRAN processor).
- **Control processors** that would accomplish functions presently done by the control programs of operating system software.
- **Service processors**, which would handle many of the subsidiary service functions of present operating system software.
- **Application processors** dedicated to the processing of major applications areas, such as sales transaction processing, electronic funds transfer processing, airline reservation processing, and the like.

Figure 4–18 illustrates the architecture of a computer with such multiprocessing components. Many of these specialized processors are already being used by present computer systems. This has led some experts to predict that the computer of the future will not be a solitary **computer system** but will be a **system of computers**.

FIGURE 4–18 An advanced multiprocessor computer system

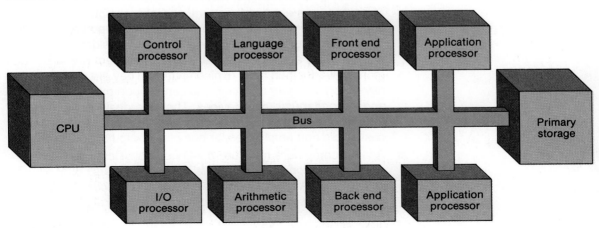

SUMMARY

- Computers are frequently classified by size (micro, mini, mainframe, and super computers) by type (digital and analog), purpose (general-purpose and special-purpose), and by processor architecture (uniprocessor and multiprocessor).

- Microcomputers are general-purpose digital computers that range in size from a computer-on-a-chip to a large typewriter plus TV-size unit. Microcomputers are being used as personal home computers, and as professional computers, intelligent workstations, and small business computers. Their personal and home uses include entertainment, personal finance, home management, education, and professional activities.

- The typical microcomputer uses a keyboard for input, a system unit containing the main microprocessor for processing and control, semiconductor RAM and ROM circuits for primary storage, floppy disk drives for secondary storage, and a video display monitor and printer for output. A wide variety of other hardware devices are also available. The software of a microcomputer system includes system software, such as operating systems, language translators, and database management systems. Thousands of application software packages are available. Most popular are packages for word processing, electronic spreadsheets, graphics, common business applications, and integrated applications.

- Selecting a microcomputer system is an important decision requiring research and analysis. Major factors that should be considered are the applications for which the microcomputer is to be used, the hardware and software required, the specific capabilities, the cost involved, and the best sources to deal with.

- Minicomputers are small general-purpose computers that are larger and more powerful than most microcomputers. They are used by small groups of users for many business data processing and scientific applications. Mainframe computers are larger and more powerful than most minicomputers. They are usually faster, have more memory capacity, and can support more input/output and secondary storage devices. They are designed to handle the information processing needs of organizations with many customers and employees, or complex computational problems.

- Analog computers measure continuous physical magnitudes, such as electronic voltage, while digital computers count discrete units (digits). A special-purpose computer is specifically designed to process a specific application, while a general-purpose computer is designed to process a wide variety of applications. Scientific computers are designed for the high-speed processing of numerical data involving complex mathematical calculations.

■ Many fourth-generation computers are multiprocessor computer systems, which have CPUs that contain several types of processing units. Some computers use microprocessors to handle subsidiary functions in support of the CPU, while others involve several separate CPUs that are interconnected and share the same primary storage. Computer manufacturers are moving toward multiprocessor architectures because of the availability of powerful low-cost microprocessors that can be dedicated to specific CPU functions.

KEY TERMS AND CONCEPTS

Microcomputer
Microprocessor
Home computer
Personal computer
Small business computer
Minicomputer
Mainframe computer
Analog and digital
  computers
Special-purpose and general-
  purpose computers.

Supercomputer
Multiprocessor computers
Personal and home
  microcomputer
  applications
Business and professional
  microcomputer
  applications
Microcomputer selection and
  evaluation factors

REVIEW AND APPLICATION QUESTIONS

1. What are the major hardware and software characteristics and uses of microcomputers? Distinguish between their use as home computers, personal computers, intelligent workstations, and small business computers.
2. Where would you buy a microcomputer? How much should you pay? Explain.
3. Outline the major factors that should be considered in acquiring a microcomputer system.
4. Can owning a personal computer be cost-justified, based on typical personal computer uses? Explain.
5. What are the major differences in the capabilities of mini and mainframe computers? How has the development of "super-mini" computers begun to blur such distinctions?

6. Are small business computers designed only for the computer applications of small business firms, or can larger organizations use such computers?
7. Are larger computer systems really necessary, given the power and versatility of modern minicomputers? Why or why not?
8. How do the following types of computers differ?
   a. Analog versus digital computers.
   b. Special-purpose versus general-purpose computers.
   c. Scientific versus business computers.
9. What are the major types of multiprocessor computer systems? Why is there a trend toward such systems?
10. Why have some experts predicted that the computer of the future will not be a *computer system*, but will be a *system of computers*?

APPLICATION PROBLEMS

1. If you have not already done so, read and answer the questions after each Real World Application in this chapter.
2. Have you used a microcomputer yet? If you have, explain what applications you accomplished. Were the microcomputer's hardware and software capabilities appropriate for the jobs you performed? Explain.
3. Have you used a mainframe or minicomputer? What jobs did you perform? Were the computer's capabilities sufficient for the jobs you had to do? Explain.
4. If you had to buy a microcomputer today, which one would you buy? Explain why in terms of the selection criteria of: applications, software, hardware, capabilities, costs, and sources.
5. Jim Klugman, the VP for Information Services of ABC Department Stores, has recommended that the company ban the purchase of microcomputers by individual stores. He feels that POS terminals and other types of terminals (tied to the firm's central mainframe computer) are sufficient. What do you think of this recommendation? Explain.
6. Joan Alvarez, a store manager for ABC Department Stores, is trying to decide on a computer purchase for her store. The top competing proposals are a proposal to purchase several microcomputer systems versus the purchase of a minicomputer system that can support up to 20 users simultaneously. What are some of the major factors that she should consider in choosing between these two proposals?

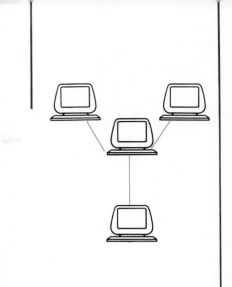

CHAPTER 5

Storage Concepts and Hardware

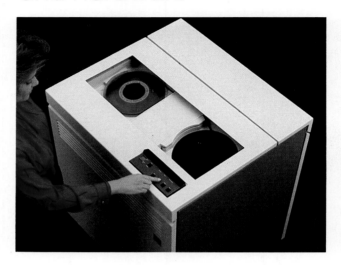

CHAPTER OUTLINE

LEARNING OBJECTIVES

The purpose of this chapter is to promote a basic understanding of computer storage hardware by analyzing (1) some important storage concepts and (2) the characteristics, functions, benefits, and limitations of major storage hardware devices.

After reading and studying this chapter, you should be able to:

1. Explain the following storage concepts:
   a. Storage media cost/speed/capacity trade-offs.
   b. CPU storage areas.
   c. Firmware versus software and hardware.
   d. Random, direct, and sequential access.
   e. Virtual memory.
2. Outline the functions, advantages, and disadvantages of semiconductor, magnetic disk, magnetic tape, and other storage hardware media and devices.
3. Identify the types of storage hardware used in your personal computer or by the computer system at your school or business. Determine the basic physical and performance characteristics of these storage devices.

SECTION I: STORAGE HARDWARE CONCEPTS

Overview of Storage Media

What storage hardware do modern information processing systems need? In Chapter Two, we introduced the concept of **storage** as one of the basic functions of any information processing system. Data and information need to be *stored* after *input*, during *processing*, and before needed as *output*. In Chapter Three, we said that a computer system accomplishes the storage function by the use of **primary storage** in the CPU, as well as in **secondary storage** hardware, such as magnetic disk and tape devices and media. Now it's time for us to take a closer look at the concepts and hardware that provide the storage function in today's computers.

Why are there so many types of storage media and devices? Take a look at Figure 5–1. It illustrates the speed, capacity, and cost of several alternative primary and secondary storage media. Notice the cost/speed/capacity trade-offs as one moves from semiconductor memories to *moving surface* magnetic media, such as magnetic disk and tape. Figure 5–1 also shows that at the present time, semiconductor memories are being used primarily for primary storage, though they are finding increasing use as high-speed secondary storage devices. Magnetic bubble memories, on the other

FIGURE

5–1 Storage media cost, speed, and capacity trade-offs

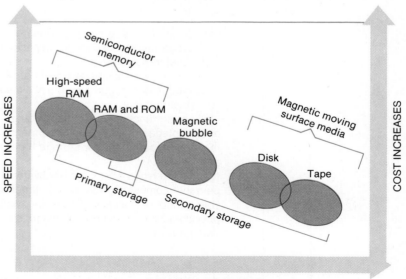

REAL WORLD APPLICATION 5-1

The Computer Memory Gap

The *primary storage* (main memory) of most modern computers consists of LSI semiconductor RAM (random access memory) circuits. Such semiconductor memory chips are fast, compact, tough, and relatively inexpensive. But their storage capacity is still limited, and they are volatile—their contents are lost if electric power is interrupted. Of course, nonvolatile ROM (read only memory) semiconductor circuit modules are available, but their use is limited to control unit microprogram storage, or infrequently changed program storage.

The *secondary storage* of most modern computer systems consists of magnetic disk and magnetic tape devices. These electromechanical, *moving-surface* memory devices use magnetic disks or tapes as their storage media. They are high-capacity nonvolatile memory devices, which magnetically retain their contents even if electric power is interrupted. But they are quite slow, compared to semiconductor memories.

Enter *bubble memory*. Magnetic bubble memory stores and moves data magnetically as tiny magnetic spots—which look like bubbles under a microscope—on the surface of a special type of semiconductor chip. Bubble memory is slower than regular semiconductor memory, but it can be produced using conventional semiconductor manufacturing processes. Bubble memory chips can store much more data than most semiconductor memory chips (1 million bits versus 64,000 bits, for example), and they are nonvolatile memory devices. Bubble memory is thus competitive with magnetic disk and tape memories in terms of nonvolatility, storage capacity, and price. It is also much faster and more reliable, since it has no moving parts, uses very little power, and is quite shock and temperature resistant. Thus magnetic bubble memory promises to fill the present computer memory gap.

- What is the computer memory gap?
- Why might magnetic bubble memories fill this gap in modern computer systems?

hand, are currently being used primarily in secondary storage applications, as are magnetic disk and tape devices.

Figure 5–1 should emphasize that the "perfect memory" does not exist—yet. High-speed storage media costs more per byte and provides less capacity. Large capacity storage media costs less per byte but is slower. That's why we have different kinds of storage media. Semiconductor and magnetic bubble memory and magnetic disk and tape devices all play specific roles in modern computer systems. We'll take a look at each of them in this chapter. But first, there are some other important computer storage concepts you need to understand.

CPU Storage Areas

Several types of storage exist within the CPU, depending on the particular storage function being performed. Figure 5–2 is a conceptual illustration of the types of storage areas that might exist within the CPU of modern computers. Let's examine each of them briefly.

Primary Storage Areas

The primary storage unit can be conceptually subdivided into input storage, output storage, program or instruction storage, and working storage. *Input storage* receives data from input devices, program storage contains program instructions, and *output storage* contains information waiting for transfer to output devices. *Working*

FIGURE 5–2 Types of CPU storage areas

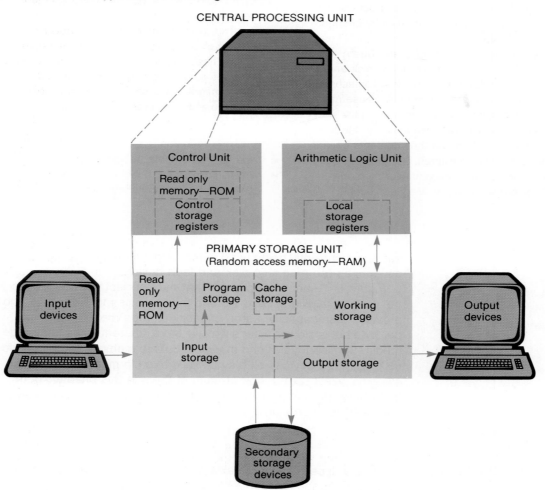

storage holds information being processed, as well as intermediate processing results. The primary storage units of many larger computers also include a small, very high-speed **buffer** or **cache** storage area. It is sometimes called *scratch pad memory*, because it is used to temporarily store data, instructions, and intermediate results during processing.

Arithmetic-Logic and Control Storage Areas

Other categories of CPU storage include *local storage*, which consists of the high-speed *registers* of the arithmetic-logic unit, and *control storage*, which consists of the *registers* and *read only storage* area of the control unit. Remember that **registers** are small high-speed storage circuits areas used for the temporary storage of an individual instruction or data element during the operation of the control and arithmetic-logic units. *General-purpose registers* carry out a variety of register functions, while special-purpose registers perform specific functions. In Chapter Three we saw the use of several types of registers in the execution of an instruction. For example, a *storage register* temporarily holds data or instructions taken from or being sent to primary storage. An *address register* may hold the address of the storage location of data, or the address of an input/output device or a control function. An *instruction register* contains the instruction being executed by the CPU. An *accummulator register* accumulates the results of arithmetic operations.

Firmware Storage

The CPUs of most computers today contain special storage circuitry modules where certain programs (**software**) are permanently stored in semiconductor ROM chips (**hardware**). This permanent storing of selected programs or instructions in ROM storage circuits is known as **firmware**. Remember from the previous chapter that ROM (read only memory) consists of microelectronic memory circuit chips whose contents have been permanently recorded into the storage circuitry. You should also realize that variations of ROM exist that are not permanent and can be changed under certain conditions. We will discuss them shortly. Important programs that do not need frequent changes are placed in ROM to protect them from accidental erasure or loss if electric power is interrupted. ROM also significantly increases the speed of program execution since programs are stored in high-speed microelectronic circuits in the form of machine language instruction codes, or even more elementary *microcode*.

It appears that firmware will continue to take over many current hardware and software functions. Electronic **logic circuitry**, which is designed to accomplish a particular task (such as perform an arithmetic operation), can be replaced by microprograms stored in microelectronic **memory circuits**. Thus firmware is also called *solid-state software*, since machine language instructions are permanently stored in semiconductor memory circuits. Given the steadily decreasing cost of microelectronic memory circuitry, many experts are predicting that firmware modules will continue to take over many functions now performed by both hardware logic circuitry or software packages. Let's look at what is happening in microcomputers.

Remember from the previous chapter that many current microcomputers (and other computers) contain ROM chips in which selected programs or parts of programs have been permanently stored. In microcomputers, this usually consists of parts of the *operating system* program of the computer, a *programming language translator* program (typically a BASIC *interpreter*), and selected application programs. For example, here's what is stored in the form of firmware in the ROM chips of three current microcomputers:

- The IBM Personal Computer has 40K bytes of ROM storage. This contains part of the PC-DOS operating system, that is, the basic input/output system (BIOS). It also uses more than half of the ROM to store a BASIC language *interpreter* (translator program).
- The Apple Macintosh microcomputer has 64K bytes of ROM storage. This contains its operating system program and the NotePad, Calculator, ScratchPad, Puzzle, and Calendar application programs.
- The Hewlett-Packard HP 110 Portable microcomputer contains 384K bytes of ROM storage. The ROM of this nine-pound *lap-sized* portable stores its MS- DOS operating system, the Lotus 1-2-3 integrated application package, a Personal Application Manager program, a MemoMaker word processing program, and a terminal communication program!

Firmware and Microprogram Storage

The control units of many current computers contain ROM modules or other read-only storage areas, where elementary machine instructions called *microinstructions* or *microcode* are stored. Sets of microinstructions (called **microprograms**) interpret the machine-language instructions of a computer program and decode them into elementary microinstructions, which are then executed. Thus, elementary functions of the control unit that had formerly been executed by *hardware* (hardwired) *logic circuits* are now executed by **firmware**.

Firmware and **microprogramming** (the use of microprograms) increase the versatility of computer systems by allowing various degrees of "customizing" of the *instruction set* of a CPU. For example, firmware enables one type of computer to **emulate** (act like) other types of computers and process programs written for them. The emulated computers are called *virtual machines*, because they are not *real* computers. Remember, all of this is possible because firmware allows various control functions formerly performed by hardwiring to be performed by easily changed microprograms. Firmware is frequently used to enable newer computers to process programs written for older models, thus helping users **migrate** (move up) from old computers to new ones.

Random, Direct, and Sequential Access

Primary storage media, such as microelectronic *semiconductor* storage chips or *magnetic core* memory, are called *direct access* or *random access* memories (RAM). Magnetic disk devices are frequently called *direct access storage devices* (DASD). On the other hand, media like magnetic tape and punched cards are known as *sequential-access devices*. Then there are *magnetic bubble* and other devices that have a combination of direct access and sequential access properties. What do the concepts of *random access*, *direct access*, and *sequential access* mean in terms of the capabilities of storage media? Let's see.

■ **Random access** and **direct access** both describe the same concept. They both mean that any element of data or instructions (bit, byte, word) can be *directly* stored and retrieved by *randomly* selecting and using any of the locations on the storage media. It also means that each storage position has a unique address and can be individually accessed in approximately the same length of time without having to search through other storage positions. For example, each memory cell on a microelectronic semiconductor **RAM** chip can be individually sensed or changed in the same length of time. The same holds true for magnetic disk media. Any data record stored on such a **direct access storage device** (DASD) can be accessed directly in *approximately* the same time period.

An example of direct access from the world of popular music media might clarify this concept. Consider what happens when you decide to play a stereo phonograph record on a record turntable unit. The direct access process is similar to directly selecting a specific song on a phonograph record that is spinning on a turntable. To select a certain song you pick up the tone arm and move it directly to the track where the song you want to hear begins. That's direct access.

■ **Sequential access storage devices** use secondary storage media, such as *magnetic tape* or punched cards whose storage locations do not have unique addresses and cannot be directly addressed. Instead, data must be stored and retrieved using a *sequential* or *serial* process. Thus data is recorded one after another in a predetermined sequence (such as a numerical or alphabetical order) on a storage medium, such as magnetic tape. Locating an individual item of data requires starting at the beginning of a tape and searching all of the recorded data until the desired item is located. This is similar to having to "fast forward" or rewind a home tape recorder/player to find a specific song or conversation. See Figure 5–3.

Virtual Memory

Virtual memory is the ability to treat *secondary storage* devices as an extension of the *primary storage* of a computer. This gives the "virtual" appearance of a larger main memory than actually exists. Data and programs are subdivided into *pages*, which are transferred between main memory and secondary storage devices by the computer's operating system. Thus it appears that the com-

FIGURE

5–3 Sequential versus direct access storage

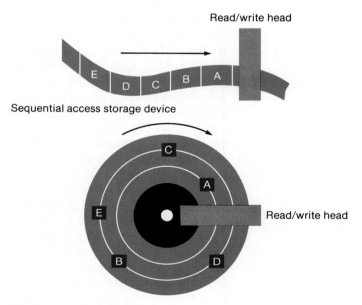

Sequential access storage device

Direct access storage device

puter has a larger *real memory* than it actually does. Therefore, the computer system can be used as if it had "virtually" unlimited primary storage. For example, one recent computer model with a real memory (primary storage) capacity of 512,000 bytes can act as though it has a memory size of 16 million bytes through its use of secondary storage on magnetic disks and its virtual memory operating system. See Figure 5–4.

Virtual memory requires a form of dynamic relocation called *paging*. Primary storage is segmented into a large number of *pages* whose contents and location are automatically controlled by the virtual memory operating system and the use of special hardware registers. Programs and data are subdivided automatically into pages and moved to and from secondary storage devices and retrieved as needed. This paging is "transparent" to the computer user. A program may appear to be stored and processed in a single section of primary storage, when in reality it is subdivided into pages that are scattered throughout primary and secondary storage.

With virtual memory, large programs can be easily processed, since programs do not have to reside entirely in main memory and subdividing large programs into segments or overlays is no longer necessary. Efficient use is made of primary storage, since pages of programs can be placed wherever space is available. Many more programs can be run simultaneously when paging is used. For example, the third-generation multiprogramming operating system of one computer manufacturer allowed from 6 to 14 user programs to run concurrently. However, its fourth-generation virtual memory operating system has a theoretical maximum of 250 concurrent users! This difference is primarily because virtual memory systems require that only a few pages of a program being processed be in primary

FIGURE

5–4 The virtual memory process

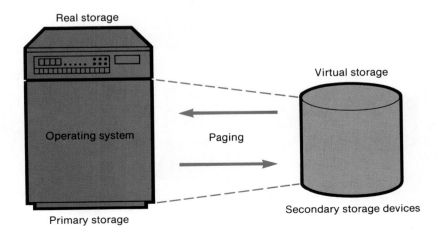

Real storage

Operating system

Primary storage

Paging

Virtual storage

Secondary storage devices

storage. Only those parts of a program containing the specific instructions and data actually being processed are required.

Virtual memory systems have several limitations that should be mentioned. Many users of virtual memory systems found that applications took longer to process and used more total memory space. Thus the easier programming of a virtual memory system seems to have been gained at the expense of some throughput time and some waste of the memory resources of the computer system. In some systems, the problem can become so acute that a *thrashing*

FIGURE 5–5 Example of the virtual machine concept

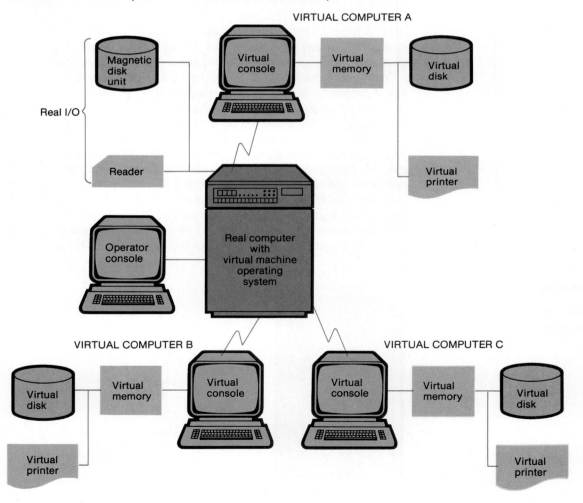

condition occurs where the operating system must spend most or all of its time moving pages or segments between primary and secondary storage units. Proper systems and programming controls are needed to minimize the increase in "overhead" (i.e., time and memory space) that can result from the use of virtual memory systems.

The concept of virtual memory has expanded to include the concept of virtual computer systems or **virtual machines**. A combination of virtual memory operating systems and microprogramming is required. Several different configurations of computers can then be simulated by a single computer system. These simulated computers, called *virtual machines*, provide one or more computer users not only with virtual memory but with complete virtual computer systems, including both virtual hardware and software. See Figure 5–5.

SECTION II: TYPES OF STORAGE HARDWARE

PRIMARY STORAGE MEDIA

Semiconductor Storage

The primary storage of most modern computers consists of microelectronic semiconductor circuits. Groups of these circuits (each group representing eight bits or one byte, for example) make up each position of storage. Thousands of **semiconductor storage** circuits are etched on large-scale integrated (LSI) circuit chips. Remember that the chips originated from *semiconducting* silicon crystal *wafers*. Each memory chip may be less than an eighth of an inch square and contains thousands of storage positions. For example, many current memory chips are 64K bit chips containing 65,536 bit positions for a storage capacity of 8K bytes. Memory chips with a 256K bit capacity (32K bytes) are now being produced and 1 million bit chips (1 megabit or 128K bytes) have been announced. See Figure 5–6.

Each storage position (cell) consists of a microelectronic switch or "flip-flop" circuit. The direction of the electronic current passing through each cell determines whether the switch is in an *ON* or *OFF* position. Thus the binary digits 0 and 1 can be represented. The *state* of each storage position (*ON* or *OFF*) can be electronically sensed without altering that state. Semiconductor storage is known as a *random access memory* (*RAM* or *direct access storage*) medium because each memory cell can be individually sensed or changed in the same length of time irrespective of its location. Figure

FIGURE

5–6 Semiconductor memory chips

A 64K bit chip.

B One million bit chip.

A

B

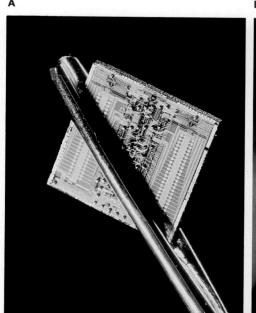

5–7 illustrates an eight-by-eight array that can store 64 bits (8 bytes). The individual bit being sensed or changed (dark shaded) is at location 53 (column 5, row 3).

Semiconductor memories currently use two basic types of LSI technology, *bipolar* and *metal oxide semiconductor* (MOS), with many variations of these two technologies being used. High-speed semiconductor memory uses bipolar circuits that are faster but more costly and, therefore, are used primarily for very high-speed *buffer (cache)* storage. Most semiconductor main memories use MOS type circuits. Access times for high-speed memories are below 50 nanoseconds and into the picosecond range. Speeds from 70 to 300 nanoseconds are common for regular semiconductor memories.

FIGURE

5–7 Diagram of a semiconductor memory chip

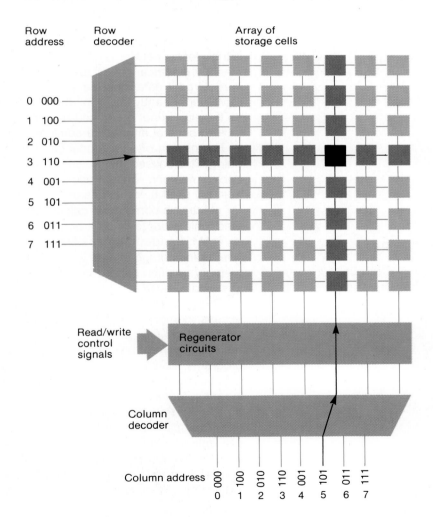

Research and development is continuing on improving present silicon chip performance, or developing substitutes for silicon. One new silicon technology is CMOS (complimentary metal oxide semiconductor) which allows production of microprocessor and memory chips that are smaller, faster, and consume much less power than standard MOS chips. The most promising silicon substitute is a chip made from a costly rare mineral called *gallium*. The *gallium-arsenide* chip offers speeds up to five times faster than silicon, doesn't overheat as much, and uses a fraction of the power that silicon chips need.

Some of the major attractions of microscopic semiconductor storage are small size, great speed, shock and temperature resistance, and low cost due to mass production capabilities. One major disadvantage of most semiconductor memory is its **volatility**. Uninterrupted electric power must be supplied or the contents of memory will be lost. Therefore, emergency transfer to other devices or standby electrical power (battery packs or emergency generators) is required if data must be saved. Another alternative would be to more permanently "burn in" the contents of semiconductor devices so they could not be erased by a loss of power. Let's take a closer look at several alternative semiconductor memories.

The growth of semiconductor storage and microelectronic technology has caused the development of two basic types of semiconductor memory: random access memory (RAM) and read only memory (ROM). Variations of these two basic types are being used for electronic computers, calculators, and other devices requiring electronic storage of data or instructions.

- RAM: **Random Access Memory**. Used for primary storage (i.e., temporary storage of data and instructions during processing). Each memory position can be both sensed (read) or changed (write) so it is also called *read/write memory*. This is a *volatile* memory.

- ROM: **Read Only Memory**. This is a type of *nonvolatile* random-access memory used for permanent storage. Can only be read, not "written" (i.e., changed). Frequently used control instructions (as in the control unit of the computer) and other more permanent programs, such as programming language translators and mathematical routines, are permanently written into the memory cells during manufacture.

- PROM: **Programmable Read Only Memory**. This is a type of ROM that can be programmed after manufacture. Several versions can only be written in (programmed) once after their manufacture.

- EPROM: **Erasable Programmable Read Only Memories**. These are a type of ROM that can be erased and reprogrammed indefinitely. Erasure of memory requires a special technique, such as exposing the circuits to ultraviolet light. These memories are useful for storage of contents that will be changed infrequently. A version that can be erased by applying a larger electrical charge is known as *electronically erasable read only memory*, or EEPROM.

Other Primary Storage Media

Magnetic Core Memory

Magnetic cores were a widely used primary storage media in second- and third-generation computers. Magnetic cores are tiny doughnut-shaped rings composed of iron oxide and other materials that are strung on wires, which provide an electrical current that magnetizes the cores. A string of several cores represents one storage position (eight cores plus one for a check bit for all computers using the EBCIDIC code). Thousands of cores strung on wires make up a core "plane," and several core planes make up a core "stack." See Figure 5–8.

Magnetic cores are a binary or two-state device, since they can be magnetized in a clockwise or counterclockwise direction, producing the binary *ON* or *OFF* state, which is used to represent the binary digits 0 and 1. The direction of electric current in the wires running through the center of the cores determines their magnetic direction. This magnetic direction can easily be changed, though the magnetic core can retain its magnetism indefinitely if so desired. Thus magnetic core memories retain their contents even when electric power is interrupted. The magnetic direction of each core can be individually sensed or changed at speeds in the nanosecond range. Magnetic core storage is, therefore, an extremely fast direct access storage medium.

FIGURE

5–8 Magnetic core plane

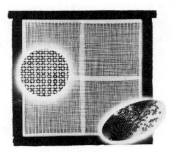

Cryoelectronic Storage

Cryoelectronic storage devices are under development that will be much faster and smaller than semiconductor storage. Though IBM recently ended a 20-year development program, the Japanese are still interested in developing this technology. *Cryoelectronic* devices consist of materials which become superconductors at extremely low temperatures. There is still a possibility that a new generation of supercomputers using cryoelectronic circuits called *Josephson Junctions* will be developed. Such circuits (also called *super conductive tunnel junction circuits*) have demonstrated speeds in the 10 picosecond range.

Laser Storage

Laser storage devices (including devices called *holographic* memories), which utilize crystalline material to change the polarization of light, are being developed. Changes in the polarity of light captured by these *photonic* circuit chips would provide a binary storage device operating at the speed of light.

SECONDARY STORAGE HARDWARE

There isn't enough room (yet) in the primary storage circuits of any computer to store all the data and programs required to meet the information processing needs of most users. That's why computers have a secondary storage capability. *Secondary storage hardware* consists of media and devices (such as magnetic disks and magnetic disk units) that are used to store data and programs in support of the primary storage unit of the computer system. Thus secondary storage hardware (also called *auxiliary storage*) greatly enlarges the storage capacity of the computer system. However, as we have noted earlier, the contents of secondary storage devices cannot be processed without first being brought into the main memory of the CPU. Figure 5–9 summarizes the functions, speed, storage capacities, advantages, and disadvantages of important secondary storage peripherals and media. Let's take a closer look at each of them.

Magnetic Disk Hardware

Magnetic disk media and equipment are now the most common form of secondary storage for modern computer systems. They provide a direct access capability and high storage capacities at a reasonable cost. The two basic types of magnetic disk media are conventional (*hard*) metal disks and flexible (*floppy*) diskettes. Several types of magnetic disk peripheral equipment are used as direct access storage devices (DASDs) in both small and large computer systems.

Characteristics of Magnetic Disks

Magnetic disks are thin metal or plastic disks that resemble phonograph records and are coated on both sides with an iron oxide recording material. Several disks may be mounted together on a vertical shaft, which typically rotates the disks at speeds of 2,400 to 3,600 revolutions per minute (rpm). Electromagnetic *read/write heads* are positioned by access arms between the slightly separated

FIGURE 5–9 Overview of characteristics: Secondary storage peripherals and media

Peripheral Equipment	Media	Primary Functions	Typical I/O Speed Range	Typical Storage Capacity	Major Advantages and/or Disadvantages
Magnetic disk drive	Magnetic disk Disk pack Disk cartridge Fixed disk	Secondary storage (direct access) and input/output	Data transfer: 100,000– 3,000,000 bytes per second Access time: 15– 200 microseconds	Over 300 million characters per disk pack and a billion characters per drive	Large capacity, fast direct access storage device (DASD), but expensive
Floppy disk drive	Magnetic diskette 8, 5¼, 3½, and 3¼ inch diameters	Secondary storage (direct access) and input/output	10,000–20,000 bytes per second Access time: 100–300 milliseconds	150,000 to 3,500,000 characters/ disk	Small, inexpensive and convenient, but slower and smaller capacity than other DASDs
Magnetic tape drive	Magnetic tape reel	Secondary storage (sequential access) and input/output	15,000– 1,250,000 bytes per second	Up to 180 million characters per tape reel	Inexpensive with a fast transfer rate, but only sequential access
Magnetic tape cartridge and cassette drives	Magnetic tape cartridge and cassette	Secondary storage (sequential access) and disk backup	3,000–85,000 bytes per second	1–20 million characters per cassette 10–200 million characters per cartridge	Small, inexpensive and convenient, but only sequential access
Magnetic strip storage unit	Magnetic strip cartridge	Mass secondary storage (direct/ sequential access)	Data transfer: 25,000–55,000 bytes per second Access time: up to several seconds	Up to 500 billion bytes per unit	Relatively inexpensive, large capacity, but slow access time

disks to read or write data on concentric circular **tracks**. Data is recorded on tracks in the form of tiny magnetized spots to form binary digits arranged in serial order in a code such as EBCDIC. Thousands of bytes can be recorded on each track, and there are several hundred data tracks on each disk surface. Each track contains the same number of bytes, because data is packed together more closely on the small inner tracks than on the large outer tracks.

Figure 5–10 illustrates some of the physical storage characteristics of magnetic disks. This illustration shows a disk assembly consisting of 11 disks, which provide 20 recording surfaces since the unprotected top surface of the top disk and bottom surface of the bottom disk are not used to record data. An access mechanism with 20 read/write heads is shown, providing one head for each recording surface. This illustration shows a **moving-head** access mechanism that moves in and out between the disks to position the read/write heads over the desired track. Other types of magnetic disk units may use **fixed-head** (or *head-per-track*) access mechanisms, which do not move because they provide a read/write head for each track of each disk.

Figure 5–10 also illustrates the concept of a **cylinder**, which is one of the basic methods of organizing data on magnetic disks. In this illustration, each cylinder is composed of the 20 circular tracks that are on the same vertical line, one above the other, on each of the 20 recording surfaces. Thus a cylinder is sometimes defined as the collection of tracks that can be read when the read/write heads are stationed in a position between the disks. In Figure 5–10, each disk surface contains 200 tracks, which means that the disk units shown can store data in 200 cylinders. When the cylinder

FIGURE 5–10 Characteristics of magnetic disks

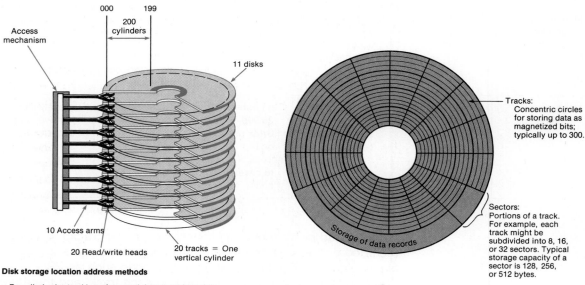

Disk storage location address methods

- By cylinder (or track), surface, and data record number.
  Example: Cylinder 199, surface 15, record 08.
- By sector and data record number.
  Example: Sector 74, record 02.

method of organization is used, the location of an individual data record is determined by an address consisting of the cylinder number, the recording surface number, and an individual data record number.

Another popular method of disk organization used for floppy disks and some large disk units is shown in Figure 5–10. Each track on a disk is subdivided into a fixed number of **sectors** or *fixed blocks*. This is sometimes called *fixed block architecture*. Typically, tracks are subdivided into 8, 16, or 32 sectors. Sector storage capacities are usually 128 bytes per sector (single density), 256 bytes per sector (double density), or 512 bytes per sector (quad density). Sectors seem to subdivide the disk surface into pie-shaped or wedge-shaped areas, since sectors at the large outer tracks are larger than sectors at the smaller inner tracks. However, each sector has the same storage capacity since data is packed together more closely on the inner tracks of a disk. When the sector method of organization is used, each sector in the entire disk unit is assigned a unique number. Thus, the location of data is identified by an address consisting of the sector number and an individual data record number.

Types of Magnetic Disks

There are several types of magnetic disk arrangements including removable disk packs and modules as well as fixed disk units. The removable disk devices are the most popular, because they can be used interchangeably in magnetic disk units and stored *offline* when not in use.

■ **Disk packs** are easy to handle; one popular type contains 11 disks, each 14 inches in diameter, is about 6 inches high, weighs about 20 pounds and can store over 300 million characters. See Figure 5–11.

■ **Winchester disk modules** combine magnetic disks, access arms, and read/write heads into a sealed module or cartridge. This Winchester technology reduces exposure to such airborne contaminants as smoke or dust and significantly increases speed, capacity, and reliability, compared to regular open disk packs. One typical disk module contains four magnetic disks, each eight inches in diameter and can store over 70 million bytes. See Figure 5–12.

■ **Fixed disk**, nonremovable magnetic disk assemblies are used in some magnetic disk units. This allows higher speeds, greater data-recording densities, and closer tolerances within a sealed, more stable environment. Fixed disks typically use a fixed-head access mechanism (one read/write head per track) and thus have great speed as well as high storage capacity and reliability. One typical

FIGURE

5–11 Magnetic disk media and devices

A Left to right: 60 MB backup magnetic tape cartridge, half-height 10 MB hard disk drive, half-height 2.8 MB floppy disk drive, and full-height 33 MB Winchester hard disk drive.

B Magnetic disk cartridges, disk packs, and floppy disks (8 inch and 5¼ inch).

A

B

FIGURE

5–12

A Inside a Winchester Hard Disk Drive.

B Loading a hard disk cartridge.

fixed disk unit contains six eight-inch disks and has a storage capacity of more than 500 megabytes.

Sealed disk modules and fixed disk drives have grown in popularity because their control of the disk environment results in a faster, more reliable operation and more compact, high-density storage capacity, as well as very low read/write head "flying heights." The read/write heads in magnetic disk devices "float" or "fly" on a cushion of air and do not touch the surface of the disk. The clearance between the read/write head and the disk surface is usually less than 50 microinches (millionths of an inch). Thus all magnetic disk units have air filtration systems to remove airborne particles, such as smoke or dust. Such particles could cause the read/write head to come in contact with the disk (called a *head crash*) which usually results in the loss of data on that portion of the disk. This explains the increased use of both fixed and removable Winchester-type disks, since they are sealed and filtered to eliminate all particles greater than 17 microinches. Thus the read/write head of many Winchester-type disk devices flies less than 20 microinches above the disk surface which improves the quality and density of its data recording capability. Figure 5–13 illustrates the size of airborne particles compared to the flying height of conventional magnetic disk devices.

Capabilities of Magnetic Disks

The speed of magnetic disk units is expressed by their *average access time* and *data transfer rate*. The average access time refers to the time it takes a read/write head to access a specific data location on a magnetic disk. The **average access time** of moving-head disks includes both the time required to move the read/write head into position over the track where the data is stored (*seek time*), and the time it takes the disk to rotate until the desired data

FIGURE

5–13 Comparative size of magnetic disk contaminants

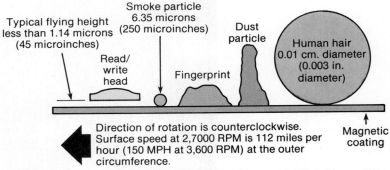

Typical flying height less than 1.14 microns (45 microinches)

Smoke particle 6.35 microns (250 microinches)

Dust particle

Human hair 0.01 cm. diameter (0.003 in. diameter)

Read/write head

Fingerprint

Magnetic coating

Direction of rotation is counterclockwise. Surface speed at 2,7000 RPM is 112 miles per hour (150 MPH at 3,600 RPM) at the outer circumference.

Source: Adapted from Ronald Rosenberg, "Hard Disk Drives," *Mini-Micro Systems*, February 1979, p. 47.

is under the read/write head (*rotational delay*). Of course, since fixed-head disks provide a read/write head for every track on the disk, seek time is eliminated, so the average access time equals the rotational delay time. Average access times for moving-head disks range from about 30 to 60 milliseconds and from 15 to 30 milliseconds for fixed-head disk units. The **data transfer rate** of magnetic disk units refers to the speed by which data can be transferred between the disk unit and the CPU. Data transfer rates vary from 100,000 to over 3 million bytes per second (bps).

Storage capacity of *magnetic disk units* varies depending on the type, number, and arrangement of magnetic disks in a unit. Magnetic disk units may contain one or more disk drives, each of which accommodates one removable disk pack or module, or contain a permanent grouping of fixed disks. The storage capacity of individual disk packs, modules, or fixed disk drives range from several million bytes to over 500 megabytes, while large magnetic disk units containing multiple disk drives can store several billion bytes (gigabytes). The use of microcomputers has encouraged increases in the capacity of both hard and floppy disks, while their size has been reduced. *Half-height* drives that are half the height of full size drives are in use. See Figure 5–14.

Floppy Disks

The magnetic *diskette*, or **floppy disk**, is a small, flexible magnetic disk that resembles a small phonograph record. It consists of a polyester film covered with an iron oxide compound. A single disk is mounted and rotates freely inside a protective plastic jacket,

FIGURE

5–14 Large magnetic disk unit with multiple disk drives

which has access openings to accommodate the read/write head of a floppy disk drive unit. Floppy disk drives rotate the disks at between 300 to 400 revolutions per minute. Average access time is 100 to 300 milliseconds. Data can be recorded on one or both sides (single or double-sided disks). Data can also be recorded at 3,200 bits per inch (on the innermost track), 6,400 bpi, or 12,800 bpi. This is known as *single density*, *double density*, and *quad density*. Thus, a double-sided quad density disk will hold eight times as much data as a single-sided single density disk.

Standard-size floppy disks have an eight-inch diameter and have storage capacities from over 1 million bytes to over 2.5 million bytes. *Minifloppy* disks have a 5 ¼-inch diameter and typically provide from 150,000 to 750,000 bytes of storage, with super minifloppies storing in excess of 3 megabytes. "Microfloppy" disks 3¼ or 3½ inches in diameter have appeared with from 400,000 bytes to over 1 megabyte of storage. (Remember that 150K bytes is equivalent to about 60 double-spaced typewritten pages.) Floppy disks have become a popular secondary storage and input/output medium for microcomputer and minicomputer systems. They provide an economical and convenient form of direct access storage. They are also removable and interchangeable with other diskettes and can be conveniently stored offline when not being used. See Figure 5–15.

FIGURE 5–15 Characteristics of a mini-floppy disk

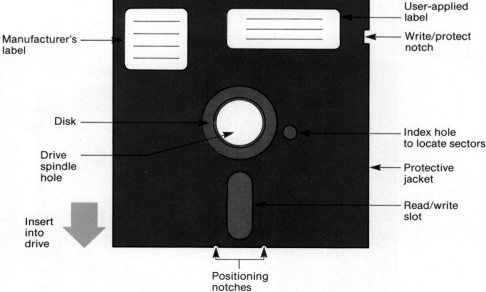

Manufacturer's label

User-applied label

Write/protect notch

Disk

Drive spindle hole

Index hole to locate sectors

Protective jacket

Read/write slot

Insert into drive

Positioning notches

REAL WORLD APPLICATION 5-2

Richard T. Rodgers, Attorney at Law

As a lawyer, I've got a lot invested in my computer system. Not just money, but information. Programs, data, and access to specific information when I need it have turned my computer into the cornerstone of my law operation.

As I came to depend on my computer for more of my daily activities, my need for data storage increased proportionately. It wasn't long before I outgrew the storage capacity of my TRS-80 Model 12 with its 8-inch floppy disks. In spite of relentless efforts to keep my floppy-disk library organized, I could never be certain that I'd be able to locate the data I needed or the form letter I was looking for.

A hard disk, I thought, would be the answer. One disk could store *all* my programs and data in one place and keep them from being lost on a little-used floppy. So I transferred everything to a hard disk—Visicalc, Scripsit, Profile Plus, dictionaries . . . everything. And when the process was complete, I still had nearly 6 million bytes of storage space left. It was just too good to be true.

But now I had the opposite problem. I had to play "Where Is It?" on a disk with a massive directory. Although I could use wild-card searches and other tricks that gave me more selective access to the directory contents, locating information was still overwhelming. The situation was even worse when my operator wanted to run something. My hard disk, which was supposed to make life easier for me, actually increased the amount of time I spent messing around in the disk operating system (DOS), pulling directories, and so on. In one stroke, the hard disk had obliterated the neat divisional lines I had established between the floppy disks in my library.

I needed a way to organize my hard disk so I could find and run the programs I wanted without becoming too chummy with the DOS. After some thrashing around, I found I could do it with Profile Plus, my all-purpose database system. You can probably do the same thing with your own database system. I divided my disk into sections that an operator can invoke by simply pressing one key. The programs and data on my hard disk fall into seven categories. Using these categories, I developed a main menu with these options: Accounting, Word Processing, Information Management, Communication, Substantive System, Games/Recreation and Utilities, and an option to exit to DOS. Each option on the main menu leads to a submenu that I also created. This has saved an enormous amount of time and, as an added benefit, has made the hard-disk system easier to use than floppy disks.

- Why did Mr. Rodgers switch from floppy disks to a hard disk drive?
- What problems arose when he began using a hard disk drive? How did he solve those problems?

Source: Richard T. Rodgers, "How to Organize Hard Disk Data," *Popular Computing*, May 1984, p. 123. Reprinted with permission.

Advantages and Disadvantages

The major attraction of magnetic disks is that they are superb direct access secondary storage devices. They are thus superior to magnetic tape for many current applications that require the immediate access capabilities of direct access files. Removable disk devices provide large storage capacities at a relatively low cost, and they can be easily stored offline. One of the limitations of hard magnetic disks is their higher cost, compared to magnetic tape. Thus a large magnetic disk pack or Winchester module may cost over $1,000, while a large-capacity magnetic tape reel may cost less than $100. Of course, this limitation does not apply to floppy disks, which cost only a few dollars. Magnetic disks may also be slower and more expensive than magnetic tape for applications where large sequential access files are used.

Magnetic Tape Hardware

Magnetic Tape

Magnetic tape is a widely used input/output and secondary storage medium. Data is recorded in the form of magnetized spots on the iron oxide coating of a plastic tape somewhat similar to that used in home tape recorders. Magnetic tape is usually subdivided into nine horizontal tracks or channels to accommodate a check bit and the eight-bit EBCDIC Code. Blank spaces known as "gaps" are used to separate individual data records or **blocks** of grouped records. Most magnetic tapes are 4 inches wide and 2,400 feet long and are wound on plastic reels 104 inches in diameter. The density of the data that can be recorded on such tape is frequently either 1,600 or 6,250 bytes per inch. Thus, a reel of magnetic tape could contain over 180 million bytes, which is the equivalent of over 2 million punched cards. See Figure 5–16.

FIGURE

5–16 Magnetic tape data storage format

NINE-TRACK TAPE (EBCDIC CODE)

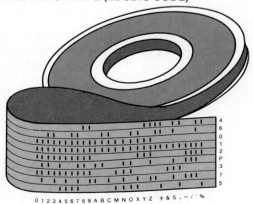

0 1 2 3 4 5 6 7 8 9 A B C M N O X Y Z + & S . — / ' %

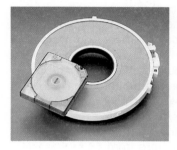

Magnetic Tape Cartridges and Cassettes

Magnetic tape also comes in the form of small *cassettes* and *cartridges*. Cassettes have a capacity of 0.5 to 20 megabytes, while cartridges can store from 10 to 200 million characters. Magnetic tape cassette decks are being used as low-cost input/output units for minicomputer and microcomputer systems and "intelligent" terminals. Magnetic tape cartridges are becoming a popular means of providing a **backup** capability for microcomputers using hard disk drives. See Figure 5–17.

Magnetic Tape Peripherals

Devices that can read and write data on magnetic tapes are called *magnetic tape drives*. Electromagnet read/write heads record data on each channel in the form of magnetic spots on the tape during writing operations. The read/write heads are also used in the reading operation to sense the magnetized spots on the tape and convert them into electronic impulses that are transmitted to the CPU. Reading and writing speeds range from 15,000 to 180,000 bytes per second using standard magnetic tape and up to 1,250,000 bytes per second for high-density tape. Small magnetic tape *cartridge drives* can read data at the rate of 85,000 characters per second, while magnetic tape *cassette decks* can read or write data at speeds ranging from 300 to 5,000 characters per second. See Figure 5–18.

Magnetic Strip Hardware

Magnetic strip hardware combines the inexpensive high-capacity benefits of magnetic tape with the direct access advantages of magnetic disks. These advantages are offset to some extent by a slower access time. Magnetic strip units offer **mass storage** capacity random access storage at a lower cost than magnetic disks. They are used for applications that do not require fast access times, such as for a large inventory file in a batch processing system.

For example, the IBM 3850 Mass Storage System uses magnetic strips similar to magnetic tape but about 3 inches wide and up to 770 inches long. Several hundred strips are mounted in removable cartridges and stored in a "honeycomb-like" arrangement of "cells." The magnetic strip *mass storage system* allows the computer to select an individual strip, move it under a read/write head, and return it to its cartridge. Such units may store from 16 to 500 billion bytes of data! Access times are quite slow, however, ranging from a fraction of a second to several seconds. Data transfer rates vary between 25,000 to 55,000 characters per second. See Figure 5–19.

Advantages and Disadvantages

Magnetic tape is a high-speed input/output medium as well as a high-density secondary storage medium. In comparison to punched cards, magnetic tape is less expensive since one reel of tape can replace hundreds of thousands of cards, occupy a lot

FIGURE

5–19 Magnetic strip cartridge in a data cell unit

less storage space, and can be reused many times because data can be easily erased and new data recorded. The limitations of magnetic tape include the fact that it is not human-readable, that it is vulnerable to dust particles, and that it is a sequential access storage medium and thus slower than direct access media like magnetic disks.

Other Secondary Storage Devices

Several other secondary storage devices which are coming into wider use should also be mentioned.

Magnetic Bubble Storage

Magnetic bubble storage chips have been developed that use thin slices of garnet crystals on which tiny magnetized areas known as magnetic bubbles or "domains" can be generated. The data is represented by groupings of these magnetic bubbles, which can be moved across the surface of the crystal slices by electrical currents or magnetic fields. Magnetic bubble chips with capacities of 32K bytes to 1 megabit (1 million bits) are now in use. Though magnetic bubble memory is slower than semiconductor memory, it has the important advantage of retaining data being stored even when electric power is cut off. Though it has not been able to compete in the past with magnetic disk devices, its use as a secondary storage medium is growing.

The first major applications of bubble memory chips have been in numerical control of machine tools, where dust and chemicals in the atmosphere make moving magnetic media unsuitable, and in portable terminals, where resistance to shock is important. It is being used as either a built-in or removable cartridge type of secondary storage medium in microcomputers, and as "buffer" memory for such devices as data entry terminals. For example, the Sharp PC-5000 portable microcomputer offers 128K bytes of secondary storage in the form of a plug-in magnetic bubble cartridge, while the Grid portable microcomputer has 384K bytes of built-in magnetic bubble secondary storage. Larger magnetic bubble devices that will replace some current magnetic tape or disk units for large-capacity secondary storage are still under development. See Figure 5–20.

Semiconductor Secondary Storage

Semiconductor storage chips are now being used as direct access secondary storage media for both large and small computers. For example, if you own an IBM PC or similar microcomputer, you

FIGURE

5–20 One million bit magnetic bubble memory chips

could add a plug-in circuit board containing up to 384K of semiconductor storage chips (a *RAM card*). You could use this for additional **primary storage**, but you could also use it for **secondary storage**. Additional control circuitry and software makes the main microprocessor and the operating system program think that you have added another floppy disk drive to your system! What you have instead is a very high-speed semiconductor secondary storage capability, sometimes called a *RAM disk*. See Figure 5–21.

Some semiconductor secondary storage devices are marketed as competition for magnetic disk units used on mainframe computers. They are called *semiconductor disk* or *solid state disk* units. They are significantly faster and less expensive than *electromechanical*, *moving surface* direct access storage devices, such as magnetic disk units, but have smaller storage capacities. They are competitive with most fixed-head, fixed-disk devices, which are needed for high-speed transfer *(paging)* of programs and data between primary and secondary storage devices in large computer systems. Data transfer rates range from 1.5 to 4 megabytes per second, and these units provide from 10 to 100 megabytes of storage.

FIGURE

5–21 Multifunction circuit board and software that adds 384K bytes of semiconductor storage to an IBM PC

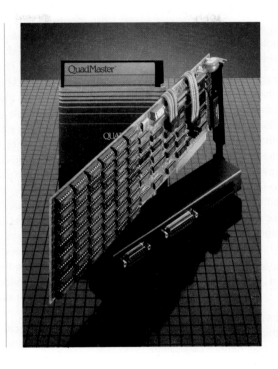

Optical Disks

Research and development work is continuing on a new mass storage medium using optical disks (also called *laser optical disk* or *video disk*) technology. Video disks are being introduced commercially for entertainment and educational use in homes, schools, and industry. In these applications, video disks compete to some extent with video cassette systems, especially prerecorded educational and entertainment video cassettes for television viewing. Video disks can hold several hours of high-quality television pictures and sound or the equivalent of over 50,000 35mm photographic slides. Thus an individual disk could contain the text and picture contents of the entire *Encyclopaedia Britannica*!

However, the use of optical disks as a secondary data storage medium for information processing is still in its early stages. One version uses a laser to burn microscopic pits arranged in 54,000 circular tracks in a recording layer sandwiched between two transparent 12-inch plastic disks. This *laser-optical* system then uses laser beams to read the information stored on the disk. Capacities of several billions of bytes are now available. One of the major limitations of present systems is that data cannot be erased, so

The Laser Optical Disk

The laser optical disk is a major new development in computer technology. It has three major advantages over the traditional magnetic disk:

- The information-storage density on a laser disk is much higher than on a magnetic disk, permitting up to 10 times or more information to be stored on similarly sized disks.
- An optical disk together with the information stored on it can be mass replicated inexpensively—unlike a magnetic disk.
- The laser disk can be removed from its drive, allowing the disk itself to be used for archival storage. On the other hand, the hard disk associated with a magnetic disk drive cannot be removed on most microcomputers.

The laser disk drive also has two major disadvantages compared to the traditional magnetic disk drive:

- It can write only *once*, since information (at least with today's optical disk technology) once written onto the disk cannot be erased. Erasable optical disks are still under development.
- It has an access time that is much longer than that of a magnetic disk drive. Access times for optical drives range from 100 to 500 milliseconds. By contrast, the access times for high-performance magnetic disk drives vary from 16 to 30 milliseconds.

Given these facts and other characteristics of both optical and magnetic disk drives, where will the optical disk drive fit in? Will it displace the magnetic disk drive?

Even if the write-only-once limitation of the optical disk drive did not exist, it is unlikely it would displace the traditional magnetic disk drive in many cases. Especially for a high-performance computer system, having a disk drive with fast access time is important. With access times of 100 to 500 milliseconds, the laser optical disk drive is simply too slow.

For such high-performance computer systems, the laser disk drive, though, could still have an important role. That role is *not* to displace the magnetic disk drive—but to supplement it. The magnetic disk drive is, of course, *on-line secondary storage*. The laser optical disk drive would become a new type of storage: *on-line tertiary storage*. (There are on-line mass storage devices available that can be considered tertiary storage. But these are very costly, are aimed mainly at the mainframe market, and have longer access times.) Information that in the past would have been copied from a magnetic disk and stored off-line on reels of tape can now be stored on-line on a laser optical disk drive. With the high storage capacity of laser disk drives, tremendous amounts of archival information can be stored on-line ready for access in milliseconds. Such information would be much more rapidly accessible than if stored on tape off-line. Also, since the optical disk can be removed from its drive, a platter can also be used for off-line storage.

The laser optical disk drive will not displace the traditional magnetic disk drive—but will supplement it. What the laser disk will really displace is magnetic-tape storage. Information once stored off-line on magnetic tape will now be stored on-line on a laser optical disk drive or off-line on laser disks. The laser disk will also be used for storing information now stored on paper in endless file draws, on microfilm, on photographs, and on photographic plates, such as x-rays.

- What are the advantages and disadvantages of laser optical disks compared to magnetic disk drives?
- Will the laser optical disk supplant magnetic disks? magnetic tape? microfilm? Explain. Be sure to mention the concept of *online tertiary storage* in your answer.

Source: Larry Fujitani, ''Laser Optical Disk: The Coming Revolution in Online Storage,'' *Communications of the ACM*, June 1984, pp. 547–48. Reprinted with permission.

FIGURE

5–22 Optical data disk

One side of this 1.2 gigabyte optical disk can hold all the data stored on more than 50 reels of magnetic tape.

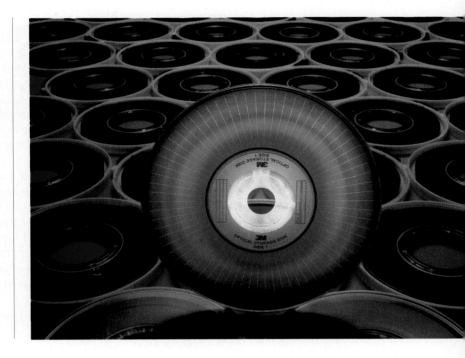

optical disks are being used primarily for long-term *archival* storage where historical files must be maintained. However, new *erasable* optical disk systems have been announced, so this technology looks promising. See Figure 5–22.

SUMMARY

Figures 5–1 and 5–9 should be used to summarize the many types of computer storage hardware discussed in this chapter. These figures show there are many types of storage media and devices, each with their own cost/speed/capacity characteristics. This includes integrated circuit semiconductory memory for primary storage, and magnetic disk, magnetic tape, and other devices for secondary storage.

Besides the primary storage unit, the arithmetic-logic and control unit contain small temporary storage areas called registers. The CPUs of most computers today contain special storage circuitry modules, where selected programs are permanently stored in semiconductor ROM chips. This is called firmware. This includes the storing of microprograms of elementary machine instructions in ROM modules of the control unit. Such use of firmware and microprogramming increase the versatility of computer systems.

KEY TERMS AND CONCEPTS

Direct access	RAM and ROM memories
Sequential access	Volatility
Semiconductor storage	Firmware
Magnetic core memory	Microprogramming
Magnetic bubble memory	Optical disk

Refer to Figures 5–1, 5–9, and 5–10 for other key storage hardware terms.

REVIEW AND APPLICATION QUESTIONS

1. Why are there so many types of storage media and devices?
2. Which storage devices are the fastest? Which have the greatest capacity? Which have the lowest cost? Taking cost/speed/capacity trade-offs into consideration, which storage device do you think is the best? Explain.
3. Explain the functions of the various types of storage areas that exist within the CPU of modern computers.
4. Is firmware like hardware or software? Explain.
5. What is microprogramming? How does it increase the versatility of modern computer systems?
6. What are the advantages and disadvantages of random, direct, and sequential access memories?

7. What are the major advantages and disadvantages of semiconductor storage?
8. What are the major types of semiconductor memory?
9. If you were to design a computer, would you use magnetic bubble circuits for primary storage or secondary storage? Why?
10. What are the major types of magnetic disk hardware? What are the major advantages and disadvantages of such hardware?
11. What are the major types of magnetic tape hardware? What are the major advantages and disadvantages of this media?
12. What is the most widely used primary storage media? Secondary storage media? Explain why this is so.

APPLICATION PROBLEMS

1. If you have not already done so, read and answer the questions after each Real World Application in this chapter.
2. Outline the functions, advantages, and disadvantages of semiconductor, magnetic disk and magnetic tape storage hardware, and indicate the equipment and the media involved.
3. Give the biggest advantage of using magnetic disks over magnetic tape. Then give two reasons why one might still use magnetic tape instead of magnetic disks.
4. How would you answer each of the following arguments for using magnetic tape instead of magnetic disk?
    a. No backup files exist when one uses magnetic disk.
    b. Disks are more expensive than tapes.
    c. Disks are too expensive for historical storage.
    d. Disks require the use of terminals.
    e. Disks can be easily damaged by dust, and fingerprints.
5. Joan Alvarez, a store manager for ABC Department Stores, is trying to decide whether to replace one of the floppy disk drives on her microcomputer with a 10 MB hard disk drive. She says she needs more storage capacity, but is worried about backing up the files and programs stored on the hard disk. What would you advise Joan to do? Explain your recommendation.
6. Indicate which secondary storage medium you would use for each of the following storage tasks. Choose among the following: (1) magnetic hard disk, (2) floppy disk, (3) magnetic tape, (4) magnetic bubble, (5) semiconductor storage, and (6) optical disk.
    a. Long-term archival storage.
    b. Small business microcomputer storage.
    c. Personal computer files.
    d. Large files for occasional processing.
    e. Secondary storage for portable computers.
    f. High-speed secondary storage.

CHAPTER 6

Input/Output Concepts and Hardware

CHAPTER OUTLINE

SECTION I: INPUT/OUTPUT CONCEPTS
  The User Interface
DATA ENTRY CONCEPTS
  Traditional Data Entry
  Source Data Automation
  Computer-Assisted Data Entry
DATA OUTPUT CONCEPTS
  Changing Output Methods
  Computer Graphics
SECTION II: INPUT/OUTPUT HARDWARE
COMPUTER TERMINALS
VISUAL HARDWARE
PRINTED OUTPUT HARDWARE
MAGNETIC MEDIA DATA ENTRY
PUNCHED CARD HARDWARE
VOICE HARDWARE
OCR HARDWARE
MICR HARDWARE
MICROGRAPHICS HARDWARE
I/O INTERFACE HARDWARE

LEARNING OBJECTIVES

The purpose of this chapter is to promote a basic understanding of computer input/output by analyzing (1) important input/output concepts and methods, and (2) the characteristics, functions, benefits, and limitations of major input/output hardware devices.

After reading and studying this chapter, you should be able to:

1. Explain several major input/output concepts, including:
   - *a.* Traditional data entry versus source data automation.
   - *b.* Computer-assisted data entry.
   - *c.* Changing output methods, including the use of computer graphics.
2. Outline the functions, advantages, and disadvantages of several major input/output hardware devices.
3. Identify the input and output hardware of the microcomputers you use, as well as the computers used by your school or business. Also, determine their basic physical and performance characteristics.

SECTION I: INPUT/ OUTPUT CONCEPTS

How do you communicate with a computer? Typically, you will (1) ask questions, (2) give commands, and (3) supply data to your computer and it will respond in a variety of ways. Such communication relies on the information processing system functions of *input* and *output*. Data has to be collected, converted to a form the computer can understand, and entered into the computer system in the **input** function. After processing is completed, information has to be converted to a form you can understand and be presented to you by the computer in the **output** function. To perform these functions, an information processing system needs the resources of **hardware** (equipment and media), **software** (programs and procedures), and **people** (specialists and users). We will discuss how this occurs in this chapter, concentrating on some important input/output concepts and on the wide variety of input/output equipment and media that enable us to communicate with computers.

Why are there so many types of input/output media and devices? Look at Figure 6–1. Notice how many types of media and devices

FIGURE 6–1 Overview of input/output hardware

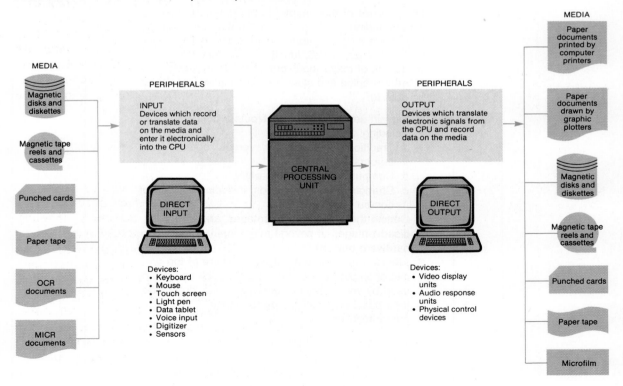

MEDIA

Magnetic disks and diskettes

Magnetic tape reels and cassettes

Punched cards

Paper tape

OCR documents

MICR documents

PERIPHERALS

INPUT
Devices which record or translate data on the media and enter it electronically into the CPU

DIRECT INPUT

Devices:
• Keyboard
• Mouse
• Touch screen
• Light pen
• Data tablet
• Voice input
• Digitizer
• Sensors

CENTRAL PROCESSING UNIT

PERIPHERALS

OUTPUT
Devices which translate electronic signals from the CPU and record data on the media

DIRECT OUTPUT

Devices:
• Video display units
• Audio response units
• Physical control devices

MEDIA

Paper documents printed by computer printers

Paper documents drawn by graphic plotters

Magnetic disks and diskettes

Magnetic tape reels and cassettes

Punched cards

Paper tape

Microfilm

are used to communicate with computers. Then take a look at Figure 6–2. It shows you the equipment, media, major functions, speed, advantages, and disadvantages of several important input/output devices. Look specifically at the advantages and disadvantages summarized in the last column. This should emphasize that the perfect input/output device does not exist. They all have their advantages and disadvantages, especially given the many different users and environments that we have for computers. So the computer industry has responded by developing the many different input/output devices we will discuss in this chapter.

The User Interface

The computer industry is making a major effort to develop better input/output methods and devices for users. Their goal is to develop a better **user interface** between users and computers. (An *interface* is a connection or boundary between systems or parts of systems.) In this chapter, we will show you how the computer industry is using such developments as source data automation, computer-assisted data entry, keyboard aids, video display aids, computer graphics, and many other input/output devices and methods to assist you in using computers. A major effort is being made to use the science and technology of **ergonomics** (also called *human factors engineering*) to produce hardware and software that will be **user-friendly** (i.e., safe, comfortable, and easy to use). Figure 6–3 summarizes many of the input/output features being developed to improve the interface between users and computers.

DATA ENTRY CONCEPTS

In Chapter Two we mentioned that the **input** function in information processing systems was also known as *data collection*, *data capture*, or *data entry*. In particular, the term **data entry** is widely used to convey the concept of a *process* in which data is *captured* by *recording*, *coding*, and *editing* activities, then *converted* to a form that can be *entered* into a computer system. Data entry activities have always been a bottleneck in the use of computers for information processing. We have always had a problem getting data into computers quickly and *correctly* enough to match their awesome processing speed. Thus traditional *manual* methods of data entry that make heavy use of *data media* are being replaced by more *direct automated* methods known as **source data automation**. Let's take a look at these methods.

FIGURE 6–2 Overview of selected input/output peripherals and media

Peripheral Equipment	Media	Primary Functions	Typical I/O Speed Range*	Major Advantages and/or Disadvantages
Video display terminal	No tangible media	Keyboard input and video output	250–50,000 characters per second output	Conventional and inexpensive, but limited display capacity and no hard copy
Line and page printers	Paper	Printed output of paper reports and documents	200–3,000 lines per minute: line printer 250–20,000 lines per minute: page printer	Fast hard copy, but inconvenient and bulky
Character (serial) printer	Paper	Printed paper output	10–400 characters per second	Low-cost hard copy, but low speed
Card reader/punch	Punched cards	Input and output	Input: 150–2,700 characters per minute Output: 80–650 characters per minute	Low cost, but slow speed and bulky media
Paper tape reader/punch	Paper tape	Input/output	Input: 50–2,000 characters per second Output: 10–300 characters per second	Simple and inexpensive, but fragile and bulky
Magnetic ink character reader (MICR)	MICR paper documents	Direct input of MICR documents	700–3,200 characters per second 180–2,000 documents per minute	Fast, high-reliability reading, but documents must be preprinted and the character set is limited
Optical character reader (OCR)	Paper documents	Direct input from written or printed documents	100–3,600 characters per second 180–1,800 documents per minute	Direct input from paper documents, but limitations on input format

FIGURE 6–3 Major development in user interfaces: Improving the interface between users and computers

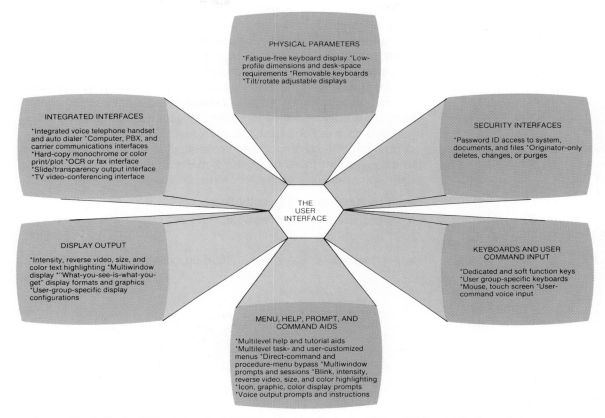

Source: John K. Murphy, "Office Automation," *Mini-Micro Systems,* December 1983, p. 222. Reprinted with permission.

Traditional Data Entry

Traditional methods of data entry typically rely on the *users* of the information processing system to capture data on **source documents**, such as purchase orders, payroll time sheets, and sales invoices. The source documents are then usually accumulated into *batches*, and transferred to *data processing professionals* who specialize in data entry. Periodically, the source documents are subjected to one of the following additional data entry activities:

■ The data is converted into a *machine-readable media*, such as punched cards, magnetic tape, or magnetic disks. Typically, this means using such devices as keypunch machines, key-to-tape machines, and key-to-disk systems. The media are then read by input devices to enter the data into the computer.

■ The data from source documents could alternatively be *directly* entered into the computer system, using a *direct input* device (such as the keyboard of a video terminal) without the use of machine-readable media.

Figure 6–4 illustrates this traditional data entry process, using sales transaction processing as an example. Notice the use of sales forms as source documents, and their conversion to magnetic tape media. Notice also the following data entry activities: source documents are (1) manually edited, (2) batched, (3) converted to another media, (4) entered into a computer system, (5) edited again, (6) rejected data is corrected and reentered, (7) sorted, and (8) accepted into the computer system. It should not be surprising, then, to discover that there has been a major shift away from traditional data entry because of the following factors:

■ It requires too many **activities**.

■ It requires too many **people**.

FIGURE 6–4 A traditional data entry example: Sales transaction processing

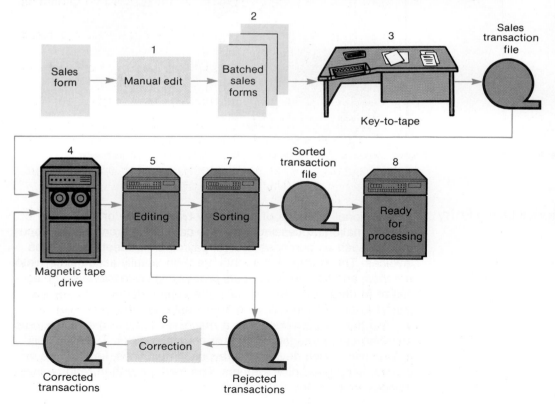

- It requires too many forms of **data media**.
- It incurs high **costs**.
- It increases the potential for **errors**.

Therefore, the response of both users and the computer industry has been to move toward *source data automation*.

Source Data Automation

The use of automated methods of data entry is known as **source data automation**. Several methods have been developed to accomplish this automation, though very few completely automate the data entry process. They are all based on trying to reduce or eliminate many of the *activities*, *people*, and *data media* required by traditional data entry methods. Source data automation attempts to:

- Capture data as *early as possible* after a transaction or other event occurs.
- Capture data as *close as possible* to the *source* that generates the data.
- Capture data by using *machine-readable media* initially, instead of written source documents.
- Capture data that rarely changes by *prerecording* it on machine-readable media, or by *storing* it in the computer system.
- Capture data directly *without the use of data media* if possible.

Figure 6–5 is an illustration of an automated data entry process, using the entry of sales data into a computer system as an example. Notice that:

1. Sales data is captured as soon as sales occur by *POS (point-of-sale) terminals*. They are not batched for later processing, and no sorting is necessary.
2. Sales data is captured by sales personnel right at the store, not by data processing personnel at another location. They edit their own input just once.
3. Sales data is captured partially by the use of machine-readable data media, on which product or customer data has been prerecorded. This includes bar-coded merchandise tags, which are read by *optical scanning wands*, and a plastic credit card with a *magnetic stripe*, which can be read by POS terminals. Thus no written source documents are used.
4. Other sales data is entered directly into the computer system without the use of any type of data media by using the *keyboard* of the POS terminal.

FIGURE 6–5 An automated data entry example: Sales transaction processing

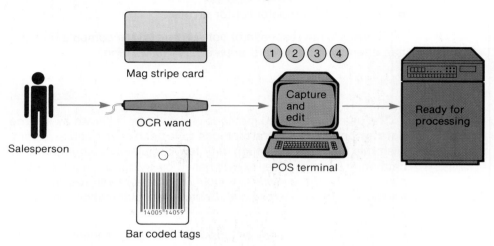

The example in Figure 6–5 reveals some of the types of equipment and media used in current source data automation. Major types of such hardware include:

- *Transaction terminals* and *data collection terminals*, such as POS terminals and keyboard/video display terminals.
- *Optical character recognition* (OCR) devices, such as optical scanning *wands*.
- *Magnetic ink character recognition* (MICR) devices, such as MICR reader/sorters used in banking for check processing.
- Other technologies, including the *electronic mouse*, *light pens*, *magnetic stripe cards*, *voice input*, and *tactile input*. We will discuss each of these technologies in more detail in the rest of this chapter.

Computer-Assisted Data Entry

Besides attempts to automate data entry, the computer industry is continually developing methods and devices to use the computer itself to assist a user or data entry operator. *Computer-assisted data entry* (CADE) can assist traditional methods of data entry, as well as source data automation systems. Let's take a look at the many ways this can be accomplished using computer terminals, microcomputers, and other computer systems.

Keyboard Aids

Most keyboards now provide specialized *function keys* and *control keys*, which reduce the number of keystrokes needed to accomplish data entry tasks. Pressing one or two keys may accomplish what formerly took several keystrokes to accomplish. The functions of these keys may be controlled by hardware circuits, firmware modules, or software. The advantage of function keys controlled by software (*soft keys*) is that they can be controlled to accomplish different tasks, depending on the application program being processed. Examples of function keys are *deposit* and *withdrawal* keys on a bank teller terminal, and *boldface* or *italics* keys on a microcomputer using a word processing package. Examples of typical control keys include *cursor control* keys, and *delete*, *backspace*, and *numeric mode* keys. See Figure 6–6.

Video Display Aids

Most video display units have a point-of-light called a **cursor** to assist the user in the input of data. The cursor may look like a *dot* or short *underline* or other shape that indicates the position of data to be entered or changed. Many other display features that an operator can control are available in video display units. These features include blinking cursors and characters, underlining displayed material, highlighting, split screen windows, scrolling, and of course, multiple color displays.

■ *Highlighting* or *reverse video* is a feature which highlights areas of the screen where data is to be entered by having light characters on a dark background or dark characters on a light background. The entire screen, or just certain sections, can be

FIGURE 6–6 Special keys on the keyboard of the IBM personal computer

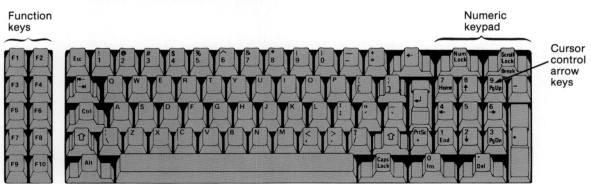

reversed to highlight specific information, or to *format* the screen to assist operators in entering data.

- *Scrolling* allows the operator to move lines of displayed information either up or down the screen.
- *Windows* or *split-screen* functions divide the screen into several sections or windows and allow different material to be shown in each section.
- *Color* is a feature that adds multiple colors to video displays. This makes the display more pleasing and easier to understand.

The display features mentioned above have made video terminals widely used *data entry* devices. Keyed-in data can be displayed and visually edited and corrected before input into a computer system. The terminal can be programmed to project a **formatted screen,** which displays a document or report *format* on the CRT. An operator can then *fill out* this electronic form by using the keyboard to *fill in the blanks,* guided by the cursor. When both the computer and user agree the form is properly filled out, the data is entered into the computer system. See Figure 6–7.

Many data entry tasks using video display are also **menu driven**. Software packages provide *menu displays* and operator prompting to support use by the regular clerical staff or by other users. A **menu** is a display of a *list of available options* from which users can select the functions they wish to perform. Each time the operator makes a choice, another more specific menu from which to choose may be displayed until the selected processing function is per-

FIGURE

6–7 A formatted screen assists data entry

formed. At this point, many terminals provide operator **prompts**, which are helpful messages that assist the operator in performing a particular job. This would include error messages, correction suggestions, prompting questions, and other messages that guide an operator through the work in a series of structured steps. Thus the computer uses the logic of a computer program and its memory capability to make the task as easy and as friendly as possible for the operator. See Figure 6–8.

A more recent development is the display of **icons**, which are small figures that look like familiar devices, such as a file folder (for storing a file), a wastebasket (for deleting a file), a calculator (for switching to a calculator mode),and so on. Icons were developed by Xerox for the STAR line of *workstation* computers in 1978. The Apple Lisa and Macintosh computers also emphasize the use of icons. An electronic *mouse* is used to move the cursor to an icon for the task you wish to accomplish. The use of icons to help simplify data entry and computer use is expected to increase in the future. See Figure 6–9.

Other Aids

Other devices and methods are used to simplify data entry. These include **audio prompts**, in which an audio "beep" or other sound

FIGURE

6–8 A menu and prompt display

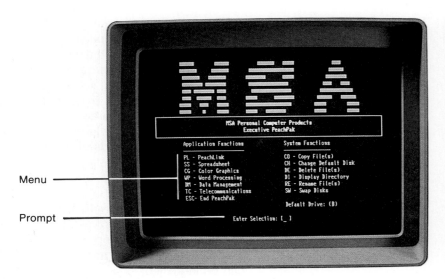

Menu

Prompt

FIGURE

6–9 A display of icons

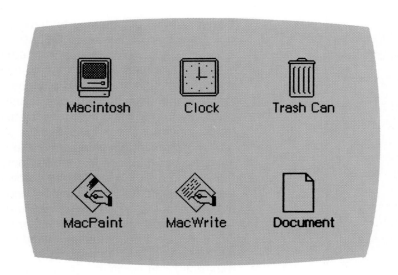

(including computer-generated speech) alerts the user. Also included in this category are several specialized input devices we will describe shortly, such as *voice input*, the *electronic mouse*, *light pen*, *joystick*, and *touch-sensitive screen*. All of these devices are designed to simplify the job of entering data into computer systems by reducing the use of manual keyboard methods for data entry.

DATA OUTPUT CONCEPTS

The **output** function involves converting processed data (information) from electronic impulses or magnetic media into a form that users can understand. It also involves presenting such information to users in a variety of *information products* or forms, such as paper documents and reports, visual displays or audio responses. Forms and methods of output are changing in computerized information processing systems, paralleling the changes taking place in data entry. Let's take a brief look at several major developments that are occurring in methods of output.

Changing Output Methods

The goal of the changes taking place in output methods is to reduce the bottleneck of output activities that slows the speed of computerized processing, as well as making computer-generated output more attractive and easy to use. Several important trends can be identified:

■ Replacing printed paper output with **visual displays** from video

REAL WORLD APPLICATION 6–1

Hubert Distributors

After Michigan's third largest beer wholesaler acquired 25 battery-powered, hand-held Route Commander data-entry terminals, sales errors no longer surfaced.

"We wholesale about two million cases of beer a year," says Alice B. Shotwell, vice president and general manager of Pontiac-based Hubert Distributors. "With Route Commanders, we've virtually eliminated sales-ticket errors that previously averaged two per driver per day—or 250 per week—for our 25 routes."

Data stored on a magnetic tape cassette in each Route Commander is put into Hubert's in-house computer system when each of the 25 drivers check in; a complete report is available before the end of each business day. It shows total sales by dollars, total sales by product, where each product was delivered, how much cash was taken in, and a wealth of other information.

"Previously," says Shotwell, "we had to key-punch every sales ticket into our computer system, which took too much time. Normally, we wouldn't have figures for one day's business unit until about the middle of the following day—even though we were using computers."

Now the data on cassettes from the Route Commander terminals is read by a magnetic tape unit of an IBM Series One computer. An operator uses a CRT to monitor this conversion process. The information is put onto a diskette that goes into an IBM System 34 computer. When all the information is captured, a high-speed printer prints Shotwell an immediate daily report on one entire day's business.

- Why is the use of hand-held data entry terminals better than the previous methods used by Hubert Distributors? Is this an example of source data automation? Explain.
- What other types of computer hardware do they use? Explain. What you think their functions are?

Source: "Beer Distributor's Portable Computers Lift Accuracy," *Computer Decisions*, November 1980, p. 114. Copyright 1980, Hayden Publishing Company. Reprinted with permission.

---

display terminals or **voice output** from audio response devices.

- Replacing punched paper cards and tapes, as well as printed paper output with machine-readable media, such as magnetic tape and disks or **microfilm** media. They are faster to use for retrieval or processing, and take up much less space.
- Reducing the amount of standardized printed paper reports produced on a *regular basis* with visual displays *tailored* to users and furnished to them *instantly, but only at their request*.
- Reducing the use of *monochrome* displays of *numeric data* or *text material* with **color displays** of various forms of **graphics**, such as line, bar, and pie charts, or other more attractive graphics displays.

Figure 6–10 illustrates the variety and changes taking place in the methods, equipment, and media found in modern information

FIGURE

6–10 Output methods
example: Sales transaction
processing

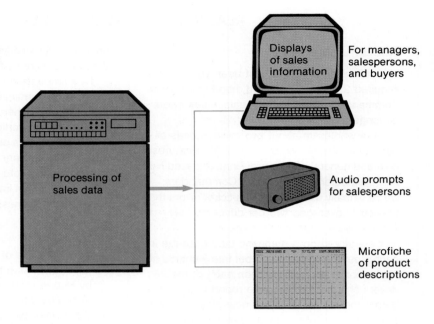

Displays of sales information — For managers, salespersons, and buyers

Processing of sales data

Audio prompts for salespersons

Microfiche of product descriptions

processing systems. Notice how printed sales documents and reports are being replaced by visual displays, audio responses, and
magnetic and microfilm media. We will discuss the equipment and
media used in traditional and newer methods of output in this chapter. But first, lets take a closer look at one of the major developments
in computer-generated output, *computer graphics*.

Computer Graphics

Which type of output would you rather see—columns of figures
or a graphic display of the same information? Most people find it
difficult to quickly and accurately comprehend numerical or statistical
data that is presented in a purely numerical form (such as rows
or columns of figures). That is why charts and graphs are typically
used in technical reports and business meetings. This graphics capability is now being offered by **graphics terminals** using video displays as well as *graphics plotters* and *graphics printers*, which draw
or print graphs on paper and other materials. Most computer systems
now offer some degree of graphics capability, including most microcomputer systems. However, many graphics features require additional hardware capabilities and special **graphics software
packages**. For example, advanced graphics terminals use special
microprocessor chips, called *display processors*, and additional
buffer memory. However, the rapid decrease in the cost of micropro-

REAL WORLD APPLICATION 6–2

Federal Express

Fast delivery is what Federal Express is all about. So management could appreciate the ability of Tektronix Graphics to deliver information quickly and concisely. "Prior to Tektronix we'd draw a few graphs by hand," says analyst David White, "and they weren't exactly pretty. Most graphic reports we now provide routinely we never had time to do at all."

Graphics terminals and plotters are now in use throughout the company. They're in Flight Operations, helping clarify flight schedules. In Management Information and Market Analysis departments, turning statistical printouts into line graphs and pie charts. In Operations Research, helping draft more efficient intracity courier routes. Color graphics may soon move into the corporate boardroom.

Using Tektronix Easy Graphing software, secretaries with no previous terminal experience are producing graphic reports every day. Analysts are constructing multicolor, fine-line graphs on plotters for final presentations.

■ What are the advantages of computer graphics to Federal Express? What graphics hardware and software are they using?

Source: Tektronix, Inc.

cessor and memory chips has moved computer graphics capabilities from large, expensive computer systems down to the range of small, low-priced systems, including microcomputers and their relatively inexpensive printers.

Color graphics displays are replacing monochrome (one color) displays of graphics. This, too, requires additional hardware and software capabilities. Color displays provide a more normal and natural people-computer interface. This should make using a video terminal a more attractive and comfortable experience and should result in fewer errors and more productivity. Color is a very effective way of categorizing displayed information. Color helps draw attention more easily to selected items and can be used to link related items in the display. For example, if a terminal operator changes a data item that affects other data items in a display, the affected data items can be programmed to change color, alerting the operator to the relationships that exist.

Computer graphics has been used for many years for complex engineering design applications called *computer-aided design* (CAD) used in the aircraft, automobile, machine tool, electronics, and other industries. Computer graphics assists engineers in designing complex structures, researchers in analyzing volumes of data, and process control technicians in monitoring industrial processes. However, its use to help managers analyze business operations and make better decisions is now being emphasized. Instead of being overwhelmed by vast amounts of computer-produced data, graphics displays assist managers in analyzing and interpreting data. Trends, problems, or opportunities hidden in data are easier to spot. For example, computer graphics would make it easier for a marketing manager to see complex market trends and analyze market problems and opportunities, such as product line, sales outlet, and salesperson performance. Also, graphics displays can be done on an *interactive* basis and thus provide immediate *decision support* to management. These capabilities and developments indicate that computer graphics will be a management tool of growing importance in the years to come. See Figure 6–11.

SECTION II: INPUT/OUTPUT HARDWARE

We have now examined several important input/output concepts and how they affect you and other computer users. We can thus begin our coverage of input/output hardware, both the equipment involved and the media they utilize. Notice that in each case we also briefly analyze the advantages and disadvantages for computer users of each major hardware category.

COMPUTER TERMINALS

Computer terminals of various types are the most widely used form of input/output hardware. Any input/output device that can directly enter data into a computer or directly receive computer output is called a **terminal**. It should be emphasized that most terminals use a **keyboard** for direct entry of data into a computer system without the use of input media. The major categories of computer terminals are summarized below, and illustrated in Figure 6–12.

■ **Visual Display Terminals**. Terminals that use a keyboard for input and a TV-like screen for visual output are called visual (or *video*) display terminals (VDT) or, more popularly, CRT (cathode ray tube) terminals. They allow the display of alphanumeric data and graphic images. They are the most widely used type of computer terminal.

■ **Printing Terminals**. These typewriter-like terminals have a keyboard for data input and a printing element for output. They print one character at a time and are slower than visual display terminals or high-speed computer printers and so are usually connected to low-speed communication lines.

■ **Intelligent Terminals**. *Smart terminals* have built-in microprocessors so they can perform their own error checking and input/output communications control functions. *Intelligent terminals* are really microcomputers or minicomputers with input/output and data

FIGURE 6–11 Business graphics displays

Notice the use of line and bar graphs, pie charts, three dimensional graphs, and multiple window graphics.

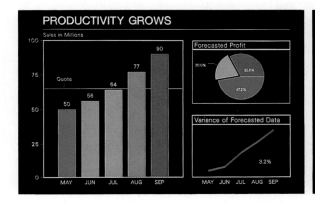

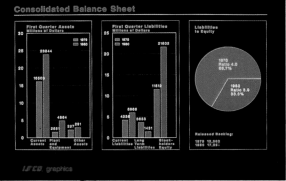

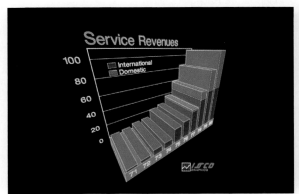

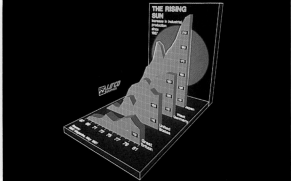

communications capabilities, which can also act as *stand-alone* computers and independently perform some data processing tasks.

■ **Data Entry Terminals**. Typically used for traditional data entry tasks, these terminals use a keyboard for entry of data and a CRT screen so data can be displayed and corrected before it is recorded on magnetic disks or tapes or entered into a computer system. These terminals differ from *transaction terminals* (see below) in that they may be offline to the main computer system, and they are typically used to convert data taken from source documents

FIGURE 6–12 Computer terminals

A CRT terminal.

B Portable printing terminal.

C Graphics terminal.

D Financial transaction terminal.

into computer-readable media (such as floppy disks) for later entry into a computer system. They are primarily used for data entry in *batch processing systems*, where transaction data from source documents are grouped into *batches* before being processed by the computer.

■ **Graphics Terminals**. Graphics terminals and graphics programs allow operators to transform numeric data into graphics displays. Numeric data can be entered through the use of the terminal keyboard or be retrieved from the memory of the computer system. Numeric data can be transformed into bar charts, pie charts, line graphs, three-dimensional graphs, or the multitude of drawings found in engineering design, architecture, and even *computer art*! Advanced graphics terminals allow the operator to *zoom* in and out, to *pan* (turn) the drawing up or down, right or left, in order to better analyze and modify the graphic display. This can be done with buttons on the terminal keyboard or by the use of a graphics control lever or *joystick*.

■ **Transaction Terminals**. These terminals are widely used in banks, retail stores, factories, and other worksites for source data automation. They are used to capture *transaction data* at its point-of-origin. They typically use a keyboard or small *pad* for data entry and either a printer or video display unit for output, as well as a variety of other input/output methods and media. Thus most of these terminals can be classified as *special-purpose* terminals. For example, many transaction recorders might include a slot into which badges, plastic cards, inventory tags, or prepunched cards can be inserted for data input. Some terminals may use an OCR (optical character recognition) *wand* to directly enter printed data into a computer system. Three specific examples are:

Automated teller machines (ATMs), also called *cash machines,* are a major type of transaction terminal that seems to be everywhere. Typically, they require you to insert a bank card with a magnetic stripe into the machine and use a small keypad to enter a security code plus data on your transaction. Output is by a small video display and printed receipts.

A transaction terminal in a factory could use an employee's plastic badge, prepunched cards, and a keyboard to enter data directly into a manufacturing control system.

Point-of-sale (POS) terminals connected online to a computer serve as electronic cash registers and allow instant credit verification and immediate automated capture of sales transaction data for entry into the computer system. Magnetic stripe credit cards and OCR wands are typically used to capture sales data.

VISUAL HARDWARE

Visual Output Devices

■ **Cathode ray tubes (CRT)** are used in most visual display monitors and terminals for display of output. They use a "picture tube" similar to those used in home TV sets, though a variety of technologies are used to provide different levels of picture clarity. These video display devices are available in *monochrome* (typically white, green, blue, or amber displays) or multiple color models. Usually, the clarity of a color display depends on whether you use a regular color TV set (poor), a *composite-video* monitor (better), or a RGB (red-green-blue) monitor (best). Of course, the cost of these devices increases with the level of picture clarity or the number of colors provided.

Most CRT video monitors use a **raster-scan** process in which an electron gun generates an electron beam which *scans* across a phosphor-coated screen in a series of parallel lines known as a *raster*. The computer sends signals to circuits (including a display control microprocessor) which control the direction and the intensity of the electron beam. This causes the phosphors to emit light of various intensities and colors, thus causing images to form on the screen. This scanning process must be repeated 30 to 60 or more times per second to *refresh* the image so that it will not flicker or fade away. Most standard monitors show a display of 25 lines (rows) with 40 to 80 characters (columns) per line. Each character on the screen is composed of *picture elements* called **pixels**.

Video monitors used primarily for displays of text material (numeric, alphabetic, and special characters) are less expensive but have lower *resolution* (clarity) than monitors used primarily for graphics displays. Low-resolution monitors typically use a *character addressable* display, where the screen is divided into a specific number of addressable character locations, and each character is composed of a predefined matrix of pixels. High-resolution monitors usually rely on a *bit-mapped display*, where each pixel is a directly addressable bit or dot location on the screen. The clarity of this *dot addressable* display is therefore much higher and is limited only by the number of pixel locations provided. For example, a medium-resolution display might contain 64,000 pixels (200 × 320 pixels), while a high-resolution graphics workstation might display over one million pixels (1,000 × 1,000 pixels)! Such displays require special microprocessor control and significant amounts of additional primary storage.

FIGURE

6–13 Alternative visual output technologies: Liquid crystal and plasma displays

A Portable terminal with OCR wand and LCD display.

B A flat panel plasma display terminal.

A

B

■ **Liquid crystal displays (LCDs)**, such as those used in electronic calculators and watches, are also being used to display computer output in a limited number of applications, including small *pocket* and portable microcomputers and terminals.

■ **Plasma display** devices are replacing CRT devices in providing visual displays in a limited number of applications. Plasma displays are generated by electrically charged particles of gas (*plasma*) trapped between glass plates. Plasma display units are becoming more popular, but are still more expensive than CRT units. However, they are being used in applications where a compact, flat visual display is a critical factor, such as in portable terminals and micro-computers. See Figure 6–13.

Visual Input Devices

The video display screens of microcomputers and many video terminals can now be used for input as well as output. A variety of devices allow graphic or alphanumeric data to be entered directly into the computer system by "writing" directly on the video screen or on the surface of other devices. Visual or graphic input has been used for many years in military applications, engineering and archi-tectural design, scientific research, cartography (mapmaking and analysis), and is now being used in many business applications.

■ The **electronic mouse** was described briefly in Chapter Four as a recent input device for microcomputers. It is also being used with some video display terminals of large computer systems. The *mouse* is used to move the cursor on the screen, as well as to issue commands and make responses and menu selections. It is connected to the computer and contains a roller ball, which moves the cursor in the direction the ball is rolled. For example, you would move the mouse on your desktop with your hand in the direction you want the cursor to go on the screen. You then move the cursor next to the item you want to select from a menu displayed on the screen. Then press a button on the mouse to make your selection.

■ The **joystick** is another device that is used to move the cursor on the display screen. It looks like a small gear shift lever set in a box. Joysticks are widely used for computer-assisted design, and are also popular control devices for microcomputer video games.

■ The **light pen** is a pen-shaped device that uses photoelectric circuitry to enter data into the computer through the CRT screen. A user can *write* on the CRT display, because the light-sensitive pen enables the computer to calculate the coordinates of the points on the screen being touched by the light pen, even though the CRT screen may contain over one million points of light.

■ **Touch-sensitive screens** are *tactile input* devices that allow operators to enter data into a computer system by touching the surface of a sensitized video display screen with a finger or pointer. For example, you could indicate your selection on a menu display by just touching the screen next to that menu item.

- **Digitizers** of several types are used to convert drawings and other graphic images on paper or other materials into digital data and enter it into a computer system. Digital data can then be displayed on a CRT screen and be processed by the computer system. One form of digitizer is the **graphics tablet**, which has sensing devices embedded in a special tablet on which material to be digitized must be placed. A **graphics pen** (also called an *electronic stylus*) is pressed on the material placed on the graphics tablet to draw or trace figures that appear simultaneously on the CRT screen. A small hand-held device called a *spatial cursor*, with a small round viewing window with cross hairs etched on the glass, is another form of digitizer. It can be passed over the surface of a drawing or graphic image and convert it to digital data. Some graphic pens are *sonic digitizers*, which use sonic impulses (sound waves) to digitize drawings laid on a graphics tablet. See Figure 6–14.

Advantages and Disadvantages

Visual display units are much faster and quieter than printing devices and do not flood users with rivers of paper. A specific piece of information or an entire page of data can be displayed instantly in either alphanumeric or graphic form. The ability to correct or edit input data displayed by a VDT before entry into a computer system is a major benefit. The light pen and other digitizers provide a valuable method of visual/graphic input.

Visual input/output units are major advances in people-computer communication, but they do have several limitations. Special hardware circuits or software are needed to refresh the image of most CRT units or the data being displayed will fade away. Additional equipment is required to produce the hard copy that visual display units do not provide. In addition, there has been some controversy concerning the possible harmful effects of radiation generated by CRT units. Recent studies have shown that such radiation is minimal and not harmful, but research is continuing to investigate these and other complaints concerning the long-term use of visual display devices.

PRINTED OUTPUT HARDWARE

After video displays, **printed output** is the most common form of computer output. Most computer systems use printing devices to produce permanent (*hard copy*) output in human-readable form.

FIGURE 6–14 Visual input devices

A Using a mouse with Macintosh.

B Using a light pen with the HP200 Computer-Aided-Design workstation.

C Using a touchscreen microcomputer, the HP 150.

D Using the graphics tablet, keyboard, and joystick of the MEDUSSA engineering workstation.

You need such printed output if you want copies of output to take with you away from the computer and to share with others. Hard copy output is also frequently needed for legal documentation. **Printers** are used to produce printed reports and documents, such as sales invoices, payroll checks, bank statements, and forms of all kinds. Printers can be classified as impact or nonimpact printers; as character, line, or page printers; and as slow-speed and high-speed printers. **Plotters** that draw graphics displays on paper are also included.

Character, Line, and Page Printing

All computer printing devices print a character at a time, a line at a time, or a page at a time. **Character printers** (also called *serial printers*) print *serially* (one character at a time) as typewriters do. Thus most character printers print at the slow speed of between 15 to 200 characters per second. **Line printers** print an entire line at a time (up to 132 characters) and, therefore, are much faster than a character printer, reaching speeds of 3,000 lines per minute. **Page printers** print an entire page at a time and reach speeds exceeding 20,000 lines per minute.

Impact Printers

Impact printers form characters and other images on paper through the impact of a printing mechanism that presses a printing element (such as a print wheel or cylinder) and an inked ribbon or roller against the face of a continuous paper form. Multiple copies can be produced because the impact of the printing mechanism can transmit an image onto several layers of multiple copy forms.

Slow-speed impact printers are typically used in microcomputer and minicomputer systems and as slow-speed printing terminals. They cost much less than high-speed printers (from a few hundred to a few thousand dollars) and yet are fast enough for most small computer applications. Speeds of such printers range from 15 to 400 characters per second for character printers and up to 3000 lines per minute for line printers. Many slow-speed printers are character impact printers, which use a rotating wheel (**daisy wheel**), a **dot matrix**, or other type of printing element. The daisy wheel printing element rotates to print a solid character. A dot matrix printing element consists of short *print wires* that are struck by a hammer to form a character as a series (or *matrix*) of dots. Solid character printing is usually of higher quality than dot matrix printing. Thus, printers with solid character (*solid font*) print mechanisms (like the daisy wheel) are frequently used for *correspondence quality* or *letter quality* printing jobs, while dot matrix printers are used for *draft quality* printing. However, dot matrix printing is much faster, and it is considered more reliable and versatile than *solid font* printing.

High-speed line impact printers can print up to 3,000 lines per minute using a moving metal chain or cylinder of characters as the printing element. Costs for such printers depend on speed and print quality but can range from $3,000 to over $100,000. Figure 6–15 illustrates several types of computer printing methods.

Nonimpact Printers

Nonimpact printers may use specially treated paper that forms characters by thermal (heat), electrostatic, or electrochemical processes. Other nonimpact printers use plain paper and inkjet, laser, or xerographic technologies to form an image. Nonimpact printers are usually much quieter than impact printers, since the sound of a printing element being struck is eliminated. However, they cannot produce multiple copies like impact printers.

Slow-speed nonimpact printers include **ink-jet printers**, which spray tiny ink particles from fast-moving nozzles against paper. Electrostatic charges placed on the paper attract the ink, which forms characters of high-print quality. Ink-jet printers can print at speeds of over 200 characters per second. **Thermal printers** are slow-speed nonimpact character printers that print a character on heat-sensitive paper by using heated wires to produce a character similar to the dot matrix printing element.

High-speed nonimpact xerographic page printers use Xerox copier technology and microprocessor intelligence to print up to 4,000 lines per minute on plain paper. IBM, Xerox, and several other companies have developed large high-speed **laser printers** that can print over 20,000 lines per minute. These page printers use laser beam technology and require a built-in minicomputer to control the printing process. Costs for such printers range from $150,000 to $300,000. However, less-expensive but slower laser printers are now available, at prices ranging from $3,000 to $20,000; with speeds from 5 to 120 pages per minute. The lowest priced laser printers print 5 to 12 pages per minute, and have become popular high-performance printers for microcomputer systems. See Figure 6–16.

Hard Copy Graphics Devices

Hard copy graphics devices reproduce graphic computer displays on paper or other materials. This requires such equipment as printers, plotters, copying machines, or photographic devices. **Plotters** produce graphic displays using a pen-and-ink process, electrical inscribing, or electrostatic nonimpact techniques. Some plotters have mechanical arms containing one or more pens: they draw lines on paper as directed by a computer. See Figure 6–17.

Printers can also produce hard copy graphics of reasonable quality. Thus graphics software packages allow even dot matrix printers

FIGURE 6–15 Computer printing methods

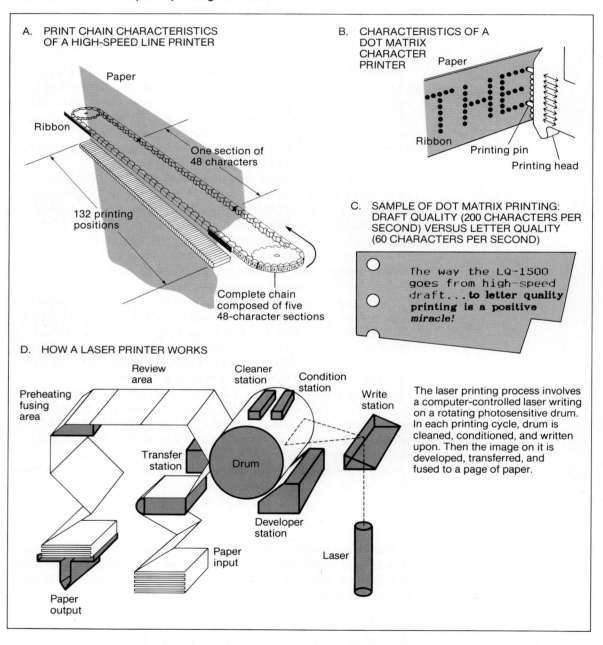

A. PRINT CHAIN CHARACTERISTICS OF A HIGH-SPEED LINE PRINTER

Paper

Ribbon

One section of 48 characters

132 printing positions

Complete chain composed of five 48-character sections

B. CHARACTERISTICS OF A DOT MATRIX CHARACTER PRINTER

Paper

Ribbon

Printing pin

Printing head

C. SAMPLE OF DOT MATRIX PRINTING: DRAFT QUALITY (200 CHARACTERS PER SECOND) VERSUS LETTER QUALITY (60 CHARACTERS PER SECOND)

The way the LQ-1500 goes from high-speed draft...**to letter quality printing is a positive miracle!**

D. HOW A LASER PRINTER WORKS

Review area

Cleaner station

Condition station

Write station

Preheating fusing area

Transfer station

Drum

Developer station

Paper input

Laser

Paper output

The laser printing process involves a computer-controlled laser writing on a rotating photosensitive drum. In each printing cycle, drum is cleaned, conditioned, and written upon. Then the image on it is developed, transferred, and fused to a page of paper.

FIGURE 6–16 Computer printers

A Small ink-jet printer—the Quad Jet.

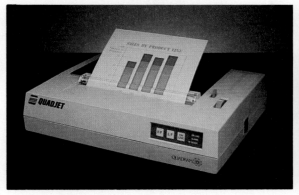

B Small laser printer—the HP Laser Jet.

C A dot matrix printer.

D A high-speed line printer.

to produce hard copy graphics. Ink-jet and laser printers are also used to produce high-quality printed graphics.

Input Preparation Function

Computer output peripherals, such as printers, can also perform an *input preparation* function. High-speed printers can produce output in the form of documents printed in OCR or MICR characters.

FIGURE

6–17 Computer plotters

A A large electrostatic plotter.

B A small pen plotter for a micro-computer system.

A

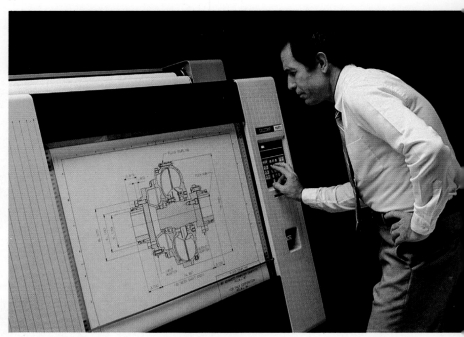

B

REAL WORLD APPLICATION 6–2

Computer Printers Are Changing

Someday, in the automated offices of tomorrow, video screens may take the place of ink and paper. Today, however, office automation is producing more paper, not less. The printers that help computers create much of this paper have become a $2.4 billion industry, and printer sales should more than double before this decade ends.

But the nature of printers is changing. During the next several years, printers that write with heat, beams of light, or jets of ink are expected to supplant those that work like typewriters. "The change will be almost complete by the end of the decade," says Roger Kiel, a Xerox Corporation vice president.

At present, almost all printers use what is called *impact technology*. In some machines, a hammer strikes a piece of metal or plastic type, pressing it against a ribbon and transferring its image to paper. Other impact machines replace the type with a matrix of needles. By hitting the needles in the appropriate patterns, hammers print arrays of dots that look like letters or numbers.

Impact printers are simple. Some sell for as little as a few hundred dollars. But they are slow and noisy. Nonimpact printers, all those that don't rely on hammering, are fast and quiet but, until recently, much more expensive.

Consider the most well-developed of the nonimpact technologies, laser printing. Laser printers work like copying machines. In a copier, light reflecting from an original document creates a pattern of electrical charges on a rotating drum. The drum turns through a tray of black powder. The powder adheres to the charged pattern and is transferred to paper, creating a copy. A copier is transformed into a printer by replacing the light-reflecting mechanism with a laser beam that, under the control of a computer, can write directly on the rotating drum.

Although prices have been dropping since the first laser printer was introduced about 1978, the machines were still far too costly for most data processing or word processing installations. The fastest laser printers cost nearly a half-million dollars, and even the slowest machines cost about $20,000. However, several computer companies have begun selling laser printers (such as Hewlett-Packard's *Laser Jet*) using technology developed by Canon USA, Inc., at prices between $3,000 and $5,000.

Prices of other kinds of nonimpact printers are falling, too. Hewlett-Packard introduced a $495 ink-jet printer that operates by spraying ink on paper. Delphax and C. Itoh of Japan have devised a $5,000 machine that prints with a stream of ions, or charged particles. Epson American has developed a printer using liquid crystals that should sell for a few thousand dollars.

Dataquest, a California market research company, predicts that sales of impact printers will peak during the next two years. Annual sales will be about $2.5 billion in 1988, only slightly higher than in 1983. By contrast, sales of printers using alternative technologies are expected to rise to about $2.6 billion in 1988, from about $44 million last year. According to the forecast, the laser will be the dominant nonimpact technology.

- What is the dominant printer technology today? What will it be by 1990?
- How does a laser printer work? Why is it expected to become so popular?

Source: Richard A. Shaffer, "Laser Printers for Computers May Soon Dominate Industry," *The Wall Street Journal*, March 16, 1984, p. 25.

Forms produced in this manner are known as **turnaround documents** because they are designed to be returned to the sender. For example, many computer-printed invoices consist of a turnaround portion, which is returned by a customer along with his or her payment. The turnaround document can then be automatically processed by OCR or MICR readers. Thus the high-speed printer has performed an input preparation function.

Advantages and Disadvantages

Printing devices provide a computer system with the ability to produce printed reports and forms of all kinds. Printing of excellent quality can be done at high speeds. However, the speed factor is the cause of two contradictory problems. Computers can now produce printed reports so quickly that managers can be "buried" in mountains of paper. The ability of managers to use the information in computer-printed reports to assist their decision making is diminished by the rapid flow of volumes of paper. On the other hand, high-speed printers are not fast enough output devices for most computer systems, thus causing an "output-bound" condition. The data transfer rate of high-speed printers is over 4,000 characters per second, which is quite slow compared to over 300,000 characters per second for magnetic tape output. This problem is being solved by the use of visual display terminals, offline magnetic tape to printer operations, and microfilm output devices.

MAGNETIC MEDIA DATA ENTRY

Key-to-Disk Devices

Magnetic disk and floppy disk systems can be used for the *data entry* function, in which data from source documents (such as sales invoices) is recorded on magnetic disk media. Large **key-to-disk** systems use many keyboard/CRT terminals, which input data simultaneously to a central magnetic disk unit. These systems are usually offline from a large computer system but are controlled and supported by a minicomputer. Key-to-disk systems are expensive and can only be justified for applications with large volumes of data from many sources, in which immediate processing of data is not required. The major advantage of these systems over key-to-tape methods is that they do not require the merging and sorting of magnetic tapes that is characteristic of key-to-tape systems. Floppy disks are also used for data entry by microcomputer, minicomputer, and small business systems. Data is typically entered via a keyboard, visually verified by display on a CRT, and recorded on a diskette. Floppy disks provide an inexpensive data entry medium for such small computer systems.

Key-to-Tape Devices

Key-to-tape devices enter data directly from a keyboard onto magnetic tape. The aim of such data entry devices is to bypass the process of first recording data into punched cards or punched paper tape and then converting these media into magnetic tape. These devices produce magnetic tape in the form of standard-size magnetic tape reels, small cartridges, and cassettes. Data recorded on standard-size magnetic tape reels can be used by the magnetic tape units of a computer system, while small magnetic cartridges and cassettes require special computer peripheral equipment, such as tape cartridge readers and cassette decks. Key-to-tape devices are being phased out and replaced by direct entry and key-to-disk data entry methods.

PUNCHED CARD HARDWARE

The Punched Card

Punched card hardware was widely used in electronic data processing because of the prior use of punched cards in electromechanical data processing systems. One type of punched card still used in some computer systems is the 80-column punched card also known as the "Hollerith" card. Up to 80 individual data elements, such as alphabetic, numeric, and special characters, can be punched into such a card, using the *Hollerith* code shown in Figure 6–18. Notice that numeric characters require the punching of only a single hole, while alphabetic and special characters require the punching of two or three holes in a column. Also used is a 96–column punched card. Data is punched as round holes in three sections of this smaller card, with each section containing 32 characters. This card uses the six-bit BCD computer code.

Card Readers and Punch Units

Punched card peripheral equipment for computer systems include *card readers* and *card punch units*. These units use photoelectric cells to sense the holes in the punched cards and convert the data into electric pulses, which are then converted into the internal code of the computer. Cards are read by two different reading stations in card reader units as a check on the accuracy of the operation. Card punch machines punch output data into cards under the control of the computer, and they include a reading station to check on the accuracy of the punching process. The *card read-punch* combines the functions of reading and punching into a single unit. The reading speed of card reading devices varies from 160 to 2,700 cards per minute, while card punching speed varies from 80 to 650 cards per minute.

FIGURE 6–18 Punched card coding

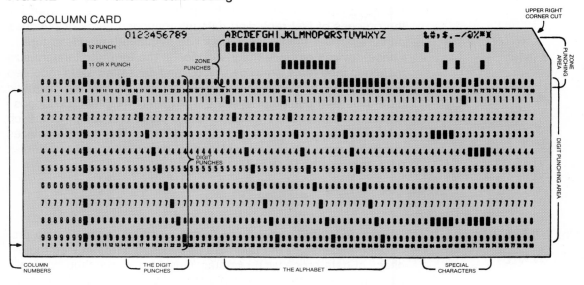

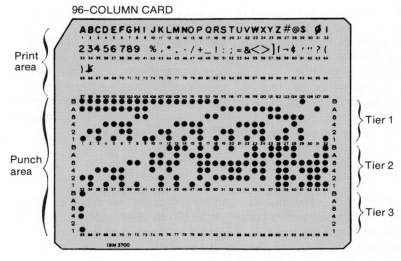

Punched Card Data Entry Equipment

The *keypunch* machine records data in punched cards by punching holes in the cards. An operator uses a keyboard similar to that of a typewriter. Accuracy of the punching process is checked by a *verifier* which is similar in appearance to the keypunch. Instead of punching holes, it electrically senses whether a discrepancy exists between the keys being depressed and the holes punched in the

FIGURE

6–19 Punched card hardware

A Read/punch units.

B Keypunch machine.

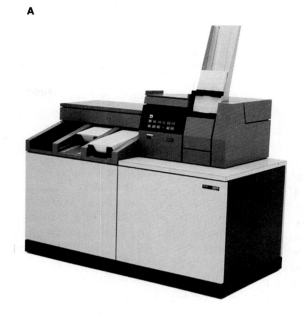

A

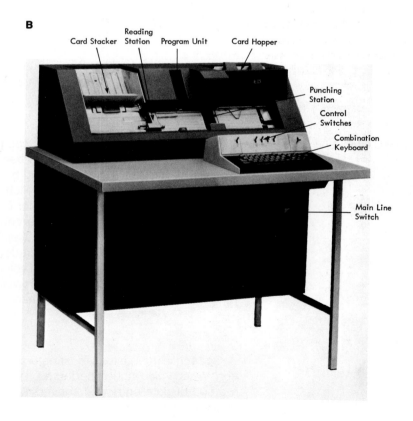

B

Card Stacker

Reading Station

Program Unit

Card Hopper

Punching Station

Control Switches

Combination Keyboard

Main Line Switch

card during the keypunching operation. If a discrepancy exists, a hole is punched in the top of the card above the incorrectly punched column. Machines called *card data recorders* are available that perform both the punching and verifying functions. See Figure 6–19.

Advantages and Disadvantages

Punched cards are an inexpensive and simple input/output and secondary storage medium. Data in a file of cards can easily be changed by adding, deleting, or repunching a card. Punch card output can be in the form of a human-readable document, which can later be used as input to an electronic data processing system. Punched card paychecks and utility bills are familiar examples. However, cards are bulky, can hold only a limited amount of data, and provide a very slow method of computer input/output, compared to magnetic media. For instance, an inch of high-density magnetic tape can hold as many characters of data as 80 punched cards, and magnetic tape input speeds range up to 350,000 characters per second, compared to a maximum of about 2,500 characters per second with punched cards. Another major limitation of punched cards is the keypunching, verifying, and other *input preparation* activities that are required before data can be entered into the computer system. Thus the use of punched cards is declining rapidly.

VOICE HARDWARE

Have you talked or listened to a computer recently? Applications of voice input/output devices have been limited in the past but are now growing rapidly and should be widely used in the future. Rapid advances in microelectronic technology have developed *talking chips*. These are microprocessor chips that synthesize human speech and are being used to give **voice output** capabilities to everything from children's toys to telephone communication systems. Voice input hardware has not developed as fast as voice output devices. However, the use of voice input terminals with limited speed recognition capabilities is growing steadily in applications ranging from sales data entry to manufacturing quality control.

Voice Input

Speech is the easiest, most natural means of human communication. When voice input is perfected, it will be the easiest, most reliable method of data entry and conversational computing. Voice input of data into a computer system is now at the frontier of people-computer communication, but it has become technologically and economically feasible for a variety of applications. **Voice data entry terminals** are now being used that allow the direct entry of data into a computer system by verbal communication of a human operator. A typical configuration might consist of one or more portable voice recognition units, microphones, and a CRT terminal for visual display of spoken input. This system can have over a 1,000-word vocabulary and support several users simultaneously. Other voice-recognition *modules* have all of the required circuitry on a single circuit board, including a vocabulary of several hundred words, and are being incorporated in visual display terminals and microcomputer systems. See Figure 6–20.

Voice input units rely on **voice recognition** (or *speech recognition*) microprocessors, which analyze and classify acoustic speech patterns and transform them into electronic digital codes for entry into a computer system. The process is directed by speech recognition programs that compare the speech input to previously stored voice reference patterns that are kept on a secondary storage device, such as a magnetic disk. Most voice input systems require "training" the computer to recognize a limited vocabulary of standard words for each individual using the system. Operators train the system to recognize their voices by repeating each word in the vocabulary about 10 times. Trained systems regularly achieve over a 99 percent word recognition. **Speaker-independent** voice recognition systems are being developed that allow a computer to understand a voice it has never heard before. Development of such systems would eliminate the need for training.

FIGURE

6–20 Using a voice data entry system with the Texas Instruments professional computer

Voice input devices are now being used in work situations where operators need to perform data entry without using their hands to key in data or instructions, or where it would provide faster and more accurate input. For example, voice recognition systems are being used by several manufacturers for the inspection, inventory, and quality control of a variety of products, and by several airlines and parcel delivery companies for voice-directed sorting of baggage and parcels. In another application, a major U.S. oil company uses a voice recognition system to receive oil exploration data over the telephone that are called in from exploration centers around the country. This application demonstrates that voice recognition technology can transform the telephone into a voice input terminal. Voice recognition units for microcomputers have recently become available that enable users to develop and use electronic spreadsheet and other standard software packages using voice input.

Besides data entry and computerized machinery control, other voice recognition applications include information retrieval from data banks, telephone network control, and **speaker recognition** systems. In speaker recognition applications, voice input to a computer is analyzed to verify the identification of a speaker for security purposes. The speaker's voice is compared to a file of previously recorded voice patterns (sometimes called *voice prints*) to establish the identification of the speaker.

Voice Output Devices

Voice output devices have changed dramatically as a result of the microcomputer revolution. Computer **audio-response** units have shrunk dramatically in size and cost. Microelectronic **speech synthesizers** are now being used that fit the devices necessary to synthesize human speech onto a single integrated circuit chip. Texas Instruments was the first to develop a "talking chip" and introduced it in 1978 with an educational toy called Speak and Spell. It holds the patents for an integrated circuit that digitally synthesizes human speech, a speech synthesis filter that electronically models the human voice tract, and a converter that drives the speaker so audible speech can be generated. National Semiconductor produces a talking chip that breaks a human voice into "wave form" fragments and then patches these forms together into words to form synthetic speech. Several other semiconductor companies are producing such chips, and they are rapidly being used to provide computerized speech for toys, games, greeting cards, consumer appliances, automobiles, elevators, and a variety of other consumer, commercial, and industrial uses. Such speech synthesizing microprocessors are also being used in electronic calculators, in digital watches, and

REAL WORLD APPLICATION 6–3

Interstate Electronics Corporation

Interstate Electronics' high-accuracy VRT300 voice recognition terminal circuit board instantly adds new capabilities to DEC VT100 and C.ITOH CIT-101 terminals for $1,295. The need for special programming has been eliminated by resident voice recognition firmware, which enables spoken works to be transmitted to the host computer as if they had been keyed in. The VRT300 has a 100-word vocabulary and over 99 percent accuracy. The price includes mike and cable. And the system has proved itself in a variety of real world applications.

In factory automation, Interstate increased final inspection productivity up to 60 percent with hands-free operation. And in the process of delivering real-time quality control data, it demonstrated that direct voice data entry is a workable concept in noisy plant environments.

Interstate also talks medical applications—in depth. For example, its menu-driven system uses less than an 80 word input vocabulary to let hospital patients order more than 10,000 services.

In computer-aided design, Interstate doubled productivity and showed that voice and graphics can work perfectly together. In security, it has proven that voice recognition offers a highly accurate, low-cost means of speaker identification. Interstate is also involved with office automation, banking, and other applications.

- What capabilities does the VRT300 circuit board give to computer terminals?
- What are some of the uses of voice recognition technology? What benefits have resulted?

Source: Interstate Electronics Corporation.

in hand-held computers and foreign language translators. See Figure 6–21.

Voice output devices allow the computer to verbally guide an cperator through the steps of a task in many types of activities. They are widely used to allow computers to respond to inquiries and other input over the telephone. In many present applications, input of data is accomplished by pressing the buttons of a *Touch Tone* telephone while output is in the form of a voice produced by an audio-response device controlled by a computer system and transmitted over the telephone lines. This application is found in bank *pay-by-phone* bill-paying services, stock quotation services, and customer credit and account balance inquiries.

Advantages and Disadvantages

Voice input/output devices provide the quickest and easiest method of people-computer communications. Every telephone becomes a potential computer terminal. Voice output devices are small

FIGURE

6–21 A talking chip

Also shown is a diagram of the operation of the chip, with an enlarged view of the chip circuitry in the background.

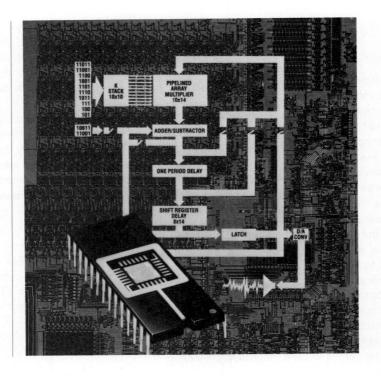

and inexpensive, while voice input devices are now feasible for many applications. Chief limitations concern the quality of synthetic speech and the limited vocabulary and training required by most voice recognition systems. These limitations should be overcome with the continued development of electronic voice technology.

|| OCR HARDWARE

FIGURE

6–22 USA standard character set for optical character recognition

ABCDEFGHIJKLMNOPQRS
TUVWXYZ0123456789·,
'-{}%?♪⌐⌐:⌐=+/$*"&

Optical character recognition (OCR) equipment can read alphabetic, numeric, and special characters that are printed, typed, or handwritten on ordinary paper. OCR is an attempt to provide a method of direct input of data from *source documents* into a computer system. There are many types of optical readers, but they all employ photoelectric devices to scan the characters being read and to convert reflected light patterns of the data into electronic impulses that are accepted as input into the computer system. Documents that contain characters not meeting the character design standards of the optical reader are rejected. OCR devices can now read many types of printing, and progress is continually being made in improving the reading ability of OCR equipment. A widely used character design for OCR is shown in Figure 6–22.

Optical character recognition devices can read preprinted characters produced by typewriters, word processors, computer printers, cash registers, calculators, credit card imprinters, as well as handwriting, provided the characters meet OCR standards. Thus OCR readers are being used to read pages of text for entry into advanced word processing systems, as well as into the more traditional reading of documents printed in OCR standard characters. OCR equipment can also read pencil marks made in specific positions of a form. This variation is called **mark-sensing**. OCR devices, such as handheld **wands**, are being used to read data on merchandise tags and other media. OCR devices can read documents that contain **bar coding**, which is a code that utilizes bars to represent characters. **Universal product code** (UPC) bar coding on packages of food items and other products has become commonplace, since it is required for the *automated checkout* "scanners" installed at many supermarkets and retail stores.

Supermarket scanners (like that shown in Figure 6–23) emit laser beams, which are reflected off a universal product code. The reflected image is converted to electronic impulses that are sent to the in-store minicomputer, where they are matched with pricing information. Pricing information is returned to the terminal, visually displayed, and printed on a receipt. It happens as fast as the item can be moved past the scanning window. Take a look at the universal product code (UPC) in Figure 6–23. It identifies the item as a grocery product (the 0 on the left) of the Green Giant Company

FIGURE 6–23

A Supermarket OCR scanner.

B The Universal Product Code: An example.

B

A

(specified by the 20000), which in this instance is a 10-ounce frozen package of baby lima beans in butter sauce (specified by the 12190).

Advantages and Disadvantages

The major benefit of OCR is that it provides a method of direct input of data from a source document into a computer system. It thus eliminates much costly input preparation activity and increases the accuracy and speed of an electronic information processing system. OCR is extensively used in the credit card billing operations of credit card companies, banks, and oil companies. It is also used to process utility bills, insurance premiums, airline tickets, and cash register and adding machine tapes. OCR is used to automatically sort mail, score tests, and process a wide variety of forms in business and government. The major limitation of OCR has been its stringent character design requirements. Other major limitations for some applications were high document rejection and error rates. However, recently developed OCR readers can read typewriter, word processor, or computer printing of a variety of type fonts with satisfactory accuracy.

II MICR HARDWARE

Magnetic ink character recognition (MICR) allows the computer systems of the banking industry to magnetically read checks and deposit slips and thus sort, tabulate, and post them to the proper checking accounts. Such processing is possible because the identification numbers of the bank and the customer's account number are preprinted on the bottom of checks with an iron-oxide based ink. The first bank receiving a check after it has been written must encode the amount of the check in magnetic ink on its lower right-hand corner. The MICR system uses 14 characters (the 10 decimal digits and four special symbols) of a unique design.

MICR characters can be preprinted on documents or can be encoded on documents using a keyboard-operated machine called a *proof-inscriber*, which also segregates checks into batches and accumulates batch totals. Equipment known as MICR *reader-sorters* read a check by first magnetizing the magnetic ink characters and then sensing the signal induced by each character as it passes by a reading head. The check is then sorted by directing it into one of the pockets of the reader-sorter while the data is electronically captured by the computer system. Reader-sorters can read over 2,000 checks per minute, with a data transfer rate of over 3,000 characters per second. See Figures 6–24 and 25.

FIGURE

6–24 A check with MICR encoding

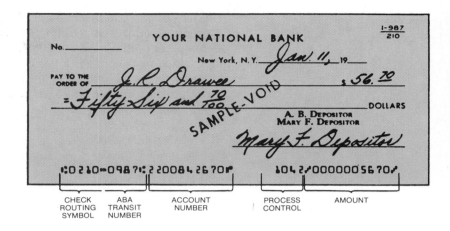

FIGURE

6–25 MICR reader-sorter

Advantages and Disadvantages

MICR processing has greatly benefitted the banking industry. Banks would be hard pressed to handle the processing of checks without MICR and computer technology. MICR documents are human-readable as well as machine-readable. MICR has proved to be a highly accurate and reliable method for the direct entry of data on a source document. Major limitations of MICR are the lack of alphabetic and other characters and the necessity to encode the amount of the check in a separate manual processing step.

MICROGRAPHICS HARDWARE

The use of computers in the field of **micrographics** involves:

■ **Computer-output-microfilm**, or COM, in which microfilm is used as a computer output medium. High-speed microfilm recorders are used to electronically capture the output of computer systems on microfilm, microfiche, and other *microforms*.

■ **Computer-input-microfilm**, or CIM, where microfilm is used as an input medium. CIM systems use OCR devices to scan microfilm for high-speed input of data.

■ **Computer-assisted-retrieval**, or CAR, in which special-purpose computer terminals or minicomputers are used as micrographics

FIGURE 6–26 How COM works

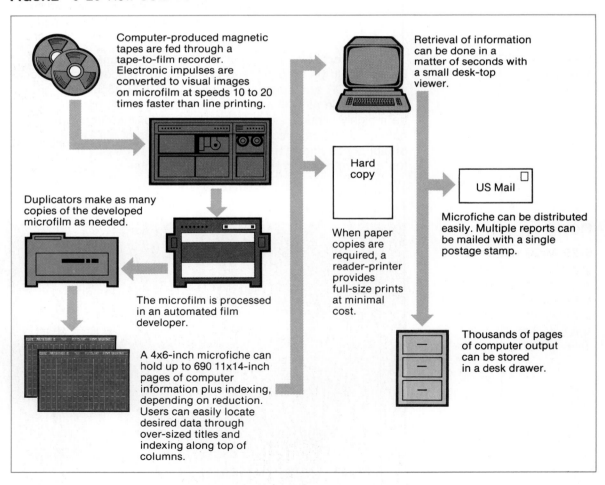

Computer-produced magnetic tapes are fed through a tape-to-film recorder. Electronic impulses are converted to visual images on microfilm at speeds 10 to 20 times faster than line printing.

Duplicators make as many copies of the developed microfilm as needed.

The microfilm is processed in an automated film developer.

A 4x6-inch microfiche can hold up to 690 11x14-inch pages of computer information plus indexing, depending on reduction. Users can easily locate desired data through over-sized titles and indexing along top of columns.

Retrieval of information can be done in a matter of seconds with a small desk-top viewer.

Hard copy

When paper copies are required, a reader-printer provides full-size prints at minimal cost.

US Mail

Microfiche can be distributed easily. Multiple reports can be mailed with a single postage stamp.

Thousands of pages of computer output can be stored in a desk drawer.

terminals to locate and retrieve automatically a microfilm copy of a document.

Micrographics hardware includes microfilm recorders, hard copy printers, microfilm readers, and micrographics terminals. See Figures 6–26 and 6–27.

Advantages and Disadvantages

Micrographics hardware is widely used to replace computer printing devices that are too slow and produce too much paper. COM recorders can have a data transfer rate up to 500,000 characters per second and "print" up to 60,000 lines per minute, which is much faster than most high-speed printers and equals or exceeds the output rate of magnetic tape or disk units. Microfilm output also takes up only 2 percent of the space of paper output. Micrographic output thus is a lot faster and takes up much less space than paper output. The storage, handling, and retrieval of microfilm files are substantially easier and cheaper than paper documents. COM is used to sharply reduce the volume of computer-printed paper, even though some COM users record *all* transaction data instead of merely producing printed "exception reports." Such users claim that they can provide better customer service and better information for management because the computer provides them with up-to-date microfilm records of all transactions, recording only exception items on paper. The major limitation of COM has been its high hardware cost, which limited it to high-volume applications or the

FIGURE

6–27 A computer output-microfilm installation including a magnetic tape drive and minicomputer unit, tape-to-film recorder and developer, and an operator console.

COM facilities of computer service centers. However, advances in *microimage* technology have made micrographics much more cost effective and a fast-growing area of computer use.

I/O INTERFACE HARDWARE

Several computer system devices exist that are difficult to classify since they can be physically part of the CPU, a separate unit, or can be built into an input/output or storage device. The main purpose of devices, such as *buffers, channels,* and *input/output control units*, is to assist the CPU in its input/output assignments. These devices have been developed to provide a uniform, flexible, and efficient *interface* between the CPU and its input/output units. They provide modern computer systems with the ability to carry out many input and output functions simultaneously, while at the same time allowing the CPU to carry out other processing functions, since it no longer must directly control I/O devices. See Figure 6–28.

Buffers

Buffers are high-speed storage units that are used for the temporary storage of input or output data to reduce the demands of input/output operations on the CPU. Buffers are sometimes built into the

FIGURE 6–28 Input/output interface devices

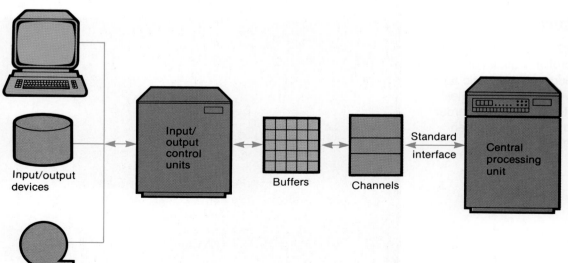

Input/output devices

Input/output control units

Buffers

Channels

Standard interface

Central processing unit

CPU or into the input/output device, or they may be housed separately in a peripheral unit. When buffers are used, the CPU does not have to wait for the input or the output of data but can initiate an input or output command and then return to other processing. Data can then move from the input device into the buffer or from the buffer into an output device without tying up the CPU. High-speed transfer of data occurs when an input buffer transfers data to a CPU or when a CPU can transfer data into an output buffer.

Channels

Channels are special-purpose microprocessors or miniprocessors that control the movement of data between the CPU and input or output devices. Channels are housed within the CPU or can be separate peripheral units and may contain buffer storage. Once the channel receives an input or output command from the CPU, it can control the operations of several input/output units simultaneously without disturbing the CPU. Only when the input or output operation is completed will the channel "interrupt" the CPU to signal the completion of its assignment. There are two main types of channels, each of which can handle several input or output units. The *selector channel* selectively allows each input or output device temporarily to monopolize the entire channel in what is called the "burst mode" of data transmission. *Multiplexor channels* can control data input or output from several slower devices simultaneously in a *multiplex mode*. Most multiplexor channels can also operate in a burst mode to service high-speed input/output devices. Some multiplexor channels are called *block multiplexor channels*, since they can transmit or receive data in "blocks" of several bytes of data, rather than one byte at a time. The high-speed data transmission of these units is called "data streaming."

Input/Output Control Units

Channels are normally not connected directly to an input/output device but to an *input/output control unit*. A control unit can be built into an input/output device or be housed as a separate unit (frequently called a *controller*) that controls several input/output devices. The job of the controller is to decode the input/output commands from the CPU or the channel and to control the operation of the appropriate input/output device, including the coding, decoding, and checking of data transmitted from the CPU. Buffer storage units are part of the controllers of some input/output devices.

SUMMARY

- Traditional data entry methods that require too many activities, people, and forms of data media are being replaced by more direct automated methods known as source data automation. The high cost and potential for errors of traditional data entry methods can be minimized if source data automation is used to capture data as early and as close as possible to the source that generates the data. Data is captured by using machine-readable media, prerecording data, or capturing data directly without the use of data media.

- Whether traditional or automated methods of data entry are used, the computer can still be used to assist the data entry process. Special keyboards can be used, and video displays can provide such features such as cursors, menus, prompts, and icons. Or other devices and methods can be used, such as audio prompts, the electronic mouse, touch-sensitive screens, etc. All of these devices are designed to simplify the job of entering data in the computer systems by reducing the use of manual keyboard methods for data entry.

- Computer output methods are also changing. Printed paper output is being replaced by visual displays. Magnetic tape and disks or microfilm media are replacing punched paper cards and tapes, as well as printed paper reports and documents. Standardized printed reports produced on a regular basis are being replaced by visual displays tailored to users and furnished to them at their request. Finally, displays of numeric data or text material are being replaced by colored graphics displays.

- Figures 6–1, 6–2, 6–3 and 6–28 should be used to help you summarize the types of input/output hardware and methods which have been discussed in this chapter.

KEY TERMS AND CONCEPTS

User interface	Direct input/output
Ergonomics	Computer-assisted data entry
User-friendly	Cursor
Traditional data entry	Menu
Source data automation	Color graphics
Source document	Icons
Batch	Intelligent terminal
Machine-readable media	Prompt

Transaction terminal
Computer graphics
Cathode ray tube (CRT)
Computer terminal
Plasma display
Data entry terminal
Light pen
Point-of-sale (POS) terminal
Digitizers
Liquid crystal displays (LCD)
Character, line, and page
  printers
Electronic mouse
Touch-sensitive screen

Turnaround documents
Impact and nonimpact printers
Plotters
Key-to-tape, key-to-disk
Voice input/output
Magnetic ink character
  recognition (MICR)
Optical character recognition
OCR scanner and wand
Punched card hardware
Audio-response
Micrographics
Input/output interface
  hardware

REVIEW AND APPLICATION QUESTIONS

1. Why are there so many types of input/output media and devices?
2. Why have data entry activities always been a bottleneck in the use of computers for information processing?
3. Why is there a movement away from traditional data entry methods?
4. What are the five major objectives of source data automation? Give an example of each one.
5. How can the computer assist you in data entry? Can you think of other ways that data entry could be made easier for you?
6. What are four important trends in changing output methods? Give an example of each one.
7. Why is the use of computer graphics becoming popular? What are some limitations to the use of graphics displays?
8. What is the difference between a data entry and a transaction terminal? Give an example of the use of each type.
9. Explain the use of the following data entry display aids: cursor, menu, prompt, and icon. Which one do you find most helpful?
10. Explain the use of the following visual input devices: electronic mouse, light pen, touch-sensitive screen, and digitizer. Which one of these would be most helpful to you?
11. How does a turnaround document assist the data entry function?
12. Why hasn't voice input become a more common method of data entry?
13. Distinguish between the characteristics and functions of the following:
    a. VDT and printing terminals.

     b. Visual and voice input/output hardware.
     c. Character and line printers.
     d. Magnetic tape and disk data entry.
     e. MICR and OCR hardware.
     f. I/O devices and I/O interface devices

14. What are the reasons for the increasing use of micrographics?
15. Which of the input/output hardware devices described in this chapter do you personally use? Which devices are most widely used by people in organizations with whom you come into contact on a regular basis? Evaluate such devices from this personal perspective.

APPLICATION PROBLEMS

1. If you have not already done so, read and answer the questions after each Real World Application in this chapter.
2. Outline the functions, advantages, and disadvantages of several input/output devices, indicating whether they perform input, output, and secondary storage functions and the type of media they use.
3. A chain of eight department stores processes sales by recording each sale on a sales order form. Daily these forms are sent to the central computer department for keypunching. Monthly customers are billed, and inventory and sales reports are sent to store managers. The managers receive their reports about 7 days after the end of the month. The managers have been complaining about the infrequency and untimeliness of these reports. Could new input/output hardware alleviate the problem? Justify your answer.
4. Robertson Manufacturing has been using the medium of printed paper output in its computer systems. Now it is facing mountains of paper. What other devices could be used to cut down on this excessive volume of paper?
5. Intelligent terminals cost more than *dumb* terminals. Name two advantages of using intelligent terminals that help to justify the added cost.
6. Name two devices that can read characters printed on source documents and convert these characters directly into computer-usable format. Identify a current use for each device.

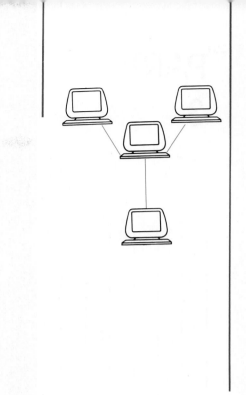

PART
3

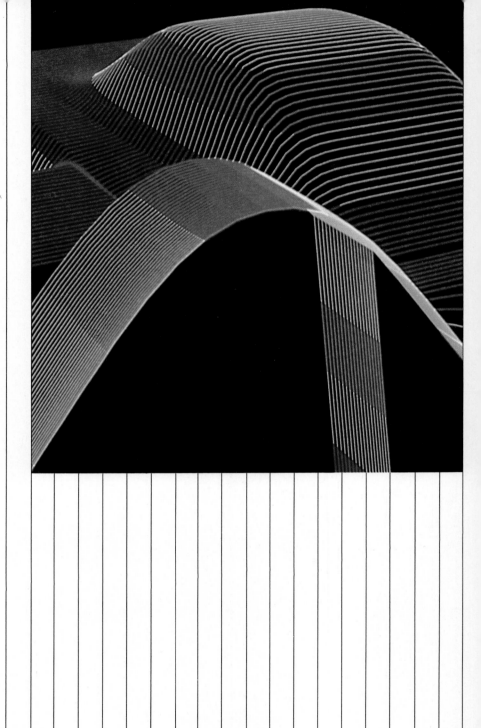

Computer Software
and Programming

CHAPTER 7

System and Application Software

CHAPTER OUTLINE

LEARNING OBJECTIVES

The purpose of this chapter is to promote a basic
understanding of computer software by analyzing the
functions, benefits, and limitations of major software
packages. After reading and studying this chapter, you
should be able to:

1. Differentiate between the following terms:
   a. System software versus application software.
   b. Software packages versus user-developed
      software.
   c. Control programs versus service programs.
   d. Database management systems versus data
      communications monitors.
2. Identify several major categories of system and
   application software.
3. Outline the functions of an operating system.
4. Describe the role of programming language
   translator programs.
5. Identify and explain the purpose of several popular
   microcomputer software packages.
6. Explain the purpose and benefits of electronic
   spreadsheet packages.
7. Determine the various types of system and
   application software available for use on your
   microcomputer system, or at your computer center.

INTRODUCTION

By now, you should have a good idea of the role of **software** in information processing systems and computer systems. In this chapter, we will explore in more detail the major types of software you will depend on as you work with computers. We'll discuss their major characteristics and purposes, and give examples of their use. This should provide you with the knowledge you need to learn to use the many types of software that are an indispensable part of modern computer systems.

First, let's summarize three different ways that software can be categorized to give you a good overview of this important topic. We have said that information processing systems rely on **software resources,** as well as *hardware* and *people* to transform *data resources* into a variety of *information products*. In this context software resources consist of:

- **Programs** of instructions used to direct the operation of the *hardware* of computer systems.
- **Procedures** used to direct the activities of the *people* who operate and use computer systems.

We have also emphasized that computer software consists of two major types of programs:

- **System software**—programs that control and support the operations of a computer system as it performs various information processing tasks.
- **Application software**—programs that direct the performance of a particular use or *application* of computers to meet the information processing needs of users.

Finally, you should realize that computer software can be subdivided into two other categories, depending on whether it is developed by users themselves or acquired from external sources.

- **Software packages**—programs acquired by users from various software vendors that are developed by computer manufacturers, independent software companies, or other users.
- **User-developed software**—programs developed by users or the professional programmers of a computer-using organization.

Let's begin our analysis of software by looking at an overview of the major types and functions of software available to computer users. First of all, don't forget that all software must support the *input*, *processing*, *output*, *storage*, and *control* functions of a computer system. Refer back to Figure 3–14 to refresh your memory concerning this important software role. Now look at Figure 7–1. This figure summarizes the major categories of system and applica-

FIGURE 7–1 Overview of system and application software

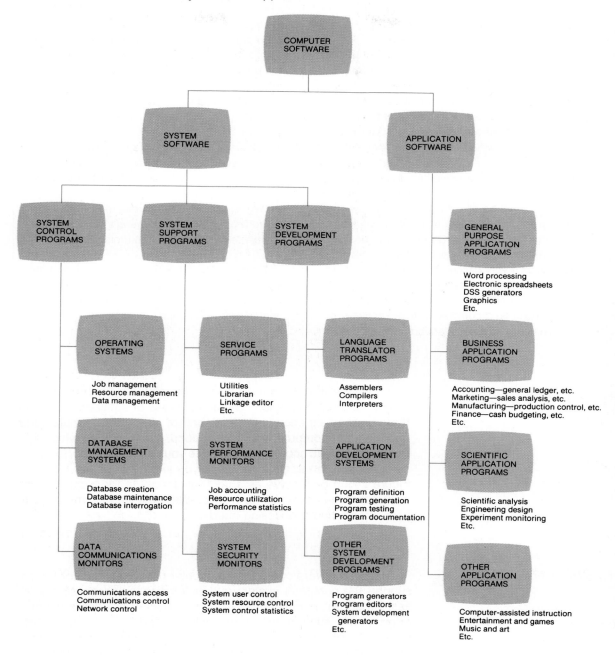

REAL WORLD APPLICATION 7–1

Physician's Microcomputer, Inc.

Dr. Greg Berlin of San Francisco wanted to buy a microcomputer system when he set up his practice, but couldn't find one he liked. "As I learned more about microcomputers," Berlin recalls, "I began to realize that most of the microcomputer systems available for physicians made the office more difficult to manage. They solved a few problems but introduced many others. There's no reason for computers to be that difficult to operate. It shouldn't take any training at all. You should be able to say, This is how you turn the machine on, and this is how you insert a diskette,' and that's it. So I began to design software that teaches users as they go along, that makes it very difficult to destroy something or do something accidentally."

For four years, Berlin spent about half of his time working on a complete office-practice system. The program uses standard medical codes to keep patients' health records, does the billing, even processes insurance claims. To work the bugs out of it, Berlin invited friends to try to make the program "crash." He now markets his system, through Physician's Microcomputer, Inc., for under $25,000.

- Why did Dr. Berlin develop his own software? Why does he think other doctors will buy his software package, rather than develop their own programs?
- Would you say that he has tried to develop software that: Is *user-friendly*? Is *well documented*? Has *built-in* controls? Explain.

Source: "The Data Game: Business and the Microcomputer," *Passages*, May 1981, p. 24. Copyright 1981 by The Webb Company. Reprinted with permission.

tion software that we will discuss in this chapter. Of course, this is a conceptual illustration. The actual types of software categories that you may experience depend, first of all, on the manufacturer and model of computer you use. Second, it depends on which additional software is acquired to increase your computer's performance or to accomplish specific tasks for you and other users. However, Figure 7–1 should serve as a good guidepost to the wealth of software resources available to help operate and apply computers to your information processing needs.

SYSTEM SOFTWARE

System software consists of computer programs that control and support the computer system and its information processing activities. As shown in Figure 7–1, system software includes a variety of programs, such as operating systems, database management systems, communications monitors, service programs, and programming language translators. Notice, however, that such programs can be grouped into three major functional categories:

■ **System Control Programs**—programs that *control* the use of the hardware, software, and data resources of the computer system during its execution of the various information processing jobs of users. Major control programs are operating systems, database management systems, and communications monitors.

■ **System Support Programs**—programs that *support* the operations, management, and users of a computer system by providing a variety of support services. Major support programs are service programs, performance monitors, and security monitors.

■ **System Development Programs**—programs that help users *develop* information processing programs and procedures and prepare user programs for computer processing. Major development programs are language translators and application development systems.

Each of these programs perform important functions in modern computer systems and should be understood by knowledgeable computer users. They serve as a vital **software interface** between computer system hardware and the application programs of users. See Figure 7–2.

Operating Systems

The most important system software package for any computer is its **operating system**. An operating system is an integrated *system* of programs that supervises the *operations* of the CPU, controls the input/output and storage functions of the computer system,

FIGURE

7–2 The software interface between users and computer hardware

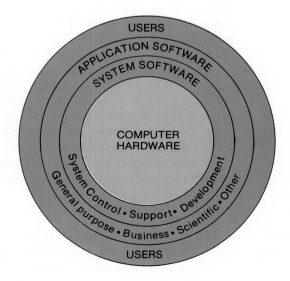

and provides various support services as the computer executes the application programs of users.

The primary goal of the operating system is to maximize the productivity of a computer system by operating it in the most efficient and effective manner possible. An operating system minimizes the amount of human intervention required during processing by performing many functions that were formerly the responsibility of the computer operator. An operating system also simplifies the job of the computer programmer, since it includes programs that greatly simplify the programming of input/output and storage operations and many other standard processing functions. If you have done any of the hands-on exercises of the Appendix or any other jobs on a computer, you know that you must load and use the operating system before you can accomplish any other task. This emphasizes that operating systems have become the most indispensable component of the software interface between users and the hardware of their computer systems.

Most operating systems are designed as a collection of program *modules*, which can be organized in several combinations to form operating systems with various capabilities. An operating system, therefore, can be tailored to the requirements of a particular computer system and user. Thus a mix of operating system capabilities can be acquired to fit the processing power and memory capacity of a computer system and the type of processing jobs that need to be done. For example, many operating system packages include a selected number of service programs, languages translator programs, and even some application programs! Other operating systems support the ability to process several tasks or programs at the same time (*multitasking* and *multiprogramming*). Users who want such additional capabilities must acquire appropriate programs from their operating system supplier or other vendors.

Figure 7–3 is an example of the programs that are or can be included in two popular operating systems. The UNIX operating system was developed by AT&T. Versions of UNIX are being used in many mainframe, super-mini, and super-micro computers because UNIX is such a powerful and *portable* operating system. Of course, most operating systems for microcomputers would not include so many different programs. Like PC-DOS, they usually consist of a main control program and several service and utility programs.

Control Programs in an Operating System

The control programs of an operating system perform three major functions in the operation of a computer system.

1. **Job management**—preparing, scheduling, and monitoring of jobs for continuous processing by the computer system. The job

FIGURE 7–3 Programs in an operating system

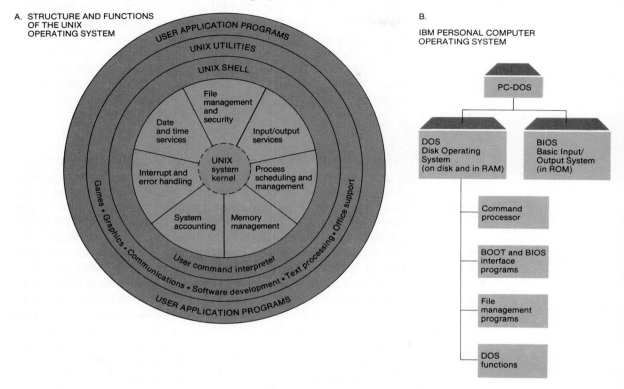

A. STRUCTURE AND FUNCTIONS OF THE UNIX OPERATING SYSTEM

B. IBM PERSONAL COMPUTER OPERATING SYSTEM

management function is provided by an integrated system of programs that schedules and directs the flow of jobs through the computer system. Job management activities include interpreting job control language (JCL) statements, scheduling and selecting jobs for execution by the computer system, initiating the processing of each job, terminating jobs, and communicating with the computer operator.

2. **Resource management**—controlling the use of computer system resources by the other system software and application software programs being executed by the computer system. These resources include primary storage, secondary storage, CPU processing time, and input/output devices. Since these resources must be managed to accomplish various information processing tasks, this function is also called *task management*.

3. **Data management**—controlling the input/output of data as well as their location, storage, and retrieval. In some operating systems, the programs that perform this function are called the *input/output control system (IOCS)*, since they are a collection of pro-

grams that perform all of the functions required for the input and output of data. Data management programs control the allocation of secondary storage devices, the physical format and *cataloging* of data storage, and the movement of data between primary and secondary storage devices. Since most business computer applications require a great deal of input/output and secondary storage activity, the use of data management programs greatly simplifies the job of programming business applications.

The Supervisor

In some operating systems, some of the functions of resource, job, and data management are handled by a group of control programs called the *supervisor* (also known as the *executive*, the *monitor*, or the *controller*). The supervisor directs the operations of the entire computer system by controlling and coordinating (1) the other operating system programs, (2) other system and application software packages, and (3) the activities of all of the hardware components of the computer system. Portions of the supervisor reside in primary storage whenever the computer is operating, while other supervisor segments are transferred back and forth between primary storage and a *systems residence* direct-access storage device. The supervisor monitors input/output activities and handles interrupt conditions, job scheduling and queuing, program fetching, and primary storage allocations. It coordinates the use of other system control software, such as communications monitors and database management systems. The supervisor also communicates with the computer operator through the computer console concerning the status of computer system operations, and records information required for proper job accounting. See Figure 7–4.

Database Management Systems

A *database management system* (DBMS) is a set of computer programs that control the creation, maintenance, and use of the *databases* of users and computer-using organizations. A DBMS is a system software package that helps you use the integrated collections of data records and files contained in *databases*. It allows different user application programs to easily access the same database. DBMS also simplifies the process of retrieving information from databases in the form of displays and reports. Instead of having to write computer programs to extract information, users can ask simple questions in the *query language* provided by most DBMS. Examples of popular mainframe DBMS include IDMS-R by Cullinet and TOTAL by CINCOM. Popular microcomputer database management systems are dBASE II and III by Ashton-Tate and R:base

FIGURE

7–4 The role of system control software

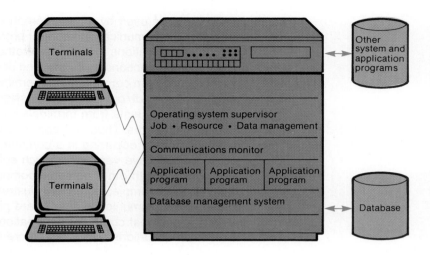

4000 by Microrim. We will explore the use of DBMS in modern information processing systems in Chapter Eleven. A hands-on tutorial on the use of microcomputer DBMS packages is presented in the Appendix at the back of the book. Figure 7–5 illustrates the use of two popular microcomputer DBMS packages.

Communications Monitors

Modern information processing relies heavily on data communications systems, which provide for the transmitting of data over electronic communication links between one or more computer systems and computer terminals. This requires data communications control programs called *communications monitors* (or *teleprocessing* moni-

FIGURE

7–5 Using DBMS packages

A Using dBASE III by Ashton-Tate to establish a database file.

B Using R:base 4000 by Microrim for information retrieval.

tors). They are used by a main computer (called the *host*) or in specialized communications control processors (*front-end* computers). Communications monitors and other similar programs perform such functions as connecting or disconnecting communication links between computers and terminals, automatically checking terminals for input/output activity, assigning priorities to data communications requests from terminals, and detecting and correcting transmission errors. Thus they control and support the data communications activity occurring in a communications network. Even microcomputers have versions of such software that help them communicate with other personal computers and mainframes in a network. For example, Figure 7–6 illustrates the main menu displays of two data communications software packages that help users access a personal computer information network. (We will discuss data communications software in more detail in Chapter Twelve.)

Language Translator Programs

Language translators (or *language processors*) are programs that translate other programs into *machine language* instruction codes the computer can execute. They also allow you to write your own programs by providing program creation and editing facilities. Computer programs consist of sets of instructions written in programming languages like BASIC, COBOL, FORTRAN, or Pascal, which must be translated into the computer's own *machine language* before they can be processed by the CPU. Most programming language translator programs are called either **assemblers, compilers,** or **interpreters.** Interpreters translate and execute each program statement one at a time, instead of first producing a complete ma-

FIGURE 7–6 Accessing personal computer information networks

A PFS: Access by Software Publishing Corporation.

B OPEN ACESS communications by Software Products International.

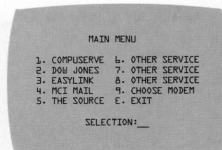

chine language program, like compilers and assemblers do. The language translation process is called *interpreting* when an interpreter is used, *compiling* when a compiler is used, and *assembling* when an assembler is used.

Figure 7–7 illustrates the typical language translation process. A program written in a language like BASIC or COBOL is called a *source program*. When the source program is translated into machine language, it is called the *object program*. The computer then executes the object program. Besides the object program, most translators can produce a listing or display of the source program, and error messages (called *diagnostics*), which identify program-

FIGURE

7–7 The language translation process

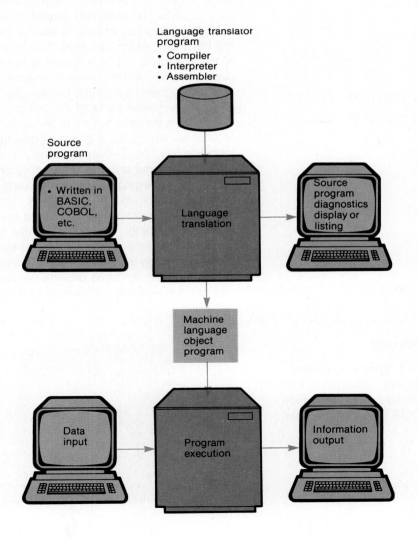

ming errors recognized by the translator program. The major categories and types of programming languages are covered in Chapter Nine.

Service Programs

Service programs are specialized programs that perform common routine and repetitive functions and are made available to all of the users of a computer system. For example, service programs, language translators, and most control programs and applications programs are usually maintained in *program libraries*. In addition, there is usually a *system library* of commonly used programs and subprograms (*subroutines*) shared by all users of the computer system. Therefore, an important service program usually provided is the **librarian,** which catalogs, manages, and maintains a directory of the programs that are stored in the various libraries of the computer system. Another service program is the **linkage editor,** which edits a program by defining the specific storage locations it requires and links together parts of the program which require subroutines.

Finally, a major category of service programs is **utility programs** or *utilities*, which are a group of miscellaneous programs that perform various "housekeeping" and file conversion functions. *Sort-merge* programs are important utility programs that perform the sorting and merging operations on data which are required in many information processing applications. Utility programs also clear primary storage, load programs, record the contents of primary storage (memory dumping), and convert a file of data from one storage medium to another, such as card-to-tape, tape-to-disk, etc. Many of the *operating system commands* used with microcomputers and other computer systems provide users with utility programs and routines for a variety of chores. See Figure 7–8.

FIGURE

7–8 Typical operating system commands for utilities of the Microsoft DOS Operating System

```
          DOS COMMANDS
A> =  DOS Prompt:  Enter
      a DOS Command such as:
BASIC = Load BASIC Interpreter
COPY = Copy file
DIR = Display directory
DISKCOPY = Copy disk
ERASE = Delete file
FORMAT = Format disk
MODE = Change display option
RENAME = Change file name
TYPE = Display file contents
```

REAL WORLD APPLICATION 7–2

Spectra-Physics, Inc.

A manufacturer of high-technology products (lasers and electro-optical instruments), Spectra-Physics, Palo Alto, California, has grown dramatically over the last five years, from $25 million to $140 million in sales, and growth continues at a rate of some 25 percent per year. The firm operates eight divisions, each having a separate production capability involving thousands of parts, assemblies, and operations, and many suppliers of components, ranging from nuts and bolts to microprocessors and rare gases.

Company management realized that the explosive growth required highly developed production control. Early in the growth phase, controls were centralized and handled by a small computer. As growth progressed, the firm learned that turnaround time was not responsive to fast-moving events. A corporate decision was made to decentralize operations, making each division an accountable profit center, and to install divisional manufacturing information systems that are linked to an overall corporate management information system (MIS).

Roy Daheb was brought in as corporate director of MIS to design and install the system, which had to include not only manufacturing but marketing and financial as well. He considered this a challenge, since it was mandatory for all production operations to continue unimpeded during MIS implementation, and complete control of inventory and financial status had to be maintained during the changeover from old to new.

Daheb took an interesting approach to accomplish his goals. Rather than take on the huge task of developing all the elements of a complete MIS in-house, he opted to purchase existing packages and link them together with programs developed by his staff, such as an online, front-end module, which allows terminal-independent linking of all present and future MIS modules. The catalyst for the direction taken was set by the selection of MAC-PAC/HP, a modular online manufacturing control package, jointly developed by accounting firm Arthur Andersen & Company and by Far-West Data Systems, Inc., of Irvine, California.

The package runs on Hewlett-Packard 3000 computers operating in COBOL environments. With the decision to use MAC-PAC/HP came the requirement to operate the entire MIS in an HP 3000-COBOL environment. A McCormack & Dodge financial package was selected for the financial portion of the MIS and converted to HP3000-COBOL by Far-West Data Systems. The HP 3000 systems selected also use the multiprogramming executive (MPE) operating system and the Image/3000 database management system (DBMS).

■ Identify the system and application software packages selected by Spectra-Physics.
■ What are the functions of these packages?
■ Why didn't Spectra-Physics develop these programs themselves?

Source: "Software Package Leads to Online System," *Infosystems*, November 1980, p. 92. Copyright 1980, Hitchcock Publishing Co. Reprinted with permission.

Other System Software Packages

Let's take a brief look at several other important system software packages which we will explain in greater detail in later chapters of the book.

Application development systems provide interactive assistance to programmers in the development of application programs. Software tools, such as DEC's Adminis-11 application generator, or IBM's DMS (development management system), help simplify and automate the programming process. An application development system does this by providing programs that support interactive program editing, coding, testing, debugging, and maintenance by programmers using video display terminals. We will discuss application development systems further in the next chapter.

System performance monitors are programs that monitor the processing of jobs on a computer system. They monitor computer system performance and produce reports containing detailed statistics concerning the use of system resources, such as processor time, memory space, I/O devices, and system and application programs. Such reports are used to plan and control the efficient and effective use of a computer system. We will discuss the role of such programs again in Chapter Nineteen.

System security monitors are programs that monitor the use of a computer system to protect the computer system and its resources from unauthorized use, fraud, and destruction. Such programs provide the *computer security* needed to allow only authorized users to access the system. For example, identification codes and passwords are frequently used for this purpose. Security monitors also control use of the hardware, software, and data resources of a computer system. For example, even authorized users may be restricted to the use of certain devices, programs, and data files. Finally, such programs monitor use of the computer and collect statistics on any attempts at improper use. They produce reports to assist in maintaining the security of the system.

APPLICATION SOFTWARE

Application software or **application programs** consists of programs that direct the computer system to perform specific information processing activities for users. These programs are called *application programs* because they direct the processing required for a particular use or *application* of computers. Remember that a **computer application** is the use of a computer to solve a specific problem or to accomplish a particular job for a computer user. Thousands of application programs are available because there are thousands of different jobs that users want computers to do. Refer back to Figure 7–1. Notice that application software includes a variety of programs that are segregated into general-purpose, business, scientific, and other application program categories.

- **General-purpose application programs**—programs that can perform common information processing jobs for users from all application areas. For example, word processing programs, electronic spreadsheet programs, and graphics programs can be used by individuals for home, education, business, scientific, and many other purposes.
- **Business application programs**—programs that can accomplish the information processing tasks needed to support important business functions or industry requirements. Examples of several business functions and corresponding applications are: accounting *(general ledger)*, marketing *(sales analysis)*, finance *(cash budgeting)*, manufacturing *(material requirements planning)*, operations management *(inventory control)*, and personnel *(employee benefits analysis)*.
- **Scientific application programs**—programs that perform information processing tasks for the natural, physical, social, and behavioral sciences, for mathematics, engineering, and all other areas involved in scientific research, experimentation, and development. Some broad application categories include scientific analysis, engineering design, and monitoring of experiments.
- **Other application programs**—there are so many other application areas of computers that we lump them all into this category. Thus we can talk of computer applications in education, entertainment, music, art, law enforcement, medicine, etc. Some specific examples are computer-assisted instruction (CAI) programs in education, video game programs in entertainment, and computer-generated music and art programs.

Popular Application Packages

We have mentioned several types of application programs in previous chapters that are very popular with computer users, especially users of microcomputers. Let's take a brief but closer look at their purposes and requirements. Then let's examine one important package more closely, the electronic spreadsheet program. We have already introduced you to three popular system software packages in this chapter: operating systems, database management systems (DBMS), and data communications monitors. These and the other packages are explained in more detail in later chapters of the book.

Word Processing Packages

Word processing programs automate the creation, editing, and printing of **documents** of all kinds, including letters, memos, reports, etc. They electronically process **text data** (words, phrases, sentences, paragraphs) you provide through the keyboard of a microcomputer or terminal. The text material is simultaneously stored in memory and displayed on your video screen so you can easily correct, change, and manipulate it. You can then print a document on your printer and save a copy of it on your system's magnetic disk unit. Sounds simple, doesn't it? It is, with a little bit of study and practice. Word processing is discussed again in Chapter Thirteen in the context of office automation. The use of word processing packages (like WordStar, Easy Writer, VolksWriter, MultiMate, etc.) is described in detail in the Appendix at the back of the book. Figure

FIGURE

7–9 Using word processing packages

A Wordstar by Micropro.

B OPEN ACCESS Word Processor by Software Products International.

A

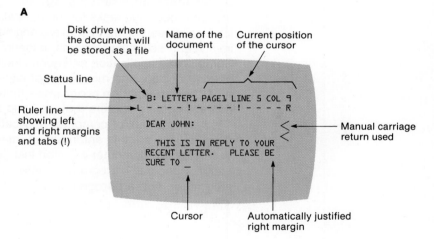

Disk drive where the document will be stored as a file

Name of the document

Current position of the cursor

Status line

Ruler line showing left and right margins and tabs (!)

B: LETTER1 PAGE1 LINE 5 COL 9
L - - - - ! - - - - ! - - - R

DEAR JOHN:

    THIS IS IN REPLY TO YOUR
RECENT LETTER.   PLEASE BE
SURE TO _

Manual carriage return used

Cursor

Automatically justified right margin

B

7–9 illustrates video displays generated by two popular word processing packages.

Graphics Packages

Graphics packages transform numeric data into **graphics displays,** such as line charts, bar charts, and pie charts. These are displayed on your video monitor, or printed copies can be made on your system printer or plotter. Not only are such graphic displays easier to comprehend then numeric data but multiple color displays can more easily emphasize strategic differences and trends in the data. To use some graphics packages (like BPS Graphics, PFS: GRAPH, and GraphPlan), you merely enter through the keyboard the categories of data you want plotted in response to prompts displayed on your screen. The graphics program then analyzes the file of data you specify and generates the requested graphics. See Figure 7–10.

Integrated Packages

Integrated packages combine the ability to do several general-purpose applications in one program. This really benefits you if you wish to perform a variety of information processing jobs using the same file of data. The alternative would be to use separate programs, entering each program and the same data file each time you used a different program. To make it worse, some programs will refuse to work with data files created by other programs! Integrated packages have solved the problems caused by the inability of individual programs to communicate and work together with common files of data. However, most integrated packages require significant amounts of additional memory capacity. Also, they have had to compromise on the speed, power, and flexibility of some of their functions in order to achieve integration. Therefore, users may prefer single function packages for applications that they use heavily.

Integrated packages, like Lotus 1-2-3, Symphony, Framework, Open Access, and Corporate MBA, may combine some of the general-purpose application software functions of **electronic spreadsheets, word processing,** and **graphics** with the system software functions of **database management** and **data communications.** Thus you could process the same file of data with one package, moving from one function to the other by pressing a few keys on your computer keyboard and viewing displays from each one together on multiple **windows** on your video screen. For example, you could:

- Create a file of data using database management functions.
- Analyze and manipulate this file using an electronic spreadsheet.

FIGURE 7–10 Using graphics packages

A Entering graphics specifications using BPS Graphics.

B The bar chart produced.

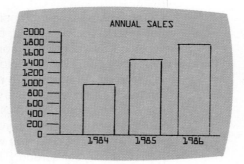

C Selecting a type of graph using Microsoft CHART.

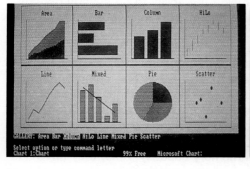

D 3-dimensional bar graph produced by OPEN ACCESS graphics.

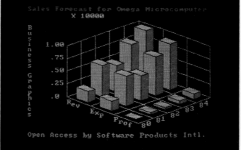

- Transfer part of the spreadsheet to a report you are creating using word processing functions.
- Create a graph of the spreadsheet data to include in your report using the program's graphics function.
- Transmit a copy of the report by *electronic mail* to another user with the help of the program's data communications facilities!

Some of the advantages of integrated packages can be derived by using an **operating environment** package, like TopView, VisiOn, Windows, and DESQ. They provide an additional *software interface* between users, the operating system, and their application programs. These packages serve as a *shell* to interconnect several

FIGURE

7–11 Integrated multiple window packages

A Corporate MBA by Context Management Systems. This is a revised version of the first integrated package, Context MBA. It provides more program functions than the Symphony or Framework packages.

B TopView by IBM. This new operating environment package can integrate the concurrent operations of several individual application packages.

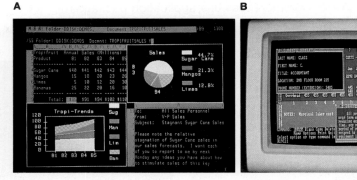

A   **B**

separate application packages so they can communicate and work together and share common data files. They also allow the outputs of several programs to be displayed at the same time in *multiple windows.* Finally, several of these packages support some type of *concurrent processing,* where several programs or tasks can be processed at the same time. (Concurrent processing is explained in Chapter 10.) These *software integrator* packages have become popular with users who prefer to use a variety of single function programs. See Figure 7–11. The use of an integrated package for spreadsheet analysis, database management, and graphics is demonstrated in the Appendix at the back of this book.

Common Business Packages

These business application programs accomplish the information processing tasks required by common accounting and other business functions. You need to perform functions like sales analysis, accounts receivable and payable, inventory control, order processing, general ledger, and payroll whether your business is large or small. So you need software packages that accomplish these functions, such as those from Peachtree software, MAI/Basic Four, Excalibur, and IBM, to name a few. Let's take a brief look at some of these application areas. They are all discussed in more detail in Chapter Sixteen. See Figure 7–12.

■ **Sales analysis** programs analyze sales data (provided by a sales transaction processing program) to produce management reports analyzing the sales generated by each salesperson, customer, product, region, and so on.

FIGURE 7–12 Common business application packages

A Menu of common business application packages.

B Main menu of the MSA fixed assets application package.

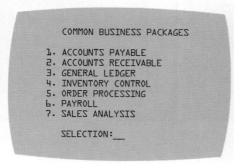

- **Order processing** programs process sales orders received from customers and produce information needed for production, inventory control, and sales analysis.
- **Inventory control** programs record all changes to inventory, notify management of items needing reordering, and provide management with comparative inventory status reports.
- **Accounts receivable** programs keep records of amounts owed by customers, prepare monthly customer statements, and produce various credit management reports.
- **Account payable** programs keep track of purchases made and amounts owed to suppliers, produce checks to pay suppliers, and sometimes produce cash management reports.
- **Payroll** programs maintain employee work records and produce employee paychecks, earnings statements, and other documents, as well as various payroll and tax reports to management and government agencies.
- **General ledger** programs process data furnished by the other common business programs to produce several major financial statements and reports, including the general ledger trial balance, the balance sheet, and the income statement of the business firm.

SPOTLIGHT ON ELECTRONIC SPREADSHEET PACKAGES

What is an **electronic spreadsheet package**? How does one use such programs? This section will provide some of the answers to these questions about one of the most important application software packages available today. For a hands-on tutorial on how to use such packages, see the section on using a spreadsheet package in the Appendix at the back of the book.

An electronic spreadsheet package is an application program used as a computerized tool for analysis, planning, and modeling. It is an electronic replacement for more traditional tools, such as a paper worksheet, pencil, and calculator. It generates an *electronic spreadsheet*, which is a worksheet of rows and columns that is stored in the computer's memory and is displayed on its video screen. The computer's keyboard or other devices, such as an electronic *mouse* or *touch screen*, are used to enter data and to command the computer to manipulate the data in the worksheet. The spreadsheet package performs many functions traditionally performed by programs written in high-level programming languages (such as BASIC or COBOL). However, results are accomplished in a significantly different way: A user develops a spreadsheet, enters data, and the computer performs necessary calculations based on the relationships the user defined in the spreadsheet. Then results are immediately displayed. Thus electronic spreadsheet packages allow users to do **nonprocedural programming** using a **visible processor.**

VisiCalc was the first spreadsheet program, and it is one of the biggest selling microcomputer programs of all time. VisiCalc (*visible calculator*) was developed in 1978 by Robert Frankston and Daniel Bricklin. Bricklin, a student at Harvard Business School, was frustrated with the tedious and repetitive task of analyzing numerous business cases each week, many of them requiring complicated financial analysis. With the programming help of Frankston, Bricklin developed VisiCalc, a spreadsheet program that automates the recording and computation of data in a worksheet format. VisiCalc has since been followed by many other spreadsheet packages, such as *SuperCalc, Multiplan,* and the spreadsheet modules of integrated packages, such as *Lotus 1-2-3.* See Figure 7–13.

Spreadsheet Format and Use

All electronic spreadsheet programs draw a worksheet on the video screen of your personal computer. How is this worksheet organized? The typical electronic spreadsheet is a matrix or grid of many rows and columns (254 rows and 63 columns in VisiCalc and many other packages). Since an electronic spreadsheet is so large, only a section (called a **window**) is displayed on the video screen at any one time. For example, the standard window in VisiCalc allows you to view only 8 columns and 21 rows of the spreadsheet in memory. However, this window can be moved around for you to see and work on any part of the spreadsheet that you wish. Also, most electronic spreadsheet programs allow you to split the screen into two or more smaller windows. This allows you to view

FIGURE

7–13 Electronic spreadsheet displays

A VisiCalc by Visicorp.

B Multiplan by Microsoft.

A

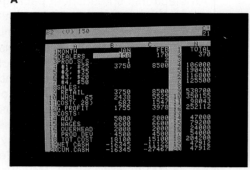

B

two or more parts of the spreadsheet at the same time, and thus you can more easily use the spreadsheet.

The spaces formed by the intersection of rows and columns are called **cells**. Thus a VisiCalc spreadsheet contains over 16,000 cells. Cells are typically identified by their column-row coordinates (i.e., the number or letter of the column and row in which the cell is located). In VisiCalc, rows are numbered and columns are specified by letters, with the column of a cell mentioned first, then its row. For example, cell C12 identifies a cell at the intersection of the 3rd column and the 12th row of the spreadsheet. Thus in VisiCalc, rows are numbered from one to 254, while the 63 columns are specified by the letters A through Z, AA through AZ, and BA through BK. Spreadsheet programs, such as MultiPlan, however, use numbers to designate both rows and columns.

How do you use the worksheet created by electronic spreadsheet packages? You use the worksheet to set up and manipulate rows and columns of numbers, titles, and formulas. The worksheet thus becomes a *visual model* of a particular business activity or other operation. It can, therefore, be used not only to record and analyze past and present activity but as a decision-making tool to answer **what-if** questions. For example, "**what** would happen to net profit **if** advertising expense increased by 10 percent?" To answer this question, you would simply change the advertising expense figure on an income statement worksheet, and the affected figures would be recalculated, including a new net profit figure. Once an electronic spreadsheet has been developed, it can be stored on a floppy disk or other storage device for later use, or be printed out as a paper report on your computer's printer. Figure 7–14 is a display of a simple financial spreadsheet developed with the VisiCalc electronic spreadsheet package.

Look closely at Figure 7–14. A financial analyst for the ABC Com-

FIGURE

7–14 Simple financial spreadsheet using VisiCalc

```
C12  {V}  +C8-C10
Move:  From. . .To
C12. . .D12
        A       B       C       D       E       F
  1
  2                   SPREADSHEET EXAMPLE
  3
  4               ABC COMPANY:  FINANCIAL PERFORMANCE
  5
  6                   1983    1984    1985    TOTAL  AVERAGE
  7                   ----    ----    ----    -----  -------
  8  REVENUE         1,000   1,100   1200    3300    1,100
  9
 10  EXPENSES         600     660     720    1980     660
 11
 12  PROFIT           400    [440]    480    1320     440
 13
 14  TAXES            160     176     192     528     176
 15                   ----    ----    ----    -----  -------
 16  PROFIT           240     264     288     792     264
 17  AFTER TAXES
 18
 19
```

pany developed this simple spreadsheet of the company's recent financial performance. If you were the analyst, you could build and use this spreadsheet in the following manner:

■ Load the **spreadsheet program** into the computer from a floppy disk. Immediately, the spreadsheet format of rows and columns are displayed on the computer's video screen.

■ Enter the **titles and headings** of this spreadsheet, using the keyboard of the computer.

■ Then enter **data** (dollar amounts) into the cells of categories where you already know the values that should be displayed. For example, revenue for 1983 was $1,000.

■ Then you begin entering **formulas** into the remaining cells that express the relationships between each category of values on the spreadsheet. For example, if you know that expenses are 60 percent of sales, you would enter the formula (B8*.6) into cell B10. (Note that 1983 revenue is in cell B8, and 1983 expenses are in cell B10.) The computer immediately calculates $600 as the value for 1983 expenses ($1,000 × .6) and displays it in cell B10. You would continue this process until all cells contain appropriate formulas and display values calculated by the computer.

■ Then you could **save** the spreadsheet you created on a floppy disk for use at another time and **print** out a copy for your records.

■ This process is not as burdensome as it sounds. The spreadsheet program provides special built-in **functions** for calculations like the Total and Average amounts. It also automatically fills in cells (at your command) with similar data and formula relationships with its **replication** ability.

■ Then you could make **what-if** assumptions, and the spreadsheet program would automatically perform calculations based on these assumptions and display the results. For example, you could change 1983 sales to $2,000 and the computer would instantly calculate and display $480 as the profit after taxes for 1983 based on that assumption. In this way you could analyze the effect of various changes on the past, present, and future financial performance of the ABC Company.

Advances in Electronic Spreadsheets

Improvements are continually being made to electronic spreadsheet programs. The first generation of electronic spreadsheet packages (*VisiCalc* and *SuperCalc,* for example) have been challenged by a second generation of electronic spreadsheet programs (*Multiplan* and *Perfect Calc*), which have advanced features, such as many built-in functions, the ability to link several spreadsheets, and more user-friendly and flexible formats. However, a third generation of software packages has just been mentioned (*Lotus 1-2-3* and *Corporate MBA,* for example), which integrate advanced electronic spreadsheet capabilities with *graphics, data management, word processing,* and *data communications* functions. These developments indicate that electronic spreadsheet capabilities will continue to improve, but they will also continue to be integrated with other functions into more *general-purpose* application programs.

A major advance in the use of electronic spreadsheet programs is the availability of special-purpose spreadsheet models called **templates.** Templates are electronic spreadsheet forms that have been developed for specific occupations, operations, or classes of problems. Column and row headings are already set up, and formulas and special functions defining mathematical and logical relationships between the elements in the spreadsheet are already included. These worksheet models have been developed for specific business applications, such as accounting, real estate, banking, engineering, and the like. They are available as separate programs or are included in advanced spreadsheet packages. For example, you can buy electronic spreadsheet programs designed for tax accounting, financial analysis, or real estate investment applications. Users do not have to develop these models themselves, but only need to enter data to produce results; for example, a completed tax return. The use of such templates is growing rapidly, since it allows unsophisticated users to use the power of electronic spreadsheets without having to develop the worksheet models themselves.

Advantages of Spreadsheet Packages

The electronic spreadsheet is a valuable tool not only for accounting, finance, marketing analysis and planning, but for the solution of any problem which requires comparison, projections, or the evaluation of alternatives. Therefore, electronic spreadsheets are used for many applications. Typical business uses include sales forecasting, profit and loss analysis, product pricing, investment analysis, development of budgets, cash flow analysis, financial statement preparation, construction bidding, real estate investment, bank loan analysis, and many other applications for individuals, business firms, and other organizations.

Electronic spreadsheet packages have made it dramatically easier to create and use models of business operations and problems. You can build a model by entering the data and relationships (formulas) of a problem into an electronic worksheet, make a variety of changes, and visually evaluate the results of such changes. Once you define all of the mathematical and logical relationships in your spreadsheet model, computations are calculated instantly and accurately at your command every time you enter data or make any changes to the spreadsheet. Just think of how much time and effort is saved and how many errors are avoided, compared to a manual spreadsheet process! Because repetitive calculations are made so quickly and accurately, electronic spreadsheets allow users to make comparisons, projections, and evaluations that they might never have tried using manual methods. Thus electronic spreadsheet programs have revolutionized the use of computerized models for business analysis and planning.

The electronic spreadsheet's "what-if" capability makes an electronic spreadsheet program a simple but important type of **decision support system** (DSS) package. It allows managers to interact with a computerized model by comparing the effects of alternative proposed decisions. This interactive evaluation process significantly assists managers in the making of many business decisions. After setting up a spreadsheet model, managers can ask "what-if" questions to quickly and easily discover the effect any change will have on the "bottom line" of their model. For example, what if we give employees an increase in salary? What if shipping costs increase? What if interest rates go up? What if we purchase, rather then lease, a new piece of equipment? What if we cut the recruiting budget? What if we add additional production capacity? Such questions should give you an idea of the variety of uses, the computational power, the modeling capability, and the decision-making support provided by electronic spreadsheet packages. Best of all, electronic spreadsheet programs are available for only a few hundred dollars on most microcomputer systems.

REAL WORLD APPLICATION 7–3

Popular Software Packages

VisiCalc Electronic Spreadsheet Package

Solve complicated numerical problems with this electronic spreadsheet program—even if you're a novice computer user. VisiCalc combines the convenience and familiarity of a pocket calculator with the powerful memory and electronic screen capabilities of your personal computer. Specially designed to train you in its own use, VisiCalc will soon have you building your own numerical spreadsheets. Later modifications are automatically recalculated throughout the entire spreadsheet. With a simple change of data elements, you can also compute a variety of "what-if" situations and organize the results for quick and easy comparisons.

dBASE II Database Management System

Use your personal computer to do jobs that normally only large computers can do. With dBASE II, you'll be able to work with up to 15 command files at once; manipulate a database; update and revise data; and deactivate, reactivate, or delete files entirely. Use the report function to organize data by the month. Match output to your business forms, instead of redesigning your forms to match output. Even untrained office personnel can do all this, because dBASE II has the added advantage of operating through simple English commands.

BPS Business Graphics Package

Quickly and easily produce multicolored charts and graphs that help speed decision making. Use simple commands to key in data or extract input from programs, reports, and documents. Create your own graphic formats with the color display; then store the commands to automatically update or generate graphic reports.

LOTUS 1-2-3 Integrated Package

Get this one powerful package and you'll have data management, electronic worksheet analysis, and sophisticated graphics in a single program. With 1-2-3 you get a flexible worksheet of up to 256 variable-length columns and 2,048 rows. You also get dedicated function keys, expanded mathematical functions, extensive customizing capability, "what-if" analysis, flexible text manipulation capability, and instant HELP. 1-2-3 has interactive lessons that use immediate feedback to demonstrate entries and menu selections.

Crosstalk Communications Package

Crosstalk lets you dial into a host computer system and act as terminal to that system. You can also easily exchange or transfer any size or type of file with compatible systems. Crosstalk supports most popular autodial modems.

WordStar Word Processing Package

WordStar provides comprehensive word processing capabilities. Your editing commands are easily accomplished: insert, delete, move and copy text, and read and write text to and from different files. You can choose page breaks, margin variations, or justifications. WordStar's flexibility even allows the simultaneous printing of one document while another is being edited.

- Which of these software packages would you (or do you) find most useful? Why?
- Have you used any of these or similar packages? Which were easiest to use? Why?

Source: VisiCorp (VisiCalc); Ashton-Tate (dBASE II); Business and Professional Software (BPS Graphics); Lotus Development Corporation (LOTUS 1-2-3); Microstuff, Inc. (Crosstalk); and Micropro International Corporation (WordStar).

SUMMARY

- The software resources of an information processing system consist of (1) programs of instructions used to direct the operation of the hardware of a computer system and (2) procedures used to direct the activities of the people who operate and use computer systems. Computer software consists of two major types of programs: (1) system software, which controls and supports the operations of a computer system as it performs various information processing tasks; and (2) application software, which directs the performance of a particular use or application of computers to meet the information processing needs of users. Computer software can also be subdivided into (1) software packages, which are acquired by users from various software vendors; and (2) user-developed software, which are developed by users or professional programmers of a computer-using organization.

- System software can be subdivided into system control programs, system support programs, and system development programs. System control programs control the use of the hardware, software, and data resources of the computer system during its execution of information processing jobs. Major control programs are operating systems, database management programs, and communications monitors. System support programs support the operations, management, and users of computer system by providing a variety of support services. Major support programs are service programs, performance monitors, and security monitors. System development programs help users develop information processing programs and procedures and prepare user programs for computer processing. Major development programs are language translators and application development systems.

- The most important system software package for any computer is its operating system. An operating system is an integrated system of programs that supervises the operation of the CPU, controls the input/output and storage functions of the computer system, and provides various support services. The control programs of an operating system perform the three major functions of job management, resource management, and data management. Other programs that could be part of the operating system, or that can be acquired as separate programs, are language translators and service programs. Language translator programs convert programming language instructions into machine-language instruction codes. Service programs are specialized programs that perform common support functions for the users of a computer system.

- Database management systems control the creation, maintenance, and use of database. A DBMS simplifies the use of the data and information in a database for both users and programmers. Data communications monitors monitor, control, and support the data communication activities between the computers and terminals in a data communications network.

- Application software includes a variety of programs that can be segregated into general-purpose, business, scientific, and other application program categories. General-purpose application programs can perform common information processing jobs for users. Examples are word processing, electronic spreadsheet, and graphics programs. Business application programs can accomplish information processing tasks that support important business functions or industry requirements. Scientific application programs perform information processing tasks for the sciences, engineering, and all other areas involved in scientific research, experimentation, and development. The other application programs category includes programs in education, entertainment, music, and art. Popular application packages include word processing packages, graphics packages, integrated packages, common business packages, and electronic spreadsheet packages.

- An electronic spreadsheet package is an application program used for analysis, planning, and modeling. It generates an electronic spreadsheet, which is a worksheet of rows and columns where a user can insert data and formulas that represent a model of the user's problem. The programs then automatically manipulate the data in the spreadsheet in response to commands of the user. An electronic spreadsheet package allows users to do nonprocedural programming and perform "what-if" analysis, which makes it an important decision support system package for managers.

KEY TERMS AND CONCEPTS

System software	Supervisor
Application software	Language translator program
Software packages	Service program
Operating system	Database management system
Control program	User-developed software

System control programs
System support programs
System development programs
Data communications monitor
Job management
Resource management
Data management
Application development
   system
System performance monitor

System security monitor
Computer application
General-purpose application
   program
Electronic spreadsheet
   package
Word processing package
Graphics package
Integrated package
Common business package

REVIEW AND APPLICATION QUESTIONS

1. What is the distinction between system software and application software? Between software packages and user-developed software? Give examples of each.
2. What are the three major categories of system software? Give examples of each.
3. What is an operating system? What are the three major functions of control programs in an operating system? Explain the role of these functions in the operation of a computer system.
4. What is a database management system (DBMS)? What is the advantage of a DBMS to a computer user?
5. If you wrote a simple program in the BASIC language and wanted to execute it, how would the BASIC language translator program (interpreter) be involved?
6. One of the best-selling packages for the IBM PC is a group of utility programs called the *Norton Utilities*. Why do you think that IBM did not include these utilities in its DOS operating system?
7. How do the roles of service programs differ from that of control programs?
8. Don't we have programs that can help us develop our own programs, asks a user? How would you answer this question?
9. A word processing package is used to write a financial report for a school district. Is this an example of a business application program? Educational application program? General-purpose application program? Explain.
10. What are some of the popular application packages for microcomputers? Give examples of how each of them are used.
11. What are the benefits of integrated application packages? Which functions would you find most useful?
12. What are the common business application packages? Provide examples of what several of them do.

13. What is an electronic spreadsheet package? What uses does it have?
14. How does one develop an electronic spreadsheet? How do you use it once you have developed it.?
15. What are several advantages of electronic spreadsheet packages? Give examples to demonstrate these benefits.

APPLICATION PROBLEMS

1. If you have not already done so, read and answer the questions after each Real World Application in this chapter.
2. Have you completed any of the exercises or assignments in the use of software packages from the Appendix? Remember, you need hands-on experience with these packages to be a knowledgeable computer user. Briefly describe the advantages and disadvantages of one of the packages you have used so far, such as Mortgage, WordStar, VisiCalc, dBASE II, and Lotus 1-2-3, or similar packages.
3. Have you used VisiCalc or some other electronic spreadsheet package yet? How would such a package help you in a present or future job situation? How would you improve the package you used?
4. Make a list of 10 of the major types of software packages mentioned in this chapter. Then briefly explain (one sentence each) the purpose of each package.
5. ABC Department Stores would like to acquire system software that could do the following tasks: *(a)* Control data communications with many remote terminals. *(b)* Control access and use of the hardware, software, and data resources of the system. *(c)* Monitor and record how the system resources are being used. *(d)* Make it easier to update and interrogate its databases. Explain what system software packages they need.
6. A software commentator stated recently that integrated packages like Symphony, Framework, and Corporate MBA were not a new generation of software, but the last of the present software generation. He feels that operating environment packages like TopView and DESQ, which make it easy for users to integrate the operations of a variety of individual packages, are the real wave of the future. What do you think? Explain.

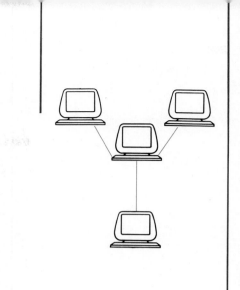

CHAPTER 8

Computer Programming Concepts and Methods

CHAPTER OUTLINE

LEARNING OBJECTIVES

The purpose of this chapter is to promote a basic understanding of computer programming by analyzing (1) the changing methodology of computer programming, (2) the activities of the six stages of programming, (3) the concepts and applications of structured programming, and (4) the construction and use of several program design aids. After reading and studying this chapter, you should be able to:

1. Explain why users should have a basic knowledge of computer programming.
2. Identify three major changes taking place in computer programming and explain how this affects both users and professional programmers.
3. Summarize the functions of the six stages of computer programming.
4. Outline several ways that structured programming affects program design, coding, and debugging.
5. Briefly explain the purpose of structure and HIPO charts, layout forms, flowcharts, pseudocode, and decision tables.
6. Prepare simple system and program flowcharts.
7. Identify the basic types of computer instructions.
8. Identify several types of programming errors and describe some checking and testing activities of program debugging.
9. Discuss the purpose and content of program documentation and maintenance.

WHY LEARN COMPUTER PROGRAMMING?

Understanding the fundamentals of computers and their hardware and software is an important achievement. However, it is equally important that you have a basic understanding of how computers are *programmed* to do what we want them to do (i.e., **computer programming**). That is the purpose of this chapter, of the following chapter on programming languages, and of any practice in actual computer programming that you may be required to do in an introductory computer course.

However, an important "fact of life" of modern computer use is this: **most people who use computers don't develop their own programs**. Instead, they use software packages developed by external sources, or they use programs developed by the professional programming staff of their own organizations. So why learn computer programming? Because of these other "facts of life":

■ Business people, managers, and other computer users must understand computer programming if they are to communicate effectively with programmers, concerning computerized solutions to business problems.

■ The development of microcomputers, time-sharing terminals, and simpler computer languages make it possible for many computer users to be their own computer programmers.

■ Many computer users still do computer programming, but this no longer involves detailed coding of information processing instructions in a traditional programming language. Instead, they develop an application program using a conversational *nonprocedural* language in an interactive "dialogue" with a computer. However, other more traditional programming activities still need to be accomplished.

Therefore, most people don't have to become expert *computer programmers*. However, they need to have a basic knowledge of computer software and programming to become *knowledgeable computer users*. In your case, this means that you should:

■ Learn the fundamentals of the **computer programming** process.

■ Know the basic characteristics of several popular **programming languages**.

■ Develop some simple programs of your own using a **high-level programming language**.

■ Learn to use several important types of **software packages**.

The resources you need to accomplish these goals are provided by the three chapters in this part of the book, the Appendix at the end of the text, and the Study Guide. They should help you learn to use software to transform computer hardware into a productive tool for your information processing needs.

CHANGES IN COMPUTER PROGRAMMING

Before we get too far into our discussion of computer programming we should acknowledge the fact that computer programming is changing. Why? Because major computer-using business firms, government agencies, and other organizations recognized that major problems had developed with the programming process and the programs that were being produced. Here's what they saw:

- **Programmer productivity.** Professional programmers were taking too long to develop correct programs. Programs were not being produced on time. The backlog of unfinished and unstarted programming projects required by users was getting too large. Users were being asked to wait too long (several years!) for their programming projects to be completed.
- **Programming quality.** Completed programs still contained too many errors and did not meet user's requirements. Programs were too complex. Programs were not well documented. Programs were difficult to test. Programs were difficult to maintain (i.e., it was difficult to make corrections or changes).
- **Programming cost.** The cost of developing, testing, correcting, and maintaining programs was too high and was continuing to increase.

The response of major computer users and the computer industry was to sharply increase the use of pre-programmed **application packages,** and to develop new ways of programming. Three of the most important changes in modern programming, **structured programming**, **computer-assisted programming,** and **user programming** have been developed to try to solve these major programming problems. Let's take a look at them now. See Figure 8–1.

FIGURE

8–1 The new programming

```
APPLICATION PROGRAM DEVELOPMENT

  • Acquire and modify application
    packages

  • Use structured programming
    methods

  • Use computer-assisted
    programming tools and
    fourth generation languages

  • Support user programming
```

REAL WORLD APPLICATION 8-1

PPG Industries

Inefficiencies were evident. Maintenance requirements were growing. A new system was needed.

PPG Industries Chemical Group, located in Pittsburgh, rewrote its entire order processing and invoicing system (OP&I) using MANTIS, the fourth-generation application development system from Cincom Systems. The new OP&I system was operational in less than one year, and required 50 percent of the code and less than 25 percent of the development time of its predecessor. The OP&I system is now in full production throughout the Chemical Group's network of North American sales office and manufacturing plants.

In addition to helping PPG update the core of its business activities, MANTIS has delivered productivity gains in other areas. Programmer productivity increased 35 percent during the first year, and the ratio of application development to program maintenance increased to 80 percent for application development and only 20 percent for maintenance.

"MANTIS has also provided PPG with major benefits that can't be quantified numerically," explains Michael Crowley, manager, Management Information Systems. "MANTIS has helped MIS send a positive signal to our user community. We are now more flexible, can deliver new applications more cost-effectively, and can react to change more quickly.

"The strong points of MANTIS, as we see them," Mr. Crowley continues, "are the ability to develop applications both quickly and interactively. We are able to show our end-users exactly what the application will do in a production environment while we are still in the prototype stage."

- How has MANTIS helped PPG solve its problems with programming productivity, quality, and cost? Explain.
- What other benefits has MANTIS provided to users?

Source: Courtesy of Cincom Systems.

Structured Programming

Structured programming is a programming methodology that is part of a renewed emphasis on **software engineering,** which involves the systematic design and development of software and the management of the software development process. Software engineering views the development of a program as a coordinated activity involving people, tools, and practices, using modern design, development, and management methods in an integrated approach. Structured programming involves such methods as *top-down* program design and uses a limited number of *control structures* in a program to create highly structured *modules* of program code. Structured programming includes program design, coding, and testing techniques, such as *top-down design*, *modularity*, *stepwise refinement*, and *chief programmer teams*. It also includes such tools as *structure* and *HIPO charts, structured coding, pseudocode*, and *structured walkthroughs*. We will discuss the role of these computer programming techniques in this chapter.

Why has structured programming become popular? Primarily because it promises to reduce the cost of developing and maintaining computer programs by standardizing program development and structures. This increases their simplicity and accuracy and minimizes programming cost and maintenance. Software engineering and structured programming are methodologies that enable computer programming to become more of a *science* than an *art*. Traditional ways of programming rely on the creativeness of each programmer to write "efficient" programs that require a minimum of instructions, storage, and computer time to perform a specific data processing assignment. However, this flexible and creative environment frequently results in complex and difficult-to-read programs, which require much testing before they are error free, and are costly to develop and maintain. Structured programming, on the other hand, emphasizes group responsibility for program development with *team programming* and *egoless programming* approaches. It also emphasizes a standardization of programming design concepts and methods, which significantly reduces program complexity. Therefore, organizations using structured programming have shown the following results:

- *Programming productivity*—programmers write more program instructions per day with fewer errors.
- *Programming economy*—The cost and time of program development and maintenance are reduced.
- *Programming simplicity*—programs are easier to write, read, correct, and maintain.

With these potential results, it's easy to see why structured programming continues to be a popular programming methodology.

Computer-Assisted Programming

Another way to increase productivity, quality, and economy is to automate. Thus for many users and programmers, computer programming is becoming an automated, interactive process. A computer user or programmer can design and code the processing logic of a computer program with substantial realtime assistance from a computer system. This involves using a microcomputer or computer terminal to code, translate, test, debug, and develop alternatives for a new program in a realtime interactive process. Thus **computer-assisted programming** has become feasible through the use of software tools such as **application development sys-**

tems (or *application generators*), which provide interactive assistance to programmers (including menus, prompts, and graphics) in their development of application programs. Application development systems (ADS) simplify and automate the programming process, just as *database management systems* (DBMS) simplify and automate the creation, maintenance, and extraction of data and information from the databases of an organization.

Application development systems contain programs called **programming tools,** which support interactive and automated program logic design, editing, coding, testing, debugging, and maintenance. Look at Figure 8–2. It illustrates the variety of programming tools in two application development systems: NATURAL by Software AG and MANTIS by Cincom. Look at the names of each program in NATURAL and each function in the MANTIS menu. This should give you a good idea of the many different types of automated assistance these software packages can provide to users and programmers. Of course, you should realize that many of the programs in a application development system can be acquired separately or in other combinations. Thus such programming tools as *program generators, report generators*, and *screen generators* are being used to automate parts of the programming process.

Another major development in computer-assisted programming is the emergence of **fourth-generation languages** (4GL), or *nonprocedural languages*. This new breed of programming languages allows users and professional programmers to specify the *results* they want and let the computer determine the *sequence of instructions* that will accomplish those results. This differs from traditional programming languages, which require users and programmers to develop the sequence of instructions the computer must follow to achieve a result. This greatly simplifies and accelerates the programming process. These languages typically rely on the support of DBMS and ADS packages to provide easy database access and interactive program development support. We will discuss nonprocedural languages further in the next chapter.

Finally, many firms have established specialized **development centers** to provide expert organization support to their professional programming staff, as well as to advanced user-programmers. The members of the development center serve as consultants to the application development group of the firm. Their role is similar to that of an industrial engineering group in a manufacturing company. Thus they analyze programming productivity and quality, recommend better methods or resources, and help implement their recommendations.

Computer-assisted programming can be summarized in the concept of the **programmer workstation** (or *workbench*), which pro-

FIGURE 8–2 Programming tools in application development systems

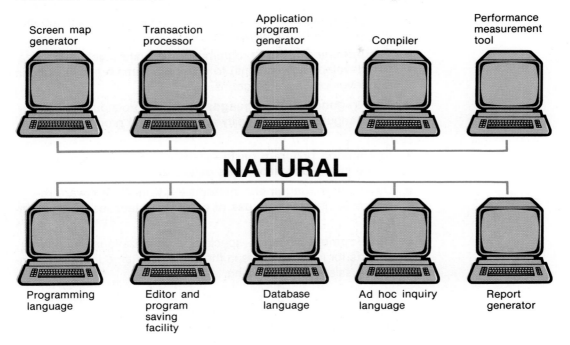

NATURAL BY SOFTWARE AG

Screen map generator

Transaction processor

Application program generator

Compiler

Performance measurement tool

NATURAL

Programming language

Editor and program saving facility

Database language

Ad hoc inquiry language

Report generator

MANTIS BY CINCOM

```
                          MANTIS


                     FACILITY SELECTION


RUN A PROGRAM BY NAME . . . . . . . . 1   RUN A PROGRAM BY MENU . . . . . . 10
DISPLAY A PROMPTER . . . . . . . . . 2   SIGN ON AS ANOTHER USER . . . . . 11
DESIGN A PROGRAM . . . . . . . . . . 3   DIRECTORY OF PROGRAMS . . . . . . 12
        "   SCREEN . . . . . . . . . . 4         "   SCREENS . . . . . . 13
        "   FILE . . . . . . . . . . . 5         "   FILES . . . . . . . 14
        "   PROMPTER . . . . . . . . . 6         "   PROMPTERS . . . . . 15
        "   INTERFACE . . . . . . . . 7         "   INTERFACES . . . . . 16
        "   TOTAL FILE VIEW . . . . . 8         "   TOTAL VIEWS . . . . 17
        "   EXTERNAL FILE VIEW . . . . 9         "   FILE VIEWS . . . . . 18


        TERMINATE . . . . . . . . . . . . . . . . PA2

              : :
```

vides users and professional programmers with programming support (illustrated in Figure 8–3). This includes:

- **Hardware support**—an intelligent terminal with advanced display and graphics capabilities.
- **Programming tools**—programming software (such as application development systems) to provide automated assistance in the development of programs.
- **Fourth-generation languages**—new nonprocedural programming languages that simplify and accelerate program development.
- **Application program parts**—standard program segments stored in an application parts database.
- **Database management systems**—a valuable software resource for the realtime use of common databases by programmers.
- **Development centers**—specialized organizational support by experts for improvements in the quality and productivity of computer-assisted programming.

FIGURE 8–3 Support provided for computer-assisted programming

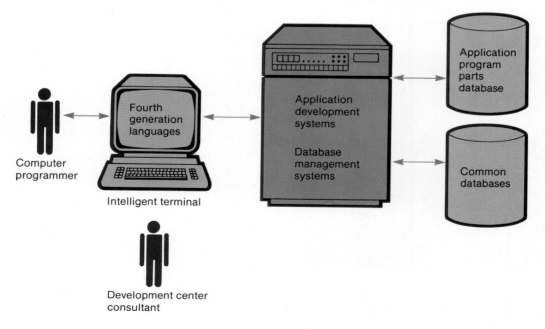

Continuing developments in computer-assisted programming will have a significant effect on the computer programming process in the future. Some experts even predict that such developments will one day make most current programming practices obsolete. However, it is still important for knowledgeable computer users to understand the major activities that must be accomplished to develop workable computer programs.

User Programming

There is another important way whereby major computer-using organizations and the computer industry have responded to problems with programming productivity, quality, and cost. They have begun to encourage and support more programming by **users**. Instead of depending on professional programmers, users are encouraged to develop their own application programs with the assistance of several hardware, software, and organizational resources. *For example*:

- **Hardware support**. Users are provided with **intelligent workstations**, i.e., microcomputers tied into data communications networks to central databases and mainframe computer resources. Users can use these personal computers to access the power of mainframe computers and extract data and software from these central resources to help them program their own applications.

- **Software support**. Users are provided with many of the same **programming tools** available to the professional programming staff. This includes application development systems, fourth-generation nonprocedural languages, and database management system query and report generator languages. Also provided are general-purpose application packages, such as electronic spreadsheet, graphics, and integrated packages, as well as more specialized business application packages.

- **Organizational support**. Users are provided with a major new source of organizational support—the **information center**. These are centrally located support facilities for the computer users of an organization. They allow users to develop their own application programs and to accomplish their own information processing tasks. They provide *hardware support* for users who need it by providing the use of microcomputers, intelligent terminals, advanced graphics terminals, word processors, high-speed printers, plotters, etc. *Software support* is provided with advanced software packages, such as application development systems, nonprocedural languages, database management systems, and a variety of application software packages. *People support* is provided by a staff of *user consultants*. They are systems analysts/programmers who are trained to educate and help users take advantage of the hardware and software resources of the information center.

THE PROGRAMMING PROCESS

The Systems Development Cycle

One of the most important things you can learn about computer programming is that it is just one of several major activities that must take place to develop computerized information processing systems. The process of developing information processing systems is called the **systems development cycle**, though other names, such as *application development* or *systems analysis and design*, are also used. We learned in Chapter Two that *software* is but one of the resources of an information processing system. *Hardware* and *people resources* are also needed to transform *data resources* into *information products*. Therefore, you should realize that the **programming process** deals primarily with the development of *software resources*. The *systems development process*, on the other hand, is concerned not only with the development of software resources but also with the development of hardware, people, and data resources and information products.

Figure 8–4 shows you that software development through computer programming is just one of six major steps in the systems development cycle. Some people even contend that computer programming is just one part of the design stage or the implementation stage (or both) of systems development. However, programming is such an important process that software development deserves to be spotlighted as a separate systems development step. Figure 8–4 also summarizes the stages of the systems development cycle from: (1) when an information processing need is first conceived (**investigation**); (2) an analysis of its *functional requirements* (**analysis**); (3) the development of hardware, software, people, data, and information *specifications* (**design**); (4) development of the computer programs required (**software development**); (5) implementing the new system, (**implementation**); and finally, (6) the maintenance of the established system (**maintenance**). We will discuss this cycle in detail in Chapter Seventeen.

The Stages of the Programming Process

Computer programming is a process that results in the development of a *computer program*, the set of detailed instructions which outline the information processing activities to be performed by a computer. However, it is important for you to understand that the

FIGURE 8–4 The systems development cycle

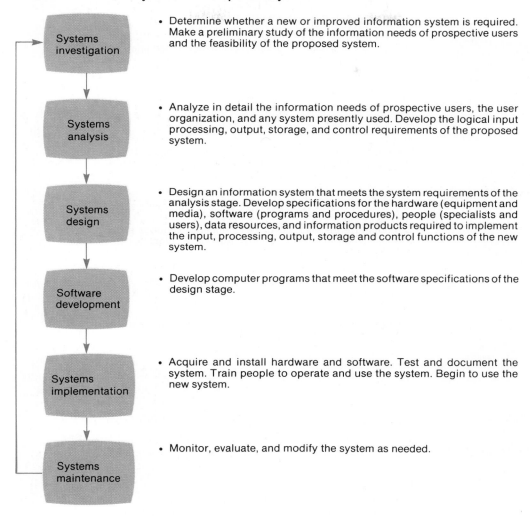

Systems investigation

- Determine whether a new or improved information system is required. Make a preliminary study of the information needs of prospective users and the feasibility of the proposed system.

Systems analysis

- Analyze in detail the information needs of prospective users, the user organization, and any system presently used. Develop the logical input processing, output, storage, and control requirements of the proposed system.

Systems design

- Design an information system that meets the system requirements of the analysis stage. Develop specifications for the hardware (equipment and media), software (programs and procedures), people (specialists and users), data resources, and information products required to implement the input, processing, output, storage and control functions of the new system.

Software development

- Develop computer programs that meet the software specifications of the design stage.

Systems implementation

- Acquire and install hardware and software. Test and document the system. Train people to operate and use the system. Begin to use the new system.

Systems maintenance

- Monitor, evaluate, and modify the system as needed.

computer programming process involves more than the writing of instructions in a programming language. Computer programming may be subdivided into several stages: program *analysis, design, coding, verification, documentation,* and *maintenance.* Each stage of the traditional and computer-assisted programming process is summarized in Figure 8–5. In this chapter, we will discuss some of the tools and activities needed to accomplish these programming stages.

FIGURE 8–5 The stages of the programming process

A. THE TRADITIONAL PROGRAMMING PROCESS

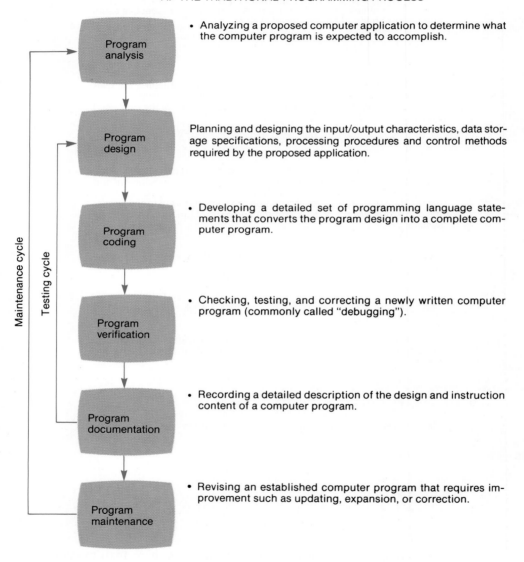

- Analyzing a proposed computer application to determine what the computer program is expected to accomplish.

Planning and designing the input/output characteristics, data storage specifications, processing procedures and control methods required by the proposed application.

- Developing a detailed set of programming language statements that converts the program design into a complete computer program.

- Checking, testing, and correcting a newly written computer program (commonly called "debugging").

- Recording a detailed description of the design and instruction content of a computer program.

- Revising an established computer program that requires improvement such as updating, expansion, or correction.

B. THE COMPUTER-ASSISTED PROGRAMMING PROCESS

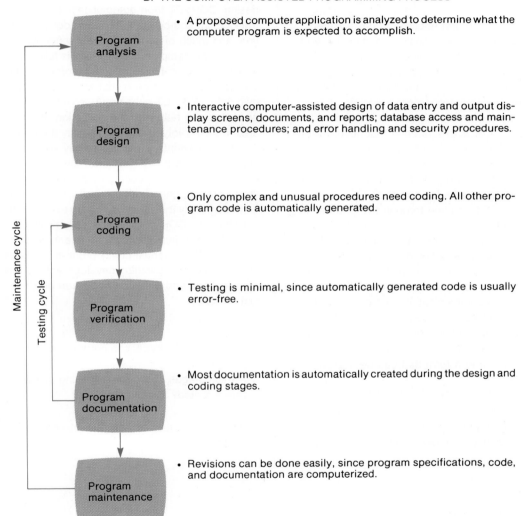

- A proposed computer application is analyzed to determine what the computer program is expected to accomplish.

- Interactive computer-assisted design of data entry and output display screens, documents, and reports; database access and maintenance procedures; and error handling and security procedures.

- Only complex and unusual procedures need coding. All other program code is automatically generated.

- Testing is minimal, since automatically generated code is usually error-free.

- Most documentation is automatically created during the design and coding stages.

- Revisions can be done easily, since program specifications, code, and documentation are computerized.

Program analysis

Program design

Program coding

Program verification

Program documentation

Program maintenance

Maintenance cycle

Testing cycle

REAL WORLD APPLICATION 8–2

CORVET Computerized Programming

CORVET is the first application development tool designed to allow analysts and users, working directly with the computer, to develop fully operational COBOL programs for virtually any business need. It is an automated COBOL programmer—computerized programming, if you will.

It is a COBOL programmer that never misunderstands or miscommunicates and never commits any coding errors. It is a COBOL programmer that never gets sick, never takes a day off, and never asks for a raise.

CORVET takes you through five phases. In the LAYOUT phase, you use the graphics capability of the terminal to paint a picture of the task/program description or logic flow described in your function specs, no matter what design methodology you used. It is an excellent way to avoid miscommunication, because both the user and analyst can see and agree on the logical flow of the application/task/module. LAYOUT translates the task you are trying to accomplish into a form that can be used by CORVET.

The FILE, SCREEN, and REPORT phases allow you to either create new or use existing input and output structures. Finally, in the PROCESS phase, you answer a series of simple business English questions to complete the detailed design. CORVET then automatically produces the COBOL source code, program documentation, and much of your job control language.

Since the completed application is fully operational, true prototyping is an economic reality. The application can be tested with the user's own data. CORVET even produces a batch program that can help with the collection of test data. If the prototype does not satisfy the user's exact requirements, it can be quickly and easily changed by using CORVET's MODIFY mode. It is designed like an editor, so you can move things around, change them easily. You simply go through only the steps necessary to complete the changes. CORVET automatically produces a new code to implement those changes. This eliminates the potential costly program rewrites of conventional application development. Future modifications and enhancements can be done just as easily.

- How does CORVET computerize programming?
- Which stages of the programming process are affected? Explain how.

Source: Courtesy of Analysts International Corporation.

PROGRAM ANALYSIS

"What is the proposed program supposed to do?" Program analysis is an important first step in computer programming, which answers that question. The amount of work involved is directly related to the type of application being programmed and to the amount of *systems development* work that has previously been accomplished. Program analysis may be relatively simple for short problems or for complex mathematical problems whose arithmetic form clearly defines the problem to be solved. Even complex problems and systems may not require extensive program analysis if a thorough job of systems development has been accomplished. If the application to be programmed is viewed as a *problem* that requires a solution, then program analysis is really a process of *problem definition* and *problem specification*. If the application to be programmed is considered to be an information processing *system*, then program analysis should involve analyzing the **software specifications** produced by the design stage of the systems development cycle, or developing your own set of required *program specifications*.

Whether the application to be programmed is simple or complex, and whether the proposed application has been subjected to an extensive systems development effort, the program analysis stage requires the programmer to determine what the program is supposed to accomplish. Thus (1) the **output** required, (2) the **input** available, (3) the data held in **storage** that will be provided or updated, (4) the **processing** (mathematical, logical, and other procedures) that may be required, and (5) the **control** procedures that will be needed should be determined in a preliminary way. See Figure 8–6.

ǁ PROGRAM DESIGN

The *program design* stage of computer programming involves the planning and design of the specific **input/output characteristics**, **processing procedures**, **data storage specifications**, and **control methods** required by the proposed application. As in the case of the programming analysis stage, the amount of effort required in the program design stage depends on the complexity of the application and the amount of systems development work that has previously been performed. Traditional program design requires the development of a logical set of rules and instructions that specify the operations required to accomplish the proposed data processing application. This aspect of program design is known in computer science as the development of an **algorithm**, which can be loosely defined as a set of rules or instructions that specify the operations required in the solution of a problem or in the accomplishment of a task. Of course, most algorithms are automatically generated when computer-assisted programming methods are used.

In traditional programming design, the program is usually divided into several main subdivisions, or *modules,* such as a beginning **initialization** module, **input, processing,** and **output** modules, as well as ending **termination** module. Most programs also have **control** modules that deal with the testing and control of (1) the order of processing, (2) the repetition of processing steps (*looping*), (3)

FIGURE

8–6 Program analysis:
A system function
approach

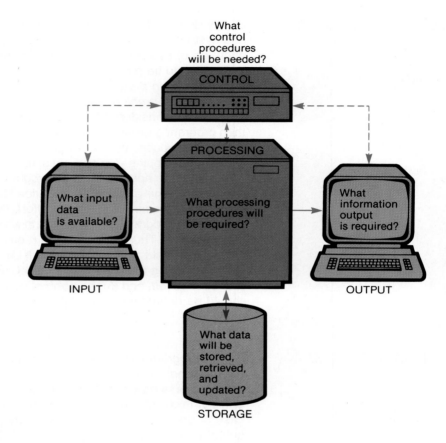

What
control
procedures
will be needed?

CONTROL

PROCESSING

What input
data
is available?

What processing
procedures will
be required?

What
information
output
is required?

INPUT

OUTPUT

What data
will be
stored,
retrieved,
and
updated?

STORAGE

exceptional conditions, such as errors, and (4) other deviations from
normal processing requirements. The use of *subroutines* or subprogram modules that may be used to perform common processing
operations required by the program must also be considered during
the design stage. See Figure 8–7. In computer-assisted programming, application development software emphasizes the interactive
design of input/output and storage program components first, automatically generating the necessary code. Then the processing and
control components may be designed (and coded) using a very
high-level programming language. Figure 8–8 outlines how the
IDEAL application development system accomplishes this process.

Top-Down Design

Top-down design is a method of program design that is a major
part of structured programming. Let's take a look at the steps involved.

FIGURE

8–7 Program modules with examples of typical activities

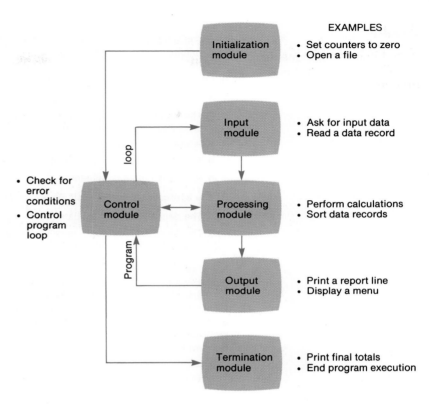

- The programmer must define the *output* that is to be produced, the *input* required, and the *major processing tasks* that are necessary to convert input into output.
- The major processing tasks are then *decomposed* into independent *functional modules*, which define the processing structure of the program.
- Finally, the processing *logic* or algorithm for each module is defined. The programmer designs the *main module* first, then the lower-level modules.

Design tools, such as *structure charts*, *HIPO charts*, *flowcharts*, *pseudocode, decision tables*, and input/output and storage *layout forms*, are used to accomplish the design of each module. We will discuss these analytical tools shortly. Each program module in a top-down design process is usually limited in its contents by the following restrictions:

- Each module should have only one entrance and one exit point.
- Each module should represent only one program function; for example, "read master record."

FIGURE

8–8 Program components in computer-assisted programming

IDEAL's framework divides a commercial application program into the following components:

I. General declarative information, including—

- A declaration of the application and its inputs and outputs.
- The logical database definition (or traditional file record layout for applications that use conventional file access methods).
- Possible report definitions.
- Screen panel layouts and definitions for online screen-oriented applications.
- Input and output parameters.

II. The application program itself, consisting of—

- The definition of working data (data local to the program).
- The logic, computations, terminal interaction and database maintenance rules, procedures, and actions.

Since all but the last component are highly declarative or descriptive in nature, the approach in IDEAL is to use special-purpose, fill-in-the-blank screen formats, or "panels." These panels are processed interactively and eliminate the need for a textual language. All logic, computations, and database maintenance are expressed in a language, IDEAL/PDL, and in a manner that solves traditional problems by offering a comprehensive, yet simple, unified, structured, and very high-level language.

Source: Courtesy Applied Data Research.

- Each module should not require an excessive amount of program code. Some experts place this at no more than one page of program code, which is about 50 lines of programming language instructions.

The purpose of these restrictions is to simplify and standardize the programming process by making programs easier to read, test, and correct. Dividing a lengthy program into modules facilitates not only the design process but also coding, testing, and documentation.

Structure and Hierarchy Charts

A program designed by a top-down method consists of a series of modules related in a hierarchical "treelike" structure. A **structure chart or hierarchical chart** may be used to show the program modules, their purpose, and their relationships. Such charts show the flow of logic in a program using a "tree" of interconnected program modules. The **visual table of contents** is related to the structure chart and hierarchy chart, but each module is numbered so that its position in the structure chart and its operations can be more easily referred to by other program documentation methods. See Figure 8–9.

HIPO Charts

Another aid in top-down design is the *HIPO chart* or HIPO diagram (hierarchy + input/processing/output). It is used to record the input/processing/output details of the hierarchical program modules. The HIPO chart aids the programmer in determining:

- The *output* required—its format, media, organization, volume, frequency and destination.
- The *input* available—its source, format, media, organization, volume, and frequency.
- The *processing* needed—the mathematical, logical, and other procedures required to transform input into output.

A HIPO chart for the main program module (also called the *main control module*) is done first and gives an overall view of the input/processing/output of the program. The HIPO charts or diagrams can then be constructed for the other-lower level modules in the program. Figure 8–10 is an example of a HIPO chart for a gross pay calculation. (It is part of module 2 in the visual table of contents of Figure 8–9).

FIGURE 8–9 A visual table of contents for a payroll program

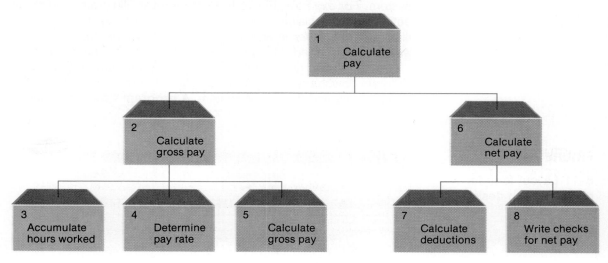

FIGURE

8–10 A HIPO chart for a gross pay calculation

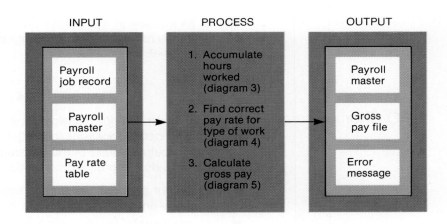

INPUT

Payroll job record

Payroll master

Pay rate table

PROCESS

1. Accumulate hours worked (diagram 3)

2. Find correct pay rate for type of work (diagram 4)

3. Calculate gross pay (diagram 5)

OUTPUT

Payroll master

Gross pay file

Error message

Layout Forms

Layout forms are used to design the format of input, output, and storage media. They usually consist of preprinted forms on which the form and placement of data and information can be "laid out." Layout forms are used to design source documents, input/output and storage records and files, and output displays and reports. See Figure 8–11.

Flowcharts

The flowchart is an important tool for computer programming and systems analysis. A *flowchart* is a graphic representation of the steps necessary to solve a problem, accomplish a task, complete a process—or it may be used to illustrate the components of a system. *For example*, Figure 8–12 humorously illustrates the many activities and decisions "Oscar" faces each morning. The flowchart illustrates the *order* in which a variety of *decisions* are made and *activities* performed in the *process* of Oscar's early morning *routine*.

The two basic types of flowcharts are system flowcharts and program flowcharts. A **system flowchart** is a representation of the components and flows of a system. A **program flowchart** repre-

FIGURE

8–11 Layout form for display screen design

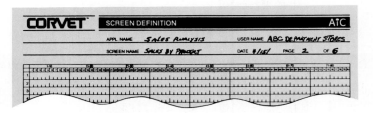

FIGURE 8–12 A flowchart of Oscar's morning

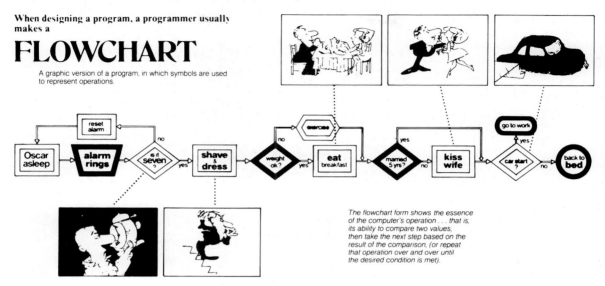

When designing a program, a programmer usually makes a

FLOWCHART

A graphic version of a program, in which symbols are used to represent operations.

The flowchart form shows the essence of the computer's operation . . . that is, its ability to compare two values, then take the next step based on the result of the comparison, (or repeat that operation over and over until the desired condition is met).

sents the information processing steps (algorithm) to be performed within a computer program. Commonly used system and program flowcharting symbols are illustrated and described in Figure 8–13.

System Flowcharts

The **system flowcharts** used in information systems development show the flow of data among the components of a data processing system or information system. Such flowcharts were used several times in the preceding chapters of this book to illustrate components and flows of data in various systems. The system flowchart emphasizes how data moves in various forms through the stages of input, processing, output, and storage. It does not show the details of the processing that takes place in the computer program. System flowcharts can vary in their degree of complexity. *For example*, Figure 8–14 illustrates a payroll system, using just the three basic flowcharting symbols that indicate input/output (a parallelogram), processing (a rectangle), and the direction of data flow (an arrow). A more detailed system flowchart of the payroll system is shown in Figure 8–15. Notice that the flowchart illustrates the flow of data in the system and the input/output and storage media that are used and does not present the details of computer programs that will be required.

FIGURE 8–13 Flowchart symbols

PROGRAM FLOWCHART SYMBOLS

SYMBOL	REPRESENTS
	PROCESSING
	A group of program instructions which perform a processing function of the program.
	INPUT/OUTPUT
	Any function of an input/output device (making information available for processing, recording processing information, tape positioning, etc.).
	DECISION
	The decision function used to document points in the program where a branch to alternate paths is possible based upon variable conditions.
	PREPARATION
	An instruction or group of instructions which changes the program.
	PREDEFINED PROCESS
	A group of operations not detailed in the particular set of flowcharts.
	TERMINAL
	The beginning, end, or a point of interruption in a program.
	CONNECTOR
	An entry from, or an exit to, another part of the program flowchart.
	OFFPAGE CONNECTOR
	A connector used instead of the connector symbol to designate entry to or exit from a page.
∧∨<>	**FLOW DIRECTION**
	The direction of processing or data flow.

SUPPLEMENTARY SYMBOL
FOR SYSTEM AND PROGRAM FLOWCHARTS

	ANNOTATION
	The addition of descriptive comments or explanatory notes as clarification.

SYSTEM FLOWCHART SYMBOLS

PROCESSING		INPUT/OUTPUT	
A major processing function.		Any type of medium or data.	
PUNCHED CARD		**PUNCHED TAPE**	
All varieties of punched cards including stubs.		Paper or plastic, chad or chadless.	
DOCUMENT		**TRANSMITTAL TAPE**	
Paper documents and reports of all varieties.		A proof or adding machine tape or similar batch-control information.	
MAGNETIC TAPE		**ONLINE STORAGE**	
OFFLINE STORAGE		**DISPLAY**	
Offline storage of either paper, cards, magnetic or perforated tape.		Information displayed by plotters or video devices.	
COLLATE		**SORTING**	
Forming two or more sets of items from two or more other sets.		An operation on sorting or collating equipment.	
MANUAL INPUT		**MERGE**	
Information supplied to or by a computer utilizing an online device.		Combining two or more sets of items into one set.	
MANUAL OPERATION		**AUXILIARY OPERATION**	
A manual offline operation not requiring mechanical aid.		A machine operation supplementing the main processing function.	
KEYING OPERATION		**COMMUNICATION LINK**	
An operation utilizing a key-driven device.		The automatic transmission of information from one location to another via communication lines.	
FLOW	< >∨∧	The direction of processing or data flow.	

Program Flowcharts

A **program flowchart** illustrates the detailed sequence of steps required by a computer program. A program flowchart can be used to: (1) visualize the logic and sequence of steps in an operation, (2) experiment with various programming approaches, and (3) keep track of all processing steps, including procedures for alternatives and exceptions. Once final versions of the flowcharts for a program are completed, they serve as a guide during the program coding, testing, documentation, and maintenance stages of computer programming. Program flowcharts can also vary in their complexity, ranging from *general* flowcharts to *detailed* program flowcharts.

FIGURE

8–14 Simple system flowchart—payroll

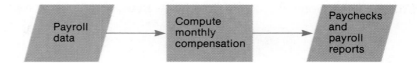

Figure 8–16 is a general program flowchart of a *sales personnel payroll report* program, which is a simplified example of one of the computer programs that might be required in a payroll system. It outlines the steps that result in the printing of the Salesperson Payroll Report. This process would ordinarily be just a segment of a larger payroll program but has been modified to illustrate the use of program flowcharting symbols.

FIGURE

8–15 System flowchart—payroll

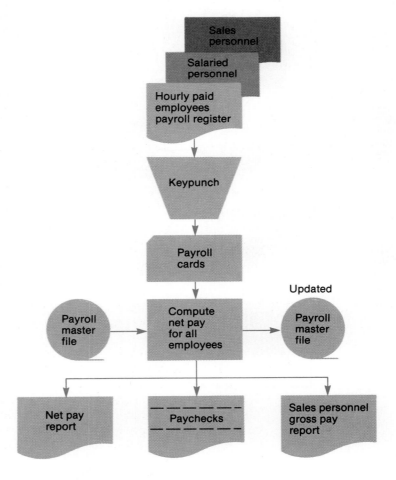

FIGURE 8–16 General program flowchart—salesperson payroll report

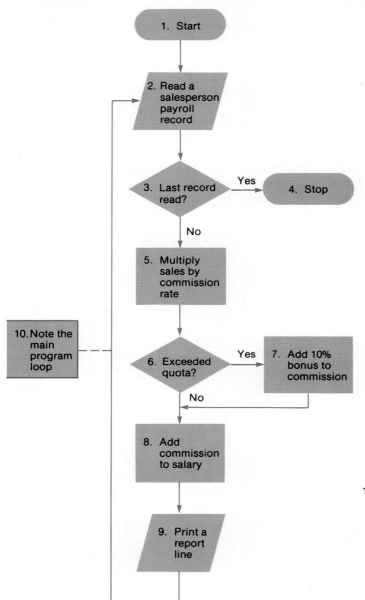

1. This is the start of the program.
2. A salesperson payroll record is read as illustrated by the input/output symbol. It should contain data "fields" like the name, monthly salary, commission rate, and sales quota of each salesperson. The data record could be in the form of a punched card, or could be stored on magnetic tape or disk.
3. This is the "last record" decision point. Has the last data record been read?
4. If the answer is yes, the program comes to a stop.
5. If the answer is no, the processing symbol indicates that the sales amount on this data record should be multiplied by the commission rate to compute the sales commission earned.
6. Another decision point. Has the sales made exceeded the sales quota set for this salesperson?
7. If the answer is yes, a 10 percent bonus (10 percent of the normal commission) is added to the commission earned.
8. If the answer is no (and also whenever completing step 7) the sales commission earned is added to the regular monthly salary to compute the monthly *gross pay* for the salesperson.
9. A line on the Salesperson Payroll Report is printed. This would probably include the name, quota, sales, commission, salary, and gross pay for each salesperson.
10. This *comment* symbol points out the main *loop* of the program.

In the example of Figure 8–16, salesperson payroll data records are read and commissions and gross pay are calculated and included in a printed report. Each symbol in the flowchart has been numbered so that we can explain the function of each symbol and show the flow of processing and control activities in this program.

A **program loop** (see function 10 in Figure 8–16) allows any computer program to repeat automatically a series of operations. In this example, the main program loop of input, processing, and output operations is repeated until the last payroll record is read. The *looping* process is then ended by the program modification feature, which allows computer programs automatically to modify themselves by *branching* to another routine. In this example, when the last record is read, the program *branches* to a stop. The looping process is shown in this flowchart by an arrow that connects the beginning and ending symbols of the loop, though two connector symbols (see Figure 8–13) could have also been used.

Structured Flowcharts

Structured flowcharts are another development of structured programming. They illustrate the steps in a computer program using basic program *control structures* (that we will cover shortly) and use a "box-within-a-box" format to show what is to be done and in what order. Many people find them easier to understand than regular flowcharts. Use of structured flowcharts emphasizes the top-down and structured process within a computer program. Figure 8–17 is a compact, structured flowchart revision of the traditional flowchart shown in Figure 8–15.

Pseudocode

Another tool in detailed program design that is part of the top-down design of structured programming is *pseudocode*. **Pseudocode** is the expression of the processing logic of a program module in ordinary English language phrases. Like decision tables, pseudocode was developed as an alternative to flowcharts. In many programming assignments, flowcharts were found to be an unsatisfactory way of expressing the flow and logic of a program. Pseudocode allows a programmer to express his or her thoughts in regular English phrases, with each phrase representing a programming process that must be accomplished in a specific program module (as detailed in a HIPO chart). The phrases almost appear to be programming language statements; thus the name "pseudocode." However, unlike programming language statements, pseudocode has no rigid rules; only a few optional *keywords* for major processing functions

FIGURE

8–17 Structured program flowchart—salesperson payroll report processing

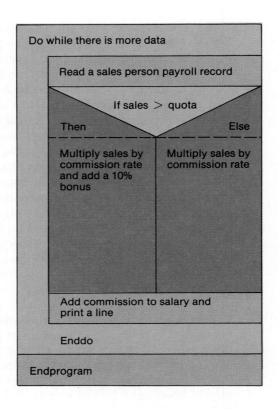

are recommended. Therefore, programmers can express their thoughts in an easy, natural, straightforward manner, but at a level of detail which allows pseudocode to be directly convertible into programming language coding. Figure 8–18 provides an example of pseudocode for the same salesperson payroll program that we have flowcharted earlier.

FIGURE

8–18 Pseudocode example for salesperson payroll report processing

```
Begin Program
  Read a salesperson payroll record
  Do while there is more data
    multiply sales by commission rate
    If sales greater than quota
      then add 10% bonus to commission
    End-If
    Add commission to salary
    Print a report line
    Read a sales person payroll record
  End-Do
End Program
```

Decision Tables

Decision tables are another important tool of the systems analyst and computer programmer and are used in conjunction with, or in place of, flowcharts. Using flowcharts for the analysis and design of complex programs involving many specified conditions and decision paths becomes an extremely difficult and frequently unsatisfactory process. The flow of data and the logical sequence of the program or system becomes hard to follow, and errors or omissions may result. Therefore, decision tables may be used in such cases as a tool for the analysis and design of programs and systems involving complex conditional decision logic. A *decision table* is a tabular presentation of system or program logic. The general format of a decision table is shown in Figure 8–19. It shows that there are four basic parts to the decision table:

■ The *condition stub*, which lists conditions or questions similar to those contained in a flowchart decision symbol.

■ The *action stub*, which lists statements describing all actions that can be taken.

■ The *condition entry*, which indicates what conditions are being met or answers the questions in the condition stub.

■ The *action entry*, which indicates the actions to be taken.

Most decision tables also include a table heading and decision rule headings or numbers. The columns in the condition entry and action entry section of the table (called the "body" of the table) illustrate various **decision rules**, since they specify that **if** certain conditions exist, **then** certain actions must be taken. Depending on the complexity of the decision logic, condition entries are indicated by a Y (yes), or a N (no), comparison symbols such as $< \leq = \geq >$, quantities, codes, or are left blank to show that the condition does not apply. Action entries are usually indicated by an X. When a decision table is completed, each rule indicates a different set of conditions and actions. A simple example should help clarify the construction and use of a decision table. Figure 8–20 illustrates a decision table based on the payroll system and program examples flowcharted in the preceding pages. The decision

FIGURE

8–19 General format of a decision table

Table Heading	Decision Rule Heading
Condition statements	Condition entries
Action statements	Action entries

logic has been made more complex than in the previous example to illustrate the usefulness of decision tables for the analysis of decision logic. Examine Figure 8–20 to see what actions are taken when various possible conditions occur.

For example: decision rule Number 6 concerns the case of a salesperson who has made sales for the month but has not exceeded his or her sales quota. Given these conditions, the payroll processing actions that must be taken are to compute his or her salary and commission (but not a bonus), perform other salesperson payroll processing, and perform net pay processing common to all employees. The information in Column 6 of the decision table can therefore be expressed in words by the following decision rule statement:

If an employee is a salesperson who has had sales for the month

FIGURE

8–20 Payroll decision table

Payroll Table No. 1		Decision Rule Numbers						
		1	2	3	4	5	6	7
Conditions	Hourly paid employee	Y						
	Salaried employee		Y					
	Executive employee			Y				
	Unclassified employee				Y			
	Salesperson					Y	Y	Y
	Made sales?					N	Y	Y
	Exceeded quota?					N	N	Y
Actions	Compute wages	X						
	Compute salary		X					
	Compute sales salary					X	X	X
	Compute commission						X	X
	Compute bonus							X
	Salesperson gross pay processing					X	X	X
	Net pay processing	X	X			X	X	X
	Go to payroll table number:			2	3			

but has not exceeded his or her sales quota, **then** compute his or her salary and commissions, and complete salesperson payroll processing and all-employee net pay processing.

PROGRAM CODING

Program coding is the process that converts the logic designed during the program design stage into a set of programming language statements that constitute a computer program. The term *programming* is frequently used to refer only to the program coding stage, but, as we have seen, five other important steps are also necessary. Depending on the programming language used, coding involves a rigorous process that requires the computer programmer to strictly follow specific rules concerning format and syntax (vocabulary, punctuation, and grammatical rules).

Structured Coding

Structured coding is an important part of "top-down structured programming," which stresses that only three basic "control structures" should be used for program coding: (1) *sequence*, (2) *selection*, and (3) *repetition* (or loop). Using just these three basic control structures simplifies and standardizes program coding and makes the resulting programs easier to read and understand. Figure 8–21 illustrates the three basic control structures of structured programming in both traditional and structured flowcharts.

Sequence Structure

This structure expresses the fact that program instructions are usually executed in the order in which they are stored in the computer. Figure 8–21 illustrates that program statements in function A will be executed before those for function B. Thus we say that "control" flows from function A to function B.

Selection Structure

This structure is also called the *decision* or IF-THEN-ELSE structure. It expresses a *choice* between two program control paths based on a *test* that results in either a true or false condition. Figure 8–21 shows that, if the test is true, control will flow to function A and its statements will be executed; if the test is *false*, function B will be done.

FIGURE 8–21 The three basic program control structures

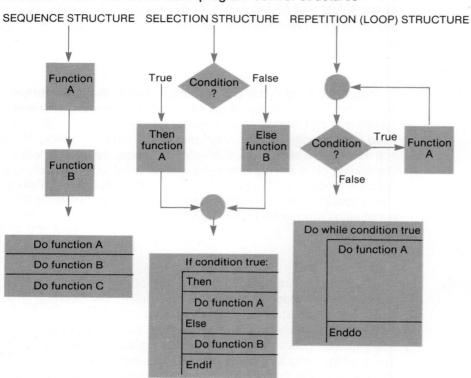

Repetition (Loop) Structure

This structure is also called the DO-WHILE or DO-UNTIL structure. It expresses the performing of a program function *while* or *until* a condition is *true*. Figure 8–21 shows the flow of program control that can be expressed as "do function A *while* the condition is true." The opposite control flow can be expressed by a variation of this structure, which would say "do function A *until* the condition is true."

Structured coding can be implemented to some extent in many current programming languages. However, it is easier to implement in some languages (such as PL/1, Pascal, and COBOL) than in others (such as FORTRAN and BASIC). Structured "top-down" programming and coding are designed to simplify the flow of program control and eliminate or minimize *branching* forward and backward from the main flow of the program. Thus the main control module (also called the *mainline*) should clearly show that control flows from the top down (i.e., top to bottom without being transferred to earlier program modules). The cause of much of this unnecessary branching is blamed on the "GO TO" statement found in many programs. Therefore, this aspect of structured programming is sometimes called "GO TO-less" programming.

Types of Instructions

The types of instructions available to a computer programmer for program coding depend on the program language used and the *command repertoire* or *instruction set* of the computer CPU. However, computer instructions can usually be subdivided into six categories: (1) specification, (2) input/output, (3) data movement, (4) arithmetic, (5) logical, and (6) control.

■ *Specification instructions* are descriptive instructions which describe the data media to be used, the size and format of data records and files, the constants to be used, and the allocation of storage. Many of these instructions are based on the input/output and storage layout forms completed during the program design stage. The "FORMAT" statement of FORTRAN or the "PICTURE" statement of COBOL are examples of specification instruction statements.

■ *Input/Output instructions* transfer data and instructions between the CPU and input/output devices. "READ" or "PRINT statements are examples of such instructions.

■ *Data movement instructions* involve rearranging and reproducing data within primary storage. "MOVE," "SHIFT," or "STORE" instructions are examples.

■ *Arithmetic instructions* are instructions that accomplish mathematical operations, such as "ADD" and "SUBTRACT."

■ *Logical instructions* perform comparisons and test conditions and control some branching processes, as illustrated in the decision symbol of program flowcharts. Examples are "IF, THEN," or "COMPARE" statements.

■ *Control instructions* are used to stop and start a program, change the sequence of a program through some branching processes, and control the use of subroutines. "DO," "RETURN," and "STOP" statements are examples of control instructions.

Figure 8–22 shows the statements and flowchart of a very simple BASIC program. The program reads an undetermined number of student test scores, computes an average test score, and prints the result. Examples of similar programs coded in several widely used programming languages are included in the next chapter.

PROGRAM VERIFICATION

Program verification, more commonly known as **debugging**, is a stage of programming that involves checking, testing, and correction processes. These activities are necessary because newly coded

FIGURE 8–22 Statements and flowchart of a simple BASIC program

```
*10 REM AVERAGE EXAM SCORE PROGRAM
*20 LET C = 0
*30 LET T = 0
*40 READ S
*50 IF S = 9999 THEN 100
*60 PRINT S,
*70 C = C + 1
*80 T = T + S
*90 GO TO 40
*100 A = T/C
*110 PRINT "NUMBER OF STUDENTS TAKING EXAM = "; C
*120 PRINT "AVERAGE EXAM SCORE = "; A
*130 DATA 87, 64, 95, 77, 82, 73, 98, 70, 63, 91, 9999
*140 END
*RUN
87 64 95 77 82 73 98 70 63 91
NUMBER OF STUDENTS TAKING EXAM = 10
AVERAGE EXAM SCORE = 80.0
*
```

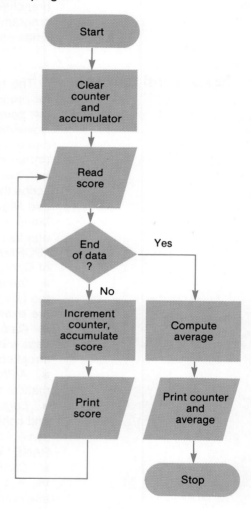

programs frequently contain errors (*bugs*) that must be identified and corrected by a debugging process.

Programming Errors

Programming errors are of three major types: syntax, logic, and systems design errors.

Syntax errors are caused by violating the rules of the programming language in which the program is coded, or by making mistakes in the organization and format of data. These errors can be as simple as a misplaced decimal point or a comma and can be made by the programmer or be the result of an error made in the terminal entry of the source program.

Logic errors are errors that occur because of mistakes in the logical structure of a program. Necessary procedures may have been omitted or incorrect procedures included in a program. For example, a payroll program that did not distinguish between hourly paid employees and salaried employees or which used an incorrect commission for salespersons would produce logic errors.

Systems design errors are errors in the design of a computer application that result in a program that produces unsatisfactory results for a computer user. A program may be free of clerical and logic errors and still not meet all the requirements of a proposed information processing application. Such errors are caused by failures in communication between the programmer and the systems analyst or computer user.

Syntax errors are easier to detect than logic errors, because they are usually identified during the language translation process when *diagnostic messages* identifying such errors are produced. Syntax errors may also cause the computer to reject a program during this process or later processing. Logic errors are harder to detect, since they will not be identified by the translator diagnostics, and the complete program may be processed by the computer without being rejected. The output of such a program, however, will be incorrect.

Checking

Program checking must take place during the program design, program coding, and program verification stages. Checking should take place during and after the development of program design aids, such as HIPO charts, pseudocode, flowcharts, and decision tables. The purpose of this procedure is to verify that all program requirements are being met and to determine that the design aids correctly represent the processing logic required by the program. Checking should take place at the completion of the program coding stage to ensure that the instructions correctly translate the logic of the flowcharts and decision tables and that any syntax errors have been identified. This "desk checking" process is facilitated if top-down design and structured programming have been used, because they significantly simplify and standardize program logic and coding, thus making programs easier to read and correct.

The final checking process involves attempting to have the program or program module translated into a machine language program that is acceptable to the computer. An *assembler, compiler,* or *interpreter* (language translator program) is used to accomplish this process. (Refer back to Figure 7–7.) During or after such a translation process, *diagnostic messages* will be printed, identifying any syntax errors in the program. The programmer makes necessary corrections to the program and then makes another translation attempt. This process must be repeated until an error-free "pass" is accomplished and the resulting machine language program is ready for a test period.

Structured Walkthroughs

Structured walkthroughs are an aid to good programming design, coding, and debugging, and are one of the tools of structured programming. A structured walkthrough is a methodology that requires a *peer* review (by other programmers) of the program design and coding to minimize and reveal errors in the early stages of programming. Its aim is to promote errorless and *egoless* programming by having other programmers formally involved in any programming process. Thus structured walkthroughs may involve the *team programming* concept, where several programmers are assigned to develop the same program under the direction of a *chief programmer*. Team members review each other's design and coding at regular intervals as each program module is designed and then coded. Structured walkthroughs are an attempt to minimize the cost of program verification by catching errors in the early stages of programming, rather than waiting until the program has reached the testing stage, where corrections are more difficult and costly to make.

Testing

A properly checked program is tested to demonstrate whether it can produce correct results using *test data*. This *testing* should attempt to simulate all conditions that may arise during processing. Therefore, test data must include unusual and incorrect data as well as the typical types of data that will usually occur. Such test data is needed to test the ability of the program to handle exceptions and errors,as well as more normal forms of data. The programmer must have previously prepared the test data by manually (and carefully) calculating and determining the correct results. After the object program has processed the test data, the output is compared to the expected results. If correct results are produced, the program or program module is considered properly tested and ready for use.

In structured programming, the higher-level modules of a program are supposed to be coded and tested first. Since the lower-level modules are not ready for testing, "dummy modules" are created in their place so each higher-level module can be tested. As lower-level modules are tested, higher-level modules are tested again. This allows coding and testing modules separately and from the "top down." This process simplifies finding errors, because errors can be isolated in specific modules. Then, when even the lowest-level program modules are successfully tested, the program is considered fully tested as an individual program. However, one final *systems test* step remains. The program must be tested together with other programs that are part of the same information processing system. Only when these programs show that they can properly work together are they considered fully tested.

The final phase of program verification is a temporary period, in which actual data is used to test a computer program. If the program has been designed to replace an older data processing method, this procedure is known as "parallel processing." The parallel run allows the results of the new program to be compared to the results produced by the system it is to replace. If the results agree over a brief specified time, the old operation is then phased out.

PROGRAM DOCUMENTATION

Program documentation is a process that should occur throughout all other stages of computer programming. Program documentation is the detailed description of the design and the instruction content of a computer program. Program documentation is extremely important in diagnosing program errors, making programming changes, or reassembling a lost program, especially if its original programmer is no longer available. Descriptive material produced in the previous stages of computer programming should be collected and refined, and new material developed. A "program documentation manual" should be assembled, which might include contents as shown in Figure 8–23.

PROGRAM MAINTENANCE

The final stage of computer programming begins after a computer program has been accepted as an operational program. *Program maintenance* refers to the revision of computer programs that is needed if they are to be improved, updated, expanded, or corrected. The requirements of information processing applications are subject to continual revisions due to changes in company policies, business operations, government regulations, etc. Also, changes in the capabilities of newly acquired computer hardware and the continual development of new versions or "releases" of system or application

FIGURE

8–23 Contents of program documentation

Program Specifications

Describe what the program is supposed to do.

Program Description

Consists of structure charts, HIPO charts, pseudocode, input/output and storage layout sheets, program flowcharts, decision tables, program listing, and a narrative description of what the program does.

Verification Documentation

Includes listings of test data and results, memory dumps, and other test documents.

Operations Documentation

Consists of operating instructions which describe the actions required of the computer operator during the processing of the computer program.

Maintenance Documentation

A detailed description of all changes made to the program after it was accepted as an operational program.

---

software by vendors are a major cause of programming maintenance requirements. Recent studies have shown that programming maintenance uses a major part of the budget of the information processing departments of many computer-using organizations. Much more time, effort, and money is spent by these organizations in maintaining present programs than in developing new ones! Solving this problem is another major reason for the trend toward structured programming, computer-assisted programming, and user programming.

Program maintenance is, therefore, an important stage of computer programming—involving the analysis, design, coding, verification, and documentation of changes to operational computer programs. Large computer users frequently have a separate category of application programmers, called *maintenance programmers,* whose sole responsibility is program maintenance. Theirs is a difficult assignment, since they must revise programs they did not develop. This should emphasize the importance of the structured programming approach, since it provides simplified, standardized, and structured documentation that is easy to read and understand. Such documentation is essential for proper program maintenance. Inadequate documentation may make program maintenance impossible and require the rewriting of an entire program.

REAL WORLD APPLICATION 8–3

Monsanto Company

Programmers at the Monsanto Company are using IBM's Application Development Facility (ADF) and report impressive productivity gains. Time savings for three large systems amounts to an estimated $1.5 million over using COBOL.

"We've found, though, that there are times to resort to COBOL, especially when a heavy transaction rate is expected and CPU resources are a concern," says Mr. G. L. Bratsch, director, MIS Department. "ADF'S conversational' mode uses from 50 percent to 100 percent more CPU resources than IMS/COBOL, while the nonconversational mode uses about 20 percent to 50 percent more CPU resources.

"When the programmer gets into a situation where one transaction will occur very frequently, he branches off and writes it in COBOL to get the best CPU efficiency. This is the case for the plant procurement system, which is expected to generate 120,000 transactions a day, twice as many IMS transactions as all other Monsanto IMS systems put together. Even so, this approach gives us a 4-to-1 or 5-to-1 productivity gain." Major ADF features include:

Automated generation of message format service. "In the past an experienced programmer would spend one to two days writing this portion of the program and then spend varying amounts of time debugging and testing. With ADF, we now spend one half to four hours and no testing is necessary. It works as is."

Automated database access. "Previously, generating an efficient database call structure would take up to several days, based on the experience of the programmer. We now spend almost no time on this at all. ADF does most

of it automatically, and in many cases, much more efficient call patterns result."

Mapping of data to or from screen and databases. "We have cut about ten days from the cycle and, just as significant, we encounter very few errors in an area that was highly error-prone with straight IMS/COBOL. Further, most of the errors tended to be logic errors, instead of syntax, which were much more difficult to debug."

Effective key selection menus. "These are provided to coach the user for proper database selection, step-by-step, level-by-level, until the user gains the proficiency that allows him to bypass steps as desired."

A 90 to 95 percent reduction in total code. "Only the more complex procedures need coding."

Testing is minimal.

Maintenance is significantly reduced. "In fact, none has been required to date, and when it is required, we expect it will be greatly simplified. Also, we need much less documentation; much editing is automatic, and conversational ADF provides some automatic security features."

"We estimate that it takes two years to become a journeyman IMS/COBOL programmer, but only about three to four months to becomes a journeyman ADF programmer."

- How has ADF affected each of the stages of computer programming?
- What are the major benefits and limitations of using ADF for programming?

Source: "Application Development Aids," *Computing Newsletter*, April 1983, p. 6. Reprinted with permission.

SUMMARY

- Computer programming is a process that results in the development of a detailed set of instructions, which outline the information processing activities to be performed by a computer. Computer programming may be subdivided into the six stages summarized in Figure 8–5. However, the programming process is only one major stage of the systems development cycle summarized in Figure 8–4.

- Computer programming is changing, due to major problems in productivity, quality, and cost that developed with traditional programming methods. Structured programming, computer-assisted programming, and user programming have been developed as solutions to these problems.

- Structured programming is a programming methodology that involves the use of a top-down program design and uses a limited number of control structures to create highly structured modules of program code. Structured programming includes program design, coding, and verification techniques, such as top-down design, structure and HIPO charts, pseudocode, structured coding, and structured walkthroughs.

- Computer-assisted programming involves the use of such software tools as application development systems and other hardware, software, and organizational resources to make computer programming an automated, interactive process.

- User programming is being encouraged by computer-using organizations by providing users with hardware support (intelligent workstations), software support (such as application development systems, data base management systems, fourth generation languages, and application packages), and organizational support (such as information centers).

- Program design aids, such as structure charts, HIPO charts, flowcharts, pseudocode, and decision tables, are important techniques used not only in program design but also assist in program coding, debugging, documentation, and maintenance.

- Once a computer program has been coded, it may be verified by a debugging process, documented with suitable program documentation, and revised when necessary by the program maintenance activity.

KEY TERMS AND CONCEPTS

Programming cycle	Program flowcharts
Systems development cycle	Layout forms
Stages of programming	Structured flowcharts
Structured programming	Program loops
Computer-assisted programming	Pseudocode
User programming	Decision tables
Application development systems	Program coding
Information centers	Basic control structures
Programming tools	Types of computer instructions
Program analysis	Program verification
Program design	Debugging
Algorithm	Syntax errors
Top-down design	Logic errors
Program modules	System design errors
Structured charts	Program checking
HIPO charts	Structure walkthroughs
System flowcharts	Program testing
	Program documentation
	Program maintenance

REVIEW AND APPLICATION QUESTIONS

1. Why is knowledge of computer programming desirable for computer users?
2. Why and how is computer programming changing? How will these changes affect professional programmers? Users?
3. What is structured programming? What benefits are claimed for its use?
4. What is computer-assisted programming? What hardware and software resources does it require? Will it make traditional programming methods obsolete? Why or why not?
5. What hardware, software, and organizational support is being provided to encourage more user programming?
6. How does computer programming fit into the systems development cycle?
7. Identify each of the stages in the computer programming process.
8. What is top-down design? How is it accomplished? What benefits are supposed to result from its use?
9. What is the purpose of structure charts, HIPO charts, layout forms, decision tables, and pseudocode?

10. What is the purpose of a flowchart? How do system flowcharts differ from program flowcharts?
11. What are the basic system and program flowcharting symbols which represent input, processing, output, decision points, etc.?
12. How does a decision table show the decision rules that are possible in a given situation? Give an example.
13. What are the three basic control structures of structured coding? What benefits are supposed to result from their use?
14. What are the six basic types of computer instructions? What functions are performed by each basic type of instruction?
15. What is program debugging? What activities are involved?
16. Is program debugging always necessary? Explain.
17. Differentiate between syntax, logic, and system design errors. What type of error is easier to detect?
18. What are structured walkthroughs? How do they assist the program verification process?
19. Why is program documentation important?
20. What is the purpose of the program maintenance stage?

APPLICATION PROBLEMS

1. If you have not already done so, read and answer the questions after each Real World Application in this chapter.
2. Construct a simple system flowchart and a program flowchart that illustrate the flow of data and some of the processing steps required to accomplish an information processing task. Use an information processing task of your choice, such as the processing of payroll records, student grades, sales transactions, or mathematical computations.
3. Figure 8–24 is a program flowchart for a COBOL program. The program produces a report, listing each individual sale and the total sales for a restaurant. In addition, any sale over $100 is flagged with an exception message. Each record contains the dollar amount of the sale and whether the sale was for breakfast, lunch, or dinner. Structured program coding allows three structures: sequence structure, selection structure, and repetition or loop structure. In Figure 8–24, the letter next to parts of the flowchart represents a specific one of these structures. For each letter identify the appropriate structure.
4. In order to develop a structured program, you could produce a structure chart before you developed a program flowchart. The structure chart breaks the program into functional modules and shows their hierarchical relationship. For the program flowchart in Figure 8–24, one could identify the following modules:

FIGURE 8–24 COBOL program flowchart for sales report

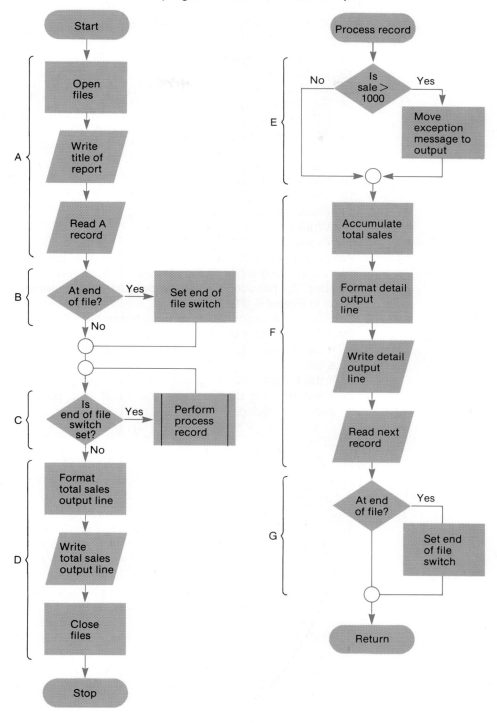

1. Produce sales report.
2. Open files.
3. Write title of report.
4. Get first record.
5. Process record.
6. Format exception message.
7. Accumulate total sales.
8. Format detail output line.
9. Write detail output line.
10. Get next record.
11. Format total sales output line.
12. Write total sales output line.
13. Close files.

Produce a structure chart using these modules, using the flow-chart and the number of the modules to help you.

5. Develop the pseudocode for the program expressed as a flow-chart in Figure 8–24.

6. Construct a decision table for a customer billing program given the following requirements:

   a. If the balance due is less than or equal to zero, do not send a bill.

   b. If the balance due is greater than zero send a bill.

   c. If the balance due exceeds the credit limit, print customer exception report.

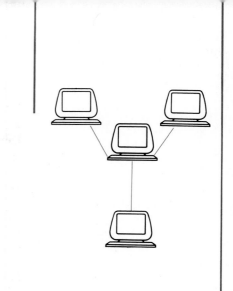

CHAPTER 9

Overview of Programming Languages

CHAPTER OUTLINE

LEARNING OBJECTIVES

The purpose of this chapter is to promote a basic
understanding of computer programming languages
by analyzing the fundamental characteristics and use
of several major types and widely used versions of
programming languages. After reading and studying
this chapter you should be able to:

1. Explain the differences between machine,
   assembler, high-level, and fourth generation-
   languages.
2. Discuss the trends in the development of
   programming languages.
3. Summarize several major characteristics, benefits,
   and limitations of BASIC, COBOL, FORTRAN,
   PL/1, Pascal, APL, and RPG.

TYPES OF PROGRAMMING LANGUAGES

Programming languages allow computer instructions to be written in a language that is mutually understandable to both people and computers. To be a knowledgeable computer user, you should know the basic characteristics of several popular programming languages and be capable of using one to develop at least a few simple programs of your own. Many different programming languages have been developed, each with its own unique vocabulary, grammar, and uses. A brief description of several languages is outlined in Figure 9–1. We will briefly analyze several of these languages later in this chapter. However, let us first examine the four major types of computer programming languages:

- **Machine** languages.
- **Assembler** languages.
- **High-level** languages.
- **Fourth-generation** languages.

Figure 9–2 illustrates the multilevel structure of programming languages, which ranges from microprogram machine languages to fourth- generation languages. Notice also the types of language translation needed at each level before machine language instruction codes or microinstructions can be executed by the logic circuitry of the CPU.

Machine Languages

Machine languages are the most basic level of programming languages. In the early stages of computer development, instructions were written that used the internal binary code of the computer. This type of programming involved the extremely difficult task of writing instructions in the form of coded strings of binary digits. Programmers had to have a detailed knowledge of the internal operations of the specific CPU they were using and had to write long series of detailed instructions to accomplish even simple data processing tasks.

Programming in machine language requires specifying the storage locations for every instruction and item of data used. Instructions must be included for every register, counter, switch, and indicator that is used by the program. These requirements made machine language programming a slow, difficult, and error-prone task. Depending on the internal code used by the particular computer being programmed, machine language instructions could be expressed in pure binary form, binary, octal, or hexadecimal codes, or even codes using decimal numbers and/or alphabetical characters (which were then decoded by the circuitry of the CPU into pure binary

FIGURE

9–1 A summary of several major programming languages

Ada: Named after Augusta Ada Byron, considered the world's first computer programmer. Developed in 1980 for the U.S. Department of Defense as a standard "high-order language." It resembles an extension of Pascal.

ALGOL: (ALGOrithmic Language). An international algebraic language designed primarily for scientific and mathematical applications. It is widely used in Europe.

APL: (A Programming Language). A mathematically oriented interactive language originated by Kenneth Iverson of IBM. It utilizes a very concise symbolic notation designed for efficient interactive programming.

BASIC: (Beginners All-Purpose Symbolic Instruction Code). A simple procedure-oriented language developed at Dartmouth College. It is used for interactive programming on time-sharing systems and has become a popular language for minicomputer and microcomputer systems for small business use and personal computing.

C: A low-level structured language developed by Bell Laboratories as part of the UNIX operating system. It resembles a machine-independent assembler language and is presently popular for system software programming.

COBOL: (COmmon Business Oriented Language). Designed by a committee of computer manufacturers and users (CODASYL) as an English-like language specifically for business data processing. It is the most widely used programming language for business applications.

FORTRAN: (FORmula TRANslation). The oldest of the popular high-level languages. It was designed for solving mathematical problems in science, engineering, research, business, and education. It is still the most widely used programming language for scientific and engineering applications.

LOGO: An interactive graphical language used as a tool for learning a variety of concepts (color, direction, letters, words, sounds, and the like) as well as learning to program and use a computer. Forms and figures are used (*sprites* and *turtles*), which a child learns to move around on the screen to accomplish tasks.

Pascal: Named after Blaise Pascal. Developed by Niklaus Wirth of Zurich as a powerful successor to ALGOL, and designed specifically to incorporate structured programming concepts and to facilitate top-down design. Pascal has become a popular language for both small and large computers.

PILOT: (Programmed Inquiry, Learning Or Teaching). A special-purpose language designed to develop CAI (computer-aided-instruction) programs. It is a simple interactive language that enables a person with minimal computer experience to develop and test interactive CAI programs.

PL/1: (Programming Language/1). A general-purpose language developed by IBM. It was designed to combine some of the features of COBOL, FORTRAN, ALGOL, and other special languages. It is thus a highly flexible "modular" general-purpose language that can be used for business, scientific, and specialized applications.

RPG: (Report Program Generator). A problem-oriented language that generates programs that produce reports and perform other data processing tasks. It is a popular language for report preparation, file maintenance, and other business data processing applications of small computer users.

form). For example, a machine language program that would add two numbers together in the accumulator and store the result (X = Y + Z) might take the form shown in Figure 9–3. Like many computer instructions, these instructions consist of an "operation code," which specifies what is to be done, and an "operand," which specifies the address of the data or device to be operated upon.

FIGURE

9–2 Levels of programming languages

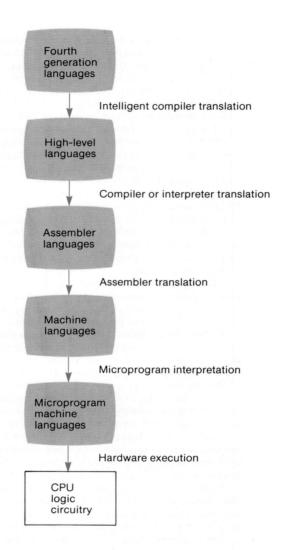

The three machine language instructions shown merely compute the sum of two one-digit numbers and store the results in a single storage location. Many more instructions would be needed to complete a computer program that would accept data from an input device, perform the addition operation, and transmit the results to an output device.

Assembler Languages

Assembler languages are the next level of programming languages and were developed to reduce the difficulties in writing ma-

FIGURE

9–3 Examples of four levels of programming languages

MACHINE LANGUAGE

Operation Code	Operand	
1010	11001	(Replace the current value in the accumulator with the value Y at location 11001.)
1011	11010	(Add the value Z at location 11010 to the value Y in the accumulator.)
1100	11011	(Store the value X in the accumulator at location 11011.)

ASSEMBLER LANGUAGE

Operation Code	Operand	
LD	Y	(Load Y into the accumulator)
AD	Z	(Add Z to the accumulator)
ST	X	(Store the result X)

HIGH-LEVEL LANGUAGE

FORTRAN: $X = Y + Z$
   COBOL: COMPUTE $X = Y + Z$

FORTRAN: GROSPAY = SALARY + COMMIS
   COBOL: ADD SALARY, COMMISSIONS GIVING GROSSPAY

FOURTH-GENERATION LANGUAGE

SUM THE FOLLOWING TWO NUMBERS
COMPUTE THE GROSSPAY OF ALL SALESPERSONS BY
SUMMING THEIR SALARY AND COMMISSIONS

Note: These programming language instructions might be used to compute the sum of any two numbers, as expressed by the formula $X = Y + Z$. The last two levels also demonstrate how English-like instructions can be, if X is defined as GROSSPAY, Y as SALARY, and Z as COMMISSIONS.

chine-language programs. The use of assembler languages requires the use of language translator programs called *assemblers*, which allow a computer to convert the instructions of such languages into machine instructions. Language translator programs were discussed in Chapter Seven. Assembler languages are frequently called "symbolic" languages, because symbols are used to represent operation codes and storage locations. Convenient alphabetic abbreviations called *mnemonics* (memory aids) and other symbols are used to represent operation codes, storage locations, and data elements. For example; the computation ($X = Y + Z$) in an assembler-language program might take the form shown in Figure 9–3.

Notice how alphabetical abbreviations that are easier to remember are used in place of the actual numeric addresses of the data.

This greatly simplifies programming, since the programmer does not need to know or remember the exact storage locations of data and instructions. However, it must be noted that an assembler language is still *machine-oriented,* since assembler-language instructions correspond closely to the machine-language instructions of the particular computer model being used. Also, notice that each assembler instruction corresponds to a single machine instruction so the same number of instructions are required in both illustrations. This "one for one" correspondence between assembler instructions and machine instructions is a major limitation of some assembler languages.

Assembler languages are still widely used as a method of programming a computer in a machine-oriented language. Most computer manufacturers provide an assembler language that reflects the unique machine-language *instruction set* of a particular line of computers. This characteristic is particularly desirable to *systems programmers*, who program systems software (as opposed to *applications programmers*, who program applications software) since it provides them with greater control and flexibility in designing a program for a particular computer. They can then produce more *efficient* software i.e., programs that require a minimum of instructions, storage, and CPU time to perform a specific data processing assignment.

Macro Instructions

Many assembler languages have been improved by the development of a **macro instruction** capability, which is also a basic concept in the design of high-level languages. A macro instruction is a single instruction that generates one or more machine instructions when it is translated into machine language. Macro instructions are provided by the software supplier or are written by a programmer for such standard operations as arithmetic computations and input/output operations. The format and sequence of instructions that will be generated by the "macro" must first be defined, but from then on a single macro can be written each time the desired sequence of instructions is required in a program. The development of a macro instruction capability for modern assembler-languages reduces the number of instructions required in an assembler language program, thereby reducing programming time and effort and the potential for programming errors.

For example; an assembler language with a macro instruction, capability would probably include a macro for the process of addition. The computation of $(X = Y + Z)$ might then take the form of a single macro instruction which would later be translated into the three machine instructions required for addition. The macro instruction might take the form: ADD Y, Z, X.

Subroutines

Assembler languages were further improved by the development of the **subroutine** concept, which is also used by all compiler languages. A *routine* is a sequence of instructions in a program that performs a particular data processing activity, such as an "input" routine, an "addition" routine, and "sort" routine. The term *subroutine* is used to describe a special-purpose routine or small program that can be made part of a larger "main" program to perform a standard data processing task. Subroutines eliminate the necessity of programming a particular data processing operation each time it is required in a computer program. For example, many input/output activities and mathematical and statistical calculations can be performed by using standard "preprogrammed" subroutines. Subroutines that check input data for errors or compute the square root of numbers are examples of the many types of subroutines that are frequently used.

A subroutine can be defined at the beginning of a program and then used whenever needed in the program by the use of a specific macro instruction, which causes the program temporarily to "branch" to the subroutine, perform necessary operations, and then return to the regular sequence of the program. A more widely used method of using subroutines involves storing many standard subroutines in an online *subroutine library* that is available to all computer users. In this method, the main program of a computer user would "call" a subroutine by the use of a particular macro instruction whenever the subroutine was needed. The computer would then branch to the specific subroutine in the subroutine library, perform necessary operations, and then return to the main program. The subroutine is, therefore, a powerful tool that minimizes programming effort and provides different computer users with an efficient method of performing common but special-purpose information processing operations.

High-Level Languages

High-level languages are also known as *compiler languages*. The instructions of high-level languages are called *statements* and closely resemble human language or the standard notation of mathematics. Individual high-level language statements are really macro instructions, since each individual statement generates several machine instructions when translated into machine language by high-level language translator programs called *compilers*, or *interpreters*. Most high-level languages are designed to be *machine-independent* (i.e., a high-level language program can usually be processed by computers of different sizes or manufacturers, depending on the compiler used).

High-level language statements do not resemble machine- or assembler-language instructions. Instead, they resemble the English language or mathematical expressions required to express the substance of the problem or procedure being programmed. The *syntax* (vocabulary, punctuation, and grammatical rules) and the *semantics* (meanings) of such language statements do not reflect the internal code of any particular computer but instead are designed to resemble English or mathematical expressions as closely as possible. For example, the computation $(X = Y + Z)$ would be programmed in the high-level languages of FORTRAN and COBOL as shown in Figure 9–3. It also illustrates how close to the English language high-level language statements can be.

Advantages of High-Level Languages

A high-level language is obviously easier to learn and understand. It takes less time and effort to write an error-free computer program or to make corrections and revisions that may be required. However, high-level language programs are usually less efficient than assembler language programs and require a greater amount of computer time for translation into machine instructions. These characteristics were considered serious limitations when high-level languages were first developed. However, the savings in programmer time and training, the increased speed and storage capacity of third- and fourth-generation computer hardware, and the efficiency and versatility of modern computer software have made high-level languages the most widely used programming languages for business, scientific, and other applications.

Since many high-level languages are machine-independent, programs written in a high-level language do not have to be reprogrammed when a new computer is installed, and computer programmers do not have to learn a new language for each computer they program. High-level languages have less-rigid rules, form, and syntax, thus reducing the potential for errors. Compiler- language translators include extensive diagnostic capabilities that assist the programmer by recognizing and identifying programming errors.

Types of High-Level Languages

High-level languages are frequently subdivided into "procedure-oriented" languages and "problem-oriented" languages. *Procedure-oriented languages* are general-purpose languages that are designed to express the "procedure" or logic of a data processing problem. Programmers do not have to concern themselves with the details of how the computer will process a program. Popular procedure-oriented languages are FORTRAN, COBOL, PL/1, BASIC, and Pascal.

Problem-oriented languages are designed to provide an efficient programming language for specialized types of data processing problems. The programmer does not even specify the procedure to be followed in solving the problem but merely specifies the input/output requirements and other parameters of the problem to be solved. Such programming simplicity is possible because the specialized nature of the language allows the problem-solving procedure to be "preprogrammed." Some examples of problem-oriented languages are: RPG, which is used to produce reports and update files, GPSS, which is used for simulation applications; LISP, which is used to process lists of symbolic data; and COGO, which is used for the solution of civil engineering problems.

Fourth-Generation Languages

The term **fourth-generation languages (4GL)** is used to describe a variety of computer-using languages. Other names used include: *natural language*; *very high level language* (VHLL); *nonprocedural* language, *actoral* language, *application-oriented* language; *user-oriented* language; and so forth. *Application* and *program generators* are also considered to be fourth-generation languages, as are the *query, report generator*, and *data manipulation* languages provided by most current database management systems. They allow users and programmers to interrogate and access the databases of a computer system using English-like statements. We will discuss DBMS related languages in Chapter 11. These languages are called *fourth-generation languages* (*4GL*) to differentiate them from machine languages (first generation), assembler languages (second generation), and high-level languages (third generation).

Natural languages are a type of 4GL that are very close to English or other human languages. Much research and development activity is still underway to develop languages that are as easy to use as ordinary conversation in one's *natural* language. Development of the complex language translator programs (sometimes called *intelligent* compilers) required to translate such natural languages into structured machine-language programs is also involved. Fourth-generation languages are called **nonprocedural languages,** because they do not require users to write detailed *procedures* that tell the computer *how* to do a *process* to produce a desired result. Instead, such languages allow users to simply tell the computer *what* result they want. Most fourth-generation languages are designed to support interactive programming and conversational computing using a personal computer or online computer terminal. They are also more tailored to users and user applications.

Figures 9–3 and 9–4 compare fourth-generation languages with earlier generation languages. In Figure 9–4, notice how brief and nonprocedural NOMAD is compared to BASIC to accomplish the same task; which is finding the average of a set of 100 numbers. Then notice how brief, nonprocedural, and conversational INTEL-LECT is compared to COBOL, or even to a formal query language, when you wish to accomplish a simple sales analysis task. Many other fourth-generation languages are available, such as SAVVY, FOCUS, SQL/DS, CLOUT, and RAPPORT, including several micro-computer versions. Many more are being developed and will be introduced in the coming years. Thus as we pointed out in the previous chapter, indications are that such languages will one day make computer programming as easy for you as ordinary conversation. Of course, there are major differences in the ease of use and technical sophistication of these products. For instance, INTELLECT and CLOUT impose no rigid grammatical or syntax rules, while SQL/DS requires concise structured statements. Figure 9–5 outlines some of the major categories of fourth-generation languages.

FIGURE 9–4 Comparing third and fourth generation languages

```
BASIC

  10 DIM X {100}
  20 LET S = 0
  30 READ N
  40 FOR I = I TO N
  50 READ X {I}
  60 LET S = S + {I}
  70 NEXT I
  80 LET A = S/N
  90 PRINT A
 100 DATA

     - - - - -
     - - - - -
 XXX END

NOMAD

     READ DIGITS LIST AVG{DIGITS}
```

```
COBOL {PROCEDURE DIVISION}:
ON ENDFILE {EMPLOYEE_FILE} GOTO WRAP_UP:
PUT SKIP LIST {'1982 MAY ACT SALES', '1982 MAY EST SALES',
   'DIFFERENCE', '% CHANGE'}'
DO WHILE {'1'B}:
   READ FILE {EMPLOYEE_FILE} INTO {EMPLOYEE_RECORD}
   IF EMPLOYEE_RECORD.DEPT = 'MEN'
      :EMPLOYEE_RECORD.DEPT = 'WOMEN'
   THEN DO:
      DIFFERENCE = Y1982_MAY_ACT_SALES - Y1982_MAY_EST_SALES;
      CHANGE = 100 *{Y1982_MAY_ACT_SALES - Y1982_MAY_EST
        _SALES}/ Y1982?MAY? ACT?SALES;
   PUT SKIP LIST{Y1982_MAY_ACT_SALES, Y1982_MAY_EST_SALES,
      DIFFERENCE, CHANGE};
   END;
 END;
WRAP_UP

FORMAL QUERY LANGUAGE:
PRINT 1982-MAY-ACT-SALES, 1982-MAY-EST-SALES,
   {1982 - MAY-ACT-SALES - 1982-MAY-EST-SALES},
   {100 {1982-MAY-ACT-SALES - 1982.MAY-EST-SALES}/
   1982-MAY-ACT-SALES}
WHERE {DEPT = 'MEN' OR DEPT = 'WOMEN'};

NATURAL LANGUAGE {INTELLECT}:
FOR THE MENS AND WOMENS DEPARTMENTS, COMPARE THE ACTUAL
AND FORECASTED SALES FOR LAST MONTH.
```

Sources: James Martin, *Application Development without Programmers* (Englewood Cliffs, N.J.; Prentice-Hall, 1982), p. 83; and Vincent C. Rouzino, "Natural Language Processor, *Computerworld,* September 5, 1983, pp. 45–52. Reprinted with permission.

FIGURE   9–5 Selected fourth-generation languages

	Suitable for End Users		Suitable for DP Professionals	
		Vendor		Vendor
Database query languages	QUERY-BY-EXAMPLE ON-LINE ENGLISH INTELLECT EASYTRIEVE CLOUT	IBM Cullinet Artificial Intelligence Pansophic Microrim	SQL QWICK QWERY GIS MARK IV DATATRIEVE	IBM CACI IBM Informatics DEC
Information retrieval systems	STAIRS CAFS	IBM ICL		

Report generators	NOMAD2
	
	QWICK QWERY
	EASYTRIEVE
	ORACLE
		D&B Computing
		  Services
		CACI
		Panasophic
		Distribution
		Man. Systems
			NOMAD2
			
			GIS
			RPG II and III
			ADRS
			MARK IV/
			  REPORTER
				D&B Computing
				  Services
				IBM
				Various sources
				IBM
				Informatics

Decision support tools	VISICALC MULTIPLAN LOTUS 1-2-3 SYSTEM W EXPRESS	Visicorp Microsoft Lotus Compuserve Management Decisions Inc.		
Application generators	MAPPER RAMIS II FOCUS NATURAL LINC	Univac Mathematica, Inc. Information Builders Software AG Burroughs	ADF RAMIS II DMS ADMINS II MANTIS IDEAL ADS	IBM Mathematica IBM ADMIN Inc. CINCOM ADR Cullinet

Very high-level programming languages	APL/DI
	NOMAD2
	
	NPL
	
	AME
		IBM
		D&B Computing
		  Services
		Desktop
		  Software
		IBM
			APL
			ADRS
			NOMAD2
			
			MANTIS
				Various sources
				IBM
				D&B Computing
				  Services
				CINCOM

Source: Adapted from James Martin, *An Information Systems Manifesto* (Englewood CLiffs, N.J.: Prentice-Hall, 1984), p. 34. Reprinted with permission.

REAL WORLD APPLICATION 9–1

4GL Productivity in the Real World

■ In the Chase Manhattan Bank an end-user department created a complex system for on line analysis of the Chase's management accounting data, using ADMINS 11. They accomplished this in 4 months with two people and claim that the DP department had estimated that they would take 18 months with 20 people and cost $200,000.

■ IBM in its own internal DP achieved a 27:1 improvement in development productivity with ADF over what would have been achieved with COBOL and IMS.

■ Playtex, Inc. claimed to have increased its rate of code writing from a small number of lines of COBOL per programmer per day to more than 1,000 equivalent lines per day using IBM's ADF/IMS.

■ The state of Connecticut used IBM's DMS to implement a Medicaid system with one systems analyst on his first assignment, one programmer, one trainee, and a medical social worker. The system was implemented in 18 person-months. Their head of analysis and programming estimates at least 10:1 productivity improvements over CICS on future applications.

■ The Bank of America has over 500 NOMAD applications running, almost all put up by end-users. Half a dozen NOMAD consultants and instructors supported them.

■ A benchmark version of a management reporting system, which had taken six months to program in COBOL in Heublein, was created in half a day with FOCUS.

■ Karsten, the golf club manufacturer, installed that company's most complex application (on-line order entry) in six weeks with IBM's DMS.

■ End-users at the Santa Fe Railroad created applications with Univac's MAPPER, bypassing the DP department, on such a scale that it resulted in Univac's largest computer order ever. The system has about 2,000 display terminals and printers.

■ John Deere, Inc., rewrote three existing CO-BOL applications using IBM's ADF. A new employee inexperienced in programming did the work. He achieved a productivity twice that of the COBOL team on the first application, 32 times that of the COBOL team on the second application, and 46 times that on the third.

■ Why do you think that the use of 4GL for program development shows such great gains in productivity over third generation languages such as COBOL?

■ Identify each 4GL mentioned above by relating it to the categories in Figure 9–5. What types of 4GL are mentioned?

Source: James Martin, *Application Development without Programmers* (Englewood Cliffs; N.J., Prentice-Hall, 1982), p. 30. Reprinted by permission.

POPULAR PROGRAMMING LANGUAGES

Hundreds of programming languages have been developed, many of them with humorous names, ranging from FRED and LOLITA to STRUDL and SYNFUL! However, the seven high-level languages most widely used for the coding of business application programs are FORTRAN, COBOL, PL/1, BASIC, Pascal, APL, and RPG. A brief analysis and illustration of each language is presented in the remainder of this chapter.

BASIC

BASIC (Beginner's All-purpose Symbolic Instruction Code) is a widely used programming language for time-sharing applications and microcomputer systems for small business use and for personal computing. BASIC was developed in the early 1960s at Dartmouth College as a simple, easily learned language that would allow students to engage in interactive (conversational) computing, using a time-sharing computer system. BASIC resembles a shortened and simplified version of FORTRAN. With only a few hours of instruction, a computer user can solve small problems by "conversing" with a computer, using a time-sharing terminal or small computer. BASIC has proven so easy to learn and use that it has quickly become a widely used programming language.

Several versions of BASIC have been developed. Such "extensions" of BASIC have transformed it into a more powerful language that can handle a wide variety of data processing assignments, using either batch processing or realtime processing. The extensions of BASIC have not been standardized, and differences exist in the BASIC compilers developed by many computer manufacturers and large computer users. However, the specifications for the most essential and widely used parts of BASIC (called Standard Minimal BASIC) were standardized in 1978. Versions with more advanced features (frequently called "Extended" BASIC) are more likely to contain differences in specifications and usage.

BASIC is a "friendly" language that is easy to learn and use, for several reasons. Entering data is easy because input is comparatively "free form" (i.e., no rigid input format is necessary). Output formats are also provided, if desired. Most BASIC compilers are really interactive *interpreters* which translate each BASIC statement immediately after it is typed in, and provide helpful diagnostics immediately if an error is sensed in a statement. Correcting an erroneous BASIC statement is also easy. Retyping the line number of such a statement and a corrected version of the statement is all that is necessary. All of these benefits must be balanced against the lack of a standard extended version of BASIC and its limited ability to handle large database processing applications.

BASIC Statements

There are five major categories of statements in fundamental versions of BASIC:

- *Arithmetic statements*. Arithmetic operations can be accomplished through the use of LET statements such as LET X = Y + Z. Arithmetic expressions may also be contained in a PRINT statement.

- *Input/output statements*. Fundamental input/output statements are READ, DATA, INPUT, and PRINT. READ statements read the contents of specific data fields from input data provided by DATA statements. INPUT statements accept input data directly from the terminal, while PRINT statements type output onto a terminal.

- *Control statements*. Fundamental control words are GO TO, IF . . . THEN, FOR, NEXT, and END. GO TO and IF . . . THEN statements alter the sequential execution of program statements by transferring control to another statement. FOR statements command the computer to repeatedly execute a series of statements (a "program loop") that are part of the computer program. NEXT statements are used to end program loops formed by the FOR statement, while an END statement terminates a BASIC program.

- *Other statements*. Two other BASIC statements are frequently used even in simple BASIC programs. REM statements are not translated by the compiler or executed by the computer. They are merely remarks and comments of the programmer that help document the purpose of the program and only appear in the program listing. The DIM statement is used in BASIC to specify the "dimensions" (rows and levels) or "arrays" of data items. It reserves the memory locations required to store each element in an array.

- *System commands*. BASIC system commands are not BASIC program statements but are "commands" to the operating system of the computer. They control the use of the BASIC compiler and the processing of BASIC programs. Two examples are:
  RUN: Tells the computer to execute a program.
  LIST: A listing of the statements in the program is printed or displayed.

Sample BASIC Program

Figure 9–6 illustrates the "realtime" programming of a simple BASIC program that computes an average exam score (arithmetic mean) of the scores received on an exam by students in a class. It outlines system commands of the user, responses of the computer, the statements of the BASIC program, the input data of exam scores, and the output of the computed average exam score. Student exam scores are contained in the two DATA statements used. The computer reads these one at a time until all are read and then automatically branches to statement 90 to compute the exam average, print it, and terminate the program.

FIGURE

9–6 Sample BASIC
program

```
*
/ EXECUTE BASIC
* BASIC OLD OR NEW? NEW
* NEW PROGRAM NAME? AVERAGE
READY
*10 REM PROGRAM TO COMPUTE AN AVERAGE EXAM SCORE
*20 LET C = 0
*30 LET T = 0
*40 READ X
*50 IF X = 999 THEN 90
*60 LET C = C + 1
*70 LET T = T + X
*80 GO TO 40
*90 LET A = T/C
*100 PRINT ""AVERAGE SCORE IS' ';A
*110 DATA 64,87,43,95,66
*120 DATA 75,59,97,67, 999
*130 END
*RUN
AVERAGE SCORE IS 72.5555
*BYE
```

A brief analysis of the program reveals the following activities:
1. A REM statement (10) documents the purpose of the program.
2. Two values, a counter (C) and an accumulator, (T) are cleared to zero. (Statements 20 and 30.)
3. Input of exam scores (X) is by a READ statement (statement 40) from exam scores contained in two DATA statements (statements 100 and 120).
4. After each score is read, it is tested to see whether the last item of data has been read. The 999 value serves as an end of data "flag" or "sentinel" for this purpose. (Statement 50.)
5. The counter (C) keeps track of the number of scores being read, while a running total (T) of scores is accumulated. (Statements 60 and 70.)
6. The program "loops" back to read another score. (Statement 80.)
7. When the computer senses the end-of-data condition (statement 50) it will transfer control or "branch" to statement 90.
8. The average exam score (A) is calculated by dividing the total scores accumulated (T) by the number of exam scores (C) tallied. (Statement 90.)
9. The average exam score is printed as output and the program terminates. (Statements 100 and 130.)

COBOL

COBOL (COmmon Business Oriented Language) is the most widely used programming language for business data processing.

It is an English-like language that was specifically designed to handle the input, processing, and output of large volumes of alphanumeric data from many data files that is characteristic of business data processing. COBOL was developed and is maintained by the Conference on Data Systems Languages (CODASYL), which is composed of representatives of large computer users, government agencies, and computer manufacturers. The specifications of the COBOL language are, therefore, subject to periodic revision and updating. The American National Standards Institute (ANSI) has developed standards for COBOL that recognize different "levels" and "modules" of COBOL. Standards for a "Minimum Standard" COBOL and "Full Standard" COBOL have also been developed.

COBOL's use of English-like statements facilitates programming, makes it easy for a nonprogrammer to understand the purpose of a particular COBOL program, and gives a "self-documenting" capability to COBOL programs. Of course, COBOL does have several limitations. It is a "wordy" programming language, which is more difficult for nonprofessional programmers to use than other languages such, as FORTRAN or BASIC. Since it has a business data processing and batch processing orientation, it is limited in its applicability to scientific data processing and interactive processing.

The COBOL Divisions

Every program written in the COBOL language must contain four major parts called "divisions," which are summarized below.
1. *The Identification Division*. Identifies the program by listing such information as the name of the program, the name of the programmer, the date the program was written, and other comments that identify the purpose of the program.
2. *The Environment Division*. Specifies the type of computer and peripheral equipment that will be used to process the program.
3. *The Data Division*. Describes the organization and format of the data to be processed by the program.
4. *The Procedure Division*. Contains the COBOL statements (called "commands") that describe the procedure to be followed by the computer in accomplishing its data processing assignment.

COBOL Procedure Division Statements

The Procedure Division is the section of a COBOL program that is most like programs written in languages like FORTRAN or BASIC. The major statements in this division of COBOL can be grouped into the following four categories:

REAL WORLD APPLICATION 9–2

Automobile Club of Michigan

"Our goal was to enable end-users to design and perform their specialty in their own way and to keep smaller, low-priority job requests out of this department," says Charles L. Cone, director of data processing for the Automobile Club of Michigan in Dearborn.

"To achieve this we gave terminals to a number of nonprogrammer accountants, actuaries, and others. They learned to use APL on those terminals, and within three months one of them even wrote a program that we sold.

"You can see, we began realizing our goal right from the start," he adds, "and today our end-users do a range of work that could not be accomplished through conventional data processing operations.

"Typically, we would get requests from our actuaries to revise new rating programs," says Cone. "We'd assign an analyst who studied the need, developed program specifications, and send them to the actuaries for agreement. They would come back with new requirements. The process would continue back and forth until we could finally agree on exactly what was needed.

"Now, we still run new rating programs because COBOL handles them more efficiently, but the actuaries develop and refine their own specs and formats through APL" he continues. "They come to us with a job that's ready for coding, and we save countless hours all around."

■ How are APL and COBOL being used in the example above? What are the benefits of such use?

Source: "Proof of the Pudding . . . ," *Data Processer*, September–October 1980, pp. 17–18. Reprinted with permission.

■ *Input/output statements*. The OPEN statement is used to prepare files to be read or written. The CLOSE statement terminates the processing of a file in a program. The READ statement reads a single record from a file that is named in the statement. The WRITE statement writes a single record that is named in the statement onto an open output file.

■ *Data movement statements*. The MOVE statement transfers data from one area of storage to another.

■ *Arithmetic statements*. The COMPUTE statement is used to perform arithmetic operations that are expressed in the form of a mathematical formula. The ADD, SUBTRACT, MULTIPLY, and DIVIDE statements also perform arithmetic computations.

■ *Control statements*. GO TO and IF statements alter the sequential execution of program statements by transferring control to another statement. The PERFORM statement transfers control temporarily to another part of the program, while the STOP statement halts the execution of the program.

Sample COBOL Program

Figure 9–7 illustrates the statements of a simple COBOL program that computes an average exam score similar to the previous BASIC example. Notice the large number of statements required by the first three COBOL divisions. However, notice how easy it is to read the English-like statements that detail the data processing procedures required by the program.

FIGURE

9–7 Sample COBOL program

```
 1 IDENTIFICATION DIVISION.
 2 PROGRAM-ID. SIX.
 3 AUTHOR. STEVE RUNDELL.
 4 ENVIRONMENT DIVISION
 5 INPUT-OUTPUT SECTION.
 6 FILE-CONTROL.
 7 SELECT CARD-FILE ASSIGN TO SYSIPT.
 8 SELECT PRINT-FILE ASSIGN TO SYSLST.
 9 DATA DIVISION
10 FILE SECTION.
11 FD CARD-FILE
12 RECORDING MODE IS F
13 LABEL RECORDS ARE OMITTED
14 DATA RECORD IS CARD-IN
15 01 CARD-IN.
16 02 NAME-IN PIC X(40).
17 02 SCORE PIC 999.
18 02 FILLER PIC X(37).
19 FD PRINT-FILE
20 RECORDING MODE IS U
21 LABEL RECORDS ARE OMITTED
22 DATA RECORD IS PRINT-LINE
23 01 PRINT-LINE PIC X(133).
24 WORKING-STORAGE SECTION.
25 77 STORE-NUMBER PIC 999 VALUE IS ZEROS.
26 77 STORE-SCORE PIC 99999 VALUE IS ZEROS.
27 01 PRINTER-LINE.
28 02 FILLER PIC X.
29 02 NAME-OUT PIC X(40).
30 02 FILLER PIC X(5).
31 02 SCORE-OUT PIC ZZ9.
32 02 FILLER PIC X(84).
33 01 AVERAGE-LINE.
34 02 FILLER PIC X(46).
35 02 AVERAGE PIC ZZ9.99.
36 02 FILLER PIC X(81).
37 PROCEDURE DIVISION.
38 OPEN-FILES.
39 OPEN INPUT CARD-FILE.
40 OPEN OUTPUT PRINT-FILE.
41 READ-CARDS.
42 READ CARD-FILE AT END GO TO END-OF-JOB.
43 ADD SCORE TO STORE-SCORE. ADD 1 TO STORE-NUMBER.
44 MOVE-DATA.
45 MOVE NAME-IN TO NAME-OUT.
46 MOVE SCORE TO SCORE-OUT.  WRITE PRINT LINE
47 FROM PRINTER-LINE. GO TO READ-CARDS.
48 END-OF-JOB.
49 DIVIDE STORE-NUMBER INTO STORE-SCORE
50 GIVING AVERAGE-SCORE. MOVE AVERAGE-SCORE
51 TO AVERAGE. WRITE PRINT-LINE FROM AVERAGE-LINE
52 AFTER ADVANCING 2 LINES.
53 CLOSE CARD-FILE.
54 CLOSE PRINT-FILE.
55 STOP RUN.
```

II FORTRAN

FORTRAN (FORmula TRANslation), developed in 1957, is the oldest of the popular high-level languages. As its name indicates, FORTRAN was designed primarily for solving the mathematical problems of scientists, engineers, and mathematicians. Therefore, FORTRAN programs use many mathematical statements consisting of algebraic types of expressions. Since FORTRAN cannot express certain input/output and nonnumeric operations, it is not suitable for many business data processing applications that require extensive processing of alphanumeric data files stored on many secondary storage devices. FORTRAN IV and FORTRAN 77, the latest versions of FORTRAN, are the most widely used programming languages for scientific and engineering data processing. However, FORTRAN is also used to program business computer applications that involve many mathematical calculations. For example, FORTRAN is frequently used to program quantitative business applications in operations research and management science that require such techniques as statistical analysis, mathematical models, network analysis, and linear programming.

Many versions of FORTRAN have been developed by computer manufacturers, and large computer users have added special features to their FORTRAN compilers. For example, several versions of FORTRAN have been developed to simplify the teaching of FORTRAN in schools or to facilitate interactive programming in FORTRAN. One of the most noticeable features of some versions (such as WATFOR, WATFIV, XTRAN, and FASTRAN) is that they allow "free form" input/output statements similar to the BASIC programming language. FORTRAN now exists in two standard forms: FORTRAN and Basic FORTRAN. These standard versions were developed by the American National Standards Institute in cooperation with the computer industry. Basic FORTRAN is a shorter and simpler version of standard FORTRAN and is probably the most widely used form of the FORTRAN language. The full standard version of FORTRAN is an extension of Basic FORTRAN, with advanced features and a greater variety of instructions.

FORTRAN Statements

There are five major categories of FORTRAN statements.

- *Arithmetic statements*. Arithmetic operations to be performed are described by statements closely resembling mathematical expressions.
- *Input/output statements*. Fundamental input/output words are READ and WRITE, which read or write the contents of specific data fields from or to a specified input/output unit.

■ *Specification statements*. The fundamental specification words are FORMAT and DIMENSION. FORMAT statements specify the "format" (size, type, number, etc.) of input or output data fields and records, while DIMENSION statements specify the dimensions (rows, columns, levels) of "arrays" of data items, and reserve the memory locations required to store each element in an array.

■ *Control statements*. Fundamental control words are GO TO, IF, DO, STOP, and END. GO TO and IF statements alter the sequential execution of program statements by transferring control to another statement, while DO statements command the computer to repeatedly execute a series of statements (a "program loop" or "DO loop") that are part of the computer program. STOP and END statements terminate a program.

■ *Subprogram statements*. Subprogram statements include CALL, RETURN, FUNCTION, and SUBROUTINE statements. Such statements allow programmers to develop and use the "preprogrammed" functions and subroutines that are stored in the "subroutine library" of the computer system.

Sample FORTRAN Program

Figure 9–8 illustrates the statements and flowchart of a short and simple FORTRAN program that computes the average (arithmetic mean) of the scores received on an exam by students in a class. Note that variable names like "COUNTR" are abbreviated due to one of the restrictions of FORTRAN. Notice how similar it is to the previous BASIC example program.

PL/1

PL/1 (Programming Language 1) was developed by IBM in 1965 as a general-purpose language that could be used by new generations of "general-purpose" computers for both business and scientific applications. PL/1 was designed to include the best features of FORTRAN and COBOL as well as some of the capabilities of assembler languages and ALGOL. PL/1 is not as widely used as COBOL and FORTRAN, primarily because other software suppliers were slow to develop PL/1 compilers. However, growth in the use of PL/1 is expected to continue as more computer users adopt it as their primary programming language. PL/1 has been criticized as being difficult to learn and inefficient to program. However, even its critics agree that it is a highly flexible "modular" general-purpose language, which is better suited to the requirements of "structured programming" than many other languages.

FIGURE 9–8 Sample FORTRAN program

```
01 COUNTR = 0.0
02 TOTAL = 0.0
03 READ (1,04,END=09) SCORE
04 FORMAT (F6.2)
05 COUNTR = COUNTR+1.0
06 TOTAL = TOTAL+SCORE
07 WRITE (2,04) SCORE
08 GO TO 03
09 AVRAGE = TOTAL/COUNTR
10 WRITE (2,11) COUNTR,AVRAGE
11 FORMAT (1X,F10.2,F6.2)
12 STOP
13 END
```

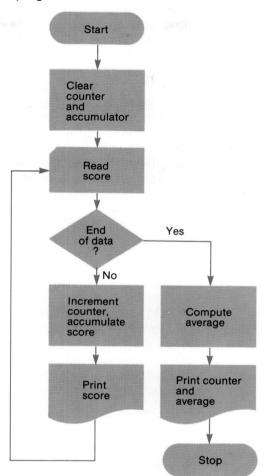

PL/1 attains its flexibility by providing features that support business, scientific, realtime, and systems programming applications and by using a "modular" design and a "default interpretation" capability. Thus PL/1 is organized into modules (or "subsets"), which are tailored to specific applications or levels of complexity similar to the levels and modules of ANSI COBOL. The default interpretation feature simplifies PL/1 programming, since it allows a programmer to ignore the specifications of the PL/1 modules not being used. The PL/1 compiler will automatically select the "default interpretation" for each specification that is required by a program unless it is specified by the programmer. Such "default specifications" are typically used by programs that do not require the advanced features of PL/1.

The modular design and default interpretation features of PL/1 facilitate its use by former users of FORTRAN, COBOL, and ALGOL, and by computer users with either simple or complex requirements. PL/1 can also be used by both large and small computers, since PL/1 compilers are available in modules that are tailored to the various PL/1 language subsets. Another feature of PL/1 that contributes to its flexibility and that facilitates program coding is a *free-form format* for program coding. No special coding form is required, and more than one statement can be written on a line. Also, different "modes" of data (integer, real, etc.) can be mixed in an expression. The PL/1 compiler automatically performs the necessary conversions so proper results are obtained. Finally, PL/1 allows free-form formatting of input and output (as in BASIC), though the format of the data can also be specified as in FORTRAN and COBOL.

PL/1 Statements

A PL/1 *statement* is defined as a string of characters terminated by a semicolon. A PI/1 program consists of several statements that are grouped into "blocks" or "groups." One or more blocks make up a "procedure"; while one or more procedures make up a complete PL/1 *program*. Five basic categories of statements used in simple PL/1 programs are outlined below:

- *Assignment* or *arithmetic* statements assign values and perform arithmetic and logical operations.
- *Input/output* statements transfer data between the CPU and input/output devices. When input/output is in the form of discrete data records in a file, the READ or WRITE statements are used. When input/output takes a "free form" format in the form of a continuous "stream" of characters, the GET and PUT statements are used.
- *Control* statements (such as DO, GO TO, and IF-THEN statements) control the execution sequence of the statements in a program. They perform comparisons and test conditions, transfer control within a program through a branching process, and direct the repetitive execution of statements by forming program loops.
- *Data declaration* statements specify the mode and format of data variables. For example, DECLARE statements specify the number of rows and columns in "arrays" of data and the "levels" of data fields in a data record.

■ *Program structure* statements identify and specify the types of program segments being used. A procedure "label" identifies a procedure. For example, the label "PAYROLL" might be used for a payroll calculation procedure. The procedure statement: PROCEDURE OPTIONS (MAIN), identifies a program as a simple "main" program, as opposed to a complex program with several procedures (subroutines) and other options. The END statement is the last statement of a PL/1 program.

Sample PL/1 Program

Figure 9–9 illustrates a simple PL/1 program to compute an average exam score, which is similar to programs in the previous programming language sections. Note the similarity of some of the statements to FORTRAN and COBOL. Also, a free-form "stream" format is used for input and output, which is reminiscent of BASIC. Note also the use of the "DO WHILE" statement, which forms a loop that is one of the basic program control structures of structured programming.

|| PASCAL

Pascal is a general-purpose language named after the noted mathematician and philosopher Blaise Pascal (1623–1662), who invented a practical calculating machine at age 19. Pascal was in-

FIGURE

9–9 Sample PL/1 program

```
AVERAGE: PROCEDURE OPTIONS (MAIN);
        /* PROGRAM FOR AVERAGE OF STUDENT SCORES */
        /* END OF SCORES IS INDICATED BY A NEGATIVE NUMBER */

        DECLARE (AVERAGE, TOTAL, VALUE, SCORE, COUNTER)
         FIXED DECIMAL;

          COUNTER = 0;
          TOTAL = 0;
          GET LIST (SCORE);
          DO WHILE (SCORE >=0);
           COUNTER = COUNTER + 1;
           TOTAL = TOTAL + SCORE;
           GET LIST (SCORE);
           END;
          AVERAGE = TOTAL/SCORE;
          PUT LIST ('AVERAGE SCORE IS', AVERAGE);
        END AVERAGE;
```

vented in the late 1960s by Professor Niklaus Wirth of Zurich, who was looking for an ideal language to teach the concepts of structured programming and top-down design. The small number of types of Pascal statements and the simplicity of its syntax have enabled systems programmers to write very efficient and "bug-free" Pascal compilers, which occupy a minimal amount of memory. This, together with its appeal as a logically complete and easy-to-learn language, explains the growing popularity of Pascal especially as implemented on microcomputers.

One of the major contributions of Wirth's work is his formalization of the concept of "type" as used in Pascal. Each item of data must have its *type* specified explicitly or implicitly in the module in which it appears. As data is passed from one module to another, their type must not change, and any attempt to write a program which violates this principal should result in an error message generated by the compiler. The main disadvantages of Pascal, in the opinion of many programmers, are the lack of a variable dimension facility for arrays and the lack of flexible file handling capabilities. Some implementations of Pascal, however, have provided extensions to the language that overcome these deficiencies. A notable achievement in the implementation of Pascal is a complete single-user software system for interactive use on microprocessors, developed by Kenneth L. Bowles of the University of California, San Diego, called UCSD Pascal.

Pascal Statements

A Pascal program consists of a program statement followed by declaration statements, which in turn are followed by executable statements. Statements are separated by semicolons, and the program is terminated with a period. Declaration statements are used to assign constants to identifiers, to declare the "type" of each variable, and to define procedures and functions (which, in turn, contain declarations and executable statements). Executable statements are described below:

- *Assignment* statements are used to assign a new value to a variable, usually as a result of a calculation.
- *Input/Output* statements move data between variables and either external devices or internal files defined by the user. Files are declared, specifying the "type" of data they are to contain. *Textfiles* represent data as a string of characters, such as English letters, or as decimal digits. Other files may hold numerical data with internal (binary) representation.
- *Compound statement*—a sequence of statements enclosed be-

tween BEGIN and END is considered to be a single statement in the logic of a program.

■ *Conditional statements* choose alternative flow of control based on the value of some expression. PASCAL includes the IF-THEN, the IF-THEN-ELSE and, for multiple alternatives, the CASE statement.

■ *Repetitive statements* repeat the execution of a statement or sequence of statements until some condition is met. These "structured statements" include the WHILE-DO, the REPEAT-UNTIL, and the FOR statement.

■ *GOTO statement*—there is rarely a need to transfer control from one place in a block of code to another using a GOTO, and it is considered poor programming practice to overuse this statement. Its presence often complicates attempts to verify the correctness of a program and violates structured programming concepts. However, the GOTO statement can be effectively used to abandon a section of a program from deep within a set of "nested" loops.

Sample Pascal Program

To illustrate Pascal programming, Figure 9–10 contains yet another program that finds the average of exam scores. It should be apparent from studying this program that Pascal bears more

FIGURE

9–10 Sample Pascal program

```
PROGRAM averagescore {infile,outfile};

VAR score, sum, average, count : real;
    infile, outfile : text;

BEGIN
    sum:=0.0; count:0.0;
    REPEAT
        read{infile,score};
        sum:=sum + score;
        count:=count + 1.0
    UNTIL eof{infile};
    average:=sum/count;
    write {outfile, ' Average score is', average}
END.
```

resemblance to PL/1 than to the other languages we have discussed. When comparing with the PL/1 program note that the Pascal program uses the control structure REPEAT-UNTIL; rather than the WHILE-DO, and that the repetition is terminated by the use of the standard function *of*, which returns the value "true" when an "end-of-file" has been reached.

‖ APL

APL (A Programming Language) is an interactive language originated by Kenneth Iverson of IBM. It is a sophisticated *problem-oriented* language designed for interactive problem solving. It uses a very concise symbolic notation, representing a large number of built-in functions and operators. This makes it possible to write complicated programs in a simple, concise form. APL uses a special character set, illustrated in Figure 9–11. This requires a terminal with an APL keyboard or APL character capability.

APL is a powerful language that can specify the processing of complex operations with just a few *operators* and variables. APL allows very efficient, interactive programming. Only a few operators are needed to define and manipulate large arrays of data. APL does not require the programmer to specify the detailed procedures needed to construct and control program loops that would be required in other high-level programming languages. IBM has offered an APL compiler since 1968. APL compilers are also available for other computer systems, including one offered by the Digital Equipment Corporation. APL is especially popular in time-sharing systems, and thus is available from several nationwide time-sharing networks. APL's concise, symbolic notation make its programs difficult to read, and it requires a large amount of primary storage. However, it is not difficult to learn to use APL for many common mathematical operations. The availability of APL from time-sharing networks has increased its use as a programming language.

FIGURE

9–11 A typical APL character set and keyboard

FIGURE

9–12 Examples of APL statements

APL Statement	Function
A ← □	Provide input data for A
A + B	A plus B
A ⌈ B	Find the larger of A and B
A ← 1 2 3	Assign this list (vector) of numbers to A
3 2 ρ A	Create a 3 × 2 matrix or two-dimensional array from the vector A

APL Statements

There are over 50 APL *operators* that can be used to construct APL statements. A few simple examples are shown in Figure 9–12.

Sample APL Program

Figure 9–13 illustrates a simple APL program to compute an arithmetic mean (average) of a group of numbers. As soon as the program was entered at a computer terminal, it asked for and was supplied with input data, and immediately computed the average.

FIGURE

9-13 Sample APL program

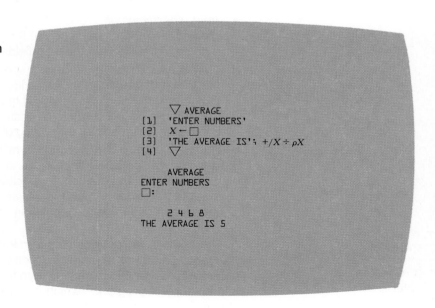

```
        ▽ AVERAGE
[1]  'ENTER NUMBERS'
[2]  X ← □
[3]  'THE AVERAGE IS'; +/X ÷ ρX
[4]  ▽

     AVERAGE
ENTER NUMBERS
□:

     2 4 6 8
THE AVERAGE IS 5
```

RPG

RPG (Report Program Generator) is a simple *problem oriented* language that was originally designed to generate programs that produced printed reports. However, several versions of RPG have been developed (such as RPG II and RPG III), which have made RPG a widely used language for report preparation, file maintenance, and other applications of small computer users. Since it is *problem-oriented*, rather than *procedure-oriented*, RPG does not require the use of statements that outline the procedure to be followed by the computer. Instead, a person using RPG fills out a few simple *specification forms* (or screens) which are used to describe (1) the form of the input data, (2) the input/output devices and data files to be used, (3) the format of output reports, and (4) the calculations that are required. Given these specifications, the RPG translator program generates a machine-language program that can perform the necessary processing and produce required reports.

RPG Specification Forms

Programming in RPG usually involves the use of at least three of the four specifications forms described below.

- *File description specifications*. This form defines the data files to be used. It identifies a file as input and/or output, specifies its characteristics, and assigns it to an input/output device.
- *Input specifications*. This form specifies the format of data records contained in an input file. It identifies and describes the records in the file, and the data fields that make up each record.
- *Output specifications*. This form specifies the format of the output report. It identifies and describes output data records and their fields. It may also specify (1) the use of titles and headings, (2) printer carriage control, (3) editing operations, and (4) the conditions which govern the writing of each type of output record.
- *Calculation specifications*. This form is used whenever a program requires mathematical operations, such as addition, subtraction, multiplication, and division. It specifies the mathematical operations to be performed and identifies the types of data which are to be used in each calculation.

The completed specifications forms represent the RPG "source program." Each line of a specifications form is entered into a computer system. The RPG compiler then translates the source program into an "object program," which consists of machine-language instructions that represent the data processing procedures required by the specifications forms. Thus the RPG compiler has "generated a program" that can produce reports and carry out other data processing assignments when appropriate input data are entered into the computer system.

REAL WORLD APPLICATION 9-3

The Department of Defense

Confronted with a costly and at times chaos-producing array of more than 1,000 computer languages, the Pentagon several years ago decided to develop a single tongue for the thousands of computers in the Department of Defense that aim weapons, watch for Soviet ballistic missiles, guide patrolling submarines and bombers, and relay critical information to battlefield commanders. The language has now made its debut, and the Pentagon hopes it will eventually spell the end of computer babel.

Called Ada, in honor of Augusta Ada Byron, considered the world's first computer programmer and the only legitimate daughter of English poet Lord Byron, the language will cut the Pentagon's cost of developing and maintaining computer programs and will increase the reliability and speed of computer networks.

Pentagon experts say that Ada, unlike many other languages, is simple to use since it mimics human languages by incorporating common words and phrases in its programming and printed answers. Further, it has the functional richness for a diverse and demanding set of applications and can be used on almost any computer. Ada is a "high-order" language, one in which a single command initiates a series of low-level computer operations. In most applications, a high-order language, such as Ada, is easier to use than a low-order one. Ada and the unique characteristics that make it so attractive to the military are the result of a two-year international competition held by the Pentagon, the first of its kind. It resembles an extension of the Pascal programming language and was submitted by Jean Ichbiah of Honeywell Bull in Paris and of the Honeywell Systems and Research Center in Minneapolis.

The Pentagon hopes to entice all computer users—not just the military. It wants universities to use Ada for teaching computer programming and software engineering, wants companies to exploit Ada in the commercial marketplace, wants foreign vendors to adopt Ada, and wants the NATO allies to accept it. The benefits for the U.S. military would be many, including easier hiring of programmers and easier purchasing of program-compatible equipment.

- What benefits are expected from the use of the Ada programming language by the Department of Defense? By other computer users?
- Do you think that Ada should become a standard computer language like COBOL? Explain.

Source: William J. Broad, "Pentagon Orders End to Computer Babel," *Science* 211, January 1981, pp. 31–33. Copyright 1981 by the American Association for the Advancement of Science. Reprinted with permission.

Sample RPG Program

We will conclude our introductory analysis of RPG by showing a simple RPG program that computes the same average of student test scores as the examples for previous languages. However, since many RPG compilers limit the size of data names and file names to six characters, data names are shortened to comply with such restrictions. Figure 9–14 illustrates the specifications forms of a simple RPG program that (1) reads an undetermined number of student test scores (SCORE), (2) calculates (AVRAGE by dividing TOTAL by COUNTR), and (3) prints the average score and its heading.

FIGURE

9–14 Sample RPG program

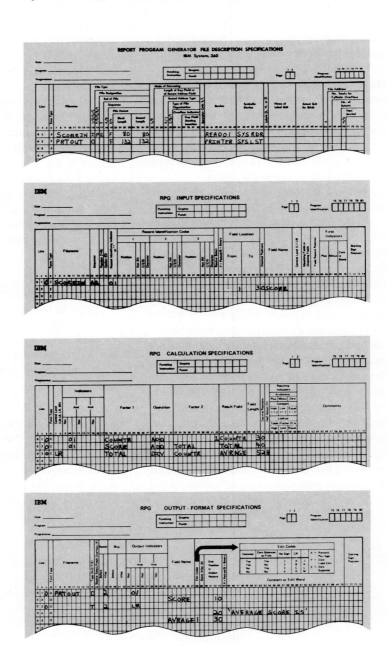

SUMMARY

- Programming languages are a major category of system software. They allow computer instructions to be written in a language that is understandable to both people and computers. The four major levels of programming languages are machine languages, assembler languages, high-level languages, and fourth-generation languages. Language translators, such as compilers and assemblers, are needed to convert assembler or high-level programming language instructions into machine-language instructions. High-level languages such as FORTRAN, COBOL, BASIC, PL/1, Pascal, APL, and RPG, are the most widely used programming languages for business applications.

- BASIC (Beginner's All-purpose Symbolic Instruction Code) is a simple, widely used programming language for time-sharing applications and microcomputer systems for small business use and for personal computing.

- COBOL (COmmon Business Oriented Language) is the most widely used language for business data processing. It is an English-like language specifically designed to handle the input, processing, and output of large volumes of alphanumeric data from many data files that is characteristic of business data processing.

- FORTRAN (FORmula TRANslation) is the most widely used language for scientific and engineering data processing. However, it is also used to program business computer applications that involve many mathematical calculations.

- PL/1 (Programming Language 1) is a general-purpose language designed for both business and scientific applications. It is a modular language that is better suited to the requirements of structured programming than many other languages.

- Pascal was designed specifically to incorporate structured programming concepts and to facilitate top-down design. It has become a popular programming language for microcomputers as well as for larger computer systems.

- APL (A Programming Language) is a sophisticated problem-oriented programming language designed for interactive problem solving. It uses a concise, symbolic notation and is especially popular for time-sharing applications.

- RPG (Report Program Generator) is a simple problem-oriented language primarily designed to generate programs that produce business reports. It uses specification forms instead of program statements.

KEY TERMS AND CONCEPTS

Machine language	Subroutine
Assembler language	BASIC
High-level language	COBOL
Fourth-generation language	FORTRAN
Natural language	PL/1
Procedural language	Pascal
Nonprocedural language	APL
Problem-oriented language	RPG
Macro instruction	

REVIEW AND APPLICATION QUESTIONS

1. How do machine, assembler, high-level and fourth-generation languages differ? Which type is easier to program and understand?
2. What is a macro instruction? How does it differ from a subroutine?
3. What are the advantages and limitations of high- level languages?
4. What is the difference between a procedural and nonprocedural language?
5. What is a fourth generation language? How is it used?
6. Will we ever be able to program a computer using a natural conversational language? Explain.
7. What are the major characteristics and uses of BASIC?
8. What are the major categories of BASIC statements? Give an example of each.
9. What are the major characteristics and uses of COBOL?
10. What are the functions of the major divisions of COBOL?
11. What are the major characteristics and uses of FORTRAN?
12. What are the major categories of FORTRAN statements? Give an example of each.
13. What are the major characteristics and uses of PL/1?
14. What are the major categories of PL/1 statements? Give an example of each.
15. What are the major characteristics and uses of Pascal?
16. What are the major categories of Pascal statements? Give an example of each.
17. What are the major characteristics and uses of APL?
18. How do APL statements differ from those of more conventional programming languages?
19. What are the major characteristics and uses of RPG?

20. How does programming in RPG differ from that required by the other languages described in this chapter?

APPLICATION PROBLEMS

1. If you have not already done so, read and answer the questions after each Real World Application in this chapter.
2. Compare and contrast the major characteristics of the programming languages discussed in this chapter. Which language would you recommend for business data processing? Explain.
3. The PL/1 language is supposed to have the best features of COBOL and FORTRAN and more. Yet it is still not a widely adopted language. Explain what you think the reasons for this are.
4. Have you used a programming language to write a simple program yet? Evaluate this language in terms of how much it facilitates structured programming, business applications, and user programming.
5. Look at Figure 9–2. Explain what it tells you about the different types of programming languages and about language translation processes. Where does the language you have used fit in?
6. Have you used a fourth-generation language yet? Explain how it differs from the high-level language you have used. Do 4GLs make other types of languages obsolete? Explain.

PART
4

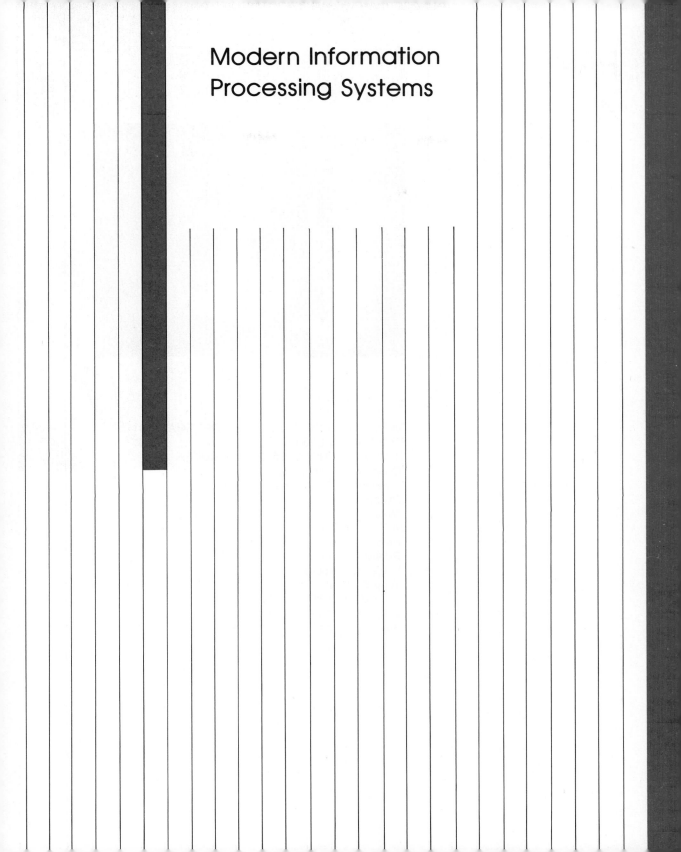

Modern Information
Processing Systems

CHAPTER 10

Introduction to Electronic Information Processing

CHAPTER OUTLINE

LEARNING OBJECTIVES

The purpose of this chapter is to promote a basic
understanding of electronic information processing by
analyzing the basic concepts, functions, and
capabilities of computer-based information processing
systems. After reading and studying this chapter, you
should be able to:

1. Identify several major types and capabilities of
   electronic information processing systems.
2. Provide several reasons for the use of batch
   processing and realtime processing systems,
   interactive processing, and time-sharing systems.
3. Use examples to illustrate several levels of realtime
   processing systems.
4. Explain the concept of distributed processing and
   the reasons for its importance in today's computer
   environment.

CAPABILITIES OF ELECTRONIC INFORMATION PROCESSING SYSTEMS

Do you realize that several basic types of electronic information processing systems are available to satisfy your information needs? That each of these can use several basic processing methods? That each system or method has several advantages and disadvantages? In this chapter, we will begin to clarify the many capabilities of modern electronic information processing systems.

Look at Figure 10–1. Its purpose is to emphasize the processing capabilities of modern information processing. It spotlights the changes that have occurred since manual data processing systems were replaced by electronic data processing systems, which relied on *batch processing* methods. In the late 50s and early 60s *realtime* EDP systems began to appear, along with *remote-access* batch processing systems. This trend accelerated with third- and fourth-generation developments, which made possible *distributed processing systems* of microcomputers, minicomputers, intelligent terminals, and other computers dispersed throughout an organization and interconnected by *data communications networks*. Other developments included *database processing systems*, which integrate the use and storage of data, and computerized *word processing systems*, where computers automate typing and other office communications. These developments emphasize the mutual dependence of data and information processing, storage and communications. Modern information processing systems have integrated *data processing* and *word processing*, and, with the help of advanced *telecommunications systems*. have begun to integrate the transmission and processing of data, words, images, and voices.

The diversity of information processing capabilities mentioned in the preceding paragraph and illustrated in Figure 10–1 can seem overwhelming. It is the cause of some of the confusion concerning the use of computers. However, such diversity is really the key to the amazing versatility of computers and the wide range of problems that they can handle. Therefore, you should realize that several varieties of electronic information processing may be needed to meet the information requirements of an organization. We will explore each of the major types of information processing systems and their capabilities in the four chapters of this part of the book.

COMPUTER PROCESSING CAPABILITIES

As Figure 10–1 illustrates, computer systems can have several basic processing capabilities, such as *concurrent processing, overlapped processing, dynamic job processing, multitasking, multiprogramming, and multiprocessing*. It is important that you gain a basic understanding of these capabilities, since they make possible the

FIGURE 10–1 Capabilities of electronic information processing systems

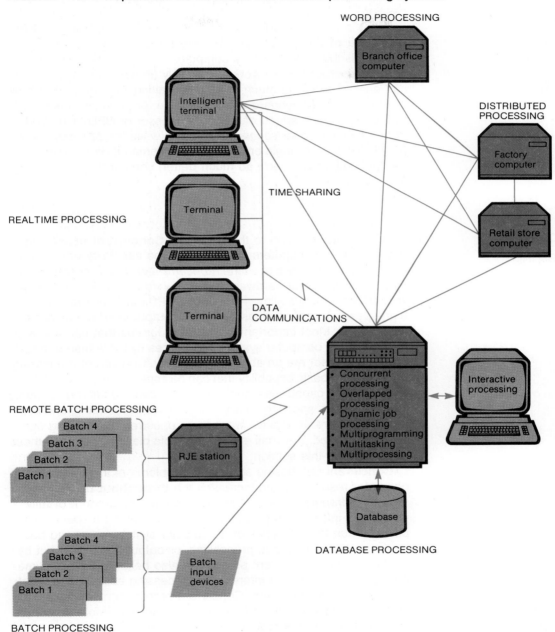

efficient and effective use of computers for modern information processing.

What is the basic objective of these different capabilities? **Efficient use of computer system resources**, is the answer. The problem is this. The CPU of a computer system or the microprocessor of a microcomputer works so quickly (in nanoseconds) that it can easily spend too much of its time waiting. Do you realize how slow the fastest keyboard user, disk drive, or printer is, compared to the processing speed of a microprocessor or CPU? Hundreds of thousands of *nanoseconds* can go by while the processor waits for you to key in a single one-character command! High-speed printers and disk drives don't do much better, comparatively speaking.

Concurrent Processing

What is the solution to this problem? **Concurrent processing** is the answer. Computers can be given the capability of working on more than one task at a time (*concurrently*). This is accomplished by a combination of hardware and software resources. Hardware with advanced capabilities—advanced CPUs and microprocessors, high-speed storage devices, and input/output interface devices— are needed. Most importantly, control programs that can manage the use of the computer system's resources by more than one task, program, or user are an absolute necessity. Concurrent processing, however, is a basic capability that can be implemented several ways. More specific capabilities, such as overlapped processing, dynamic job processing, spooling, multitasking, multiprogramming, and multiprocessing, are alternative ways that concurrent processing can be implemented. We shall examine the role played by each of these capabilities in this section.

Concurrent processing solves the problems of inefficient use of computer resources, and increases the **throughput** of a computer system. *Throughput* can be defined as the total amount of fully completed information processing occurring during a specific time period. Thus the efficiency of a computer system is gauged not by the speed of its input, processing, or output equipment but by its throughput. Concurrent processing also helps reduce the time it takes to complete an information processing assignment, which is called **turnaround time.** Concurrent processing techniques greatly increase the throughput of most business information processing systems and reduce turnaround time because most business applications require many input/output operations that can waste large amounts of CPU time.

Overlapped Processing

A computer system with an **overlapped processing** capability can increase the use of its central processing unit by overlapping input/output and processing operations. Input/output interface hardware (such as buffers, I/O control units, and channels) and *system software* (data management programs of an operating system) make such processing possible. Overlapped processing is the opposite of *serial processing*, where the processing function cannot take place until the input function is completed, and the output function must wait until the processing function is completed. As a result, the input, processing, and output equipment of a computer system are idle for large portions of the time necessary to complete a data processing assignment. A computer system is *input/output bound* if its CPU must wait while its input/output equipment carries out its functions, and it is *process-bound* (or CPU-bound) if the input/output devices have to wait while the CPU is involved in computations and other operations. See Figure 10–2.

FIGURE 10–2 Serial and overlapped processing

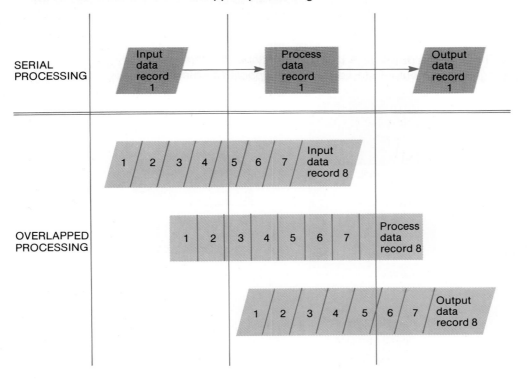

Overlapped processing frequently involves an activity known as **spooling** (simultaneous peripheral operation online), which allows input and output operations to occur simultaneously with processing operations. Input data from low-speed devices is stored temporarily on high-speed secondary storage units. On large computer systems, this is typically magnetic disk or tape units. On microcomputers, it may be magnetic bubble devices or a reserved section of RAM circuits. Data forms a *queue* (waiting line), which can be quickly accessed by the CPU. Output data can also be transferred quickly by the CPU to high-speed, storage units and form another queue waiting to use slow-speed devices such as a printer or a card punch. The operating system needs to have a special utility program to control the spooling process, or it must be purchased as a separate software package. See Figure 10–3.

Dynamic Job Processing

Some operating systems allow computers to perform **stacked job processing**, in which a series of data processing jobs are executed continuously without operator intervention being required between each job. Necessary information is communicated to the operating system through the use of a *job control language* (JCL),

FIGURE 10–3 The spooling process: A user can continue to interact with an application program while output stored on disk is *spooled* to the printer.

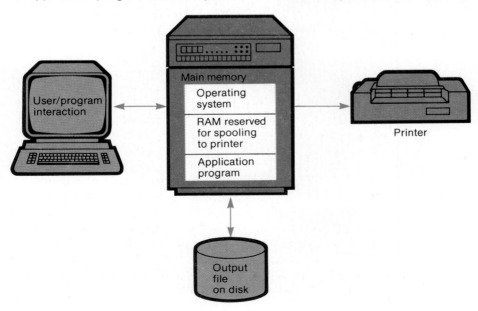

consisting of various job control statements. JCL statements provide the operating system with such information as the sequence in which jobs are to be processed and the input/output devices required for each job.

Dynamic job processing is a term used to describe the constantly changing computer operations required by modern electronic information processing and provided by many current operating systems. In dynamic job processing, jobs are not processed sequentially in stacks but are processed according to a constantly changing *priority interrupt system*. A system of priorities is established for jobs, job steps, and various operational situations, which indicate when the CPU can be "interrupted" in its processing and diverted to another task. For example, an error indication or a signal from the computer operator would have a higher priority than a payroll processing computation.

A priority interrupt system usually requires *time slicing,* in which each job is allocated a specified "slice" of CPU time (frequently a fraction of a second) as measured by the electronic clock of the computer. Jobs are interrupted if they exceed their allocated time slice, are replaced with a waiting job, and are assigned another priority for later processing. A priority interrupt system usually results in a waiting line, or *queue*, of jobs that may be stored in primary storage or in direct access storage devices called "swapping" storage. Thus, dynamic job processing involves the continual swapping of jobs and job steps between the primary storage and the swapping storage on the basis of a continually revised queuing and priority interrupt schedule maintained by the operating system.

Multiprogramming versus Multiprocessing

Multiprocessing—the ability of a multiprocessor computer system to execute several instructions simultaneously—should not be confused with the concept of *multiprogramming*. **Multiprogramming** can be defined as the ability of a uniprocessor computer system to process two or more programs in the same period (i.e., *concurrently*). But only one instruction at a time is executed by the central processing unit. However, the CPU switches so quickly from the execution of instructions from one program to another that it gives the effect of simultaneous operation. Multiprogramming is accomplished by storing all or part of several programs in primary storage and then switching from the execution of one program to another in an *interleaving* process. This is done by an enhanced operating system or operating environment program, which transfers entire programs or segments of programs and data into and out of main memory from secondary storage devices. It also allows

REAL WORLD APPLICATION 10–1

The Reserve Fund

Mutual funds require an extraordinary degree of transaction processing and information control. The Reserve Fund, Inc., is no exception. This $2 billion money market fund handles more than 5,000 transactions a day. Brokers and customers are calling constantly to check the status of their accounts to make certain that their temporary cash balances are always working.

To meet this demand for data, Reserve Fund has turned to Honeywell's transaction processing system, TPS-6. Together with four Level 6 computers, TPS-6 makes it possible to do immense amounts of production work while simultaneously developing new programs. The four Level 6 systems give Reserve Fund all the flexibility and back-up it needs. Information flows easily.

For example, terminals are used to enter purchase orders and to provide quick answers to customer inquiries. At the same time, the system is also maintaining an ongoing record of all transactions.

As you'd expect, security is a great concern. But thanks to features built into TPS-6, Reserve Fund has developed effective safeguards. Every operator has an ID number, a password, and a specific security clearance. Access is carefully regulated. As a further precaution, the system has a built-in time-out feature that automatically clears the screen after a specified period.

Thanks to capabilities like screen data formatting and multiple key access to files, Reserve Fund has been able to tailor a system that's both effective and efficient. Current information is always available. When it's needed. Where it's needed.

- What processing capabilities does the Reserve Fund need for its transaction processing system?
- What controls are features of this system?

Source : Courtesy Honeywell.

---

arithmetic or logic operations for one program to be performed while simultaneously performing input/output or storage operations for several other programs.

Also considered a form of multiprogramming is **multitasking**, which involves the concurrent use of the same computer to accomplish several different information processing *tasks*. Each task may require the use of a different program, or the concurrent use of the same copy of a program by several users. Each *task* in this context is defined as a unit of work that may involve the execution of a separate program, subprogram, subroutine, I/O operation, etc. A multiprogramming capability allows a computer system to better utilize the time of its central processing unit, since a large part of a CPU's time can be wasted as it waits between jobs. When dynamic job processing involves multiprogramming, the operating system must allocate portions of primary storage among various jobs and job segments. The operating system subdivides primary storage into several fixed or variable *partitions* or into a large number of

FIGURE

10–4 Multiprogramming
with fixed partitions

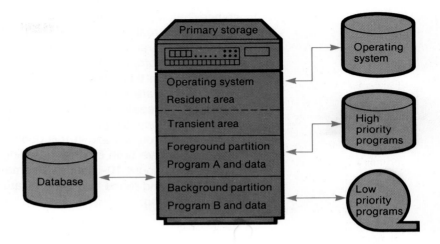

pages. This allows several programs to be processed during the same period of time.

Figure 10–4 shows the allocation of primary storage into three *fixed partitions*: one for the operating system, a *foreground* partition for high-priority programs, and a *background* partition for low- priority programs. Typically, high-priority programs have extensive input/ output requirements but require only small amounts of CPU processing time. Low-priority jobs usually have extensive CPU processing requirements or are routine jobs that do not require immediate processing. For example, a time-sharing system with many remote terminals may use the foreground partition, while stacked job processing might take place in the background partition. Figure 10–4 shows that application programs and parts of the operating system are stored on direct access storage devices, such as magnetic disk units, so they can be shuttled back and forth between primary and secondary storage devices. Notice that only part of the operating system "resides" continuously in the *resident area* of primary storage. Other programs of the operating system are transferred to a *transient area* of primary storage from a magnetic disk *system residence device* whenever they are needed.

BATCH AND REALTIME PROCESSING

There are two basic types of electronic information processing: **batch processing** and **realtime processing.** All electronic information processing systems in use today usually have a combination of characteristics that fall into *one* or *both* of these two categories, though many other terms may be used to describe them. For instance, batch processing is also known as *sequential, serial*, or *offline*, while realtime processing may also be called online, inline, direct access, random access, interactive, transaction, or even *online, realtime* processing! Though even experts disagree in using these terms, in this book **batch processing systems** are those in which *data are accumulated* and *processed periodically*, while **realtime processing systems** are those which *process data immediately after they are generated and can provide immediate output to users*. As you will see in this book, many forms of information processing have both batch processing and realtime processing capabilities. Figure 10–5 outlines some of the important concepts, capabilities, and terms that differentiate batch processing and realtime processing.

Batch Processing

In a batch processing system, data are accumulated over a period of time and then processed periodically. Batch processing usually involves:

- Gathering *source documents* such as sales orders or invoices into groups called *batches*.
- Recording transaction data on an *input medium*, such as floppy disks, punched cards, or magnetic tape.

FIGURE 10–5 Batch versus realtime processing

Characteristics	Batch Processing	Realtime Processing
Processing of transactions	Transaction data is recorded, accumulated into batches, sorted, and processed periodically	Transaction data is processed as generated
File update	When batch is processed	When transaction is processed
Response time/turnaround time	Several hours or days after batches are submitted for processing	A few seconds after each transaction is captured
Processing mode	Periodic processing of batches when scheduled	Interactive processing
Access to processor	Primarily local access Some remote access	Primarily remote access using data communications Some local access
File access method	Sequential access	Direct access
File organization method	Sequential Indexed sequential	Random Indexed sequential
File storage medium	Magnetic tape Some magnetic disk	Magnetic disk
File status between processing	Offline, some online	Online
Control logs and backup files	Created as part of processing	Capability must be added to the system

- Sorting the transactions in a *transaction file* into the same sequence as the records in a sequential *master file*.
- Computer processing that results in an updated master file and a variety of *documents* (such as customer invoices or paychecks) and *reports* (such as control and management reports).

In batch processing, not only are the data for a particular application or job accumulated into batches but usually a number of different jobs are accumulated into batches and *run* (processed) periodically (daily, weekly, monthly). The rationale for batch processing is that data and jobs should be grouped into batches and processed periodically according to a planned schedule to efficiently use the computer system, rather than allowing data and jobs to be processed in an unorganized, random manner. Of course, this efficiency, economy, and control are accomplished by sacrificing the immediate processing of data for computer users. In a typical example of batch processing, the banking industry usually accumulates all checks that are deposited at banks during the day into batches for later processing each evening. Thus, customer bank balances are updated on a daily basis and many management reports are produced daily.

Figure 10–6 illustrates a batch processing system where batches of data, computer programs, and master files for several different jobs are processed periodically according to a schedule set up by the computer operations department of an organization. The master files are updated by making any necessary changes to the records in the files based on the contents of the batches of input data. Output takes the form of required reports and updated master files. For example, the data could be in the form of batches of sales transactions, income and expense figures, or units of production. Reports produced could be reports required by management, such as sales analysis reports, income and expense reports, or production status reports.

Remote Access Batch Processing

Batch processing systems can have a *remote access capability*, frequently called **remote job entry** (RJE). Batches of data can be collected and converted into an input medium at *remote* locations that are far away from the computer. Input/output devices at these locations (called RJE stations) are then used to transmit data over communications circuits to a distant computer. The batches of data are then processed, thus producing updated master files as well as information that is transmitted back to the remote terminal. Remote access batch processing can also involve *remote offline input/output*. For example, data can be transmitted from the keyboard

FIGURE 10–6 A batch processing system example

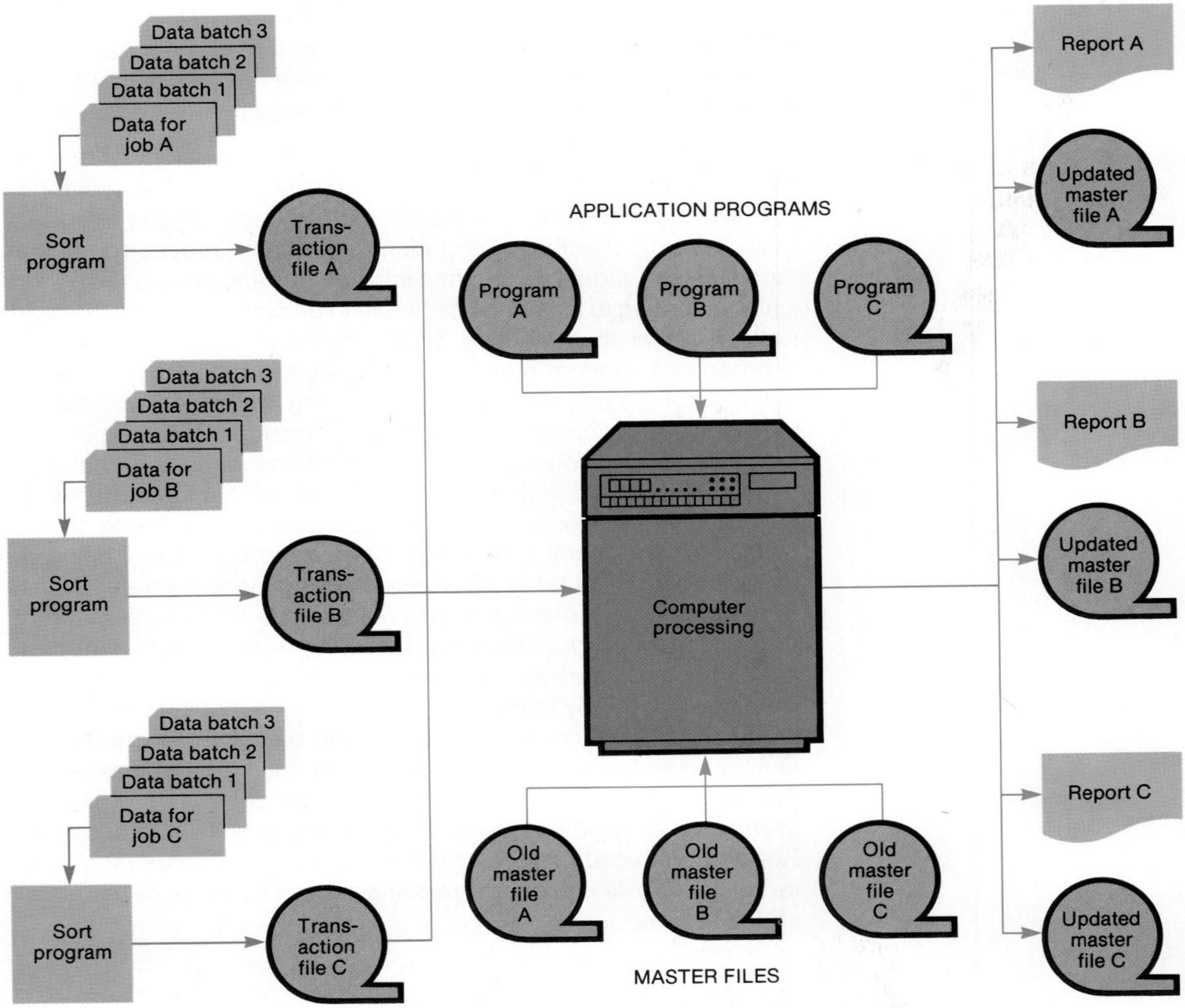

of a terminal to an offline magnetic tape unit where they are accumulated for subsequent batch processing.

Advantages and Disadvantages

Batch processing is an economical method when large volumes of data must be processed. It is ideally suited for many applications where it is not necessary to update files as transactions occur, and where documents and reports are required only at scheduled intervals. For example, customer statements may be prepared on a monthly basis, while payroll processing might be done on a weekly basis. Many batch processing systems still make heavy use of magnetic tape, which is a low-cost medium for simple sequentially organized files. A final advantage of batch processing is the fact that transaction files and old master files, which are created as part of regular processing, also serve as excellent control and backup files.

Batch processing has some real disadvantages. Much of them stem from the use of sequentially organized files stored on sequential access media, such as magnetic tape. Transactions must be sorted and an entire file must be processed, even if only a few records are affected. Also, master files are frequently out-of-date between scheduled processing, and immediate updated responses to inquiries cannot be made. For these reasons, more and more computer applications use realtime processing systems. However, batch processing systems are still widely used, and some of their disadvantages are overcome by using direct-access files and realtime processing for some data processing functions. *For example,* many information processing systems with large volumes of transactions use the indexed sequential method of file organization (ISAM) to store data sequentially on direct access storage devices such as magnetic disks. They then use batch processing to update the files on a periodic basis, but they can give immediate responses to user inquiries concerning information stored in the file.

Realtime Processing

In full-fledged realtime processing systems, data are processed as soon as they are originated or recorded, without waiting to accumulate batches of data. Data are fed directly into the computer system from *online terminals*, without having to be sorted, and are always stored *online* in *direct access files*. The master files are always up-to-date since they are updated whenever data are originated, regardless of its frequency. Responses to user inquiries are immediate, since information in the direct access files can be retrieved almost instantaneously. Heavy use is made of *remote terminals* connected to the computer using *data communications* links. The realtime processing system concept is shown in Figure 10–7.

An example of a realtime processing system is shown in Figure 10–8. Notice how POS terminals are connected by data communications links for immediate entry of sales data and control responses (such as customer credit verification). The online direct access customer, inventory, and sales master files are all immediately updated to reflect the effect of sales transactions. The application programs required for sales transactions processing, file updates, and inquiry/

FIGURE

10–7 Realtime processing
system concept

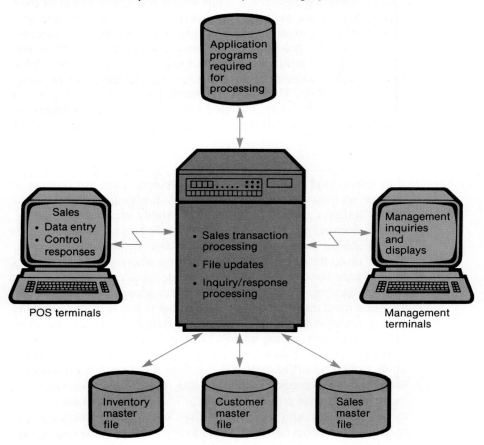

INPUT/OUTPUT PROCESSING SECONDARY
STORAGE

FIGURE 10–8 Example of a realtime processing system

response processing are brought into the CPU from a direct-access program file as needed. Finally, management personnel use data communication links to terminals located throughout the organization to make inquiries and receive displays concerning customer sales potential, inventory status, and salesperson performance.

Realtime processing is frequently called **online**, or **direct access processing**, since both of these capabilities are required of realtime processing systems. However, use of such terms can be misleading because we have seen that **batch processing systems** can use *online direct access files* in the processing of batches of data. As a compromise, experts may use the term *online realtime* (OLRT) processing. Part of the reluctance to use the term *realtime* stems from its former narrow meaning as promoted by the U.S. Department of Defense. In that context, not only had data to be processed immediately but the results of processing had to be instantly available to control an ongoing process. That definition could then be used to describe only a limited number of applications, typically process control and military defense systems. However, advances in computer hardware and software capabilities have made a realtime capability applicable to many of the functions of modern information processing systems. In this context, **realtime processing** means that not only is input data processed immediately but output results are available fast enough to meet the immediate information needs of users. Many modern information processing systems can easily meet this criterion, whether they rely on microcomputers or mainframe computer systems.

Other writers use the term **interactive processing** to emphasize the interactive capability of many realtime systems, or the term **transaction processing** to emphasize that individual transactions are processed as they occur and are not accumulated into batches. Some of the semantic confusion arises from the fact that there can be different combinations of realtime and batch processing capabilities, depending on the information processing functions to be performed. Thus many current information processing systems are combinations of batch and realtime processing subsystems. Again, a typical example is the banking industry, which updates checking accounts on a daily batch basis, but uses realtime processing to allow immediate response to inquiries concerning customer bank balances stored on online direct-access files. To help clarify this situation, you should understand that realtime processing systems can be subdivided into the five levels illustrated in Figure 10–9 and summarized below.

■ **Inquiry/Response Systems**. The main function of an inquiry system is information retrieval. The user of a realtime inquiry system

FIGURE

10–9 Levels of realtime processing systems, with examples

Level of Realtime Processing	Business Examples
Inquiry/response	Request customer balance in bank checking accounts using online audio-response terminals.
	Request number of parts on hand in inventory using on-line visual display terminals.
Data entry	Collect sales data with online terminals and record on magnetic tape for later processing.
	Capture checking account transactions handled by bank tellers and record on temporary file for control purposes.
File processing	Update customer files due to sales transaction data captured by online terminals.
	Update work-in-process inventory files due to production data captured by data recording terminals on the factory floor.
Full capability	Process airline reservations using online terminals and update online flight reservation files.
	Process data arising from the purchase or sale of securities using online terminals and update online securities transaction files.
Process control	Control petroleum refinery process with online sensing and control devices.
	Control of electric power generation and transmission.

wishes a quick response to a request for information; *for example*, the current balance in a particular bank checking account.

■ **Data Entry Systems**. The main function of a data entry system is the immediate but temporary collection and recording of data until they can be processed at a later date. Thus the realtime data entry system is designed to perform only the collection, conversion, and storage functions of information processing, leaving the manipulation function to a batch processing system. *For example*, some retail stores use online "point-of-sale" terminals to capture and record sales data on magnetic tape or disk during the day for subsequent remote batch processing at night.

■ **File Processing Systems**. File processing realtime systems perform all of the system functions of information processing except the communication function. Thus, data are collected, converted, manipulated, and then stored— resulting in an immediate and continual updating of files. The communication function may be performed by subsequent batch processing, which produces reports and other output, or by a realtime inquiry system, which interrogates the files.

For example, customer files could be updated immediately by POS terminals, but customer statements and credit reports could be done only on a periodic basis.

■ **Full Capability Systems**. The full capability realtime processing system provides immediate and continuous performance of all of system functions of information processing. It can thus perform the services of any of the other levels of realtime systems. *Example*: the reservation systems of the major airlines are full capability systems, since they process passenger reservations in realtime using online terminals at airline offices and airports. Realtime processing systems with a full processing capability are being installed or developed by almost all users of large or medium-scale computers.

■ **Process Control Systems**. A particular type of full capability realtime processing system is the process control system, which not only performs all information data processing functions but, in addition, uses its information output to control an ongoing physical process. *Examples* are industrial production processes in the steel, petroleum, and chemical industries.

Advantages and Disadvantages

Realtime processing systems provide immediate updating of files and immediate responses to user inquiries. Realtime processing is particularly important for applications where there is a high frequency of changes that must be made to a file during a short time to keep it updated. Nonsequential methods of file organization are used, and data are stored on direct-access storage devices. Thus, input data does not need to be sorted, and only the specific records affected by transactions or inquiries need to be processed. Also, several files can be processed or updated concurrently, since transaction data does not have to be sorted into the sequence of any particular file.

Realtime processing has its disadvantages. Direct access storage devices such as hard magnetic disks are still more expensive than the magnetic tape used in many batch processing applications. Because of the online, direct access nature of realtime processing, special precautions must be taken to protect the contents of data files. Thus many realtime systems have to use magnetic tape files as *control logs* (to record all transactions being made) or as *backup files* (by periodically making a magnetic tape copy of a file). Also, more controls have to be built into the software and data processing procedures to protect against unauthorized access or accidental destruction of data. Thus the many advantages of realtime processing must be balanced with the extra costs and security precautions that are necessary. However, most computer-using firms are willing

REAL WORLD APPLICATION 10–2

Commercial Office Products Company

Commercial Office Products (COPCO) is a large distributor of office supplies in the Midwest. Based in Denver, the firm handles receiving, order processing, and distribution from four different locations. With the business growing at over 35 percent per year, David Elliott, president, noticed that his batch system could not keep pace with the demands of his business. After extensive investigation, Mr. Elliott chose an HP 3000 system along with an application package, developed in conjunction with Information Resources of Denver to solve his data processing needs.

"We chose the HP 3000 because of its data base capability, QUERY, virtual memory for multiprogramming, in general for the capabilities of the entire system. The system is able to do multiple tasks, such as batch and transaction processing at the same time. It also has the ability to do multiple language processes.

"We use the system interactively in every area of our business. Twenty-eight terminals are distributed in order entry, purchasing, receiving, will-call department, cash receipts, collection, program development, and in the executive offices. We even have two customers who have terminals in their offices. They simply phone into the system and place the orders themselves. This saves us considerable cost.

"The system has benefited COPCO in a number of ways. Orders are taken and entered into the system over the telephone. Within seconds our customers can get information on stock and price as well as getting definitive answers about the status of their orders. The system has given us the flexibility to get immediate departmentalized reports, allowing me to keep better track of the business. With the HP 3000 I am now able to predict nearly 100 percent of our annual purchases and sales.

"QUERY (the data base inquiry language) is fantastic. We do all of our reporting with it. QUERY gives me instant access to all of the information relating to my company. Sales, total sales per salesman, per market, by Zip code, whatever, QUERY makes it easy to do. And it takes but a few hours on instruction, at the most, to learn to use.

"Our programmers love the system. Because it is an interactive system, they have access to all of the capabilities of the machine at every terminal. The system is easy to use and the capabilities proved unreal. The software and data base components have great flexibility in allowing users to develop their own applications.

"The HP 3000 has been the solution for COPCO. We can now process an order in a matter of minutes and send the bill out with the order. Because of this, accounts receivable has dropped from 48 days to 38 days. At the same time, inventory turnover has climbed from about five to eight times per year. In addition, we have saved money by reducing our inventory from 21,000 to 7,000 items while, at the same time, our order-fill efficiency has gone up to 96 percent. With the new system we are beating our competition by responding quicker to customer needs."

- Why did COPCO switch from a batch processing system to a realtime, interactive system? What benefits have occurred?
- What levels of realtime systems and types of interactive processing are demonstrated in this example?

Source: Courtesy Hewlett-Packard.

to pay this price, since the use of realtime processing continues to increase in modern information processing systems.

Interactive Processing

An important characteristic of many realtime processing systems is that they provide an **interactive processing** capability. You can use a microcomputer or online terminal to interact with a computer on a realtime basis. This is frequently a **menu-driven** process (i.e., you select options from a series of menus until you accomplish your particular information processing task). See Figure 10–10. The four major types of interactive processing are:

- **Inquiry/response** applications, where a request for information is entered through the keyboard and the answer is immediately displayed on the screen.
- **Conversational computing**, which uses *interactive software packages* to carry on a dialogue and help a user solve a problem or accomplish a particular job on the computer.
- **Online data entry**, which provides sophisticated data entry as-

FIGURE 10–10 An example of menu-driven interactive processing

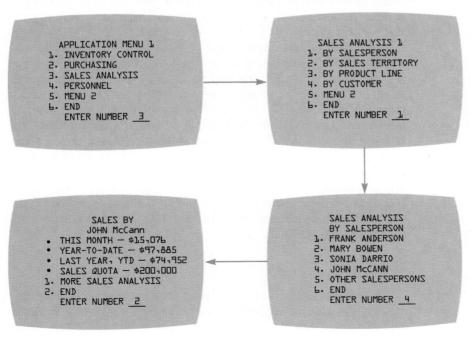

sistance to operators. For example, a data entry system is usually a *menu-driven* approach, which *prompts* and guides the data entry operator with menu-selecting choices, specialized formats that help an operator with prompting messages, and sophisticated editing with error-control reminders.

- **Interactive programming**, where a programmer uses a terminal to develop and test the instructions for a program with the real-time assistance of the computer. It is an important form of interactive processing that has become the primary form of programming for professional programmers.

Time-Sharing

Want to share the use of a computer in realtime? You can by using a **time-sharing system**. Time-sharing is the sharing of a computer system by many users in different locations at the same time through the use of online input/output terminals. Time-sharing systems "interleave" the data processing assignments of many users by giving each user a small, frequently repeated "slice" of time. Time-sharing systems operate at such fast speeds that each user has the illusion that he or she alone is using the computer, because of the seemingly instantaneous response. The ability of time-sharing systems to service many users simultaneously is sometimes hard to comprehend. However, one must remember that a computer operating in nanoseconds speeds can process millions of instructions per second.

Remote batch processing and *realtime processing* can be accomplished using time-sharing systems. A time-sharing user could accumulate batches of data and periodically process them, using input/output devices ranging from small terminals to larger batch processing stations, to small satellite computer systems. However, time-sharing systems are currently used primarily for realtime processing applications. Time-sharing systems can easily handle the inquiry/response, data entry, and file processing types of realtime processing assignments from users at work sites throughout an organization or geographical area. Time sharing thus relies heavily on data communications hardware and software to provide instantaneous responses to many users using remote terminals and personal computer workstations.

Types of Time-Sharing

Special-purpose time-sharing systems exist that have been designed for a specific application, such as airline reservation systems. The American Airlines Sabre systems or the United Airlines Apollo system are examples. More prevalent, however, are general-purpose time-sharing systems, which can be used internally within an organization, such as a large business firm or university, where many remote time-sharing terminals allow simultaneous use of the computer by many users throughout the organization. The other major form of general-purpose time sharing is the time-sharing service offered by data processing service centers and national time-sharing companies. Time-sharing services are provided to many subscribers, representing various business firms and organizations. Subscribers pay for time-sharing by paying an initial installation charge, basic monthly charges, and transaction charges, which vary according to the amount of computer resources used. Firms offering such time-sharing services are sometimes referred to as computer or information "utilities." Nationwide time-sharing services are offered to business firms by such companies as General Electric, Control Data, Tymeshare, and Telenet. Time-sharing services are also available to personal computer users from networks like *The Source* and CompuServe.

DISTRIBUTED PROCESSING

Distributed processing, also called **distributed data processing** (DDP), is a form of information processing made possible by a network of computers "dispersed" throughout an organization. Processing of user applications is accomplished by several computers interconnected by a data communications network, rather than relying on one large *centralized* computer facility, or on the *decentralized* operation of several completely independent computers. Computers may be dispersed over a wide geographic area, or may be distributed to user departments in a limited *local area network* at a major user location, such as a large building or manufacturing plant. Distributed processing systems rely heavily on a network composed of microcomputers, minicomputers, and intelligent terminals controlled by computer users throughout an organization. These computer users can perform many of their own data processing and word processing tasks with their own *local processors*, and they can communicate with similar computers (*processing nodes*) in the network if necessary. See Figure 10–11.

Distributed processing is a movement away from a **centralized processing** approach, which relys on large central computers and a centralized information processing department. However, it is not the same as traditional **decentralized processing**. That would involve completely independent user computer systems with independent databases, programs, applications, budgets, and information system development efforts. Instead, distributed processing is:

FIGURE 10–11 Centralized, decentralized, and distributed data processing

CENTRALIZED DATA PROCESSING

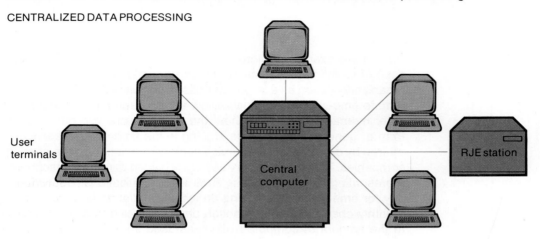

DECENTRALIZED DATA PROCESSING

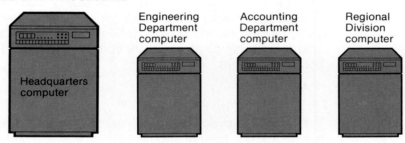

DISTRIBUTED DATA PROCESSING

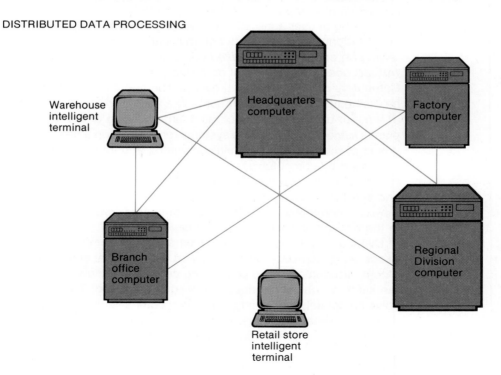

- A *system* of user department and headquarters computers,
- *Interconnected* by a data communications network,
- *Integrated* by a common database-oriented approach,
- *Coordinated* by an organization-wide *information resource management* plan.

Distributed Processing Applications

The use of distributed processing systems can be subdivided into six application categories: (1) distributed information processing, (2) central site processing, (3) distributed data entry, (4) distributed database processing, (5) distributed word processing, and (6) distributed communications networks. Figure 10–12 illustrates these applications.

- **Distributed Information Processing.** Local users can handle a broad range of information processing tasks. This ranges from data entry processing, to local database inquiry and response systems, to fully independent transaction processing, which includes updating local databases and generating necessary output reports. One rule of thumb states, that if 70 percent to 80 percent of the information needed by users can be produced locally, then users should have their own computer systems. Thus data can be com-

FIGURE 10–12 Distributed processing applications

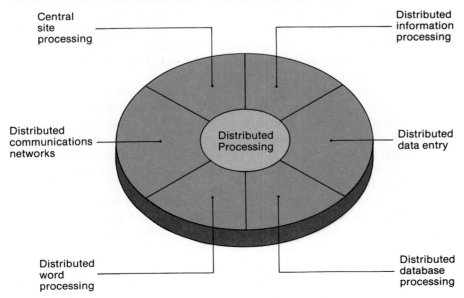

Central site processing

Distributed information processing

Distributed communications networks

Distributed Processing

Distributed data entry

Distributed word processing

Distributed database processing

pletely processed locally, where most input and output (and errors and problems) must be handled, anyway. This should provide computer processing more tailored to the needs of users, and increase information processing efficiency and effectiveness as users become more responsible for their own application systems.

■ **Central Site Processing**. With DDP, large central site computers can be applied to those jobs they can best handle, like large highly structured and repetitive batch applications, communications control for the entire distributed processing network, maintaining large corporate databases, and providing sophisticated planning and decision-making support for corporate management. Users at local sites might typically access a central computer to receive corporate-wide management information or transmit summary transaction data reflecting local site activities.

■ **Distributed Data Entry**. Data entry using intelligent terminals (or dumb terminals connected to a local computer) helps generate *clean data* from source documents at their point of origin for local processing or transmittal to a central site. Data which contain errors and requires editing and preprocessing (*dirty data*) can usually be cleaned better at the site where it originated. Local personnel are more familiar with the local conditions, which may have caused the errors, and feel more responsible for having them corrected.

■ **Distributed Database Processing**. There are many kinds of data that may be of interest to only one local site. Thus specialized *local databases*, containing data unique to user departments, can be *distributed* to local sites. In such *distributed database processing systems*, all transaction data, or just summary data, may be sent to a central computer for storage in a common database. Distributed database systems can provide faster response times, better user control of data structures and access, and lower communication costs, because data are closer to users.

■ **Distributed Word Processing**. Computerized word processors or terminals connected to a local computer with word processing software can easily automate the preparation of internal and external correspondence, business documents, and management reports. Such *local word processing* can improve productivity and timeliness, while providing the flexibility to make last-minute changes to official documents and reports.

■ **Distributed Communications Networks**. Several computers and many terminals can typically be interconnected by local area networks (LAN) at each large local site. These LANs can be connected by communications channels to each other and to headquarters computers. We will discuss these and other distributed processing networks in Chapter Twelve when we analyze data communications networks.

Advantages and Disadvantages

What are the advantages and disadvantages of the distributed processing approach? Figure 10–13 summarizes the advantages and disadvantages of distributed processing systems. This figure should emphasize that distributed processing systems can provide many benefits to new generations of computer users by providing them with their own computer resources to help them control and manage their operations. The additional problems arising from the use of distributed processing systems can be solved if managing information processing functions and resources is made a major

FIGURE

10–13 Advantages and disadvantages of distributed processing

Advantages:

- Communication costs can be reduced, since there is less need for users to communicate with a central computer and database.
- Response time and turnaround time to the users are improved, because processing is carried out at the user's location.
- Input errors are minimized, because computerized data entry supports and controls user input and simplifies the capture of clean data.
- Productivity of end users can be increased by shortening and reducing the need for communications links, improving the accessibility of data, and providing interactive computing power for user applications that had been performed manually or handled by a central batch processing system.
- Computer applications can be more flexible and tailored to a user's requirements, since hardware and software can be developed to fit the user's organizational and operational requirements.
- Reliability and availability are improved, because malfunctions do not have to affect the information processing operations of the entire organization. Unaffected local computers can act as backup systems and function as *stand-alone* systems, since they are not totally dependent on a large central computer.

Disadvantages:

- Building a complete distributed processing network for an entire organization is a complex task. Hardware, software, data communications facilities, database design, data processing methods, and application systems will tend to become incompatible between computer-using sites unless advance planning and coordination is emphasized.
- Inefficient use and unnecessary duplication of information processing resources may occur and make it difficult to achieve the economies of specialization that are possible in distributed systems.
- Distributed processing has the potential for a loss of consistency in the data and information needed to run the organization. Additional controls and security measures are required to preserve the integrity of the distributed databases in the organization.
- Inadequately trained users may result, unless there are adequate training methods, documentation, and other forms of user support. This is a major reason for the development of *information centers*, where users can go to get help in developing and implementing their own computer applications from internal information processing consultants.

REAL WORLD APPLICATION 10-3

The Veterans Administration

The Veterans Administration is the largest independent agency of the United States government, providing service to 30 million veterans and their families. In one year alone, the portion of the VA responsible for compensation, pensions, and educational benefits will disburse over $14 billion. One would expect an operation this big to be a bureaucratic nightmare. But the truth is, it runs like clockwork. A Honeywell distributed processing system with a database-orientation provides instant control of the work flow and nearly 15 million records. Online access now enables VA people to answer in seconds questions that once took weeks. As a result of this new system, the efficiency with which veterans receive their benefits has been enhanced. And taxpayers are saving millions.

The VA's distributed processing system is called TARGET. And it includes four Honeywell large-scale host computers, 100 small computers, 3,000 terminals, and 800 printers. Naturally, the system is spread throughout the country, operating in 57 cities in the United States. There are databases in Chicago and Austin, and regional data processing centers are located in Philadelphia, Chicago, and Los Angeles. But from the user's point of view, it's all a single system with a single database.

A veteran's file stored in Chicago can be on a CRT in Miami faster than claims developers could pull it from a stack on their desks. Providing quick, uncomplicated service is TARGET's prime function. Currently, the system is processing 200,000 complex transactions a day. Response time per transaction? A few seconds. TARGET was designed this way so veterans could be served quickly and easily from whatever VA regional office they walk into.

- Is the VA's TARGET system a distributed processing system? Explain.
- Do you agree that TARGET is the best approach for the VA? Explain.

Source: Courtesy Honeywell Information Systems.

responsibility of the managers of user departments. Since distributed processing allows information processing resources to follow an organization's functional and geographic structure, user managers should be able to accomplish the management of information processing along with their other management responsibilities.

SUMMARY

- Several types of electronic information processing capabilities are available to meet the information needs of an organization. This includes concurrent processing—the ability of a computer system to work on more than one job at the same time. Concurrent processing can be implemented by such techniques as overlapped processing, spooling, dynamic job processing, multiprocessing, multiprogramming, and multitasking.

- The two basic categories of electronic information processing systems are batch processing systems, in which data are accumulated and processed periodically, and realtime processing systems, which process data immediately. Realtime processing systems can be subdivided into several levels: inquiry, data entry, file processing, full capability, and process control systems.

- Realtime processing systems provide an interactive processing capability, in which users at online terminals can interact with a computer on a realtime basis. This may take the form of inquiry/response, conversational computing, online data entry, or interactive programming. Most interactive processing systems are menu-driven to assist users. Time-sharing systems are a major form of realtime processing systems, which allow many users in different locations to share a computer system at the same time through the use of online input/output terminals.

- Distributed processing is a new form of decentralization of information processing made possible by a network of computers dispersed throughout an organization. Processing of user applications is accomplished by several computers interconnected by a data communications network, rather than relying on one large centralized computer facility, or on the decentralized operation of several completely independent computers. Distributed data processing constitutes a system of user department and headquarters computers, which are interconnected by a data communications network, integrated by a common database-oriented approach, and coordinated by an organization-wide information resource management plan.

- Distributed data processing systems are found in six major application areas: (1) distributed data processing, (2) central site processing, (3) distributed data entry, (4) distributed database processing, (5) distributed word processing, and (6) distributed communications networks. Distributed processing systems can reduce communication costs, improve response time, minimize input errors, and improve user productivity. Computer reliability and availability are also improved. However, building a complete distributed processing network for an organization is a complex task. It requires significant additional planning and controls by both corporate and user management.

KEY TERMS AND CONCEPTS

Concurrent processing

Batch processing systems

Overlapped processing

Realtime processing systems

Dynamic job processing

Interactive processing

Multiprocessing

Menu-driven

Multiprogramming

Time-sharing

Multitasking

Distributed processing

REVIEW AND APPLICATION QUESTIONS

1. How are modern information processing systems related to data processing and word processing systems? Do you think that the trend toward the integration of the transmission and processing of data, words, images, and voices will continue into the future?
2. What is the difference between batch processing and realtime processing? Use examples to illustrate your answer.
3. Realtime processing can be subdivided into several levels of processing. What examples can you think of to illustrate this concept?
4. What is interactive processing? Explain the use of interactive processing for inquiry/response, conversational computing, on-line data entry, and interactive programming.
5. Why are most interactive processing systems menu-driven? What are several characteristics of a menu-driven system?
6. What is time-sharing? Can time-sharing be used for remote batch processing as well as realtime processing?
7. What are the major types and sources of time-sharing services? Can individuals as well as business firms make use of nationwide time-sharing networks?
8. What is distributed processing? How does it differ from centralized data processing? From traditional decentralized data processing?
9. Why did the trend toward distributed data processing develop? Do you expect this trend to continue? Why or why not?
10. What are several major types of distributed processing applica-

tions? Use examples to illustrate how these applications use the distributed processing concept.

11. What are several advantages and disadvantages of the distributed processing approach? Do you expect the trend toward distributed processing to continue?

12. "Problems arising from the use of distributed processing systems can be solved if managing information processing functions and resources is made a major responsibility of the managers of user departments." Do you agree with this statement? Why or why not?

APPLICATION PROBLEMS

1. If you have not already done so, read and answer the questions after each Real World Application in this chapter.

2. Match the term below with the appropriate sentence:

   a. Stacked job processing.   e. Dynamic job processing.
   b. Multiprocessing.   f. Virtual memory.
   c. Multiprogramming.   g. Time sharing.
   d. Multitasking.   h. Interactive processing.

   _____ 1. One operating system in control of more than one CPU.
   _____ 2. One copy of a program used interactively by several users.
   _____ 3. Several users access the same CPU via terminals and receive what seems to be simultaneous results.
   _____ 4. The ability to switch from one program to another so rapidly that is appears that many programs are running at the same time.
   _____ 5. Works on the basis of an interrupt feature.
   _____ 6. Works on the basis of a paging feature.
   _____ 7. A conversational type of computing.
   _____ 8. Allows for automatic job to job transition.

3. For each example below of an information system, state whether the system is most probably batch or realtime. If realtime, specify the level of realtime processing: inquiry/response, data entry, file processing, full capability, or process control.

   a. A computerized tax program designed to catch up with individuals and businesses who have evaded city tax payments has resulted in the collection of millions of dollars in New York City. The system matches various types of files; the city has been able to detect evaders of the commercial rent tax, or of unpaid business income taxes and delinquent individual taxpayers.

b. A large chain of pharmacies has automated its order entry and customer billing functions. Pharmacists enter orders via terminals located in each retail store. When an order is entered, charge information is automatically generated, captured, and stored by the computer. The information is passed to the main computer on a daily basis. The main computer reads pharmacy data, posts charges to the proper accounts, and generates customer bills.

c. In an accounts payable system, all transaction are currently driven by interactive user menus. It takes about one minute to update an invoice.

d. A large warehouse is taking inventory. The stock clerks carry small handheld terminals. As they count the number of items in each bin, they enter the stock code and the quantity on hand onto the terminal. The handheld terminals are then linked to the computer to update the inventory.

4. Match the term below with the appropriate sentence:
   a. Centralized processing.
   b. Decentralized processing.
   c. Distributed processing.

   _____ 1. The accounting, marketing, and engineering departments each have their own independent computer systems and databases.

   _____ 2. The accounting, marketing, and engineering departments have video display terminals and remote printers tied in a time-sharing network to the headquarters computer and central database.

   _____ 3. The accounting, marketing, and engineering departments each have computer systems and local databases interconnected by a data communications network to other users and the headquarters computer and central database.

5. New operating systems, operating environment programs, and 32-bit microprocessors have caused such terms as *multiuser*, *multitasking*, and *concurrent processing* to be applied to some recent microcomputers. Explain what you think is going on, and what it means to users of such microcomputer systems.

6. ABC Department stores uses POS terminals connected to a minicomputer in each store to capture sales data immediately and store them on a magnetic disk unit. Each night the central computer in Phoenix *polls* each store's minicomputer to access and process the day's sales data, update the corporate database,

and produce management reports. The next morning, managers use their terminals to interrogate the updated store and corporate databases. Describe what is going on using the following terms: *a.* batch, *b.* realtime, *c.* online, *d.* transaction, *e.* interactive, *f.* data entry, and *g.* distributed.

CHAPTER 11

Data Organization and Database Systems

CHAPTER OUTLINE

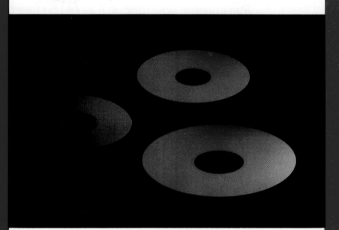

LEARNING OBJECTIVES

The purpose of this chapter is to promote a basic
understanding of how data are organized, stored, and
accessed in modern information processing systems
by analyzing the basic concepts, functions, and
capabilities of file and database processing systems.
After reading and studying this chapter, you should
be able to:

1. Provide examples to illustrate each of the common
   data elements.
2. Differentiate between the following concepts:
     a. Physical versus logical elements.
     b. Sequential versus random file organization.
     c. Sequential access versus direct access file
        processing.
     d. File processing systems versus database
        processing systems.
3. Discuss the development and use of database
   processing systems.
4. Explain the functions of a database management
   system in terms of users, programmers, and
   database processing systems.

SECTION I: DATA ORGANIZATION AND FILE PROCESSING

Just imagine how difficult it would be for you to get any information from an information processing system, if data and information were stored in an unorganized way, and if there was no systematic way to retrieve them! Therefore, in all electronic information processing systems, data must be organized and structured in some logical manner so that it can be processed efficiently. That's why the topics of **data organization, file processing,** and **database processing** are so important. **Data structures** ranging from simple to complex have been devised to logically organize data in electronic information processing.

Common Data Elements

A *hierarchy* of several levels of data has been devised that differentiates between the most simple elements of data and more complex data elements. Thus, data are organized into *characters*, *fields*, *records*, and *files*, just as writing may be organized in letters, words, sentences, and paragraphs. We introduced you to these **common data elements** in Chapter Two. Now lets review and expand our knowledge of these concepts. Examples of the common data elements are shown in Figure 11–1.

Character

The most basic data element is the **character**, which consists of a single alphabetic, numeric, or other symbol. One could argue that the *bit* or *byte* is a more elementary data element. But remem-

FIGURE 11–1 Examples of the common data elements

Employee record 1			Employee record 2			Employee record 1			Employee record 2		
Name field	SS no. field	Salary field	Name field	SS no. field	Salary field	Name field	SS no. field	Insurance field	Name field	SS no. field	Insurance field
Jones T. A.	575-32-3874	20,000	Klugman J.L.	649-88-7913	18,000	Jones T. A.	575-32-3874	90,000	Klugman J.L.	649-88-7913	50,000

ber that those terms refer to *computer data elements* (along with *words* and *pages*) as explained in Chapter Three. From a user's point of view, the character is the most elementary element of data that he or she can observe and manipulate.

Field

The next higher level of data is the **field**, which consists of a grouping of characters, such as the grouping of alphabetical characters in a person's name, which forms a *name field*, or the grouping of numerical characters in a sales amount, which forms a *sales amount field*. The field is sometimes also called an *item* or *word*. A data field represents an **attribute** (a characteristic or quality) of some **entity** (objects, people, places, or events). For example, a person's age could be a data field that represents one attribute of an individual.

Record

Related fields of data are grouped to form a **record**. Thus a record represents a collection of *attributes* that describes an *entity*. An example is the *payroll record* for a person, which consists of data fields, such as his or her name, social security number, and rate of pay. *Fixed-length* records contain a fixed number of data fields, whereas *variable-length* records may contain a variable number of fields.

File

A group of related records is known as a **data file** (or *data set*). Thus a *payroll file* would contain the payroll records for all of the employees of a firm. Files are frequently classified by the data processing application for which they are primarily used, such as a *payroll file* or an *accounts receivable file*. Files are also classified by their permanence. For example, a *payroll master file*, as opposed to a payroll *weekly transaction file*. A **transaction file**, therefore, would contain records of all transactions occurring during a period and would be used periodically to update the permanent records contained in a **master file**. A *history file* is an obsolete transaction or master file retained for *backup* purposes or for long-term historical storage called *archival storage*. A **program file** (as opposed to a *data file*) is a file that contains a computer program. For example, floppy disks for microcomputer systems are frequently used to store both data files and program files.

Database

In the early years of electronic information processing, the data file was the most complex element in the data hierarchy. However, a level of data organization known as the **database** has now become an important data element in modern information processing. A database is a *nonredundant* collection of logically related records or files. A database so consolidates records previously stored in separate files that a common pool of data records serves as a single *central file* or *database* for many data processing applications. For example, a *personnel database* consolidates data formerly segregated in separate files, such as a payroll file, personnel action file, and employee skills file. The term **data bank** is sometimes used to describe a collection of several databases.

Logical and Physical Data Elements

A distinction should be made between "logical" and "physical" data elements. The common data elements just discussed are *logical* data elements, not *physical* data elements.

- **Physical data elements** are related to the individual physical data media or devices on which logical data elements are recorded. For example, a single punched card is a *physical record*, while a single reel of magnetic tape represents a frequently used *physical file* or "volume."
- **Logical data elements** are independent of the data media on which they are recorded. Thus a punched card can contain several logical records, while several reels of magnetic tape may be used to store a single logical file. *For example*, a punched

FIGURE

11–2 Logical versus physical data elements

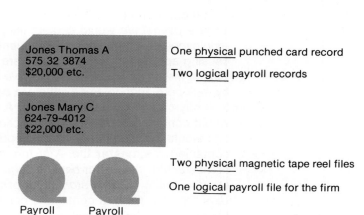

Jones Thomas A
575 32 3874
$20,000 etc.

Jones Mary C
624-79-4012
$22,000 etc.

One physical punched card record

Two logical payroll records

Two physical magnetic tape reel files

One logical payroll file for the firm

Payroll file Volume I

Payroll file Volume II

card may contain payroll data concerning two different employees (two logical records), while several reels of magnetic tape may be needed to store the payroll data file (one logical file) of a large business firm. See Figure 11–2.

Another example: A magnetic tape or disk file may contain blank spaces (*gaps*) between groups (**blocks**) of logical records. A *block* of logical records on magnetic tape or disk is considered a *physical record*. Interrecord or interblock gaps are required, since a certain amount of blank space between records or blocks is needed to allow for such mechanical operations as the start/stop time of a magnetic tape unit. Most files group logical records into blocks to conserve file space instead of leaving gaps between each logical record. See Figure 11–3.

File Organization: Access and Processing

Files are stored on various types of *storage media* and are usually *organized* in some manner to make it easier to **access** (store, locate, and retrieve) the data records they contain. Let's review several important concepts of file organization, access and processing.

- In Chapter Five we described two basic types of storage media, *sequential access storage devices* such as magnetic tape, and *direct access storage devices* (DASDs) such as magnetic disks. Refer back to Figure 5–3 to refresh your memory if necessary. In this chapter, we will discuss several ways that data can be organized, accessed, and processed when stored on such devices.

- The data records in a file can be physically organized on a storage device in two basic ways, **sequential file organization** (in a physical sequence next to each other) and **random file organization** (in no particular physical sequence). The random file orga-

FIGURE

11–3 Unblocked and blocked records

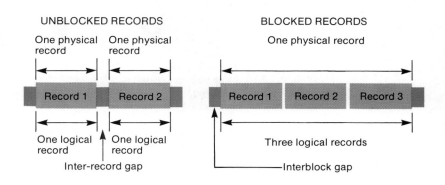

nization is also called the *direct* or *nonsequential* method of file organization.

■ Various methods have been developed to access data records stored in files. These **file access methods** include the *sequential access method* and the *indexed sequential access* method for files organized sequentially, and the *key transformation* method, the *linked list* method, and various *indexing* methods for files using a random method of organization.

In common usage, *file access* methods are frequently called *file organization* methods. For example, one popular file access method that is typically called a method of file organization, is the indexed sequential file access method (ISAM). It is a way to directly access records stored sequentially on a direct access storage device using an index. Thus, file access methods can be viewed as methods which *logically* organize the records in a file. That is why file access methods are frequently referred to as methods of *logical* file organization. You should keep this fact in mind when looking at Figure 11–4. It summarizes some of the major concepts involved in file (and database) organization and processing. We will discuss these concepts and their use in information processing in this chapter. However, let's first explain four basic tools used to help organize data in files and databases.

Key

Each record in a file or database contains one or more *identification fields* or **keys**, which are used when searching or sorting a

---

FIGURE

11–4 Important file concepts

File Storage Media
  Sequential access storage devices
  Direct access storage devices
File Organization Methods
  Sequential organization
  Random organization
File Access Methods
  Sequential
  Indexed sequential
  Key transformation
  Indexed
  Linked list
  Inverted file
File Processing Methods
  Sequential access
  Direct access

file. For example a social security number might be used as the *key* for identifying each employee's data record in a payroll file.

Pointer

Records may contain other identifying fields (called **pointers**) that help in cross-referencing the contents of a file or database. Thus each record could contain a *pointer field*, which contains the storage location address of a related record in the file or database. For example, the payroll record of an employee could include the address of the payroll record for another employee who works on the same project.

Index

A file or database may contain an **index**, somewhat similar to an index in a book. The index is an ordered reference listing of record keys and their associated storage location addresses,which helps locate records in the file or database. For example, an index could consist of a listing of employee social security numbers (record keys) along with the corresponding storage address for each employee's payroll record.

Directory

A **directory** is a listing of the names and other characteristics of data files and programs files stored on some type of storage device. For example, microcomputer users can easily find out which files are stored on a floppy disk. They insert it in a disk drive and then issue a directory command that displays the files stored on that disk. (Note: sometimes an *index* is called a directory.)

Sequential File Organization and Processing

Sequential File Organization

One of the basic ways to organize the data in a file is to use a *sequential* methodology. Records can be physically stored in a predetermined sequence. Records are arranged in a specified order according to a *record key*. For example, payroll records could be placed in a payroll file in a *sequential* manner according to a numeric order based on employees' social security numbers or an alphabetical order based on employees' last names. The sequential file organization is a simple method of data organization that is fast and efficient when processing large volumes of data that do not need to be processed except on a periodic basis. However, the sequential file organization requires that all records be sorted into the proper sequence before processing, and the entire file must be searched to locate, store, or modify even a small number of data records. Thus this method is too slow to handle applications requiring immediate updating or responses.

Sequential Access File Processing

When sequentially organized files are stored on sequential access storage devices, they must be processed using a methodology called *sequential access file processing*. Figure 11–5 illustrates sequential access file processing. In this example:

■ The input data from source documents (such as sales invoices)

FIGURE

11–5 Sequential access file processing

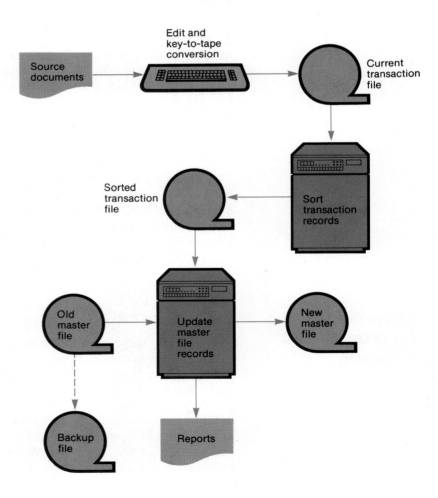

is captured and edited for correctness using a key-to-tape device, which records the data on a magnetic tape *transaction file*. Editing is important in insuring that incorrect data is not entered into the processing system. (Remember GIGO—garbage in, garbage out!)

■ The current transaction file is then sorted into the same sequence as the master file (such as a sales order master file).

■ A *master file* update program uses the transactions data from the sorted transaction file to update the records in the old master file. This requires sequentially reading the entire master file.

■ A new updated master file is produced, which incorporates all the changes to records that were affected by the data in the transaction file. *Updated master files* are then usually stored *offline* (away from the computer) until the next time transactions are scheduled for processing. The old master file may also be stored offline for backup purposes. Usually, several *generations* of master files are kept for control purposes. Thus, for example, if the sequential access file processing is being done on a weekly basis, master files from the three most recent weeks' processing (known as the *child, parent, and grandparent files*) might be kept for backup purposes. Depending of the application, even more backup files might be required.

■ Various reports are also produced, such as control listings, activity reports and analytical reports for management.

Random File Organization and Processing

Random File Organization

This method is also called *direct, nonsequential*, or *relative* file organization. Records are physically stored in a file in a *random* or nonsequential manner; that is, they are not arranged in any particular sequence. However, the computer must keep track of the storage location of each record in the file using such data organization aids as *keys, pointers, indexes*, and other methods so data can be retrieved when needed. For example, payroll records could be placed in a payroll file in no particular sequence. The computer system could use each record's *key field* to assign and keep track of the storage locations of each record in the file. In the random file organization, input data does not have to be sorted, and processing that requires immediate responses or updating is easily handled. There are a number of ways to *access* (assign storage locations, locate, and retrieve) the records in the random file organization. Let's take a look at each of them.

Key Transformation Access Method

One common technique of file access is called **key transformation**. It uses a *transform algorithm* (also called a *randomizing* or *hashing* algorithm), which involves performing some arithmetic computation on a record key and using the result of the calculation as an address for that record. Thus the process is also known as a *key transformation*, since an arithmetic operation is applied to a key to transform it into a storage location address. To use a simple example, the transform algorithm might involve dividing the key field of a record (such as an employee number) by the maximum number of records that might be stored in a file, and using the resulting number as the storage location address for that record. Thus if the random file organization is used, the computer could use record keys and a key transformation process to randomly store and directly locate the data records in a file.

Sometimes the transformation computation results in the same address (the same answer) for two different keys. This occurrence is called a *collision*, and the keys with the same address are called *synonyms*. One method of handling such collisions is to place the record in the next available storage location. To minimize collisions, randomly organized files may be kept only 60 to 70 percent full. Thus the speed of this method of accessing a file must be balanced with the file space that is wasted.

Indexed Access Method

Another basic access method used to store and locate records for a random file organization involves the use of an **index** of record keys and storage addresses. A new record is stored at the next available location and its key and address are so placed in an index that a list of occupied and available storage locations is maintained. See Figure 11–6.

Indexed Sequential Access Method

In this method, records are stored **sequentially** on a direct access storage device (such as a magnetic disk) based upon the key field of each record. However, each file also contains an **index** that references the key field of each data record to its storage location

FIGURE

11–6 Example of an index

Record Key (employee number)	Record Address
28541	101
35879	102
47853	103
50917	104

address. Thus any individual record can be directly located by using its key to search and locate its address in the file index.

The indexed sequential access method (ISAM) combines the advantages of both the sequential and random file organizations. The sequential organization provided by this method is used when large numbers of records must be processed periodically, as in *batch processing systems*. However, if a few records must be processed quickly (as in *realtime processing*), the file index is used to directly access the records needed. The indexed sequential organization does have several disadvantages. It is slower than the direct organization, because the index is usually stored on secondary storage devices and not in main memory. Another disadvantage is the cost of creating, storing, and maintaining the indexes, including the extra storage space this requires.

List Access Method

This method uses **pointers** to locate related records stored in a nonsequential manner. This data structure is called a **list** (or *linked list*), because pointers (also called *link fields*) are used to express data relationships as *lists* of data records. Each data record contains a pointer field, which gives the address of the next logical record. Thus all logically related records can be linked together by means of pointers. A grouping of records related by pointers is called a *list*, or **chain**. Since the records in a file can have many possible relationships (for example, employees' ages, sex or department), each record can contain several pointers. These pointers form *chains* throughout the file or database. This allows records with the same particular attributes (such as all male employees over age 55) to be located. In many cases, an index containing the addresses of the first record in each list is used. The pointer in the first record will point to the address of the next logical record in the list, thus allowing the computer to follow a chain of pointers to locate specific records in a file.

A pointer field may also indicate the address of a related record in another file. For example, the payroll record for an employee in the *payroll file* might include a pointer linking it to the same employee's record in a *personnel action file*. Figure 11–7 demonstrates how pointers can link an employee record in a personnel file with the same employee's record in the payroll file. It also shows a pointer linking two records in the payroll file for employees who belong to the same department. In summary, the list organization uses pointers to easily access records having multiple logical data relationships. A disadvantage of this method is that pointers may

FIGURE 11–7 Pointers linking records in files

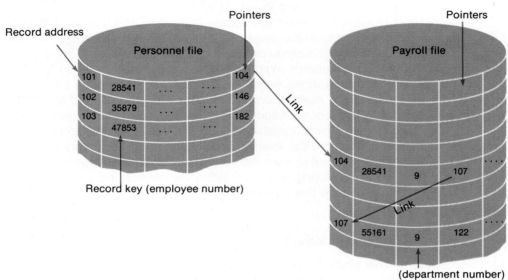

become too numerous and the lists or chains may become too long, thus increasing access time and storage requirements.

Inverted File Access Method

This approach uses an index called an *inverted file* (also called an *inverted index* or *inverted directory*). Each inverted file lists the addresses or keys for all records having the same attribute. For example, an inverted index might indicate the record addresses of all employees between the ages of 18 to 25, 26 to 30, 31 to 35, and so forth. Several inverted files would be needed, if we wish to locate the records for multiple alternatives (such as age, sex or marital status). Thus inverted files allow efficient access to records having multiple logical relationships. This greatly facilitates searching a file for records sharing one or more attributes. However, it must be emphasized that these advantages are attained at the cost of creating, storing, and continually updating multiple large inverted files. The data needed to express relationships and addresses of the records referenced by inverted files is known as *overhead data*. Such overhead data may be several times as great as the original data it describes! Figure 11–8 provides an example of an inverted file.

FIGURE

11–8 Inverted file example

Portion of Personnel File			Inverted File by Age	
Record Address	Employee Number	Age	Age	Record Address
101	28541	43	18–25	104, . . .
102	35879	27	26–35	102, 103, . . .
103	47853	32	36–45	101, . . .
104	50917	24		

Direct Access File Processing

We have now explained several major ways that the records in sequentially or randomly organized files can be accessed directly. Such files are processed, using *direct access file processing* methods similar to that illustrated in Figure 11–9. Notice the following:

FIGURE

11–9 Direct access file processing

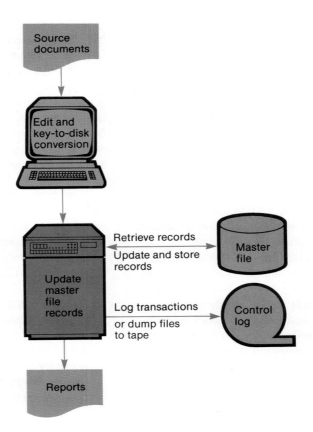

REAL WORLD APPLICATION 11–1

Bearings, Inc.

Greater productivity among personnel, an easily identifiable savings in disk storage space on its main-frame computer, and faster access to more information are three principal benefits that Bearings, Inc., has derived from its database management system. The Cleveland-based distributor of more than 250,000 different parts of 3.2 million stock-keeping units has converted to a relational database management system, Applied Data Research's (ADR) DATACOM/DB, to reorganize and modernize its accounts receivable and product inventory files. "ADR provided a utility to unload our old files and reload them into DATACOM/DB," Brian Sanders, Director of DP, explained. "We kept the record and file sizes the same, except for some numerical field sizes."

One feature of the ADR database system is its creative use of disk space for data storage. "It's very stingy on space," Robert Falkowski, Assistant DP Director, said. "It compresses spaces, zeros and multiple characters. It's an excellent feature that saves a lot of disk space. Using full data compression, we now use only 39 percent of the space we used before. We ended up using one and one half disk drives less than before." That is 1.5 times 317M bytes of information, or about 475M bytes, he noted. The savings postponed acquisition of additional disk storage equipment.

The accounts receivable files were reduced to two files from five, and the product files were reduce to one file on 4,000 disk tracks from three files on 13,000 disk tracks. Nightly updating of the receivables took four to six hours, and all files were reorganized every two months in a 26-hour, over-the-weekend, nonproduction environment. Now, the receivable database is updated and reorganized nightly, and it takes from 60 to 65 minutes. Updating of the product file used to take two and one half to three hours. Now it takes less than 15 minutes.

"We can do concurrent multiple updates. Any program, online or batch, can access any file for review or updating," Falkowski said. "We're able to get more things done," Sanders added. "We get more work done in a more timely manner. We used to run seven days, 24 hours. Now there is time available." Alexis Corrado, supervisor in accounts receivable department in which CRT terminals are used for daily check postings and other related work, commented that "response time is a lot faster. The work is easier and the features are fantastic. Downtime is practically nil."

Within the computer system, there are about 700,000 invoice records related to customers-a three-month historical record; and about 170,-000 customer records. Bearings, which operates two similar subsidiary companies, also has an IBM 370/155 main-frame computer in Atlanta, Georgia and Perkin-Elmer 7/32 minicomputers in seven branch warehouse locations. The headquarters computer in Cleveland supports about 50 local CRT terminals and printers. The networks for sales and order entry support about 300 CRTs and printers in about 225 branches in 32 states.

"The database is the vehicle that will enables us to grow with the future," Sanders stated. "We will be able to develop a true management information systems department. We will be able to give our users and our management timely information based on current information. "

- How many different types of data records, files, and databases can you identify in this example?
- What benefits has Bearings, Inc., experienced by changing from the use of files to a database approach using a database management system?

- Input source documents, such as sales orders or sales invoices are edited and entered into the system by a key-to-disk conversion process using a *data entry* terminal with a keyboard and CRT display.
- Since a direct access master file is used, there is no need to sort input data before updating the master file. Thus the master file is immediately updated.
- The master file update program also produces several reports, such as control listings, summary reports, exception reports, and analytical reports for management.
- Direct access file processing does not result in old master files that can be used for backup purposes. Therefore, **backup copies** of the direct access files are obtained by periodically copying or *dumping* the contents of a direct access file to a magnetic tape file. This backup file is then stored for *control* purposes. Another control method is to keep a magnetic tape *control log*, which records all transactions.

SECTION II: DATABASE PROCESSING SYSTEMS

How would you feel if you were the president of a computer-using company and were told that some information you wanted about some of your employees was too difficult and too costly to obtain? Suppose your vice-president of Information Services gave you the following reasons:

INTRODUCTION

- The information you want is stored in several different files, each organized a separate way.
- Each file has been organized to be used by a different application program, none of which produces the information you want in the form you need.
- No application program is available to help get this information from these files.

Figure 11–10 shows a summary of the information you want and its related files and programs.

FIGURE

11–10 Example of files and programs for information on employees

Information Requested	File	Application Program
Employee salary	Payroll file	Payroll program
Educational background	Employee skills file	Skills inventory program
Salary increases and promotions	Personnel action file	Personnel action program

As a company president, you would probably be frustrated and disenchanted with computer-based processing if it could not provide you with information for such a simple request. Well, that's just the way electronic information processing frustrated users when it relied on **file processing systems**, such as those described in the previous section. Data are organized, stored, and processed in *independent files* when file processing systems are used. In **database processing systems**, on the other hand, files are consolidated into a common pool of records available to many different application programs. In addition, an important system software package called a **database management system** (DBMS) serves as a software interface between users and databases. This helps users easily access the records in a database. For example, if all data about an employee was stored in a common database, you could use the query language feature of a DBMS and a computer terminal to easily obtain the employee information you want. See Figure 11–11. Thus database processing systems have significantly improved the performance of electronic information processing systems.

Reasons for Database Processing

For many years, electronic information processing had the *file processing* orientation illustrated in the previous example. Data needed for each user application was stored in independent data files. Data processing consisted of using separate computer programs that updated these independent data files and used them

FIGURE

11–11 Example of data inquiry and response

```
INQUIRY:    Display Name, Salary, Degrees, Last
            Promotion For Employee = 575-38-6473
RESPONSE:   Employee = 575-38-6473
            Name = Joan K. Alverez
            Salary = $45,000
            Degrees = BA: 1972, MBA: 1974
            Last Promotion = Store Manager: 1982
```

to produce the documents and reports required by each separate user application. This file processing approach had several major problems, which limited the efficiency and effectiveness of electronic information processing.

Data Redundancy

Independent data files include a lot of duplicated data. The same data (such as a customer's name and address) was recorded and stored in several files. This caused problems when data had to be updated, since separate *file maintenance* programs had to be developed and coordinated to insure that each file was properly updated. This was a time-consuming and costly process, which increased the secondary storage space requirements of computer systems.

Unintegrated Data

Independent data files made it difficult to provide users with information that required processing data stored in several different files. Special computer programs would have to be written to retrieve data from each independent file. This was so difficult, time consuming, and costly for some organizations that it was impossible to provide users or management with such information. Some users had to manually extract the required information from the various reports produced by each separate application.

Program/Data Dependence

Computer programs typically contained references to the specific *format* of data stored in the files that they used. Thus any changes to the format and structure of data and records in a file required that changes be made to all of the programs that used that file. This *program maintenance* effort, due to changes to the format of data, is a major burden of file processing systems.

The Database Concept

The concepts of *databases* and *database processing* were developed to solve the problems of file processing systems. We have defined a **database** as a nonredundant collection of logically related records or files that consolidates records previously stored in independent files, so that it serves as a common pool of data to be accessed by many different application programs. The data stored in a database is independent of the computer programs using it and of the type of secondary storage devices on which it is stored. **Database processing systems** are a major type of modern information processing systems. They consist of electronic information processing systems which use a *database orientation* for both the *storage* and *processing* of data.

Database Storage

The data needed by many different data processing applications in an organization are consolidated and integrated into several *common databases*, instead of being stored in many independent data files. For example; customer records and other data needed for several different applications in banking, such as check processing, automated teller systems, bank credit cards, savings accounts, and installment loan accounting, can be consolidated into a common *customer database*, rather than being kept in separate files for each of those applications.

Database Processing

Electronic information processing no longer consists of updating and using independent data files to produce information needed by each user's application. Instead, information processing with a database orientation consists of three basic activities:

- Updating and maintaining a common database.
- Providing information needed for each user's application by using computer programs that share the data in the common database.
- Providing an inquiry/response capability so users can easily interrogate the database and receive quick responses to their requests for information.

Example: Traditionally, an individual computer program for each banking application mentioned above would be used to update a special data file for each application, as well as producing desired reports and documents. Thus Figure 11–12 illustrates the use of separate computer programs and independent data files in a file processing approach to the savings, installment loan, and checking account applications.

However, in a database processing system, the computer programs needed for each banking application would be designed to use a common *customer database* to produce information in a variety of forms. In addition, the programs of a *database management system* package would be used to control the updating of the database and to provide an inquiry/response capability for users. Thus Figure 11–13 illustrates how the savings, checking, and installment

FIGURE 11–12 Examples of banking file processing systems

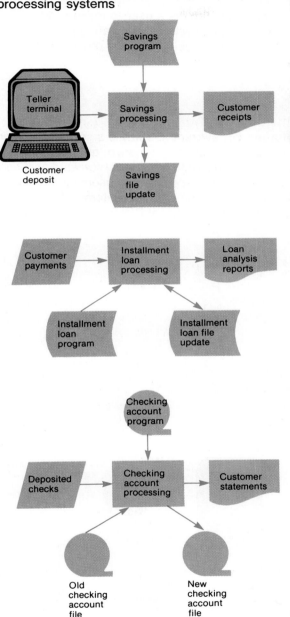

FIGURE 11–13 A banking database processing system example

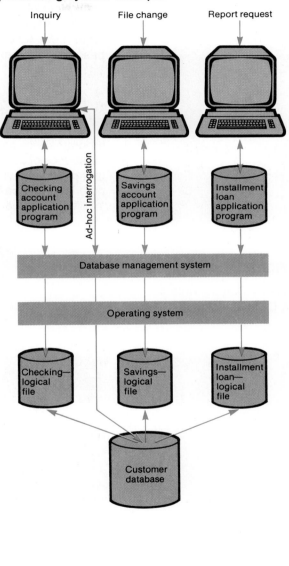

loan programs use a *database management system* to share a customer database, as if it were organized into separate *logical files*. Note also that the DBMS allows a user to make a direct *ad hoc interrogation* of the database without using an application program. Let's take a closer look at the capabilities provided by database management systems.

Database
Management
Systems

A **database management system** (DBMS) is a set of computer programs that control the creation, maintenance, and use of the databases of computer users. A DBMS is a system software package that provides a vital *software interface* between users and the computerized databases of database processing systems. Figure 11–14 illustrates the components of a typical DBMS.

FIGURE

11–14 Components of a DBMS

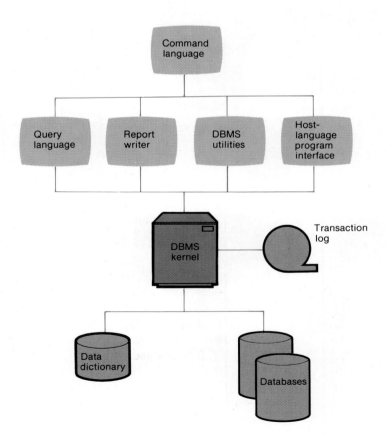

A DBMS helps users perform the following tasks:

- **Database creation**—defining and organizing the content, relationships, and structure of the data needed to build a database.
- **Database interrogation**—accessing the data in a database to support various information processing assignments that require information retrieval and report generation.
- **Database maintenance**—adding, deleting, updating, correcting, and protecting the data in a database.

A database management system controls all use of the databases of a computer-using organization. It works in conjunction with the data management control programs of the operating system, which are primarily concerned with the physical input, output, and storage of data during processing. Advanced computer systems may even use a **back-end processor** or *database machine*, which is a special-purpose computer that contains the DBMS. Use of a DBMS has four important characteristics, which are illustrated in Figure 11–15.

- End-users can use a DBMS by asking for information from a database using a simple English-like **query language** or **report writer**. They can receive an immediate response in the form of a video display or a printed report. No difficult computer programming is required. This database processing capability is a major benefit to ordinary end users. The *query language* feature reduces their reliance on information provided by periodic reports produced by a traditional information processing system. Managers and other computer users do not have to write complete programs in order to easily obtain immediate responses to spontaneous inquiries concerning the operations and management of their organization. Instead, they can key in a few short statements on a microcomputer or computer terminal using a simple, English-like query language provided by most data base management systems. See Figure 11–16.

- A DBMS facilitates the job of programmers, because they do not have to develop detailed data-handling procedures using a conventional programming language (a *host* language, such as COBOL) each time they write a program. Instead, they can include several simple **data manipulation language** (DML) statements in their application programs, which let the DBMS perform necessary data handling activities. Figure 11–17 is a sample of DML statements in an actual COBOL program segment.

- Users and the information services department can access and update the data in selected databases of the organization. This is accomplished by the use of business application programs contain-

FIGURE   11–15 Role of a database management system

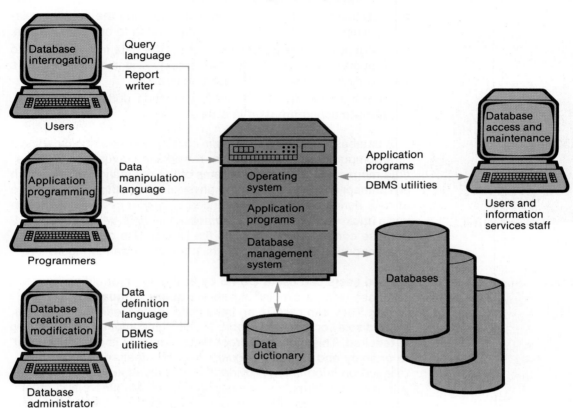

ing DML statements or various *utilities* (specialized service programs), which are provided by the DBMS.

■ A DBMS removes the database from the control of individual programmers and computer users and places responsibility for it in the hands of a specialist called a **database administrator** (DBA). This improves the integrity and security of the database. The database administrator uses a data definition language (DDL) to specify the content, relationships, and structure of the database and to modify it when necessary. Such information about the database is stored in a special file called a **data dictionary**, see Figure 11–18, which is maintained by the DBA. Figure 11–19 lists some of the popular DBMS programs available today.

FIGURE 11–16 Using a query language

A A formal mainframe query language: PROLOG.

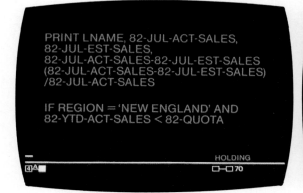

B A natural mainframe query language: INTELLECT.

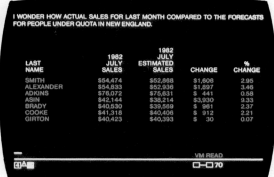

C A formal microcomputer query language: dBASE II.

D A natural microcomputer query language: CLOUT.

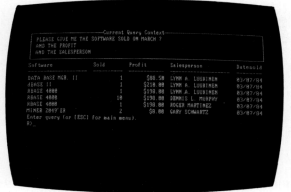

Microcomputer DBMS Packages

Many database management packages are available for microcomputer systems. They allow users to set up a database of files and records on their personal computer systems. Most DBMS microcomputer packages are used to perform three primary jobs:

- Create and maintain (change or update) data files.
- Selectively retrieve and display records from one or more files to provide users with information they need.

404

FIGURE

11–17 Using data manipulation language statements in a COBOL program segment

COBOL/DL Data Manipulation Language statements of the Datacom/DB, Database Management System.

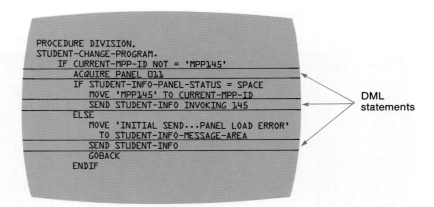

```
PROCEDURE DIVISION.
STUDENT-CHANGE-PROGRAM.
    IF CURRENT-MPP-ID NOT = 'MPP145'
        ACQUIRE PANEL 011
    IF STUDENT-INFO-PANEL-STATUS = SPACE
        MOVE 'MPP145' TO CURRENT-MPP-ID
        SEND STUDENT-INFO INVOKING 145
    ELSE
        MOVE 'INITIAL SEND...PANEL LOAD ERROR'
            TO STUDENT-INFO-MESSAGE-AREA
        SEND STUDENT-INFO
        GOBACK
    ENDIF
```

DML statements

FIGURE

11–18 A display of part of the information in a data dictionary

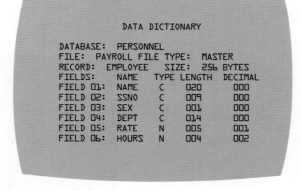

```
               DATA DICTIONARY

DATABASE:  PERSONNEL
FILE:  PAYROLL FILE TYPE:  MASTER
RECORD:  EMPLOYEE   SIZE:   256 BYTES
FIELDS:       NAME  TYPE LENGTH  DECIMAL
FIELD 01:    NAME    C    020      000
FIELD 02:    SSNO    C    009      000
FIELD 03:    SEX     C    001      000
FIELD 04:    DEPT    C    014      000
FIELD 05:    RATE    N    005      001
FIELD 06:    HOURS   N    004      002
```

FIGURE

11–19 Examples of current Database Management Systems

Microcomputer DBMS	Supplier
Condor III	Condor
dBase II and III	Ashton-Tate
Knowledgeman	Micro-Data Base Systems
R:base 4000 and 6000	Microrim
Revelation	Cosmos

Mainframe DBMS	Supplier
ADABAS	Software AG
DATACOM DB	Applied Data Research
IDMS, IDMS-R	Cullinet
IMS, SQL/DS, DB2	IBM
Model 204	Computer Corp. of America
RAMIS II	Mathematica
System 2000	INTEL
TIS, TOTAL	CINCOM

REAL WORLD APPLICATION 11–2

Best Western International

The world's largest lodging chain is meeting its needs for timely, accurate and end-user accessible information using TIS, the new generation of integrated database technology from Cincom Systems, Inc. Using TIS, Best Western International is building a fully integrated corporate information system, where users maintain and retrieve their own data in a completely online, realtime environment. The first component—the Payroll/Personnel System—has already been developed and is in production under TIS. When the complete corporate information system is in place, decision makers will have access to databases for such areas as reservations, financial, marketing,and computer equipment repair.

Best Western already utilizes a sophisticated reservation network based on the airline control program (ACP). But it's goal is to create online interactive systems in all other business areas, and then integrate these with the reservation system. This ambitious project is under the direction of a three-person data processing department.

"We found only one software technology that fulfills all our needs—and is practical and implementable without adding more staff," says Ray Siggins, MIS manager at Best Western. "That technology is TIS. We were one of the first installed users of the product when TIS became commercially available last year. We had no previous database system in place, so we are building a state-of-the-art information system from the ground up with TIS," he explains.

The TIS In-Line Directory (data dictionary) provides the integration necessary to bind all TIS components together as one complete database system. Fully active, the TIS In-Line Directory is the central brain of TIS and controls every aspect of data access, security, integrity, and application development. "We believe the In-Line Directory is the way to build and control fully integrated systems," states Mr. Siggins. "With the In-Line Directory, we avoid the old-style piecemeal approach to building systems. We don't need clumsy interfaces to allow users to access corporate data. Through the Logical User View, all users—both within and outside Data Processing—access information without having to know how it is physically stored. All logical views are assigned by the database administrator and controlled by the TIS directory," he says.

The unique architecture of TIS encompasses the complete needs of an integrated information system, such as Best Western's. TIS answers the physical structure requirements of data processing as well as the logical requirements of end-users and programmers. Using the powerful relational approach of the TIS Logical user View, Best Western's Data Processing Department was able to bring up the payroll/personnel system in only six months. Previously implemented on a minicomputer, the new TIS payroll/personnel system is fully interactive, online and real-time. Users maintain and access their own information using TIS Intelligent Query (I.Q).

- What are the major components and functions of the TIS database management system?
- How is Best Western benefiting from the use of TIS?

Source: Courtesy of Cincom Systems, Inc.

■ Print information from these files in various formats to provide printed reports and documents.

Some DBMS microcomputer packages provide a fourth major capability. They contain their own built-in programming language, which allows users to write programs that use the database for more complex jobs. For example, users can develop programs for inventory, payroll, and accounting systems involving multiple files, menu-driven input, and complex reports. The Appendix at the back of this book includes a section, "Using Database Management Packages," which introduces you to the use of such microcomputer packages.

Database Structures

The databases of many modern computer-using organizations are collections of integrated records and files involving complex record relationships. They may use many variations of the data organization and access methods we described in the first section of this chapter. The complex relationships between the many individual records stored in large databases can be expressed by several **logical data structures** or **models**. Database management systems are designed to use a specific data structure to provide computer users with quick and easy access to information stored in both small and large databases. The three fundamental database structures or models are **hierarchical, network,** and **relational.** Simplified illustrations of these three database structures are shown in Figure 11–20.

Hierarchical Structure

In this model, the relationships between records form a *hierarchy* or *tree* structure. In this structure, all records are dependent and arranged in multilevel structures, consisting of one *root* record and any number of *subordinate* levels. Thus all of the relationships between records are *one-too-many*, since each data element is related to several records below it, but only one data element is above it. The data element or record at the highest level of the hierarchy (the *department* data element in this illustration) is called the *root* and is the point of entry into the hierarchy. Data elements are stored and located by moving progressively downward from a root and along the *branches* of the tree until the desired record (for example, the *employee* data element) is located.

FIGURE 11–20 Three fundamental database structures

HIERARCHICAL STRUCTURE

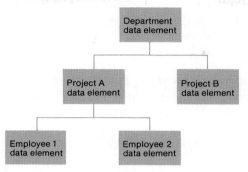

NETWORK STRUCTURE

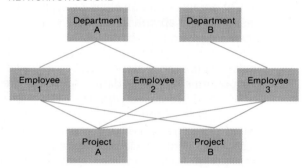

RELATIONAL STRUCTURE

General form of the relational database structure

Departmental records

Dept No	D Name	D Loc	D MGR
Dept A			
Dept B			
Dept C			

Employee records

Emp No	E Name	E Title	E Salary	Dept No
Emp 1				Dept A
Emp 2				Dept B
Emp 3				Dept A
Emp 4				Dept B
Emp 5				Dept C
Emp 6				Dept B

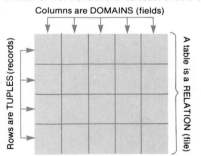

Network Structure

This model can represent more complex logical relationships between records by allowing *many-to-many* relationships between records. Thus the network structure allows entry into a database at multiple points, because any data element or record can be related to any number of other data elements. For example, in Figure 11–20, departmental records can be related to more than one employee record and employee records can be related to more than one project record. Thus one could locate all employee records for a particular department, or all project records related to a particular employee. The network structure is also called the CODASYL model, because the Conference On Data Systems Languages formed a subcommittee which developed specifications and standards for a network database structure. (CODASYL is the same group that developed the COBOL programming language.)

Relational Structure

The relational model is the most recent of the three database structures. It was developed in an attempt to simplify the representation of complex relationships between data elements in large databases. In this approach, all data elements within the database are viewed as being stored in the form of simple tables. Figure 11–20 shows the general form of the relational database model and two tables representing departmental and employee records. Note the unique terminology this database model uses. Tables are equivalent to files and are called **relations.** Rows are equivalent to records and are called **tuples.** Columns are equivalent to fields and are called **domains.** Other relations for this organization's database might represent the data element relationships between projects, divisions, product lines, etc. Database management systems based on the relational model are used to link data elements from various tables to provide information with multiple relationships to users.

Developing a Database

Developing a large database based on the hierarchical and network models is a complex task. Even the more simple relational model may require the development of hundreds of tables of record relationships in a large database. So there is much work to do by users, programmers, and systems analysts. In many companies, developing and managing the database is the primary responsibility of a *database administrator* (DBA), and database design analysts. They work with users, programmers, and analysts to determine what data should be included in the database and what structure or relationships exist between the data elements. Figure 11–21 outlines the major stages of logical database design.

Schema

Defining the structure of the logical relationships between data in a database results in the development of a database **schema.**

FIGURE 11–21 Designing a database

A. STEPS OF LOGICAL DATABASE DESIGN

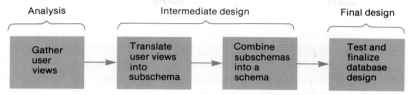

B. COMPUTER-ASSISTED DATABASE DESIGN USING DATA DICTIONARY AND DATABASE DESIGN
SOFTWARE PACKAGES FROM APPLIED DATA RESEARCH (ADR)

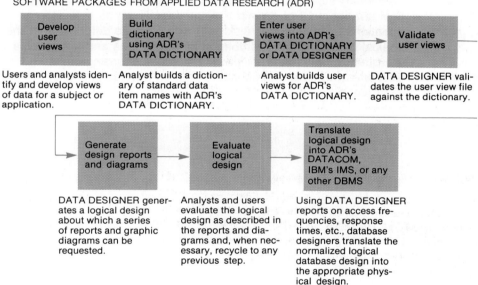

The schema is an overall *conceptual* or *logical* view of the relationships between the data in the database. For example, the schema would describe what types of data elements (fields, records, files, etc.) are in the database, the relationships between the data elements (pointer fields, linking records, etc.), and the structure of data relationships (hierarchical, network, or relational database structures).

Subschema

Once the schema is designed and documented, the database administrator must define a **subschema** for each user application program that will access the database. A subschema is a subset or transformation of the logical view of the database schema that is required by a particular user application program. Obviously, each program does not have to access the entire database, but only a portion (subschema) of its logical data elements and relationships. For example, the subschema for a bank's checking account program would not include all of the record types and relationships in a customer database but only those records and files that were related to the operation and management of the checking account activity.

It must be emphasized that both the schema and subschema are *logical* views of the data and relationships of the database. The *physical* view of the data (also called the internal view) describes how data is physically arranged, stored, and accessed on secondary storage devices of the computer system. The actual physical arrangement of data in the database (such as their storage locations on a magnetic disk unit) may be quite different from the logical data relationships defined in the schema and subschema (frequently called *user's views*). The physical arrangement and placement of data on secondary storage devices is one of the pri-

FIGURE

11–22 Examples of multiple database views and software interfaces

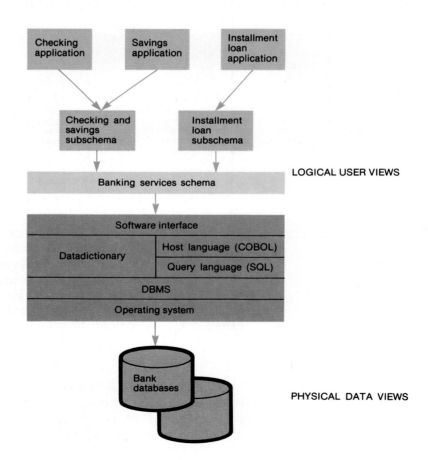

mary tasks performed by the data management control programs of an operating system. Figure 11–22 shows the multiple database views and software interface of a bank database processing system.

Types of Databases

Modern database processing systems require more than one set of databases for an entire organization. The growth of distributed processing, microcomputer-based executive workstations, and decision support systems has caused the development of several major types of databases. Figure 11–23 illustrates five major types of databases for computer-using organizations:

■ **Common operational databases.** These databases store detailed data generated by the operations of the entire organization. Thus they are also called *transaction databases* or *production databases*. Examples might include a customer database, personnel database, accounting database, and other common databases containing data generated by business operations.

■ **Common user databases.** These databases store data and information extracted from selected operational and external databases. They consist of summarized data and information most needed by the organization's managers and other end users. Thus they are also called *information databases* or *management databases*. These are the common databases accessed by personal computer/executive workstation users as part of the *decision support systems* (DSS) that support managerial decision making, discussed in Chapter Fourteen.

FIGURE

11–23 Types of databases

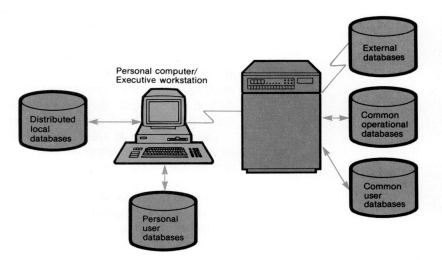

■ **Distributed local databases.** These are databases at local workplaces such as regional offices, branch offices, and manufacturing plants. These databases can include segments of both common operational and common user databases, as well as data generated and used only at a user's own site. The next section discusses several important concepts of such *distributed databases*.

■ **Personal user databases.** These local databases consist of a variety of data files developed by personal computer/executive workstation users to support their individual professional activities. For example, they may have their own electronic copies of documents they have generated by using word processing packages or received by electronic mail. Or they may have their own data files generated from using electronic spreadsheet and microcomputer DBMS packages.

■ **External databases.** Access to large, privately owned databases are available for a fee to an organization's computer users. These **data banks** contain a wealth of economic information that can help support the management of an organization if it is properly analyzed and presented. Figure 12–15 in the next chapter summarizes the types of information provided by such data banks.

Distributed Databases

The concept of **distributed databases** is a major consideration when developing databases for an organization that uses *distributed processing systems*. As we mentioned in Chapter Ten, data as well as computing power must be distributed to the user departments in the organization. Thus data that needs to be used and processed only at a user's site (called *local data*) is stored in *local databases*, while data needed by all or several of the local and central computer systems (called *global data*) is frequently stored in *common databases*. However, part or all of the common database can be duplicated at one or more local sites. Thus global data can be *centralized* in one common database, or *partitioned* into *segments* which are distributed to several processing sites. Also, all or part of the global data in the common database can be duplicated (*replicated*) and distributed to various processing sites.

Obviously, any of these methods of distributing databases has its advantages and disadvantages and requires careful planning and design. For example, centralizing all global data is the simplest arrangement but may involve potential problems of performance and reliability, since all computers in the network are dependent on the computer system where the common database is stored. These problems can be eliminated if the global data are replicated and copies of the data are distributed to several processing sites.

However, this arrangement involves potential problems in insuring that all copies of the global data are properly and concurrently updated every time they are affected by transactions or other changes. Thus developing a distributed database system frequently requires trade-offs between service to users, processing and communications costs, and processing performance and control. See Figure 11–24.

Advantages and Disadvantages

Database processing systems supported by DBMS software are steadily replacing traditional file processing systems. The superior service and performance of database processing is a result of the integration of data required by the database concept, the availability of fast and high-capacity direct access storage devices, and the use of powerful database management systems that greatly facilitate the control and use of databases. These resources provide computer users with easy access to specific information derived from manipulating the data in an updated database. Updating and maintaining the database, producing documents and reports required by various user application programs, and responding to user inqui-

FIGURE 11–24 Example of a distributed database system

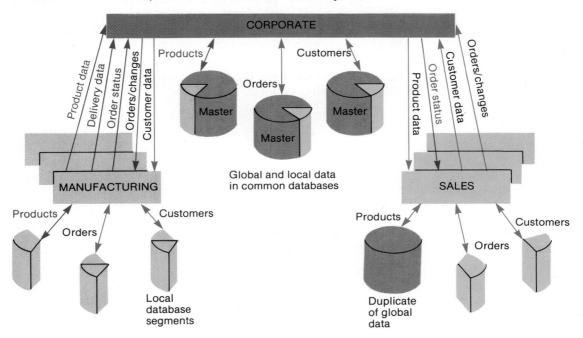

ries with immediate video display responses are easily handled by modern database processing systems.

Several other advantages of database processing systems have already been mentioned. Database processing systems reduce the duplication of data and integrate data so they can be accessed by multiple programs and users. Programs are not dependent on the format of data and the type of secondary storage hardware being used. Users are provided with an inquiry/response capability, which allows them to easily obtain information they need without having to write computer programs. Computer programming is simplified, because programs are not dependent on either the logical format of data or its physical storage location. Finally, control and security of the data stored in databases is significantly increased, since all access to data is controlled by a database management system and a database administrator.

Disadvantages and limitations of database processing systems arise from the increased complexity of the database concept. Developing a large database and installing a DBMS can be difficult and expensive. More hardware capability is required, since storage requirements for the organization's data, *overhead control data*, and the DBMS programs are greater. Finally, if an organization relies on one central database, its vulnerability to errors and failures is increased.

In most cases, the benefits of database processing systems far outweigh their limitations. Database processing systems increase the productivity of users by providing information more efficiently and effectively than file processing systems. Users can more easily get the data they need in less time using the database approach. Thus the use of database processing is increasing in modern information processing systems.

REAL WORLD APPLICATION 11–3

Aetna Life and Casualty Company

The Employee Benefits Division (EBD) of the Aetna Life and Casualty Company in Hartford, Connecticut, utilizes the equivalent of seven IBM 3033 processors, several hundred IBM 3350 disk drives, a full complement of printers and peripheral devices, and a full-time staff of 400 programmers. Considering the possibilities for large-scale data management, EBD concluded their most cost-effective choice would be purchasing a DBMS from an outside vendor. A thorough survey of major DBMSs on the market quickly narrowed the field to four systems: System 2000, ADABAS, DL/1, and Cullinet's Integrated Database Management System (IDMS).

"In the end, we went with IDMS for two overriding reasons: its superior backup and recovery facilities and its CODASYL network oriented database organization," says EBD Database Administrator Bob Yellin. "The IDMS backup and recovery capabilities are by far the best offered by any commercially available DBMS, and its building-block CODASYL structure has made it possible to design large operational databases, reduce our administrative overhead, and implement a variety of complex data structures."

EBD purchased IDMS in 1978, along with Cullinet's CULPRIT and OnLine Query (OLQ) packages. EBD has since implemented or enhanced a number of extremely ambitious systems using IDMS, the largest of which is an enhancement to AECCLAIMS, an online application that processes group health claims. AECCLAIMS presently utilizes four dedicated IBM 3033 large mainframe computers, and some 275 IBM 3350 disk drives to process claim transactions from over 4,000 terminals spread throughout the United States.

AECCLAIMS is an interactive system reportedly processing over 300,000 IDMS transactions per day. "During our first three months of 13-hour-per-day online operations, we didn't experience a single volume-related failure through IDMS. In fact, from what we've seen of it so far, I'd have to say that IDMS is more reliable than any other software product I've ever seen," Mr. Yellin says.

IDMS has enabled EBD to streamline its operation and keep up with a mounting workload. The schema/subschema relationships designed into the system have reduce administrative overhead by eliminating the need to build a distinct database descriptor for each program. "On the manpower side," Robert Lee points out, "we can effectively assign programmers who normally work with less-complex tasks to projects involving more-complex tasks without retraining. Also, the IDMS-Directory has been extremely useful as a central repository of data definitions."

- Why did Aetna choose the IDMS database management system? Which database structure does it use? What information processing applications are involved?
- What benefits have resulted from the use of IDMS? What benefits has the "schema/subschema relationships designed into the system" produced for Aetna?

Source: Courtesy Cullinet Software Inc.

SUMMARY

- Data must be organized in some logical manner so that it can be efficiently processed. Thus data is commonly organized into characters, fields, records, files, and databases, and can be described as either physical or logical elements. Data files can be organized in either a sequential or random manner, and files can be processed by either sequential access or direct access file processing methods.

- Access methods for the two basic file organization methods include the indexed sequential access method, in which records are organized sequentially but referenced by an index; the list file organization, which uses pointers to locate related records stored in a nonsequential manner; and the inverted file access method. Database structures are used to organize the complex relations between the individual records stored in large databases. Three fundamental database structures are the hierarchical, network, and relational models.

- For many years, electronic information processing had a file processing orientation, in which separate computer programs were used to update independent data files and produce the documents and reports required by each user application. This caused problems of data redundancy, unintegrated data, and program/data dependence. The concepts of databases and database processing were developed to solve these problems.

- Database processing systems use a database orientation for both the storage and processing of data. The data needed by different data processing applications is consolidated and integrated into several common databases, instead of being stored in many independent data files. Also, information processing consists of updating and maintaining a common database, having users application programs share the data in the database, and providing an inquiry/response capability so users can easily receive quick responses to requests for information from the database.

- Database management systems are system software packages which control the creation, use, and maintenance of a database. They provide a software interface between users and programmers and the database.

- Developing a large database is a complex task, which is the responsibility of users, programmers, systems analysts, and the database administrator. The schema or structure of the logical relationships between data elements in the database must be developed, as well as the subschema, which is a subset of the schema required for a particular user application. Developing distributed databases requires trade-offs between service to users, processing and communications costs, and processing performance and control. Security of the data stored in databases can be significantly improved. However, vulnerability to errors and failures may be increased unless stringent controls and security are developed.

KEY TERMS AND CONCEPTS

Common data elements:
    character, field, record, file,
    database
Logical and physical data
    elements
Data organization aids: key,
    pointer, index
File organization:
    random, sequential, indexed
    sequential, list, inverted file
Sequential access file
    processing

Direct access file processing
Database structures: hierar-
    chical, network, relational
Data base processing
Schema
Subschema
Distributed databases
Types of databases: opera-
    tional, user, local, external
Data banks

REVIEW AND APPLICATION QUESTIONS

1. Provide examples to illustrate each of the common data elements.
2. Can a single physical record contain more than one logical record? Explain.
3. What is the difference between sequential and random methods of file organization, and between sequential access and direct access file processing?
4. What are the functions of keys, pointers, and indexes? How are these data organization aids used in the indexed sequential, list, and inverted file methods of file organization?
5. Why are database structures necessary? Use the concepts of the hierarchical, network, and relational data structure models to illustrate your answer.
6. What are database processing systems? Are they superior to file processing systems? Explain.
7. Explain how database processing systems use a database approach for both the storage and processing of data.

8. What are a schema and subschema? What role do they play in the development of a database?
9. Which of the five basic types of databases is most important for managers? Explain.
10. Should databases be centralized or distributed? Explain.
11. What database processing capability is of most benefit to ordinary end users? Use an example to substantiate your answer.
12. What are several advantages and disadvantages of database processing systems? Do the benefits of database processing outweigh its limitations? Explain.

APPLICATION PROBLEMS

1. If you have not already done so, read and answer the questions after each Real World Application in this chapter.
2. Given the following examples of files, what file organization and access method would most likely be in use? Why?
   a. A payroll masterfile.
   b. A checking account masterfile at a bank.
   c. An accounts receivable masterfile at a large retail store.
   d. A student registration file used for on-line registration at a major university.
3. Refer to Figure 11–7, which shows a personnel and payroll file being linked together via pointers. Assume that using this pointer method has become too cumbersome. Numerous pointers are being stored and the access time has doubled. Therefore, the company is preparing to combine its payroll and personnel files into a single file. For producing paychecks, the file will be processed in a batch mode once a week. For meeting personnel needs, the file will be accessed on an ad hoc basis to answer such questions as "which of our data processing personnel can speak Spanish?"
   a. What type of file (by permanence not by organization) will the combined payroll and personnel file be?
   b. Can one file be used or accessed in the two different ways indicated? Why or why not?
   c. When processing payroll in batch mode, should sequential or random access be used? What criteria must be considered to make this decision?
   d. What file organization should be used in establishing the combined file? Why?
   e. On what medium should the file be stored?
4. A partial inventory file is shown on the next page. Complete the forward and backward links (pointers) for this file.

Inventory Item Number	Warehouse Number	Quantity	Unit Price	Forward Warehouse Link or Pointer	Backware Warehouse Link
438	3	50	1.50		
450	2	610	6.00	463	472
452	1	750	7.50		
463	2	112	.50	472	450
469	3	425	9.00		
472	2	62	4.75	450	463
473	3	30	3.25		

5. Using the partial inventory file in problem 4, create an inverted file:
   a. By warehouse
   b. By unit price using two categories 0-5.00,5.01-10.00
6. A database management system (DBMS) has three different types of languages: data manipulation language (DML), data definition language (DDL), and query language. For each of the examples given below, identify which of these three languages would most probably be used:
   a. A programmer writes a COBOL program to update fields of accounts receivable records contained in the database.
   b. The field for ZIP code in the database is expanded to handle a 10 digit number.
   c. The president of the company requests and receives an ad hoc report detailing the company's debt structure.
   d. The database administrator documents the content, relationships, and structure of the database.
7. What database structures do the diagrams in Figure 11–25 represent? Explain your answer.

FIGURE

11–25 Two database structures

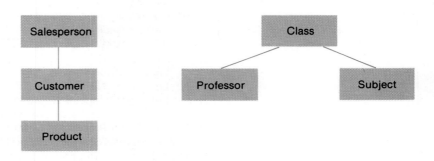

CHAPTER 12

Data Communications Systems

CHAPTER OUTLINE

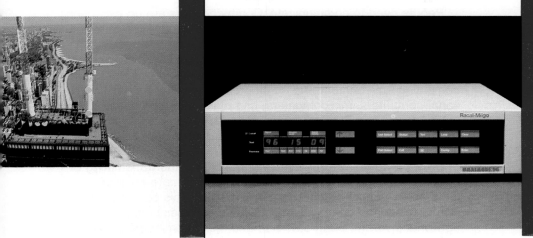

LEARNING OBJECTIVES

The purpose of this chapter is to promote a basic understandingof data communications and the role it plays in electronic information processing systems. After reading and studying this chapter, you should be able to:

1. Identify the functions and components of a data communications system.
2. Explain the functions of data communications hardware and software.
3. Identify the major types of communications channels, carriers, and networks.
4. Use examples to illustrate the benefits and limitations of data communications for electronic information processing.

INTRODUCTION

People need to communicate. Computer users are no exception. They need to transmit and receive data and information between themselves and their computer systems. This wasn't possible in the early years of computing, when all the computer resources of an organization may have been located in a single room. But today's computing environment is a lot different. Computer terminals, personal computers, minicomputers, and mainframe computers seem to be everywhere. They are *dispersed* both geographically and organizationally throughout computer-using organizations. That's why we need *data communications*.

Data communications systems provide for the transmitting of data over communication links between one or more computer systems and a variety of input/output terminals. This can range from simple telephone communication links to complex communications networks involving earth satellites and many communications control computers. We will discuss data communications systems, networks, and applications in this chapter. You should also realize that data communications are part of the general area of **telecommunications**. That term refers to all types of long-distance communication (i.e., voice, data, and images) including telephone, radio, and television transmissions. Finally, you should note the frequently used term of **teleprocessing**. It is a combination of the terms *telecommunications* and *data processing* and has more of an information processing emphasis. However, in this text, we will continue to use the more popular term of *data communications*. Let's now look at the major components of a data communications system. Then we will discuss the major ways such data communications systems are used in today's dynamic computer environment.

A DATA COMMUNICATIONS SYSTEM MODEL

It would be easy for you to be overwhelmed by the large numbers of devices and complex technologies involved in modern data communications. What you need is a simple *system model* to help you organize and understand this important area of computer use. Look at Figure 12–1. It shows you that a data communications system consists of the following five major components:

■ **Terminals,** such as video display terminals, or any input/output device that uses communications channels to transmit or receive data.

■ **Data communications interface devices** (such as *modems, multiplexers and front-end processors*), which support data transmission between terminals and computers. These devices perform a variety of support functions on both ends of a communications channel between terminals and computers. For example, they con-

FIGURE 12–1 The five basic components of a data communications system

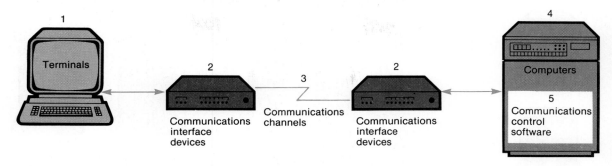

Data communications hardware consists of a variety of computer

vert data from digital form to analog and back, code and decode data, and control and maximize the communications flow between computers and terminals in a data communications network.

■ **Communications channels** over which data are transmitted and received. Communications channels can consist of combinations of *media*, such as telephone lines, coaxial cables, fiber optic cables, microwave systems, or earth satellite systems.

■ **Computers** of all sizes and types use data communications to carry out their information processing assignments. Many times there is one larger general-purpose computer that serves as the *host* computer and contains the main data communications control programs which control the data communications network.

■ **Communications control software** consists of control programs which reside in the host computer system and other communications control computers in the data communications system. They control input/output activities involving the data communications system, and they manage the functions of communications networks.

DATA COMMUNICATIONS HARDWARE

Data communications hardware consists of a variety of computer terminals, several types of data communication interface devices, communications channel equipment and media, and the computers that operate in the data communications network. Let us examine these hardware devices more closely. See Figure 12–2.

Terminals

In Chapter Six we discussed the many types of computer terminals that can be used in information processing systems. These

FIGURE 12–2 Communications hardware in a data communications network

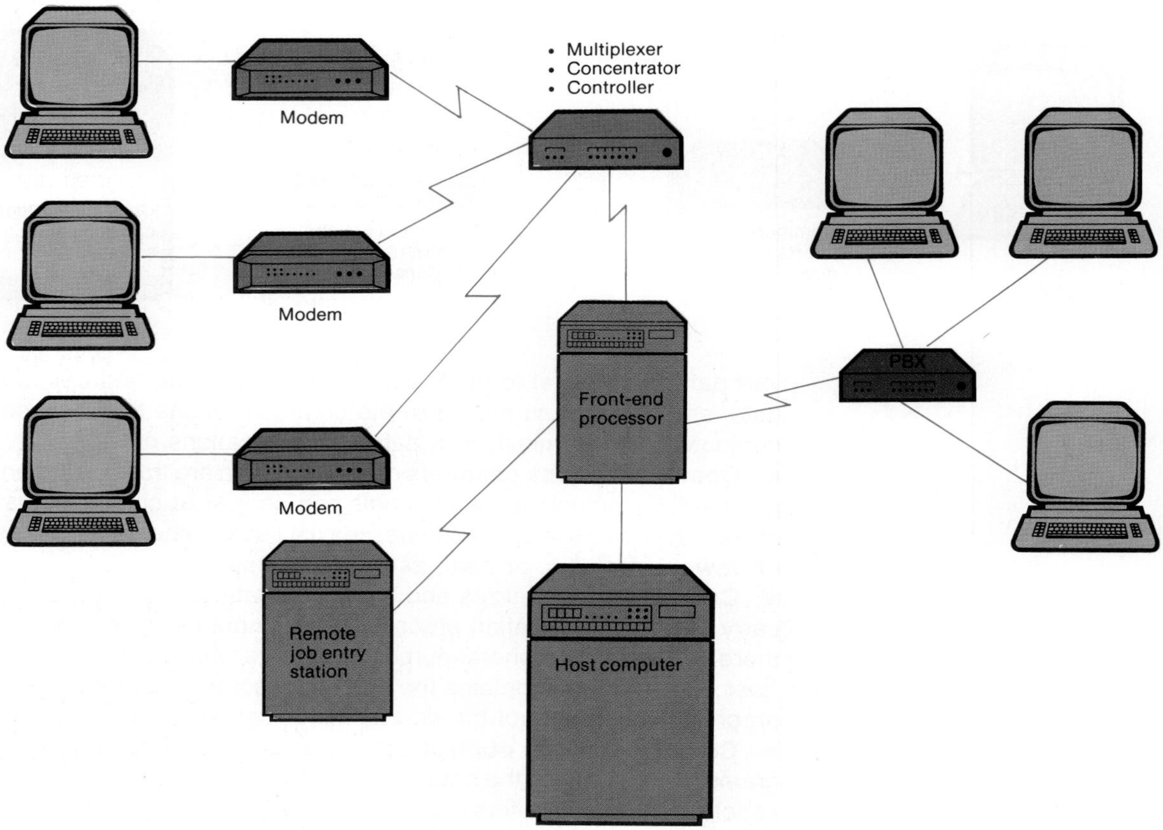

included *video display terminals*, *printing terminals*, *transaction terminals*, and *intelligent terminals*. However, any input/output device that has data communications capabilities is a terminal. Thus personal computers, push-button *smart* telephones, and other information processing equipment may have the capability to act as terminals. Even small dedicated computer systems can act as terminals in a data communications network. Such *remote job entry* (RJE) *stations* are used for remote-access batch processing, where they collect and transmit batches of data and receive the output of the host computer in a batch processing system.

Modems

Modems convert the **digital** signals from a computer or transmission terminal at one end of a communications link into **analog** frequencies, which can be transmitted over ordinary telephone lines. A modem at the other end of the communications line converts the transmitted data back into digital form at a receiving terminal. This process is known as *modulation* and *demodulation*, and the word *modem* is a combined abbreviation of these two words. Modems are necessary because ordinary telephone lines were primarily designed to handle continuous analog signals, such as the human voice. Since data from computers are in digital form, devices are necessary to convert digital signals into appropriate analog transmission frequencies and vice versa. However, *digital communications networks* that transmit digital signals are rapidly developing. Modems that only perform the digital/analog conversion function are not required when such channels are used. See Figure 12–3.

Intelligent modems use special-purpose microprocessors to support additional capabilities, such as simultaneous data and voice transmission, transmission error detection, automatic dialing and answering of calls to and from remote terminals, conversion from EBCDIC to ASCII codes and back, and automatic testing and selection of transmission lines. Modems can also vary in their data communications speed capacity. Typically, speeds vary from 300 *bits per second* (BPS) for connecting low-speed printing terminals, to 1,200 BPS, for use with medium-speed video terminals, and up to 9,600 BPS or higher, for high-speed peripheral devices.

If you have a **microcomputer** you will need a modem if you want to communicate with other computers or use some of the personal computer networks and data banks. To connect to a modem, your computer will have to have a communications interface circuit board with a *serial* (one bit at a time) interface *port* and an *RS23C* interface. RS232C is a standard 25-pin connector arrangement needed to connect modems to terminals and personal computers. It includes pins for data, control signals, and timing circuits. You will need either a 300 or 1,200 BPS modem (or one that provides both speeds). Cost typically ranges between $200 and $700 but can go higher.

Modems come in three major forms: (1) stand-alone, (2) board-level, and (3) acoustic coupler. The stand-alone modem is a separate

FIGURE 12–3 The modulation-demodulation process

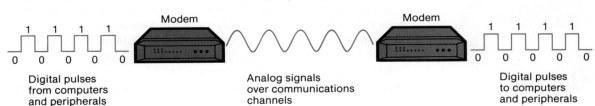

Digital pulses
from computers
and peripherals

Analog signals
over communications
channels

Digital pulses
to computers
and peripherals

unit that is connected between a terminal or microcomputer and the telephone line. The board-level modem consists of a circuit board, with appropriate chips and circuits, that plugs into one of the expansion slots inside the microcomputer or terminal. The acoustic coupler modem has a special holder or cradle into which the telephone handset is placed. This *acoustically* connects the modem to the telephone line so the modem can process audible analog tones. See Figure 12–4.

Multiplexers and Other Communications Processors

There are many types of data communications interface devices besides modems. These include devices known as *multiplexers, concentrators, communications controllers, cluster controllers, protocol converters, data encryptors, communications processors,* and *front-end processors!* However, the fastest growing communications control device is the **multiplexer.** A multiplexer is an electronic device that allows a single communications channel to carry simultaneous data transmissions from many terminals. Typically, a multiplexer merges the transmissions of several terminals at one end of a communications channel, while a similar unit separates the individual transmissions at the receiving end. This is accomplished in two basic ways. In *frequency division multiplexing* (FDM), a multiplexer effectively divides a high-speed channel into multiple slow-speed channels. In *time division multiplexing* (TDM), the multiplexer divides the time each terminal can use a high-speed line into very short-time slots or time frames. The most advanced and popular type of multiplexer is the *statistical time division multiplexer*, most commonly referred to as a **statistical multiplexer** or *stat mux*. Instead of giving all terminals equal time slots, it dynamically allocates time slots to only active terminals based on priorities assigned by a user.

Statistical multiplexers are rapidly making all other types of multiplexers obsolete. They are also being used to perform the functions of other devices. By their use of microprocessors and memory circuits, **intelligent multiplexers** can now perform many communications interface functions. For example, advanced models have capabilities, such as error monitoring, diagnostics and correction, modulation-demodulation, data compression, data coding and decoding, protocol conversion, message switching, port contention, buffer storage, use of internally stored programs, and serving as an interface to satellite and other advanced communications networks! Many of these capabilities were formerly found only in other advanced devices. For example, devices known as **concentrators** and **communications controllers** use microprocessor intelligence,

FIGURE

12–4 A stand-alone modem

stored communications programs, and buffer storage to *concentrate* many slow-speed lines into a high-speed line and to *control* transmission activities among several terminals. However, since some intelligent multiplexers can now perform such functions, they are being called *concentrators* and *controllers* by their manufacturers. Thus several vendors have already begun to use the more generic term **communications processors** to describe their advanced statistical multiplexers. See Figure 12–5.

Front-End Processors

A **front-end processor** is typically a special-purpose minicomputer that is dedicated to handling the data communications control functions for large mainframe computer systems. It can perform many of the functions of other data communications interface devices and can be programmed to perform additional necessary functions. For example, it has its own memory, which is used to store its data control programs and to provide temporary buffer storage. Its functions may include coding and decoding data, error detection, recovery, recording, interpreting, and processing of control information which is transmitted (such as characters that indicate the beginning and end of messages). It can also *poll* remote terminals to determine if they have a message to send or are ready to receive a message.

However, a front-end computer has more advanced responsibilities. It controls access to a network and allows only authorized users to use the system, assigns priorities to messages, logs all data communications activity, computes statistics on network activity, and routes and reroutes messages among alternative communi-

FIGURE

12–5 Communication processors

A Multiplexers.

B A communications controller.

A

B

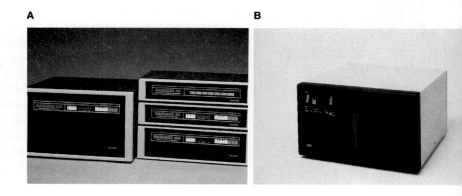

cation links. Thus the front-end processor can relieve the host computer of its data communications control functions. It has been estimated that the use of front-end processors and other advanced data communications interface devices can provide up to 30 percent additional processing time for a host computer system.

Private Branch Exchange

Large offices and other work areas have been using a telephone switching device called the **private branch exchange (PBX)** for decades. A PBX is a *switchboard* that serves as an interface device between the many telephone lines within a work area and the local telephone company's main telephone lines or *trunks*. In recent years, PBXs have become electronic computerized devices with built-in microprocessor and stored program intelligence. They not only route telephone calls within an office but also provide other services, such as automatic forwarding of calls, conference calling, and *least-cost routing* of long-distance calls.

However, the PBX has recently become a major new *data communications interface device* to connect and control the terminals, computers, and other information processing devices in modern offices and other work areas. These computerized PBXs can handle the switching of both **voice** and **data** in the *local area networks* (*LANs*) that are needed in such locations. They allow computer users to share data and information processing capabilities with each other. The computerized PBX is being called a variety of names, including PABX (private automatic branch exchange), CBX (computerized branch exchange), and DPBX (digital private branch exchange), though the PBX term is still the most widely used.

A computerized PBX typically consists of five major components: (1) a main microprocessor, (2) semiconductor memory, (3) a stored program, (4) interface circuits, and (5) switching circuits. The main microprocessor or MPU controls the network by following a program of instructions stored in the memory unit. Interface circuits and *support microprocessors* perform such functions as *digitizing* analog voice communications before transmission over digitial networks. Then they convert such **digitized voice** messages back into normal analog form. They also handle feedback and control messages between the MPU, the other components of the PBX, and the telephone devices in the system. Lastly, the switching circuits and support microprocessors in the PBX are used to switch both voice and data calls between internal and external telephone lines. We will discuss the role of the PBX further in an upcoming section on local area networks. See Figure 12–6.

FIGURE

12–6 A computerized PBX: The Rolm CBX II

DATA COMMUNICATIONS SOFTWARE

Software is a vital component of all data communications systems. Data communications software consists of computer programs stored in the *host computer* or in *front-end computers* and other communications processors that control and support the communications occurring in a data communications network. Data communications system software packages are frequently called **communication monitors**, or **teleprocessing** (TP) **monitors**. They include **communications access programs**, which establish the connection between terminals and computer systems, and the link between user application programs and the communications network. Most microcomputer communications packages are of this type. They also include **network control programs**, which manage the functions of a communications network. They may reside in the host computer or in front-end computers or other communications processors. Figure 12–7 illustrates the tasks performed by one major type of communications monitor, which includes:

- Connecting and disconnecting communications links.
- Detecting and correcting errors.
- Polling the terminals in a network.
- Forming "waiting lines" (*queuing*) of data and program tasks.
- Routing (switching) messages in the network.
- Logging statistics of errors and other network activity.

DATA COMMUNICATIONS CARRIERS

Common Carriers

Data communications and other telecommunications services are provided by many companies. Several companies have traditionally offered a broad range of communications services, including American Telephone and Telegraph (AT&T), the new operating companies that were formerly part of the Bell system, General Telephone and Electronics, Western Union, and the many independent telephone companies. These **common carriers** provide a variety of communications channels that are used by most computer-using firms and individuals. They have traditionally been authorized by government agencies to provide public communications services. However, as Figure 12–8 shows, many of communications carriers are authorized to provide a wide variety of communication services. For example, besides voice and data communications, many communications carriers provide standard radio and television transmission, facsimile, teleconferencing, electronic mail, and cellular radio services. We will discuss these services in this chapter and the next.

FIGURE 12–7 Communications monitor activities

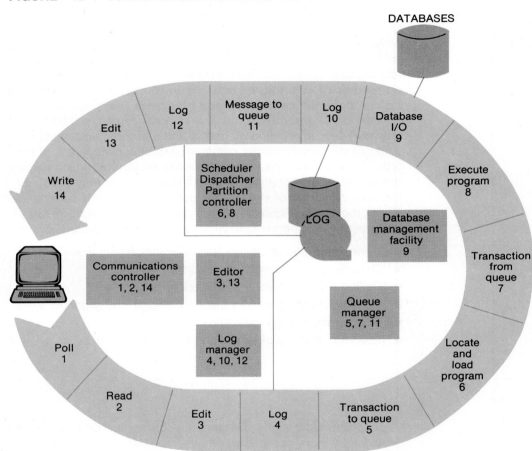

Source: Myles E. Walsh, *Database and Data Communications Systems* (Reston, Va.: Reston Publishing Company, 1983), p. 103. Reprinted with permission.

Specialized Carriers

Private communications networks used by major business firms and government agencies are a growing communications alternative. However, most data communications activity still takes place in public networks. This includes companies known as *specialized common carriers*, which sell high-speed voice and data communications services in selected high-density areas of the country. Examples of such specialized carriers are ITT World Communications, Southern Pacific Communications Company, MCI Communications Corporation, American Satellite Company, and Satellite Business Systems. In addition, there are companies called *value-added carri-*

FIGURE 12–8 A guide to communications carriers and services

CARRIERS	Local telephone	Long-distance telephone	Satellite networks	Local area networks	Cellular radio	Telex & TWX	Data communications	Information services*	Facsimile	Teleconference
American Satellite		■	■				■		■	■
American Telephone & Telegraph		■	■	■	■		■			■
Bell Operating Companies	■			■	■		■	■	■	
Communications Satellite			■							
CompuServe							■	■		
Continental	■			■	■		■	■		
General Telephone & Electronics	■	■	■	■	■		■	■		
Graphic Scanning					■	■			■	
Hughes Communications			■							
International Telephone & Telegraph		■		■			■	■	■	
MCI Communications		■				■	■			
RCA		■	■			■	■		■	
Satellite Business Systems		■	■				■	■	■	■
Southern Pacific Communications		■	■				■	■		
The Source							■	■		
Tymnet							■	■		
United Telecom	■	■		■				■		
Western Union		■	■		■	■	■		■	■
Xerox						■	■	■	■	

* Electronic mail, public data banks, personal computing, timesharing, and so on.

ers, which lease communications facilities from the common carriers and combine messages from customers into groupings called *packets* for transmission. These **packet switching** networks (also known as **value-added** networks—VAN) add "value" to their communications facilities by adding advanced hardware and software to provide packet switching and other data communication services. Examples of value-added companies include GTE Telenet and Tymnet by Tymeshare. We should also not forget two major communications carriers that provide networks for personal computing. As we mentioned in Chapter Four, these are *CompuServe* (owned by Compu-Serve, Inc., and H&R Block, Inc.) and *The Source* (owned by Source Telecomputing Corporation—a subsidiary of *Reader's Digest*). We will discuss the services of these specialized carriers later in the chapter.

DATA COMMUNICATIONS CHANNELS AND MEDIA

We have discussed all but one of the major components of a data communications system (terminals, interface devices, computers, and control software). Now let's discuss the last major component: **communications channels**. A communications channel (also called a communications *line* or *link*) is the means by which data and other forms of communications are transmitted between the sending and receiving devices in a communications network. A communications channel makes use of a variety of **communications media**, such as ordinary telephone lines, coaxial cables, fiber optic cables, microwave systems, and earth satellite systems to transmit and receive data. You should have a basic understanding of the major types of communications media that are used in modern data communications channels.

Standard Telephone Lines

Ordinary telephone lines, consisting of copper wire twisted into pairs **(twisted pair wire),** are used extensively for data communications. These lines are widely used in established communications networks throughout the world for both voice and data transmission. This includes privately leased lines, which can be *conditioned* to reduce distortion and error rates and thus allow faster transmission rates.

Coaxial Cables

Coaxial cable consists of groups of copper and aluminum wires that are wrapped to insulate and protect them and thus minimize interference and distortion of the signals they carry. These high-quality lines are usually buried underground or laid on the floors of lakes and oceans. They allow high-speed data transmission and are being used as replacements for twisted pair wire lines in high-service metropolitan areas, for cable TV systems, and for short-distance connection of computers and peripheral devices. They are thus being widely used in office buildings and other work sites for *local area networks*. There are two basic coaxial cable technologies: **baseband**, in which all devices share one communications channel, and **broadband**, which provides over 10 times the channels of baseband cable but costs up to twice as much.

Fiber Optics

FIGURE

12–9 Glass fibers from a fiber optics cable conducting light from a laser

Fiber optics uses cables consisting of thousands of very thin filaments of glass fibers, which can conduct light pulses generated by **lasers** at transmission frequencies that approach the speed of light. *Lasers* are very concentrated high-frequency beams of light that are capable of transmitting about 100,000 times as much information as microwaves. Fiber optics has demonstrated digital transmission speeds about a thousand times faster than microwave transmission. Fiber optic cables provide substantial size and weight reductions as well as increased speed and greater carrying capacity. A half-inch diameter fiber optics cable can carry up to 50,000 channels compared to about 5,500 channels for a standard coaxial cable. In another comparison, a one and one-half pound fiber optics cable can transmit as much data as 30 pounds of copper wire. Fiber optic cables have already been installed in several major cities, including high-speed lines between New York and Washington D.C. Lasers and fiber optics are expected to seriously compete with other communications media in the near future. See Figure 12–9.

Microwave Systems

Terrestrial (earth-bound) microwave systems transmit high-speed radio signals in a line-of-sight path between relay stations spaced approximately 30 miles apart. Microwave antennas are usually placed on top of buildings, towers, hills, and mountain peaks, and are a familiar site in many sections of the country.

Communication Satellites

The most exciting data communications development at the present time is the use of **communications satellites** for microwave transmission. There are several dozen communication satellites from several nations placed into stationary "parking orbits" approximately 22,000 miles above the equator. Most satellites are launched by NASA, weigh several thousand pounds, are powered by solar panels, and can transmit microwave signals at a rate of several hundred million bits per second. They serve as relay stations for communication signals transmitted from *earth stations*. Earth stations beam microwave signals to the satellites, which amplify and retransmit the signals to other earth stations thousands of miles away. While communication satellites were used initially for voice and video transmission, they are capable of high-speed transmission of large volumes of data. Present communication satellite systems are operated by several firms, including AT&T, Western Union, RCA, American Satellite Company, Satellite Business Systems (SBS), which is owned jointly by IBM, Aetna Insurance, and the Communications Satellite Corporation (COMSAT), and Intellsat, an international consortium of over 100 nations. See Figure 12–10.

Cellular Radio

Cellular radio is a new radio communications technology that divides a metropolitan area into a honeycomb of **cells**. This greatly increases the number of frequencies and thus the users that can take advantage of mobile phone service. Each cell has its own low-power transmitter, rather than having one high-powered radio transmitter to serve an entire city. The number of radio frequencies available for mobile phone service using this technology increases dramatically: from 14 to 333! However, a powerful central computer and other communications interface equipment is needed to coordinate and control the transmissions of thousand of mobile phone users as they drive from one cell to another. Cellular radio is ex-

FIGURE 12–10

A Westar communications satellite. **B** A communications satellite system.

A

B

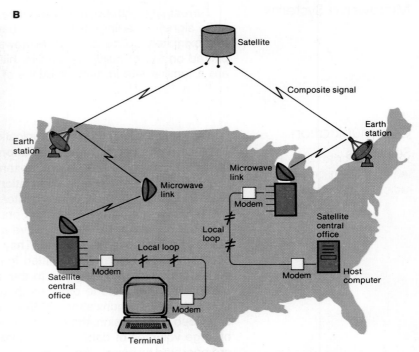

Source: P. D. Moulton, "Satellite Communications," Auerbach series on distributed processing management, Auerbach Publishing Company. Reprinted with permission.

pected to become an important communications medium for mobile voice and data communications. See Figure 12–11.

DATA COMMUNICATIONS NETWORKS AND APPLICATIONS

Most data communications systems are not solitary single-user, single-purpose systems, but complex **data communications networks**. These networks consist of interconnected hardware, software, and communications channels, which support many types of data communications activity for many users. Thus we can speak of *public* data communications networks, *private* networks which support the data communications activity of individual business organizations, *international* networks which span the globe, and so on. We will now look at several applications of modern data communications networks in business. (Technical network characteristics are discussed in the supplement at the end of this chapter.) First, let's summarize basic types of electronic information processing that rely heavily on a data communication capability.

- *Inquiry/response systems* allow inquiries and responses to be transmitted electronically to and from a realtime processing system, thus providing up-to-date information for business operations and management.

- *Online data entry and remote job entry*, in which data are captured and transmitted to a computer system immediately after

FIGURE

12–11 A portable data terminal using cellular radio technology

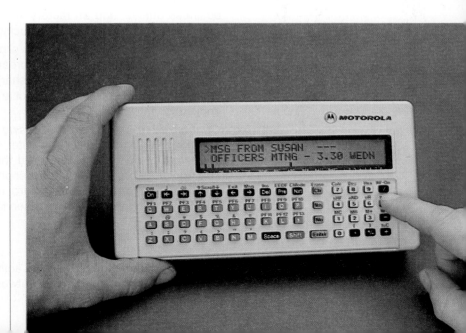

REAL WORLD APPLICATION 12-1

First Interstate Bank Corporation

First Interstate Bank Corporation has developed and now operates what *Business Week* has described as "the most sophisticated network of interstate electronic terminals yet built," the Teller Item Processing System (TIPS), which connects more than 825 banking offices in 11 western states. This system currently processes more than 300,000 account inquiries every day by means of IBM 3604 terminals located at teller work stations. The terminals work during the daytime under the control of distributed data processors. At night, that whole data base is turned around by satellite channels into the Los Angeles facility to update the central data base and then transmit the data back.

An American Satellite Company network, consisting of three 5-meter stations and one 10-meter station, connects the three largest regional computer processing centers with the TIPS center in Los Angeles, where the larger station is located. A total of eight satellite channels are being used, and the satellite network now handles about 40 million of the 60 million bits transmitted over the entire network every day. The sensitive financial information transmitted is protected by cryptographic equipment, which codes and decodes data before and after transmission. Over a three-year period, First Interstate expects to save nearly $1 million in communications costs.

- Why did First Interstate Bank Corporation develop a communications satellite network? Explain the advantages (and disadvantages) of this approach.

Source: "Satellite Data Exchange Service," *American Satellite Capabilities and Service*, American Satellite Company.

---

it is generated at its point of origin. Terminals in retail stores, business offices, and on factory floors minimize manual data entry, thus cutting costs and reducing errors.

- *Remote realtime computer use* is provided by linking users, terminals, and computer systems spread over a large geographic area. This not only includes timesharing systems and personal computing but also process control and interactive programming applications.
- *Centralized or distributed processing* is made possible. Users can be linked to a central computer system or be serviced by a network of computers dispersed throughout the organization. The choice depends on the philosophy of management and the needs of the organization for control of computer use and costs, and the quality and flexibility of service to user departments.

Large Networks

How much information processing activity depends on data communication? Data communications networks are becoming a necessity for carrying out many business, government, and individual activities. Let's look at several examples.

■ The *electronic funds transfer* (EFT) systems of commercial and savings banking would not exist without data communications. Bank data communications systems support *teller terminals* in all branch offices, *automated teller machines* (ATMs) at remote locations throughout a city or state, and *pay-by- phone* services, which allow bank customers to use their Touch-Tone telephones as computer terminals to electronically pay their bills.

■ Airline and hotel reservation systems are another example. Computer terminals are installed all over the world at airline offices and ticket counters, in the offices of travel agents, rental car agency offices, and hotels and motels. The SABRE system of American Airlines or the Holidex system of Holiday Inns are examples. These national and international data communications systems provide realtime inquiries and responses concerning the status of travel reservations and realtime file updating to reflect reservations made or other transactions.

■ In other examples, data communications systems allow insurance agencies across the country to access and update insurance policy files in realtime, retail stores to use *point-of-sale* terminals to capture sales data when a sale is made, and national and multinational corporations to communicate with all of their branch offices, manufacturing plants, and distribution centers throughout the country and the world. See Figure 12–12.

Local Area Networks

Why can't you just plug your microcomputer or terminal into a wall outlet and communicate with other computers in your office building or anywhere in the world? You can in many organizations. One of the bottlenecks was right in the office. But this is changing because of the rapid growth of privately owned **local area networks** (LAN). Local area networks connect information processing devices within a limited physical area, such as an office building, manufacturing plant, or other worksite. LANs use either regular telephone lines and a computerized PBX, or coaxial cables and other devices as communications channels and interface devices. Local area networks were originally developed to interconnect word processing terminals but have been expanded to include computer terminals personal computers, other computer systems, and a variety of office information processing equipment. These local networks are connected to larger external networks by communications interface devices that form a common interface called a *gateway*. See Figure 12–13.

FIGURE 12–12 A large-scale communications network

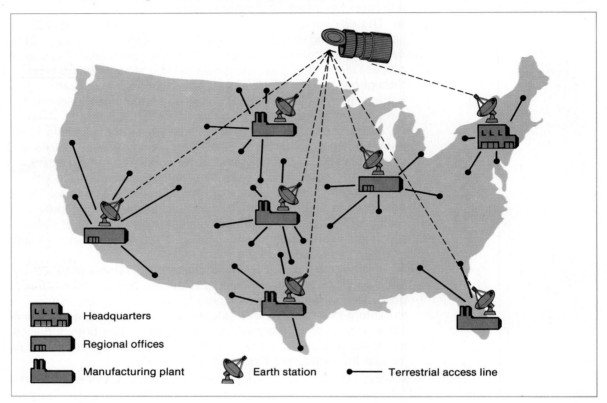

Several competing technologies are vying for dominance in providing the communications channels for local area networks. Two major types are coaxial cable and PBX-based networks. **Coaxial cable** networks rely on baseband or broadband cable strung throughout an office building or other worksite. Computers, interface devices, and other office equipment are connected to this cable and can thus communicate with each other. **PBX-based** systems use standard telephone wiring to interconnect all devices, and they rely on advanced computerized PBXs to control both voice and data communications. However, the technology for LANs is still developing.

Ethernet, a joint development of Xerox, Digital Equipment Corporation, and Intel Corporation, and ARC by Datapoint Corporation are examples of local area networks using baseband coaxial cable technology. Many companies are also experimenting with broad-

FIGURE   12–13 A local area network

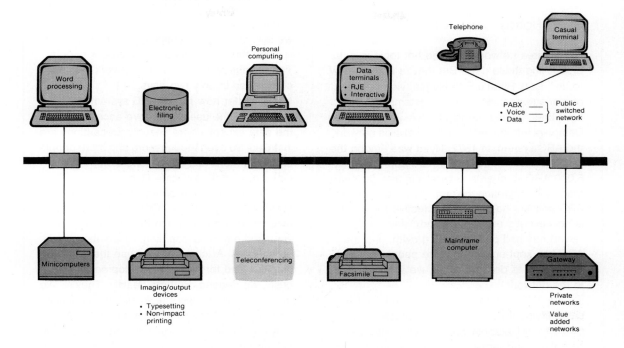

band technology, including the use of channels provided by cable TV companies, whose cables are of the broadband type. Wangnet by Wang Laboratories and Videodata Lan/1 by 3M Corporation are examples of broadband networks. Many other companies are turning to computerized PBX-based networks, because they allow use of regular phone lines instead of the expensive installation of coaxial cable. Examples of advanced computerized PBXs are CBX II by Rolm Corporation and SLI by Northern Telecom. The ability of computerized PBXs to control both voice and data transmission is growing rapidly. However, baseband or broadband coaxial channels are still needed to handle high-speed/high-capacity applications, such as mainframe-to-mainframe computer input/output, or CAD/CAM and video teleconferencing transmissions.

Personal Computer Networks

Another fast-growing group of communications networks is the personal computer networks, which were mentioned in Chapter Four and Chapter Seven. They range from networking several microcomputers together in a local area network, to the large public networks

REAL WORLD APPLICATION 12–2

Hyatt Hotels Corporation

"Local area networks are the hot topic in data processing these days. But they're nothing new to us," says Hyatt's Bob Regan, vice president of management information systems. "Ours have been up and running for five years." When Datapoint introduced the first local area network, the ARC system, in 1977, Hyatt was among the first to install it. Today there are approximately 5,000 ARC local area networks in use, far more than any competing system. "One reason the ARC network has been so effective for Hyatt is because it's easy to expand," says Regan. "Hyatt has had phenomenal growth, and the ARC has kept up. When more people needed the system to do more work, we simply added to the network."

The ARC local area network can be expanded virtually without limit by simply plugging in additional Datapoint processors, printers, storage disks, and terminals. Each new processor adds power to the network so new users get the same fast response the original users were getting. Companies can closely match the power of an ARC system to their needs, expanding in small, inexpensive, increments instead of buying more computers than they need to have room for growth.

What's more, Datapoint systems can be expanded or upgraded without replacing software. "We run some programs on ARC networks that were originally written for our first Datapoint computer more than 10 years ago," says Regan.

"That means we didn't lose any of the money we invested in programming and training. And it made the growth steps easy on our people. The changeover to the ARC network was accomplished in only two days."

No matter how far an ARC system is expanded, all the users can have access to all the data except where security precautions are installed. So even though more and more people are using more and more computers, there's never a need to duplicate files.

"At present, Hyatt operates forty-five ARC systems," Regan says. "Others are in the planning stages right now. On the operations side we use them for accounting, reservations, and group sales. At corporate we use them for accounting and for systems development. Obviously, we depend on them heavily. They're like the meters where we check our own financial performance. They simply have to work. And they do. "Hyatt has stayed with the ARC system because it's been cost-effective. That's the bottom line. I can recommend a certain system to a hotel, but in the end, the system has to sell itself. And keep selling itself after it's installed. Our Datapoint ARC systems have done that."

- What types of LAN technology is Hyatt using?
- What benefits have the ARC local area networks brought to Hyatt?

Source: Courtesy Datapoint Corporation.

provided by value-added carriers, such as CompuServe, and The Source. These networks offer a wide variety of information services to anyone with an appropriately equipped personal computer or computer terminal. They offer such services as electronic mail, financial market information, use of software packages for personal computing, electronic games, home banking and shopping, news/ sports/weather information, and a variety of specialized *data banks*.

How do you gain access to such services? It's easy if you have a personal computer; but it must be equipped with a communications interface board, a modem, and a communications software package. First, you load the communications package from a diskette into your computer. Then the program takes over, leading you by the hand with a series of menus. You can dial the number of the network, using the keyboard of the computer, or with the proper software and an automatic dialing modem, your computer will dial it for you! Then you pick a service, such as electronic mail or stock market quotes. Finally, you perform whatever tasks are necessary, such as information retrieval, or composing and sending an electronic message. Figure 12–14 shows you a series of menus furnished by CompuServe that lead you to their electronic mail service. It should also give you a good idea of the variety of services available on such personal computer networks.

Data Banks and Videotex Networks

What do you do if you want a computer to give you data and information on a variety of topics? Use data communications and a *data bank* or *videotex* service. **Data banks** are large, privately owned computerized databases available to the computer-using public for a fee. All you need is a computer terminal or microcompu-

FIGURE 12–14 Using a personal computer for electronic mail

Once your personal computer or terminal is connected to a modem you're ready to connect to the CompuServe Information Service. The procedure is simple. Dial the access number for your area. When you hear a continuous, high-pitched tone, connect the phone to the modem. Simple instructions will appear on your screen; by following these, you can easily reach your "destination."

To get here, you entered #1 from the main menu. Now, enter #3 and. . .

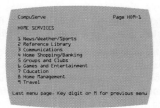

. . .CompuServe will guide you to Electronic Mail's main menu.

. . .this will appear: Select #1 (Electronic Mail) and. . .

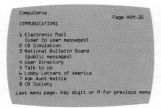

Now you're ready to read or send mail, electronically!

ter with data communications capability. Data and information are available in the form of statistics on all types of economic and demographic activity from *statistical data banks*, or in the form of abstracts from hundreds of newspapers, magazines, and other periodicals from *bibliographic data banks*. Some of the data bank services even provide software for a fee that allows you to manipulate their data for such purposes as investment analysis or economic forecasting. Figure 12–15 shows you the contents of some of the major computerized data banks.

Another way you can get information using a computerized telecommunications system is **videotex**. In its simplest form (*teletext*)

FIGURE

12–15 Computerized data banks

CompuServe and The Source. Personal computer networks providing statistical data banks (business and financial market statistics) as well as bibliographic data banks (news, reference, library, and electronic encyclopedias). CompuServe is the largest supplier of such services to personal computer users.

Data Resources Inc. A large vendor offering statistical data banks in agriculture, banking, commodities, demographics, economics, energy, finance, insurance, international business, and the steel and transportation industries. DRI economists maintain a number of these data banks. Standard & Poor's is also a source.

Dow Jones Information Service. One of the largest data bank services in number of users. It provides statistical data banks on stock market and other financial market activity, and in-depth financial statistics on all corporations listed on the New York and American stock exchanges, plus 800 selected other companies. Its Dow-Jones News/Retrieval system provides bibliographic data banks on business, financial, and general news from *The Wall Street Journal, Barron's,* the Dow Jones News Service, Wall Street Week, and the 21-volume American Academic Encyclopedia.

Interactive Data Corporation. A large statistical data bank distributor covering: agriculture, autos, banking, commodities, demographics, economics, energy, finance, international business, and insurance. Its main suppliers are Chase Econometric Associates, Standard & Poor's, and Value Line.

Lockheed Information Systems. The largest bibliographic distributor. Its DIALOG system offers over 75 different data banks in: agriculture, business, economics, education, energy, engineering, environment, foundations, general news publications, government, international business, patents, pharmaceuticals, science, and social sciences. It relies on many economic research firms, trade associations, and governmental groups for data.

Mead Data Central. This large data bank service offers two major bibliographic data banks. *Lexis* provides legal research information, such as case law, court decisions, federal regulations, and legal articles. *Nexis* provides a full text (not abstract) bibliographic database of over 100 newspapers, magazines, newsletters, new services, government documents, and so on. It includes full text and abstracts from the *New York Times* and the complete 29-volume Encyclopaedia Brittanica. Also provided is the Advertising & Marketing Intelligence (AMI) data bank, and the National Automated Accounting Research System.

it is a one-way, repetitive television broadcast of pages of text and graphics information to your TV set, using cable, telephone lines, or standard TV transmission. A control device allows you to select the page you want to display and examine. Videotex, however, is meant to be an *interactive* information service provided over phone lines or cable TV channels. Not only can you select specific video displays of data and information (such as electronic *Yellow Pages*, or your own personal bank checking account register), but you can use a special terminal or personal computer to do your banking and shopping electronically! Many banks, telephone companies, large retailers, newspaper publishers, television networks, and equipment manufacturers are testing videotext services. Such services are already available from several sources, including personal computer networks (such as the CompuServe Bank-at-Home and Shop-at-Home services). See Figure 12–16.

Distributed Processing Networks

In Chapter Ten, we described how distributed processing involves *dispersing* smaller computers throughout an organization, rather than relying on one central computer facility. These distributed computers (microcomputers, minicomputers, or mainframe computers) are typically interconnected by data communications channels to form *distributed processing networks*.

FIGURE

12–16 Using Videotex for shopping at home

Figure 12–17 illustrates the two basic structures of distributed processing networks: a **star network**, with end-user computers tied to a large central computer, and a **ring network**, where local computer processors are tied together on a more equal basis. In many cases, star networks take the form of *hierarchical networks* with a large headquarters computer at the top of the company's hierarchy connected to medium-sized computers at the divisional level, which, in turn, are connected to smaller computers at the departmental or local level. Ring networks are also called *peer networks*, because in most cases computers operate autonomously for local processing, but also cooperate as equal partners or *peers*. A variation of the ring network is the *mesh network*, where direct communication lines are added to connect some or all of the computers in the ring to each other.

In most cases, distributed processing systems use a combination of star and ring approaches. Obviously, the star network appears to be more centralized, while the ring network is a more decentralized approach. However, this is not always the case. For example, the central computer in a star configuration may be acting only as a **switch** or message-switching computer, which handles the data communications between primarily autonomous local computers. Figure 12–18 illustrates a simple combination of star and ring approaches, while Figure 12–19 outlines the hierarchical DDP network of a large manufacturing firm.

Star and ring networks differ in their performance, reliability, and cost depending on the type of organization structure and information processing required. There is no simple answer to what network will provide the best performance. A pure star network is considered less reliable than a ring network, since the other computers in the star are heavily dependent on the central host computer. If it fails, there is no backup processing and communications capability, and the local computers will be cut off from the corporate headquarters and each other. Therefore, it is essential that the host computer be highly reliable, including having some type of *multiprocessor architecture* to provide a backup capability.

Star network variations are most common, because they can support the *chain-of-command* and hierarchical structure of most organizations. Ring networks are most common in the form of *local area networks*, which tie together several computers at one local site. Ring networks are considered more reliable and less costly if there is a minimum of communication between the computers in the ring. Also, if one computer in the ring *goes down*, the other computers can continue to process their own work as well as communicating with each other. If there is a lot of communications within a distributed processing network, computers in a ring network will need to have sophisticated communications control hardware and

FIGURE

12–17 Star and ring network structures

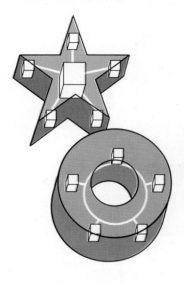

FIGURE 12–18 Distributed processing network combining star and ring structures

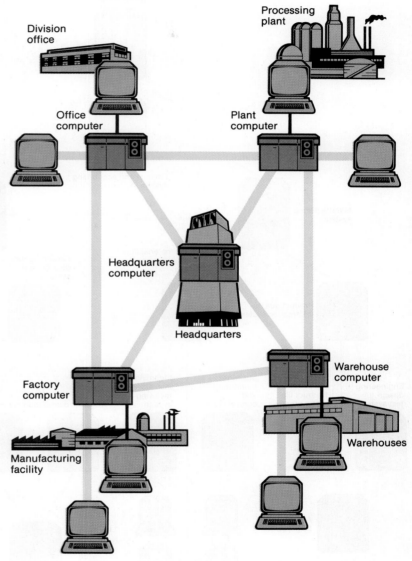

software, compared to the local computers in a star network, where the host computer or switching computer handles communications control assignments. Thus if most communication is with a central site, a star network is the most simple and practical approach. In any event, the performance, reliability, and cost of each type of

446

FIGURE 12–19 A hierarchical distributed processing network

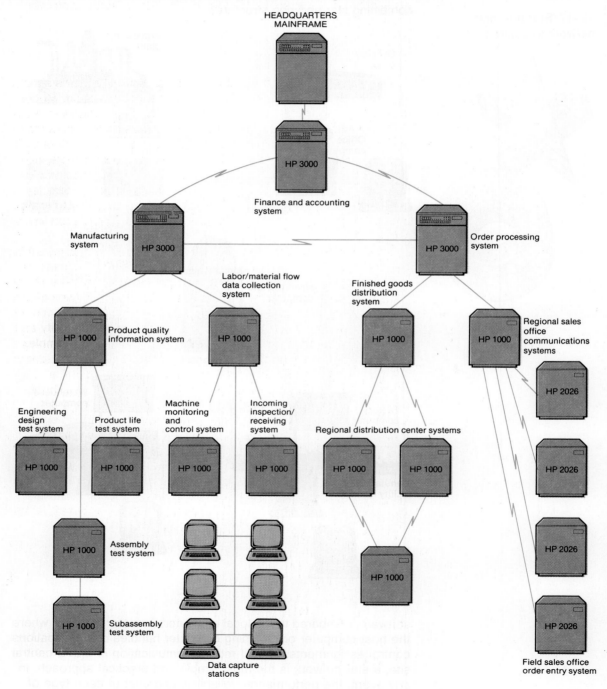

network is dependent on the organizational structure, geographic dispersion, and information processing needs of each computer-using organization.

ADVANTAGES AND DISADVANTAGES

The many advantages of the use of data communications should be quite evident to you after reading the previous section. Modern computing relies heavily on the sharing of computer hardware, software, and data resources that data communications networks make possible. Even personal computer users, who can do much of their information processing tasks with their own microcomputers, can greatly increase their computing power by using data communications. They can tie into networks of other personal computers, large mainframe computers, and data banks. However, you should realize that data communications systems do have several significant limitations.

Unauthorized persons can gain access to the data that is transmitted over communications lines or stored in secondary storage devices of computer systems tied into communications networks. Many instances of tampering and theft of data from data communications systems have been reported recently in the press. Significant control methods and measures must be taken to protect the integrity and security of data communications systems. For example, complex coding techniques called **encryption** are applied to data by special communications control circuitry and decoded upon arrival at a receiving terminal. Many data communications systems use the national Data Encryption Standards (DES) as the basis for the encryption of data. Data communications systems are subject to a small degree of error and do cause additional costs for required hardware, software, and communications channel use. However, the benefits of data communications outweigh its costs and limitations. The use of data communications networks is expected to accelerate in the future as more data communications terminals and microcomputers move into business offices, warehouses, factories, retail stores, banks, and other organizations.

448

Hewlett-Packard Company

Most Hewlett-Packard North American manufacturing plants and regional offices have HP 3000s to handle their local data processing needs, reducing the burden on the company's central computers. Major offices are linked with HP headquarters in Palo Alto by computer-based communications systems. These are powerful enough to give the smaller sales offices plenty of EDP capability for such things as order processing and maintaining customer files.

In Brazil, the Campinas manufacturing plant is linked by computer to the main office in Sao Paulo. This, in turn, communicates with headquarters in California. Sales offices in Venezuela and Mexico have computer-based communications systems with sufficient computer power to handle local accounting and inventory management.

Most data from Europe are funneled through the European headquarters in Geneva. Data from sales offices are generally "queued" in the Geneva computers, waiting for the twice-daily call from the United States. All three manufacturing facilities in France, Germany, and Scotland also use HP computers for accounting, order processing, management information, and the like.

The two major factories in Southeast Asia (more than 2,000 people), reduce communications costs by linking the Penang plant with the Singapore facility. Here data are consolidated for transmission to the United States. Accounting, payroll and inventory are handled locally by HP computers. A similar situation exists in Japan, with the plant in Hachioji connected with the main sales office in Tokyo. In Australia and New Zealand, HP sales offices are equipped with computers for both local data processing and long-distance communications. See Figure 12–20.

■ Would you say that Hewlett-Packard needs a worldwide data communications network? Is this also a distributed processing network? Explain.
■ What are the benefits and limitations of this approach?

Source: Courtesy Hewlett-Packard.

FIGURE

12–20 A worldwide communications network

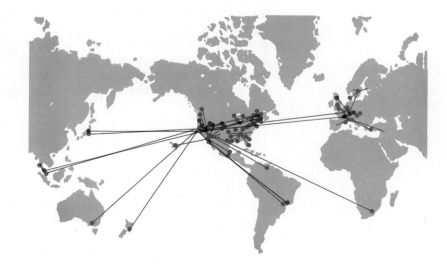

SUMMARY

- Data communications systems provide for the transmitting of data over electronic communications links between one or more computer systems and a number of input/output terminals at some physical distance away from the computer. Modern use of computers is heavily dependent on data communications systems for remote access batch processing, most realtime processing, and many word processing and office communication systems.

- The major components of a data communications system consists of (1) terminals, (2) data communications interface units, (3) communications channels, (4) computers, and (5) communications control software. Data communications hardware consists of a variety of computer terminals, modems, multiplexers, and various communications processors. Data communications software consists of computer programs that control and support the communications occurring in a data communications network.

- Communications channels include such media as ordinary telephone lines, coaxial cables, fiber optics cables, microwave systems, cellular radios and communications satellite systems. Use of these channels is provided by companies called common carriers and specialized carriers. They offer a variety of communications services including several types of data communications services.

- Data communications systems are becoming more prevalent in carrying out business and individual activities. They range from the worldwide networks of multinational operations to regional distributed processing networks, to local area networks in office buildings and other worksites, personal computer networks, and videotex and data bank networks. Data communications make inquiry/response systems, online data entry and remote job entry, remote computer use, and either centralized or distributed processing possible. Data communications systems also require controls over unauthorized use, such as data encryption.

KEY TERMS AND CONCEPTS

Data communications system
Communications interface
  devices

Modems
Multiplexers
Communications processors

Front-end processors
Communications channels
Fiber optic cables
Communications satellites
Communications control
  software
Communications carrier
Star and ring networks
Communications network
  architecture
Digital networks

Local networks
Personal computer networks
Encryption
Protocol
Packet switching
Facsimile
Teleconferencing
Coaxial cable
Cellular radio
Private branch exchange
Videotex

REVIEW AND APPLICATION QUESTIONS

1. What are data communications systems? Why are they necessary in today's computer environment?
2. What are the five major components and functions of a data communications system?
3. What are the major types and functions of data communications hardware and software?
4. What are communications carriers? What services do they provide?
5. What are the major types of communications media and channels? Will communication satellite systems become the primary channel for data communications?
6. What are local area networks? What are the major competing LAN technologies?
7. What are the major types of distributed processing networks? What are their advantages and disadvantages?
8. What are some examples of the use of data communications by business firms and individuals?
9. Can personal computers use data communications? Explain how.
10. Would you be willing to pay for videotex or data bank services? Explain.
11. What are some of the advantages and disadvantages of data communications systems? Do you expect the use of data communications to increase in the future? Why or why not?

APPLICATION PROBLEMS

1. If you have not already done so, read and answer the questions after the Real World Applications in this chapter.
2. Apply the data communications system model to the data com-

munications networks of First Interstate Bank, Hyatt Hotels, and Hewlett-Packard as described in the Real World Applications of this chapter. That is, identify as many of the five basic components of a data communications system that you can find in these networks.

3. Users of the mainframe computer at ABC Department Stores are experiencing very slow response times at their terminals. Some users are speculating that the modems they are using are too slow. The mainframe vendor's sales rep says that it needs more ports so more terminals can be directly connected. Somebody from the Information Services Department says that ABC needs to add a front-end processor. A data communications consultant advises ABC to purchase several multiplexers. Who do you think is right? Why?

4. The corporate headquarters for ABC Department Stores wants to install a local area network in its present 10-year-old, five-story office building. They are trying to decide between a baseband or broadband coaxial cable network, or a PBX-based LAN. They want to tie together the word processors, personal computers, and terminals in the building. What would you advise them to do? Explain your recommendation and the assumptions you had to make.

5. The data communications network used by Hewlett-Packard (described in Real World Application 12–3) must use a variety of communications channels and media. Describe how they could use almost all of the communications media mentioned in this chapter in their communications channels.

6. A personal computer user tells you that she uses a local area network to share resources in her office, a private network to communicate with the corporate headquarters computer, and a public network to access several data banks. Do you know what she is talking about? Explain what she is doing and the benefits she is probably deriving from using such networks.

CHAPTER SUPPLEMENT

DATA COMMUNICATIONS—TECHNICAL CHARACTERISTICS

Data communications is a highly technical, rapidly developing field of computer technology. Most business computer users will not become involved in decision making about data communications alternatives and, therefore, do not need a detailed knowledge of its technical characteristics. However, it is important that business computer users who wish to become better managers of the computer resources of their organizations become familiar with the basic characteristics of data communications channels and networks. This supplement should help you achieve that goal.

Communications Network Architectures

Until quite recently, there was a lack of sufficient standards for the interface between the hardware, software, and communications channels of data communication networks. Therefore, it is quite common to find a lack of compatibility between the data communications hardware and software of different manufacturers. This situation has hampered the use of data communications, increased its costs, and reduced its efficiency and effectiveness. Since the mid-1970s, computer manufacturers and national and international organizations have developed standards called **protocols** and have been working on master plans called **network architectures** to support the development of advanced data communications networks.

The goal of network architectures is to promote an *open, simple, flexible*, and *efficient* data communications environment. This will be accomplished by the use of standard protocols, standard communications hardware and software interfaces, and the design of a *standard multilevel interface* between end users and computer systems. The International Standards Organization (ISO) has developed a seven-layer *Open System Interconnection* (OSI), model to serve as a standard model for network architectures. By dividing data communications functions into seven distinct layers, the ISO hopes to promote the development of modular network architectures. This would greatly facilitate the development, operation, and maintenance of data communications networks consisting of many types of communications devices and users. Network architectures currently being developed and implemented include IBM's System Network Architecture (SNA), Univac's Distributed Communication Architecture (DCA), Honeywell's Distributed Systems Architecture (DSA), and the Digital Network Architecture (DNA) of the Digital

Equipment Corporation. Figure S12–1 illustrates the multilevel interface of IBM'S SNA as compared to the OSI model.

Protocols

A **protocol** is a standard set of rules and procedures for the control of communications in a network. However, these standard procedures may be limited to just one manufacturer's equipment, or to one type of data communications. Thus there are many competing and incompatible protocols in use today. Part of the goal of communications network architectures is to create more standardization and compatibility in communications protocols. We have already mentioned one example of a protocol; the RS232C standard for physical connection of terminals and computers to modems and communications lines. Another example is the X.25 protocol for *packet switching* networks described in the next section. Figure S12–2 summarizes many of the protocols in use today and shows

FIGURE S12–1 Communications network architectures

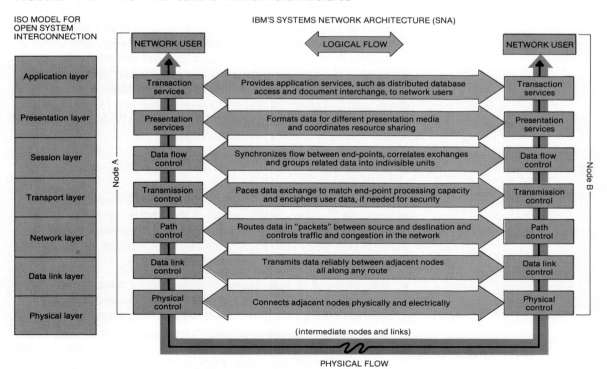

FIGURE S12–2 Protocols used in data communications networks

Physical interconnection protocols (layer one)	Data link control protocols (layer two)	Network connection management protocols (layer three)	End-to-end data transport protocols (layer four)
RS232C MIL-STD-188 RS449 V.24 X.21 bis X.21 V.35 303 (All specify the characteristics of interconnecting devices.)	Start-Stop BSC: Binary Synchronous HDLC ⎫ SDLC ⎬ High-level UDLC ⎬ data link BDLC ⎭ control ADCCP CSMA ⎫ CSMA/CD ⎬ LAN Token ⎭ control	X.21: Circuit switching X.25: Packet switching Request-Response Autodial Gateway Protocols X.75: Packet networks IP: Internet Protocol GGP: Gateway-to-Gateway	TCP: Transmission Control Protocol TP: International Transport Protocol

Source: Adapted from Eric D. Steel, "Your Pocket Protocol Primer," *Datamation,* March 1984, p. 152. Used with permission.

how they apply to communications activity in the layers of the OSI model.

Local Area Network Control

Another major area of LAN technology that is still developing has to do with techniques of controlling communications within a local area network. Three basic technologies are now vying for supremacy: (1) **collision detection** and **avoidance** systems, such as the Ethernet system, (2) **token passing** systems, such as those developed by Datapoint and endorsed by IBM, and (3) **star** systems, which have been developed by AT&T. Figure S12–3 describes and illustrates these three LAN technologies.

Transmission Speed

The communication capabilities of communication channels can be classified by *bandwidth*, which is the frequency range of the channel and which determines its maximum transmission rate. Data transmission rates are typically measured in bits per second (BPS). This is sometimes referred to as the **baud** rate.

- **Narrowband** or **low-speed** channels allow transmission rates of up to 300 bits per second (BPS) and are used primarily for teletypewriters and other low-speed printing terminals.
- **Voiceband** or **medium-speed** channels are "voice grade" communication lines commonly used for voice communications. Data transmission rates of up to 4,800 BPS are attainable while rates

FIGURE S12–3 Three competing LAN communications control technologies

THREE WAYS TO LINK TOGETHER THE AUTOMATED OFFICE AND FACTORY

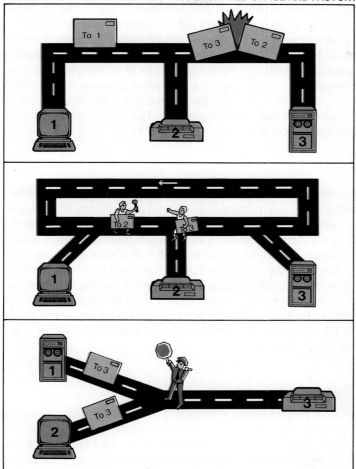

Collision avoidance and detection: This scheme, pioneered by Xerox Corp.'s Ethernet, operates like a one-lane highway with two-way traffic. It requires all computer equipment to monitor the network, then send a message on to the data highway in packages whenever the road appears clear. If two packages collide, they must go back and try again. Because the electronics controlling this net are simple, it is relatively inexpensive. But when traffic is heavy, it is more difficult to send a package down the highway. **Suppliers:** AT&T, Bridge, Corvus, DEC, 3Com, Ungermann-Bass, and Xerox.

Token passing: Computer equipment attached to this kind of network must wait for a coded electrical signal, called a token, to pass by. Then the equipment attches its information package to that token and moves it on to the data highway. After delivering the package, the token is passed along to the next device. The token scheme comes in two configurations: a linear approach pioneered by Datapoint and a ring design expected to be adopted by IBM. **Suppliers:** Concord Data, Datapoint, IBM, Prime Computer, Proteon and Nestar.

Star: All information packages must pass through a central controller, which directs them to their final destination. Because this network functions much like a central telephone switchboard, it is easy to piggyback on to existing office telephone systems without having to do any new wiring. This scheme is somewhat easier to maintain than the others because of centralized control, but if the central switch fails, the network does too. **Supplier:** AT&T.

Source: "Linking Office Computers: The Market Comes of Age," *Business Week,* May 14, 1984, p. 144. Used with permission.

of up to 9,600 BPS are achieved with the use of specially conditioned leased lines. These medium-speed lines are typically used for CRT terminals, microcomputers and medium-speed printers.

■ **Broadband** or **high-speed** channels allow transmission rates at specific intervals from about 20,000 BPS to more than 200,000 BPS and typically use microwave or satellite transmission. These channels are primarily used for high-speed data transmission between computer systems.

Transmission Mode

The two modes of transmitting data are called *asynchronous* and *synchronous* transmission. **Asynchronous** transmission transmits one character at a time with each character preceded by a *start bit* and followed by a *stop bit*. Asynchronous transmission is normally used for low-speed transmission at rates below 2,000 BPS. **Synchronous** transmission transmits groups of characters at a time, with the beginning and ending of a character determined by timing circuitry of a modem or other data communications control unit. Synchronous transmission is normally used for high-speed transmission exceeding 2,000 BPS.

Transmission Direction

Communications channels can provide for three types of data transmission direction. A **simplex** channel allows data to be transmitted in only one direction, such as just receiving transmissions or just sending transmissions. A *half-duplex* channel allows transmission in either direction, but in only one direction at a time. This is usually sufficient for many low-speed terminals (such as transaction terminals) where alternating sending and receiving is characteristic of normal communications activities. The **full duplex** channel allows data to be transmitted in both directions at the same time. It is used for high-speed communications between computer systems. See Figure S12–4.

FIGURE

S12–4 Simplex, half-duplex, and duplex channels

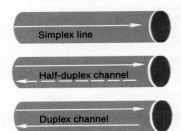

Packet Switching

Packet switching involves subdividing communications messages into groups called **packets,** typically 128 characters long. The packet switching network carrier uses minicomputers and other communications processors to control the packet switching process and transmit the packets of various users over its leased lines. Packet switching networks are also known as *X.25 networks*, which is the international standard or *protocol* governing the operations of public packet switching networks. Protocols frequently establish the communications control information needed for *handshaking*, which is the process of exchanging predetermined signals and characters to establish a connection between two data communications terminals or stations.

Point-to-Point versus Multidrop Lines

The two basic types of communication links in data communications networks are *point-to-point* and *multidrop*. When **point-to-**

point lines are used, each terminal is connected by its own individual line to the computer system. When **multidrop** lines are used, several terminals share each data communications line to a computer system. Obviously, point-to-point lines are more expensive than multidrop lines, because all of the communications capacity and interface equipment of a data communications line is being used by a single terminal. Thus a multidrop line decreases communications costs, because each line is shared by many terminals. Thus point-to-point lines are used only if there will be continuous communications between a computer and a terminal or other computer system.

Multidrop lines allow more than one terminal on the line to receive data at the same time, but only one terminal at a time can transmit data to the computer system. There are several ways to get around this limitation. In the **contention** approach, line use is on a first-come, first-served basis, where a terminal can transmit data if the line is not in use, but must wait if it is busy. In the **polling** approach, the computer or communications processor polls contacts each terminal in sequence to determine which has a message to send. The sequence in which the terminals are polled is based upon the communications traffic expected from each terminal. Thus the transmission of each terminal is based on a "roll call" of each terminal on the line. Polling is widely used, because the speed of computers allows them to poll and control transmissions by many terminals sharing the same line without any apparent slowdown in response time. The typical terminal user would not be aware that many terminals were using the same line. Thus users at many terminals can share the same line, if their typical communications consist of brief messages and inquiries. See Figure S12–5.

Leased versus Switched Lines

Multidrop lines are usually *leased lines* (or *direct lines*), in which a specific communications circuit is leased (or acquired) and used to connect terminals with a computer system. Typically, a user can begin using a terminal on a leased line by merely turning the terminal on and entering appropriate identification messages. Point-to-point lines may use leased lines or a *switched line*, which uses the telephone lines and switching service of the regular telephone system. A user wanting to begin using a terminal on a switched line must dial the telephone number assigned to the communications processor, which establishes contact with the computer system.

Communications Codes

Data communications systems typically use the American Standard Code for Information Interchange (ASCII) to represent the char-

FIGURE

S12–5 Multidrop versus point-to-point lines

MULTIDROP LINES

POINT-TO-POINT LINES

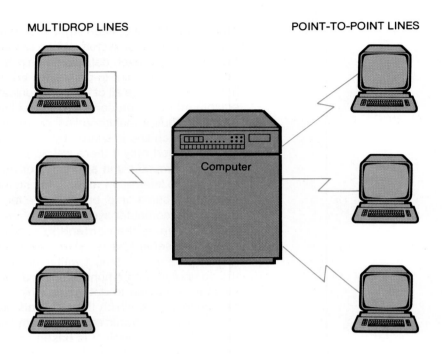

acters of data being transmitted. Since most computers use the Extended Binary Coded Decimal Interchange Code (EBCDIC), the ASCII code is typically translated into the EBCDIC code by communications control units prior to entry into a computer system. These computer codes were illustrated in Chapter Three.

Communications Control Information

Communications control units and communications processors control errors in transmission by several processes, including *parity checking*. As described in Chapter Three, parity checking involves determining whether there is an odd or even number of *binary one* digits in a character being transmitted and received. If a transmission error is detected, it is usually corrected by retransmitting the message. Besides parity bits, additional *control information* is usually added to the message itself. This includes information indicating the destination of the data, their priority, the beginning and ending of the message, plus additional error detecting and correcting information. For example, in packet switching networks, packets are preceded and followed by control information, which is necessary to manage their routing through the network and to detect transmission errors. Thus a *protocol layer*, or *envelope*, of control information "packages" the user data during transmission. See Figure S12–6.

FIGURE   S12–6 An envelope of protocol layer control information

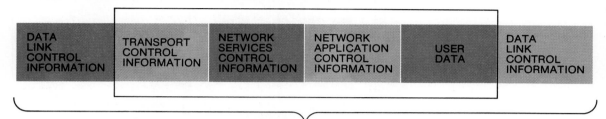

Complete envelope transmitted
from one node to an adjacent node

CHAPTER 13

Word Processing and Automated Office Systems

CHAPTER OUTLINE

LEARNING OBJECTIVES

The purpose of this chapter is to promote a basic understanding of the role played by word processing and other automated office systems in modern information processing. After reading and studying this chapter, you should be able to:

1. Identify the functions and components of word processing as a system, and the major types of word processing hardware.
2. Explain the functions of word processing packages.
3. Discuss the functions of the major types of automated office systems.

INTRODUCTION TO AUTOMATED OFFICE SYSTEMS

Would you like to work in an office where all information processing activities were done manually? Of course not. Office machines, such as electric typewriters, copying machines, and dictation machines, have made office work a lot easier and productive. But the *mechanized office* is giving way to the *automated office*. The computer and its tiny cousin, the microprocessor, are changing the equipment and work habits of today's office workers. This has resulted in the development of *word processing* and other *automated office systems*, which are substantially changing the information processing activities of the modern office.

Word processing is the automation of the transformation of ideas and information into a readable form of communication. It involves the manipulation of **text data** (characters, words, sentences, and paragraphs) to produce office communications in the form of **documents** (letters, memos, messages, forms, and reports). **Word processing systems** are information processing systems that rely on automated and computerized typing, dictation, copying, filing, and telecommunication systems used in many offices and other work areas of modern organizations. Word processing systems are a primary component of **office automation**, in which the application of computer and communications technology to most office activities is transforming them from manual to automated forms of information processing. This development is creating several types of **automated office systems** such as those summarized in Figure 13–1. We will discuss such automated office systems in this chapter, concentrating our attention on word processing and office communications systems. See Figure 13–2.

FIGURE

13–1 Overview of systems in the automated office

Word Processing Systems
Computer-assisted document and text creation and editing systems. Automated text entry through dictation and OCR systems.

Office Communications Systems
Electronic mail, voice mail, facimile and teleconferencing systems.

Document Management Systems
Document storage, reproduction, and retrieval through records management, micrographics (microfilm media), and reprographics (copying and duplicating) systems.

Office Support Systems
Electronic calendar, tickler file, scheduling, and task management systems.

Personal Computing Systems
Interactive computing, graphics, information retrieval, and modelling at intelligent workstations in offices or other work sites (telecommuting).

FIGURE 13–2

Computers have become an integral part of the modern office. Illustrated is the Desktop Generation of networked microcomputers by Data General.

A WORD
PROCESSING SYSTEM
MODEL

Like all types of information processing, the activities of word processing can be viewed as an **information processing system**. This is illustrated in Figure 13–3. Notice that *hardware resources* (word processing equipment and media), *software resources* (word processing programs and procedures, and *people resources* (users and word processing specialists) are required. These three system resources transform text data resources into finished information products using the system functions of input, processing output, storage, and control. Let's first look at the most basic form of these functions.

- **Input** activities include the *creation* or *origination* of ideas expressed in words—by writing on paper or by using the keyboard of a word processor. One may also dictate ideas to a secretary who records them in *shorthand* coding, or more commonly by speaking into *dictation* equipment which records spoken words on magnetic media.

- **Processing** activities include the *transcription* (conversion) of words recorded on written material or magnetic media using the keyboard of the word processor. This *keyboarding* activity converts words into electronic impulses in the circuitry of the

FIGURE 13–3 The word processing system model

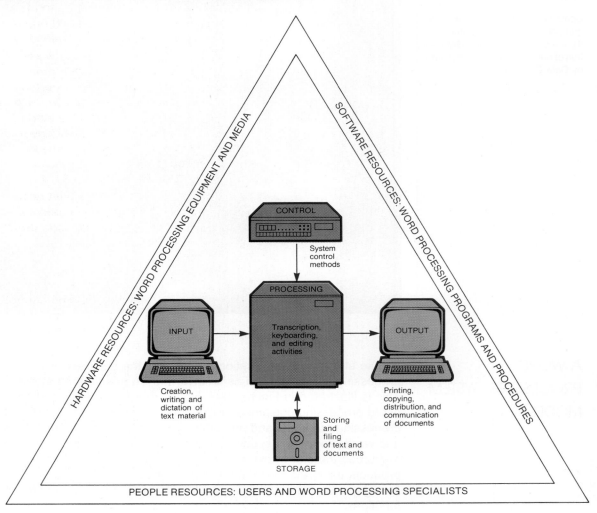

word processor, records them on electronic media such as floppy disks and simultaneously displays them on a video screen. At this point, the *editing* activity is performed in which the displayed material is visually checked or proofed by the operator or electronically proofed by the word processor and corrections and other changes are made. Errors can be corrected by electronically typing over the error, and characters, words, sentences, paragraphs, and pages can be inserted, moved around, and deleted.

- **Storage** activities include (1) *storing* typed material on magnetic floppy diskettes for temporary storage before printing, and (2) *filing* which involves storing material in a structured and organized manner so that it can be retrieved easily when needed.
- **Control**. All word processing activities are directed by word processing programs, and by manual word processing procedures. Some word processing functions can be *hardwired* in the electronic circuitry of the processor, or stored as *firmware* in ROM modules. Most word processing programs are stored on secondary storage media such as floppy disks until needed for processing. A great number of word processing software packages are available for word processors as well as microcomputers, minicomputers, and mainframe computer systems.
- **Output** activities typically involve using a printer to print documents on paper and distributing them to appropriate persons. Multiple copy forms may be used or copies can be made using office copying machines.

Advanced System Functions

Besides the basic input, processing, output, storage, and control functions just described, many word processing system have the capability of performing several advanced system functions. For example:

- Input. Some word processing systems use remote, pooled dictation in which users dial a central transcription service and dictate by telephone into magnetic tape recorders. Another technology that is being introduced to automate word processing input is the use of OCR (Optical Character Recognition) devices that can read typewritten text material and convert it into electronic input and enter it into the word processing CPU. Thus the printed paper output of ordinary typewriters and computer printers promises to be another source of automated input for word processing systems.

- Processing. Automatic *text editing* includes a **global editing** feature which searches through the entire recorded text material for a particular word or phrase. The operator can then automatically correct or replace a word wherever it is used in the text material. For example, every occurrence of a particular word or phrase can be changed automatically throughout an entire document with a single instruction from the operator. Word processing may also involve use of a **spelling dictionary** to automatically correct the spelling of all words in the typed material. For example, most word processing packages have optional spelling dictionaries of 50,000 to 100,000 words. The words in the typed material are electronically compared to entries in the dictionary and highlighted on the video display so they can be corrected by the operator. Some word processors even include multilingual dictionaries which can be used to help translate from one language to another!

Other **text processing** activities include the automatic typing of letters and documents according to a predetermined format. The word processor stops at predetermined places for the manual or electronic insertion of variable information such as names and addresses on a *form letter* sent to a firm's customers. Standard phrases and paragraphs (nicknamed *boilerplate*) stored on floppy disks are retrieved and automatically typed. The operator then inserts names, dates, and other information at appropriate points in the text to produce form letters, legal documents, and all types of reports. Text processing also includes *hyphenation*, which automatically hyphenates words and adjusts word spacing and line endings, as well as many other features, such as automatic margins, spacing and indentation.

Advanced word processing systems also include **list processing** capabilities which allow long mailing lists of names and addresses (and other lists) to be automatically merged with previously created standard text (such as form letters). They also may include a built-in math program package which lets the operator do on-the-spot arithmetic calculations on data as it is entered into the system and inserts the resulting figures in the appropriate spot on the document being typed.

■ Storage. The storage and retrieval of office records is called **records processing** or *records management*. It allows a finished document to be stored and retrieved under several different categories as if there were several copies stored in multiple files, though only one copy may exist on a magnetic disk. A finished document might be given a *document number* which describes the location of the *physical file* where it will be stored (typically on a magnetic diskette) and describes it as a *record* which can be stored (*filed*) by subject matter, title, author, document category, or other descriptive or identifying characteristic. Some word processing systems use **micrographics** equipment which can store a microfilm (or microfiche) copy of a document, display a full-size image on a screen, prepare a full-size paper copy, and transmit an electronic image to another terminal in the word processing system. Micrographic media are frequently used for long term *archival* storage.

■ Output. Multiple copies of documents created by word processing systems can be made using *intelligent copiers* and other

reprographics equipment such as copying and duplicating machines. Documents can be transmitted in electronic digital form over telecommunications channels to other word processors, personal computers, computer terminals, intelligent workstations, and other intelligent office machines (like *intelligent copiers*). Thus, advanced word processing output is a major form of **electronic mail**.

Office Word Processing Example

Figures 13–4 and 13–5 illustrate many word processing activities that take place in a modern office. These figures show how a personnel department responds to inquiries concerning employment opportunities with a personal letter composed of variable information and standard paragraphs. The following word processing activities take place:

1. A member of the personnel department (called the *principal*) dictates a listing of names and addresses of persons applying for employment and also indicates the appropriate standard paragraphs which should be selected from those stored in the system.
2. The word processing *operator* creates a *document* (letter) from the variable information and the chosen standard paragraphs.
3. If this was a more complex document, the operator could visually and electronically proof the letter, print out a *draft copy* for the principal to review and approve, and make all necessary revisions electronically.
4. A personalized letter and an envelope are printed for each applicant. (If an *electronic mail* system was in use, an electronic version of the letter could be sent to each applicant!)
5. A copy of each letter is transmitted to the word processing terminal of the personnel department, which can electronically store the letter on a magnetic disk file, print a paper copy if requested, or electronically store and display a short message that tells the principal that this particular letter was sent.

WORD PROCESSING HARDWARE

Word processing began with the automation of the office typewriter. One of the first major developments was the introduction of the IBM magnetic tape Selectric typewriter (MTST) in 1964. It had electronic circuitry and used magnetic tape to store what was being typed. Changes could be made electronically without retyping, and the finished copy could be typed automatically on paper. Other automatic typewriter systems began to appear, including some which used CRT units to display keyed-in material so it could be visually edited before typing a final copy. Finally, *electronic typewriters* with video displays, computerized features, and even telecommunica-

FIGURE

13–4 Steps in a word processing application

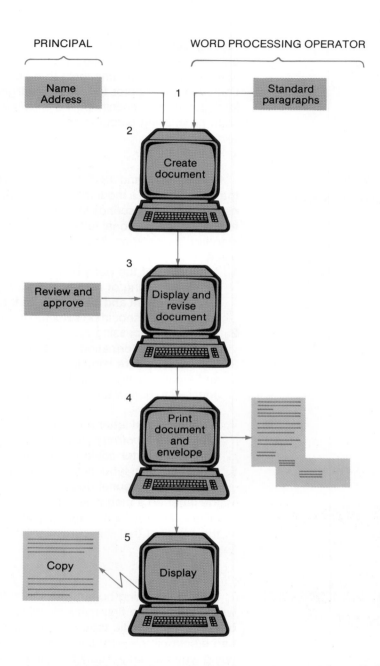

PRINCIPAL

WORD PROCESSING OPERATOR

Name Address

Standard paragraphs

1

2 Create document

3 Display and revise document

Review and approve

4 Print document and envelope

5 Display

Copy

tions capabilities were developed. Today, many **word processors** are full-fledged microcomputers, minicomputers, or computer terminals, although there is still a big market for "dumb" *electric* typewriters and "smart" *electronic* typewriters, which are not full-fledged computers.

FIGURE

13–5 A personalized letter produced by word processing

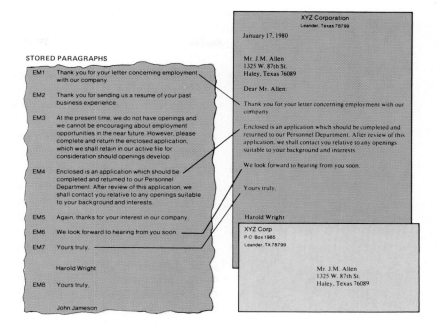

STORED PARAGRAPHS

EM1 Thank you for your letter concerning employment with our company.

EM2 Thank you for sending us a resume of your past business experience.

EM3 At the present time, we do not have openings and we cannot be encouraging about employment opportunities in the near future. However, please complete and return the enclosed application, which we shall retain in our active file for consideration should openings develop.

EM4 Enclosed is an application which should be completed and returned to our Personnel Department. After review of this application, we shall contact you relative to any openings suitable to your background and interests.

EM5 Again, thanks for your interest in our company.

EM6 We look forward to hearing from you soon.

EM7 Yours truly.

Harold Wright

EM8 Yours truly.

John Jameson

XYZ Corporation
Leander, Texas 78799

January 17, 1980

Mr. J.M. Allen
1325 W. 87th St.
Haley, Texas 76089

Dear Mr. Allen:

Thank you for your letter concerning employment with our company.

Enclosed is an application which should be completed and returned to our Personnel Department. After review of this application, we shall contact you relative to any openings suitable to your background and interests.

We look forward to hearing from you soon.

Yours truly,

Harold Wright

XYZ Corp
P.O. Box 1985
Leander, TX 78799

Mr. J.M. Allen
1325 W. 87th St.
Haley, Texas 76089

FIGURE

13–6 A stand-alone word processing system: The IBM Displaywriter

The hardware of a typical word processing computer system is pictured in Figure 13–6. Notice that this **work station** consists of a video monitor, keyboard, floppy disk drives, and main system unit. The visual display unit may be larger than many CRT units so it can display a full page (8½ × 11 inches or larger) of text. Floppy disks are used for secondary storage. Typically, a floppy disk unit with at least two disk drives is included, so that one floppy disk contains the word processing programs and space for documents that are currently being processed, while the second disk holds documents recorded for storage. Floppy disks can hold hundreds of pages of typed material. Large capacity and more expensive hard disk cartridges can also be used, and can hold thousands of pages of documents.

Word processing systems typically include a *letter quality* printer, which provides better quality printing than most printing terminals or high-speed computer printers. *Daisy wheel, dot matrix,* or *ink jet* printers are often used. More expensive systems may use a *laser printer* or an **intelligent copier** as output devices. These copying machines use microprocessor intelligence and can be linked by communication lines to the CPU and terminals of a word processing system. Thus, though they can still make copies from paper documents, they also provide a **facsimile** capability, since they can receive documents electronically from word processing terminals and print them on paper in multiple copies. There are five major categories of computerized word processing systems.

- **Intelligent electronic typewriters**. These smart typewriters use microprocessors to perform many basic word processing functions at a lower cost than full-fledged computerized word processors. They can have built-in electronic memory, small video *minidisplays*, and even built-in minidiskette drives. Intelligent typewriters are typically priced from $2,000 to $3,000.
- **Stand-alone word processors** consist of a keyboard, CRT screen, floppy disk or hard disk storage, and a printer. Stand-alone word processing systems sell for between $5,000 to $15,000, depending on the capabilities required.
- **Shared logic systems** consist of several CRT terminals that share the processing power and storage capacity of a minicomputer. These minicomputer systems include printers for hard copy output and magnetic disk units for secondary storage, and are quite similar to the key-to-disk data entry computer systems used in electronic data processing.
- **Shared resource systems** use intelligent terminals as word processing *workstations*, which are part of a distributed local area network (LAN) in a large building or other large worksite. These workstations are essentially microcomputers that share expensive *system resources*, such as large- capacity disk drives and high-speed printers that are part of the network.
- **Time-sharing systems** consist of computer terminals connected by telecommunications lines to a central computer, which has word processing software as well as programs for other applications. Many users can share the computer at the same time for both word processing and data processing jobs. Thus any computer system with data communications and time- sharing capabilities can use word processing program packages to provide word processing services to its users.

Figure 13–7 illustrates a word processing system in a large office building that combines the features of shared logic, shared resource, and time-sharing systems. The number of word processing computers and terminals has grown rapidly in the last ten years. However, many experts predict that most will eventually be replaced by general-purpose computer systems and terminals which can integrate both *word processing* and *data processing*. These predictions seem accurate since word processing software packages are now readily available for most microcomputer, minicomputer, and full-sized computer systems.

FIGURE 13–7 A word processing system with shared logic/resource and time-sharing features

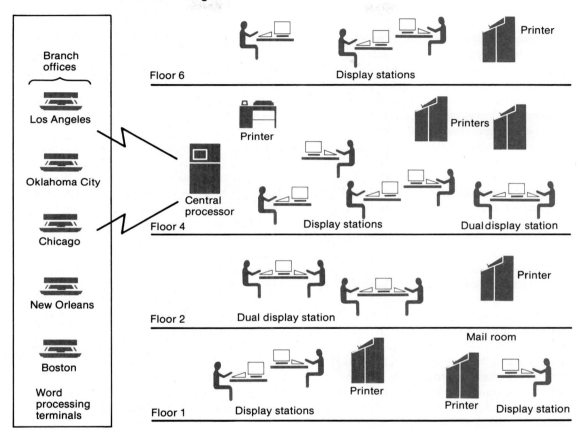

WORD PROCESSING SOFTWARE

Most word processing hardware, whether a dedicated word processor, a microcomputer, or a video terminal connected to a large computer system, need word processing programs to accomplish their word processing tasks. In this section, let's concentrate on the features of microcomputer software packages. Dozens of word processing packages are now available to turn your microcomputer into a topflight word processing machine. Such word processing programs have become the most popular type of application software package available for use with personal computers. A word processing package allows you to use a microcomputer or other computer to develop **documents** (i.e., letters, memos, reports, etc.). It helps you accomplish three primary jobs:

REAL WORLD APPLICATION 13–1

Eastman Kodak

At Eastman Kodak's Rochester, New York, headquarters, word processing equipment is helping to streamline the time-consuming job of text preparation and is providing for significant increases in the volume of work completed, without significant increases in labor.

Kodak's Central Correspondence and Reprographics Department (CC&R) is currently using multiple word processing systems from Wang Laboratories, Inc. Yet, word processing equipment has been in use at Kodak's corporate headquarters since the 1940s, when typing devices that utilized paper tape were installed in the central correspondence area to supplement the existing typing staff and help automate the work flow. Magnetic media typing equipment with more sophisticated editing capabilities was installed during the late 1960s.

A few years ago, a study was undertaken to review the editing and typing needs in the CC&R Department. Although the whole range of potential solutions to the text-editing problem was studied, three basic approaches to word processing were scrutinized most carefully: "stand-alone" systems, the broad range of shared-logic systems, and large-scale computerized, text-editing systems.

The feasibility study ruled out the stand-alone approach as offering little more text-editing flexibility than the magnetic media equipment. Large-scale, computerized systems could not be justified in terms of the hardware support and software development required for such an operation. Shared-resource, multiterminal systems, the study reasoned, seemed best suited to handle Kodak's immediate applications because of their self-contained power, modularity, and flexibility. Numerous minicomputer-based, multiterminal systems were investigated by the study group. Of the units judged appropriate to handle Kodak's applications, three Wang word processing systems were recommended as the best-suited.

The Central Correspondence and Reprographics Department is currently using one Wang System 20 and one Wang System 30. The System 20 supports one CRT-based workstation. The System 30 supports seven workstations and three daisy wheel printers. A Wang System 10A has also been installed as an offline editing station for use by the Business and Technical Personnel Department.

Another System 10A is being used by the Business Systems Markets Division (BSMD), one of the six market divisions within the Kodak organization. Storage of data on the 10A and the larger Wang System 20 word processing systems is on floppy diskettes, while the Wang System 30 uses a larger-capacity fixed disk. Thus, BSMD often will use the three daisy wheel printers in the CCR Department to prepare documents it has "stacked up" in a background mode on System 10A disks. This playout process is typically done at night, unattended.

- How does the capabilities of Eastman Kodak's present word processing system compare to what they have used in the past? To the other two basic WP approaches they considered?
- Identify each of the basic hardware components in Kodak's word processing system.

Source: *Word Processing—At Kodak*, Wang Laboratories, Inc.

- Create, edit, and format documents.
- Store and retrieve documents.
- Print documents.

Word processing packages also do a fourth major job: the creation and editing of data and program files. Though most operating systems provide their own *editors* for such tasks, they are usually very limited *line editors*, which allow you to enter data only on a line-by-line basis within a very restricted format. Therefore, computer users who have word processing packages may use their more powerful editing features to build data files or to write and edit application programs using a variety of programming languages. Section II: Using Word Processing Packages is in the Appendix at the end of the book. It provides you with an introductory tutorial on how to use a word processing package to create documents and data files.

Features of Word Processing Packages

A word processing package is a valuable writing tool that allows you to type a document using the keyboard of your computer. You see the document on your video monitor and can manipulate it in a variety of ways. Then you can store the document on your computer's magnetic disk as a *text file*, retrieve it later and make whatever changes you wish, and then print as many copies you need. Thus word processing has made manual typing using a conventional typewriter obsolete.

A typical word processing package consists of an integrated set of programs, including an editor program, a formatting program, a print program, an optional dictionary, and mailing list programs. Most popular word processing packages provide menus to help the user select commands. They are *menu-driven* (i.e., much of their operation comes from you selecting from a list of choices provided by a series of menus). They also organize the video display screen into several specialized areas (such as a menu area, file directory area, and text area) to help you in your word processing tasks.

Word processing packages can be classified into two basic types: *screen-oriented* programs and *command-oriented* programs. Screen oriented programs display the text material on the screen almost exactly as it will look on the final printed page, since they perform both the document creation and editing functions at the same time. Thus the document appears with such features as indentations, line widths, underlining, and page breaks clearly showing on the screen. Command-oriented programs intersperse commands within the text of the document to indicate such printing features as spacing, indenting, boldface, and italics. Therefore, you do not see exactly how the text will look until it is printed on your system printer.

Obviously, screen-oriented word processing packages are much easier to use. However, command-oriented programs usually provide a larger set of commands and thus are more powerful and flexible. Today, most word processing packages combined features of screen oriented and command oriented programs. Thus some of the text is displayed as it will appear, while other features are displayed as commands within the text. For example, while a word processing package like Wordstar is primarily a screen-oriented program, it has more command-oriented features then some other word processing packages, such as Microsoft's Word package. Figure 13–8 illustrates many typical features of microcomputer software packages

Benefits of Word Processing Packages

The benefits of word processing over manual typing really stand out when you consider the editing and revising activities that are so common in any writing task. Computers and word processing packages allow you to:

■ Move to any point in a document, and add, delete, or change words, sentences, or paragraphs,

FIGURE 13–8 Typical features of microcomputer software packages: The opening menu and on-screen tutorial menu of the Select word processing package illustrate its many word processing features.

OPENING MENU OF ACTIVITIES   ON-SCREEN TUTORIAL MENU

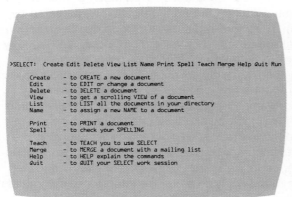

- Move a block of text from one part of the document to another,
- Insert standard information from another text file,
- Selectively change all occurrences of a particular word or phrase,
- Check you document for spelling or grammatical errors, and
- Print the contents of a text file according to a variety of predesigned formats!

Thus word processing has made writing and printing documents dramatically easier. Also, it can substantially increase the quality of your writing because it makes editing, correcting, and revising so much easier to do.

Computers and word processing programs have thus automated word processing activities. The advantages of word processing over conventional typing add up to a major improvement in people's capacity to prepare documents. Compared to manual typing methods, the major advantages of computerized word processing can be summarized as follows:

- Preparation of documents is significantly easier and faster because computer software and hardware can perform many tasks normally done by a typist.
- Documents are easier to edit and change because they are stored on magnetic disks and displayed on video screens.

Developments in Word Processing Packages

Many word processing packages are available, of which *WordStar* is the best known and best selling of them all. It was designed to provide microcomputer users with all of the features formerly found only on computers dedicated exclusively to word processing. WordStar was first introduced in 1981, and versions now exist for virtually every microcomputer system. Compared to other word processing programs, WordStar may be slightly more awkward to use, but provides superior control over the format of documents. Other popular word processing packages include *Easy Writer, Word, Multimate, Volkswriter,* and *Word Perfect*.

Improvements and enhancements continue to be made to microcomputer word processing packages. Progress continues in making them easy to use, more powerful, and combining them with other programs (such as spreadsheets and graphics) into *integrated packages*. Improved packages are more menu-driven, reduce the number of commands needed to carry out any operation, and support system devices, such as the *electronic mouse* and the *touch screen*. Another top priority is improving their "what you see is what you get" capabilities so that features such as boldface and italics appear

REAL WORLD APPLICATION 13–2

Sunset Magazine

Although *Sunset* has been involved in electronic data processing for years, we approached the age of computer text editing with some skepticism. But we took the big leap a while back and on this page in September 1982 we gave you a first look at our new computerized system for processing, editing, and formatting pages. As we write this (on a computer terminal, of course), the system has undergone its second diagnostic maintenance—akin to a 15,000-mile checkup—through a telephone line to Boston. After one memory circuit board was replaced, the system was given a clean bill of health. Just as important is the report card given by our writers and editors who have used the terminals daily to produce 16 issues of *Sunset*—more than 1,800 articles—since that September. It took us a while to jettison old ways and get use to the new. We had to learn new words, a seemingly endless number of abbreviations and acronym codes, and how to use the extra keys that buttress the VDT keyboard. But once the mysteries were unveiled, writers abandoned their once-beloved typewriters so readily that more terminals had to be ordered, in a hurry.

A *Sunset* article usually goes through many drafts before the writer feels it's good enough to turn in. The words don't come any easier on a computer, but it does make revision simple and lightning fast. With just a couple of keystrokes, we can move a paragraph, copy it, or delete it. Another keystroke and the machine sets the text to the width of a magazine column and tells how long it is. These instant results give workers more time to research, write, and polish their articles. Then they push a few more keys and their articles go to our copy department for editing and fine-tuning, again on VDTs. (Most editing pencils have gone the way of typewriters.) Soon each article is ready for electronic formatting: positioning the text, photographs, and captions on the page. This step has given us a flexibility in page makeup that we never had before. With complex commands and minute adjustments, we strive for the best visual balance, from headline and caption placement to the white space around each photograph. These changes, though not apparent to our readers, make for a more readable magazine.

We're still coming up to speed, but the benefits of electronic publishing are evident to our staff. Just ask our writers how many would trade back their VDTs for a typewriter.

- What benefits has word processing (computer text editing) brought to *Sunset Magazine*?
- What problems did they experience?
- What word processing system functions can you identify?

Source: "Into 1984 with Our Computers," *Sunset Magazine*, January 1984, p. 136. Reprinted with permission.

on the screen as well as the final printout. In addition, new packages include such features as global search and replacement of word and phrases, hyphenation, and paragraph justification. Others provide several preformatted document styles called *style sheets*. This capability automatically formats what you type into letters, memos, contracts, or other formats. Also available are subsidiary programs that check spelling and grammar and process form letters and mailing lists. Thus the capability of word processing packages will continue to grow to meet the needs of personal computer users for easy, flexible and powerful word processing functions.

AUTOMATED OFFICE SYSTEMS

Word processing systems are just the tip of the automated office iceberg. They are the forerunner of other **automated office systems**, which many experts predict will lead to the *automated office*, the *electronic office*, or the *office-of-the-future*. Word processing systems are being joined by a number of major automated systems that combine word processing, data processing, telecommunications, and information systems technologies. Automated office systems collect, process, store and transmit data and information in the form of electronic office communications produced by the employees of an organization. This also includes the use of computerized *administrative workstations* and *management workstations* in the office and other workplaces. Figure 13–1 outlined these automated office systems. Figure 13–9 summarizes the functions of the major types of automated office systems. Following is a brief description of several major systems that will be integrated in future automated office systems. We will then discuss several major developments in electronic office communications in more detail.

- **Advanced word processing systems** include communicating word processors and the interconnection of intelligent office machines, such as intelligent copiers, printers, micrographics systems, OCR systems, and photocomposition systems.
- **Electronic mail and message systems** allow for the transmission and distribution of text material in electronic form over computerized data and communication networks. This practice would drastically reduce the present flow of paper messages, letters, memos, documents, and reports which flood our present interoffice and postal systems. Voice and video message systems will be another part of this development.
- **Electronic audio/visual systems** will make heavy use of communications satellite systems for electronic facsimile (printed image) transmission, but more importantly for **teleconferencing**, which integrates video and voice communications so that geographically separated users can conduct ordinary business meetings.
- **Office support systems** will provide support services to managers, such as electronic calendars, scheduling, *tickler files*, tele-

FIGURE 13–9 The functions of automated office systems

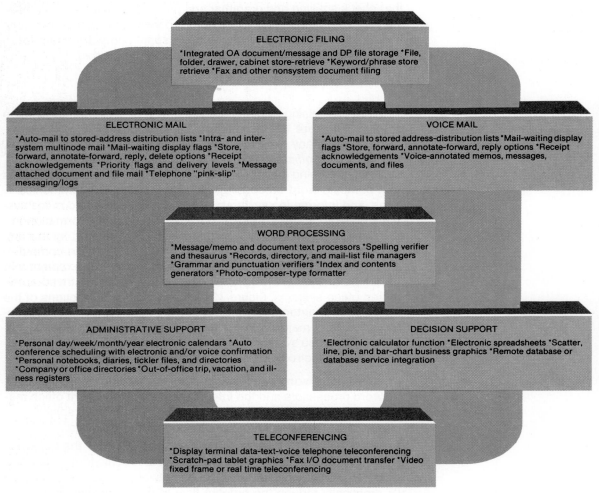

ELECTRONIC FILING
*Integrated OA document/message and DP file storage *File, folder, drawer, cabinet store-retrieve *Keyword/phrase store retrieve *Fax and other nonsystem document filing

ELECTRONIC MAIL
*Auto-mail to stored-address distribution lists *Intra- and inter-system multinode mail *Mail-waiting display flags *Store, forward, annotate-forward, reply, delete options *Receipt acknowledgements *Priority flags and delivery levels *Message attached document and file mail *Telephone "pink-slip" messaging/logs

VOICE MAIL
*Auto-mail to stored address-distribution lists *Mail-waiting display flags *Store, forward, annotate-forward, reply options *Receipt acknowledgements *Voice-annotated memos, messages, documents, and files

WORD PROCESSING
*Message/memo and document text processors *Spelling verifier and thesaurus *Records, directory, and mail-list file managers *Grammar and punctuation verifiers *Index and contents generators *Photo-composer-type formatter

ADMINISTRATIVE SUPPORT
*Personal day/week/month/year electronic calendars *Auto conference scheduling with electronic and/or voice confirmation *Personal notebooks, diaries, tickler files, and directories *Company or office directories *Out-of-office trip, vacation, and illness registers

DECISION SUPPORT
*Electronic calculator function *Electronic spreadsheets *Scatter, line, pie, and bar-chart business graphics *Remote database or database service integration

TELECONFERENCING
*Display terminal data-text-voice telephone teleconferencing *Scratch-pad tablet graphics *Fax I/O document transfer *Video fixed frame or real time teleconferencing

Source: John K. Murphy, "Office Automation," *Mini-Micro Systems*, December 1983, p. 224. Reprinted with permission.

phone logs, and even an *electronic in-tray* which records nonelectronic documents that are received. See Figure 13–10.

Electronic Office Communications Systems

Would you like to use computers to send a message in text or voice form, send a copy of a document, or send video pictures of a meeting to participants all over the globe? And do it in seconds, not hours or days? If you do, you are interested in one of the major

FIGURE

13–10 Electronic office support systems

A An electronic calendar.

B An electronic address card file.

These functions are part of the time management module of the OPEN AC-CESS integrated package.

A

B

new areas in computer-based communications: **electronic office communications systems**. This concept covers a variety of electronic communication services, such as *electronic mail, voice mail, facsimile* and *teleconferencing*. These services have been developed to meet two basic objectives: (1) more *cost-effective* communications and (2) more *time-effective* communications than traditional written and telephone communications methods.

Electronic communications systems are designed to minimize *information float* and *telephone tag*. **Information float** is the time (at least several days) when a written letter or other document is in transit between the sender and receiver, and thus unavailable for any action or response to occur. **Telephone tag** is the process of (1) repeatedly calling people, (2) finding them unavailable, (3) leaving messages, and (4) finding out later that you were unavailable when they finally returned your call! Electronic office communications systems can also eliminate the effects of mail that is lost in transit, or phone lines that are frequently busy. They can also reduce the cost of labor, materials, and postage of office communications (from more than $5 for written message to less than 50 cents for an electronic message is one estimate). Also, the amount of time wasted in regular phone calls can be reduced (by one-third is another estimate). Let's take a brief look at the communications methods that promise such results.

Electronic Mail

We have used various forms of electronic mail for a long time. Western Union's *telegram* and *mailgram* services are an example. So are their *TWX, Telex* and *Teletype* services, which have provided long distance-communications (using printing terminals) for news media services and large organizations for many years. Another long-standing form of electronic mail is **facsimile**. It is a remote copying process in which copies of photographs, documents, and reports can be transmitted and received in hard copy form anywhere in the world. Also, we have been able for many years to use computer terminals, word processors, and data communications channels to transmit and print reports and documents at remote sites.

So what is new about **electronic mail**? New, easy to use and lower-cost systems have been developed. Computer manufacturers and software suppliers have taken advantage of advances in computer technology (such as low cost and more powerful personal computers, word processors, and video terminals) and advances in digital communications technology (such as local networks and intelligent communications interface devices).

Today, you can send an electronic message to one or more individuals in an organization for storage in their *electronic mailboxes* on magnetic disk devices. Whenever they are ready, they can read their electronic mail by displaying it on the video screen on their terminals, personal computers, or *intelligent workstations*. So with only a few minutes of effort (and a few microseconds of transmission) a message to one or many individuals can be composed, sent, and received. Many large computer-using business firms and government agencies are using electronic mail. Even the U.S. Postal System has started a variation of electronic mail service called E-COM. Communications companies such as GTE, TELE-NET, and MCI, are also offering this service. Personal computer networks like CompuServe offer electronic mail services, including an **electronic bulletin board** service where electronic messages can be posted for other subscribers to read. Figure 13–11 shows you video displays provided by the MCI electronic mail service.

Another variation of electronic mail is **voice mail** (also called *voice store-and-forward*) where *digitized voice messages*, rather than electronic text, are used. In this method you first dial the number of the voice mail service and enter your identification code. Once you are accepted, you dial the voice mail number of the people you wish to contact and speak your message. Your analog message is digitized and stored on magnetic disk devices of the voice mail computer system. Whenever anyone wants to hear their voice mail, they simply dial their mailbox number and listen to the stored messages, which the computer converts back into analog voice form.

Teleconferencing

Why do people have to spend travel time and money to attend meetings away from their normal work locations? They don't have

FIGURE   13–11 Using electronic mail: Main menu and electronic mail being created
using the MCI Mail Service

MCI MAIL MAIN MENU

```
MCI Mail Version 1.14

   There are no messages waiting in your INBOX.

Press <RETURN> to continue

You may enter:

   SCAN         for a summary of your mail
   READ         to READ messages one by one
   PRINT        to display messages nonstop
   CREATE       to write an MCI Letter
   DOWJONES     for Dow Jones News/Retrieval
   ACCOUNT      to adjust terminal display
   HELP         for assistance

Command (or MENU or EXIT):  create
```

ELECTRONIC MAIL EXAMPLE

```
                     MCI Mail
   _____

You currently have an unsent DRAFT.
Do you wish to delete it?
YES or NO : yes

TO:  J. BAKER
cc:  C. ALVAREZ
SUBJECT:  SALES PERFORMANCE
TEXT:  (TYPE/1 ON A LINE BY ITSELF TO END)

JENNIFER:

LOOKS LIKE WE HAVE OUR WORK CUT OUT
FOR US.  WE NEED TO BUILD A FIRE UNDER
OUR SALES REPS. ANY SUGGESTIONS? J.J.
/
NAME OF TEXT FILE TO SEND:  B:  SALES
PRIVACY CODE:  2
```

to if they use **teleconferencing**, a growing type of electronic office communications. Teleconferencing is the use of video and audio communications to allow conferences and meetings to be held with participants who may be scattered across a country, a continent, or the globe. Teleconferencing is being promoted as a way to save employee time and thus increase productivity. Less travel to and from meetings should also reduce travel expenses and energy consumption. However, some corporations have found that teleconferencing is not as effective as fact-to-face meetings, especially when

FIGURE

13–12 Teleconferencing
at Martin-Marietta

important participants are not trained in how to communicate using this new media.

There are several variations of teleconferencing. In some versions, participants key in their presentations and responses whenever convenient from online terminals connected to a central conference computer. Since all participants don't have to do this at the same time, this form of teleconferencing is closer to the electronic mail methodology. In the other variation of teleconferencing (sometimes called *video conferencing*), sessions are held in *realtime*, with major participants being televised, while other participants may take part with voice input of questions and responses. Several major communications carriers and hotel chains now offer teleconferencing services for such events as sales meetings, new product announcements, and employee education and training. See Figure 13–12.

ADVANTAGES AND DISADVANTAGES

Word processing and other automated office systems significantly improve the simplicity and efficiency of typing and other office communication processes. Correcting errors and making revisions and changes no longer mean long hours of mechanically typing the same text over and over again. Word processing makes it easy to correct typographical errors, make changes and revisions, and automatically type standard paragraphs and pages while allowing insertion of variable information. Studies have shown that word processing reduces typing time by about 50 percent. This allows growth in typing work loads to be handled by fewer typists and frees secretaries for more productive work. Besides improving typing productivity, word processing has also upgraded the quality of the typing task by reducing the drudgery in error correction, revisions, proofing, and typing long sections of standard text material.

In addition, automated office systems can increase the productivity of executives and other **knowledge workers** by significantly reducing the time and effort needed to produce, access, and receive office communications. (Knowledge workers include executives, managers, supervisors, and professionals, such as planners, engineers, analysts, scientists, and other staff personnel.) Studies made of how knowledge workers spend their time have determined that office automation can save a significant amount of a knowledge worker's time (15 percent is one estimate). The major areas that could be improved include *less-productive activities*, such as seeking information, waiting, organizing work, scheduling, and filing, as well as more-productive activities, such as meetings, telephone calls, and creating documents. See Figure 13–13.

In summary, word processing and automated office systems can:

- Increase the productivity of secretarial personnel and reduce the costs of creating, reviewing, revising, and distributing written office communications.
- Shorten the turnaround time between the preparation and receipt of a document by moving information quickly and efficiently to the people who need it.
- Reduce the frustration, expense, and errors involved in typing or retyping variable or standard text material.
- Store, retrieve, and transmit documents and other written office communications quickly and efficiently.
- Increase the productivity of executives and professionals who are heavy users of office communications.

Of course, all of these advantages are not acquired without some negative effects. First, the cost of automated office hardware is significantly higher than the equipment it replaces. Another limitation is less obvious. Automated office systems can disrupt traditional office work roles and work environments. For example, some word processing systems have caused employee dissatisfaction by giving some secretaries nothing but typing to do, and isolating them from other employees. Such problems must be solved before employees will accept and cooperate with a technology that significantly changes their work roles, processes, and environment. Only then will the promises of increased productivity and job satisfaction be fulfilled. See Figure 13–14.

FIGURE

13–13 How knowledge workers spend their time

This multiple window display of the Corporate MBA software package shows the activities of knowledge workers (K-Ws). Also shown is the savings potential of teleconferencing (Video), electronic mail (E-Ma), access to computerized databases (DB-A), various office productivity tools (Tool), and personal computers and calculators (Calc).

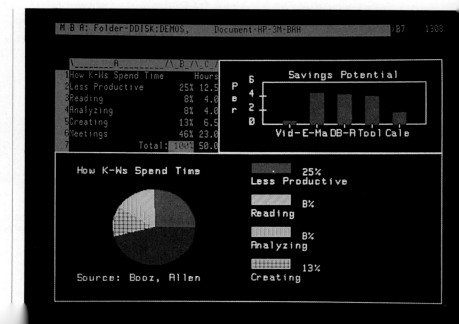

FIGURE 13–14 Major factors affecting the success of automated office systems: Environmental, communication, and processing factors are *economically* and *technologically* feasible. However, people and management factors may limit the *operational* feasibility of automated office systems.

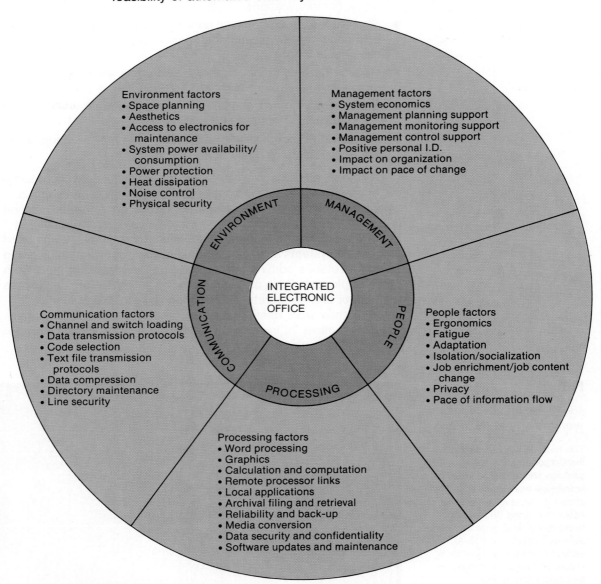

TRW Incorporated

In 1980, TRW, a Fortune 500 manufacturer of large-scale communication systems, chose the Software and Information Systems division of the Electronic Information Systems (EIS) group to conduct a pilot study of office automation. Digital's ALL-IN-1 office information system was installed at four locations in August 1981. The 40 participants were EIS managers, senior professionals, secretaries, and an in-house programmer dedicated to developmental work on the system. TRW's ALL-IN-1 menu included electronic mail, word processing, calendar management, phone directories, personal computing, and computer-based instruction. See Figure 13–15.

The EIS project ended in December 1982, but its findings have encouraged other TRW groups to see how ALL-IN-1 can work for them. "Our latest data," project manager Guy Talbott says, "shows that office automation is saving managers and professionals about half a day from routine paperwork, allowing more time for administrative and managerial tasks. Communication by electronic mail has eliminated some meetings, but more important, we're cutting down on missed phone calls, message writing, and the numerous other frustrations that are associated with telephone tag. In addition, the calendar function eliminates the phoning and paperwork normally required to arrange meetings."

The improved interdepartmental communication that has resulted from electronic mail justifies TRW's investment in ALL-IN-1, Talbott believes. The study findings showed that managers spend 65 percent of their system time using electronic mail. Other frequently used features are the calendar, word processing, and the phone directory. Talbott says that conclusive productivity findings from the pilot are not yet in. "However," he says, "we anticipate that employees using electronic mail as a telephone and meeting substitute will spend an average of 4.8 hours a day communicating, a decrease from the 5.5 hours previously needed. Furthermore, if they increase their reliance on automatic filing, retrieval, and word processing features, they can reduce the two-and-a-half hours a day spent on paperwork to two hours. Saving as little as an hour a day on routine tasks adds 15 percent more time for planning and administration. And this type of productivity boost leads to financial savings in the long run."

- What functions are provided by the office automation system used by TRW?
- What benefits have resulted from the use of such automated office systems?

Source: "TRW Tests ALL-IN-1, Finds It Delivers on Promise of Office Automation," *Insight*, July–August 1983, pp. 10–11. Reprinted by permission.

FIGURE

13–15
The main menu of the office automation system used by TRW

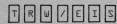

E. G. Talbott IR&D Project Manager 20-Sep-'82

T R W / E I S

Office Automation System

EM Electronic Mail   AI Action Item
WP Word Processing   PC Personal Computer
CM Calender Management   ID User ID Changes
PD Phone Directories   SB Suggestion Box
UM User's Personal Menu   TI Display Current Time

LO Log Out of {Leave}   NU Instructions
   OAS   for New Users

Please enter code from the list above and then press the RETURN key, OR press the HELP keys {PF2 and/or keypad , key}.

SUMMARY

- Word processing automates the transformation of ideas and information into readable forms of communication, such as letters, memos, messages, reports, and other documents. Word processing systems are information processing systems which rely on automated and computerized typing, dictation, copying, filing, and telecommunication systems. The activities of word processing can be viewed as a system of input, processing, output, storage, and control components. Ideas are expressed in words and recorded (input); keyed into a word processor (processing); stored and filed electronically, or on magnetic, micrographic, or paper media (storage); under the direction of a word processing program (control); and communicated electronically or on paper to a recipient (output).

- The five major types of computerized word processing systems include intelligent electronic typewriters, stand-alone word processors, shared logic systems, shared resource systems, and time- sharing systems. Word processing systems increase the productivity of secretarial personnel and reduce the costs of written office communications. They shorten the turnaround time between the preparation and receipt of a document, reduce the expense and errors involved in typing standard text material, and increase the productivity of executives and professionals who are heavy users of office communications. However, the cost of word processing hardware is significantly higher than the equipment it replaces, and word processing may disrupt traditional office work roles and work environments.

- Automated office systems combine word processing, data processing, telecommunications, and information systems technologies to develop computerized administrative and management work stations in the office and other work places. The automated office systems that are being developed will include advanced word processing systems, electronic mail and message systems, electronic audiovisual systems, and advanced office support systems.

KEY TERMS AND CONCEPTS

Word processing	Word processor
Word processing system	Shared logic systems
Word processing package	Shared resource systems

Office automation
Automated office systems
Electronic mail
Voice mail
Teleconferencing

Facsimile
Information float
Telephone tag
Knowledge worker

REVIEW AND APPLICATION QUESTIONS

1. What is office automation? What automated office systems are involved?
2. What is word processing? How has the computer become involved in word processing systems?
3. What are the major functions and components of a word processing system? How do these system functions differ from those of a data processing system?
4. What are the major types of word processing systems? Select one of these systems and explain which type of office could best use its capabilities.
5. What are the major functions and features of word processing packages?
6. What capabilities will be available in automated office systems?
7. Do you think that electronic mail and teleconferencing can be cost-justified in present business organizations?
8. What are information float and telephone tag? How can electronic mail and message systems solve such problems?
9. What are some of the advantages and disadvantages of automated office systems? What solutions do you have for some of the problems arising from such systems?

APPLICATION PROBLEMS

1. If you have not already done so, read and answer the questions after the Real World Applications in this chapter.
2. Have you used a personal computer (or mainframe computer terminal) and a word processing package to create and edit a document yet? The section on using word processing packages in the Appendix at the end of this book is available to help you if necessary. Analyze your word processing experience, using the word processing system model in this chapter. Explain how each system function was accomplished, using the features provided by your word processing package.
3. What word processing features and benefits do you like most? Use the word processing system model to help you suggest sev-

eral ways that each of the system functions (input, processing, output, storage, and control) could be improved to help users like yourself do a better job of word processing.

4. Which of the automated office systems (other than word processing) mentioned in this chapter would you find most useful? Why? Compare your response to the experience of TRW in Real World Application 13–3. Do you agree or disagree with their results? Explain.

5. The executives of ABC Department Stores are dissatisfied with their present telephone system. They want to purchase a new digital system with advanced features, such as *call forwarding*, which automatically switches a call to another number where an executive might be reached. Your job is to try to convince them to install an electronic mail and message system. Explain your position. Use the concepts of *information float* and *telephone tag* in your presentation.

6. Play devil's advocate. List all the things you can think of that could go wrong with various automated office systems. (Hint: for example, top executives could get stage fright and perform poorly in teleconferencing.) Now come up with a solution to each of the problems you generated. Be prepared to defend your solutions.

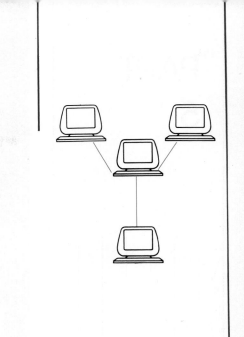

PART
5

Computer-Based
Information Systems

CHAPTER 14

Management Information and Decision Support Systems

CHAPTER OUTLINE

LEARNING OBJECTIVES

The purpose of this chapter is to promote a basic
understanding of the role of management information
and decision support systems by analyzing (1) the
business firm as a system, (2) the information
requirements of the business firm and its management,
and (3) the role of management information and
decision support systems. After reading and studying
this chapter, you should be able to:

1. Identify the basic system components of computer-
   based information systems.
2. Identify the functions of the basic system
   components of business firms.
3. Explain how the information requirements of
   management are affected by *(a)* the functions of
   management, *(b)* levels of management, *(c)*
   information quality, *(d)* internal versus external
   information, *(e)* past versus future information, and
   (f) the form and timing of information.
4. Identify the functions of the major components of
   a management information system, and discuss the
   reasons for the development of the MIS concept
   for computer use in business.
5. Explain the decision support system concept, how
   it differs from traditional operational and
   management information systems, and how it is
   related to expert systems.
6. Discuss how and why information systems should
   be integrated.

COMPUTER-BASED INFORMATION SYSTEMS

Everyone needs information to survive and thrive. Organizations and their managers are no exception. That's why organizations have several varieties of *information systems*, including *computer-based information systems*. This chapter will show you the vital role played by such information systems in modern business firms. But before we get any further, let's define some important terms.

What is an **information system**? An information system is a system that collects, transforms, and transmits information in an organization. An information system may use several kinds of **information processing systems** to help it provide information needed by the members of an organization. But this is not always necessary. For example, *informal information systems* exist in all organizations (such as the office "grapevine") which merely serve as networks to transfer information within the organization. Such information systems do not use most of the information processing system functions and activities described in Chapter Two. Therefore, you should think of information systems in a broader *organizational* or *functional* context (i.e., *business* information systems, *management* information systems, *marketing* information systems). You can then think of information processing systems in more of a *technological processing* context (for example, *manual* information processing systems, or *electronic* information processing systems).

What, then, is a **computer-based information system**? A computer-based information system can be defined as a system which uses the computer hardware, software, people, and data resources of electronic information processing systems to collect, transform, and transmit information in an organization. Figure 14–1 illustrates a system model of modern computer-based information systems. Notice the following system components:

- **Input**—Data and information from within the organization or from the societal environment are entered into the system.
- **Processing**—Information processing systems use computer hardware (equipment and media), software (programs and procedures), and personnel (information specialists and users) to transform data and information into a variety of information products.
- **Output**—Transaction processing is accomplished by *operational information systems* (OIS).

    —Office communications are accomplished by *automated office* systems (AOS).

    —Management reporting is accomplished by *management information systems* (MIS).

FIGURE   14–1 A system model of computer-based information systems

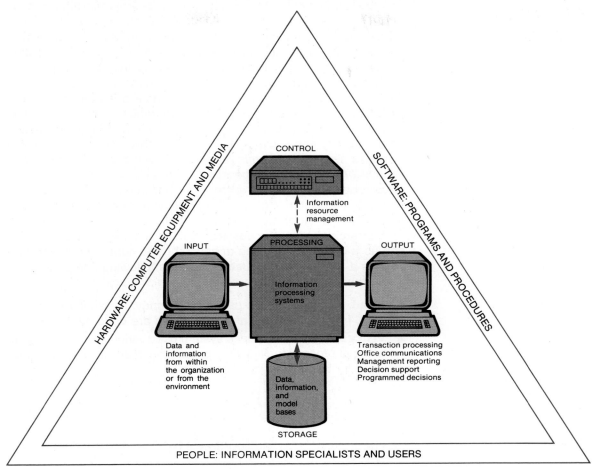

—Managerial decision support is accomplished by *decision support systems* (DSS).

—Automatic programmed decision making is accomplished by *programmed decision systems* (PDS).

■ **Storage**—Data, information, and models for analysis and decision-making are stored for retrieval and processing.

■ **Control**—The *information resource management* function monitors and adjusts information system performance for optimum efficiency and effectiveness.

THE BUSINESS FIRM AS A SYSTEM

In this chapter we will examine the various types of computer-based information systems found in business firms and other organizations. Understanding such systems is necessary if you are to effectively use computers in business management. In particular you need to visualize the unique *feedback* role played by information systems in business organizations. However, this is not possible until you first learn to understand the business firm as a *system*. Figure 14–2 illustrates the business firm as a **business system** which consists of interrelated components which must be controlled and coordinated toward the attainment of organizational goals such as profitability and social responsibility. In this simple model of the business system, *economic resources* (input) are transformed by various *organizational processes* (processing) into *goods and services* (output). *Information systems* provide information on the operations of the system (feedback) to *management* for the direction and maintenance of the system (control).

We can also view the business firm as a subsystem of society, and as a system composed of several basic subsystems. Figure 14–3 is a more detailed illustration of the following components of the business firm as a system:

- **Input**. Resources such as people, money, material, machines, land, facilities, energy, and information are used by the firm.
- **Processing**. The business system uses various kinds of organizational processes, including production, marketing, finance, and

FIGURE

14–2 The business firm as a system

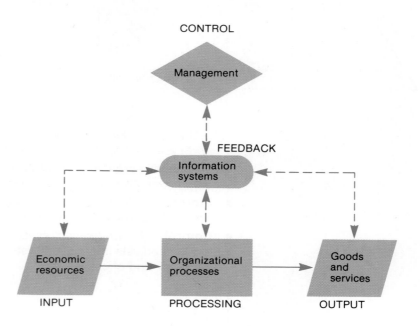

personnel, known as the **functions of business**, and other processes that help transform input into output (such as engineering, research and development, and legal services).

- **Output**. The firm produces products, services, payments (such as employee benefits, dividends, interest, taxes, and payments to suppliers), contributions, information, and other effects.
- **Feedback. Operational information systems** collect, process, and store data generated by the operations of the business and produce feedback (data and information) for input into a programmed decision or management information system. **Automated office systems** collect, process, store, and transmit data and information in the form of electronic office communications within the organization and to the business environment. **Programmed**

FIGURE 14–3 The business firm as a system: Components and environment

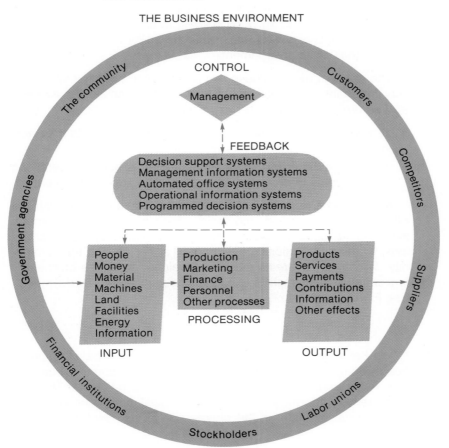

decision systems accept operational information and produce decisions that *control* an operational process such as inventory reordering or production process control. **Management information systems** and **decision support systems** play a vital feedback role in support of the management of a business firm. They refine the data and information provided by the operational information systems of the firm, gather information from the business environment, and provide information to support structured and unstructured management decision making.

- **Control**. The management of an organization consists of managers at all organizational levels who are engaged in planning, organizing, staffing, directing, and controlling activities (called the **functions of management**). They control the operations of the business system based on feedback provided by the firm's information systems.

- **Environment**. A business firm is a *subsystem* of society and is surrounded by the other systems of the **business environment**. It exchanges inputs and outputs with its environment, and is therefore called an *open system*. In addition, a business firm is an *adaptive system* (i.e., it has the ability to adjust to the demands of its environment).

The concept of a business firm as an open, adaptive system is very important, for it means that a business firm can use its *feedback and control* components in two ways:

- It monitors and regulates its operations to achieve its predetermined goals.
- It monitors the environment and can change both its operations *and its goals* in order to survive in a changing environment.

A business firm must maintain proper interrelationships with the other economic, political, and social subsystems in its environment, including customers, suppliers, competitors, stockholders, labor unions, financial institutions, governmental agencies, and the community. *Information systems* must be developed to help a business firm shape its relationships to each of these *environmental systems*. See Figure 14–4.

TYPES OF INFORMATION SYSTEMS

We have identified five major types of computer-based information systems that perform the vital feedback function in a business firm. Automated office systems were discussed in Chapter Thirteen. Management information systems and decision support systems will be discussed later in this chapter. So let us now briefly look

FIGURE

14–4 Information requirements of the business environment

Customer Systems. Information systems should help the business firm understand what consumers want and why they want it, so *consumers* can be converted into *customers*. Such "marketing information systems" support marketing activities such as advertising, selling, pricing, distribution, product development, and market research.

Competitor Systems. Information systems must provide management with information on present and potential *competitors,* why they are competitors, and what their competitive activities are and will be. Such information helps management shape its competitive strategy.

Supplier Systems. *Suppliers* provide a business firm with goods and services. Information systems must support the purchasing function so that the business firm can minimize its purchasing cost and maximize the value of goods and services that it procures.

Labor Union Systems. Though employees are a vital component of the business firm they are frequently represented by an environmental system—the *labor union*. Information systems must provide management, employees, and labor unions with information on employee compensation and labor productivity within the firm and competing business systems.

Stockholder Systems. Though *stockholders* are the owners of business firms that are organized as corporations, they can be considered as an environmental system because many business firms are owned by many different and distant stockholders. Information systems must provide information concerning dividends and financial and operating performance to management and stockholders.

Financial Institution Systems. Financial institutions (such as banks) provide the business system with money, credit and various financial services. Information systems must provide management and financial institutions with information on the financial and operating performance of the firm, and the state of the financial markets.

Governmental Systems. Business firms are governed by laws and regulations of *government agencies* at the city, county, state, federal, and foreign government levels. The information systems of a business firm must supply a wide variety of information to various governmental agencies concerning many aspects of the operations of the firm. Management also needs information on political, legal, and legislative developments so that it can effectively deal with changes in laws and regulations.

Community Systems. The business firm resides in local, regional, national, and world *communities*. Information systems must provide the management of business firms with information concerning how well they are meeting their responsibilities as "good citizens" of these communities.

at operational information systems and programmed decision systems.

Operational Information Systems

Operational information systems process data that is generated by business operations (sales transactions, production results, employee payroll, etc.) but do not produce the kind of information that can best be used by management. Further processing by a management information system is usually required. Operational information systems are sometimes called **transaction processing systems**, because they frequently process data resulting from the occurrence of *business transactions* (i.e., sales, purchases, inventory changes, etc.). However, operational information systems may also process data resulting from the monitoring of physical production processes, or data caused by making miscellaneous adjustments to the records in a file or database. Figure 14–5 illustrates an integrated group of information systems for a manufacturing firm built upon the basic *operational* system of a manufacturing firm.

Programmed Decision Systems

Programmed decision systems accept operational information and produce decisions that control an operational process. Programmed decisions are decisions that can be automated (programmed)

FIGURE 14–5 Selected information systems of a manufacturing firm

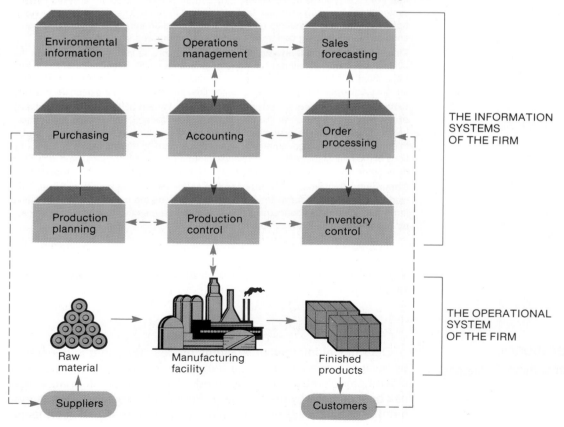

by basing them on a "decision rule," which outlines the steps to take when confronted with the need for a specific decision. A programmed decision does not have to be part of a computer program, though this is usually the case since the computer is the usual method for automating information systems. For example, programmed decisions might involve the inventory reorder process. Thus, many computerized inventory systems involve economic order point and order quantity decision rules in their computer programs. This allows automatic ordering of inventory items when amounts in inventory reach predetermined levels. Another example involves process control decisions, where decisions adjusting a physical production process are automatically made by computers.

INFORMATION REQUIREMENTS OF MANAGEMENT

The Functions of Management

Before we discuss the information requirements of management we should define what the term **management** means. Management is traditionally described as a process of leadership involving the functions of **planning, organizing, staffing, directing**, and **controlling**. These traditional functions can be used in response to the question, "What does a manager do?" A manager should *plan* the activities of the organization, *staff* it with required personnel, *organize* its personnel and their activities, *direct* the operations of the organization, and *control* its direction by evaluating feedback and making necessary adjustments. *Planning* involves the development of long- and short-range plans that requires the formulation of goals, objectives, strategies, policies, procedures, and standards. It also involves the perception and analysis of opportunities, problems, and alternative courses of action, and the design of programs to achieve selected objectives. *Organizing* involves the development of a structure which groups, assigns, and coordinates activities by delegating authority, offering responsibility, and requiring accountability. *Staffing* involves the selecting, training, and assignment of personnel to specific organizational activities. *Directing* is the leadership of the organization through communication and motivation of organizational personnel. *Controlling* involves observing and measuring organizational performance and environmental activities and modifying the plans and activities of the organization when necessary.

Management as a System

Figure 14–6 illustrates management as a system. Information from management information and decision support systems is the *input* to this system. Information is subjected to *analysis and synthesis*, utilizing data, models, and techniques from the MIS/DSS data-

FIGURE 14–6 Management as a system

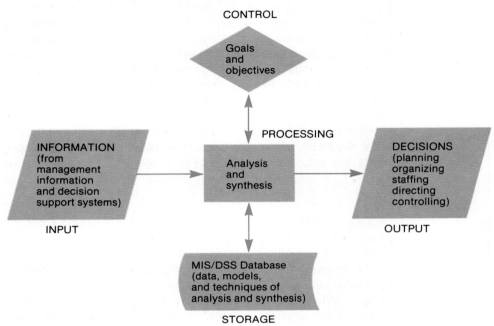

base. Alternative decisions are evaluated in the light of the *goals and objectives* of the firm. *Output* is in the form of planning, organizing, staffing, directing, and controlling *decisions*.

Figure 14–6 emphasizes why information is an indispensable ingredient in management. Each of the management functions requires *the analysis and synthesis of information* before a specific decision can be made. This information must be accurate, timely, complete, concise, and relevant or the quality of the decisions being made will suffer. Of course, even the best information cannot guarantee good decisions if managers do not have the ability to use it effectively. This is why information must be presented in a form which is easy to understand and use. Figure 14–6 also emphasizes the importance of information systems since they supply management with the *feedback* and *database* required for decision making.

Management Information Requirements

What information does management need? First of all, it must be emphasized that managers cannot possibly absorb all of the information that can be produced by information systems. Therefore, systems developers must determine not only (1) what information management *wants* but (2) what information management *needs*.

The factors that are important in making each decision must be identified. *What* decisions must be made, *who* should make them, and *when, where,* and *how* they should be made in the organization must be determined. Only then can we identify the types of information required to support each decision. Several concepts which guide the determination of the information needed by management are outlined in this section and illustrated in Figure 14–7.

Information Quality

Managers need information of high quality, not of great quantity. High-quality information must possess several major characteristics in order to effectively support managerial decision making. For example, information should have the following qualities:

- **Timely**. Information must be provided when needed by the manager.
- **Accurate**. Information must be free from errors.
- **Complete**. All of the information needed to make a decision must be provided.
- **Concise**. Only the information needed to make a decision must be provided. This avoids flooding the manager with unnecessary information.

FIGURE   14–7 Information requirements of management

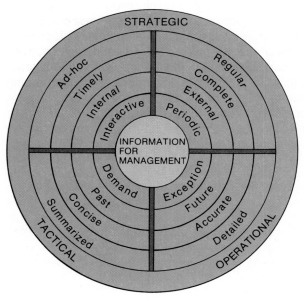

Past versus Future Information

Future information is another important concept that has to be emphasized in determining the information needs of management. It means that managers must be provided with information that helps them see future trends and determine their impact on their decision-making responsibilities. It's not enough to provide managers with historical (backward-looking) information and analysis. Future (forward-looking) information and analysis concerning trends developing inside the organization or in the business environment must also be provided. *For example*, an analysis of past sales performance does not provide management with adequate information. Sales management reports should provide forecasts of expected trends in sales and factors that might affect sales performance.

Internal versus External Information

Management should be provided with information (and *information analysis techniques*) about the internal operations of the business firm as well as the developments in the business environment. Refer back to Figure 14–4 and ahead to Figure 14–9. They summarize the types of external and internal information need by management.

Information Form and Timing

How do managers want and need their information? Do they prefer periodic scheduled reports or a quick response on demand? How about a report whenever an exceptional condition occurs? Or would an interactive modeling session with a computer be preferable? These are some of the choices facing system designers. They know that modern computer-based information systems can produce information to suit the timing and form preferences of most managers. For example, information can now be provided in the form of reports or video displays of *numeric data, text material*, or *graphics*. The major timing alternatives are summarized below.

- **Periodic scheduled reports**. For example, weekly sales analysis reports or monthly financial statements.
- **Exception reports**. Reports are produced only when exceptional conditions occur and only contain information about these exceptional conditions. For example, the credit manager is notified only if and when customers exceed their credit limits. Such *exception reporting* promotes *management by exception*, instead of overwhelming management with periodic detailed reports.

- **Demand reports and responses**. Information is provided whenever a manager demands it. For example, online video terminals and DBMS query languages and report generators allow managers to get immediate responses or reports as a result of their requests for information.
- **Interactive responses**. Information is provided in an interactive session between a manager and a computer containing an interactive program or a modeling package. For example, using an electronic spreadsheet package results in a series of answers in response to alternative "what if?" questions from a manager.

Levels of Management

Finally, the information requirements of management depend heavily on the *management level* involved. Figures 14–8 and 14–9 illustrate how a management system can be subdivided into three

FIGURE 14–8 Levels of management information needs

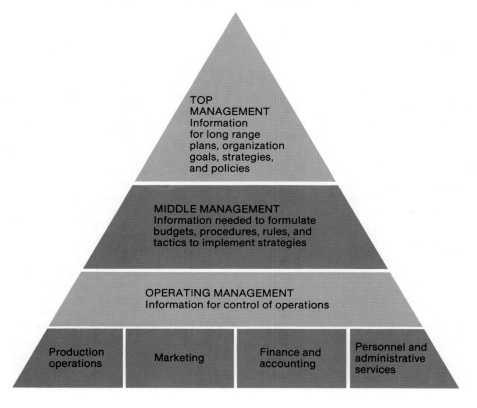

TOP MANAGEMENT
Information for long range plans, organization goals, strategies, and policies

MIDDLE MANAGEMENT
Information needed to formulate budgets, procedures, rules, and tactics to implement strategies

OPERATING MANAGEMENT
Information for control of operations

Production operations

Marketing

Finance and accounting

Personnel and administrative services

major subsystems: (1) *strategic management*, (2) *tactical management*, and (3) *operational management*. These subsystems are related to the traditional management levels of top management, middle management, and operating management. The activities and results of each management subsystem are summarized, as well as the types of information required by each subsystem.

Figure 14–9 emphasizes that the information requirements of management are directly related to the types of activities that predominate in each level of management. For example, the strategic management level requires more summarized special one-time reports, forecasts, and external reports to support its heavy planning and policymaking responsibilities. The operational management level on the other hand, may require more regular internal reports emphasizing detailed current and historical data comparisons which support its control of day-to-day operations.

FIGURE 14–9 Management activities and information requirements

Management Levels	Primary Activities	Activity Results	Activity Examples	Information Requirements
STRATEGIC MANAGEMENT	Long-range planning. Determine organizational resource requirements and allocations.	Goals. Objectives. Policies. Long-range plans and other strategic decisions.	Policy on diversification. Social responsibility policy. Major capital expenditure policy.	Forecasts. Simulations. Inquiries. External reports. One-time reports. Condensed internal reports.
TACTICAL MANAGEMENT	Allocate assigned resources to specific tasks. Make rules. Measure performance. Exert control.	Budgets. Procedures. Rules and other tactical decisions.	Personnel practices. Capital budgeting. Marketing mix.	Forecasts and historical data. Regular internal reports. Exception reports. Simulations. Inquiries.
OPERATIONAL MANAGEMENT	Direct the utilization of resources and the performance of tasks in conformance with established rules.	Directions. Commands. Actions and other operational decisions.	Production scheduling. Inventory control. Credit management.	Regular internal reports. Detailed transaction reports. Procedures manuals. Current and historical data. Programmed decisions.

REAL WORLD APPLICATION 14–1

Thermo Electron Corporation and Westinghouse Electric Corporation

It's 7:30 A.M. Do you know where your chief executive is? Managers at Thermo Electron and at Westinghouse Electric strongly suspect, that at their companies, the boss is already pecking away at a computer terminal to monitor the business and, they fear, to check up on them. Depending on their boss's style, they are beneficiaries or victims of a new wrinkle in computer technology—executive information systems.

These systems, also called decision support systems, allow executives to bypass the usual intelligence channels and quickly discover for themselves how the company or industry is faring. Depending on the system's complexity and their own needs, a boss unfazed by computers can call up information as detailed as the name of a bank officer who authorized a specific loan and as general as total corporate sales.

Even the executives using the new systems generally don't actually sit down at a computer terminal and punch in instructions themselves; most use an assistant to fetch the data they want and to run the analysis. However, some executives run the system themselves and even write their own programs. Among them are George Hatsopoulos, Thermo Electron's chairman. "When I sit down at a terminal, I get ideas on how to analyze things that I'd never get otherwise," Mr. Hatsopoulos says.

In most big companies, general-ledger, accounting-type information has long been funneled through the data processing department. The market research department handles outside sources of information, such as Nielsen data, consumer surveys and census reports. In short, top executives are flooded with data—but often not in useful or comparable formats. An answer to an executive inquiry that cuts across several sources of information might take a busy data processing department several weeks or longer and produce already outdated figures.

With an executive information system, the executive terminals are hooked up to a computer storing vast amounts of economic, marketing, and financial data. Computer programs enable an executive, or his assistant, to test theories, challenge assumptions, and selectively analyze information in any number of ways. Current numbers can be compared with last month's, last year's, or an average of the year-to-date figures. Budgets can be stacked up against forecasts. Formats can be changed as desired.

At Westinghouse Electric, David Luce, the director of corporate database, says the company's executive information system was installed more than three years ago because executives were griping that, by the time they searched through reams of information to find what they wanted, it was ancient history. Mr. Luce says, "The complaint was, 'If we've got all this information, why can't we use it? Why do I have to wait until the end of the month to see results of last month?'" Besides getting data, a Westinghouse executive can run through "what-if analysis"— for example, what will happen to my profit if sales drop 10 percent instead of 5 percent?

The system at Thermo Electron, an energy-equipment maker, supplies not only corporate data but also customer information and economic data from the Energy and Commerce departments. A forecast of furnace sales to the auto industry, for instance, used to take a staff two weeks or more. Now, Mr. Hatsopoulos says, it takes five minutes. "Some things took so long to cross-analyze we wouldn't do them," he says.

- What management information characteristics and requirements are mentioned above? Give examples of each.
- What types of computer-based information systems are being used? Explain.

Source: Mary Bralove, "Direct Data," *The Wall Street Journal*, January 12, 1983, p. 1.

MANAGEMENT INFORMATION SYSTEMS

When information systems are designed to provide information needed for effective decision making by managers, they are called **management information systems**. The concept of management information systems (MIS) originated in the 1960s and became the byword (and the "buzzword") of almost all attempts to relate computer technology and systems theory to data processing in business. During the early 1960s, it became evident that the computer was being applied to the solution of business problems in a piecemeal fashion, focusing almost entirely on the computerization of clerical and record-keeping tasks. The concept of management information systems was developed to counteract such *inefficient* development and *ineffective* use of the computer. The MIS concept is vital to efficient and effective computer use in business for two major reasons:

- It serves as a **systems** framework for organizing business computer applications. Business applications of computers should be viewed as interrelated and integrated *computer-based information systems* and not as independent data processing jobs.
- It emphasizes the **management** orientation of electronic information processing in business. The primary goal of computer-based information systems should be the support of *management decision making*, not merely the processing of data generated by business operations.

Effective management information systems are needed by all business organizations because of the increased complexity and rate of change of today's business environment. *For example,* marketing managers need information about sales performance and trends, financial managers need information concerning financing costs and investment returns, production managers need information analyzing resource requirements and worker productivity, and personnel managers require information concerning employee compensation and professional development. Thus, effective management information systems must be developed to provide modern managers with the specific marketing, financial, production, and personnel information products they require to support their decision-making responsibilities.

The Management Information System Concept

Figure 14–10 illustrates the management information system concept. It shows that hardware resources in the form executive workstations, software resources of application packages and database management systems, and people resources in the form of information specialists, all help managers get the information they need from the data resources of the organization. Notice that the following system functions are included:

- **Input**. Collects data generated by the other subsystems of the business system and the business environment.
- **Processing**. Uses information processing systems to transform data into information products which can support managerial decision making.
- **Storage**. Maintains databases containing data and information

FIGURE 14–10 The management information system concept

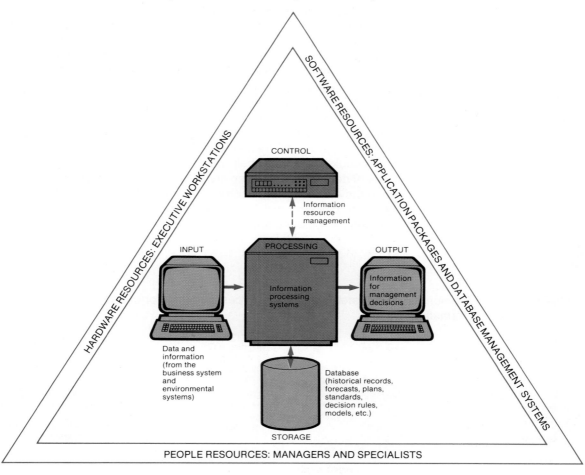

in the form of historical records, forecasts, plans, standards, decision rules, models, and other managerial and analytical techniques. Internal, external, and personal databases are used.

- **Output**. Provides a wide variety of information products needed to support the decision-making activities of management (1) on demand, (2) according to a predetermined schedule, or (3) when exceptional conditions occur.

- **Control**. Uses a continual process of *information resource management* to control the performance of the MIS, so that it efficiently and effectively meets the information needs of managers.

DECISION SUPPORT SYSTEMS

Decision support systems (DSS) are a natural progression from management information systems and earlier operational information systems. Decision support systems are interactive computer-based information systems that use *decision models* and a *management database* to provide information tailored to support specific decisions faced by individual managers. They are thus different from operational information systems, which focus on processing the data generated by business transactions and operations. They also differ from management information systems, which have primarily been focused on providing managers with structured information (reports) which could be used to help them make more effective, structured types of decisions. They also are not programmed decision systems, since they do not make decisions for managers. Figure 14–11 illustrates the place of decision support systems among the major types of computer-based information systems.

FIGURE 14–11 Decision support systems and major types of computer-based information systems

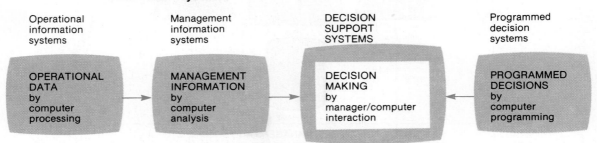

The Decision Support System Concept

Decision support systems help managers solve the *semistructured* and *unstructured* problems typically faced by decision makers in the real world. They are flexible, adaptable, quick response systems which are user-initiated and controlled and support the personal decision-making style of a manager. DSS are designed to use decision models and a decision maker's own insights and judgments in an interactive computer-based process leading up to a specific decision. Figure 14–12 illustrates the decision support system concept. Notice the following system components:

- An **executive workstation** — a personal computer or computer terminal provides the DSS *hardware interface* for managers.
- A **DSS generator** is the *software engine* that drives the system. It contains major software modules for *database management, model management*, and *dialog management*.
- **Database management software** (DBMS) provides database creation, maintenance, inquiry, and retrieval using typical database management system query languages, report generators, data manipulation languages, and data definition languages.
- **Model base management software** (MBMS) provides the ability to create, maintain, and manipulate the model base using modeling package languages or user-written programs.
- **Dialog generation and management software** (DGMS) consists of interactive input/output programs, subroutines, and nonprocedural languages. **Input**: allows users to make inquiries and responses or issue commands using a keyboard, electronic mouse, touch screen, voice input, etc. **Output**: provides output

FIGURE

14–12 The decision support system concept

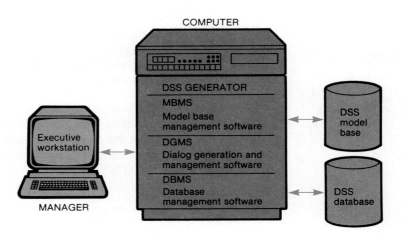

in the form of numeric, text, and graphics visual displays or printed reports. Audio responses and menus, prompts, icons, and *help* displays may also be provided.

- A **database** of data and information is stored in a special DSS database extracted from the databases of the organization, external databases, and a manager's personal database.
- A **model base** includes a library of models and analytical techniques stored as programs, subroutines, command files, and decision rules. The model base management software can combine these model components to create models for an individual manager needing support for a specific type of decision.[1]

An effective DSS should be designed to meet the following performance objectives:

- Support managerial decision making especially for semistructured and unstructured decisions. Such support should be available at all levels of the organization where it is needed.
- Enhance the coordination and communication between decision makers, especially when they must cooperate in a decision-making task, or work on related decision-making tasks.
- Support all phases of the decision-making task instead of just data gathering, analysis, comparative evaluation, or implementation. It should thus be able to communicate through an established interface with operational, automated office, and management information systems.
- Support a variety of decision making processes so that the user can direct the problem solving or decision making in accordance with his or her preferred cognitive style. This characteristic also makes DSS responsive to changes in tasks, organization environment, or the capability of the user over time.
- Be easy to use. A DSS should be a flexible user-friendly system that can be easily operated by users who are not information systems specialists. This must be a primary criterion for the software used by the decision support system.

Figure 14–13 illustrates the structure and functions of a popular DSS generator called IFPS (Interactive Financial Planning System). Figure 14–14 lists the components and capabilities of another popular DSS generator called FOCUS. Several other DSS software packages, such as EXPRESS, MODEL, EMPIRE and ENCORE, are

---

[1] This section is based in part on material from Ralph H. Sprague, Jr., and Eric D. Carlson, *Building Effective Decision Support Systems* (Englewood Cliffs, N.J.: Prentice-Hall, 1982).

available from independent consulting firms and computer manufacturers. Many are now available in microcomputer versions (e.g., PC/FOCUS or IFPS Personal). However don't forget that even lowly electronic spreadsheet packages (such as VisiCalc and Multiplan) and especially the newer integrated packages (such as Lotus 1-2-3, Symphony, Corporate MBA, and Framework) are limited DSS generators. They provide some of the model building (spreadsheet models), model manipulation (what-if analysis), database management and dialog management (menus, prompts, etc.) functions that are offered by more powerful DSS generators.

FIGURE 14–13 Structure and functions of a DSS generator: IFPS

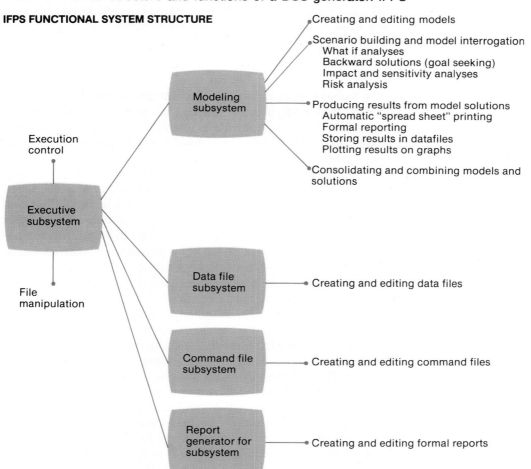

IFPS FUNCTIONAL SYSTEM STRUCTURE

- Creating and editing models
- Scenario building and model interrogation
  - What if analyses
  - Backward solutions (goal seeking)
  - Impact and sensitivity analyses
  - Risk analysis
- Producing results from model solutions
  - Automatic "spread sheet" printing
  - Formal reporting
  - Storing results in datafiles
  - Plotting results on graphs
- Consolidating and combining models and solutions

Execution control

Modeling subsystem

Executive subsystem

File manipulation

Data file subsystem — Creating and editing data files

Command file subsystem — Creating and editing command files

Report generator for subsystem — Creating and editing formal reports

FIGURE

14–14 Components and capabilities of a DSS generator: PC/FOCUS

- **Report Generator.** Creates simple or complex reports using a nonprocedural English-like language and an interactive window-driven process.
- **Dialog Manager.** Develops menu-driven interactive dialog procedures with appropriate prompts.
- **Full-Screen Editor.** Helps build and edit command and data files.
- **Screen Manager.** Develops formatted screens and windows.
- **Graphics Generator.** Produces pie charts, bar charts, line graphs, etc.
- **Database Management.** Manages the creation and maintenance of the DSS database.
- **Communications Package.** Allows microcomputer to mainframe communications.
- **Data Security Package.** Provides four levels of data security, plus encription capability.
- **Financial Modelling Language.** Creates electronic spreadsheets and allows what-if analysis, goal seeking, and other types of financial analysis.
- **Statistical Analysis Library.** Provides a library of statistical functions, including time series, regression analysis, and descriptive statistics.

Artificial Intelligence and Expert Systems

The frontiers of present DSS research are being affected by developments in **artificial intelligence** (AI). Artificial intelligence is an area of computer science that is attempting to develop computers that can hear, walk, talk, feel, and think! A major thrust is the development of computer functions normally associated with human intelligence, such as reasoning, inference, learning, and problem solving. One of the most practical applications of this area of AI is the development of **expert systems**. An *expert system* is a computer-based information system that uses its knowledge about a specific complex application area to act as an expert consultant to users. The components of an expert system consist of a **knowledge base** and software modules which perform inferences on the knowledge and communicate an answer to a user's questions. Figure 14–15 illustrates the components of an expert system.

Expert systems are also called **knowledge-based systems**. They are thus related to the development of *knowledge-based DSS*, which add a knowledge base to the database and model base of traditional decision support systems. However, expert systems are still quite different from this type of DSS. Expert systems will only provide answers to questions in a very specific problem area by making human-like inferences about knowledge contained in a very specialized knowledge base. They must also be able to explain their reasoning process and conclusions to a user.

Expert systems are being applied to many specific application areas. Examples are DENDRAL, which helps organic chemists work

REAL WORLD APPLICATION 14–2

Schwinn Bicycle Company

"Microsoft Multiplan allows me to explore more alternatives in less time. I think it leads to better management decisions," says Edward R. Schwinn, Jr., president, Schwinn Bicycle Company. "Multiplan software helps me make better business decisions. It's as simple as that. With Multiplan on my microcomputer, I can explore a number of alternatives faster. That's really important to me in planning and tracking my totally handcrafted Schwinn Paramount Bicycle. As with anything handmade, cost control and product planning are major considerations. For instance, Multiplan lets me study the effect of the learning curve on overall productivity. And although we have a mainframe computer, I find that Multiplan is a tool that allows me to personally examine my business options—without spinning my wheels."

Microsoft Multiplan is a microcomputer software program that can help you, too. In many ways. You can analyze cash flow. Plan budgets. Forecast income. Manage production. Multiplan allows you to set up an electronic worksheet for whatever your need may be. And it lets you explore alternatives faster, because when you make one change you immediately see the results of that change throughout the worksheet and on any related worksheets. Just change one number and every number that depends on it is adjusted automatically. In plain English, you won't have to learn a cryptic language to use Multiplan. It takes commands in plain English. And it will prompt you as you go along by telling you what to do next. There's even a HELP key in case you need help at any point. Press it and it gives you information to get you going again.

- Is Mr. Schwinn's use of Multiplan an example of a DSS in action? Why or why not?
- Does Multiplan sound like a DSS generator? What DSS generator features does it have? What features are missing?

Source: Courtesy Microsoft Corporation.

FIGURE

14–15 Components of an expert system

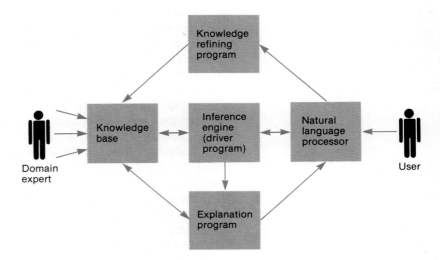

out the molecular structure of organic compounds; PUFF, which diagnoses respiratory diseases, PROSPECTOR, which interprets geological data as a guide to mineral exploration; and MYCIN, which is designed to assist physicians in the diagnosis and treatment of certain types of bacterial infection. R-1, which helps design computer systems for customers, and XSEL, which assists sales personnel in ordering computer system configurations for their customers, are expert systems being used by the Digital Equipment Corporation.

INTEGRATED INFORMATION SYSTEMS

Most business firms agree that *integration* and *coordination* should exist between the information systems of the organization and are working toward that goal in their information systems development. Integrated information systems avoid duplication, simplify operations, and produce an *efficient* information system. However, some duplication is necessary to insure *effective* information systems. For example, duplicate copies of reports may be required if several users require "hard copy" output, or duplicate storage files may be necessary if a "back-up" capability is required. *Carrying systems integration to an extreme* could result in systems that are costly, cumbersome, or unreliable. Therefore, some duplication and *redundancy* is usually required in systems design.

Business Information Systems

Business information systems support the traditional *functions of business*, such as marketing, finance, accounting, personnel, and production. You should realize that many computer-based business information systems are integrated combinations of both decision support systems, management information systems, and operational information systems. Thus most business information systems are designed to produce information and support decision making for various levels of management as well as do record-keeping and transaction processing chores.

Example. A payroll system that processes employee time cards and produces employee paychecks is an *operational* information system. An information system that uses payroll data to produce labor analysis reports, which show variances and trends in labor cost and utilization, is a *management* information system. However, in most cases, these functions are combined in an integrated payroll/labor analysis system, which not only processes employee time cards and produces paychecks but also furnishes management with labor analysis reports.

Example. Sales order/transaction processing is typically considered to be an operational information subsystem, while sales analysis is considered a management information subsystem. However, both are subsystems of the marketing information system. The sales order processing system collects and records sales transaction data and provides input to the sales analysis system, which produces management reports concerning sales generated by each salesperson, sales territory, customer, product, etc.

Example. Production and sales activity data generated by manufacturing and marketing operational information systems are utilized by the marketing MIS for sales reports and the marketing DSS for sales forecasts. These are then used by the production MIS for production reports and the production DSS for production scheduling. See Figure 14–16.

FIGURE

14–16 Interrelationships of business information systems

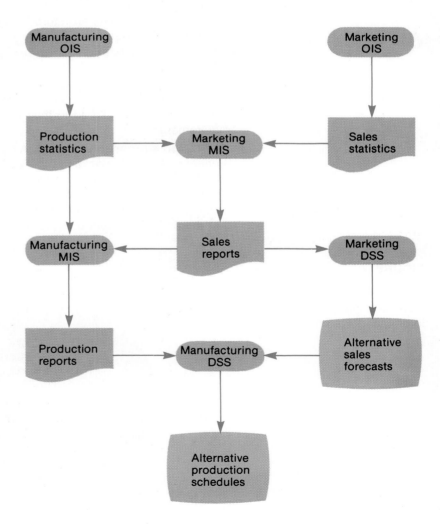

Advanced Integrated Systems

Advanced integrated information systems are being developed by many computer-using organizations which have the important characteristics summarized below. See Figure 14–17.

- **Common data flows**. Common source documents, common input/output media, and a common database are utilized so unnecessary processing activities, storage files, input data, and output information are eliminated.
- **Immediate data entry**. Data created from transactions and operations are entered directly into the computer system from their point of origin through online transaction terminals.
- **Common databases**. Current and historical data, forecasts, plans, standards, decision rules, mathematical models, and other analytical techniques are stored in direct access databases for use by all subsystems.
- **Integrated application packages**. The major types of general-purpose and business software packages are integrated into multiple-application packages, which provide users with powerful but easy-to-use tools to process data into a wide variety of information products tailored to their functional and profession requirements.
- **Decision support orientation**. A computer user uses decision-oriented software packages to evaluate the data being processed, the information produced, and the contents of data bases. As a result, the computer may make programmed decisions, specify decisions that must be made, specify actions to be taken, notify users of unusual conditions requiring decision

FIGURE

14–17 Features of advanced integrated information systems

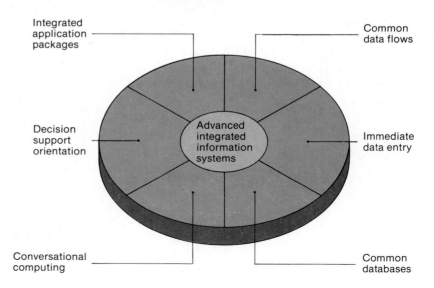

REAL WORLD APPLICATION 14-3

Anheuser-Busch Companies, Inc.

Anheuser-Busch Companies, Inc., is a diversified corporation whose subsidiaries include the world's largest brewery organization as well as operations in the fields of container/lid manufacturing and recycling, malt production, metalized label printing, international beer marketing, family entertainment, baker's yeast, real estate development, railcar repair and transportation services, major league baseball, stadium ownership, creative services, snack foods, and bakery products.

MODEL is the financial modeling tool offered by the Anheuser-Busch Companies Information Center, utilizing an IBM S/370-158AP. This activity is supported by the Information Services Department. Through the Information Center, MODEL is available to all users who have obtained security clearance, received instructions on how to gain access to the available resources, and offered and received specific training in MODEL. Currently, there are approximately 25 of the 250 users at Anheuser-Busch who use MODEL; however, four or five users account for most of the usage. The heavy users of MODEL include: Corporate Budget & Analysis, Financial Planning, Treasury Operations, and Materials Planning.

Corporate Budget & Analysis uses MODEL for analyzing monthly and year-to-date earnings versus the budget and the prior year's actual. MODEL is also used to track the monthly profit contributions of subsidiaries as well as corporate expenses. In addition, a MODEL program is utilized in projecting quarterly and annual earnings of the corporation. Financial Planning uses MODEL to determine the worth of a particular business operation in the current year and projects that information forward to determine future value. This application makes extensive use of MODEL'S financial library mixed with some user-developed subroutines to produce a flexible system for determining the future worth of a business.

Treasury Operations has used MODEL to develop a major forecasting system. When new data are loaded into the system a number of reports can be generated from this single MODEL, providing current information on cash flow analysis. The "what-if" feature, along with prompts and menu-driven reports, are included in this job. Materials Planning uses of MODEL include a system to analyze the investment potential of a major project. MODEL has proved useful for this application, since it allows the user to continuously revise the data. "What-if," goal-seeking, and the financial library have made this system very workable.

- Is MODEL being used for both MIS and DSS applications? Explain.
- Explain the features that make MODEL a DSS generator.

Source: Courtesy of Lloyd Bush and Associates

making, or integrate a decision maker's insights and judgments into an interactive decision-making process.
- **Conversational computing**. Microcomputers, intelligent terminals, database management software, fourth-generation languages, and other computer system capabilities encourage conversational computing. Computer users can simply and instantly direct the computer to solve problems, answer questions, process data, update files, and produce output in any format desired.

SUMMARY

- An information system is a system that collects, transforms, and transmits information in an organization. Computer-based information systems, such as operational information systems (OIS), programmed decision systems (PDS), automated office systems (AOS), management information systems (MIS), and decision support systems (DSS), make extensive use of the computer hardware, software, people, and data resources of electronic information processing systems.

- The business firm should be viewed as a system in which economic resources (input) are transformed by various organizational processes (processing) into goods and services (output). Information systems provide information on the operation of the business (feedback) to management for the direction and maintenance of the firm (control). The business firm is a subsystem of society and is surrounded by other systems of the business environment.

- Managers have to be provided with information that meets a variety of requirements. Information must be timely, accurate, complete, and concise. It must consist of both internal and external information, as well as information about the past and future. It should include periodic scheduled reports, exception reports, demand reports and responses, and interactive responses. Finally, information must be tailored to the strategic, tactical, or operational level of the managers who need it.

- Management information systems are systems that provide information needed for effective management decision making. Information needed by managers is provided on demand, according to a schedule, or on an exception basis. The concept of management information systems (MIS) was developed to provide a systems framework and management orientation for the development of efficient and effective computer applications in business.

- Decision support systems are interactive, computer-based information systems that use decision models and a management database to provide information tailored to support specific decisions faced by individual managers. They are designed to use a decision maker's own insights and judgments in an interactive computer-based process leading up to a specific decision.

- Decision support systems are being affected by developments in artificial intelligence. In particular, the development of expert systems has prompted the development of knowledge-based decision support systems. Expert systems are computer-based information system's that use a knowledge base about a specific complex application area to act as an expert consultant to users.

■ A major development modern information systems is the concept of integrated information systems. This concept emphasizes that the various management, decision support, and operational information systems of an organization are usually combined into integrated business information systems. For most business firms, however, the concept of integrated information systems is a goal emphasizing that integration and coordination should exist between the various information systems of the organization so they can better meet the information needs of users.

KEY TERMS AND CONCEPTS

Information system
Computer-based information
  systems
The business firm as a system
Management as a system
Environmental systems
Operational information
  systems
Programmed decision systems
Management information
  systems
Decision support systems
Expert systems
Knowledge-based systems

Functions of management
Information quality
Form and timing of information
Past versus future information
Interval versus external
  information
Periodic, exception, demand,
  and interactive information
Management levels
DSS generator
Artificial intelligence
Business information systems
Integrated information systems

REVIEW AND APPLICATION QUESTIONS

1. What are information systems? Computer-based information systems? Are they necessary in an organization? Explain.
2. Identify the basic system components of the business firm as a system and their functions as components of this system.
3. What is the difference in the role of operational and management information systems? In programmed decision and decision support systems?
4. How can a business firm use its feedback-control components as an "adaptive system"?
5. What are the functions of management? How do they affect the concept of management as a system?

6. What are several of the characteristics of information needed by management?
7. Why do the information requirements of management depend on the management level involved?
8. What are management information systems? Identify the components of a management information system.
9. Why is the MIS concept vital to efficient and effective computer use in business?
10. What are decision support systems? Explain the functions of their major components.
11. What are several performance objectives and benefits that can be gained from the use of decision support systems?
12. How do expert systems differ from decision support systems?
13. Explain how many current business information systems are integrated combinations of management and operational information systems.
14. What are several major characteristics of advanced integrated systems. Explain how they support integration of information processing.

APPLICATION PROBLEMS

1. If you have not already done so, read and answer the questions after each Real World Application in this chapter.
2. Application A has the following characteristics: relatively little data input, numerous and complex computations, infrequently run. Application B has the following characteristics: voluminous files of data, relatively simple computations, periodic program runs. Which of these systems is most likely to be an operational information system? Which is probably a decision support system?
3. The executives of ABC Department Stores currently receive some of the following types of information products: (1) monthly financial statements, (2) weekly sales analysis reports, and (3) weekly inventory status reports. The VP for Information Services is proud of how accurate and complete these reports are. But some ABC executives are complaining that these reports don't meet their information needs. Use the management information requirements summarized in Figure 14–7 to analyze what the problem is, and to suggest and defend several possible solutions.
4. Have you used a personal computer (or mainframe computer terminal) and an electronic spreadsheet package or an integrated package yet? Analyze your experience in terms of the MIS model shown in Figure 14–10 and the DSS model shown in Figure 14–

12. That is, list each systems component of these models that you can identify when using these packages.

5. Use an electronic spreadsheet or integrated package. What features do you feel would be helpful to a user in terms of decision-making support? Explain the reasons for your choices.

6. Use an electronic spreadsheet or integrated package. What features need to be added or improved to make these packages easier to use and more effective DSS generators? Explain how and why this should be done.

CHAPTER 15

Computer-Based Information Systems: Marketing, Production/Operations, and Personnel

CHAPTER OUTLINE

LEARNING OBJECTIVES

The purpose of this chapter is to promote a basic
understanding of how computers are used in business
by analyzing computer applications in marketing,
production/operations, personnel, and other areas.
After reading and studying this chapter you should be
able to identify several ways that the computer is used
to support the functions of marketing, production/
operations, and personnel, and the operations of
several industries.

HOW ARE COMPUTERS USED IN BUSINESS?

This chapter and the one that follows will attempt to answer questions concerning specific uses of the computer in business. What do computers do in business? How are computers used in business operations? How is the computer applied to business management? We will explore the answers to such questions by providing an overview as well as focusing on specific applications of the computer in business firms and other computer-using organizations. You should realize that **computer-based information systems** are frequently called *computer application systems*, or simply, **computer applications**. For example, a computer-based *payroll* information system would typically be called a payroll application. Thus you should view all computer applications in business as computer-based business information systems.

There are as many computer applications in business as there are business activities to be performed, business problems to be solved, and business opportunities to be pursued. It is, therefore, impossible to acquire a complete understanding of all computer applications in business. However, a business person should not have a *vague, unorganized* idea of business computer applications. As a present or future computer user, you should have a *basic* but *organized* understanding of the major ways the computer is used in business. You should also have a *specific* understanding of how computers affect a *particular business function* (marketing, for example) or a *particular industry* (banking, for example) that is directly related to your *career objectives*. Thus someone whose career objective is *marketing* position in *banking* should acquire a basic understanding of how computers are used in banking and how computers support the marketing activities of banks and other business firms.

Figure 15–1 illustrates how major computer applications can be grouped into business function and management level categories. Figure 15–2 gives examples of computer applications in a variety of industries. Applications in this chapter and the next will thus be discussed according to the "*business function*" they support (marketing, production/operations, finance, accounting, and personnel) or according to the *industry* in which they are utilized (retailing, banking, insurance, etc.). This should help you acquire a *basic, organized,* and *specific* understanding of how computers support the management and operations of modern business firms.

TRENDS IN COMPUTER USE IN BUSINESS

In the early years of computer use, the computer was applied to the solution of information processing problems in a piecemeal fashion. Most computer applications involved the computerization

FIGURE 15–1 Computer applications by business function and management level

STRATEGIC PLANNING SYSTEMS

Strategic and operating plan	Economic forecasting	Manpower planning	Sales and profit planning

MANAGEMENT CONTROL SYSTEMS

Manufacturing control	Marketing control	Financial control	Accounting control
• Purchasing • Time series planning • Order point planning • Inventory control • Plant loading • Master production scheduling • Demand forecasting	• Product introduction • Advertising sales promotion • Sales management • Product requirements planning • Sales forecasting and analysis • Market research	• Pricing and profitability analysis • Portfolio analysis • Capital investment analysis • Capital requirements forecasting and planning • Cash requirements forecasting	• Inventory valuation • Estimating • Cost analysis • Budgeting standard costing

OPERATIONAL SYSTEMS

Manufacturing	Marketing	Distribution	Finance	Accounting	Personnel	Administration
• Facilities and environmental protection and control • Testing and quality control • Machine control • Plant maintenance • Time reporting • Receiving • Stores control • Material movement control • Plant scheduling	• Order release • Order tracking and inquiry • Order processing • Order entry • Dealer/branch operations	• Distribution center operation • Shipping document preparation • Vehicle scheduling • Freight routing and tracking • Freight bill rating and audit • Distribution planning	• Cash management • Tax and government reporting • Auditing	• Billing and accounts receivable • Credit • Payroll • Asset accounting • Accounts payable • General ledger	• In-house education • Government reporting • Employee services • Wage and salary administration	• Library services • Stockholders relations • Legal

Source: Adapted and reprinted by permission of the *Harvard Business Review,* from "Managing the Crisis in Data Processing," by Richard L. Nolan, March–April 1979, pp. 117–21. Copyright 1979 by the President and Fellows of Harvard College; all rights reserved.

FIGURE

15–2 Computer applications by industry categories

Industry Segment	Basic Applications	Advanced Applications
Manufacturing	Accounting. Order processing. Purchasing. Inventory control.	Forecasting. Numerical control. Production scheduling. Design automation.
Business and personal services	Service bureau functions. Tax preparation. Accounting. Client records.	Econometric models. Time sharing. Engineering analysis. Database.
Banking and finance	Demand deposit accounting. Check processing. Proof and transit operations. Cost control.	Online savings. Centralized life systems. Portfolio analysis. Cash flow analysis.
Insurance	Premium accounting. Customer billing. External reports. Reserve calculation.	Actuarial analysis. Investment analysis. Policy approval. Cash flow analysis.
Utilities	Customer billing. Accounting. Meter reading. Inventory control.	Rate analysis. Line and generator loading. Operational simulation. Financial models.
Distribution	Order processing. Inventory control. Purchasing. Warehouse control.	Vehicle scheduling. Merchandising. Forecasting. Store site selection.
Transportation	Rate calculation. Vehicle maintenance. Cost analysis. Accounting.	Traffic pattern analysis. Automatic rating. Tariff analysis. Reservation systems.
Health care	Patient billing. Inventory accounting. Health care statistics. Patient history.	Lab/operation scheduling. Nurses' station automation. Intensive care. Preliminary diagnosis.
Retail	Customer billing. Sales analysis. Accounting. Inventory reporting.	Point of sale automation. Sales forecasting. Merchandising. Cash flow analysis.
Printing and publishing	Circulation. Classified ads. Accounting. Payroll.	Automatic typesetting. Home finder. Media analysis. Page layout.

Source: Adapted from Jerome Kanter, *Management Oriented Management Information Systems,* 3d ed., © 1984, p. 176. Reprinted by permission of Prentice Hall, Inc., Englewood Cliffs, New Jersey.

FIGURE 15–3 The trend in business computer applications

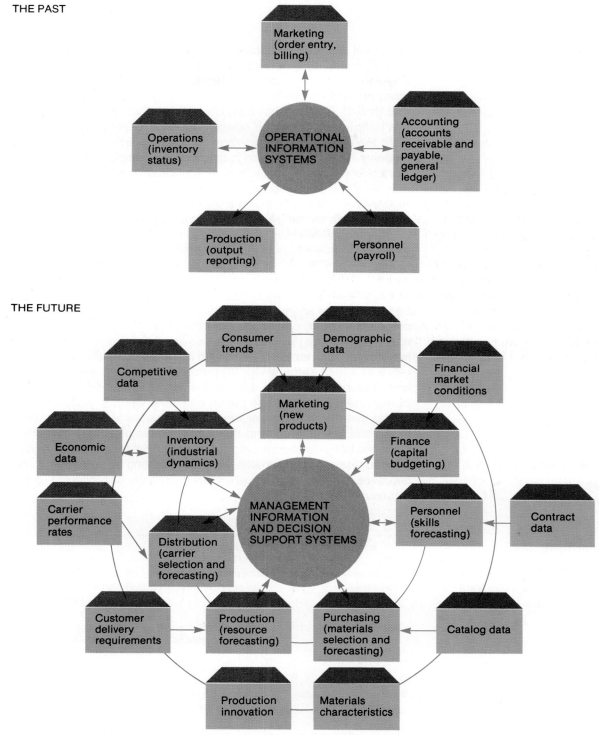

Source: Adapted from John Diebold, "Bad Decisions on Computer Use," *Harvard Business Review,* January–February 1969.

of clerical and record-keeping tasks because they: (1) were comparatively simple, (2) were already organized for manual data processing, (3) could show immediate cost savings, and (4) posed the most pressing information processing problems in terms of sheer volumes and growth. The trend of computer applications since that time has been away from such *operational information systems* and toward the concept of *management information and decision support systems*. The modern trend is to develop a computer **applications portfolio** (diversified collection of applications) whose main goal is to provide information to support management decision making. Figure 15–3 illustrates that the trend in computer applications can be viewed as a change from the *clerical record-keeping* functions of operational information systems to the *decision-making support* functions of management information and decision support systems.

Figure 15–4 illustrates three stages of computer applications in computer-using business firms. Computers are (1) applied to *record-keeping* functions (using centralized batch systems) where the payoff is frequently an immediate reduction in costs; then (2) the computer is applied to *operational* functions (using realtime distributed/ database systems) which have a less immediate payoff and whose benefits are less tangible. Firms with sufficient computer experience move to a third stage where (3) personal computers and executive workstations are used to support the *strategic planning* functions of management but whose payoff may take years to occur. Thus, as the use of the computer moves from "paper work automation" to "operations control" and then to "strategic planning" applications, the benefits of computer use change from tangible *cost reductions* to less-tangible benefits, such as operating improvements and improved decision making, which are frequently described as *profit producing* benefits.

FIGURE

15–4 Three stages of computer applications in business

Applications Stage	Applications Technology	Applications Benefits
Recording-keeping applications	Batch centralized systems	Immediate payoff. Reduced clerical cost. Improved speed and accuracy.
Operations control applications	Realtime distributed/ database systems	Intermediate payoff. Improved service and control. Reduced asset levels and operating costs.
Strategic planning applications	Interactive personal computing systems	Improved information and decisions. Slow recognition of payoff.

SECTION I: COMPUTER-BASED INFORMATION SYSTEMS IN MARKETING

The business function of **marketing** is concerned with the planning, promotion, and sale of existing products in existing markets and the development of new products and new markets to better serve present and potential customers. Thus marketing performs a vital function in the operation of a business enterprise. Performing the marketing function in business has become a much more difficult assignment because of the dynamic environment of today, which includes:

- Rapidly changing market demands.
- Steadily increasing consumer pressures.
- Shortened product life spans.
- Proliferation of new products.
- Intensified competition.
- Growing government regulations.

Business firms have increasingly turned to the computer to help them perform the vital marketing function in the face of the rapid changes of today's environment. The computer has been the catalyst in the development of *marketing information systems*, which integrate the information flows required by many marketing activities. We shall now briefly analyze marketing information systems and several computer applications in marketing. This should provide you with a basic understanding of how computers help business firms perform their marketing activities.

Marketing Information Systems

Marketing information systems provide information for the planning and control of the marketing function. *Marketing planning information* assists marketing management in product planning, pricing decisions, planning advertising and sales promotion strategy and expenditures, forecasting the market potential for new and present products, and determining channels of distribution. *Marketing control information* supports the efforts of management to control the efficiency and effectiveness of the selling and distribution of products and services.

The major types of marketing information systems are illustrated in Figure 15–5, and summarized below. Notice that these subsystems provide information needed by marketing management and other business information systems.

- **Sales order processing**. A basic form of this system will be analyzed in the next chapter. It captures and processes customer orders and produces invoices for customers and data needed for sales analysis and inventory control. In many firms, it also keeps track of the status of customer orders until goods are delivered.

FIGURE 15–5 Marketing information systems

- **Sales management**. This system provides information to help sales managers plan and monitor the performance of the sales organization. The *sales analysis* application described in the next chapter is a basic form of this system.
- **Product management**. Management needs information to plan and control the performance of specific products, product lines, or brands. Price, revenue, cost, and growth information is required for existing products and new product development. Information and analysis for *pricing* decisions is a major function of this system.
- **Advertising and promotion**. Management needs information to help it achieve sales objectives at the lowest possible costs for advertising and promotion. Information and analytical techniques are utilized to select media and promotional methods, allocate financial resources, and control and evaluate results.
- **Sales forecasting**. The basic functions of sales forecasting can be grouped into the two categories of "short-range forecasting" and "long-range forecasting." Short-range forecasting deals with forecasts of sales for periods up to one year, while long-range forecasting is concerned with sales forecasts for a year or more into the future.
- **Market research**. The market research information subsystem provides *marketing intelligence* to help management make more effective marketing decisions. It also provides marketing management with information to help plan and control the market research

REAL WORLD APPLICATION 15-1

Hayden Publishing Company

At Hayden Publishing Company in Hasbrouck Heights, New Jersey, Stacy Bearse, publisher of *Microwaves & RF* magazine, is using personal computers to enhance his salespeople's effectiveness. With three other competitors in the market and only 300 potential advertisers, Bearse is interested in knowing the amount of advertising his clients are doing with the competition. Using dBASE II software on an IBM Personal Computer, Bearse has developed a program to measure the amount of advertising appearing in all four publications to determine *Microwaves's* share of the market for each individual advertiser and for all advertisers combined. By breaking down the market by individual advertisers, Bearse can keep track of how each of his five national and five international sales representatives are doing in their respective territories

"As for salesmen, we ask that each one be the leader in their districts and regions," says Bearse. "We follow this very closely. Bonuses are given out to salesmen by their share of the market. We also look for noticeable changes in advertising budgets and to see if there are any new accounts. Or if we have been ignoring an account because they said they did not have an advertising budget and then we see they are advertising in another publication, we can return to them and sell them advertising."

Using survey data provided by *Microwave's* parent company, Hayden Publishing Company, Bearse does extensive marketing research on the computer to pinpoint specific information about the magazines' audience. From this analysis, which he calls semantic differential research,

Bearse can learn what perceptions different segments of his audience have of the publication. He can then use this research as an advertising tool.

"We had an advertiser come to us who was not satisfied with his advertising," says Bearse. "His advertising staff thought their advertising was not on target. Although the firm was only a small division in a major corporation, they were concerned that, by using the name of the company, the reader thought of the product as being high priced, but it was actually inexpensive. When we did some research, we got data back that showed the readers' impressions were in contrast to fact. The readers thought the company had expensive products. Using this data, we convinced the company to begin emphasizing its price in its advertisements."

Bearse also uses dBASE II to categorize by topic all the editorial material that appears in each edition. At the end of the year, he prints out a 50-page report identifying the exact nature of the editorial contents. Armed with this marketing and editorial information, sales representatives can give potential advertisers and advertising agencies a strong argument that advertising in *Microwaves* will get them results.

- How is a personal computer being used to improve performance in sales management? In advertising and promotion?
- Is this an example of a marketing database processing system? Explain.

Source: Richard Clucas, "Powering Up Your Sales Force," *Personal Computing*, May 1984, p. 101. Reprinted with permission.

FIGURE 15–6 Benefits of computer-based marketing information systems

	Typical Applications	Benefits	Examples
CONTROL SYSTEMS	Control of marketing costs.	More timely computerized reports.	Undesirable cost trends are spotted more quickly so that corrective action may be taken sooner.
	Diagnosis of poor sales performance.	Flexible online retrieval of data.	Executives can ask supplementary questions of the computer to help pinpoint reasons for a sales decline and reach an action decision more quickly.
	Management of fashion goods.	Automatic spotting of problems and opportunities.	Fast-moving fashion items are reported daily for quick reorder, and slow-moving items are also reported for fast price reductions.
	Flexible promotion strategy.	Cheaper, more detailed, and more frequent reports.	Ongoing evaluation of a promotional campaign permits reallocation of funds to areas behind target.
PLANNING SYSTEMS	Forecasting.	Automatic translation of terms and classifications between departments.	Survey-based forecasts of demand for complex industrial goods can be automatically translated into parts requirements and production schedules.
	Promotional planning and corporate long-range planning.	Systematic testing of alternative promotional plans and compatibility testing of various divisional plans.	Complex simulation models both developed and operated with the help of data bank information can be used for promotional planning by product managers and for strategic planning by top management.
	Credit management.	Programmed executive decision rules can operate on data bank information.	Credit decisions are automatically made as each order is processed.
	Purchasing.	Detailed sales reporting permits automation of management decisions.	Computer automatically repurchases standard items on the basis of correlation of sales data with programmed decision rules.
RESEARCH SYSTEMS	Advertising strategy.	Additional manipulation of data is possible when stored for computers in an unaggregated data base.	Sales analysis is possible by new market segment breakdowns.
	Pricing strategy.	Improved storage and retrieval capability allows new types of data to be collected and used.	Systematic recording of information about past R&D contract bidding situations allows improved bidding strategies.
	Evaluation of advertising expenditures.	Well-designed data banks permit integration and comparison of different sets of data.	Advertising expenditures are compared to shipments by county to provide information about advertising effectiveness.
	Continuous experiments.	Comprehensive monitoring of input and performance variables yields information when changes are made.	Changes in promotional strategy by type of customer are matched against sales results on a continuous basis.

Source: Adapted from Donald Cox and Robert Good, "How to Build a Marketing Information System," *Harvard Business Review* 45, no. 3 (1967), p. 146.

projects of the firm. The computer helps the market research activity collect, analyze, and maintain an enormous amount of information on a wide variety of market variables that are subject to continual change.

■ **Marketing management**. Computers assist marketing management in developing short- and long-range plans outlining product sales, profit, and growth objectives. They also provide information feedback and analysis concerning performance-versus-plan for each area of marketing. Mathematical marketing models may be used to investigate the effects of various alternative plans.

Figure 15–6 summarizes some of the major benefits of marketing information systems. Notice the specific examples of benefits generated by major types of marketing applications.

Computer Applications in Retailing

The computer has traditionally been used by many retailers for one or more of such basic applications as customer billing, accounts receivable, inventory control, general accounting, and payroll. The basic form of such applications will be analyzed in the next chapter and will not be repeated here. However, the computer is also being used for more advanced applications in retailing, such as management information systems and point-of-sale systems. Figure 15–7 illustrates the basic components of a retail management information system. Figure 15–8 depicts the kind of "customized" management report that could be provided on demand to the online terminals of retail executives.

The Point-of-Sale Revolution

Computer-based retail information systems with online *point-of-sale terminals* in retail outlets are a major computer application in retailing. Most POS systems consist of several cash-register-like terminals that are online to a data controller located somewhere in the store. The data controller could be a minicomputer with peripherals, or it can merely be a unit for storing transactions from the POS registers on magnetic tape and transmitting data over communication lines to a regional computer center.

In many POS systems, the "cash register" is an *intelligent terminal*, which can guide the operator through each transaction, step by step. These terminals can also perform necessary arithmetic operations, such as tax, discount, and total calculations. Some terminals permit online credit verification for credit transactions. Most POS terminals can automatically read information from tags or mer-

FIGURE 15–7 A retail management information system

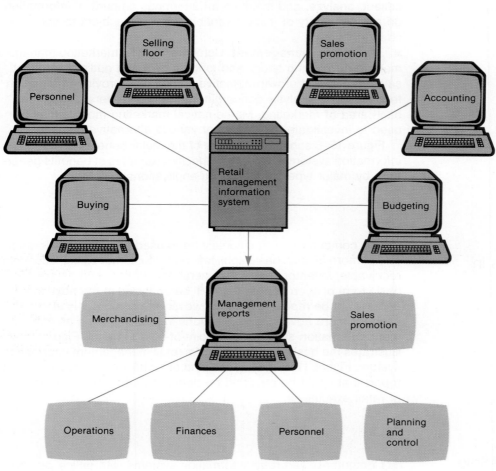

chandise labels. Hand-held "wands" or other optical reading devices are used with some terminals to scan the merchandise label and capture price and stock data. Data may be printed on the merchandise labels and tags in OCR or MICR characters or may use various optical bar-coding methods. For example, the grocery industry uses a *universal product code* and OCR bar-coding on merchandise labels that can be scanned by optical reading devices at automated checkout counters. (Refer back to Chapter Six for more on this topic.) See Figure 15–9.

Benefits of POS systems. What are the benefits of retail POS systems? Obviously, POS terminals, data controllers, and other data

FIGURE

15–8 A customized retail management report

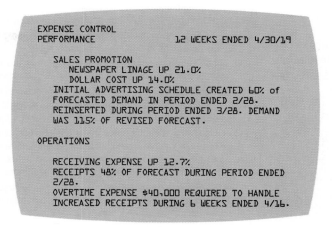

```
EXPENSE CONTROL
PERFORMANCE                    12 WEEKS ENDED 4/30/19

     SALES PROMOTION
        NEWSPAPER LINAGE UP 21.0%
        DOLLAR COST UP 14.0%
     INITIAL ADVERTISING SCHEDULE CREATED 60% of
     FORECASTED DEMAND IN PERIOD ENDED 2/28.
     REINSERTED DURING PERIOD ENDED 3/28. DEMAND
     WAS 115% OF REVISED FORECAST.

     OPERATIONS

     RECEIVING EXPENSE UP 12.7%
     RECEIPTS 48% OF FORECAST DURING PERIOD ENDED
     2/28.
     OVERTIME EXPENSE $40,000 REQUIRED TO HANDLE
     INCREASED RECEIPTS DURING 6 WEEKS ENDED 4/16.
```

communications hardware are expensive devices. One of the major benefits of such systems is their ability to produce advanced types of *sales and advertising impact analysis* by quickly providing a detailed analysis of sales by store and product, as well as such vital merchandising facts as shelf life, shelf position, displays, and the promotions and displays of competitors. Figure 15–10 summarizes the results experienced by large retail chains when they compared POS systems to traditional cash register systems.

FIGURE

15–9 A retail POS system

FIGURE

15–10 Comparison of POS systems and traditional cash-register systems

- POS terminals cost about 20 percent more than the cash registers they replaced.
- It takes only one fourth the time to complete a sales transaction on a POS terminal, compared to a conventional cash register.
- The number of checkout registers could be reduced by about one fourth with a POS system. Checkout personnel requirements can also be reduced.
- The POS terminal can perform functions either impossible or uneconomical on the conventional cash register (such as credit verification). Also, most of the input data required by retail information systems can be captured by POS terminals.
- Use of a minicomputer as a communications controller allows store managers to make online inquiries concerning merchandise availability and customer credit and to receive much faster reports on sales activity, merchandise replenishment, customer billing, clerk productivity, and store traffic.
- POS terminals demonstrate greater accuracy, increased customer service, and a significant reduction in personnel training time.

SECTION II: COMPUTER-BASED INFORMATION SYSTEMS IN PRODUCTION/OPERATIONS

The **production/operations** function includes all activities concerned with the planning, monitoring, and control of the processes that produce goods or services. Thus, the production/operations function is concerned with the management of the operational systems of all business firms. Computers are used for such *operations management* functions not only by manufacturing companies but also by all other firms that must plan, monitor, and control inventories, purchases, and the flow of goods and services. Therefore, firms such as transportation companies, wholesalers, retailers, financial institutions, and service companies must use production/operations information systems to plan and control their operations. In this section, we will concentrate on manufacturing and physical distribution to illustrate the application of the computer to the production/operations function.

Manufacturing Information Systems

Computer-based manufacturing information systems use several major subsystems to achieve *computer-aided manufacturing* (CAM). Computers are automating many of the activities needed to produce products of all kinds. For example, computers are used to help engineers design products, which is called *computer-aided-design* (CAD). Then they are used to help plan the types of material needed in the production process, which is called *material requirements planning* (MRP). Finally, they may be used to directly manufacture the products on the factory floor, by directly controlling a physical process (*process control*), a machine tool (*numerical control*) or a machine with some human-like capabilities (*robots*)! See Figure 15–11.

FIGURE

15–11 Computers in manufacturing

A Computer-aided manufacturing (CAM) systems help increase the efficiency and quality of manufacturing operations.

B Computer-aided design (CAD) systems help engineers design new products and structures.

A  **B**

Figure 15–12 illustrates the major subsystems in a manufacturing information system. Let's take a brief look at each of them.

- **Master production schedule** (MPS). Computers assist in the development of a master production schedule for a manufacturing firm. It is based on many factors, including sales forecasts (from the marketing information system) and forecasts of other production resources, such as manufacturing facilities and materials. The computer provides information required for the detailed scheduling of production. This consists of assigning production starting dates, making short-range capacity adjustments, allocating materials from production inventories, and "releasing" production orders to the plant floor.

- **Material requirements planning** (MRP). Computers are used to translate the master production schedule into a detailed plan for all material required to produce the scheduled products. The material requirements specified by the engineering subsystem for each product (called a *bill of materials*) is multiplied (*exploded*) by the number of units scheduled to be produced. The amount of material on-hand, the material needing to be purchased, and a schedule of purchases are then calculated. This helps minimize investment in material inventories while still adhering to the master production schedule.

- **Capacity requirements planning** (CRP). This subsystem uses computers to ensure that there is sufficient manufacturing capacity to meet the master production schedule. Capacity is determined by the amount of production facilities, such as equipment, supplies, buildings, and, of course, manufacturing employees.

- **Engineering**. This subsystem uses **computer-aided-design** (CAD) methods to design products and manufacturing facilities. Products are designed according to product specifications determined in cooperation with the product management subsystem of the marketing information system. One of the final outputs of this

FIGURE 15–12 Manufacturing information systems

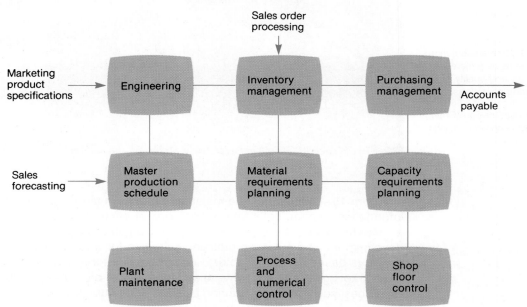

design process is the bill of materials for a product that is used by the MRP subsystem. The engineering subsystem is also frequently responsible for determining standards for product quality (i.e., *quality control*).

■ **Shop floor control**. Computers are used to monitor and control events on the shop floor during the production process. Thus this subsystem is a major focus of **computer-aided manufacturing** (CAM) activity. Computers track the status of all work in progress through a variety of data collection terminals used by production employees, and specialized devices (sensors, counters, OCR scanners, etc.). Information gathered and processed includes production counts, material usage, labor used, and machine downtime.

■ **Plant maintenance**. This subsystem provides management with information for maintenance planning, work order dispatching, maintenance costing, and preventive maintenance scheduling.

■ **Other subsystems**. The remaining subsystems are discussed in more detail in the next two sections. *Purchasing management* and *inventory management* are obviously concerned with the purchase, receipt, and storage of materials and the shipping of finished products. *Process and numerical control* involve the use of computers in the actual production process.

REAL WORLD APPLICATION 15–2

The Bullard Company

The Bullard Company of Bridgeport, Connecticut, a subsidiary of White Consolidated Industries, Inc., of Cleveland, has been known for more than a century as a manufacturer of quality machine tools. In recent years, however, the company's internal disciplines had not kept pace with the complexity of the high-tech products it produced. A serious problem developed: meeting delivery schedules. Bullard's machine tools are produced for the automotive, aerospace, and oil industries. Much of their product is built to customer specifications. Thousands of parts may be involved, and hundreds of operations may be required in the various assembly stages.

"Our major concern with the manual system was that we couldn't identify individual customer parts as they went through the shop," says Vincent Martin, president. The routing system, which defined all operations and sequences, was antiquated. No one could say for sure whether a part was in the production cycle or whether a finished product would meet its delivery date. Inventory was another problem area. "We built up a lot of surplus because we didn't have the tools to assess the number of part available or to pinpoint each part's location," Mr. Martin notes. "If a part was supposed to be here but we couldn't find it, we'd start to produce another. Since we paid for inventory through borrowing and the prime rate was up to 20 percent, it became imperative to cut back."

Not only were unnecessary parts often produced, but the production control department would schedule parts for completion eight weeks early as a cushion for lateness. "We were adding value—that is, putting in labor and purchasing materials for those parts before it was necessary," says Joseph Celotto, materials manager. "Scheduling production early gave us a distorted sense of priorities that made it difficult to establish a proper sequence for work going through the shop."

"Our new system-IBM COPICS (Communications-Oriented Production Information Control System) software driven by a 4341 computer— has brought us from 1948 to state-of-the-art," observes Mr. Celotto. Implementing the inventory accounting module enabled Bullard to develop its first accurate count of available parts. A side benefit was that many "lost" parts were located. "We've achieved 98 percent accuracy in all aspects of inventory control and location," Mr. Celotto reports. Installing the bill of materials module helped clearly specify the components of each part in production and, thereby, provided additional structure to improve scheduling. "Bills of material, coupled with inventory accounting, told us which parts we had and which we needed," Mr. Celotto explains. "The facilities' database then helped us determine which work-in-process should be assigned to which workstations for parts to be properly routed."

The materials requirement planning (MRP) module was then used to calculate the lead time associated with making each part and to indicate when each part was needed in the build cycle. Those parts that could not be produced were designated for purchase and managed by the purchasing module. Receiving also became part of the new system. Arbitrary scheduling has now been virtually eliminated. The shop floor, once cluttered with parts, has been cleaned up considerably, and engineering changes are now easier to implement and assess.

- What major manufacturing information subsystems are computerized at the Bullard Company?
- How has COPICS benefited manufacturing operations and management?

Source: "Expediting Machine Tool Manufacturing," *Viewpoint*, July–August 1983, pp. 1–2. Reprinted with permission.

Benefits

Some of the benefits of computer-based manufacturing information systems are:

- Increased efficiency due to better production schedule planning and better balancing of production workload to production capacity.
- Improved utilization of production facilities, higher productivity, and better quality control resulting from continuous monitoring, feedback, and control of plant operations.
- Reduced investment in production inventories through better planning and control of production and finished goods requirements.
- Improved customer service by reducing out-of-stock situations and producing products that better meet customer requirements.

Process Control

Process control is the use of computers to control an ongoing physical process. Process control computers are used to control physical processes in petroleum refineries, cement plants, steel mills, chemical plants, food product manufacturing plants, pulp and paper mills, electric power plants, etc. Many process control computers are special-purpose or dedicated general-purpose minicomputer systems. A process control computer system requires the use of special sensing devices that measure physical phenomena such as temperature or pressure changes. These continuous physical measurements are converted to digital form by analog-to-digital converters and relayed to computers for processing. Process control computer programs use mathematical models to analyze the data generated by the ongoing process and compare it to standards or forecasts of required results. Output of a process control system can take three forms:

- Periodic reports analyzing the performance of the production process.
- Messages and instructions which allow a human operator to control the process.
- Direct control of the process by the use of control devices that control the process by adjusting thermostats, valves, switches, etc. See Figure 15–13.

FIGURE

15–13 A process control computer system

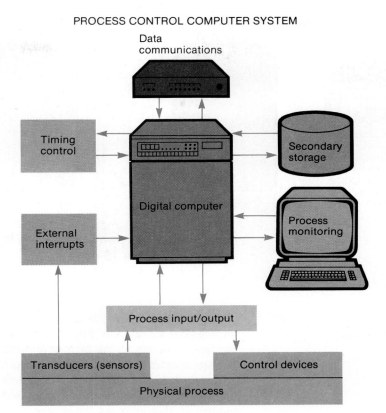

PROCESS CONTROL COMPUTER SYSTEM

Numerical Control and Robotics

Numerical control is the use of a computer to control the actions of a machine. **Robotics** is the technology of building machines with computer "intelligence" and "human-like" physical capabilities (dexterity, movement, vision, etc.). The control of machine tools in factories is a typical numerical control application, though numerical control can also be used for typesetting machines, weaving machines, and other industrial machinery. Numerical control computer programs for machine tools convert geometric data from engineering drawings, and machining instructions from process planning into a numerical code of commands, which controls the actions of a machine tool. See Figure 15–14. Numerical control can be accomplished offline by using special paper tape or magnetic tape units, which use the output of a computer to direct a machine. *Direct numerical control* is a type of numerical control involving the online control of machines by a computer. A related development is the creation of a new breed of "smart machines" and **robots** that di-

FIGURE 15–14 From computer-aided design to direct numerical control

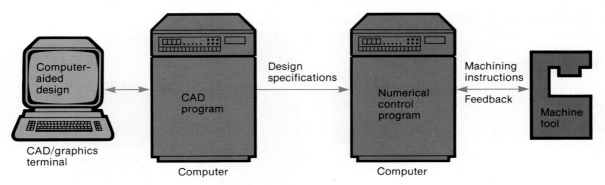

rectly control their own activities with the aid of "built-in" microcomputers. See Figure 15–15.

Physical Distribution Information Systems

A major activity of the production/operations function is known as *physical distribution*. Physical distribution is concerned with moving raw materials to the factory and moving products from the production floor to the ultimate consumer. Physical distribution involves a "distribution network," which connects raw material sources, manufacturing plants, warehouses, wholesale and retail outlets, and customers. It also involves the storage, transfer, and transportation of goods from manufacturer to customer.

Physical distribution information systems are frequently computerized. The major physical distribution information systems are illustrated in Figure 15–16. They include:

FIGURE

15–15 Computer-controlled machines in manufacturing

A This computer-controlled machine tool can automatically change 20 tools on each of its three spindles. It is used in the aircraft manufacturing industry.

B Computer controlled robots at work. This industrial robot is used in many industries for metal-cutting operations.

A

B

FIGURE

15–16 Physical distribution
information systems

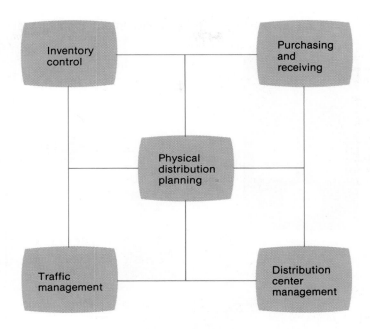

- **Physical distribution planning**. This information subsystem provides information for the planning of the physical distribution system of a business firm. Mathematical models may be used to analyze alternative distribution networks by considering such factors as customer characteristics, manufacturing locations and capabilities, the number and location of warehouses, processing and inventory management policies, and alternative transportation arrangements.
- **Inventory control**. Inventory data are processed and information is provided to assist management in minimizing inventory costs and improving customer service. For example, Figure 15–17 illustrates an advanced inventory control information system for large retail firms. This system uses mathematical decision rules, forecasting models, and simulation techniques to generate inventory replenishment decisions and various management reports.
- **Distribution center management.** This system supports the management and operations of "distribution centers," which consist of warehouses, shipping and receiving terminals, and other distribution support facilities. Its objective is to process data and provide information to assist management in the effective use of warehousing, shipping, and receiving personnel, facilities, and equipment, while maintaining a high level of customer service.
- **Traffic management**. This system supports the daily planning and control of the movement of products within the distribution net-

FIGURE 15–17 An advanced inventory control information system

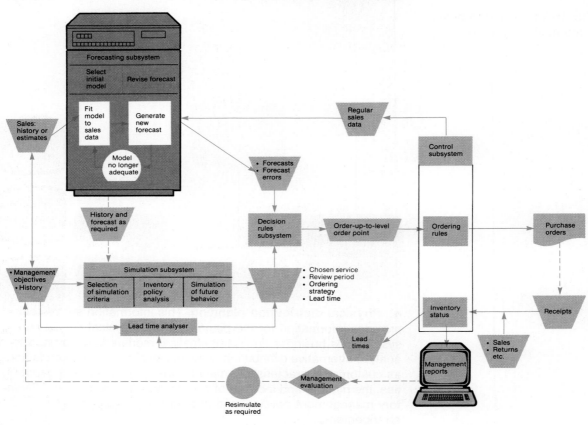

work of a firm. It must provide information required for the scheduling of transportation requirements, the tracking of freight movement, the audit of freight bills, and the determination of efficient and economical methods of transportation.

■ **Purchasing and receiving**. This system provides information to ensure availability of the correct quantity and quality of the required materials at the lowest possible price. The purchasing system assists in the selection of suppliers, placement of orders, and the follow-up activities to ensure on-time delivery of materials. The receiving system identifies and validates the receipt of materials and routes the received material to its proper destination in storage or on the production floor. Figure 15–18 illustrates a computerized purchasing information system.

FIGURE 15–18 A purchasing/receiving information system

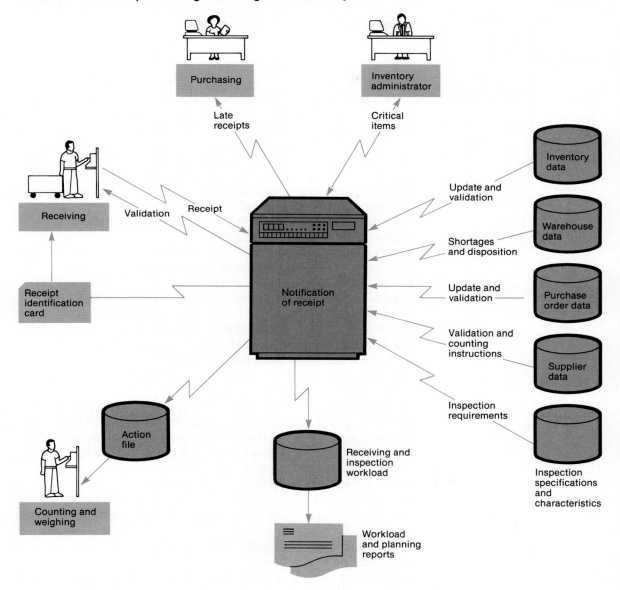

SECTION III: OTHER COMPUTER-BASED INFORMATION SYSTEMS

In this section we will briefly explore personnel information systems and several other computer-applications that should contribute to a well-rounded understanding of the use of computers in business.

Personnel Information Systems

The **personnel** function involves the recruitment, placement, evaluation, compensation, and development of the employees of an organization. **Personnel information systems** are traditionally used by business firms to (1) produce paychecks and payroll reports, (2) maintain personnel records, and (3) analyze the amounts, types, and costs of labor used in business operations. Many firms have gone beyond these traditional functions and have developed personnel information systems which support (1) recruitment, selection, and hiring, (2) job placement, (3) performance appraisals, (4) employee benefits analysis, (5) training and development, and (6) health, safety, and security. Personnel information systems support the concept of **human resource management**, which emphasizes *planning* to meet the personnel needs of the business and the *control* of all personnel policies and programs, so that effective and efficient use is made of the *human resources* of the company. The major computer applications in personnel are summarized below and illustrated in Figure 15–19.

- **Payroll and labor analysis**. Computers process data concerning employee compensation and work activity and produce paychecks, payroll reports, and labor analysis reports.
- **Personnel record-keeping**. This application is concerned with additions, deletions, and other changes to the records in the personnel database. Changes in job assignments and compensation, or hirings and terminations, are examples of information that would be used to update the personnel database.
- **Employee skills inventory**. The computer is used to locate specific human resources within a company and to maximize their use. The employee skills inventory system uses the employee skills data from the personnel database to locate employees within a company who have the skills required for specific assignments and projects. See Figure 15–20.
- **Training and development analysis**. Computers help personnel management plan and control employee recruitment, training, and development programs by analyzing the success history of present programs. They also analyze the career development status of each employee to determine whether development methods, such as training programs, or performance appraisals should be recommended.

FIGURE

15–19 Personnel information systems

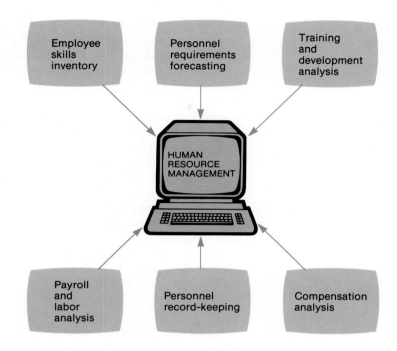

FIGURE

15–20 Skills inventory profile report

■ **Compensation analysis**. This application analyzes the range and distribution of employee compensation (wages, salaries, incentive payments, and fringe benefits) within a company and makes comparisons with compensation paid by similar firms or with various economic indicators. This information is useful for planning changes in compensation, especially if negotiations with labor unions are involved. It helps keep the compensation of a company competitive and equitable, while controlling compensation costs.

■ **Personnel requirements forecasting**. Short- and long- range planning is required to assure a business firm of an adequate supply of high-quality human resources. This application provides information required for forecasts of personnel requirements in each major employment category for various company departments or for new projects and other ventures being planned by management. Such long-range planning may use a computer-based simulation model to evaluate alternative plans for recruitment, reassignment, or retraining programs.

Operations Research Applications

Operations research (or *management science*) represents a major area of computer use. Operations research is the application of scientific techniques to organizational problems, using a methodology based on the concepts and techniques of mathematics and the natural, physical, and social sciences. Operations research techniques usually involve the formulation of *mathematical models* of the system being investigated. Mathematical models can be used for problem solving, using either *mathematical analysis* or *mathematical simulation*. Therefore, most computer applications in operations research involve the use of computer programs containing mathematical models that are then solved or "manipulated," using various types of mathematical analysis or simulation. Figure 15–21 outlines the function, effect, and software requirements of several operations research techniques.

Other Business Applications

A quick glance at how the computer is used in several industries should be sufficient to emphasize the amazing versatility of the computer and the variety of its applications in business.

■ **Airlines**. Airline reservation systems were the earliest major real-time application of computers in business. Realtime computer systems are online to terminals in airline offices both nationwide and overseas. Besides such realtime passenger reservation systems and traditional business applications, computers provide information

FIGURE 15–21 Analysis of selected operations research applications

Operations Research Technique	Application	Benefits	Software Tools Available
MATHEMATICAL ANALYSIS	Uses complex mathematics for solving engineering/research problems.	Computational processing is performed at electronic speeds. Special languages and subroutines facilitate expression and solution of problems.	Math library-precoded routines (e.g., numerical analysis, interpolation, exponential and log functions, and matrix analysis).
STATISTICAL ANALYSIS	Analysis of quantitative and statistical data for such applications as market research, sales forecasting, inventory control, research, and quality control.	Improves accuracy and validity of decision making by providing more sophisticated analysis.	Statistics library, e.g., variance, T-ratio, standard deviation, binomial distribution, random number generator, regression analysis, etc.
LINEAR PROGRAMMING	Mathematical technique for solving problems of competing demands for limited resources where there are a great number of interacting variables.	Resolves complex problems that can only be approximated or guesstimated by conventional means. Increases accuracy and improves decision making in broad class of decisions.	Linear programming (LP) packages assist in problem structuring and formulation and then provide high-speed computing power to efficiently produce solutions based on alternate decision rules.
NETWORK ANALYSIS	Scheduling, costing and status reporting of major projects.	Improves planning, scheduling, and implementing of complex projects comprising multiple events and activities. Permits continuous evaluation of projects' progress to increase probabilities of on-time, on-cost performance.	PERT (program evaluation and review technique) and CPM (critical path method) software systems for processing large networks of events and activities producing a variety of computer reports to pinpoint schedule slippages, critical events, and action needed to get back on schedule.
QUEUEING THEORY	Solving problems where it is desirable to minimize the costs and/or time associated with waiting lines or queues.	Improves management ability to improve operations like checkout counters, receiving docks, machine centers or turn-toll stations.	General-purpose simulators aid the construction and development of complex simulation models. The simulator has the ability to produce random numbers to test various activity patterns and optimize the use of resources.
SIMULATION	Determines the impact of decisions using hypothetical or historical data in lieu of incurring the expense and risk of trying out decisions in actual operations.	Business managers can test and project the effects of decisions on a wide variety of operational areas thus ensuring optimal results when the decisions and policies are put into practice.	General-purpose simulators, decision support system generators, modelling packages, and electronic spreadsheet packages.

Source: Adapted from Jerome Kanter, *Management-Oriented Management Information Systems*, 3d ed., © 1984. Reprinted by permission of Prentice-Hall, Inc., Englewood Cliffs, New Jersey.

for such functions as (1) flight plan preparation, (2) fuel loading, (3) meal catering, (4) air cargo routing, and (5) freight, supplies, and spare parts inventory control.

■ **Agribusiness**. Agriculture has become a big business—"agribusiness." Many corporate and family farms and ranches are now using the power of the computer. Major applications include (1) farm and crop record-keeping and analysis, (2) financial and tax accounting, and (3) optimal feed-blending, fertilizing, and crop-rotation programs. Computer services are provided by government agricultural extension agencies, commercial banks, computer service bureaus, and farm cooperatives. Microcomputer-based devices to automatically control farm machinery for planting, fertilizing, irrigating, and harvesting are a more recent development.

■ **Construction**. Large construction companies have been using computers for many years for traditional business applications, such as payroll and general accounting. Scientific applications requiring mathematical computations for design engineering analysis have also been used. Techniques like PERT (Program Evaluation and Review Technique) and CPM (Critical Path Method) are used for construction planning and scheduling. The computer can use such techniques to produce plans and schedules for each stage of complex construction projects.

■ **Insurance**. Like the banking industry, the insurance industry was an early user of computers. Insurance companies have a huge data processing job because of the large number of insurance policies, claims, premium notices, and dividends that must continually be processed. Large numbers of customers and complex insurance policy provisions require the maintenance of large databases. Complex actuarial computations (such as life expectancy statistics) must also be performed. Realtime inquiry systems allow branch offices to interrogate the central database for customer policy information. Another application is the use of the computer to perform part of the *underwriting* function by preparing detailed insurance coverage proposals for presentation to prospective customers.

■ **Real estate**. Real estate applications fall into several major categories. Real estate investment applications analyze financial, tax, marketing, and physical requirements data to compute rate-of-return alternatives for proposed real estate projects. Property management applications assist the management of rental property by processing rental statements, rental payments, and maintenance and utility disbursement, and by providing various management reports. Property listing applications (also called a multiple listing service) maintain up-to-date listings of all properties registered for sale with participating realtors.

REAL WORLD APPLICATION 15-3

Aetna Life & Casualty

Employee Benefits Division/Data Processing provides essential support services to Aetna's Employee Benefits Division, a leading insurer in the employee benefit and related group-coverage field. For example, Aetna annually processes more group health claims than any other insurance company, and it is the largest publicly owned insurance manager of pension fund assets. The Pension Development Section provides system development and planning services for all group pension product lines. Due to Aetna's innovation and the effect of more stringent government regulation, this business has experienced rapid growth over the past several years. This has led to development of such systems as BENEFITS, which prepared more than two million claim drafts valued in excess of $.5 billion last year; MULTIVESTOR, which managed more than 200,000 employee retirement accounts valued in excess of $1.2 billion; and to the formulation of an EDP Long-Range Plan to strategically move group pensions into the 1980s and beyond.

Insurance Development provides EDP systems support for group life and health business. In health alone, Aetna pays more than $4 billion in claims annually and provides coverage for more than 23 million workers and their dependents. The Aetna Computerized Claim System (AECCLAIMS) is one of the largest teleprocessing systems in the country. Each day this growing system processes more than 1.2 million messages from 3,600 nationwide terminals to resolve more than 120,000 claims. A nationwide online system to support more than 100 sales offices throughout the country is also being developed.

The Commercial Insurance Division markets casualty, property, and bond products and services for businesses through more than 60 field offices and 11,000 independent agents. Some 800 people within the Administration Department develop and maintain the data processing systems supporting that business. The department supports the flow of data for all coverages the division writes, from initial policy production in agencies and field offices to the combination of premium, loss, and expense data as bottom-line divisional results. A teleprocessing network connects all Commercial Insurance field offices and some agencies to the home office. By way of this network, the industry-acclaimed Systems by Aetna for Fast Access to Records and Information (SAFARI) handles nearly a quarter of a million transactions a day, performing policy-writing, billing, and claim functions for some 6.2 million active and inactive personal and commercial insurance policies.

PFSD Systems has a comprehensive set of integrated insurance, administrative, and processing systems operating in an online mode in the home office and field offices. The Life Insurance Administrative System (LIAS) processes more than 30,000 online transactions daily. It is one of the most sophisticated online systems in the industry, supporting 140 terminals in 132 agency offices. PFSD System's Consolidated New Business System is also considered one of the most sophisticated underwriting/issue systems. Further, this department also maintains individual auto and homeowners products on the industry-acclaimed SAFARI.

- Are the computer applications at Aetna personnel applications or insurance industry applications? Explain.
- Are Aetna's computer applications operational information systems? Management information systems? Distributed processing systems? Explain.

Source: Courtesy of Aetna Life & Casualty.

SUMMARY

- Business computer users should have an understanding of how the computer supports the basic functions of business and, especially, how computers affect a particular business function or a particular industry that is directly related to their career objectives. They should also be aware of the trends in business computer applications. More emphasis is being placed on MIS and DSS applications, since most operational uses are routinely computerized.

- In this chapter, we briefly described many important applications in business according to the business function they support (marketing, production/operations, and personnel) and according to the industry in which they are used (retailing, airlines, agribusiness, construction, insurance, and real estate). Refer back to Figures 15–1 and 15–2 for summaries of major business computer applications by functional and industry categories.

KEY TERMS AND CONCEPTS

Computer applications by
  business function and
  industry
Trends in business computer
  use
Marketing information systems
Retailing applications
Point-of-sale revolution
Manufacturing information
  systems

Process control
Numerical control
Robotics
Physical distribution
  applications
Personnel information systems
Operations research
  applications

REVIEW AND APPLICATION QUESTIONS

1. What kind of understanding of computer use in business should a computer user have?
2. What has been the trend in the types of business applications being computerized? What are the reasons for such trends?
3. Discuss several computer applications in marketing and the role they play in supporting the marketing function.
4. What effect does the use of point-of-sale terminals have on computer applications in retailing?

5. Discuss several computer applications in production/operations and manufacturing. How have they affected the production/operations function?
6. What effect will computer-aided manufacturing have on computer applications in production? What impact will robotics have?
7. Identify several computer applications in personnel.
8. Can computer applications in operations research be applied to any business function or industry? Explain.
9. Identify the use of computers in one of the following industries: airlines, agribusiness, construction, insurance, and real estate.

APPLICATION PROBLEMS

1. If you have not already done so, read and answer the questions after each Real World Application in this chapter.
2. Take another look at each Real World Application in this chapter. Can you identify any of the trends in computer use summarized in Figures 15–3 and 15–4? Which types of applications are these firms computerizing?
3. The marketing manager of ABC Department Stores has been told by several store managers that the company's advertising and promotion budget is too low and is not being spent to promote the right products at the right times. How should the marketing information systems shown in Figure 15–5 be used to determine if there is a problem, and the solution to that problem?
4. What has been your experience with POS terminals? Give your reaction to each of the benefits of POS terminals shown in Figure 15–10. Can you add any to that list? Can you think of any other disadvantages than higher hardware cost? Explain any of these additional benefits or disadvantages.
5. Do any of the computer-based information systems in production/operations apply to nonmanufacturing companies like ABC Department Stores? Use the information systems illustrated in Figures 15–12 and 15–16 to support your answer.
6. Explain how you would use computer-based personnel information systems to determine:
   a. The cost to the company of a proposal for an increase in fringe benefits.
   b. The amount of labor costs for a particular product line.
   c. The degree of compliance with equal opportunity and work safety laws.

CHAPTER 16

Computer-Based Information Systems: Accounting and Finance

CHAPTER OUTLINE

LEARNING OBJECTIVES

The purpose of this chapter is to promote a basic
understanding of how the computer is used in business
by analyzing computer-based information systems in
accounting and finance and seven common computer
applications in business. After reading and studying
this chapter, you should be able to summarize the
objectives, input, data base, and output of several of
these common business information systems, and to
identify several computer applications in accounting
and finance.

SECTION I: COMPUTER-BASED INFORMATION SYSTEMS IN ACCOUNTING

ACCOUNTING INFORMATION SYSTEMS

Accounting information systems are the oldest and most widely used business information systems. They record and report business transactions and other economic events. Accounting information systems are based on the double-entry bookkeeping concept, which is hundreds of years old, and other more recent accounting concepts, such as responsibility accounting and profitability accounting. Computer-based accounting systems record and report the flow of funds through the organization on a historical basis and produce financial statements, such as the balance sheet and income statement. Such systems also produce forecasts of future conditions, such as projected financial statements and financial budgets.

Operational accounting systems emphasize legal and historical recordkeeping and the production of accurate financial statements. *Management accounting systems* focus on the planning and control of business operations through the development of financial budgets and projected financial statements. In this section, we will analyze several operational accounting applications, such as accounts receivable, accounts payable, and general ledger. Other major computer applications in accounting are summarized below.

- **Fixed asset accounting.** Involves the physical control and the financial recordkeeping caused by the use and depreciation of fixed assets.
- **Cost accounting.** Involves the accumulation and apportionment of costs within a business firm. For example, costs must be grouped into specific cost categories and attributed to specific products, projects, departments, etc.
- **Tax accounting.** Involves the recording and payment of business taxes such as income taxes and inventory taxes.
- **Budgeting.** Involves the development of budgets that contain revenue and expense projections and other estimates of expected performance for the firm.

Figure 16–1 provides an overview of the relationships of various accounting information systems.

COMMON BUSINESS INFORMATION SYSTEMS

Out of all of the possible applications of the computer in business, several basic accounting and related information systems stand out because they are common to most business computer users. Most of these systems exist in both large and small computer-using business firms, whether they are experienced computer users or are using the computer for the first time. Three of these applications (accounts receivable, accounts payable, and general ledger) are

FIGURE 16–1 Computer-based accounting information systems

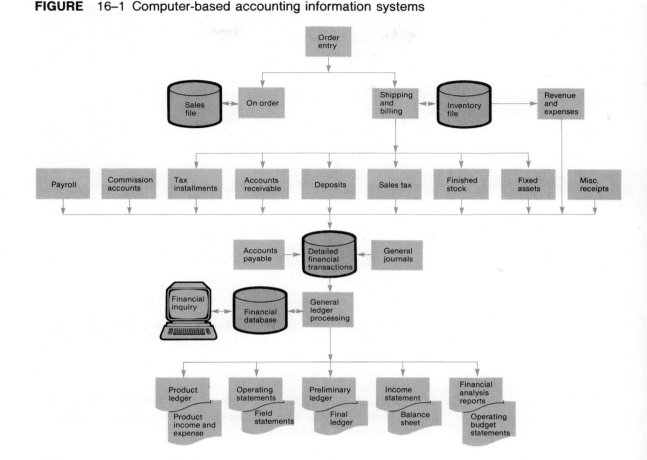

accounting information systems. The others are combinations of accounting and related business information systems in *marketing* (sales order/transaction processing and sales analysis), *production/ operations* (inventory control), and *personnel* (payroll). These **common business information systems** are summarized below and illustrated in Figure 16–2.

■ Sales Order/Transaction Processing. Processes customer orders and sales transactions. Produces sales receipts for customers and data needed for sales analysis and inventory control.

■ Inventory Control. Receives data concerning customer orders, prepares shipping documents if the ordered items are available, and records all changes in inventory.

FIGURE

16–2 How the common business information systems are related

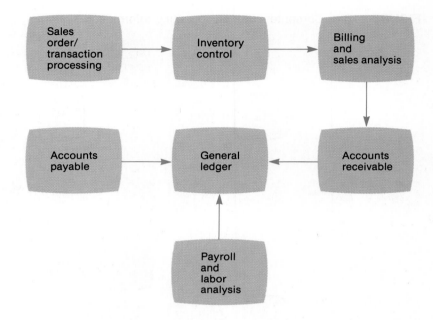

- Billing and Sales Analysis.   Receives filled- orders data from the inventory control system and produces customer invoices and management reports analyzing the sales generated by each sales- person, customer, product, and so on.

- Accounts Receivable.   Receives data concerning customer invoices and payments and produces monthly customer statements and credit management reports.

- Accounts Payable.   Receives data concerning purchases from suppliers and produces checks in payment of outstanding invoices and cash management reports.

- Payroll and Labor Analysis.   Receives data from employee timecards and other records and produces paychecks, payroll re- ports, and labor analysis reports.

- General Ledger.   Receives data from accounts receivable, accounts payable, payroll and labor analysis, and many other busi- ness information subsystems. Produces the general ledger trial bal- ance, the income statement and balance sheet of the firm, and various income and expense reports for management.

   The description of each common business information system that follows has been simplified, since our purpose is to understand computer applications from the viewpoint of a *business computer user,* rather than that of *computer specialist.* Therefore, no attempt is made to describe all of the variations that are possible for each common computer application, since the particular form of an application will vary depending upon the type of business firm involved. For example, the sales order processing system that will be described is most often used by business firms whose customers are other business firms, rather than consumers. Another example is the inventory control system which we will describe. It is most widely used to control the inventory of wholesale or retail firms or the finished goods inventory of manufacturing firms. However, in all cases the applications we describe represent a basic form that should be understood by all business computer users.

Figure 16–3 illustrates a menu of common computer applications from which a user at a microcomputer or video terminal would select an application for processing.

The Sales Order/ Transaction Processing System

Objectives

The objectives of the **sales order/transaction processing** system are:

- To provide a fast, accurate, and efficient method of recording and screening customer orders and sales transactions.
- To provide the inventory control system with information on accepted orders so they can be filled as quickly as possible.

Figure 16–4 is a general systems flowchart that summarizes the components of the sales order/transaction processing system that should be understood by computer users.

FIGURE

16–3 A menu of common business information systems

```
10/23/8X

              ABC DEPARTMENT STORES

                    MAIN MENU

          1. Sales Order Processing
          2. Inventory Control
          3. Billing and Sales Analysis
          4. Accounts Receivable
          5. Accounts Payable
          6. Payroll and Labor Analysis
          7. General Ledger
          8. Database Query
          9. Report Writer

          ENTER NUMBER OR ESC TO EXIT:
```

FIGURE

16–4 A sales order/transaction processing system

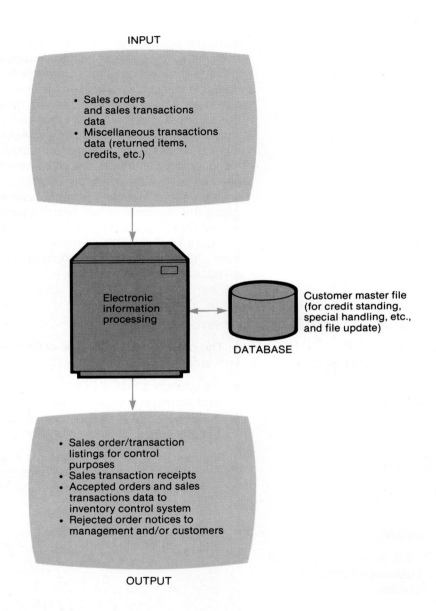

INPUT

- Sales orders and sales transactions data
- Miscellaneous transactions data (returned items, credits, etc.)

Electronic information processing

Customer master file (for credit standing, special handling, etc., and file update)

DATABASE

- Sales order/transaction listings for control purposes
- Sales transaction receipts
- Accepted orders and sales transactions data to inventory control system
- Rejected order notices to management and/or customers

OUTPUT

Input

Sales transactions and sales orders from customers or salespersons are received by mail, telephone, or are made in person. They can be recorded on sales receipt or sales order forms and then converted into other media unless OCR documents are used. Alternatively, *point-of-sale terminals* and other types of remote terminals may be used to enter sales order and sales transaction data directly into the computer system. The keyboard of such terminals or OCR *wands* might be used for such direct entry. Though sales data are the primary form of input into the system, other types of input data must also be captured. Data from "miscellaneous transactions," such as returned items and credits for damaged goods, are also entered into the system.

Database

The sales order/transaction processing system uses a *customer master file* as its database. The customer master file contains data on each customer, such as (1) name, number, address, and phone number, (2) codes indicating sales tax liability, eligibility for discounts, etc.; and (3) other information, such as location, line of business, credit limits, and assigned salespersons. This file provides information on the credit standing of customers, special handling requirements, and other information that is used to decide which orders should be accepted. The file can also be updated to reflect changes in credit standing, new customers, address changes, etc.

Output

Like most business computer applications, the output of the sales order/transaction processing system includes listings (also called logs or registers) of each sales order transaction that allow control totals and other types of data processing controls to be accomplished. The purpose of such controls is to guard against errors or fraud in the input or processing of the data and to provide an "audit trail" to facilitate the auditing of the system. One of the primary outputs of the system consists of data describing accepted sales orders and completed sales transactions. This data becomes input for the inventory control system. Figure 16–5 illustrates the types of data required to describe a single sales item.

The output of many sales order/transaction processing systems also includes notices or receipts to customers acknowledging completed sales transactions or receipt of their orders. In most nonretail business firms, sales invoices ("bills") describing filled and shipped sales orders are produced by a "billing" system, which will be described shortly. Orders not accepted by the system, because of inaccurate information, are corrected after consultation with salespersons or customers and reentered into the system. Orders rejected for exceeding credit limits or other reasons are usually referred to operating management (such as credit managers or

FIGURE

16–5 Sales transaction
record display

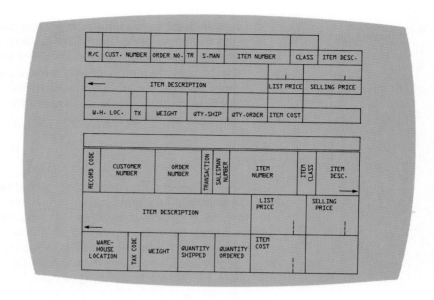

FIGURE

16–5 Sales transaction
record display

sales managers) for corrective action or may be returned to the
customer.

The Inventory Control System

Objectives

The objectives of the **inventory control** system are:

- To provide high quality service to customers by using a fast,
  accurate, and efficient method of filling customer orders and
  avoiding "stock outs."
- To minimize the amount of money invested in inventory and
  required to cover inventory "carrying costs."
- To provide management with information needed to help achieve
  the two preceding objectives.

Figure 16–6 is a general systems flowchart that summarizes the
major components of the inventory control system.

Input

Input into the inventory control system consists of accepted order
data, sales transaction data, as well as data describing stock received by the receiving department of the business firm. Input may

FIGURE

16–6 An inventory control system

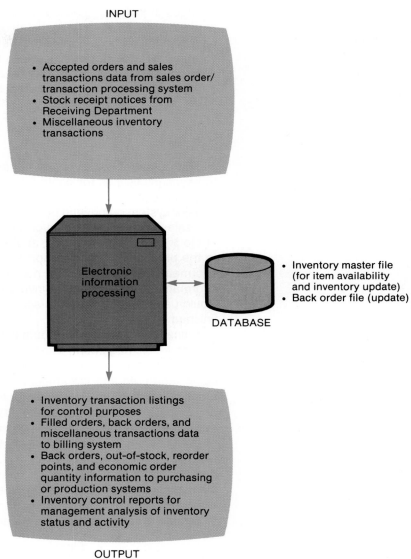

INPUT

- Accepted orders and sales transactions data from sales order/transaction processing system
- Stock receipt notices from Receiving Department
- Miscellaneous inventory transactions

Electronic information processing

- Inventory master file (for item availability and inventory update)
- Back order file (update)

DATABASE

- Inventory transaction listings for control purposes
- Filled orders, back orders, and miscellaneous transactions data to billing system
- Back orders, out-of-stock, reorder points, and economic order quantity information to purchasing or production systems
- Inventory control reports for management analysis of inventory status and activity

OUTPUT

also include *miscellaneous inventory transactions,* such as adjustments for lost or damaged stock.

Database

The database of this application consists of an *inventory master file,* which is checked for item availability and updated to reflect changes in inventory caused by filling sales orders or receipt of new stock. A *back order file* is also updated for sales orders that cannot be filled because of stockouts. Some customers are willing to wait until new stock is received. The back-order file provides data on outstanding back orders that must be filled when stock receipt notices are received for back-ordered items.

Output

The output of the inventory control system includes inventory transactions listings for control purposes. Data describing filled orders, back orders, and miscellaneous sales order transactions is a major system output and becomes the primary input into the billing and sales analysis system. Information concerning back orders, out-of-stock items, reorder points, and economic order quantities is sent to the purchasing or production departments for entry into their information subsystems. The purchasing department will use such information to procure more inventory, while a manufacturing firm would use this information to schedule the production of additional finished goods inventory.

A final major category of output consists of inventory control reports for management. These reports analyze inventory status and activity. Management must determine (1) whether the items being reordered and the amounts being reordered require adjustment, (2) the amount of unfilled orders that are occurring, (3) whether any items are becoming obsolete, (4) unusual variations in inventory activity, and (5) the items that account for the majority of the sales of the business. Figure 16–7 illustrates several inventory control reports.

Fixed order points and order quantities may be arbitrarily set by management and used by the inventory control system. However, the computer can be programmed to use mathematical techniques to calculate optimum order points and economic order quantities for use by the inventory control system. Such calculations take into account the cost of an item, its carrying cost, its annual sales, the cost of placing an order, and the length of time it takes to process, procure, and receive an item. In any case, effective inventory control can bring major benefits. Too little stock on hand may mean lost sales or excessive rush orders for stock replenishment. Too much stock may mean increased carrying costs, higher interest on invested capital, additional warehousing expenses, and greater loss due to obsolescence. In many cases, carrying costs of inventory can run as high as 25 percent per year of the investment in inventory!

REAL WORLD APPLICATION 6-1

Western Engine Company

When a trucker's diesel breaks down on the road, getting replacement parts in a hurry is of prime importance. If it happens in northern Indiana and throughout Illinois, more than likely the trucker calls one of 102 Western Engine Company dealers. "Service is crucial in our business," says Angelo Cusinato, controller of Western Engine, which distributes Detroit Diesel-Allison parts. "Our customers also include municipalities, hospitals, and manufacturers who rely heavily on diesel power. If their engines go down for any length of time, the penalties are always harsh and sometimes disastrous."

The company's System/38, with its exceptionally swift order handling procedure, keeps customer service at a very high level, Mr. Cusinato says, "For example, emergency orders—and there are many of these—are almost always turned around within 24 hours."

"However, just as crucial as maintaining a high service level, from the standpoint of impact on our bottom line, is low inventory cost," says Eileen O'Brien, vice president and treasurer. "We estimate that our system's inventory management capabilities save us at least a million dollars a year in inventory investment."

The System/38 Model 7, which data processing manager Steve Meyer calls a "very reliable, high-performance computer," runs almost continually around the clock. Some 10,000 customer orders a month flow through the system, drawing on a combined inventory of 32,000 diesel engine parts stocked at the company's headquarters in Addison, Illinois, and at a branch warehouse in Gary, Indiana. Sixty 5251 display terminals and eight printers are online to the System/38. "They support data entry and retrieval functions of order entry, order processing, inventory control and customer service inquiry response," Mr. Meyer explains.

"Our company president has a terminal in his office, as do the controller, sales manager, parts manager and other executives," he says. "These principals use them to keep tabs on orders, customers, parts and to review parts demand, service level patterns and trends." Also online is a Series/1 that functions as a communications link between the System/38 and a host computer at Detroit Diesel in Detroit, Michigan.

The system tracks every order from receipt to delivery and beyond to billing and receivables. As the order is entered, the System/38 checks inventory availability, allocates the stock, and reviews customer and parts records. It then sends the order pick list to the warehouse printer. Or, in the case of a back-ordered emergency part, it sends the order to the Series/1 for relay to Detroit. "With the system, everything moves fast under tight control," says Mr. Meyer. "Nothing gets lost or delayed. Freshly updated information on orders, parts, customers, and service level performance is always at hand via terminal inquiry. As a result, productivity in order entry, order processing and customer service is up and clerical costs are down."

When an order is processed, the system's inventory management routine records the demand against the part and the service fulfillment level. Working with this information, the computer continually adjusts part reorder points and quantities to the ongoing parts demand and service level performance to achieve the best possible inventory balance.

■ What common business information systems are used by Western Engine? How are they related to each other?
■ What benefits have occurred because of the use of computer-based information systems?

Source: "Maintaining Profitability," *Viewpoint*, March–April 1983. Used with permission.

FIGURE 16–7 Inventory control reports for management

Stock No.	Description	Opening Balance	+ Receipts	– Issue	= On Hand	PLANNING			OP
						+ On Order	= Available	Order Point	
11398	TRANSFORMER	210			210	300	510	400	
11402	MOTOR ASM 50	1205	500		1705	1500	3205	2000	
11610	CAM	10341		1423	8918		8918	9000	*
11682	LEVER	433	3500	1255	2678	500	3178	2750	

Item No.	Cumulative Count		Annual Units	Unit Cost	Annual $ Sales	Cumulative Sales	
	Number	%				$	%
T 7061	1	.01	51,553	3.077	158,629	158,629	.5
—	—	—	—	—	—	—	—
S 6832	13	.12	243,224	.317	77,102	1,652,385	5.0
K 5322	110	1.0	8,680	3.286	28,522	5,882,489	17.8
S 5678	549	5.0	244,690	.045	11,011	13,252,124	40.1
S 6121	2,198	20.0	7,239	.490	3,547	23,662,146	71.6
—	—	—	—	—	—	—	—
—	—	—	—	—	—	—	—
—	—	—	—	—	—	—	—
S 6219	6,593	60.0	15,360	.050	768	31,395,306	95.0
—	—	—	—	—	—	—	—
—	—	—	—	—	—	—	—
—	—	—	—	—	—	—	—
M 3742	10,988	100.0	0	.073	0	33,047,690	100.0

The Billing and Sales Analysis System

Objectives

The objectives of the **billing and sales analysis** system are:

- To prepare customer invoices (bills) quickly and accurately and thus maintain customer satisfaction and improved cash flow into the business.
- To provide management with sales analysis reports, which provide information concerning sales activity and trends that is required for effective marketing management.

Figure 16–8 summarizes the important components of the billing and sales analysis system.

FIGURE 16–8 A billing and sales analysis system

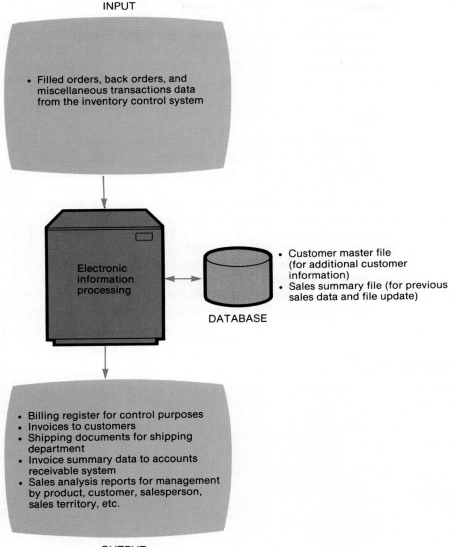

INPUT

- Filled orders, back orders, and miscellaneous transactions data from the inventory control system

Electronic information processing

- Customer master file (for additional customer information)
- Sales summary file (for previous sales data and file update)

DATABASE

- Billing register for control purposes
- Invoices to customers
- Shipping documents for shipping department
- Invoice summary data to accounts receivable system
- Sales analysis reports for management by product, customer, salesperson, sales territory, etc.

OUTPUT

Input

The input into the billing and sales analysis system consists of data from the inventory control system which describes the filled orders, back orders, and miscellaneous transactions.

Database

The database for this system consists of the *customer master file,* which is used to provide additional information about a customer that is required by a billing operation. Examples are customer "ship-to" addresses, shipping instructions, and special handling. A *sales summary file* is updated with current sales order data and provides information concerning previous sales for the sales analysis reports.

Output

The output of the billing and sales analysis system includes a *billing register,* which is a summary listing of all invoices that is used for control purposes. A major output of the system is customer invoices such as that shown in Figure 16–9. (The computer calculates all required invoice amounts.) Other output of the system includes shipping documents, such as "picking slips," shipping labels, bills of lading, and delivery receipts. The computer frequently lists the items on the invoice in a warehouse-location sequence so a copy of the invoice can be used as a *picking slip* by warehouse personnel when assembling an order for shipment. Summarized data for each invoice is entered into the accounts receivable system.

The final major output of the billing and sales analysis system

FIGURE 16–9 Customer invoice

LAURENTIAN INDUSTRIES, INC.

SOLD TO	SHIP TO	CUSTOMER NO.
S. W. STAPLES 498 RIVERVIEW STREET SAN JOSE, CALIF. 94067	RODRIGUEZ DESIGN HOMES DIVISION OF S. W. STAPLES 8363 OLIVE STREET SUNNYVALE, CALIF. 95117	430875

DATE 09/15/--	INV. NO. 138265	ORDER NO. 717690	SHIPPING INSTRUCTIONS VIA SMITH TRANSPORT	STATED TERMS 2% 15 DAYS NET 30	SALESMAN G. PEREZ

QUANTITY ORDERED	QUANTITY SHIPPED	QUANTITY B/O	DESCRIPTION	UNIT PRICE	EXTENDED AMOUNT	DISCOUNT AMOUNT	NET AMOUNT	TAX-ABLE
40	40		8500 TWINLITE SOCKET B	.60	24.00	1.20	22.80	
350	100	250	8506 SOCKET ADAPTER BRN	.32	32.00	3.20	28.80	
200	150	50	C151C SILENT SWITCH IVORY	1.20	180.00	9.00·	171.00	•
175	175		A210 PULL CORD GOLD	.42	73.50		73.50	•
60		60	1436 LAMP ENTRANCE	.50				
175	105	70	A200 FIXTURE 5 LIGHT	20.13	2113.65	211.37	1,902.28	
			FREIGHT CHARGE				18.95	
			PACKING CHARGE				45.00	

TAXABLE	TAX	FREIGHT	MISC. SPECIAL CHARGE		INVOICE AMOUNT
244.50	12.23	18.95	45.00		2,274.56

FIGURE

16–10 Sales analysis reports for management

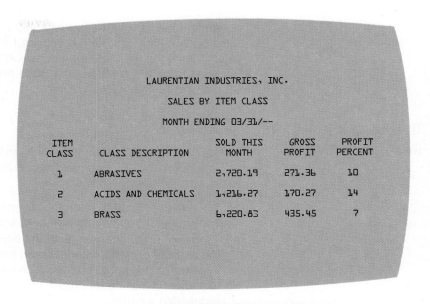

LAURENTIAN INDUSTRIES, INC.

SALES BY ITEM CLASS

MONTH ENDING 03/31/--

ITEM CLASS	CLASS DESCRIPTION	SOLD THIS MONTH	GROSS PROFIT	PROFIT PERCENT
1	ABRASIVES	2,720.19	271.36	10
2	ACIDS AND CHEMICALS	1,216.27	170.27	14
3	BRASS	6,220.83	435.45	7

LAURENTIAN INDUSTRIES, INC.

COMPARATIVE SALES ANALYSIS BY CUSTOMER

FOR EACH SALESPERSON

PERIOD ENDING 07/31/--

SLP. NO.	CUST. NO.	SALESPERSON/CUSTOMER NAME	THIS PERIOD THIS YEAR	THIS PERIOD LAST YEAR
10		A R WESTON		
	1426	HYDRO CYCLES INC	3,210.26	4,312.06
	2632	RUPP AQUA CYCLES	7,800.02	2,301.98
	3217	SEA PORT WEST CO	90.00CR	421.06
		SALESPERSON TOTALS	10,920.28	7,035.10
12		H T BRAVEMAN		
	0301	BOLLINGER ASSOCIATES	100.96	0.00

is sales analysis reports for management, such as those shown in Figure 16–10. Sales analysis reports can analyze sales by product, product line, customer, type of customer, salesperson and sales territory. Such reports help marketing management determine the sales performance of products, customers, and salespeople. They can determine whether a firm is expending too much sales effort on low-volume customers or low-profit products. For example, one business found that it had over 1,000 accounts, representing one third of all customers, who purchased less than 1 percent of their total sales volume. The firm also found that it had almost 2,000 accounts that bought at least $1,000 annually and accounted for 95 percent of their sales volume!

The Accounts Receivable System

Objectives

"Accounts receivable" represents the amounts of money owed to a company by its customers (accounts). The objectives of the **accounts receivable** system are:

- To stimulate prompt customer payments by preparing accurate and timely monthly statements to credit customers.
- To provide management with the information required to control the amount of credit extended and the collection of money owed, in order to maximize profitable credit sales while minimizing losses from bad debts. Figure 16–11 illustrates a typical accounts receivable system.

Input

Input into the system consists of invoice summary data from the billing system and source documents showing payments received from customers. The usual customer payment document is the return portion of an invoice or statement, which the customer returns by mail along with a check in payment of the account. Another type of input into this system is "miscellaneous adjustments," which are prepared by the accounting department to adjust customer accounts for mistakes in billing, the return of goods, bad debt write-offs, and so on.

Database

The database for the accounts receivable application includes the *accounts receivable file,* which provides current balances for each customer account, and which is also updated by the new billing, payments, and adjustments input data. The *customer master file* is used to provide data needed for customer statement preparation. The customer credit-standing information in this file is also updated as a result of changes in accounts receivable balances.

Output

Proper data processing control requires that listings and control totals be prepared for all cash received and for each customer

FIGURE 16–11 An accounts receivable system

INPUT

- Invoice summary data from billing and sales analysis system
- Payments from customers
- Miscellaneous adjustments data from Accounting Department

Electronic information processing

DATABASE

- Accounts receivable file (for current balances and file update)
- Customer master file (for customer data and file update)

- Accounts receivable and cash receipts registers for control purposes
- Monthly statements to customers
- Aged trial balance and delinquent account report for credit management
- Delinquency notices to delinquent customers
- Accounts receivable summary data for general ledger system

OUTPUT

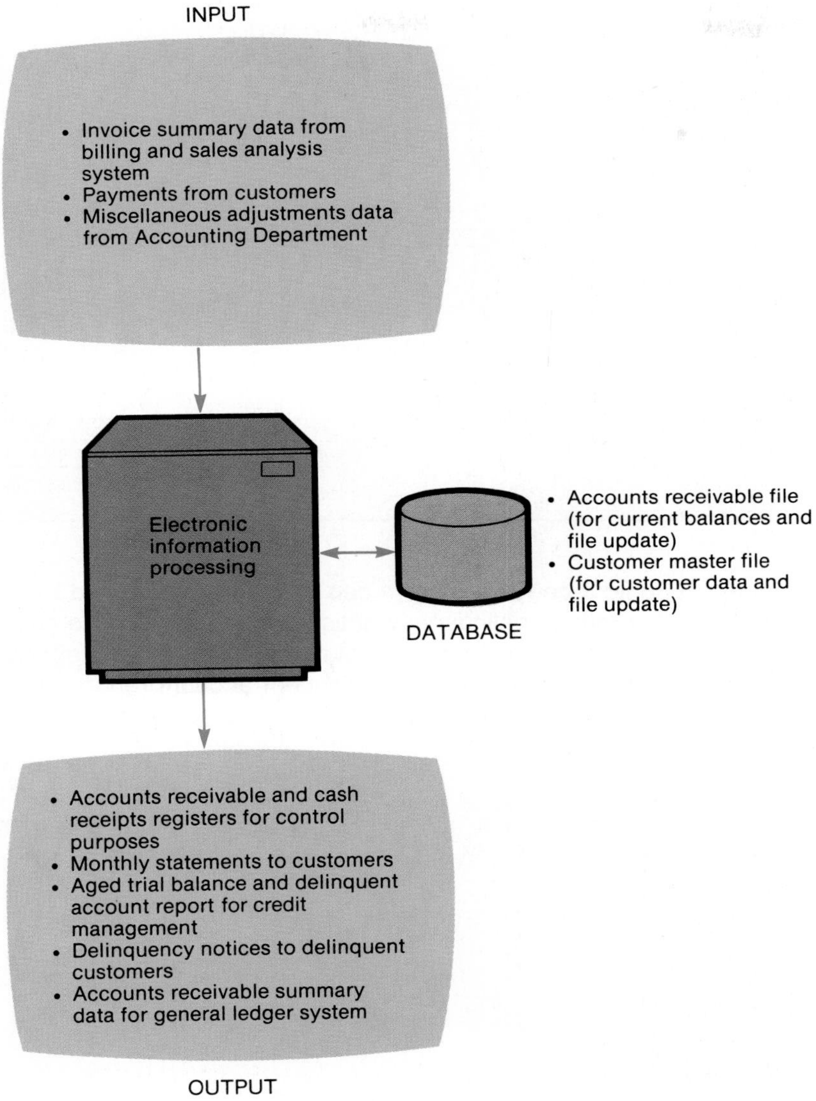

account in the accounts receivable file. Thus the output of the accounts receivable system includes an accounts receivable register and a cash receipts register. Monthly statements are also prepared for each customer that show recent charges and credits, as well as the present balance owed. See Figure 16–12. Notice that this customer statement also indicates amounts that are overdue.

FIGURE 16–12 Monthly customer statement

LANG COMPANY

STATEMENT

CUSTOMER NO.		DATE
554386	HITTON CORPORATION 138 MARSHALL DR. PO BOX 851 LONG PORT CALIF 94134	9/30/--

DATE MO	DY	YR	INVOICE NUMBER	REFERENCE NUMBER	DESCRIPTION	AMOUNT
					PRIOR BALANCE	$2,565.46
09	08	--	185163		INVOICE	1,685.91
09	10	--	075126		PAYMENT	1,856.00CR
09	15	--		091531	LC ADJUSTMENT	13.00CR
09	30	--			LATE CHARGES	8.00

CURRENT AMOUNT	30 DAYS	60 DAYS & OVER	BALANCE DUE
$1,693.91	$696.46		$2,390.37

LANG COMPANY

STATEMENT

CUSTOMER NO.		DATE
554386	HITTON CORPORATION 138 MARSHALL DR PO BOX 851 LONG PORT CALIF 94134	9/30/--

DATE MO	DY	YR	INVOICE NUMBER	REFERENCE NUMBER	DESCRIPTION	AMOUNT
					PRIOR BALANCE	$2,565.46
09	08	--	185163		INVOICE	1,685.91
09	10	--	075126		PAYMENT	1,856.00CR
09	15	--		091531	LC ADJUSTMENT	13.00CR
09	30	--			LATE CHARGES	8.00

CURRENT AMOUNT	30 DAYS	60 DAYS & OVER	BALANCE DUE
$1,693.91	$696.46		$2,390.37

RETAIN THIS PORTION FOR YOUR RECORDS

The accounts receivable system can also be programmed to automatically produce delinquency notices, which are sent to customers whose accounts are seriously overdue. Management reports produced by the system include a delinquent account report and an *aged trial balance* report (also called an *aged accounts receiva-*

FIGURE

16–13 Accounts receivable aged trial balance

ACCOUNTS RECEIVABLE AGED TRIAL BALANCE

DATE 6/30/1

CUSTOMER NUMBER	CUSTOMER NAME	[illegible]	BALANCE	CURRENT	OVER 30 DAYS	OVER 60 DAYS	90 DAYS & OVER	CREDIT LIMIT	EXCEEDS CREDIT LIMIT
13985	ANDERSON CORP.	27	1324 35	1200 00	121 50		2 85	3500 00	
14007	ARMSTRONG INTL.	27	3896 68	439 61	1911 25	499 00	1046 82	3000 00	-
37243	CONTI RENTAL	27	379 80	379 80				500 00	
48277	DELTA LIGHTING	27	241 28	65 98	175 30			500 00	
63365	FOXBORO CORP.	27	222 18	222 18				2000 00	
72466	HINDS ELECTRIC	27	2767 15	1632 09	1135 06			15000 00	
78144	INNSBRUCK ELEC.	27	861 70	27 50	54 40	127 23	652 57	1000 00	
85433	MILLER SUPPLY	27	457 90	202 60	50 70	120 70	83 90	500 00	
87542	PALMER APPL.	27	40 24	40 24				500 00	
93421	SMYTHE CO.	27	336 05	260 40		75 65		1500 00	
95642	WELLS HARDWARE	27	3195 98	469 76	325 01	151 63	2249 58	3000 00	-

ble report). Figure 16–13 illustrates an aged trial balance that helps the credit manager identify accounts seriously overdue and requiring special collection efforts. The final output of the accounts receivable system consists of accounts receivable summary data, which is used as input by the general ledger system.

The Accounts Payable System

Objectives

"Accounts payable" refers to the amounts of money that a business firm owes its suppliers. The primary objectives of the **accounts payable** system are:

- Prompt and accurate payment of suppliers to maintain good relationships, insure a good credit standing, and secure any discounts offered for prompt payment.
- Provide tight financial control over all cash disbursements of the business.
- Provide management with information needed for the analysis of payments, expenses, purchases, and cash requirements.

Figure 16–14 illustrates the accounts payable application.

Input

Input into the accounts payable system consists of invoices (bills) from suppliers and others who have furnished goods or services to the business firm. Input also may be in the form of expense "vouchers" for various business expenses and miscellaneous payments and adjustments from the accounting department. (A *voucher* is an accounting form that records the details of a transaction and authorizes its entry into the accounting system of a firm.) For example, expense vouchers may be prepared to reimburse employees for authorized expenditures. Typically, salespersons and managerial personnel request reimbursement by completing an "expense account" statement and submitting it to the accounting department. Payments from "petty cash" or adjustments from suppliers for billing errors are other types of miscellaneous input. Receiving reports from the receiving department acknowledge the receipt of goods from suppliers and are required before payment can be authorized. A copy of purchase orders from the purchasing department provides data describing purchase orders that have been sent to suppliers. This data is used to record "pending payables" and to help determine whether the business firm has been accurately billed by its suppliers.

FIGURE

16–14 An accounts
payable system

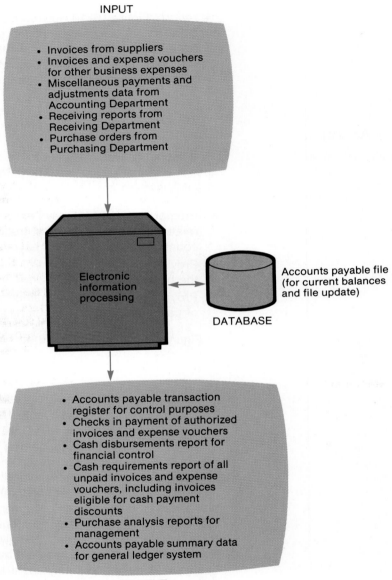

INPUT

- Invoices from suppliers
- Invoices and expense vouchers
  for other business expenses
- Miscellaneous payments and
  adjustments data from
  Accounting Department
- Receiving reports from
  Receiving Department
- Purchase orders from
  Purchasing Department

Electronic
information
processing

Accounts payable file
(for current balances
and file update)

DATABASE

- Accounts payable transaction
  register for control purposes
- Checks in payment of authorized
  invoices and expense vouchers
- Cash disbursements report for
  financial control
- Cash requirements report of all
  unpaid invoices and expense
  vouchers, including invoices
  eligible for cash payment
  discounts
- Purchase analysis reports for
  management
- Accounts payable summary data
  for general ledger system

OUTPUT

Database

The database for the accounts payable application is the *ac-counts payable file,* which provides current balances for all accounts and is updated by the new input data.

Output

As in previous applications, data processing control requires that an *accounts payable transaction register* be produced. This output document lists all system transactions and computes various control totals. A major form of output of the system are checks in payment of authorized invoices and expense vouchers. A *cash disbursements report* provides a detailed record of all checks written and contributes to proper financial control of the cash disbursements of the firm. An important output of the system for management is the *cash requirements report,* which lists or summarizes all unpaid invoices and expense vouchers, and identifies all invoices eligible for cash payment discounts during the current period. The computer also can be programmed to analyze unpaid invoices and expense vouchers so forecasts of the cash requirements for several future periods can be included in the cash requirements report. See Figure 16–15. The accounts payable system can also produce *purchase analysis reports* for management, which summarize the purchases and payments made to each supplier of the firm. (This report is sometimes produced by a separate *purchasing* system.) The final category of output consists of summarized accounts payable transaction data, which becomes input data for the general ledger system.

The Payroll and Labor Analysis System

Objectives

The primary objectives of the **payroll and labor analysis** system are:

■ Prompt and accurate payment of employees.
■ Prompt and accurate reporting to management, employees, and appropriate agencies concerning earnings, taxes, and other deductions.
■ Providing management with reports analyzing labor costs and productivity.

The payroll and labor analysis application is widely computerized. It involves many complex calculations and the production of many types of reports and documents, many of which are required by government agencies. Besides earnings calculations, many types of taxes and fringe benefit deductions must be calculated. Payroll processing is also complicated because many business firms employ hourly paid employees and salaried personnel and may have several kinds of incentive compensation plans. Figure 16–16 illustrates the payroll and labor analysis application.

FIGURE

16–15 Purchase analysis
and cash requirements
reports

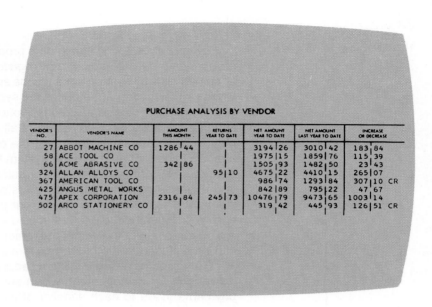

PURCHASE ANALYSIS BY VENDOR

VENDOR'S NO.	VENDOR'S NAME	AMOUNT THIS MONTH	RETURNS YEAR TO DATE	NET AMOUNT YEAR TO DATE	NET AMOUNT LAST YEAR TO DATE	INCREASE OR DECREASE
27	ABBOT MACHINE CO	1286 44		3194 26	3010 42	183 84
58	ACE TOOL CO			1975 15	1859 76	115 39
66	ACME ABRASIVE CO	342 86		1505 93	1482 50	23 43
324	ALLAN ALLOYS CO		95 10	4675 22	4410 15	265 07
367	AMERICAN TOOL CO			986 74	1293 84	307 10 CR
425	ANGUS METAL WORKS			842 89	795 22	47 67
475	APEX CORPORATION	2316 84	245 73	10476 79	9473 65	1003 14
502	ARCO STATIONERY CO			319 42	445 93	126 51 CR

KRAUSZ MANUFACTURING COMPANY

ACCOUNTS PAYABLE

CASH REQUIREMENTS STATEMENT

DATE APR 1 2 196-

ROUT TO *Mr. J. R. Crossin - Dept 100*

SHEET *1* OF *2*

VENDOR	VENDOR NUMBER	DUE DATE	INVOICE AMOUNT	DISCOUNT	CHECK AMOUNT
SOLVAY GEN SUP	1016	4/16	$ 773.30	$ 15.47	$ 757.83
ROCHESTER PR CO	1021	4/16	1,620.18	32.40	1,587.78
CALABRIA CONT	1049	4/16	143.65	2.87	140.78
ONONDAGA STL CO	1077	4/16	5,982.82	119.66	5,863.16
BLACK & NICHOLS	1103	4/16	14.25	.71	13.54
AUSTERHOLZ INC	1240	4/16	624.77	12.50	612.27
AUSTERHOLZ INC	1240	4/16	1,833.19	36.66	1,796.53
CHRISTIE & CO	1366	4/16	745.54		745.54
WILSON & WILSON	2231	4/16	2,936.12	58.72	2,877.40
CLAR. HIGGINS	2590	4/16	1,000.00		1,000.00
HONOUR BROS	3101	4/16	97.36	1.95	95.41
BASTIANI & SON	3112	4/16	3,580.85	71.62	3,509.23
DRJ WIRE CO	3164	4/16	256.90	5.14	251.76
HASTING-WHITE	3258	4/16	1,144.42	22.89	1,121.53
DARONO ART MET	3427	4/16	32.75	.66	32.09
DARONO ART MET	3427	4/16	127.52	2.55	124.97
DARONO ART MET	3427	4/16	96.60	1.93	94.67

Input

The input into the payroll and labor analysis system consists of
employee timecards or other records of time worked or attendance.
Timecards are normally used by hourly paid employees, while some
type of attendance record is usually kept for salaried personnel.
Additional input includes records of employee incentive compensation, such as factory piecework or salesperson commissions. Input
may also be in the form of miscellaneous payroll adjustments from

FIGURE

16–16 A payroll and labor analysis system

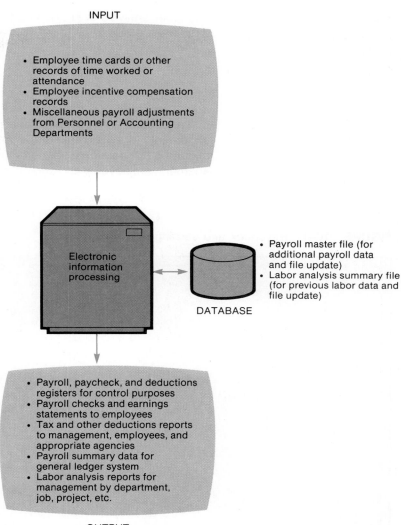

INPUT

- Employee time cards or other records of time worked or attendance
- Employee incentive compensation records
- Miscellaneous payroll adjustments from Personnel or Accounting Departments

Electronic information processing

- Payroll master file (for additional payroll data and file update)
- Labor analysis summary file (for previous labor data and file update)

DATABASE

- Payroll, paycheck, and deductions registers for control purposes
- Payroll checks and earnings statements to employees
- Tax and other deductions reports to management, employees, and appropriate agencies
- Payroll summary data for general ledger system
- Labor analysis reports for management by department, job, project, etc.

OUTPUT

the personnel or accounting departments, such as changes in wage rates, job classifications, and deductions.

Database

The database for the payroll and labor analysis application includes a *payroll master file,* which provides additional payroll data needed for payroll calculations and reports. This file is updated by the new input data. A *labor analysis summary file* provides previous labor analysis data and is also updated each time new input data are processed.

Output

All payroll transactions, all paychecks written, and all deductions made are listed and totaled on control registers. Of course, the primary output of the system consists of payroll checks and earning statements for employees of the firm. See Figure 16–17. In addition, tax and other deductions reports are prepared periodically for management, employees, and appropriate agencies. These include quarterly tax reports to the Internal Revenue Service, such as Form

FIGURE 16–17 Paycheck and earnings statement

CHECK DATE 4/30/--

90–1211
0519

J. R. SMITH & CO.

CHECK NUMBER
1303

PAY **136 DOLLARS AND 35 CENTS   **136.35

TO
THE
ORDER   A H ANKSTER
OF   SPECIMEN

COMMERCIAL TRUST BANK

⑆0210⑈0987⑉: 4121 00360⑈

EMPLOYEE NUMBER	EMPLOYEE NAME		DEPT.	PAY PERIOD	PAY PERIOD ENDED	CHECK NO.	CHECK DATE
0123	A H ANKSTER		03	8	4/30/--	1303	4/30/--

EARNINGS AND STATUTORY DEDUCTIONS

HOURS	RATE	REGULAR PAY	OVERTIME PAY	OTHER PAY	GROSS PAY	FED.W/TAX	F.I.C.A. TAX	STATE TAX
50.0	2.75	137.50	11.25	12.80	161.55	7.75	8.70	1.62

VOLUNTARY DEDUCTIONS

MEDICAL INS.	LIFE INS.	CREDIT UNION	UNION DUES	CHARITY	SAVINGS BONDS	ALL OTHERS	NET PAY
2.00		4.13	1.00				136.35

SOCIAL SECURITY AND W–2 INFORMATION

SOCIAL SECURITY NO.	EXEMPT	Y.T.D. GROSS	Y.T.D. FED. W/TAX	Y.T.D. F.I.C.A.	Y.T.D. STATE TAX	NOT NEGOTIABLE
312-32-1337	X	2,105.92	222.98	101.08	21.06	

941a and the annual W-2 form, which must be sent to employees before January 31 of each year. Reports listing and summarizing other tax and deduction information are prepared for management and various agencies, such as school districts, city, county, and state agencies, labor unions, insurance companies, charitable organizations, and credit unions.

Labor analysis reports for management are another major form of output of the payroll and labor analysis system. See Figure 16–18. These reports analyze the time, cost, and personnel required by departments of the firm or by jobs and projects being undertaken. They assist management in planning labor requirements and controlling the labor cost and productivity of ongoing projects. The final output of the payroll and labor analysis system is *payroll summary data,* which is used as input by the general ledger system.

The General Ledger System

The **general ledger** system consolidates financial data from all of the other accounting subsystems and produces the monthly and annual financial statements of the firm. The many financial transactions of a business are first recorded in chronological order in *journals*, then transferred ("posted") to *subsidiary ledgers*, where they are organized into "accounts", such as cash, accounts receivable, and inventory. The summary of all accounts and their balances is

FIGURE

16–18 Labor analysis report

DATE 8/08/-- WORK IN PROGRESS REPORT FOR JULY 19--

JOBNO	FINISH DATE	PROGRESS DATE	WORK DEPT	EMPNO	EST JOB HOURS	ACT JOB HOURS	% HRS USED	EST JOB DOLLARS	ACT JOB DOLLARS	% $ USED
11111	10/30/70	6/30/--			120.0	30.0	25.0	635.00	190.00-	30.0
		7/05/--	360	00508		8.0			40.00	
		7/10/--	360	00508		8.0			40.00	
		7/11/--	360	00604		6.0			24.00	
		7/30/--	360	00501		10.0			60.00	
TOTAL JOB 11111 TO DATE STATUS					120.0	62.0	51.7	635.00	354.00	55.7
23468	9/30/70	4/30/--			100.0	80.0	80.0	1000.00	700.00	70.0
		7/06/--	400	10105		8.0			80.00	
		7/28/--	506	36350		4.0			80.00	
		7/29/--	506	36350		4.0			80.00	
		7/30/--	506	36350		5.0			100.00	
TOTAL JOB 23468 TO DATE STATUS					100.0	101.0	101.0	1000.00	1040.00	104.0
33335	7/15/70	6/30/--			40.0	42.0	105.0	160.00	200.00	125.0
		7/14/--	500	40608		4.0			8.00	
		7/18/--	360	00508		8.0			40.00	
TOTAL JOB 33335 TO DATE STATUS					40.0	54.0	135.0	160.00	248.00	155.0
40608	11/30/70	4/30/--			200.0	120.0	60.0	1600.00	960.00	60.0
TOTAL JOB 40608 NO CURRENT ACTIVITY										

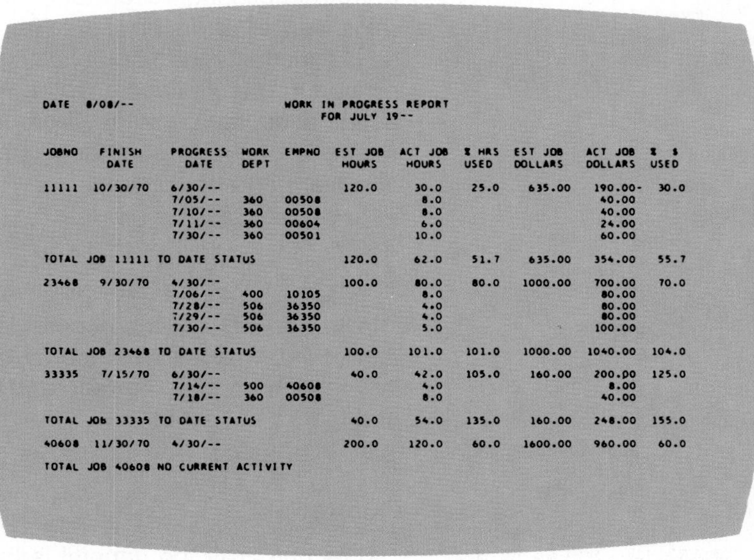

known as the *general ledger*. At the end of each accounting period (at the end of each month or fiscal year) the balance of each account in the general ledger must be computed, the profit or loss of the firm during the period must be calculated, and the financial statements of the firm (the balance sheet and income statement) must be prepared. This is known as "closing the books" of the business. The income statement of the firm presents its income, expenses, and profit or loss for a period, while the balance sheet shows the assets, liabilities, and net worth of the business as of the end of the accounting period.

Objectives

The primary objective of the *general ledger* system is to use the power of the computer to accomplish the many accounting tasks mentioned in the preceding paragraph in an accurate and timely manner. Using the computer for general ledger can result in greater accuracy, earlier closings, and more timely and meaningful financial reports for management. The computer can frequently accomplish this with less personnel and at a lower cost than manual bookkeeping and accounting methods. Figure 16–19 is a general systems flowchart of the general ledger application.

Input

Input into the general ledger system consists of summary data from the accounts receivable, accounts payable, and payroll systems, as well as financial data from other information systems (such as production control, purchasing, and engineering) that we described in the previous chapter. Another form of input is "miscellaneous accounting entries" from the accounting department that record changes to such accounts as cash, marketable securities, and plant and equipment.

Database

The database of the general ledger application is the *general ledger file,* which is updated by the new input data and provides information on past, current, and budgeted balances for each general ledger account.

Output

The output of the general ledger system includes a listing of all transactions for control purposes and *a general ledger trial balance*

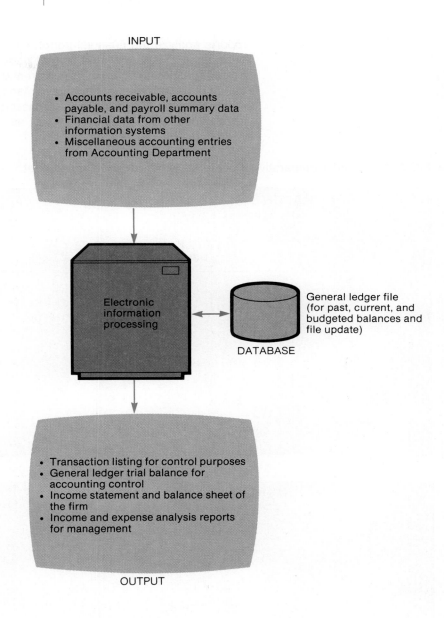

FIGURE

16–19 A general ledger system

INPUT

- Accounts receivable, accounts payable, and payroll summary data
- Financial data from other information systems
- Miscellaneous accounting entries from Accounting Department

Electronic information processing

General ledger file (for past, current, and budgeted balances and file update)

DATABASE

- Transaction listing for control purposes
- General ledger trial balance for accounting control
- Income statement and balance sheet of the firm
- Income and expense analysis reports for management

OUTPUT

report, which provides accounting control by summarizing and balancing all general ledger accounts. The *income statement* and *balance sheet* of the firm for an accounting period are major outputs of the system and are of primary importance to financial management and the top management of the firm. A final important output of the general ledger system is *income and expense analysis reports,* which can be produced for all levels of management. Such reports analyze the financial performance of a department or the business firm by comparing current performance to past and fore-casted (budgeted) figures. The difference ("variance") between actual and budgeted amounts shows managers in what area their performance is falling short or surpassing their financial objectives for a period. See Figures 16–20, 21, and 22.

FIGURE 16–20 Comparative income statement and balance sheet

HASTING-WHITE TOOL COMPANY
COMPARATIVE BALANCE SHEET

PERIOD ENDING JUNE 30. 19 —

MAJOR ACCOUNT	DESCRIPTION	PREVIOUS PERIOD THIS YEAR	CURRENT PERIOD		OVER* OR UNDER-	% OVER* OR UNDER-
			THIS YEAR	LAST YEAR		
	ASSETS					
	CASH AND RECEIVABLES					
111	CASH	$ 15,673.38	$ 16,739.73	$ 15,248.61	$ 1,491.12	9.8
112	ACCOUNTS RECEIVABLE	32,967.21	33,291.18	32,968.32	3,22.86	.9
113	RESERVE FOR BAD DEBTS	329.67–	332.91–	329.68–	3.23	.9
114	NOTES RECEIVABLE	1,000.00		1,500.00	1,500.00 –	100.0
115	MARKETABLE SECURITIES	2,164.30	5,898.13	3,673.21	2,224.9.	60.6
	TOT	$ 51,475.22*	$ 55,596.13*	$ 53,060.46*	$ 2,535.67	
	INVENTORIES					
116	INVENTORIES	183,621.83	161,298.67	149,238.61	12,060.06	8.1
	TOT	$ 193,621.83*	$ 161,298.67*	$ 149,238.61*	$ 12,060.06	
	LAND AND BUILDINGS					
121	LAND					
122	BUILDINGS		$ 50,238.96		$ 50,238.96	
123	RES. FOR DEPREC.	2,116.45–	2,363.74–	$ 1,757.88–	595.36	33.7
	TOT	$ 2,116.45–	47,875.22*	$ 1,767.88–	$ 49,643.10*	
	EQUIP. AND MACHINERY					
124	EQUIP. AND MACHINERY	$ 10,873.98	$ 8,339.61	$ 16,298.38	$ 7,958.77 –	48.8 –
125	RES. FOR DEPREC.	3,245.67–	3,469.22–	2,975.12–	494.10	16.6
	TOT	$ 7,628.31*	$ 4,870.39*	$ 13,323.26*	$ 8,452.87*–	

Routing
☐ President's Office
☑ Treasurer
☐ Comptroller
☐ Accounting
☐ Sales Manager
☐ Plant Superintendent

SOUTH LAKE SAND COMPANY
COMPARATIVE INCOME STATEMENT

PERIOD ENDING MAY 31. 19 —

ACCOUNT NUMBER	DESCRIPTION	CURRENT PERIOD		YEAR-TO-DATE		INCREASE* OR DECREASE-
		THIS YEAR	LAST YEAR	THIS YEAR	LAST YEAR	
411	SALES					
411-100	GROSS SALES	$ 1,223,195.85	$ 1,083,474.02	$ 4,739,999.14	$ 3,415,174.67	1,324,824.47 *
411-200	LESS RETURNS & ALLOW	1,726.40	1,912.71	3,245.97	3,464.22	218.25 –
	NET SALES	$ 1,221,469.45	$ 1,081,561.31	$ 4,736,753.17	$ 3,411,710.45	1,325,042.72 *
412-100	LESS COST OF SALES	581,786.15	541,950.16	2,852,146.73	2,008,762.23	843,384.50 *
	GROSS PROFIT	$ 639,683.30*	$ 539,611.15*	$ 1,884,606.44*	$ 1,402,948.22*	481,658.22 *
421	SELLING EXPENSES					
421-100	SALARIES & COMMISSIONS	$ 184,373.27	$ 179,264.43	$ 705,623.06	$ 541,579.46	164,043.60 *
421-200	TRAVELING EXPENSE	14,425.15	13,790.80	53,726.92	42,968.21	10,758.71 *
421-300	DELIVERY EXPENSE	6,140.20	5,956.00	28,364.15	16,428.19	11,935.96 *
421-400	ADVERTISING EXPENSE	1,582.00	1,450.25	18,250.00	5,225.75	13,024.25 *
421-500	OFFICE SALARIES	27,684.35	25,829.15	94,342.18	79,415.14	14,927.04 *
421-600	STATIONERY & SUPPLIES	1,380.60	1,295.00	4,982.76	3,576.82	1,405.94 *
421-700	TELEPHONE	1,315.85	1,305.62	4,148.15	3,381.26	766.89 *
421-800	BUILDING	6,725.00	6,215.10	25,175.00	18,634.55	6,540.45 *
421-900	MISCELLANEOUS	1,460.38	1,395.75	4,965.48	3,519.47	1,446.01 *
	TOTAL SELLING EXPENSE	$ 245,086.80*	$ 236,492.15*	$ 939,577.70*	$ 714,728.85*	224,848.85 *

FIGURE

16–21 General ledger summary report

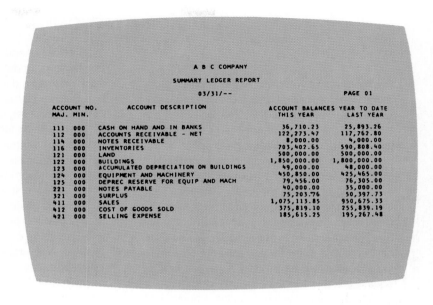

FIGURE

16–22 Income and expense analysis report for management

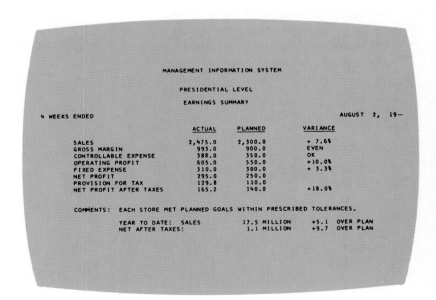

REAL WORLD APPLICATION 16–2

W. H. Shurtleff Co.

For more than five years, W. H. Shurtleff Company, Portland, Maine, used an online service bureau that helped them double their business. But when the bureau announced an increase in fees, without an increase in service, Shurtleff management decided an in-house Data General computer would provide more and better data processing power for the dollar. The resulting Chemical Management Information System (CHEMIS) was developed jointly by Shurtleff and the Computer Center of Falmouth, Maine. The hardware and software perfectly match Shurtleff's distributor data processing needs and is equally suitable for any chemical distributor.

The computer system handles a number of typical business applications, but the programs were expanded to supply employees with a wide range of comprehensive information. For example, the Order Entry program provides immediate data on credit checking, automatic pricing, bills of lading, hazardous materials classifications, priced and unpriced orders, inventory levels, and reorder points. The invoicing program can update inventory; compute line items and total invoices, gross profit margins, and percentages;

automatically handle credit memos and cash transactions; update accounts receivable; and track returnable deposit cylinders by serial number. Sales analysis is accomplished for each item by customer, customer by item, customer by item by sales territory, and more. The inventory control program handles 10 different locations and supplies data on hazardous material codes, automatic inventory expense for year-end tax reporting, unit and dollar turns, as well as pickup and delivered dollar and volume. The accounts payable program updates the payables files, produces checks for payment of amounts owed to suppliers, and produces purchase analysis reports. Of course, payroll is done by the computer, and bookkeeping, fiscal period closings, and financial statements are generated by the general ledger program.

- What common business applications are included in the CHEMIS system?
- What information is supplied by this system?

Source: *The Sensible Way to Use Computers*, Data General Corporation.

SECTION II: COMPUTER-BASED INFORMATION SYSTEMS IN FINANCE

Financial Information Systems

Computer-based **financial information systems** support management in decisions concerning the financing of the business and the allocation and control of financial resources within the business firm. Major financial information systems include cash management, portfolio management, credit management, capital budgeting, financial forecasting, financing requirements analysis, and financial performance analysis. *Accounting information systems* are also frequently included as a major group of financial information systems. Figure 16–23 illustrates that the financial performance analysis system ties together the other financial information systems to produce financial planning and control information. The characteristics and functions of these computer-based systems are summarized below.

■ **Cash management.** The computer collects information on all cash receipts and disbursements throughout a company on a real-time or periodic basis. Such information allows business firms to deposit or invest excess funds more quickly, and thus, increase the income generated by deposited or invested funds. The computer also produces daily, weekly, or monthly forecasts of cash receipts or disbursements (cash flow forecasts), which are used to spot future cash deficits or cash surpluses. Mathematical models may

FIGURE

16–23 Financial information systems

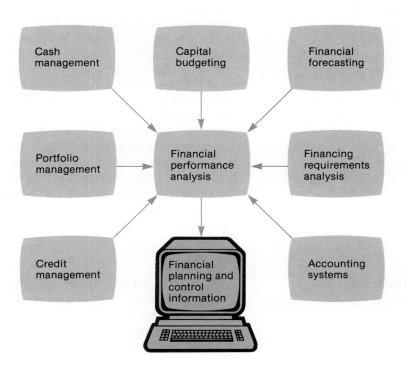

be used to determine optimum cash collection programs and to determine alternative financing or investment strategies for dealing with forecasted cash deficits or surpluses.

■ **Portfolio management.** Many business firms invest their excess cash in short-term marketable securities (such as U.S. Treasury bills, commercial paper, or certificates of deposit) so investment income may be earned until the funds are required. The "portfolio" of such securities must be managed by buying, selling, or holding each type of security so an optimum "mix" of securities is developed which minimizes risk and maximizes investment income.

■ **Credit management.** Computerized credit management information systems plan and control the extension of credit to the customers of a firm. Information is used to control credit policies to minimize bad-debt losses and investment in accounts receivable, while maximizing sales and profitability. Systems of this type use the computer to automate the "screening" of credit applications and the decision to accept or reject a credit application.

■ **Capital budgeting.** The computer is used to evaluate the profitability and financial impact of proposed capital expenditures. Long-term expenditure proposals can be analyzed using a variety of techniques, such as present value analysis and probability analysis.

■ **Financial forecasting.** This application provides information and analytical techniques that result in such economic or financial forecasts as national and local economic conditions, wage levels, price levels, and interest rates. It is heavily dependent on data gathered from the external environment and on the use of various mathematical models and forecasting techniques.

■ **Financing requirements analysis.** The computer supports the analysis of alternative methods of financing the business. Information concerning the economic situation, business operations, the types of financing available, interest rates, and stock and bond prices are used to develop an optimum financing plan for the business.

■ **Financial performance analysis.** This application uses data provided by other financial information systems. It uses *financial performance models* to evaluate present financial performance and formulates plans based upon their effect on projected financial performance.

Financial Performance Models

Advanced computer applications in finance use mathematical techniques and models for such applications as cash management, portfolio management, and capital budgeting. Another application involves the use of computerized financial models, which analyze the financial performance of the entire business firm or one of its divisions or subsidiaries. Electronic spreadsheet packages and DSS generators are frequently used to build and manipulate these models. Answers to "what-if" questions can be explored by seeing the effect of changes in data or model variables. Figure 16–24 illustrates the components of a *financial performance model* of a business firm. Computerized financial performance models are used for the following purposes:

- To control present performance by analyzing and evaluating current operations, in comparison to budgeted objectives.
- To plan the short- and long-range operations of the firm by evaluating the effect of alternative proposals on the financial performance of the firm.
- To determine the future financing requirements and the optimum types of financing required to finance alternative proposals.

Applications in Banking

Computers have had a major impact on the **banking industry.** The computer has not only affected the accounting and reporting operations required by traditional bank services but has influenced the form and extent of all such services and made possible a variety

FIGURE 16–24 A financial performance model

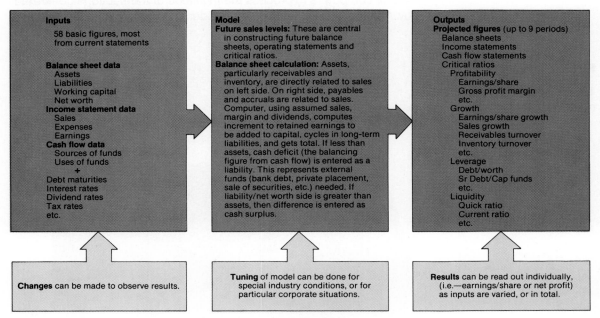

Inputs	Model	Outputs
58 basic figures, most from current statements	**Future sales levels:** These are central in constructing future balance sheets, operating statements and critical ratios.	**Projected figures** (up to 9 periods)
		Balance sheets
Balance sheet data	**Balance sheet calculation:** Assets,	Income statements
Assets	particularly receivables and	Cash flow statements
Liabilities	inventory, are directly related to sales	Critical ratios
Working capital	on left side. On right side, payables	Profitability
Net worth	and accruals are related to sales.	Earnings/share
Income statement data	Computer, using assumed sales,	Gross profit margin
Sales	margin and dividends, computes	etc.
Expenses	increment to retained earnings to	Growth
Earnings	be added to capital, cycles in long-term	Earnings/share growth
Cash flow data	liabilities, and gets total. If less than	Sales growth
Sources of funds	assets, cash deficit (the balancing	Receivables turnover
Uses of funds	figure from cash flow) is entered as a	Inventory turnover
+	liability. This represents external	etc.
Debt maturities	funds (bank debt, private placement,	Leverage
Interest rates	sale of securities, etc.) needed. If	Debt/worth
Dividend rates	liability/net worth side is greater than	Sr Debt/Cap funds
Tax rates	assets, then difference is entered as	etc.
etc.	cash surplus.	Liquidity
		Quick ratio
		Current ratio
		etc.

| **Changes** can be made to observe results. | **Tuning** of model can be done for special industry conditions, or for particular corporate situations. | **Results** can be read out individually, (i.e.—earnings/share or net profit) as inputs are varied, or in total. |

of new *computer services*. The computer is playing an even more decisive role in the operation of many banks through its use in financial models and other management science applications. Traditional and new bank services that are computerized include:

■ **Demand deposit accounting.** This application involves the automation of checking account processing. This was the first and most widely used computer application in banking. It depends heavily on the use of MICR-coded checks and deposit slips and the use of MICR reader- sorters to automate the capture of input data. Output of this system includes special reports concerning checking account activity and monthly customer statements.

■ **Realtime Banking.** Most banks use *transaction terminals* at teller windows and automated teller machines (ATMs or "cash machines") that are electronically linked to the computers in the bank. Such machines are really special-purpose *intelligent terminals*, which automatically update a customer's checking and savings account balances on the computer and perform various banking services for bank customers. Mutual savings banks and savings and loan associations are other major users of computers for realtime banking applications. See Figure 16–25.

■ **Consumer, commercial, and mortgage loans.** Banks have computerized many aspects of the data processing required by their lending activities to consumers and business firms. The widespread development of bank credit card plans has greatly increased the use of computers to process the multitude of transactions generated by millions of bank credit card holders. Output of this application

FIGURE

16–25 Automated teller machine (ATM)

includes monthly customer statements, interest and tax reports, and various loan analysis reports.

■ **Trust applications.** The trust function of banks involves the management of corporate trusts, personal trusts, pension funds, and health and welfare funds. The computer is used to handle a variety of accounting chores and produce management reports and legal documents. Advanced trust applications involve the use of computerized security analysis and portfolio selection.

■ **Computer services.** Many banks are offering computer services to other banks and financial institutions, business and professional firms, government and public organizations, and individuals. Some banks have "spun off" their information services departments into subsidiaries that compete with computer service bureaus.

■ **Electronic funds transfer (EFT) systems.** The computer is the primary component of EFT systems which will one day replace cash and checks as the primary method of payment. The banking industry is in the forefront of efforts to develop and install EFT systems. Automated teller machines (ATMs), automated clearing house (ACH) arrangements, POS terminals, computerized pay-by-phone systems, and other home banking devices are evidences of this development. See Figure 16–26.

Applications in Investments

Computers have been used by firms in the **investment industry** for many years to perform "back office operations," that is, recording transactions, billing customers, and preparing monthly statements. More recent applications of the computer in the investment industry are summarized below.

FIGURE

16–26 Forecast growth in EFT system use

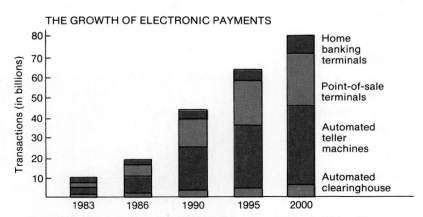

THE GROWTH OF ELECTRONIC PAYMENTS

Source: John Vacca, "Money on the Move," *Computerworld,* May 2, 1984, p. 85.

■ **The stock market.** Under the prodding of the SEC (Securities and Exchange Commission), the stock exchanges and other organizations in the investment industry are developing a computerized "central market" that will automate and centralize securities trading. Realtime computer-based information networks are currently used to facilitate the exchange of information between securities brokers, dealers, and large institutional investors. For example, the National Association of Securities Dealers (NASD) operates a nationwide realtime computer-based information network for over-the-counter (OTC) stocks, called NASDAQ.

■ **Financial information retrieval.** Investment advisory service companies now provide the investment industry with computerized data banks, computer developed reports, and specialized time-sharing services.

■ **Security analysis.** This type of analysis focuses on the financial position and prospects of a corporation to forecast the market price of its securities. Computerized security analysis uses data provided by financial advisory services and time-sharing companies. Various types of financial, economic, and market analyses are then made to forecast alternative values for a security. See Figure 16–27.

■ **Portfolio management.** Portfolio management involves the management of a combination of securities by holding, selling, or buying selected securities to minimize the risk and to maximize the return of the entire "portfolio" of investments. Computerized portfolio management relies on software containing mathematical models which can select one or more portfolios that minimize risk for specific levels of investment return while satisfying various investment constraints. In most cases, the portfolio selection process produces a list of acceptable portfolios, which are reviewed by a *portfolio manager,* who then makes the final hold, buy, and sell decisions for each portfolio managed. Figure 16–28

FIGURE

16–27 Output of Dow Jones investment analysis software packages

A Market manager.

B Market analyzer.

A

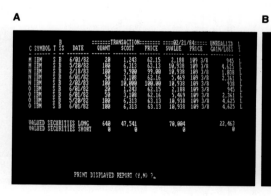

B

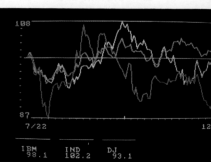

FIGURE   16–28 Integrated portfolio management system

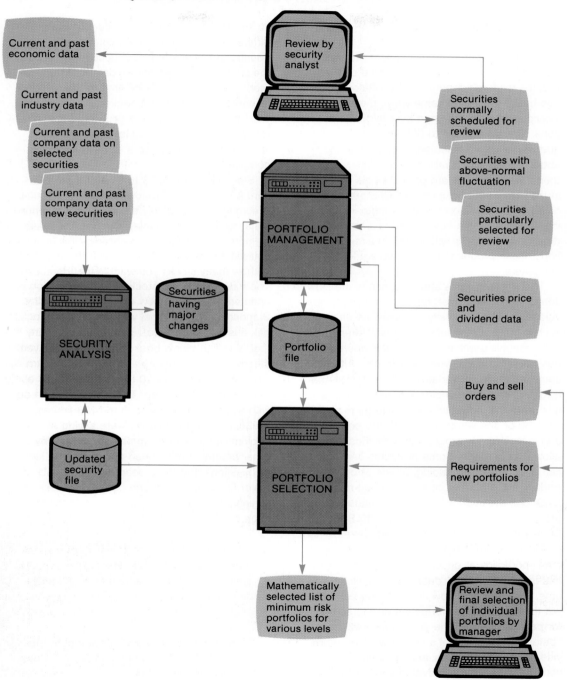

REAL WORLD APPLICATION 16–3

PC Power for Investors

There are computerized investment programs out there now that can allow a home user to rival the research department of a major brokerage house. In fact, in some ways, they give the individual investor an edge over large institutions. There are close to 300 investment programs available for personal computers and about a quarter of a million people are using them. Most of these are professionals already in the investment business but who are interested in doing their own analysis, instead of waiting to see what the boys in the research department come up with. With just a few exceptions, these programs run on Apple and IBM computers.

The biggie in sales and influence is the Dow Jones Market Analyzer, for $394, originally developed at the University of Texas. Its strength is charting. It is a beautiful program. After some initial stumbling with a manual that is not marvelously organized, it is very easy to use. Although some programs are variations of the Market Analyzer, most offer quite different capabilities, and it is up to the individual investor to think about what he or she wants to do with the computer and to look for the program that will most readily allow it to be done. Some programs are aimed just at commodities trading, others at options trading, still others at porfolio management.

One of the best of the portfolio-management programs is Net Worth, at $295, from Bullish Software, P.O. Box 853, Mansfield, Texas. This one runs on the IBM-PC and will keep track of many portfolios at once. It also permits automatic retrieval of stock data-high, low, close, volume, etc., from the Dow Jones News Wire and will then graph that information on the screen for periods of up to one year. It also will track "betas"—a measure of a stock's volatility—provide buy and sell signals, and automatically alert you when to sell for tax advantages. Each portfo-

lio set up with Net Worth can contain up to 100 different stocks, 20 different commodities accounts, and 40 different cash accounts. Because the program provides its own database management, in theory there is no limit to the number of portfolios that can be tracked—it would just depend on how many disks you're willing to handle. This is a professional-level program, and you could easily manage a small investment company with it.

Stockpak II, for $275 to $1,400, from Standard & Poor's at 25 Broadway, New York 10004, is something completely different. This is a personal database, containing much of the mass of information on stocks compiled by this famous statistical company. The price you pay depends on how many stocks you want in that database. The minimum is 800 stocks. This information is updated monthly, in new disks sent to you by Standard & Poor's. What you can do with Stockpak II is ask things like, "Find me a company that is selling below book value, has displayed steady earnings growth, and has a price-earnings ratio of less that 10-to-1." Think that's a tough order? Nonsense. The program came up with eight of them in less than two minutes.

Going back to what we were saying at the beginning, this and the problems tackled by other programs mentioned above are the kind of questions that the research departments of major firms used to spend days and weeks answering. The answer was then given to the firms' large clients first. Now it's yours for the asking.

■ Which of the three investment software packages mentioned above accomplish security analysis? Portfolio management? Financial database management? Explain how you might use each one.

Source: Bob Schwabach, "Investment Programs Rival Think Tanks of Large Firms." Copyright, Knight-Ridder, 1984.

SUMMARY

Several common business information systems exist in both large and small computer-using business firms, whether they are experienced computer users or are using the computer for the first time. The objectives, input, database, and output of the following seven common business applications were described in this chapter: (1) *sales order/transaction processing,* (2) *inventory control,* (3) *billing and sales analysis,* (4) *accounts receivable,* (5) *accounts payable,* (6) *payroll and labor analysis,* and (7) *general ledger.* In addition, important computer-based information systems in accounting, finance, banking, and investments were discussed. Figures 16–1, 16–2, and 16–23 summarize many of these systems.

KEY TERMS AND CONCEPTS

Common business information
   systems
Sales order/transaction
   processing
Inventory control
Billing and sales analysis
Accounts receivable
Accounts payable
Payroll and labor analysis

General ledger
Accounting information
   systems.
Financial information systems
Financial performance models
Computer applications in
   banking and investments
Electronic funds transfer

REVIEW AND APPLICATION QUESTIONS

1. What computer-based information systems in accounting are used by most business firms? Describe two of them.
2. Which of the common business information systems could be called accounting applications? Explain.
3. How are the common business information systems related to each other?
4. Briefly describe each of the seven common business information system discussed in this chapter.
5. Summarize the objectives, input, database, and output of one of the common business information systems.
6. What computer-based information systems in finance are used by business firms?
7. What are several traditional and new computer applications in banking?

8. What do you think will be the impact of electronic funds transfer (EFT) systems on computer applications in banking?
9. Identify several computer applications in investments. How will these applications be affected by an "electronic stock market"?
10. How are personal computers and investment application packages being used for security analysis? Portfolio management?

APPLICATION PROBLEMS

1. If you have not already done so, read and answer the questions after each Real World Application in this chapter.
2. Five examples of electronic information processing are given below. Identify the common business information system that would include these activities:
   a. Checks are printed for all employees on sick leave.
   b. A detailed listing of all products in stock is produced.
   c. Payments from customers being entered via a VDT are checked for the presence of all required fields.
   d. Out-of-date customer addresses are replaced with current addresses.
   e. A trend analysis report of overhead expenses for 5 years is produced.
3. The controller (chief accounting officer) of ABC Department Stores wants the firm to purchase a large integrated software package, which would significantly change the input and output methods for all of the common business information systems of the firm. The marketing VP objects to the changes that would result to the sales order/transaction processing system and to the sales analysis application. The director of personnel objects to the changes that would occur in the payroll and labor analysis application. The controller feels that, since these are accounting applications, she should have the final say in this decision. What do you think? What would you recommend? Defend your recommendation.
4. Which common business information system should be improved if the following complaints were brought to your attention?
   a. "Month-end closings are always late."
   b. "We are never sure how much of a certain product we have on the shelves."
   c. "Many of us didn't get a W-2 form this year."
   d. "We're tired of manually writing up a receipt every time a customer buys something."
   e. "Our suppliers are complaining that they are not being paid on time."

f. "Our customers resent being sent notices demanding payment when they have already paid what they owe."

g. "Nobody is sure which of our sales reps is our top producer."

5. List each of the computer applications in banking that you have personally experienced due to your use of specific banking services. What do you like about how each of these is computerized? What would you recommend to improve each of these services, in terms of computer hardware (equipment and media), software (programs and procedures), and people (specialists and users)?

6. The VP for finance of ABC Department Stores is pleased with its computer-based information systems in accounting. But he says its applications in finance are inadequate. What are some of the computer-based systems he might be dissatisfied with? Which of these financial applications would you select as the most important for a department store? Why?

CHAPTER 17

Information Systems Development

CHAPTER OUTLINE

LEARNING OBJECTIVES

The purpose of this chapter is to promote a basic understanding of the process by which computer-based information systems are developed. After reading and studying this chapter, you should be able to:

1. Explain what "the systems approach" means in terms of a systems *viewpoint* and *process*.
2. Discuss how methods of computer-assisted systems development are changing the traditional activities of information systems development.
3. Explain why and how users should be involved in systems analysis and design.
4. Outline the stages of the traditional information systems development cycle.
5. Describe the content of a feasibility study.
6. Outline some of the potential costs and benefits of a computer-based information system.
7. Explain the purpose and activities of systems analysis and systems design.
8. Identify several tools and techniques of systems analysis and design.
9. Identify the purpose and activities of systems implementation and maintenance.
10. Identify several input, processing, output, storage, and control considerations of systems analysis and design, and illustrate them with examples based on the computer-based information systems discussed in Chapters 15 and 16.

WHY LEARN SYSTEMS ANALYSIS AND DESIGN?

Suppose the manager of a firm where you worked asked you to **find a better way to get information** to the salespeople in your company. How would you start? What would you do? Would you just plunge ahead and hope you could come up with a reasonable solution? How would you know whether your solution was a good one for your company? Do you think that there might be a way to help you develop a good solution to your manager's request? There is. It's a developmental process called **information systems development,** or, more popularly, **systems analysis and design.**

How do you think the computer-based information systems discussed in the previous chapters are developed? Such business computer applications do not just happen. They must be conceived, designed, and implemented using a systems development process. Thus information systems development or systems analysis and design is the process in which users and systems analysts **design** information systems based on an **analysis** of the information requirements of an organization. Effective systems analysis and design is vital to the development of computer-based information systems, since ineffective and inefficient use of computers in business is frequently attributed to a failure to understand and apply basic systems concepts to the information requirements of a business firm. To a great extent, therefore, successful use of computers in business requires that **every computer user should learn to be his or her own systems analyst.**

THE SYSTEMS APPROACH

The *systems approach* is a term that describes the use of the systems concept in studying a problem and formulating a solution. The systems approach has two basic characteristics:

- "Using the systems approach" means using a **viewpoint** that tries to find systems, subsystems, and components of systems in the phenomena we are studying so all important factors and their interrelationships are considered. Therefore, the systems approach encourages us to look for the components and relationships of a **system** as we analyze a specific problem and formulate its solution.

For example, we have used a system's viewpoint throughout this text as we analyzed information processing, computers, information networks, and business firms as **systems** of **input, processing, output, storage,** and **control** components. Developing new computer applications should thus focus on the input, processing, output, storage, and control functions of the computer-based information systems that are being proposed. Systems analysis and design then becomes a process where users and systems analysts determine how these basic information processing functions *are* and *should* be accomplished. Figure 17–1 is a system function diagram that illustrates this concept. It poses basic input, processing, output, storage, and control questions (and related hardware, software, and people questions) that must be answered in the systems analysis and design process.

■ The systems approach also refers to the **process** by which we study a problem and formulate a solution. Studying a problem

FIGURE 17–1 The system's approach as a systems viewpoint: Basic questions of systems analysis and design

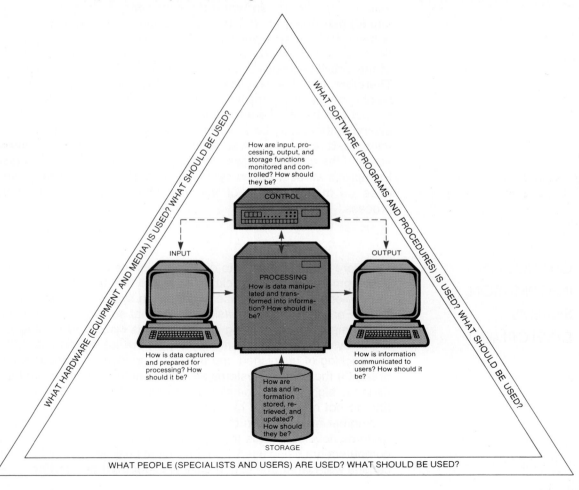

How are input, processing, output, and storage functions monitored and controlled? How should they be?

CONTROL

WHAT HARDWARE (EQUIPMENT AND MEDIA) IS USED? WHAT SHOULD BE USED?

WHAT SOFTWARE (PROGRAMS AND PROCEDURES) IS USED? WHAT SHOULD BE USED?

INPUT

OUTPUT

PROCESSING
How is data manipulated and transformed into information? How should it be?

How is data captured and prepared for processing? How should it be?

How is information communicated to users? How should it be?

How are data and information stored, retrieved, and updated? How should they be?

STORAGE

WHAT PEOPLE (SPECIALISTS AND USERS) ARE USED? WHAT SHOULD BE USED?

and formulating a solution can be considered as an organized *system* of interrelated activities (frequently called the **systems development cycle** or *systems life cycle*) composed of investigation, analysis, design, programming, implementation, and maintenance activities. Therefore, developing new computer applications should involve an **information systems development cycle** where users and systems analysts develop computer-based information systems. The rest of this chapter is spent explaining how this is accomplished.

THE SYSTEMS DEVELOPMENT CYCLE

Figure 17–2 illustrates a traditional *information systems development cycle,* which includes the stages of (1) **investigation,** (2) **analysis,** (3) **design,** (4) **software development,** (5) **implementation,** and (6) **maintenance.** It shows that developing a new user application should be a systematic multistep process based on a systems development cycle concept. You should realize however, that all of the activities involved are highly related and interdependent. Therefore, in actual practice, several developmental activities can be occurring at the same time. Also, different parts of a development project can be at different stages of the development cycle. For example, there may be a *testing cycle,* where a new system is tested and redesigned. Also typical is a *maintenance cycle,* where some of the activities of systems development are performed again to improve an established system. Figure 17–2 summarizes what goes on in each stage of the traditional systems development process.

CHANGES IN INFORMATION SYSTEMS DEVELOPMENT

Before we get too far into our discussion of information systems development, we should acknowledge the fact that the process of developing computer-based information systems is changing. Why? For the very same basic reasons that software development and computer programming is changing, as discussed in Chapter Eight. Systems development projects (1) are taking too long, (2) the backlog of unfinished and unstarted projects has become too great, (3) the costs of systems development and maintenance have risen too high, and (4) completed systems still have too many errors and do not meet users' requirements.

Another major reason for the changes occurring in information systems development is the change that has occurred in the way computers are being used. Formerly, most business computer applications were what one expert calls **prespecified computing.** Most

FIGURE 17–2 The traditional information systems development cycle

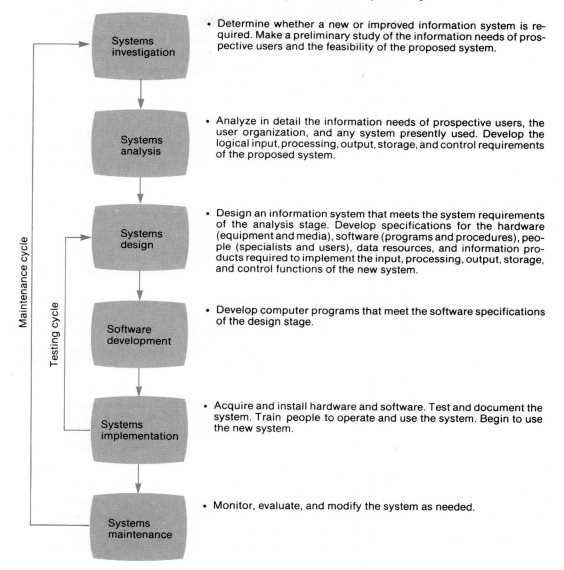

- Determine whether a new or improved information system is required. Make a preliminary study of the information needs of prospective users and the feasibility of the proposed system.

- Analyze in detail the information needs of prospective users, the user organization, and any system presently used. Develop the logical input, processing, output, storage, and control requirements of the proposed system.

- Design an information system that meets the system requirements of the analysis stage. Develop specifications for the hardware (equipment and media), software (programs and procedures), people (specialists and users), data resources, and information products required to implement the input, processing, output, storage, and control functions of the new system.

- Develop computer programs that meet the software specifications of the design stage.

- Acquire and install hardware and software. Test and document the system. Train people to operate and use the system. Begin to use the new system.

- Monitor, evaluate, and modify the system as needed.

processing requirements could be determined ahead of time. So a conventional systems development process could be used where formal determination of system requirements and system specifications could be accomplished. Now, however, many business computer applications can be classified as **user-driven computing.**

In this category, users do not know exactly what they want until they have tried a version of it, and then they change it frequently and quickly. Therefore, a conventional method of systems development is no longer effective. See Figure 17–3.

One important response of major computer-using organizations and the computer industry to these problems has been to dramatically increase the development and acquisition of application software packages where much of the systems development work has already been accomplished. The other major response has been to stress new ways of developing user applications that are closely related to the new software development methods discussed in Chapter Eight. These are **structured systems development** and

FIGURE

17–3 Prespecified versus user-driven computing

Prespecified Computing

- A formal requirements analysis is performed.
- Detailed, precise specifications are created.
- The traditional development life cycle is used, or a variant of it related to higher levels of automation.
- Programs are formally documented.
- The application development time is many months or years.
- Maintenance is formal and carefully specified.

Examples: Compiler writing, airline reservations, air traffic control, missile guidance, system software development.

User-Driven Computing

- Users do not know in detail what they want until they use a version of it and then they modify it quickly and often frequently. Consequently, formal requirement specification linked to slow application programming is doomed to failure.
- Applications are created with a generator or other software more quickly than the time to write specifications.
- The system is self-documenting, or interactive documentation is created when the application is created.
- Users create their own applications or work with an analyst who does this in cooperation with them. A separate programming department is not used.
- The application development time is days or at most weeks.
- Maintenance is continuous. Incremental changes are made constantly to the applications by the users or the analyst who assists them.
- The process may employ data models and data systems which are centrally created with information engineering processes.
- Control is imposed via the data models, dictionary, and authorization procedures.

Examples: Information systems, decision-support systems, paperwork avoidance, administrative procedures, shop floor control.

Source: James Martin, *An Information Systems Manifesto* (Englewood Cliffs, N.J.: Prentice-Hall, 1984), p. 44. Reprinted with permission.

computer-assisted systems development. Let's discuss computer-assisted systems development now, since structured systems development is discussed later in this chapter.

Computer-Assisted Systems Development

If programming can be computer-assisted, why can't systems development? It can, though the process is more complex and still not a fully developed technology. Many software packages for computer-assisted systems development are the same as those discussed in Chapter Eight for computer-assisted programming. Refer back to Figures 8–2 and 8–3. For example, such packages as **application generators** and **report generators** help a user or systems analyst develop an application or a report without going through many of the traditional stages of systems development. Other packages computerize parts of the conventional systems development process, such as packages that automatically produce systems documentation or data dictionaries. Finally, **systems development generators** provide automated tools for most of the stages of systems development. See Figure 17–4. These software tools have made two new types of computer-assisted systems development popular: **prototyping** and **user-developed systems.** See Figure 17–5.

Prototyping

This is a "quick and dirty" type of systems development where *an actual working model* (a **prototype**) of the information system needed by a user is quickly developed using an application generator

FIGURE 17–4 Examples of systems development generators

PRIDE-ASDM is an integrated and automated approach for the specification, analysis, design, development, and implementation of information systems. It includes a Computer Aided Design (CAD) tool for systems development. User information requirements are input, data flows and structures are analysed, and a design is then rendered for the entire system. If an existing system can implement the information requirements, as usage is suggested by PRIDE-ADSM. Revisions to the design can be input by the analyst until a design is agreed upon. Once a design has been decided all of the systems documentation is then generated and maintained in a reusable form by the computer.

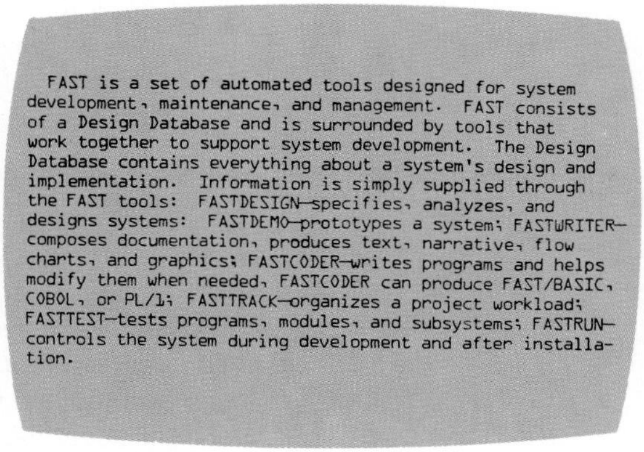

FAST is a set of automated tools designed for system development, maintenance, and management. FAST consists of a Design Database and is surrounded by tools that work together to support system development. The Design Database contains everything about a system's design and implementation. Information is simply supplied through the FAST tools: FASTDESIGN—specifies, analyzes, and designs systems; FASTDEMO—prototypes a system; FASTWRITER—composes documentation, produces text, narrative, flow charts, and graphics; FASTCODER—writes programs and helps modify them when needed, FASTCODER can produce FAST/BASIC, COBOL, or PL/1; FASTTRACK—organizes a project workload; FASTTEST—tests programs, modules, and subsystems; FASTRUN—controls the system during development and after installation.

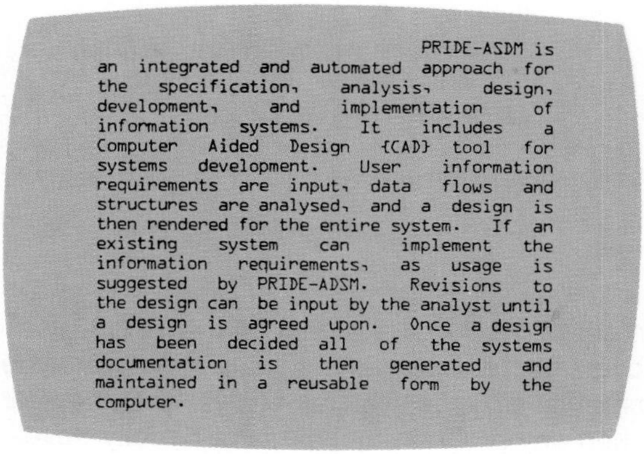

FIGURE 17–5 Differences in the activities of traditional and computer-assisted systems development

Systems Development Activities	Traditional Systems Development	Application Generator Used as a Prototyping Aid Followed by Programming	Systems Development without Professional Programmers
Requirements analysis	A time-consuming, formal operation, often delayed by long application backlog.	The user's imagination is stimulated. Users may work at a screen with an analyst to develop requirements.	The user's imagination is stimulated. Users may develop their own requirements, or work with an analyst.
System specifications	Lengthy document. Boring. Often inadequate.	Produced by prototyping aid. Precise and tested.	Disappears.
User sign-off	User is often not sure what he or she is signing off on. User cannot perceive all subtleties.	User sees the results and may modify them many times before signing off.	No formal sign-off. Adjustment and modification is an ongoing process.
Coding and testing	Slow. Expensive. Often delayed because of backlog.	The prototype is converted to more efficient code. Relatively quick and error-free.	Quick. Inexpensive. Disappears to a large extent.
Documentation	Tedious. Time-consuming.	May be partly automated. Interactive training and HELP response may be created online.	Largely automatic. Interactive training and HELP responses are created online.
Maintenance	Slow. Expensive. Often late.	Often slow. Often expensive. Often late.	A continuing process with user and analyst making adjustments. Most of these adjustments can be made very quickly—in hours rather than months.

Source: Adapted from James Martin, *Application Development without Programmers* (Englewood Cliffs, N.J.: Prentice-Hall, 1982), p. 66–67. Used with permission.

and an interactive process between a systems analyst and a user. The user can begin to use the prototype immediately. The prototype can be modified several times by the systems analyst until the user finds it acceptable. Then any program modules not directly developed by the application generator can be coded, and the final version of the system is turned over to the user. See Figure 17–6.

User-Developed Systems

This is a "do-it-yourself" type of systems development. Many users do not need systems analysts and programmers to develop

FIGURE

17–6 Information systems development with prototyping

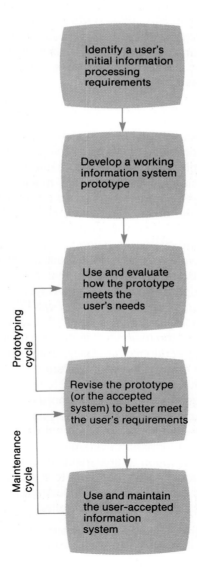

Identify a user's initial information processing requirements

Develop a working information system prototype

Use and evaluate how the prototype meets the user's needs

Prototyping cycle

Revise the prototype (or the accepted system) to better meet the user's requirements

Maintenance cycle

Use and maintain the user-accepted information system

small applications. They can do it themselves with the help of the same basic resources needed for user programming.

- **Hardware resources.** Intelligent workstations provide both microcomputer power and main-frame power through data communications links to large computers.
- **Software resources.** Computer-assisted programming and systems development packages can be used, such as application development systems and nonprocedural or natural languages, as well as general-purpose application packages, such as electronic spreadsheet programs.
- **Organizational resources.** Organizations establish **information centers** to provide users with hardware, software, and people support from systems analysts working as *consultants* to users.

User Involvement in Systems Development

Computer-assisted systems development methods make the job of information systems development easier, but do not eliminate it. Such methods help you move more quickly through the stages of systems development, by making it an automated, interactive process. There is less pressure to develop *perfect systems* the first time around. Hardware and software tools make it easier to go through several iterations of the systems development process until the system is refined to the point of acceptability. But users and systems analysts must still use **the systems approach** to build effective information systems. You cannot design a good system if you ignore how the essential system functions of *input, processing, output, storage, and control* will be performed. You cannot design a good system if you ignore the fact that you need to accomplish some of the major activities of systems development, such as determining economic feasibility, examining what your information needs really are, testing your system properly, and developing adequate documentation.

Figure 17–7 outlines in more detail the important responsibilities that users and systems analysts should assume in each stage of the conventional development of *prespecified* major computer-based information systems. Notice that users are deeply involved from inception to final installation and operation. A tongue-in-cheek reminder of what happens to a systems development project when users are not involved is illustrated in Figure 17–8. **User-involvement** has three major benefits:

- New systems should better reflect the true information requirements and capabilities of the users of the system.
- New systems will be more acceptable to users, since they are

FIGURE

17–7 Responsibilities during traditional information systems development

	Responsibilities of	
Stages	**Users**	**Information Services Staff**
INVESTIGATION	Initiate study, suggest application, sketch information needs, describe existing processing procedures.	Listen to requirements, respond to questions, devise alternatives, assess using rough estimates, prepare preliminary survey.
ANALYSIS	Help evaluate existing system and proposed alternatives, select alternative for design. Help describe existing system, collect and analyze data.	Evaluate alternatives using agreed-upon criteria. Conduct analysis, collect data, and document findings.
DESIGN	Design output, input, processing logic; plan for conversion and forecast impact on users, design manual procedures; remain aware of file structures and design. Review specifications, help develop specifications for manual procedures.	Present alternatives and tradeoffs to users for their decisions. Combine user needs with technical requirements to develop specifications, develop technical conversion plan.
SOFTWARE DEVELOPMENT	Monitor process.	Organize programming, design modules, code programs.
IMPLEMENTATION	Generate test data and evaluate results. Develop materials, conduct training sessions. Phase conversion, provide resources, conduct post-implementation audit.	Test program modules individually and in entire system. Aid in preparation of materials and train operations staff. Coordinate conversion, perform conversion processing tasks, help in post-implementation audit.
MAINTENANCE	Provide data and use output, monitor system use and quality, suggest modifications and enhancements.	Process data to produce output reliability, respond to enhancement requests, suggest improvements, monitor service.

Source: Adapted from Henry Lucas *Information Systems Concepts for Management.* (New York: McGraw-Hill, 1982). Copyright © 1982 by McGraw-Hill Book Company. Used with the permission of McGraw-Hill Book Company.

the result of a joint effort, rather than systems developed by "outsiders."

■ User involvement helps ensure the cooperation of users in solving the problems that typically arise when any new system is installed and operated.

FIGURE   17–8 Systems development without user involvement

As stated in the system requirements

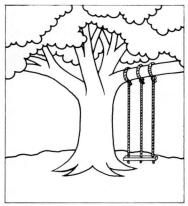

As outlined in the system specifications

As designed by the systems analyst

As implemented by information services

As operated by the user

What the user wanted

SYSTEMS INVESTIGATION

Do we have an information problem? What is causing the problem? Would a new or improved information system help solve the problem? What would be a **feasible** information system solution to our problem? These are the questions that have to be answered in the systems investigation stage — the first step in the systems development process. This stage results in the selection and preliminary study definition of the particular system that will be developed. Because the process of developing a major information system can be a costly one, this stage may require a preliminary study called a **feasibility study.** Systems investigation typically includes the steps shown in Figure 17–9 whenever a large information system is being proposed for development.

REAL WORLD APPLICATION 17–1

Borg-Warner Corporation

Increases in programmer productivity of 200-to-500 percent . . . online applications delivered to users in ½ to $\frac{1}{10}$th the time of traditional applications programming methods . . . application programming backlogs reduced dramatically. These are the kinds of benefits achieved through the use of Series 80 MANTIS, the online application development system from Cincom Systems, at Borg-Warner Chemicals, Inc., a subsidiary of Borg-Warner Corporation, in Parkersburg, West Virginia. After less than a year of use, MANTIS has exceeded the plastics and chemicals products manufacturer's expectations for increasing productivity in every area, based on benchmark studies recently completed.

In comparisons conducted at Borg-Warner, MANTIS has proven to be superior to traditional programming and systems development methods, including:
- *Learning curve time*—Programmers learned to use MANTIS in ratios that ranged from 10 to 15 times faster than learning to use COBOL or COBOL-XT.
- *Time spent developing programs*—the actual amount of time programmers spent working on developing programs is one fifth the time required using traditional methods, which involve waiting for batch processing.
- *Delivery of completed applications to end-users*—There has been an average of a 2:1 improvement in the elapsed time from the request for a new application to the time it is in the hands of the end-user.

Since MANTIS was installed at Borg-Warner, sophisticated end-users are developing applications specific to their areas, freeing MIS to concentrate on database design, data structuring, and data security.

"Series 80 MANTIS has helped our current DP staff to achieve higher productivity through state-of-the-art design methodologies such as prototyping," says Dave Yoak, manager of database administration at Borg-Warner. "Using prototyping and step-level refinement, the end-user can be involved directly in designing applications," Mr. Yoak explains. "These approaches encourage the systems analyst or programmer to sit down with the end-user at the CRT and design the application. Together, they can work with the user's own data in the proposed format to make sure it satisfies the needs for the application. The prototyping capabilities of MANTIS allow us to do in minutes what had taken hours, or even days, using traditional methods," he says.

Series 80 MANTIS has significantly reduced the application backlog at Borg-Warner already. By further increasing user satisfaction and involvement, they plan to reduce development time and backlog even further. Sophisticated end-users will be taught to do their own programming and maintenance. Systems analysts and programmers will work closely with end-users in the design of other applications.

"We are moving out of the programming business," says Dr. Thomas Purcell, who is Director of MIS at Borg-Warner. "We want to get to a point where we don't have to be concerned about writing new programs, because we already have the majority of data-capturing applications in place and in the hands of the users. We see Series 80 MANTIS as allowing us to shorten the time interval between when the user says 'I need' and we can say 'Now you can.'"

- Is Borg-Warner using Series 80 MANTIS for computer- assisted information systems development? Explain your answer.
- What benefits are MANTIS providing to Borg-Warner, compared to traditional systems development?
- How are the roles of the systems analysts and programmers changing at Borg-Warner?

Source: Cincom Systems.

Feasibility Studies

FIGURE

17–9 Activities
of the systems
investigation
stage

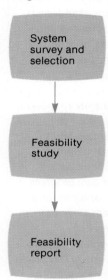

A **feasibility study** is a preliminary study that determines the information needs of prospective users and the objectives, constraints, basic resource requirements, cost/benefits, and feasibility of proposed projects. The findings of such a preliminary study are usually formalized in a written report, which is submitted to the management of the firm for approval.

Information-Gathering Methods

How do you get the information you need for a feasibility study and for the other stages of systems development? Information must be gathered from present and prospective users by:

- Personal interviews with users, operators, and managers.
- Questionnaires to appropriate individuals in the organization.
- Personal observation of the system in action.
- Examination of documents, reports, data media, procedures manuals, and other methods of systems documentation.
- Inspecting accounting and management reports to collect operating statistics and cost data for information processing operations.

Now let's look at some of the basic systems characteristics that users and analysts need to identify in a feasibility study.

Determining Information Needs

The feasibility study should make a *preliminary* determination of the *information needs* of prospective users. *Who* wants *what* information and *when, where,* and *why* they want it are the basic questions that must be answered. Users may express their information needs by describing a problem that has developed. *For example:* "We are not receiving production information early enough in our shipping department." Such statements are symptoms of an underlying information system problem, which must be identified by further study. Information needs should also be stated specifically. *For example:* "Get me all the facts" or "Give me more information than I am getting now" are not specific statements of information needs. An example of a better statement of information needs is:

- We need immediate notification concerning any products that have fallen below the minimum inventory level.

Defining Problems and Opportunities

Problems and opportunities must be identified in a feasibility study. *Symptoms* must be separated from *problems*. For example, the fact that "sales are declining" is not a properly defined problem. Examples of problem and opportunity statements that get closer to the facts are:

- *Problem:* Salespersons are losing orders, because they cannot get current information on product prices and availability.
- *Opportunity:* We could increase sales significantly, if salespersons could receive instant responses to requests for price quotations and product availability.

Determining System Objectives

Feasibility studies should determine the objectives of both the *business systems* and the *information systems* involved in a project. The basic purpose of the business activities involved (sales, purchasing, shipping, etc.) and the information systems that support those activities must be determined. Objectives should not be stated in vague terms. For example, compare the statement, "Improve efficiency," with a more specific statement, such as:

- Provide production status information to the shipping department within one hour of the end of each shift.

Identifying System Constraints

The feasibility study must identify the "constraints" of the proposed system, also known as the "restrictions" or "boundaries" of a system. *Constraints* are restrictions that limit the form and content of the system design. Constraints can be *external* to the business organization. *For example:*

- Restrictions are typically required by law or industry agreement on the format and size of source documents or output documents, such as the checks of the banking industry and the "W-2" forms required by the Internal Revenue Service.

Internal constraints may arise due to a scarcity of organizational resources or due to conflicting information needs and objectives of departments and personnel within an organization. *For example;* the objective of providing timely production status information to the shipping department may be restricted by this constraint:

- Operating costs of any new system must not exceed the costs of the present system, and no additional duties can be imposed on production personnel.

Determining Systems Criteria

An important step in systems investigation is defining the *criteria* to be used in evaluating the feasibility of the alternative systems being proposed. Criteria must also be ranked in order of their importance, because a criterion such as "low cost" may conflict with a "instant response." Typical criteria categories to be specified include:

■ Response time, operating cost, accuracy, reliability, capacity, and security.

Economic, Technological, and Operational Feasibility

The goal of feasibility studies is to evaluate alternative systems through cost/benefit analysis and other methods of evaluation. The most feasible and desirable system can then be selected for development. The "feasibility" of a proposed system can be evaluated in terms of three major categories, summarized below and illustrated in Figure 17–10.

■ **Economic feasibility**—whether expected cost savings, increased profits, and other benefits exceed the costs of developing and operating the system.

■ **Technological feasibility**—whether reliable hardware and software needed by a proposed system can be acquired or developed by the business firm in the required time.

FIGURE

17–10 Economic, technological, and operational feasibility

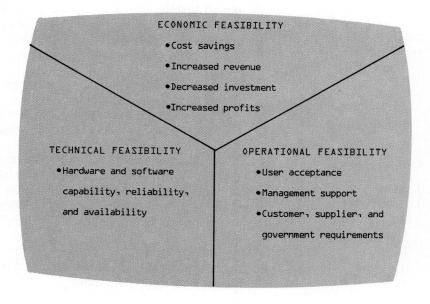

ECONOMIC FEASIBILITY
- Cost savings
- Increased revenue
- Decreased investment
- Increased profits

TECHNICAL FEASIBILITY
- Hardware and software capability, reliability, and availability

OPERATIONAL FEASIBILITY
- User acceptance
- Management support
- Customer, supplier, and government requirements

■ **Operational feasibility**—the willingness and ability of the management, employees, customers, suppliers, etc., of an organization to operate, use, and support a proposed system.

Cost/Benefit Analysis

Feasibility studies should include a *cost/benefit analysis* of the proposed system. *Costs* must include the costs of computer hardware and software, CPU time, systems analysis and design, programming, personnel, training, installation, and operations. Such **tangible costs** are comparatively easily to quantify, compared to the analysis of **intangible costs,** such as the loss of customer goodwill or employee morale caused by errors and disruptions arising from the installation of a new system.

Tangible benefits are comparatively easy to estimate, such as the decrease in payroll costs caused by a reduction in personnel or a decrease in inventory carrying costs caused by a reduction in inventory of the proposed system. **Intangible benefits** are much harder to estimate. Such benefits as "better customer service" or "faster and more accurate information for management" fall into this category. Figure 17–11 lists typical tangible and intangible benefits (with examples).

FIGURE

17–11 Benefits of computer-based information systems

Tangible Benefits

■ Increase in sales or profits. (Improvement in product or service quality.)
■ Decrease in information processing costs. (Elimination of unnecessary procedures and documents.)
■ Decrease in operating costs. (Reduction in inventory carrying costs.)
■ Decrease in required investment. (Decrease in inventory investment required.)
■ Increased operational ability and efficiency. (Improvement in production ability and efficiency; for example, less spoilage, waste, and idle time.)

Intangible Benefits

■ New or improved information availability. (More timely and accurate information, and new types and forms of information.)
■ Improved abilities in computation and analysis. (Mathematical simulation.)
■ Improved customer service. (More timely service.)
■ Improved employee morale. (Elimination of burdensome and boring job tasks.)
■ Improved management decision making. (Better information and decision analysis.)
■ Improved competitive position. (Faster and better response to actions of competitors.)
■ Improved business and community image. ("Progressive" image as perceived by customers, investors, other businesses, government, and the public.)

Return on Investment Analysis

"Will investing in a new or improved system produce a satisfactory rate of return?" This question is typically asked by management. One way to answer is to compute a percentage **rate of return on investment** for new or improved systems proposals.

$$\begin{array}{c}\textbf{Return} \\ \textbf{on} \\ \textbf{Investment}\end{array} = \frac{\text{Increased profits due to cost savings and/or increased revenue}}{\text{New investment required less any reductions in investment}}$$

The return-on-investment (ROI) concept emphasizes three potential methods of achieving *economic feasibility* for proposed systems:

- Cost reduction (such as lower operating costs).
- Increased revenue (such as an increase in sales).
- Decreased investment (such as a decrease in inventory requirements).

The Feasibility Study Report

The results of systems investigation for a major application are recorded in written form in a **feasibility study report**. This report *documents* and *communicates* the findings of the feasibility study to management and other users. Management uses the information in the feasibility report as the basis for a decision to approve or not approve the proposal. The feasibility study report typically includes:

- Preliminary specifications of the proposed new or improved system, including systems criteria and constraints.
- An evaluation of the economic, technological, and operational feasibility of the proposed system.
- A plan for the development of the proposed system.

SYSTEMS ANALYSIS

What is **systems analysis?** Whether you want to develop a new application quickly or are involved in a massive long-term project, you should still perform several basic activities of systems analysis. Systems analysis traditionally involves a study of:

- A present information system and its role in the organization.
- The information needs of the organization and its users.
- The information processing system capabilities required to meet the information needs of users.

The final product of systems analysis is the **system requirements** for proposed new or improved information system (also called the *functional specifications* or the *functional requirements*.) For large development projects, this takes the form of a *system requirements report*. It specifies the capabilities needed for each information processing system function (input, processing, output, storage, and control) to meet the information needs of users. Designing a system that meets these system requirements then becomes the goal of the *systems design* stage.

Structured Analysis

The systems analysis stage can be a *top-down* and *structured* series of activities using much of the philosophy and methodology of *structured programming* discussed in Chapter Eight. Instead of first focusing on the basic requirements of the proposed system (from the *bottom up*), **structured analysis** begins with an analysis of the organization's requirements (from the *top down*). It then moves in structured steps to the analysis of major *subsystems* or *modules* affected, then to an analysis of the information system presently used, and then finally to an analysis of the information requirements of the proposed system.

Other methods of structured analysis also emphasize a modular, top-down approach. They usually organize and name the activities of systems analysis differently. They stress a more formalized set of methodologies and tools (such as *data flow diagrams* and *data dictionaries*). We will discuss some of these tools shortly. The goal of these more formalized methods of systems analysis is to so improve the quality of the system requirements developed during this stage that more efficient and effective systems are developed. Unfortunately, this also makes this stage more time-consuming and less attractive to users. Thus, as we discussed earlier, users are attracted to faster and less formal methods.

Systems Analysis Activities

Let's briefly look at each of the major activities of systems analysis as illustrated in Figure 17–12. You should realize that many of these activities are an extension of those used in conducting a feasibility study. Some of the same information gathering methods (interviews, observations, etc.) are used, plus some new tools that we will discuss shortly. But systems analysis is not a *preliminary study*. It's the real thing.

Analysis of the User Organization

FIGURE

17–12 Activities of the systems analysis stage

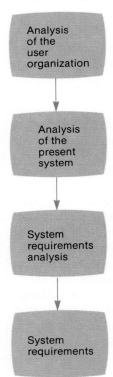

This activity can be quite complex for a systems analyst working on a big project who doesn't know much about a particular user organization. A long-time user will probably skip this step, as will systems analysts working on small projects. But it still is important. How can you improve an information system if you know very little about the **organizational environment** in which that system is located? You can't. That's why you have to know something about the organization, its management structure, its business activities, and the information systems it has installed. You also have to know this in more detail for specific user departments that will be affected by the new or improved information system being proposed. *For example,* you could not design a new inventory control system for a chain of department stores until you learn a lot about the company and the types of business activities that affect their inventory.

Analysis of the Present System

Before you design a new system, you had better study the present system that will be improved or replaced (if there is one). You need to analyze how the present system uses **hardware resources** (equipment and media), **software resources** (programs and procedures), and **people resources** (users and information system staff) to transform the **data resources** of the organization into **information products** for users. You should analyze how these system resources are used to accomplish the information processing functions of **input, processing, output, storage,** and **control.**

Look at Figure 17–13. It illustrates the system resources and system functions found in most computer-based information systems in business. You should learn to look for these *typical system components* any time you study a business computer application. Let's look at some examples.

Input

Input is frequently collected from *source documents* (such as payroll timecards) and converted to machine-sensible data by a *data entry* process (such as keypunching and key-to-tape). Other input data may be generated by online terminals (such as POS terminals). Input into the system consists of:

- **Transactions data.** *Example:* A sales transaction.
- **Database adjustments.** *Example:* Change a customer's credit limit using an online terminal in the credit department or by processing a "credit increase request form" mailed in by a customer.
- **Inquiries.** *Example:* What is the balance owed on a customer's account?

FIGURE 17–13 Analysis of the present system: Typical system components

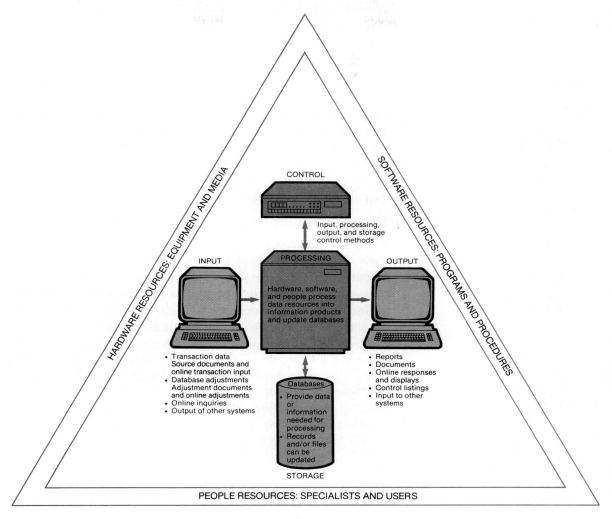

Output of other systems. *Example:* The output of a sales order/transaction processing system includes data needed as input to an inventory control system to correctly reflect transactions that change the amount of inventory on hand.

Storage

Additional data or information is supplied from the records and/or files contained in the files and databases of the system, which can also be *updated* to reflect the new transaction input. *For exam-*

ple: Current credit balances of customers are supplied in response to inquiries from sales personnel. Also, credit sales transactions will increase customer credit balances.

Processing

Computer system hardware, software, and personnel *process* data resources resulting in an updated database and output of information products. *For example:* The computer systems, computer programs, and computer specialists of a regional computer center connected to POS terminals in retail stores supply the processing power for a sales processing system.

Output

Output can take the form of:

- **Reports.** Example: A sales analysis report outlining the sales made during a period by sales territory, product, and salesperson.
- **Documents.** Example: A paycheck or sales receipt.
- **Responses or displays.** Example: A CRT terminal displays the balance owed on a customer's account. Or the same information is transmitted to a telephone by a computer audio-response unit.
- **Control listings.** Example: Each time an employee paycheck is printed, a listing known as a *payroll register* is also printed and written on magnetic tape. This helps provide an "audit trail" for control purposes.
- **Input to other systems.** Example: Part of the output of a payroll system serves as input to a labor cost accounting system and the general ledger system of the firm.

Control

Input, processing, output, and storage *controls* are provided by the hardware, software, and personnel of the system. For example, computer hardware contains *error checking* circuitry; software includes *diagnostic program routines;* and *output* includes *control listings* which can be reviewed by audit personnel.

System Requirements Analysis

This is the most difficult step of systems analysis. First, you must try to determine what your (or the users) specific information needs are. (Sometimes called *needs analysis* or *user-requirements analy-*

sis). Second, you must try to determine the information processing capabilities needed for each system function (input, processing output, storage, control) to meet these information needs. (Sometimes called *functional requirements analysis*.) Finally, you should try to develop **logical** system requirements. That means you should not tie your analysis to the **physical** resources of hardware, software, and people that might be used. That's a job for the systems design stage. The difficulty of the requirements analysis step is one of the major reasons for the development of alternative methods of systems development, such as packaged systems and prototyping. We'll discuss very shortly several tools to help you develop logical systems requirements.

The focus of requirements analysis must be on the information requirements of the prospective users of the new system. Users must answer the question: "What information is *really needed* for decision making or other purposes?" Thus users and systems analysts must distinguish between the information *requirements* and the information *preferences* of the users of the proposed system; between *essential* information and *unwanted* or *unnecessary* information. The development of management information and decision support systems requires that systems analysis focus on the information requirements of decisions that must be made within the organization. Of course, the information requirements of an organization cannot be limited to just a decision-making focus. Organizations also require information for historical, legal, and operational purposes. *For example*: Payroll tax information must be supplied to government agencies, financial information to stockholders, and sales information to customers.

System Requirements Report

For large systems projects, the system requirements are documented in a *system requirements report* that is the final step of systems analysis. Such a report should provide a detailed description of the information needs of users and the logical input/output, processing, storage, and control requirements of the proposed system. Written descriptions, data flow diagrams, system flowcharts, input/output and storage descriptions, data dictionaries, and other tools are used to document these requirements. The kinds of input data available, the contents of necessary databases or files, the control considerations required, the types of information output needs, and processing requirements, such as volumes, frequencies, and turnaround times must be described and illustrated. However,

FIGURE

17–14 System
requirements

Input Requirements
  Source, content, format, organization, volume (average and peak), frequency,
  codes, and capture and conversion requirements.

Output Requirements
  Format, organization, volume (average and peak), frequency, copies, user destinations, timing, and retention required.

Processing Requirements
  Basic information processing activities required to transform input into output. Decision rules, models, and analytical techniques. Capacity, throughput, turnaround
  time, and response time needed.

Storage Requirements
  Organization, content, and size of the database, types and frequency of updating
  and inquiries, and the length and rationale for record retention or deletion.

Control Requirements
  Accuracy, validity, safety, security, integrity, and adaptability requirements for system input, processing, output, and storage functions.

whether or not a formal report is produced, systems analysis
should determine system requirements such as those outlined in
Figure 17–14.

SYSTEMS DESIGN

Systems analysis describes **what** a system should do to meet
the information needs of users. **Systems design** specifies **how**
the system will accomplish this objective. Systems design involves
developing both a *logical* and *physical* design for an information
system that meets the *system requirements* developed in systems
analysis. **Logical systems design** involves developing general
specifications for how the basic information processing system functions of input, processing, output, storage, and control can meet
user requirements. **Physical systems design** involves the detailed
design of input/output methods and media, data bases, and processing procedures. Personnel, equipment, and software specifications are also developed for the proposed system. Designing an
efficient, economical, and effective system for major information
processing jobs is a challenging assignment. Of course for smaller
individual-user type jobs, systems design frequently consists of the
development and revision of a prototype of an information processing system.

REAL WORLD APPLICATION 17–2

The Case against the Traditional Systems Study

EXHIBIT ONE

Interviewer: What do you think is going wrong with information systems in other organizations?

Information Center Manager: I guess one thing is studying it too long.

Interviewer: So you're saying "Don't study it; get on with it."

Information Center Manager: Yes. It's often delegated down to an analyst to go and study the users' needs: what they want and don't want. They do an elaborate study that gives minimal feedback, particularly if it's in the hands of someone who does not have a great deal of experience in understanding what managers may or may not want. So they're speculating about what the needs may or may not be, which is kind of what happened with the MIS direction in the early 1970s.

Instead of that we provide the users with tools and a service. We can convert and load up any information they ask for if it's in electronic form. The time taken to get the service in action is much less than the time some people take to do a study which does not reveal the true users' needs. We add to the available data quickly as the users' needs change. The needs or perceived needs change all the time.

EXHIBIT TWO

DP Executive: We all work in different ways. You could brainstorm for years trying to find out what is the right way. The best approach is to get some people using the tools and see how they feel. You adapt to some of their feelings. Sometimes they say "No. That's no good," and that's useful feedback.

One of the reasons why this is practical now is that we've been able to get these tools into people's hands within days rather than going away for two years to develop a major system and then decide. We put up a tool and test it on the users in a few weeks. It is better to do this than to conduct a detailed study, because the study would take longer.

EXHIBIT THREE

Information Center Executive: People have got to get past the stage of becoming comfortable with the tool. Once it is a habit, like the telephone, something changes. They start to think up new ways to use it to enhance their work or how their area works. And that is infectious.

They've all got to go through the struggling transition phases, and then all of a sudden you've got everyone out there creatively thinking how to use the tools better. That's an extraordinary benefit in system development. It's light years away from what we accomplished with structured analysis.

- What major criticisms of traditional systems studies are expressed by the three information services executives?
- What benefits of a computer-assisted systems development process are revealed?
- Should all feasibility studies and systems analysis activities be abandoned? Explain.

Source: Adapted from James Martin, *Application Development without Programmers* (Englewood Cliffs, N.J.: Prentice-Hall, 1982), pp. 320–22. Reprinted by permission.

Structured Design

Systems design involves a **top-down structured approach** in designing major new systems. Structured design moves in a top-down process from (1) the development of alternative *logical design concepts,* to (2) the development of a *logical system design,* to (3) the design of the components of the *physical system,* and finally to (4) the development of *systems specifications* for the developed system. This process is applied to each of the major *subsystems* or *modules* that make up the system being developed. The tools that are used to design how available data will be transformed into required information by the new system will be discussed shortly. Detailed written and graphic **system specifications** are developed that outline the *input, processing, output, storage,* and *control functions,* and the *hardware, software, personnel* and *data resources* of the proposed system. The systems design stage can be structured into the three major steps illustrated in Figure 17–15 (unless a prototyping approach is used instead).

Logical System Design

Early in the systems investigation stage, **logical design** concepts were developed that were a *rough* or *general* idea of the basic components and flows of the proposed information system. Several alternative logical design concepts may have been developed before a single basic concept was tentatively selected. In the systems design stage, the logical design concepts are refined and finalized by a thorough analysis of alternative design concepts and their effect on the system's requirements.

Logical system design should also include the consideration of an *ideal system* and alternative *realistic systems.* Developing general specifications of an **ideal system** encourages users and systems analysts to be creative and emphasizes that meeting the information requirements of the organization is the primary goal of systems analysis and design. On the other hand, the development of **alternative realistic systems** encourages users and analysts to be flexible and realistic and emphasizes that several ways must be found to meet systems requirements, while taking into account the limited financial, personnel and other resources of most organizations.

Trade-offs may have to be made between various system design criteria. *For example;* management may demand that inventory "stockouts" never occur, which would override the criterion of minimizing inventory costs. Some criteria, on the other hand, can be adjusted to accommodate the requirements of other criteria. *For example*: The criterion of low input/output costs may be adjusted to accommodate the criterion of a user-friendly input/output interface.

FIGURE

17–15 Activities of the systems design stage

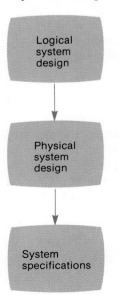

Physical System Design

Users and systems designers use their knowledge of business operations, information processing, and computer hardware and software to develop the **physical design** of an information system that meets the *system requirements* developed during the systems analysis stage. Obviously, they must relate their design to the *input, processing, output, storage,* and *control* functions of the proposed information system. They must specify what types of *hardware resources* (equipment and media), *software resources* (programs and procedures), and *people resources* (users and information systems staff) will be needed to transform *data resources* (stored in files and databases they design) into *information products* (displays, responses, reports and documents). If electronic information processing systems are to be used, they must specify the characteristics of batch processing and realtime processing systems, including the use of sequential access or direct-access files, database processing, data communications, and distributed processing networks.

System Specifications

The final step of the systems design stage is the development of the **system specifications.** For large projects, it takes the form of a report, which provides a description of the objectives and scope of the proposed system and a detailed description of the physical system design. It includes specifications for source documents, the database and output media, procedures for data preparation and collection, and information processing procedures, both manual and electronic. It includes specifications for the hardware and software that will be used by the new system, including *programming specifications,* which outline the requirements of programs that will be developed by the user organization. See Figure 17–16.

Tools of Analysis and Design

Now that we have explained the basic concepts of *logical* and *physical* analysis and design, it is time to discuss the *tools* you can use to help you perform these activities. Information collected during the feasibility study and systems analysis stages describe the information requirements of users and the input, processing, output, storage, and control components of the system being studied. After this information has been collected, it must be "analyzed and synthesized," using several tools of systems analysis and design which are summarized in Figure 17–17. Remember that such tools are used in every stage of system development—as analytical tools, design tools, and as documentation methods. For example, a flowchart can be used to *analyze* an existing system, express the *design* of a new system, and provide the *documentation* method for a newly developed system.

FIGURE

17–16 Contents of a system specifications report

System Description
The objectives, constraints, requirements, structure, and flows of the system.

Software Specifications
The required software components and the computer programming specifications of the proposed system.

Input/Output Specifications
The content, organization, and format of input/output media, and such methods as video displays, audio responses, forms, documents, reports.

Database Specifications
Content, organization format, media, distribution, and access, response, maintenance, and retention capabilities.

Hardware and Facilities Specifications
The physical and performance characteristics of the equipment and facilities required by the proposed system.

Personnel Specifications
Job descriptions of persons who will operate the system.

Procedures Manuals
Specific instructions for the personnel who will operate or use the proposed system.

FIGURE

17–17 Tools of systems analysis and design

- **System Flowcharts.** Graphically portray the flow of data media and the information processing procedures that take place in an information system. See Figure 17–19.
- **Data Flow Diagrams.** Portray the logical flow of data in a system without specifying the media or hardware involved. See Figure 17–20.
- **System Function Diagrams.** Identify the input, processing, output, storage, and control features of an information system. See Figures 17–1 and 17–13.
- **Grid Charts.** Identify each type of data element and information in the system and whether it is present in the form of input, output, and/or storage media. They are often used to identify redundant data elements and can result in the consolidation and elimination of forms, files, and reports. See Figure 17–18.
- **Structure Charts.** Show the flow of data and data processing tasks in a hierarchical "tree" structure of data processing "modules." See Chapter Eight, Figure 8–9.
- **HIPO Charts.** Show the input/processing/output characteristics of various system modules. See Chapter Eight, Figure 8–10.
- **Decision Tables.** Identify the conditional decision logic of the information system. See Chapter Eight, Figure 8–21.
- **Layout Forms.** Show the content and format of input/output and storage media. See Chapter Eight, Figure 8–11.
- **Other Tools and Techniques.** Many other types of graphic, quantitative, and written analysis can be used, such as organization charts, position descriptions, mathematical models, statistical sampling, financial statements and reports, work distribution charts, and forms that describe the content and format of data records, data files, documents, and reports.

FIGURE

17–18 A grid chart

REPORTS, DOCUMENTS, AND FILES / DATA ITEMS	Order acknowledgment	Shipping papers	Invoice	Sales by customer report	Customer credit report	Customer master file	Etc.
Customer number	√	√	√	√	√	√	
Customer name	√	√	√	√	√	√	
Customer address	√	√	√			√	
Discount code			√			√	
Credit code				√	√	√	
Salesperson name	√			√		√	
Etc.							

System Flowcharts

Figure 17–19(A) shows how a **system flowchart** is used as a tool for the **analysis** of an existing **physical** sales processing system. It graphically portrays the flow of data media and the major information processing tasks that take place. Notice how the flowchart symbols indicate the physical equipment and media (hardware) used for input, output, and storage. *For example*: Symbols and labels indicate the use of many paper documents and reports, a key-to-tape data entry device, and magnetic tape storage media.

Now look at Figure 17–19(B). It also is a system flowchart, but it is being used to illustrate the **physical design** of a new system to replace the system illustrated in Figure 17–19(A). Notice how it shows an online data entry terminal, magnetic disk storage, and several printed reports. This is obviously a physical design, because the hardware devices and media that will be used in the new system are specified. Refer back to Chapter Eight, Figure 8–13 for more examples and explanations of flowchart symbols.

Data Flow Diagrams

Figure 17–20(A) and (B) shows how a **data flow diagram** (DFD) is used as a tool for both **logical analysis** (17–20A) and **logical design** (17–20B). Notice that both portray the logical flow of data in each sales processing system without specifying the media and equipment involved. These DFDs only illustrate the *logical relationships* among *data, flows, sources, destinations,* and *stores*. The

FIGURE 17–19 Using system flowcharts

A. ANALYSIS OF THE
   PRESENT PHYSICAL SYSTEM

B. DESIGN OF THE
   PROPOSED PHYSICAL
   SYSTEM

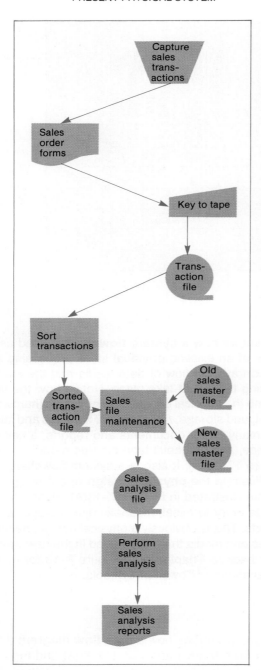

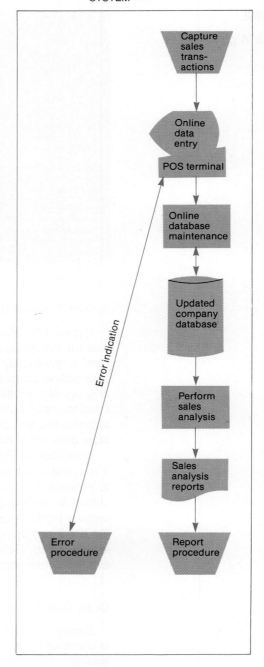

FIGURE 17–20 Using data flow diagrams

A. ANALYSIS OF THE PRESENT LOGICAL SYSTEM

B. DESIGN OF THE PROPOSED LOGICAL SYSTEM

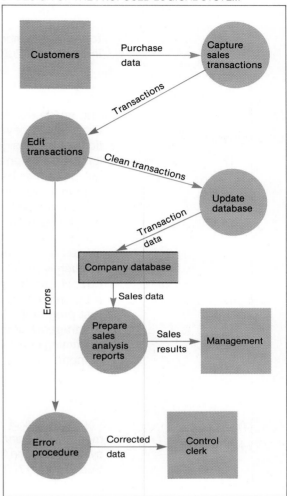

C. BASIC DFD SYMBOLS

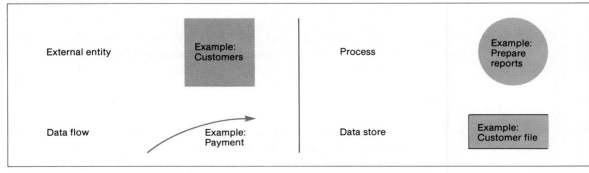

four basic symbols used in data flow diagrams are also explained in Figure 17–20(C).

SOFTWARE DEVELOPMENT

The **software development** stage involves the programming process, which develops computer programs that meet the specifications of the design stage (described in detail in Chapter 8). However, it must be emphasized that the programming stage requires continual interaction between computer users, systems analysts, and programmers who may be part of a *systems development project team* for a large system. The system specifications and system design developed by the project team may be continually refined and revised during the programming, implementation, and maintenance stages of systems development. Programmers may have to confer frequently with the other members of the project team as they dig deeper into the processing procedures and logic required by the programming specifications and when they attempt to debug and test programs. Obviously, the use of application generators and fourth-generation languages that support computer-assisted programming both simplifies and automates this stage of systems development.

SYSTEMS IMPLEMENTATION

The activities of *systems implementation* involve the testing, documenting, acquiring, installing, and operation of a newly designed system, and the training of personnel to operate and use the system. See Figure 17–21.

Planning

This activity involves the development of plans, procedures, and schedules for training, testing, acquisition, and installation. Such planning is usually part of a "project management" effort, which plans and controls the progress of information systems development projects.

Acquisition

The first step of the *acquisition* process is an evaluation of the proposals of manufacturers and other suppliers who furnish the hardware and software components required by the system specifications. (The software to be acquired are programs that will not be developed by the computer-users' own programmers.) The com-

FIGURE

17–21 Activities of the systems implementation stage

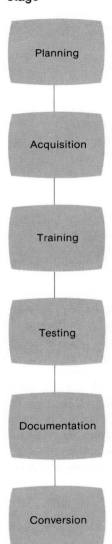

puter-user must choose from among many different models and suppliers of hardware and software components. The evaluation and acquisition of such computer resources is discussed in the next chapter.

Training

Implementation of a new system involves *orientation and training* of management, users, and operating personnel, and the "selling" of the new system to each of these groups. Users and operating personnel must be trained in specific skills to operate and use the system. If an adequate job of management and user involvement in systems development has been accomplished, the "shock effect" of transferring to a new system should be minimized. If user representatives participated in the development of the system, the problems of installation, conversion, and training should be minimized.

Testing

Systems implementation requires the *testing* of the newly designed and programmed system. This involves not only the testing and debugging of all computer programs but the testing of all other data processing procedures, including the production of test copies of reports and other output that should be reviewed by the users of the proposed systems for possible errors. System modules can also be tested by using such methods as the *structured walkthroughs* discussed in Chapter Eight. Testing does not only occur during the system's implementation stage, but should occur throughout the system's development process. *For example:* Input documents and procedures can be tested before their final form is determined by allowing them to be examined and critiqued by users and operators of the proposed system.

Documentation

Systems documentation is an important process that uses the tools and techniques of systems analysis and design to *record* and *communicate* the activities and results of each stage of information system development. Proper documentation allows management to monitor the progress of the project and to minimize the problems that arise when changes are made in systems design. Documentation serves as a method of communication between the personnel that are responsible for a project. It is also vital for proper implementation and maintenance, since installing and operating a newly designed system or modifying an established system requires a

FIGURE

17–22 Outlines of system documentation manuals

System Manual	User Manual
System summary	System summary
Organizational requirements	Operating schedule
Hardware and software specifications	Operating procedures
Input data definition	Input/output descriptions
Output data definition	Job descriptions
Database definition	System controls
Index of computer programs	Sample forms and reports
Computer operations summary	
Manual processing procedures	
Sample forms and reports	

detailed record of the systems design. Figure 17–22 outlines the types of documentation needed by systems analysts and users that can be consolidated into "documentation manuals."

Conversion

The initial operation of a new computer-based system can be a difficult task. Such an operation is usually a *conversion process* in which the personnel, procedures, equipment, input/output forms, and database of an old information system must be converted to the requirements of a new system. However, conversion problems should be minimized if an adequate job of systems analysis and design has been performed. Conversion can be done on a *parallel* basis, whereby both the old and the new system are operated until the project development team and user-management agree to switch completely over to the new system. It is during this time that the operations and results of both systems are compared and evaluated. Errors can be identified and corrected, and the operating problems can be solved before the old system is abandoned. Installation can also be accomplished by a direct *cut over* to the newly developed system, or on a *phased* basis, where only a few departments, branch offices, or plant locations at a time are converted. A phased conversion allows a gradual implementation process to take place within an organization.

SYSTEMS MAINTENANCE

Systems maintenance is the monitoring, evaluating, and modifying of a system to make desirable or necessary improvements. This includes monitoring the progress of the other stages of systems development to insure that the development plan and objectives are being accomplished. *For example:* Errors in the development,

REAL WORLD APPLICATION 17–3

RCA Corporation

In moving from the development phase into the manufacturing phase of the VideoDisc system, RCA's VideoDisc operations management, engineering, and manufacturing staffs required more and better information so a high-quality product could be released on schedule. To do this, computer programs and complete information systems had to be designed, coded, tested, and implemented in a very short time with a small programming staff and at minimal cost.

We found this could be done by using a database management system called FOCUS on the RCA time-sharing network at Cherry Hill, New Jersey. FOCUS is a member of the latest (fourth-generation) computer software.

The implementation of a new computer information system requires a development phase and then an operations phase once the system is ready. For the development phase, schedules, programmers training, preliminary studies, system design, program coding and maintenance, and costs must be considered. For day-to-day operations, required user-training, response time for reports, flexibility both for standard reports and special requests, ease of loading new data and changing existing data, and costs should be projected.

When using traditional methods, the current operations are studied, forms and reports are analyzed, costs are estimated, and the requirements for the new system are formulated. Then the system itself is designed, and file and report forms are drawn. If the user agrees to the design, the program specifications are written and the system is ready to be programmed. Once the programming has started, it is usually very difficult to make any changes to the system. Even small changes will have a major impact upon the completion date and development costs.

A new way of thinking is required when using FOCUS, beginning with the preliminary study and the system design. When using FOCUS, most of the above steps can be shortened, combined, or eliminated. For a FOCUS study, the first thing is to determine exactly what data are available. Next, a preliminary file organization is decided upon. Finally, a new database is created, load programs are written, data are loaded into the database and sample reports are generated. It is easier to create the database, load data, and write sample reports than it is to draw sample-report forms. Not only does the user have the advantage of looking at final reports but the programmer has already run a pilot project that could not have been run at all with traditional methods. If changes are requested, the programmer can easily change the reports, or, if necessary, the database structure. Also, since a large FOCUS database can be split into small systems, or vice versa, it is not even necessary to know what other systems may be added later.

FOCUS has been a tremendous tool for Product Assurance. If it had not been available, the work could not have been done as effectively with FORTRAN or COBOL even if many more people had been hired. Time and costs for program and systems development were reduced by 90 percent. Maintenance of existing programs was reduced by 98 percent. Flexibility and response to special requests were greatly increased; the timely use of the FOCUS database systems provided significant information in many decision-making processes.

- How is the traditional systems development process changed when using a tool like FOCUS? Is any stage eliminated? Explain.
- What benefits were derived from using FOCUS for systems development?

Source: W. W. Meyers, "Computer Programming and Systems Analysis in the Rapidly Changing VideoDisk Environment," *RCA Engineer,* July–August 1982. Used with permission.

operation, or use of the system must be corrected by the maintenance activity. Installation of a new system usually results in the phenomenon known as the *learning curve*. Personnel who operate and use the system will make mistakes simply because they are not familiar with it. However, such errors diminish as experience is gained with a new system. Maintenance is also necessary for unexpected failures and problems that arise during the operation of a system. Systems maintenance personnel must then perform a *trouble shooting* function to determine the causes and solutions to a particular problem.

The systems maintenance activity requires a periodic review or *audit* of a system to ensure that it is operating properly and meeting its objectives. This activity is in addition to a continual monitoring of a new system. Systems maintenance also includes making modifications to a system due to changes within the business organization or in the business environment.

SUMMARY

- Users and systems analysts should use a systems approach to help them create or improve computer- based information systems. This means having a viewpoint that looks for systems, subsystems, and components of systems in any information processing situation. They should especially look for the basic system functions of input, processing, output, storage, and control.

- However, the systems approach also means using a systematic process to create computer-based information systems, known as information systems development. The traditional information systems development cycle can be subdivided into stages of systems investigation; analysis, design, programming, implementation, and maintenance.

- The process of developing computer-based information systems is changing due to problems with traditional systems development and the growth of user-driven computing. Computer-assisted systems development methods, such as prototyping and user-developed systems, are replacing or changing many of the activities of the traditional systems development cycle.

- The traditional systems investigation stage includes the conducting of a feasibility study to determine the economic, technological, and operational feasibility of a proposed information system. The determination of economic feasibility requires a cost/benefit analysis, which focuses on the tangible and intangible costs and benefits that would result from the implementation of a proposed system.

- Systems analysis involves an in-depth analysis of the information needs of users. Its objective is to determine the information requirements and other logical system requirements of a proposed information system after analyzing the organization and its information requirements. Much of this can now be accomplished in an interactive computer- assisted prototyping process by users and systems analysts.

- Systems design is a stage of information systems development, which involves the logical and physical design of an information system that meets the systems requirements developed in the systems analysis stage. It develops specifications for a proposed system that specify the hardware, software, database, procedures, and personnel to be used by the system. Again, much of this can now be the result of a computer-assisted prototyping process.

- Once the steps of system analysis, systems design, and programming are accomplished in traditional systems development, a system is implemented by: (1) evaluating, acquiring, and installing necessary hardware and software; (2) selecting and training required personnel; (3) testing the new system; (4) completing the documentation for the new system; and (5) operating the new system; which may include converting from a previous system to the new system. Finally, the systems maintenance activity assures the continual monitoring, evaluating, and improvement of established systems.

- In traditional systems development, information about present and proposed information systems is collected by personal interviews, questionnaires, personal observations, and examination of documents and reports. This information is then analyzed and synthesized, using various tools and techniques of systems analysis and design, such as system flowcharts, data flow diagrams, layout forms, and grid charts.

KEY TERMS AND CONCEPTS

Systems approach
Systems development cycle
Information systems
  development
User involvement
User-developed systems
Prototyping
Computer-assisted systems
  development
Systems investigation
Feasibility study
Economic feasibility
Technological feasibility
Operational feasibility
Tangible/intangible costs
Tangible/intangible benefits

Return on investment
Cost/benefit analysis
Systems analysis
Systems design
Structured analysis
Structured design
Logical versus physical
  systems design
Organization analysis
Requirements analysis
System requirements
System specifications
Tools of systems analysis
  and design
Systems implementation
Systems maintenance

REVIEW AND APPLICATION QUESTIONS

1. What is systems analysis and design? Why is it necessary for the development of computer-based information systems?
2. How does one use the systems "approach" as a systems "viewpoint," and as a systems "process"?

3. Outline the stages of the traditional information systems development cycle. Are all of these steps really necessary?
4. What changes are occurring in information systems development? What are the reasons for such changes?
5. What is computer-assisted systems development? Explain its benefits and limitations.
6. How is prototyping applied to information systems development?
7. Why is user involvement important in systems analysis and design? How is it accomplished?
8. What is the purpose of the systems investigation stage of systems development? What activities are involved in this stage?
9. What is a feasibility study? What are some of the basic characteristics of information systems that must be analyzed in a feasibility study?
10. What are some of the potential costs and benefits of computer-based information systems?
11. What methods of achieving economic feasibility are emphasized by the return-on-investment concept of cost/benefit analysis?
12. What are the purpose and the activities of systems analysis? Use examples to illustrate several of these activities.
13. Explain the difference between a "physical" system and a "logical" system.
14. What are the purpose and the activities of systems design?
15. What is the difference in the purpose and content of system requirements and system specifications?
16. How is information required for systems analysis and design gathered?
17. What are some of the tools and techniques of systems analysis and design?
18. What are the purpose and the activities required by the systems implementation stage of information systems development?
19. What is systems maintenance? Why is it important to the development of effective information systems?
20. Can the tools of systems analysis and design be used as analytical tools, design tools, and documentation methods? Explain.

APPLICATION PROBLEMS

1. If you have not already done so, answer the questions after each Real World Application in this chapter.
2. Identify which statement below is most closely related to the concepts of (a) the systems approach as a viewpoint, (b) the systems approach as a process, (c) systems development with

prototyping, (*d*) user-developed systems, (*e*) user-driven computing.

(1) "We need intelligent workstations, systems development packages, and information centers."

(2) "Let's build a quick and dirty working model and try it out to see what changes are needed."

(3) "You had better show how we are going to handle the input, processing, output, storage, and control functions of this application."

(4) "First you had better do a feasibility study, then determine the system requirements, develop the system specifications, then program, install, and maintain the system."

(5) "I'm not sure exactly what information I want from the computer. Even if I did, I'd probably change my mind on what I wanted and how I wanted it in a few months."

3. Apply the system concept expressed in Figure 17–1. That is, identify several input, processing, output, storage, and control considerations of systems analysis and design. Use examples drawn from the business computer applications discussed in Chapters Fifteen and Sixteen to illustrate such considerations. *For example*, what do you think would be some input, processing, output, storage, and control considerations for a retail POS system, a manufacturing process control system, an automated bank teller machine system, a payroll system, etc.? Draw and label a system function diagram (like Figure 17–1) to organize and illustrate your answers.

4. Jim Shannon, systems analyst, was given the title of project manager to develop a new payroll system. He thought his first step should be to interview the head of the payroll department. When he met with Sara Henna, payroll manager, the first thing he asked for was an organization chart and current procedure manuals and user system documentation. Sara informed him that those items were not readily available, but she could have them for him in about a week. Not having reviewed the system documentation on the current system and now having no user documentation to discuss, Jim thought it best to reschedule another meeting with Sara in two weeks. Jim left Sara's office wondering how this two-week delay in his preliminary investigation would affect the total project. What could Jim have done to better prepare for his interview with Sara?

5. Assume a company currently has a payroll and labor analysis application as described in Chapter Sixteen. You are a systems analyst and are assigned the task of developing a cost/benefit analysis for upgrading the current system to a Personnel Information System as was described in Chapter Fifteen. Identify several

tangible and intangible costs and benefits associated with upgrading the current system. Do not assign dollar amounts.

6. Develop a system flowchart and a data flow diagram that express the flow of information processing activities as you see them in one or more of the following systems:

    a. The sales transaction processing system of ABC Department Stores described in Real World Application 2–1 of Chapter Two.

    b. The order processing/inventory control/customer inquiry system of Western Engine Company described in Real World Application 16–1 of Chapter Sixteen.

    c. One of the business information systems described in Chapters Fifteen and Sixteen. You will have to make several assumptions about how information processing activities are accomplished. Choose an application you are most familiar with.

PART
6

INFORMATION RESOURCE MANAGEMENT

CHAPTER 18

Acquiring Information System Resources

CHAPTER OUTLINE

THE COMPUTER-BASED BUSINESS
ENVIRONMENT
THE COMPUTER INDUSTRY
  Hardware Suppliers
  Software Suppliers
  External Service Suppliers
  Reasons for External Services
EVALUATING COMPUTER ACQUISITIONS
  Hardware Evaluation Factors
  Software Evaluation Factors
  Evaluation of Vendor Support
FINANCING COMPUTER ACQUISITIONS
  Rental
  Purchase
  Leasing
THE COST OF INFORMATION SYSTEM
RESOURCES
  Controlling Computer Costs

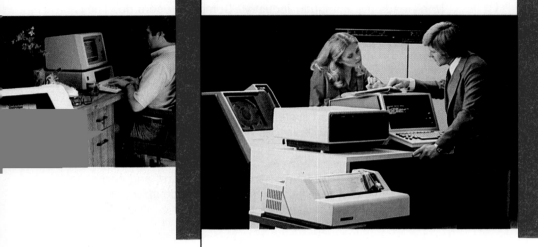

LEARNING OBJECTIVES

The purpose of this chapter is to promote a basic understanding of how computer resources should be acquired by business firms by analyzing (1) the role of the computer industry, (2) the evaluation of computer acquisitions, and (3) the financing and cost of computer resources. After reading and studying this chapter you should be able to:

1. Identify several types of firms in the computer industry and the products or services they supply.
2. Identify several benefits and limitations of using external information processing services.
3. Discuss several evaluation factors that should be considered in evaluating hardware, software, and vendor support.
4. Summarize the benefits and limitations of the rental, leasing, and purchase of computer resources.
5. Describe several major categories of information systems costs and identify several specific costs in each category.
6. Identify several methods of controlling the cost of systems development and computer operations.

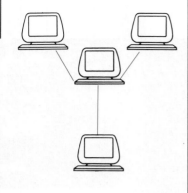

Who needs the computer industry? Computer users do. They must acquire **information system resources** (hardware, software, and personnel) and **external services** from many sources in the **computer industry**. Therefore, you should have a basic understanding and appreciation of the role of the computer industry. In this chapter we shall explore the important segments and services of the computer industry and discuss how you should evaluate the acquisition of information system resources and services. In the next two chapters, we will discuss how such resources should be managed. Thus the last three chapters of this text are dedicated to the concept of **information resource management**, which views data, information and computer hardware, software, and personnel as valuable organizational resources that should be effectively managed for the benefit of the entire organization.

THE COMPUTER-BASED BUSINESS ENVIRONMENT

The use of computers in business does not take place in a vacuum. The business firm is a system that interacts with many other systems in its environment. The computer operations of a business firm should thus be viewed as taking place in a "computer-based business environment." See Figure 18–1.

The computer hardware, software, and personnel resources of a business firm provide information services to *internal computer users*, that is, the departments in the firm that require electronic information processing. Outside of the business firm is the *computer industry*, which includes computer manufacturers, other hardware and software companies, and the suppliers of other computer-related services, such as computer service bureaus and time-sharing service companies. The information services department of a business firm relies heavily on the *hardware, software*, and *services* supplied by the computer industry. Beyond this ring of computer-support organizations are *external computer users in society*, such as customers, other business firms, governmental units, and the general public. These external groups provide input or use output produced by the computer-based information systems of the business firm or are affected in some way by the business uses of computers.

THE COMPUTER INDUSTRY

Business managers cannot effectively use their computer resources unless they have a basic understanding of the computer industry. Therefore, you should view the computer industry as a vital source of **computer hardware, software, and services**. Your

FIGURE 18–1 The computer-based business environment

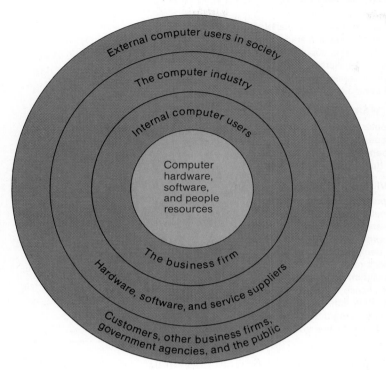

External computer users in society

The computer industry

Internal computer users

Computer hardware, software, and people resources

The business firm

Hardware, software, and service suppliers

Customers, other business firms, government agencies, and the public

effective and efficient use of computers by computer users requires the continual support of firms within the computer industry. Figure 18–2 groups the major types of firms within the computer industry into the three major categories of hardware suppliers, software suppliers, and service suppliers.

Though the computer industry consists of over 5,000 companies, only a few firms manufacture **mainframe** computers. They include the International Business Machines Corporation (IBM, which has a major share of the market for computers—defined as the dollar value of computers installed in the United States), Digital Equipment Corporation (DEC), Burroughs Corporation, Control Data Corporation (CDC), National Cash Register (NCR), the Univac Division of the Sperry Corporation, and Honeywell Information Systems.

Of course, the development of minicomputers and microcomputers has greatly increased the number of companies manufacturing computers. Important manufacturers in the **microcomputer** system and personal computer market include Apple Computer Inc., the Radio Shack Division of Tandy Corporation, and Commodore Business Machines, along with larger firms, such as IBM and Hewlett-

FIGURE

18–2 The computer
industry

HARDWARE SUPPLIERS

Computer manufacturers.
Independent peripheral manufacturers.
Original equipment manufacturers.
Data processing supplies companies.
Computer retailers.
Computer leasing companies.
Used-computer equipment companies.

SOFTWARE SUPPLIERS

Computer manufacturers.
Computer retailers.
Independent software companies.
User-developed software suppliers.

SERVICE SUPPLIERS

Computer manufacturers.
Computer service centers.
Time-sharing service companies.
Telecommunications service suppliers.
Data bank service suppliers.
Facilities management companies.
Independent consultants.
Other service suppliers:
    computer time rental, systems design services,
    contract programming, education,
    hardware maintenance, turnkey systems.

Packard, and a host of smaller firms. **Minicomputers** and small business computers are manufactured by the major computer manufacturers as well as many other companies, including Hewlett-Packard, AT&T, Datapoint, Texas Instruments, Data General, Wang Laboratories, and Prime Computer.

Figure 18–3 lists the top 10 mainframe, microcomputer, minicomputer, and office system manufacturers. Of course, there are many other firms in the computer industry that supply hardware, software, and services. For example, large companies such as Intel, Motorola, and National Semiconductor produce microprocessors, memory chips, and other devices. Companies like Management Science America, Lotus Development, Ashton-Tate, and Microsoft are major software suppliers. Finally, firms such as Automatic Data Processing, Electronic Data Systems, TRW, and Martin Marietta are examples of major suppliers of external computing services.

Hardware Suppliers

The primary sources of computer hardware are the major computer manufacturers, who manufacture many sizes of computer systems, as well as peripheral equipment and data processing supplies.

FIGURE 18–3 The top 10 mainframe, mini, micro, and office system companies

MAINFRAME SYSTEMS

Rank	Company	Revenues ($ millions)
1	IBM	$11,443.6
2	Burroughs Corp.	2,000.0
3	Honeywell, Inc.	1,020.1
4	NCR Corp.	1,000.0
5	Control Data Corp.	775.0
6	Sperry Corp.	700.0
7	Amdahl Corp.	570.7
8	National Semiconductor	200.5
9	Cray Research, Inc.	169.7
10	Nixdorf Computer Corp.	141.1

MICROCOMPUTER SYSTEMS

Rank	Company	Revenues ($ millions)
1	IBM	$2,600.0
2	Apple Computer, Inc.	1,084.7
3	Commodore	926.7
4	Tandy Corp.	598.0
5	Hewlett-Packard Co.	399.4
6	Digital Equipment Corp.	300.0
7	Texas Instruments, Inc.	150.0
8	Compaq Computer Corp.	111.2
9	Wang Laboratories, Inc.	100.0
10	NCR Corp.	83.2

MINICOMPUTER SYSTEMS

Rank	Company	Revenues ($ millions)
1	Digital Equipment Corp.	$2,700.0
2	IBM	2,627.0
3	Burroughs Corp.	950.0
4	Wang Laboratories, Inc.	892.9
5	Hewlett-Packard Co.	736.3
6	Data General Corp.	705.0
7	Prime Computer, Inc.	416.5
8	Tandem Computers, Inc.	400.0
9	Gould, Inc.	334.0
10	Honeywell, Inc.	330.0

OFFICE SYSTEMS

Rank	Company	Revenues ($ millions)
1	IBM	$1,600.0
2	Wang Laboratories, Inc.	800.0
3	Motorola, Inc.	287.8
4	Harris Corp.	275.0
5	Burroughs Corp.	250.0
6	Xerox Corp.	230.0
7	Digital Equipment Corp.	200.0
8	Exxon Office Systems, Inc.	200.0
9	CPT Corp.	192.1
10	Philips Info. Systems	175.0

Source: Adapted from Pamela Archbold, "The Datamation 100," *Datamation*, June 1, 1984, pp. 54–60. Reprinted with permission of *Datamation* magazine. Copyright by Technical Publishing Company, a Dun & Bradstreet Company, 1984; all rights reserved.

Other computer manufacturers may produce microcomputers, mini-computers, small computer systems, special-purpose computers, and a few types of peripheral devices. Other hardware suppliers can be classified as *independent peripheral manufacturers*. These firms confine themselves to the production of peripheral input, output, and storage equipment, such as video terminals or magnetic disk drives.

Two other categories of computer hardware manufacturers are the *original equipment manufacturer* (OEM) and the *plug compatible manufacturer* (PCM). OEMs manufacture and sell computers by assembling components produced by other hardware suppliers. PCMs manufacture computer mainframes and peripheral devices that are specifically designed to be compatible (by just "plugging in") to the mainframes or peripherals of major computer manufacturers, especially IBM. Such firms claim that their hardware is similar to that produced by IBM or other major manufacturers but provide better performance at lower cost. For example, the Amdahl Corporation and the National Advanced Systems Company produce large mainframe computers that are marketed as lower-priced versions of IBM mainframes.

Computer retailers sell microcomputers and peripherals to individuals and small businesses. They are an important type of hardware supplier resulting from the development of microcomputer systems used as personal computers and small business computers. Thousands of retail computer stores include independent retailers, national chains such as Computerland and The Computer Store, and some outlets owned by computer manufacturers, including Radio Shack, IBM, and Digital Equipment Corporation.

Other important sources of computer hardware are computer leasing companies, who purchase computers from computer manufacturers and lease them to computer users at rates that may be 10 to 20 percent lower than the manufacturer's rental price. Leasing companies are able to offer lower prices because they are willing to gamble that they can recover their costs and make a profit at the lower rates before their computers become obsolete. A final source of computer hardware is used-computer-equipment companies, which purchase used computers and peripheral equipment from computer users and sell them at substantial discounts.

Software Suppliers

System software and *application software* can be obtained from several sources if computer users do not wish to develop their own programs. Computer manufacturers are the largest source of software in the computer industry. They supply most of the system software (such as operating systems and other control programs and service programs) for computer users and are the major source of application packages. However, independent software companies, which specialize in the development of software packages, have become major software suppliers. Software can also be obtained from computer retailers and from other computer users. "User-developed software suppliers" are computer users who have developed application programs or service programs that are marketed to other computer users.

External Service Suppliers

The five major sources of external information processing services are computer manufacturers, computer service centers, time-sharing companies, facilities management companies, and independent consultants. They and other types of firms in the computer industry offer a variety of services. For example: Off-premise computer processing of customer jobs, time-sharing services, computer-time rental, systems design services, contract programming, consulting, "turnkey" systems, education, and hardware maintenance are offered. Many companies, especially computer manufacturers, supply several or almost all of these services. The following is a summary of three of these services.

■ *Computer service centers* (or service bureaus) provide a variety of information processing services. They process the jobs of many small firms that do not wish to acquire their own computer systems. Larger computer users also use service bureaus to handle specialized applications (such as computer-output-microfilm) or when problem situations occur, such as peak volume periods or during periods of computer "down time."

■ *Time-sharing service companies* provide realtime processing services to many subscribers using remote terminals and a central computer system. Time-sharing service companies are used by many computer users who have specialized data processing needs that require realtime processing and a large computer system.

■ *Facilities management companies* are firms that take complete responsibility for a computer user's operation. Thus a business firm may "subcontract" all information processing service needs to an outside contractor. The facilities management firm might take over all computer facilities at the user's site, using its own hardware, software, and personnel.

External services are widely used by small firms and by firms that are using computer processing for the first time. However, the majority of computers in the United States are purchased or leased by organizations for their own use. The advent of economical and easy-to-use micro- and minicomputer systems should accelerate this development. To counteract this trend, computer service centers and consultants have begun to sell computer hardware, software, and systems development services to their customers. This includes the offering of *turnkey systems*, where all of the hardware, software, and systems development needed by a user are provided by the service supplier. Ideally, the user should merely have to "turn the key" to begin operating and using the system.

Reasons for External Services

The major benefit of using external service suppliers is that computer users pay only for the information processing services that they need. Purchasing or leasing computer hardware or software and employing a staff of information services professionals creates

REAL WORLD APPLICATION 18–1

IBM versus Apple: The Year that Was

INTERNATIONAL BUSINESS MACHINES
Old Orchard Road
Armonk, NY 10504
(914) 765-1900

IBM rode the recovery to yet another record year in 1983, this time with corporate revenues topping the $40 billion mark. Once again Big Blue was the most profitable manufacturer in the country, with net earnings up 24 percent to $5.5 billion. Because IBM does not report specific product revenues, the overall dp and product category revenue listed here represent Datamation estimates. In 1983, dp revenues rose 22 percent to $35.6 billion from $29.3 billion, with most business segments performing well.

It was one of the most eventful years in IBM's history. In February, chief executive officer John Opel succeeded Frank Cary as chairman of the board, and his influence was immediately felt. IBM pursued new and existing markets with vigor, continued its push to become the preeminent low-cost producer, chased some competitors into court, and embarked on ventures it had never before tried.

The company introduced several new processors during the year, beginning with the long-awaited System/36 in May. That machine replaced the most widely installed computer in IBM's history (PCs excepted), the Systems/34. IBM also brought out two high-end models of the 4300 mainframe line and new models in the System/38 and Series/1 lines.

But the most attention was paid to a rash of new products introduced in the PC line, which in January consisted of only one model. First came the PC XT, which was announced in March. That was followed by products that allowed 3270 terminals to act as PCs and vice versa, and in October, by the 3270 PC and the PC XT/370. Finally, in November, IBM admitted to the worst-kept secret of the year, the PCjr.

IBM also introduced the 5080 color graphics system, the Database 2 mainframe DBMS, several printers, the 4730 personal banking ATM, and the 7540 manufacturing system. The year also saw the first deliveries of two major IBM products, the 3084 top-end mainframe and the MVS/XA operating system.

IBM also came closer to its goal of being the industry's low-cost supplier. While revenues increased 17 percent and income 24 percent, the payroll grew only 1.4 percent, indicating IBM was able to earn significantly more money per employee than in the past.

When it wasn't premiering new products, IBM was suing competitors, such as Hitachi and National Advanced Systems on a variety of trade secrecy charges. Both companies eventually relented under the pressure of IBM's lawyers.

IBM also got under the skins of Intel and Rolm, but in a more positive vein. The company acquired substantial chunks of both Silicon Valley firms, the first such investments in IBM's history. At year-end, IBM owned close to 20 percent of each firm.

REAL WORLD APPLICATION 18–1 *(concluded)*

APPLE COMPUTER, INC.
10260 Bandely Drive
Cupertino, CA 95014
(408) 973-3145

Growing up is hard to do, and 1983 was a very difficult year for Apple. The goal for 1983 was to crack the IBM-dominated office market in a big way with Lisa, its $10,000 PC. The results are in, and Apple failed. In the process it lost its dominance of the PC market and posted a 17 percent decline in earnings. On the brighter side, Apple's Macintosh was introduced to mostly raves and may reverse a depressing 1983.

While 1983 revenues were impressive—a 64 percent increase to $1.08 billion—earnings began falling in the September quarter and fell even faster by December. For the calendar year, earnings were $59 million, down 17 percent from 1982.

The strategy for Lisa was simple, sell to the Fortune 1,000 companies. These customers were less than enchanted with Lisa's price/performance, however, as well as with Lisa's inability to connect with their dp departments. By September, Apple revised its plans and started pushing Lisa without its software and at a substantially reduced price. The strategy, effected by Apple's new national sales force, not only failed to stimulate business but upset the company's independent dealers. While Apple was struggling with its ill-suited product and poor marketing plan, IBM took over the market.

By November, newly appointed president John Scully from PepsiCo could see red ink. Reacting quickly, he developed, then announced, a long-term strategy. The main theme was a family of 32-bit micros marketed to smaller companies through the independent dealers. The next phase was to be a new 32-bit micro, which turned out to be Macintosh. Scully stressed the importance of building communication bridges for its computers to the IBM mainframe environment. In addition, he announced plans to introduce new products for the Apple IIe to take advantages of the installed base.

These plans seem more realistic than that of tackling the Fortune 1,000 with untested Lisa. Early indications are that Macintosh is now the number one PC, thanks to Scully's carefully laid out marketing plan, which featured an intimidating tv commercial that prompted an enormous number of sales the day Macintosh was released. To really do justice to many of the advanced third-party programs being written, larger memory and storage capacities are being added. (At first, the Mac came with only 128K memory and no hard disk storage.) Apparently, though, Apple is learning that the best route to profits is through keeping the customers happy, and that's what Mac seems to be doing.

■ Why was 1983 a good year for IBM but not for Apple?
■ What new products did these firms introduce? What strategies led to these product developments?
■ How are IBM and Apple doing now? (For example, IBM's PCjr did poorly, while Apple's Macintosh was a hit in 1984.) Check the latest June issue of *Datamation* that features "The Datamation 100."

Source: Pamela Archbold, "The Datamation 100," *Datamation*, June 1, 1984, pp. 66–74.

fixed costs, such as minimum machine rental payments, depreciation charges, and the salaries of professional and managerial information processing personnel. The use of external services also eliminates the personnel and management problems caused by the employment of a group of highly paid technical professionals in a rapidly changing and highly technical field, such as computers and information processing.

The management of many organizations use external services to avoid the problems that arise from having to manage computer hardware, software, or personnel. They may also turn to external services to avoid the problems of obsolescence caused by major changes in computer technology, or user needs. In some cases the cost of external services may be lower than if the computer-using firm performed its own information processing services. This may be due to "economies of scale," since a large information processing service company may use larger and more efficient computer hardware and software to serve its many customers.

External services do have several limitations. The loss of control over information processing procedures and confidential information is one limitation. Off-premise computer processing may be inconvenient. The cost of external services may be significantly higher in some cases, because the external service company must not only meet expenses but must include a profit in its fee to computer users. Many firms are unwilling to depend on an outsider to provide vital information processing services. They want to have more control over processing procedures, report deadlines, and changes in hardware, software, and processing schedules.

EVALUATING
COMPUTER
ACQUISITIONS

How do computer-using organizations evaluate and select hardware and software? Typically, they require manufacturers and suppliers to present bids and proposals based on *systems specifications* developed during the design stage of systems development. Minimum acceptable physical and performance characteristics for all hardware and software requirements are established. Most large business firms and all government agencies formalize these requirements by listing them in a document called a **RFP (request for proposal)** or **RFQ (request for quotation)**. The RFQ is then sent to appropriate vendors, who use it as the basis for preparing a proposed purchase agreement. See Figure 18–4.

A formal evaluation process reduces the possibility of buying inadequate or unnecessary computer hardware or software. This sometimes happens because computer users or computer specialists want to keep up with their competitors and with the latest devel-

FIGURE 18–4 Example of a request for quotation (RFQ)

ABC DEPARTMENT STORES INC.

PHONE (602)323-4557   BOX 5124   PHOENIX, ARIZONA 86581-0058

REQUEST FOR QUOTATION

0001	1	1
REQUEST NO.	PAGE	OF

1
  ACME COMPUTER SUPPLY CO.
  2704 E. MCDOWELL ROAD
  PHOENIX, ARIZONA 85283

2

3

TERMS: (1) YOU ARE INVITED TO BID ON GOODS AND/OR SERVICES ITEMIZED BELOW.
(2) THIS REQUEST FOR QUOTATION IS NOT INTENDED TO BE RESTRICTIVE. BRAND NAME OR MANUFACTURER'S NAME MAY BE USED FOR PURPOSE OF DESCRIPTION AND/OR TO ESTABLISH THE QUALITY DESIRED. BIDS ARE NOT RESTRICTED TO SUCH BRAND OR MANUFACTURER.
(3) THE ATTENTION OF THE BIDDER IS DIRECTED TO THE TERMS AND CONDITIONS ON THE REVERSE SIDE WHICH ARE INCORPORATED HEREIN.

WE RESERVE THE RIGHT TO REJECT ANY AND ALL BIDS.

RETURN THIS QUOTATION TO PURCHASING DEPT. AT ABOVE ADDRESS

DATE	BUYER	REQUISITION NO.		
6/24/8X	G. WILLIAMS	0001	QUOTATION DUE DATE	7/24/8X

LINE	OBJECT CODE	QUANTITY	UNIT	PART NUMBER AND DESCRIPTION	UNIT PRICE	AMOUNT
1	08561	10	1	IMPACT DOT MATRIX PRINTER		
				MINIMUM SPECIFICATIONS:		
				FULLY COMPATIBLE WITH IBM PERSONAL COMPUTER, PC-XT, PORTABLE PC, COMPAQ PORTABLE COMPUTER, TEXAS INSTRUMENTS PROFESSIONAL COMPUTER AND HEWLETT PACKARD HP 150 TOUCHSCREEN PERSONAL COMPUTER		
				PRINTING SPEED: 100 CHARACTERS PER SECOND		
				PAPER FEED SPEED: 200 MILLISECONDS PER LINE		
				PRINTING DIRECTION: BIDIRECTIONAL, LOGIC SEEKING		
				CHARACTER MATRICES: (298 TOTAL) 96 ROMAN CHARACTERS 96 ITALIC CHARACTERS 32 ROMAN INTERNATIONAL CHARACTERS 32 ITALIC INTERNATIONAL CHARACTERS 32 GRAPHICS CHARACTERS		
				PICA CHARACTER WIDTH AND HEIGHT: 2.1 x 3.1 mm		
				COLUMN WIDTH: 80 COLUMNS PICA		
				PAPER WIDTH: 4 INCHES TO 10 INCHES ADJUSTABLE		
				PAPER FEED: ADJUSTABLE SPROCKET FEED		
				PRINT HEAD: DISPOSABLE IMPACT DOT MATRIX		
				RIBBON TYPE: CARTRIDGE RIBBON		
				FORMS HANDLING: HORIZONTAL AND VERTICAL TABS, MARGINS, FORM LENGTH, SKIP-OVER-PERFORATION, AND VARIABLE LINE FEEDS.		
				GRAPHICS CAPABILITY: HIGH-RESOLUTION GRAPHICS. SIX DENSITIES AND A GRAPHICS CHARACTER SET.		

IMPORTANT ➔ SHOW ARIZONA AND LOCAL SALES TAX WHEN APPLICABLE. IF NOT SHOWN AS SEPARATE ITEM, IT WILL BE ASSUMED TO BE INCLUDED IN UNIT AND TOTAL PRICES.

	SALES TAX	

THIS IS NOT AN ORDER

| | TOTAL | |

SHIPMENT WILL BE MADE	TERMS	F.O.B. POINT
Days after Receipt of Order		ABC DEPARTMENT STORES PHOENIX, ARIZONA

We quote as shown, except as otherwise noted. The undersigned agrees that this quotation is a firm offer which shall be irrevocable and open for acceptance for _____ calendar days (60 calendar days unless otherwise specified) from the date set for submission of quotes.

_____   _____
SIGNATURE   DATE

opments in computing. Badly organized computer operations, inadequate systems development, and poor purchasing practices may also cause inadequate or unnecessary acquisitions. Therefore, it is necessary to use various methods of evaluation to measure several key evaluation factors for computer hardware, software, and services.

Whatever the claims of hardware manufacturers and software suppliers, the *performance* of hardware and software must be demonstrated and evaluated. Independent hardware and software information services (such as Datapro Reports) should be used to gain detailed specification information and evaluations. Hardware and software should be demonstrated and evaluated either on the premises of the computer user or by visiting the operations of other computer users who have similar types of hardware or software. Other users are frequently the best source of information needed to evaluate the claims of manufacturers and suppliers. Vendors should be willing to provide the names of such users.

Large computer users frequently evaluate proposed hardware and software by requiring the processing of special "benchmark" test programs and test data. Users can then evaluate test results to determine which hardware device or software package displayed the best performance characteristics. Special simulators have also been developed that simulate the processing of typical jobs on several computers and evaluate their performances.

Computer users may use a "scoring" system of evaluation when there are several competing proposals for a hardware of software acquisition. Each evaluation factor is given a certain number of maximum possible points. Then each competing proposal is assigned part or all of the possible points for each factor, depending on how well it meets the specifications of the computer user. Scoring each evaluation factor for several proposals helps organize and document the evaluation process and spotlights the strengths and weaknesses of each proposal. See Figure 18–5.

Hardware Evaluation Factors

The evaluation of computer *hardware* includes a technical analysis of specific physical and performance characteristics for each hardware component to be acquired. For example, some of the factors that should be considered in the evaluation of the central processing unit of a computer system were shown in Figure 18–5. Evaluating hardware acquisitions should also involve the analysis of several general categories of hardware performance. These hardware evaluation factors are summarized in Figure 18–6.

FIGURE

18–5 A scoring system
for evaluating
CPU alternatives

Factor	A	B	C	D	E
CPU					
Word size	40	20	0	0	40
Cycle time	6	12	18	6	12
Instruction set	15	0	10	10	15
Arithmetic capability	4	2	0	2	4
Addressing	12	8	16	16	8
Registers	12	0	24	18	18
Communications ports	28	7	21	7	21
Input/output channels	32	24	8	16	24
Environmental requirements	4	4	4	4	4
Product life cycle	26	26	19	16	19
Subtotal	179	103	120	95	165
VENDOR					
Delivery time	14	21	28	28	28
Past performance	12	12	8	8	16
Maintenance	9	6	3	12	9
Location	4	0	8	8	8
Business position	2	4	2	2	2
Number installed	12	16	4	16	16
Training	20	15	5	10	15
Subtotal	73	74	58	84	94
Total	252	177	178	179	259

Software Evaluation Factors

Software should be evaluated according to many factors that
are similar to those used for hardware evaluation. Thus the factors
of *performance, cost, reliability, availability, compatibility, modularity,
technology, ergonomics, and support* should also be used
to evaluate the acceptability of proposed software acquisitions. In
addition, however, the factors summarized in Figure 18–7 must also
be evaluated.

Evaluation of Vendor Support

Vendor support services which assist the computer user during
the installation and operation of hardware and software must be
evaluated. Assistance during installation or conversion of hardware
and software, employee training, and hardware maintenance are
examples of such services. Some of these services are provided
without cost by hardware manufacturers and software suppliers.
Other types of services can be contracted for at a negotiated price.
Evaluation factors for vendor support services are summarized in
Figure 18–8.

FIGURE

18–6 Hardware evaluation factors

PERFORMANCE

What is its speed, capacity, and throughput?

COST

What is its lease or purchase price? What will be its cost of operation and maintenance?

RELIABILITY

What is the risk of malfunction and its maintenance requirements? What are its error control and diagnostic features?

AVAILABILITY

When is the firm delivery date?

COMPATIBILITY

Is it compatible with existing hardware and software? Is it compatible with hardware provided by competing suppliers, including PCM's?

MODULARITY

Can it be expanded and upgraded by acquiring modular "add on" units?

TECHNOLOGY

In what year of its product life cycle is it? Is it "ahead of its time" or does it run the risk of obsolescence? Has it been recently developed or is it due to be replaced by a new technology?

ERGONOMICS

Has it been "human engineered" with the user in mind? Is it "user-friendly," designed to be safe, comfortable, and easy to use?

ENVIRONMENTAL REQUIREMENTS

What are its electrical power, air conditioning, and other environmental requirements?

SOFTWARE

Is system and application software available that can best use this hardware?

SUPPORT

Are the services required to support and maintain it available?

FINANCING COMPUTER ACQUISITIONS

Computer hardware can be rented, purchased, or leased, while software is usually purchased, leased, or is sometimes made available without charge by the hardware manufacturer. Computer manufacturers offer all three methods of financing, while peripheral equipment manufacturers usually offer purchase or lease arrangements. Independent computer-leasing companies use long-term lease arrangements, while used-computer-equipment companies offer used equipment for purchase. The benefits and limitations of each method of financing computer acquisitions are analyzed below.

FIGURE

18–7 Software evaluation factors

EFFICIENCY

Is the software a well-written system of computer instructions that does not use much storage space or CPU time?

FLEXIBILITY

Can it handle its processing assignments easily without major modification?

SECURITY

Does it provide control procedures for errors, malfunctions, and improper use?

LANGUAGE

Is it written in a programming language that is used by our computer programmers and users?

DOCUMENTATION

Is the software well-documented? Does it include helpful user instructions?

HARDWARE

Does existing hardware have the features required to best use this software?

OTHER FACTORS

What is its performance, cost, reliability, availability, compatibility, modularity, technology, ergonomics, and support characteristics? (See hardware evaluation factor questions in Figure 18–6.)

FIGURE

18–8 Vendor support evaluation factors

PERFORMANCE

What has been their past performance in terms of their past promises?

SYSTEMS DEVELOPMENT

Are systems analysts and programming consultants available? What are their quality and cost?

MAINTENANCE

Is equipment maintenance provided? What is its quality and cost?

CONVERSION

What systems development, programming, and hardware installation services will they provide during the conversion period?

TRAINING

Is the necessary training of personnel provided? What is its quality and cost?

DOCUMENTATION

Are the necessary hardware, software, and applications manuals available?

BACKUP

Are several similar computer facilities available for emergency backup purposes?

PROXIMITY

Does the vendor have a local office? Are sales, systems development, programming, and hardware maintenance services provided from this office?

BUSINESS POSITION

Is the vendor financially strong, with good industry market prospects?

HARDWARE

Do they have a wide selection of compatible hardware and accessories?

SOFTWARE

Do they have a wide variety of useful system software and application programs?

Rental

Computer users may favor the *rental* arrangement for several reasons. For example, the rental price includes the cost of maintenance, and the rental agreement can be canceled without penalty by the user with only a few months notice. Thus, computer users do not have to arrange for the maintenance of the equipment and do not have to commit to a long series of lease payments or to the financing of a large purchase price. Renting computer hardware provides greater flexibility in changing equipment configurations and greatly reduces the risk of technological obsolescence, since users are not "locked in" to a purchased computer that has become obsolete due to major technological developments. The monthly rental price is commonly based on 176 hours of use per month (8 hours per day for 22 working days in an average month). Use of rented computers for second and third shifts result in additional charges, which are much lower than the rate for the first 176 hours. The major disadvantage of equipment rental is the higher total cost incurred if equipment is rented for more than four or five years. Hardware manufacturers usually base their rental prices on a two- to four-year life, during which they will recover the cost of the equipment as well as substantial profit. Therefore, if computer hardware is going to be used for a longer period (especially if it is going to be used for more than 176 hours per month) the cost of rental is higher than the cost of purchase.

Purchase

The number of computer users *purchasing* their equipment has grown in recent years for several reasons. First, the prices of microcomputers, minicomputers, and small computers are low enough to make outright purchase affordable for many computer users. Second, computer users feel that the increased capabilities and cost savings of fourth-generation computer equipment is worth the risk of technological obsolescence. Also, more computer users are using their computers for more than one shift per working day. If they purchase their computers, they do not have to pay additional charges for such "overtime" use. Purchase also has a tax advantage, since buying a computer is considered a capital investment and thus allows computer users to qualify for an investment tax credit, which reduces their income tax liability. One of the major disadvantages of the purchasing arrangement is that equipment maintenance is not included in the purchase price and, therefore, must be arranged separately with the computer manufacturer, an independent computer maintenance company, or be maintained by

REAL WORLD APPLICATION 18–2

Spalding Division

Spalding, a division of Questor Corporation, is a manufacturer of a line of sporting goods with manufacturing, sales, and distribution facilities worldwide. Their annual sales of over 15,000 items approaches $200 million. Spalding's previous batch mainframe could not provide timely solutions to the company's financial and manufacturing needs. After a lengthy feasibility study, Spalding decided to go with the HP online distributed data processing approach.

Says Joseph Mitchel, MIS director: "We chose the HP 3000 for a couple of reasons. First, we chose the Hewlett-Packard Company for its record of profitability and stability. We also chose the HP 3000 because its marketing and support orientation is geared toward the end-user and the manufacturing environment rather than being strictly an OEM machine. Another reason was Hewlett-Packard's reputation for service and all around excellence in terms of documentation and training and for not misrepresenting the capabilities of the products provided.

"We knew what we wanted. What HP has given us can best be measured in light of what we didn't have with our previous computer systems. Notably among them are a database management capability, online processing, and the in-house redundancy provided by DS/3000. HP was the only vendor we could find with computer to computer network control software that was not custom, that we could just buy and use. We also picked the HP 3000 because we felt that the IMAGE database system was easy to use and best suited to the needs of our environment.

"We presently have four HP 3000 systems connected together with DS/3000. One system is used strictly for program development. Another is used for sales and marketing type work and scientific data processing. The third system is used for order processing and accounts receivable, while the last system is used for financial applications and our manufacturing control system. Active communication takes place between all of these systems over the DS lines.

"Approximately 145 online terminals of various types are distributed in all areas of the company. We perform online data entry, inquiry, retrieval, editing, and transaction processing. We are also doing continuous program development and batch processing.

"The users are unilaterally pleased because the system makes existing information more available in terms of timeliness. We now get instant reports on operating data without having to wait for a printed batch output. With our previous batch processing system, the reports were often out of sync with our business needs. Most of these problems have gone away as a result of the online capabilities of the HP 3000.

"HP support has been very good. We haven't required much support because our computer downtime has been less than 2 percent. As for price/performance, when we made this decision we saw a price/performance advantage over a general-purpose mainframe of anywhere from 5 to 10 to 1. This advantage for the HP 3000 has held true, perhaps improved.

"The primary reason that I selected HP and would recommend it to others is that it works as advertised. The HP 3000 also eliminates some of the troublesome variables that all DP managers face: hardware reliability and operating system reliability and capability. It is also important to know that the HP organization that is here today will be around tomorrow. By selecting HP you can eliminate these as potential problems and be better able to focus your efforts on developing information systems."

- Why did Spalding select the HP 3000 system? What criteria seemed most important?
- What benefits have resulted?

Source: Hewlett-Packard.

the computer user's own personnel. Two other major disadvantages have been previously mentioned: (1) the risk of technological obsolescence and (2) the necessity to finance a large purchase price.

Leasing

Leasing computer hardware from independent computer-leasing companies was a major development of the third generation of computers. So successful did such "third-party" leasing become that computer manufacturers themselves now offer long-term lease arrangements. Leasing companies typically purchase specific equipment desired by a user and then lease it to the user for a long-term period, such as five years. Leasing arrangements include a maintenance contract, purchase and trade-in options, no charges for extra shift operation, and a reduction in lease charges after a minimum time period. However, a cancellation charge is assessed if a lease is terminated before the end of the minimum lease period. The leasing method combines some of the advantages and disadvantages of rental and purchase. Leasing does not require the financing of a large purchase price and is less expensive than renting equipment for the same period. The decline of lease charges after a minimum period, the inclusion of maintenance in the lease charges, and the absence of additional charges for overtime usage are other benefits. The major disadvantage is the long-term period of the lease contract that cannot be terminated without the payment of a substantial cancellation charge.

THE COST OF INFORMATION SYSTEM RESOURCES

Acquiring computer resources may involve substantial expenditures. **Hardware costs** have always been a major part of information processing costs but have been steadily decreasing, while **software costs** have been growing. Of course, software costs include the salary costs of systems and programming personnel who develop in-house programs, plus the cost of external software packages. Another way to look at the costs of computer resources spotlights the size of **personnel costs**. This includes salaries of systems analysts, programmers, operations personnel, and administrative staff. Figure 18–9 illustrates (based on 1984 estimates) that personnel costs are also a major cost category in providing computer services.

The growth in software and personnel costs is related to a growth in the cost of developing and maintaining new computer applications. That's because the salaries of systems analysts and programmers who develop and maintain application and systems software make

FIGURE

18–9 The cost of computer resources and services: The typical budget of computer-using organizations

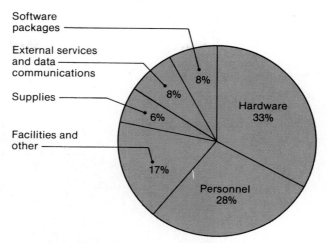

Source: Adapted from Larry Marion, "The DP Budget Survey," *Datamation,* April 15, 1984, pp. 82–86. Reprinted with permission of *Datamation* magazine. Copyright by Technical Publishing Company, a Dun & Bradstreet Company, 1984; all rights reserved.

up a sizable portion of the costs of computer services. Figure 18–10 illustrates the growth in the cost of application software development and maintenance. The size of such costs is one of the chief reasons for the major changes taking place in systems development and programming, discussed in Chapters Eight and Seventeen.

Another way to analyze the cost of providing computer services is to group costs into the functional categories of (1) systems development, (2) operations, and (3) administration. A summary of costs based on these categories is shown in Figure 18–11.

Controlling Computer Costs

The cost of providing computer services has become a major operating expense of computer-using business firms. Therefore, an extensive cost control program is necessary if computer costs are to be controlled. Some of the major *cost control techniques* that are used are summarized below.

Systems Development

The costs of systems development must be controlled by a formal *project management* program, in which a combination of plans, budgets, schedules, and reporting techniques is used to control

FIGURE

18–10 Growth in the cost of developing and maintaining computer applications

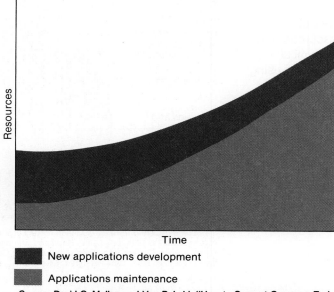

Source: David C. Mollen and Van Bahshi, "How to Support Company End Users," *Data Processor,* May–June 1981, p. 6. Reprinted with permission.

FIGURE

18–11 Computer cost categories

SYSTEMS DEVELOPMENT COSTS
  Systems development personnel.
  Systems development hardware,
    software, and supplies.
  Facilities preparation and furnishing.
  Personnel training.
  Other installation and conversion costs.

OPERATIONS COSTS
  Hardware, software, and supplies for
    operations.
  Program maintenance.
  Operations personnel.
  Occupancy and utilities.
  Communications and external services.

ADMINISTRATIVE COSTS
  Management personnel.
  Administrative staff.
  Secretarial and clerical personnel.
  Miscellaneous costs.
  Organizational overhead.

the cost and direction of a systems development project. Some computer users also find it cheaper to use contract programming or systems design services from external sources, rather than hire the additional personnel required for such systems development efforts. Other firms find that buying or leasing software packages provides a cheaper method of systems development for many applications. Of course, the trend toward the use of computer-assisted programming and systems development, user programming and systems development, and information centers is a popular solution for the control of systems development costs.

Computer Operations

Several techniques are used to control computer operations costs. A formal *cost accounting* system is a major control technique. All costs incurred must be recorded, reported, allocated, and *charged back* to specific computer users. Under this arrangement the computer services department becomes a "service center" whose costs are charged directly to computer users, rather than being lumped with other administrative and service costs and treated as an overhead cost. The use of *financial budgets* is another method of managing computer costs. Financial budgets should be required for computer operations as well as for systems development. Cost control is exercised by identifying and investigating the reasons for deviations from the budget. Finally, *external services*, such as facilities management and computer service bureaus, have been found to be a cheaper method of computer operations for some computer-using firms. Some computer users have found such services to be a decisive method of identifying and reducing the cost of computer operations.

REAL WORLD APPLICATION 18–3

Merrimack Valley Pet Supply

Merrimack Valley Pet Supply's experience reflects many of the difficulties and the benefits of putting a computer in a small business. Merrimack Valley operates a national distributorship, plus being exclusive suppliers to six Harmon family-owned retail pet stores in New Hampshire and Massachusetts. With the business expanding, owner and president Richard Harmon made the decision to computerize in 1979. He and general manager Chuck Theroux originally believed they could get a computer to do their job—they were most interested in order entry and inventory control—for about $1,500. "We ended up buying a $5,000 system," says Theroux. "We bought it as a business system, but it was really a home computer. We bought every option you could hang on the system, but after six months we knew it didn't fill our needs. We got all our money back, which says a lot for the integrity of the people we bought it from, but we had lost six months. It was just before Christmas, and we were already committed to computerizing, so we had to move fast."

Based on recommendations, they went to an independent computer retailer and bought a Data General microNOVA system. "Our first experience was valuable because we never could have been convinced we needed a computer as powerful as the microNOVA if we hadn't seen for ourselves that even a $5,000 home computer wasn't enough."

Their second effort has been far more successful. "Basically, the computer has let us keep up with the business," says Theroux. "Compared to doing everything manually, it saves time all around. We also get a lot more information than we could manually. For example, it helps when we order. We get year-to-date sales figures by item, so we know how well something is selling, and we get an up-to-date inventory level, without having to take the time to make a physical check."

One of the basic decisions Merrimack Valley made was to buy standard software packages. Says Theroux, "We had already lost six months, Christmas was coming up, and we didn't want to wait another six months to develop custom software." They haven't regretted the decision. The standard packages, plus a little imagination, have done the job. "For example," says Theroux, "we don't have an order form program per se, but we use the inventory control package to generate order forms. We stock over 6,000 items, and prices change all the time, so that's a valuable capability." Similarly, they've set up their order entry program to printout picking orders in the same sequence in which the warehouse is organized physically, reducing order picking time by 70 percent. "We've bent a little to fit the software," says Theroux, "but basically we've been able to make the system do all the things we want it to."

- Why did Merrimack have to replace their first microcomputer system after only six months?
- What acquisition criteria and methods should be emphasized to avoid such situations?
- Was buying standard software a good decision? Explain.

Source: Data General Corporation.

SUMMARY

- The computer-using business firm must acquire computer resources from many sources in the computer industry. Therefore, business computer users should have a basic understanding of the computer industry, since it is a vital source of computer hardware, software, and services. The U.S. computer industry consists of a few major computer manufacturers and many smaller suppliers of hardware, software, and services. Effective and efficient use of the computer by business firms requires the continual support of many firms within the computer industry.

- Information systems development and processing services can be acquired from sources outside the business firm instead of developing such capabilities within the organization. Many business firms use the external services provided by computer service centers, time-sharing companies, facilities management companies, etc. The major benefit of using external services is that computer users pay only for the specific services needed and do not have to acquire or manage hardware, software, and personnel. Loss of control over the information processing function, inconvenience, and higher costs are limitations that are attributed to some forms of external services.

- Computer users should have a basic understanding of how to evaluate the acquisition of computer resources. Manufacturers and suppliers should be required to present bids and proposals based on systems specifications developed during the design stage of systems development. A formal evaluation process reduces the possibility of incorrect or unnecessary purchases of computer hardware or software. Several major "evaluation factors," such as performance, cost, and reliability, should be used to evaluate computer hardware, software, and vendor support. The use of rental, purchase, or lease arrangements in financing computer acquisitions must also be evaluated.

- A major concern of computer users is the control of the cost of computer resources. Acquiring computer resources usually involves substantial expenditures for hardware, software, services, supplies, and personnel compensation. Major cost control programs are necessary to control the cost of systems development, computer operations, and administration.

KEY TERMS AND CONCEPTS

Computer-based business
  environment
Computer industry
External services
Computer service center
Facilities management
Hardware evaluation factors

Software evaluation factors
Evaluation of vendor support
Financing computer
  acquisitions
Computer cost categories
Computer cost control

REVIEW AND APPLICATION QUESTIONS

1. Why should the computer operations of a business firm be viewed as taking place in a "computer- based business environment"?
2. Identify several types of firms in the computer industry and the products or services they supply.
3. What are some of the benefits and limitations of using external services provided by computer industry firms?
4. Are speed and capacity the most important factors in evaluating hardware? Explain.
5. What factors are important in evaluating software?
6. Why is the evaluation of vendor support an important consideration for computer users?
7. Should computers be rented, leased, or purchased? Explain.
8. Is hardware, software, or personnel the most important component of the costs of information processing? Explain. What changes have been occurring in this area?
9. What are some of the typical costs incurred in developing and operating computer-based information systems?
10. Can the costs of information processing be controlled? Explain.

APPLICATION PROBLEMS

1. If you have not already done so, read and answer the questions after each Real World Application in this chapter.
2. Assume you are going to buy a personal computer system. List all of the types of firms in the computer industry that you would have to depend on directly or indirectly for hardware, software, and services. (Hint: use Figure 18–2.)
3. Assume you are going to buy a personal computer system. Make a "wish list" of the hardware, software, and vendor support fea-

tures you want this system to have. (Hint: refer to Figures 18–6, 18–7, and 18–8 but get more specific.)

4. Assume you are going to buy a personal computer system. Go to a local computer retailer and see how much it will cost you to implement the "wish list" you developed in problem 3. Are any features you wanted impossible to achieve?

5. The VP for information systems of ABC Department Stores is trying to justify a large increase in his department's budget in the coming year. He is having trouble explaining to the VP of finance why software costs and personnel costs are related. Help him out with your own explanation.

6. Joan Alvarez, a store manager for ABC Department Stores is considering buying a new personal computer and an integrated applications package that does spreadsheet analysis, graphics, database management, word processing, and communications control. Her two main evaluation criteria are (1) ergonomics and (2) technology. List several features she should consider in evaluating both hardware and software by those two criteria. (Hint: Use Figure 18–6 to help you get started.)

CHAPTER 19

Managing Information System Resources

CHAPTER OUTLINE

LEARNING OBJECTIVES

The purpose of this chapter is to promote a basic understanding of how business firms must manage their information system resources by analyzing (1) the organization and staffing of an information services department, (2) the management of systems development, computer operations, and information services personnel, and (3) the control of electronic information processing. After reading and studying this text, you should be able to:

1. Identify several activities that are involved in each of the five basic functions of an information services organization (i.e., systems development, user services, data administration, operations, and administration).
2. Outline the job responsibilities of several types of careers in computer systems development, user services, data administration, programming, and operations.
3. Identify several methods for managing the systems development function, including the concept of project management.
4. Identify some of the planning and control activities of the operations management function.
5. Outline several types of data processing controls, organizational controls, and facility controls that can be used by a computer-using organization.

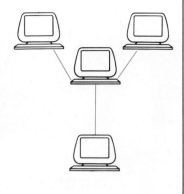

Who should manage MIS? Managers or technicians? Users or specialists? Somebody has to. Inadequate management of information services by many business firms is well-documented. Thus there is a real need for business people to understand how to manage this vital organizational function. In this chapter, we will first analyze the basic functions performed by information services groups within a computer-using firm. We will then discuss methods of managing these functions, with special emphasis given to the *planning, organizing, staffing, and controlling* activities that are required. We will also stress the **information resource management** concept, which emphasizes that managing the information system resources of a business firm has become a major responsibility of business management.

ORGANIZING FOR INFORMATION SERVICES

Information services groups in large organizations are usually given departmental or divisional status. We will use the name **information services** department, though such other names as "information systems," "information processing," "computer services," "data processing," or "EDP" department are also used. However, no matter what name is used, information services organizations perform several basic functions and activities. These can be grouped into five basic functional categories: (1) *systems development*, (2) *user services*, (3) *data administration*, (4) *operations*, and (5) *administration*. Figure 19–1 illustrates this grouping of information services functions and activities into a functional organizational structure.

The internal organizational structure of an information services organization must reflect its major functions and activities. However, the particular structure used depends on many factors, including organizational location, centralization or decentralization of information processing activities, and the size of the information services organization. Figure 19–2 illustrates the organizational structure of a medium-scale information services organization, including job titles commonly used in such organizations.

Systems Development

Systems development activities include the investigation, analysis, design, programming, implementation, and maintenance of information systems within the computer-using organization. These activities were discussed in detail in Chapter Seventeen. In addition, the systems development function frequently includes the activities of systems programming, configuration management, and communi-

FIGURE 19–1 A functional organizational structure for an information services department

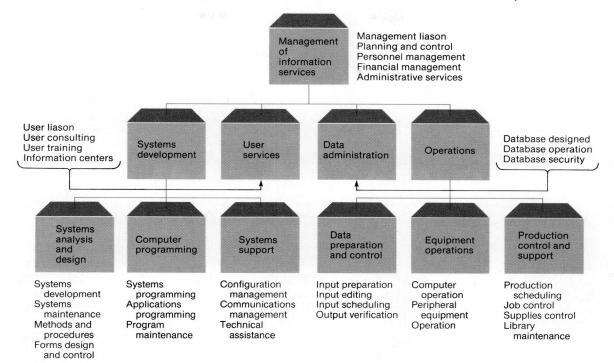

cations management. These additional systems development activities are summarized below.

■ **Systems Programming.** Design and maintenance of system software, such as operating systems and other control programs and service programs.

■ **Configuration Management.** Planning and evaluating present and proposed hardware and software "configurations". Results in recommendations for hardware and software modifications or acquisitions.

■ **Communications Management.** Planning and evaluating present and proposed data communications network hardware, software, channels, and services for the organization.

User Services

The number of people in organizations who use or want to use computers to help them do their jobs has outstripped the capacity of many information services departments. Therefore, new ways

FIGURE 19–2 Medium-scale organization structure and job titles

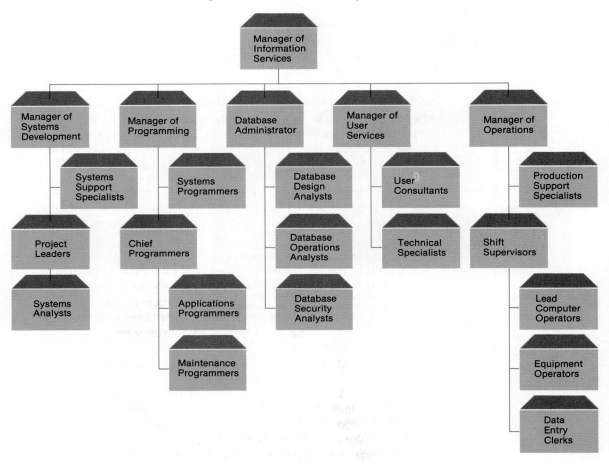

of providing hardware, software, and people support to users are being developed. The most important is the **information center**. These centrally located support facilities provide:

■ **Hardware support** for users who need it by providing the use of microcomputers, intelligent terminals, advanced graphics terminals, word processors, high-speed printers, plotters, etc.

■ **Software support** is provided with advanced software packages, such as application development systems, nonprocedural languages, database management systems, and a variety of application software packages.

■ **People support** is provided by a staff of *user consultants*. They are systems analysts/programmers who are trained to educate and help users take advantage of the hardware and software resources of the information center.

Data Administration

The widespread use of database processing systems for business information processing has made managing data and information a major information service function. Since the databases of an organization are used by many different applications, they need to be centrally coordinated and controlled by a data administration function. This usually takes the form of a **database administrator** (DBA), or a database administration department. The functions of database administration include:

- **Database Design.** Designing the structure and organization of databases. Defining and standardizing the data in the databases. Database software and hardware evaluation and selection.
- **Database Operations.** Day-to-day control and liaison with users. Maintenance of the databases. Coordination with information centers' use of databases.
- **Database Security.** Designing, monitoring, and maintaining controls for the security of databases.

Operations

The operations function of the information services department is concerned with the processing of data into information through the use of hardware, software, and personnel. The operations function includes the major activities of data preparation, equipment operation, production control, and production support. The content of these activities is summarized below.

- **Data Preparation and Control.** Includes converting input source documents into machine-sensible form by keypunching, key-to-tape or key-to-disk operations, using a variety of data entry equipment. The data control aspect of this activity refers to the continual checking and monitoring of input data and output reports to insure their accuracy, completeness, and timeliness.
- **Equipment Operation.** Includes the operation of the computer system, including the computer console, online peripheral equipment, and data communications terminals and control equipment. It also includes the operation of offline equipment, such as offline magnetic tape units and printers, and other types of offline data conversion or output support equipment.
- **Production Control.** Includes the scheduling, monitoring, and

control of facilities and processing jobs. It includes the scheduling of equipment, data files, and necessary data processing supplies, scheduling and logging job input and output, and communicating with users on scheduling requirements and the status of specific jobs.

■ **Production Support.** Activities that support information processing operations include acquisition and maintenance of processing supplies, maintaining a library of data files on magnetic tape or magnetic disks, maintaining a library of operations documentation, providing for the physical security of the computer facilities, and distribution of computer output.

Administration

The administration of information services requires the performance of several specific managerial activities. These activities include planning, controlling, managerial liaison, personnel management, financial management, and administrative services. The content of these activities is summarized below.

■ **Planning.** Includes long- and short-range planning of computer operations, systems development projects, hardware, software, and facilities acquisitions.

■ **Controlling.** Includes the monitoring and evaluating of computer operations, systems development projects, and hardware, software, facilities, and personnel utilization. Reporting systems are developed to compare performance with plans.

■ **Managerial Liaison.** This activity involves communicating and reporting to management concerning the plans and performance of the computer services department. Managerial liaison also includes meeting and maintaining proper relationships with hardware and software vendors and suppliers.

■ **Personnel Management.** Includes defining personnel requirements, recruiting, and selection of personnel, employee training and development, performance evaluation, and personnel record-keeping.

■ **Financial Management.** Includes developing and maintaining methods of financial record-keeping and financial analysis so that the cost of computer operations and systems development projects can be analyzed and controlled. This activity also includes billing computer users for information services costs, providing cost estimates for planning purposes, and purchasing required hardware, software, and services.

■ **Administrative Services.** Includes the supply of services, such as secretarial and clerical assistance, hardware maintenance scheduling, and custodial services.

Organizational Location

The location of information services within the structure of a business firm depends on the type and size of computer operations and the emphasis given to computer services by management. Large-scale operations usually become independent departments or divisions whose managers may have vice presidential status in the firm. The use of large computers with centralized databases and many remote data communications terminals support such **centralization** of information services. However, the use of microcomputers, minicomputers, intelligent terminals, and data communications in distributed processing networks supports **decentralization** of information services, since computer power is dispersed among the user departments of an organization.

The extent to which business firms should centralize or decentralize information services depends on many factors. *Centralized* computer facilities may be *more economical* and *efficient* in terms of hardware, software, and personnel cost and use. This is especially true of firms with a high volume of repetitive business data processing. In addition, centralization fosters integration and standardization of information systems within an organization. However, *decentralized* computer services are usually *more responsive* to user needs, encourage greater use of computers, and reduce the risks of computer errors and malfunctions. Therefore, many firms are turning to **information centers** as a way to get the benefits of centralized computing resources, yet make them available for end-user computing close to the users' worksites.

CAREERS IN INFORMATION SERVICES

The success or failure of an information services organization rests primarily on the quality of its personnel. Many computer users consider recruiting, training, and retaining qualified personnel as their greatest single problem. Millions of persons are employed in the information services organizations of computer users. National employment surveys continually forecast shortages of qualified services personnel (especially programmers and systems analysts) that range into the hundreds of thousands. Employment opportunities in the computer field are excellent, since the need for systems analysts, programmers, and managerial personnel is expected to expand significantly as business firms continue to expand their use of computers. Therefore, it is important to analyze the types of jobs and the managerial problems associated with information services personnel.

Figure 19–3 gives valuable insight into the variety of job types and the high salaries commanded by many computer services personnel. Of course, these figures are national averages, and actual

FIGURE

19–3 Annual salaries for computer services personnel: Departments with annual budgets over $1 million

Job Title	Average Salary
Vice President of MIS	$67,650
Director of DP or MIS	49,158
Services Coordinator/User Liaison	27,949
Manager of Systems Analysis	41,500
Senior Systems Analyst	35,100
Systems Analyst	28,278
Manager of Applications Programming	42,700
Lead Applications Programmer	38,143
Senior Applications Programmer	33,425
Applications Programmer	25,692
Junior Applications Programmer	19,530
Systems Analysis/Programming Manager	40,885
Lead Systems Analyst/Programmer	46,028
Senior Systems Analyst/Programmer	34,992
Systems Analyst/Programmer	28,478
Manager of Systems Programming	43,934
Senior Systems Programmer	35,102
Manager of Database Administration	55,000
Manager of Computer Operations	31,080
Shift Supervisor	20,864
Lead Computer Operator	19,314
Computer Operator	15,626
Control Clerk	14,518
Data Entry Supervisor	18,500
Data Entry Operator	12,740
Word Processing Supervisor	24,750
Word Processing Operator	17,537

Source: Adapted from Larry Marion, "The Big Wallet Era," *Datamation,* September 1984, p. 80. Reprinted with permission of *Datamation* magazine. Copyright by Technical Publishing Company, a Dun & Bradstreet Company, 1984; all rights reserved.

salaries can range much higher and lower, depending on such factors as the size and geographic location of the information services organization.

Careers in Systems Development

The most common type of job in this category is *systems analyst*. Larger computer service operations expand this job operation into several specialized job types. Descriptions for several jobs in this category are summarized in Figure 19–4.

Other systems development job categories are frequently classified as "systems support" occupations. These include (1) a *configuration analyst* who is responsible for evaluating and improving

FIGURE

19–4 Systems develop-
ment job descriptions

Systems Analyst
Gathers and analyzes information needed for the development or modification of information systems. Develops a statement of systems requirements and prepares detailed system specifications on which computer programs will be based. Supervises installation of new systems and evaluates existing systems for possible improvements.

Systems Designer
Translates systems requirements prepared by the systems analyst into alternative systems designs. Develops detailed systems specifications for the system being developed.

Communications Analyst
Plans, designs, and installs data communications networks, including the specification and selection of software, terminals, and communications control equipment.

hardware and software performance, (2) a *standards controller* who develops and maintains data processing standards and procedures for the organization, (3) a *technical librarian* who develops and maintains a library of system documentation and technical information, and (4) a *documentation support specialist* who assists systems analysts and programmers in developing detailed system, programming, and operations documentation.

Careers in User Services

This major new information services function has created three new job categories in the information centers of large computer-using organizations. They are being filled right now with "people who like to work with people," including former systems analysts and programmers, but also with former computer users. Figure 19–5 summarizes these job descriptions.

FIGURE

19–5 Job descriptions in user services

Information Center Manager
Manages the information center and works with the manager of information services in planning the supply of computing services to end-users.

Systems Consultant
Assists computer users in the development, prototyping, and maintenance of application systems. Trains users in the use of application development tools and application packages. Frequently serves as a liaison between computer users and the computer services department.

Technical Specialist
Evaluates, selects, installs, and maintains the hardware and software resources of the information center. Provides technical assistance to systems consultants and users.

FIGURE

19–6 Careers in data administration

Database Administrator
Designs and maintains the databases of the organization. Prepares and enforces standards for the use and security of information in databases. For large computer-using organizations, this becomes a management position, with duties delegated to other specialists.

Database Design Analyst
Designs the structure and defines the data elements in organizational databases. Evaluates database hardware and software.

Database Operations Analyst
Coordinates day-to-day use of databases with users and other information services staff. Enforces database standards. Maintains the database.

Database Security Analyst
Designs and maintains controls for the security and integrity of databases. Monitors databases to ensure proper use.

Careers in Data Administration

This is another relatively new category of information services careers in large computer-using organizations. Figure 19–6 summarizes the four major job types that have been created to implement the database administration function.

Careers in Programming

Careers in programming involve job responsibilities for the development of computer programs. The most common job title is *programmer* but several other job titles are also used that reflect the specialization in particular types of programming effort. See Figure 19–7.

FIGURE

19–7 Job descriptions in programming

Programmer
Develops program logic and codes; tests and documents computer programs.

Applications Programmer
Develops programs required for specific applications of computer users.

Maintenance Programmer
Modifies and improves existing programs.

Systems Programmer
Develops, modifies, and maintains the operating system and other system software used by an information services organization.

Analyst Programmer
A systems analyst who does his or her own application programming, or vice versa; an applications programmer who does his or her own systems analysis and design.

Chief Programmer
Leads a team of programmers all working on the same programming project. Recommended for structured programming.

Careers in Computer Operations

Operations personnel are responsible for operating or controlling the operation of information processing equipment. Operations job types can be grouped into the categories of (1) *equipment operations*, (2) *data preparation*, and (3) *production support*. See Figure 19–8.

FIGURE

19–8 Job descriptions in computer operations

Computer Operator
Monitors and controls the computer by operating the central console. Adjusts the configuration of the computer system in response to messages from the operating system or to instructions contained in the operations documentation. Operates peripheral equipment in smaller installations.

Peripheral Equipment Operator
Assists the computer operator by setting up and operating tape drives, magnetic disk drives, printers, etc. Also operates offline input/output equipment.

Data Entry Equipment Operator
Converts data on source documents into machine-sensible form by use of a keyboard-driven machine, such as a key-to-disk, key-to-tape, or video terminal.

Production Coordinator
Coordinates and controls the mix of data processing jobs to achieve optimum equipment utilization and service to users. Prepares and maintains schedules for data processing jobs and maintains records of job and equipment performance.

Careers in Administration of Information Services

Administrative personnel manage and supervise the activities of the computer services organization. They include administrative staff positions that support management in administrative planning and control. See Figure 19–9.

Other administrative positions include the managers of systems analysis and design, programming, systems support, production support, and "shift supervisors," who supervise equipment operations during each shift of a working day. Additional administrative job classifications exist in many computer services organizations due to the recognition of seniority and the assignment of supervisory responsibilities. Thus such titles as *Lead Systems Analyst, Lead Programmer,* and *Lead Computer Operator* recognize the assignment of supervisory responsibilities to these positions. Another widely used administrative job type is the position of "project manager" or "team leader." This person is frequently a senior systems analyst or programmer who supervises the activities of a systems development project team.

Manager of Information Services
Plans and directs the activities of the entire information services organization.

Manager of Systems Development
Directs the activities of systems development personnel and projects.

Operations Manager
Directs the operation of all information processing equipment and the production of all information processing jobs.

Training Coordinator
Develops and administers training programs for information services personnel and computer users.

Budget and Costing Specialist
Develops budgets for the information services organization and evaluates performance against the budget. Develops and administers a system for allocating the cost of computer services to computer users.

INFORMATION RESOURCE MANAGEMENT

Information resource management (IRM) is a concept that views hardware, software, people, data, and information as valuable organizational resources that can be effectively and efficiently managed for the benefit of the entire organization. It emphasizes that managing such resources has become a major responsibility of the management of the organization at all levels, not just of the manager of information services, the *chief information officer* (CIO) of the firm. The IRM concept also stresses that the management of an organization must apply management concepts and techniques (i.e., planning, organizing, controlling functions, management by objectives, critical success factors, etc.) to the management of information resources. Information resource management is a vital concept in today's computer environment because of two major developments:

- Information processing technology and its application to users' needs is growing and changing rapidly.
- Inadequate performance and unsatisfactory use of information systems and resources is a major and growing problem in many organizations.

Several advances in information processing technology have made implementing the IRM concept feasible. These include advances in database processing, data communications, distributed processing, and application development. Therefore, the information resource management environment (see Figure 19–10) of an organization should be viewed as:

- A *distributed system* of user department and headquarters computer facilities,
- *interconnected* by data communications networks,
- *integrated* by a common database-oriented approach
- *developed* by user-driven applications development facilities, and
- *coordinated* by an organization-wide information resource management plan.

Information Services Planning

A growing number of business firms are developing a "master information systems plan" for managing the information system resources of their organizations. This plan involves a study of how the information services function can contribute to the strategic plans and objectives of the entire organization. Assessment is made of information systems problems and opportunities, and of hardware,

FIGURE 19–10 The information resource management environment

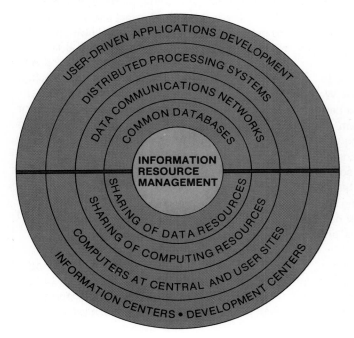

REAL WORLD APPLICATION 19–1

Bechtel Group Inc.

Last year Bechtel Group, Inc., the largest privately held construction corporation in the world, was engaged in more than 100 major engineering and construction projects ($50 million and up) in 29 countries, and each required some form of MIS support. Managing the information systems requirements for such a widely dispersed company calls not only for decentralized hardware and systems but for careful planning and—most important—a decentralized MIS organization, according to Donald E. Fowler, manager of information services at Bechtel Power Corporation, the Bechtel unit that provides MIS services for the entire $11 billion (sales) organization. Detailed strategic and tactical planning, moreover, is allowing for the smooth introduction of sophisticated communications networks, processing nodes, and applications.

MIS at Bechtel has been distributed in recent years, according to Fowler, to more accurately reflect the distributed nature of the company. Nearly half of his staff is now situated outside the headquarters complex in San Francisco. Fowler has 1,500 DP professionals in his charge. "We position support directly with the users. We give them sufficient resources to meet their daily needs, including operating people, programmers, and systems analysts," he said. The typically small staff found in each division cannot develop expertise in all areas, he noted, so the technical support group at headquarters backs them up in specialized areas like networking and training. Although each division effectively has its own DP shop, "the standards, guidelines, and procedures are developed centrally."

At Bechtel, planning stems from two functional strategies laid down in 1978: that the firm will have a worldwide communications network, and that processing will be decentralized when appropriate. From these strategies flow annual corporate objectives, which are translated within the company into divisional objectives and then into divisional operating plans, which are integrated into the corporate MIS plan. "Planning and organization," he said, allow him to "forestall knee-jerk reactions to problems."

Fowler considers the two strategies to be essential to the planning process. "Given the strategies, we set goals. First, long-range goals, which contribute directly to fulfilling the strategies. Then, each year we set objectives." For example, MIS department objectives include:

- Establish services and productivity measures for information services.
- Establish and implement training programs for executives, managers, and professionals.
- Continue implementation of the integrated worldwide communications network.
- Expand support of microcomputers.

Once the MIS objectives are set they are sent out to user divisions with a package of information. These include historic data and instructions to aid divisions in developing their own objectives and operating plans. Typically, a division will have 10 or 15 objectives and perhaps 200 activities it expects to undertake to meet those objectives. Also, the MIS department bills divisions for their use of shared MIS resources and the divisions bill customers for their DP costs.

- How is Bechtel implementing a decentralized information service organization?
- What is the role of the central MIS group?
- Does Bechtel have a master plan for information services? What are the different levels of the planning process at Bechtel?

Source: "Bechtel Disperses MIS Support", Paul E. Schindler, Jr., *Information Systems News*, March 8, 1982. Copyright 1982 by CMP Publications, Inc. Reprinted by permission.

software, and people capabilities. The master plan formulates policies, objectives, and strategies for delivering information services and allocating information system resources. It also contains a description of the information systems development projects that the business firm intends to accomplish in the future (i.e., in the next two to five years). The plan indicates a tentative timetable for the projects and provides "ball park" estimates of the resources required and the benefits to be obtained. In some large firms, long-range planning groups at the corporate level or in the information systems division are employed to gather data and formulate the alternatives required in the planning process. These alternatives are presented to top management for review and final decision making. Figure 19–11 illustrates the major activities and outputs in long-range and annual MIS planning.

Managing Systems Development

Planning, organizing, and controlling the systems development function of an information services department is a major managerial responsibility. Typically, several methods of **project management** are used to manage systems development.

FIGURE 19–11 Major activities and outputs in MIS planning

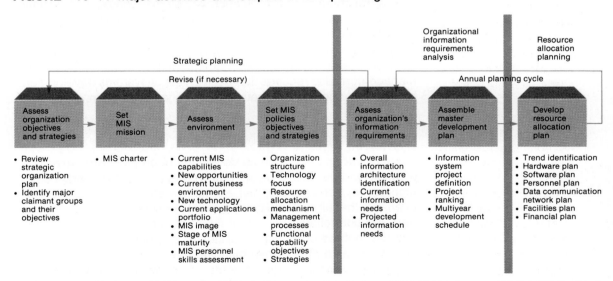

Source: James C. Witherbee, *Systems Analysis and Design,* 2d ed., (St. Paul, Minn.: West Publishing Company, 1984), p. 327. Reprinted with permission.

Project Management

Project management involves the management of the development work required by large information system projects. The concept of project management requires that each major information system be developed by a *project team* according to a specific *project plan* that is formulated during the systems investigation stage. Assigning systems analysts and programmers to specific projects headed by a project leader allows better control of the progress of systems development. The alternative is to assign personnel to work on projects on a "when available" basis. This method usually results in a lack of project control and a waste of human and financial resources.

The Project Plan

Descriptions of the tasks involved and the assignment of responsibility for each task are included in the project plan. Estimated start-up and completion dates for the entire project, as well as for major checkpoints or "milestones" in the development of the project, are also included. Specified amounts of time, money, and staff are allocated to each segment of the project. The project plan includes provisions for handling suggested changes to the proposed system. This typically includes a "design freeze" policy, which prohibits changes in systems design after specified project deadlines unless the change is formally approved by management. Provisions are usually made for revision of the project schedule due to major unforeseen developments. Record-keeping forms that report the progress of individual members of a systems development project are also used in many project management systems. Good project management also requires that each phase of systems development be properly documented before new stages are begun.

Project Management Techniques

Major information systems development projects are typically planned and controlled by several types of project management techniques. For example, many firms use special reporting forms to ensure that all systems development projects are properly authorized and controlled. The use of financial and operating budgets is another method of managing systems development projects. Budgets serve as a short-range planning device as well as a method of control. Deviations from budgeted amounts identify projects that need closer management attention. Several types of charts are used to plan and control projects, such as the Gantt chart, which specifies

FIGURE

19–12 Gantt chart showing progress of a systems development project

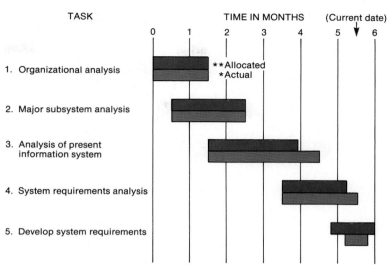

TASK

TIME IN MONTHS   (Current date)

Note: Steps 3 and 4 have exceeded their allocated time and, therefore, step 5 is behind schedule.

the times allowed for the various activities required in information systems development. See Figure 19–12. The PERT system (Program Evaluation and Review Technique), which involves the use of a network diagram of required events and activities, is also used. See Figure 19–13.

Managing Computer Operations

Planning and controlling the operations of the information services department is a major management responsibility. **Operations management** refers to the major areas of responsibility of the manager of computer operations that require planning and control activities, such as those outlined in Figure 19–14.

Production planning and control methods are necessary for effective management of computer operations. Information must be gathered concerning:

- The hardware, software, and personnel needed for each information processing job.
- Job-processing times, equipment utilization, time spent by operating personnel, and the production status of each job.
- Computer malfunctions, the number and type of reruns, processing delays and errors, and other evidences of unsatisfactory or unusual conditions.

FIGURE 19–13 PERT network segment for a systems development project

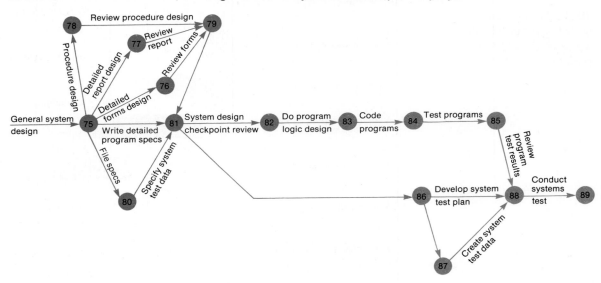

Such information is used to produce reports on computer system utilization, costs, and performance. These reports are then used as the basis for production planning, distribution of computer costs to users, control of computer system performance, and quality control of service to computer users. Software packages known as **system performance monitors** are available. They monitor the processing of computer jobs and help develop a planned schedule of computer operations that can optimize the use of a computer system. Advanced operating systems use performance monitors to monitor computer system performance and produce detailed statistics that are invaluable for effective production planning and control. *For example*, a system performance monitor could automatically generate the reports shown in Figure 19–15.

Managing Information Services Personnel

Managing information services includes **personnel management:** the management of managerial, technical, and clerical personnel. One of the most important jobs of information service managers is to recruit qualified personnel and to develop, organize, and direct the capabilities of the existing personnel. Employees must be continually trained to keep up with the latest developments in a fast-moving and highly technical field. Employee job performance

FIGURE

19–14 Computer operations management functions

Operations Planning
Forecasting changes in the volume and type of computer applications and their effect on future hardware, software, and personnel requirements.

Production Planning
Formulating daily, weekly, and monthly forecasts that schedule specific systems and applications for computer processing.

Operating and Financial Budgets
Developing budgets for operations and comparing performance to budget.

Computer System Utilization
Analysis of computer system utilization by computer users and types of applications. Determination of any excess capacity or need for additional capacity.

Computer System Performance
Analysis of computer "downtime," aborted jobs, returns, input/output errors, late reports, etc.

Computer Operations Costs
Analysis of the cost of computer hardware, software, and operating personnel.

Computer-User Service and Assessments
Evaluating the quality of user service and assessing users for the costs of computer operations.

Computer Systems Acquisition
Evaluating plans and negotiations for hardware and software changes and their effect on operations.

Systems Implementation
Planning and supervising the effect on ongoing operations of the installation and conversion of information systems or computer systems.

Controls and Security
Control of data preparation, input, processing, and output. Control of storage files and computer facilities. Fraud control.

must be continually evaluated and outstanding performance rewarded with salary increases or promotions. Salary and wage levels must be set, and "career paths" must be designed so individuals can move to new jobs through promotion and transfer as they gain in seniority and expertise.

The management and development of information services personnel poses some unique problems for management. For example, systems analysts and computer programmers are creative, professional personnel who cannot be managed with traditional work rules or evaluated by traditional performance criteria. How do you measure how well a systems analyst or programmer is doing? This question has plagued the management of many computer-using business firms. However, it should be emphasized that this question is not unique to computer professionals but is common to the management of many professional personnel, especially the scientists and engi-

FIGURE 19–15 Operations and reports produced by a computer system performance monitor

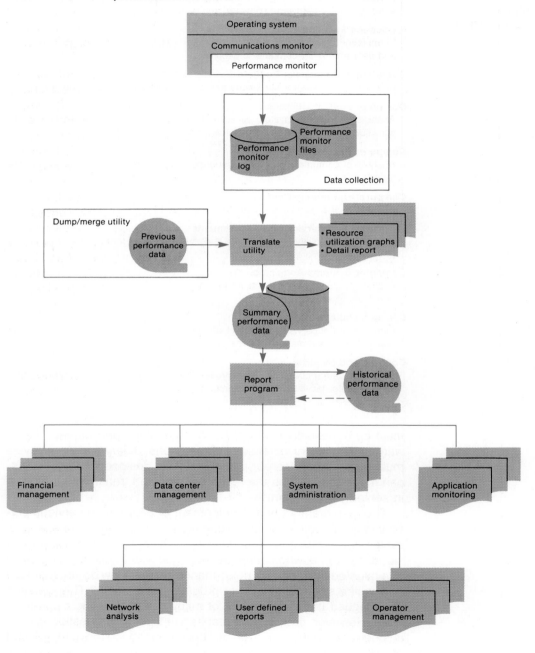

neers employed in the research and development activities of many organizations. Effective *project planning, controlling*, and *reporting* techniques (especially the modular and team approach of *structured programming, analysis, and design*) are available, which provide information required for the evaluation of systems development and programming personnel.

Another personnel management problem area is the professional loyalty of information services personnel. Like other professionals, computer specialists may have a greater loyalty to the "information processing profession" than to the organization which employs them. *For example,* computer programmers may consider themselves programmers *first* and employees *second*. When this attitude is coupled with the shortages of many types of computer specialists, a serious problem in retaining qualified personnel may arise. This problem can be solved by effective personnel management. Providing information services personnel with opportunities for merit salary increases, promotions, transfers, and attendance at professional meetings and seminars provide the flexible job environment needed to retain competent personnel. Challenging technological and intellectual assignments and a congenial atmosphere of fellow professionals are other major factors in retaining information services personnel.

COMPUTER SECURITY AND CONTROL

Does electronic information processing increase or decrease the probability of errors, fraud, and destruction of information processing facilities? Computers have proven that they can process huge volumes of data and perform complex calculations more accurately than manual or mechanical information processing systems. However, we know that (1) errors do occur in computer-based systems, (2) computers have been used for fraudulent purposes, and (3) computers and their data files have been accidentally or maliciously destroyed. There is no question that computers have had some detrimental effect on the detection of errors and fraud. Manual and mechanical information processing systems use paper documents and other media that can be visually checked by information processing personnel. Several persons are usually involved in such systems and, therefore, cross-checking procedures are easily performed. These characteristics of manual and mechanical information processing systems facilitate the detection of errors and fraud.

Electronic information processing systems, on the other hand, use machine-sensible media such as magnetic disks and tape, and accomplish processing manipulations within the electronic circuitry of a computer system. The ability to check visually the progress of information processing activities and the contents of data files is significantly reduced. In addition, a relatively small number of personnel may effectively control all of the processing activities of the entire organization. Therefore, the ability to detect errors and fraud can be reduced by computerization, and it requires the development of *information processing controls.*

Controls are needed to ensure **computer security**, i.e., the *accuracy, integrity*, and *safety* of the electronic information processing activities and resources of computer users. Controls can minimize *errors, fraud*, and *destruction* in an information services organization. Effective controls can make an electronic information processing system more free of errors and fraud than manual types of information processing. There are three major types of controls needed to achieve computer security: (1) processing controls, (2) organizational controls, and (3) facility controls. Figure 19–16 illustrates the controls needed to achieve computer security. Let's take a closer look at each of them.

FIGURE

19–16 Controls needed for computer security

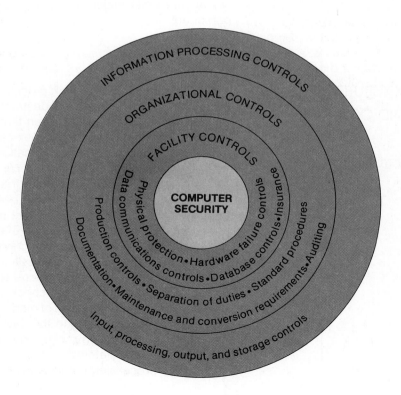

REAL WORLD APPLICATION 19–2

Guardian Life Insurance Company

Guardian Life Insurance Company has had astonishingly low turnover among its top 20 computer professionals in the past seven years. Only two of them have left during that entire period, according to John F. Kuemmerle, Guardian's senior vice-president for administration. His secret for keeping people: "You need to find out if your needs are close to their hopes and motivations. You have to find out what makes them tick."

Because computer people realize that their skills can quickly become obsolete, Kuemmerle says that one of their biggest reasons for moving on to other jobs is the opportunity to learn new skills and apply them. To counter that, "we ask our people to spend 40 percent of their time learning." That includes everything from reading magazines and books to meeting with computer vendors and discussing their new products.

But Kuemmerle's data processing staff studies more than just the latest technological breakthroughs. They also study Guardian's insurance business. "Technologists must shift their perspective and see themselves also as business people," he insists. That way, he believes, they will not only pay more attention to the bottom line but also improve their ability to see strategically how to apply technology to business problems.

Guardian encourages "individuals to make a proposal [for a technical solution to a business problem] and then in a businesslike way translate what it means for the company financially," Kuemmerle explains. "We get more than that 40 percent [education time] back in implementation because of the dedication of the individuals. They set a hot pace for themselves."

■ What motivates information services personnel on the job? To change jobs?
■ How is Guardian keeping its computer people satisfied and motivated?

Source: "Computer People: Yes They Really Are Different," *Business Week*, February 20, 1984, p. 68. Reprinted with permission.

Information Processing Controls

Information processing controls are methods and devices that attempt to ensure the accuracy, validity, and propriety of data processing functions and activities. Controls must be developed to ensure that all proper input data are collected, converted into a form suitable for processing, and entered into the computer system. Thus data processing controls can be organized according to the *input, processing, output*, and *storage* components of any information processing system. See Figure 19–17.

Input Controls

Examples of input controls that are frequently used are summarized below.

Recording Controls. Input recording aids help reduce the

FIGURE

19–17 Types of
Information processing
controls

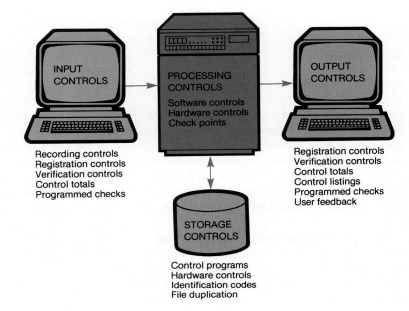

INPUT
CONTROLS

Recording controls
Registration controls
Verification controls
Control totals
Programmed checks

PROCESSING
CONTROLS

Software controls
Hardware controls
Check points

OUTPUT
CONTROLS

Registration controls
Verification controls
Control totals
Control listings
Programmed checks
User feedback

STORAGE
CONTROLS

Control programs
Hardware controls
Identification codes
File duplication

chance for error. Examples: Prepunched cards, templates over the keys of key-driven input devices, and prenumbered forms.

Registration Controls. Source documents can be registered by recording them in a logbook when they are received by data preparation personnel. External labels attached to the outside of magnetic tapes or disks are another method of registering the contents and disposition of input data. Realtime systems that use direct-access files frequently record all inputs into the system on magnetic tape *control logs.* Such logs preserve evidence of all system inputs and include *control totals,* which can be compared to control totals generated during processing.

Verification Controls. Visual verification of source documents or input media by clerical personnel and machine verification as performed by intelligent data entry terminals are examples.

Control Totals. A *record count* is a control total that consists of counting the total of source documents or other input records and comparing this total to the number of records counted at other stages of input preparation. If the totals do not match, a mistake has been made. "Batch totals" and "hash totals" are other forms of control totals. A *batch total* is the sum of a specific item of data within a batch of transactions, such as the sales amount in a batch of sales transactions. *Hash totals* are the sum of data fields that are added together only for control comparisons. For example, employee Social Security numbers could be added to produce a control total in the input preparation of payroll documents.

Programmed Checks. Computer programs can include instructions to identify incorrect, invalid, or improper input data as it enters the computer system. Computers can be programmed to check input data for invalid codes, data fields, and transactions. The computer may be programmed to conduct "reasonableness checks" to determine if input data exceeds certain specified limits or is out of sequence.

Processing Controls

Processing controls are developed to identify errors in arithmetic calculations and logical operations. They are also used to ensure that data are not lost or does not go unprocessed. Processing controls can be categorized as *software controls* and *hardware controls* and are summarized below.

Software Controls. Validity checks, reasonableness checks, sequence checks, and control total checks similar to the programmed checks on input, mentioned above, are also used during the processing stage. The computer can also be programmed to check the "internal file labels" at the beginning and end of magnetic tape and disk files. These labels contain information identifying the file as well as providing control totals for the data in the file. These internal file labels allow the computer to ensure that the proper storage file is being used and that the proper data in the file has been processed.

Another major software control is the establishment of *checkpoints* during the processing of a program. Checkpoints are intermediate points within a program being processed where intermediate totals, listings, or "dumps" of data are written on magnetic tape or disk or listed on a printer. Checkpoints minimize the effect of processing errors or failures since processing can be restarted from the last checkpoint, rather than from the beginning of the program. They also help build an "audit trail," which allows transactions being processed to be traced through all of the steps of processing. These and many other input, processing, output, and storage controls may be provided by specialized system software packages known as **system security monitors.** See Figure 19–18.

Hardware Controls. Hardware controls are special checks built into the hardware to verify the accuracy of computer processing. Hardware checks include:

■ Multiple read-write heads on certain hardware devices.
■ Parity checks (described in Chapter Three) and echo checks,

FIGURE 19–18 Overview of the features of a major software package for computer security: IBM's Resource Access Control Facility (RACF)

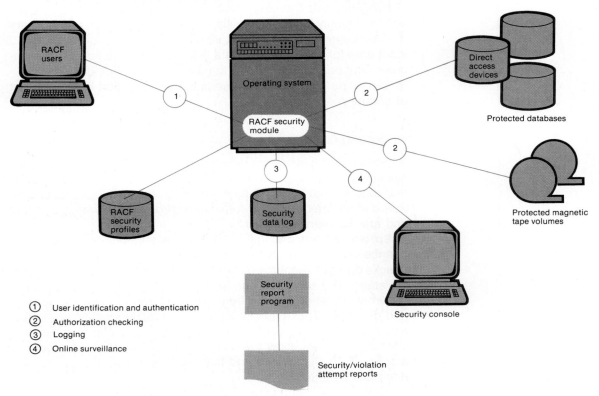

① User identification and authentication
② Authorization checking
③ Logging
④ Online surveillance

which require that a signal be returned from a device or circuit to verify that it was properly activated.

- Malfunction detection circuitry within the computer. This may include a microprocessor that is used to support remote diagnostics and maintenance.

- Switches and other devices. Switches can be set which prohibit writing on magnetic tapes or disks. On magnetic tape reels, a removable plastic or metal ring can be removed to prevent writing on a tape. The write/protect notch on floppy disks has a similar function.

- Miscellaneous hardware controls. There are many other kinds of hardware controls, such as duplicate arithmetic load checks, overflow checks, sign checks, and CPU timing and voltage checks.

Output Controls

Output controls are developed to ensure that output information is correct and complete and is transmitted to authorized users in a timely manner. Several types of output controls are similar to input control methods. For example, output is frequently logged, identified with route slips, and visually verified by input/output control personnel. Control totals on output are compared with control totals generated during the input and processing stages. Control listings provide hard copy evidence of all output produced. Prenumbered output forms are used to control the loss of important output documents, such as stock certificates or payroll check forms. Distribution lists help input/output control personnel ensure that only authorized users receive output. Access to the output of realtime processing systems is controlled by hardware or software that identifies who can receive output and the type of output they are authorized to receive. Finally, persons who receive output should be contacted on a regular basis for feedback on the quality of output.

Storage Controls

Many data files are protected from unauthorized or accidental use by control programs that require proper identification before a file can be used. Hardware devices and software routines are used to protect the database of realtime processing systems from unauthorized use or processing accidents. "Lock words" (also called "pass words") and other identification codes are frequently used to restrict access to authorized users. A catalog of authorized users enables the computer system to identify eligible users and determine which types of information they are authorized to receive.

Organizational Controls

Organizational controls are methods of organizing and performing the functions of the information services organization that facilitate the accuracy and integrity of computer operations and systems development activities. Some of these controls are discussed below.

Production Control. A production control section should monitor the progress of information processing jobs, data entry activities, and the quality of input/output data.

Separation of Duties. A basic principle of organizational control is to assign the duties of systems development, computer operations, and control of data and program files to separate groups. For example, systems analysts and computer programmers may not be allowed to operate the computer console or make changes to data or programs being processed. In addition, the responsibility for maintaining a library of data files and program files is assigned to a *librarian* or *database administrator.*

Standard Procedures. Manuals of standard procedures for systems development, computer programming, and computer operations should be developed and maintained. Following standard procedures promotes uniformity and minimizes the chances of errors and fraud.

Documentation. System, program, and operations documentation must be developed and kept up-to-date to ensure the correct processing and maintenance of each computer application.

Authorization Requirements. Requests for systems development, program changes, or computer processing must be subject to a formal process of review before authorization is given. For example, program changes generated by maintenance programmers should be approved by the manager of programming after consultation with the manager of computer operations and the manager of the affected user department.

Conversion Scheduling. Conversion to new hardware and software, installation of newly developed information systems, and changes to existing programs should be subjected to a formal notification and scheduling procedure to minimize their detrimental effects on the accuracy and integrity of information services.

Auditing of Information Services. The information services organization and its activities must undergo periodic examinations or "audits" to determine the accuracy, integrity, and safety of all computer-based information systems. We will discuss this important aspect of organizational control shortly.

Facility Controls

Facility controls are methods that protect physical facilities and their contents from loss or destruction. Computer centers are subject to such hazards as accidents, natural disasters, sabotage, vandalism, industrial espionage, and theft. Therefore, physical safeguards and various control procedures are necessary to protect the hardware, software, and, most importantly, the vital information and records of computer-using organizations. Several important facility controls are described below.

Database Controls

Control over files of computer programs and data must be maintained. A librarian or database administrator is responsible for maintaining and controlling access to the libraries and databases of the organization. Many firms use *backup files,* which are duplicate files of data or programs. Such files may be stored "off premise," that is, in a location away from the computer center, sometimes in special storage vaults in remote locations. Many realtime processing systems use duplicate files that are updated by data communication links. Files are also protected by "file retention" measures, which involve storing copies of master files and transaction files from previous periods. If current files are destroyed, the files from previous periods are used to reconstruct new current files.

Data Communications Controls

The communications control hardware and software described in Chapter Twelve play a vital role in the control of data communications activity. In addition, data can be transmitted in "scrambled" form and unscrambled by the computer system only for authorized users. This process is called **encription.** It transforms digital data into a scrambled code before it is transmitted and then decodes the data when it is received. Special hardware and software must be used for the encription process.

Computer Failure Controls

A variety of controls are needed to prevent computer failure or minimize its effects. Computers fail or "go down" for several reasons, such as power failure, electronic circuitry malfunctions, mechanical malfunctions of peripheral equipment, hidden programming errors, and computer operator errors. Therefore, the information services department must take steps to prevent equipment failure and to minimize its detrimental effects. Computers with automatic and remote maintenance capabilities should be acquired. A program of *preventive maintenance* of hardware must be developed. Adequate electrical supply, air conditioning, humidity control, and fire prevention standards must be set. A *backup computer system* capability should be arranged with other computer-using organizations. Major hardware or software changes should be carefully scheduled and implemented. Computer operators must have adequate training and supervision. Finally, consideration should be given the acquisition of **fault-tolerant** computer systems, which include multiple major processors and special software that provide *fail-safe* or *fail-soft* capabilities. That is, the computer system either will continue to operate at the same level, or at a reduced but acceptable level, even if there is a major hardware or software failure.

Physical Protection Controls

Providing maximum security and disaster protection for the computer installation requires many types of controls. Only authorized personnel are allowed access to the computer center through such techniques as identification badges for information services personnel, electrical door locks, burglar alarms, security police, closed-circuit TV, and other detection systems. The computer center should be protected from disaster by such safeguards as fire detection and extinguishing systems; fireproof storage vaults for protection of files; emergency power systems; electromagnetic shielding; and temperature, humidity, and dust control.

Insurance

Adequate insurance coverage must be secured to protect the business firm from substantial financial losses in the event of accidents, disasters, fraud, and other risks. Several insurance companies offer special computer security policies, which include insurance against fire, natural disasters, vandalism and theft, liability insurance for data processing errors or omissions, fidelity insurance for the bonding of information services personnel as a protection against fraud, etc. The amount of such insurance should be large enough to replace computer equipment and facilities. Insurance is also available to cover the cost of reconstructing data and program files.

Auditing Electronic Information Processing

The information services organization should be periodically examined or *audited* by internal auditing personnel of the business firm or by external auditors from professional accounting firms. Such audits should review and evaluate whether proper and adequate *information processing controls, organizational controls*, and *facility controls* have been developed and implemented. There are two basic approaches for auditing the information processing activities of computer-based information systems. They are known as (1) "auditing around the computer" and (2) "auditing through the computer."

Auditing around a computer involves verifying the accuracy and propriety of computer input and output without evaluating the computer programs used to process the data. This is a simpler and easier method that does not require auditors with programming experience. However, since this auditing method does not trace a transaction through all of its stages of processing and does not test the accuracy and integrity of the computer program, it should not be the only method used for large-volume, sophisticated computer applications.

Auditing through the computer involves verifying the accuracy and integrity of the computer programs that process the data, as well as the input and output of the computer system. Auditing through the computer requires a knowledge of computer operations and programming. Some firms employ special "EDP auditors" for this assignment. Special *test data* may be used to test processing accuracy and the control procedures built into the computer program. The auditors may develop a special *test program* or use **audit software packages** (such as that illustrated in Figure 19–19) to process the data of the business firm. They then compare the results produced by their audit program with the results generated by the computer users' own programs. One of the objectives of such testing is to detect the presence of unauthorized changes or *patches* to computer programs. Unauthorized program patches may be the cause of "unexplainable" errors or may be used by an unscrupulous programmer for fraudulent purposes.

Auditing through the computer may be too costly for some computer applications. Therefore, a combination of both auditing approaches is usually employed. However, both auditing approaches must effectively contend with the changes caused by electronic information processing to the "audit trail." The **audit trail** can be defined as the presence of information processing media and proce-

FIGURE

19–19 Audit information management system

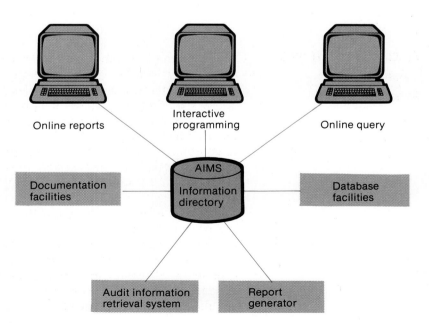

dures that allow a transaction to be traced through all stages of information processing. This begins with a transaction's appearance on a source document and ends with its transformation into information on a final output document. The audit trail of manual information processing systems was quite visible and easy to trace. However, electronic information processing has changed the form of the audit trail. Information formerly available to the auditor in the form of visual records is no longer available or is recorded on media which can be interpreted only by machines. Realtime processing systems have increased the "invisibility" of the traditional audit trail. Paper documents and historical files are frequently eliminated when remote terminals and direct access files are used.

Such developments make the auditing of such systems a complex but vital assignment. Therefore, auditing personnel should be included on the project team of all major systems development projects and consulted before smaller systems projects are implemented. In addition, auditing personnel should be notified of all changes to computer programs caused by the program maintenance activity. Such procedures give the auditor the opportunity to suggest methods of preserving the audit trail and providing adequate information processing controls in systems that are being developed or modified.

REAL WORLD APPLICATION 19-3

Martin Marietta Corporation

"It's like having a chain link fence charged with electricity around your files." Jim Elliott is talking about data security at Martin Marietta Data System's massive computer center in Orlando, Florida, one of the world's largest. More precisely, he's talking about the Resource Access Control Facility, or RACF, an IBM program product designed to protect data files from unauthorized disclosure, modification, or destruction. Basically an access control mechanism, RACF controls who may use a system, what parts of the system they may access, and how each user may access those resources. In effect, the customer defines users, groups, and resources and builds profiles to verify them, check authorizations, and provide an audit trail.

Protecting data is of course, just one aspect of security for the division. But it is an area in which the Orlando facility has done more than most. "Overall security is something we have to live with, part of the job," says Mr. Elliott. "There are all kinds of things that can be done, from palm prints to cipher locks. We've always been on the leading edge, with closed-circuit TV, fire and smoke detection, and redundant diesel-powered generators for our own uninterruptible power supply. RACF has helped make us state-of-the-art in the security of data as well—for anyone who wants to use the service."

This belief has helped to foster new relationships at the Data Systems Division—particularly between DP auditing and security. These two areas are combined in the division's quality assurance function under Chuck Elliott. "Quality assurance here functions in a number of capabilities," he explains. "Among other things, we are a form of substitute for DP auditing. We interface with the corporation's internal and external auditors. Now, through this interface, our internal auditors have an avenue to DP they never had before. Our outside CPA firm recognizes both the interface and RACF utilization as desirable and has recommended to the internal audit staff that they assess how our corporate customers are using RACF. Quality assurance is being more formally aligned with the corporate internal audit team. The services complement each other."

"It goes all the way to the board of directors level," adds Jim Elliott. "Security is not a one-man show here. Everybody is concerned about it. Protection and control are the key to this whole operation. We want to protect ourselves as well as our customers."

- What types of controls are used by Martin Marietta for computer security?
- What control functions are provided by the RACF software package?

Source: "Getting a Lock on Data Security," *Data Processor*, December 1979, pp. 9–12. Reprinted with permission.

SUMMARY

- Managing the computer resources of a business firm has become a major new responsibility of business management, known as information resources management (IRM). Business computer users must learn how to plan, organize, and control the hardware, software, people, data, and information resources of their firms. The major activities of information services organizations can be grouped into five basic functional categories: (1) systems development, (2) user services, (3) data administration, (4) operations, and (5) administration.

- The organizational structure, location, and staffing of an information services department must reflect these five basic functions and activities. However, many variations exist, which reflect the attempts of business computer users to tailor their organizational and staffing arrangements to their particular business activities and management philosophy, as well as to the capabilities of centralized or distributed information processing.

- There is a wide variety of career choices and job types in many computer-using organizations. However, computer services personnel can be grouped into six occupational categories: systems development, user services, data administration, programming, operations, and administration. Managing the technical personnel in an information services department is a major personnel management assignment.

- Another major managerial responsibility in computer-using business firms is the development and implementation of plans to manage their information systems resources. This requires long-range planning and project management techniques. Managing computer operations requires many applications of operations management, including various production planning and control techniques.

- One of the most important responsibilities of the management of computer-using business firms is the security and control of its information services activities. Controls are needed that ensure the accuracy, integrity, and safety of the electronic information processing activities and resources of computer users. Such controls attempt to minimize errors, fraud, and destruction in the information services department. Such controls can be grouped into three major categories: (1) information processing controls, (2) organizational controls, and (3) facility controls.

- The information services department should be periodically audited to review and evaluate whether proper and adequate information processing controls, organizational controls, and facility controls have been developed and implemented. Information systems auditing, therefore, plays a vital role in ensuring proper managerial control of computer resources and information processing activities.

KEY TERMS AND CONCEPTS

Organizational functions of information services
Centralization or decentralization of information services
Careers in information services
Job categories of information services personnel
Project management
Information resource management

Information services planning
Operations management
Computer security and control
Information processing controls
Organizational controls
Facility controls
Auditing information processing
Audit trail

REVIEW AND APPLICATION QUESTIONS

1. Why has managing the computer and information resources of a business firm become a major responsibility of management?
2. What are some of the activities that are involved in information systems development, user services, data administration, operations, and administration in a computer services organization?
3. Where do you think the information services department should be located within the business firm? Why?
4. Should information services be centralized or decentralized within a business firm? Explain.
5. What are some of the career choices and job responsibilities of information services personnel? Which job type is most appealing to you? Why?
6. Why does the management and development of information services personnel pose some unique problems for management?
7. What are some of the solutions to the personnel management problems in information services organizations?
8. What is the role of information resource management (IRM) in a computer-using firm?

9. What are some of the major activities of information services planning?
10. What is project management? How can it be applied to systems development projects?
11. Identify some of the planning and control activities of operations management.
12. Does electronic information processing increase or decrease the probability of errors, fraud, and destruction of processing facilities? Explain.
13. Distinguish between information processing controls, organizational controls, and facilities controls. Provide several examples of each type of control.
14. Is "auditing through the computer," always superior to "auditing around the computer"? Explain.
15. What is meant by the "audit trail"? How has it been affected by electronic information processing?

APPLICATION PROBLEMS

1. If you have not already done so, read and answer the questions after each Real World Application in this chapter.
2. ABC Department Stores has a large mainframe computer and a 40-person MIS department at corporate headquarters. POS terminals at each department store, as well as video display terminals for store managers and buyers, are connected in a data communications network to the host computer. Also, a few store managers use personal computers at work. Several store managers feel that ABC should move to a more decentralized information services organization. The VP for MIS says that a distributed processing approach would not work for a department store chain. What do you think? How would you decentralize information services? What problems can you foresee?
3. Jim Klugman, the VP for MIS at ABC Department Stores says that IRM is just another buzzword like MIS. He says that any organization has information processing jobs to do, and his job is to see that they get done efficiently. Do you agree with Jim? What would Jim's attitude be if he believed in the IRM concept? Finish the following sentence for him: "Since I believe in the IRM concept, I feel that the job of the MIS department is to . . ."
4. There is a two-year backlog of user systems development requests at ABC Department Stores. The VP for MIS wants to hire more programmers and systems analysts to reduce this backlog. Top management is resisting this proposal, saying that new ways should be found to solve this problem. Jim Klugman, the

VP for MIS says that concepts like information centers and distributed processing wouldn't work at ABC, because each department store is too small to support their own computer facilities and information centers. What do you think? What solution do you have?

5. There has been a rash of resignations of programmers and systems analysts from the MIS department at ABC Department Stores in recent months. One analyst says she is leaving because computing at ABC isn't challenging enough. Another says he feels isolated from developments taking place in the computer industry. A third analyst says she doesn't have enough contact with computer users at ABC. What are these analysts revealing about what motivates information services personnel? How would you solve some of these problems?

6. An information systems auditor has written a report criticizing the controls ABC Department Stores has implemented in its payroll and accounts payable applications. His report states that these two applications should have more stringent controls than other common business applications? Why? What risks are involved? What controls can you suggest to minimize such risks?

CHAPTER 20

Computers, Management, and Society

CHAPTER OUTLINE

LEARNING OBJECTIVES

The purpose of this chapter is to promote a basic understanding of the major challenges that computers present to business management by analyzing (1) the challenge of computer performance, (2) the challenge to management performance, and (3) the social challenge of the computer. After reading and studying this chapter, you should be able to:

1. Explain how the problem of poor computer performance can be solved by management involvement in planning and control.
2. Identify several reasons for user resistance to computerization.
3. Discuss how and why solving the problems of user resistance requires meaningful user involvement.
4. Explain how the computer can support either the centralization or decentralization of (a) information processing, (b) management, and (c) operations.
5. Discuss how the computer can be a "catalyst" for the systems approach to management.
6. Identify several ways that the computer can enlarge and enrich the job of management.
7. Discuss the impact of computers on society in terms of several socioeconomic effects.
8. Identify several social applications of the computer that have helped to solve social problems.

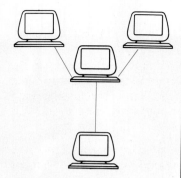

The preceding chapters of this book should have emphasized that the computer is a valuable and powerful resource presenting a major challenge to business management. Figure 20–1 illustrates that we will conclude our study of computers in business management by focusing on three major challenges of the computer:

- The challenge of computer performance.
- The challenge to management performance.
- The social challenge of the computer.

THE CHALLENGE OF COMPUTER PERFORMANCE

Computers are used by business firms to reduce costs, increase profits, provide better service to customers, and provide better information to management. Computers should reduce the cost of doing business by automating the processing of data and the control of operations. Better customer service and improved management information are supposed to result from the speed and accuracy of the computer. Thus computers should improve the competitive position and profit performance of business firms. However, this has not occurred in many documented cases. Studies by management consulting firms, computer-user groups, and others have shown that many business firms moved too far and too fast into computer processing without adequate personnel resources and management involvement, and that many computer users and computer professionals have not yet learned how to manage this vital but expensive business resource.

Poor Computer Performance

There can be no doubt that the computer has become an indispensable tool for modern business management. Without computers, managers could not plan, operate, and control the operations of most of the businesses of today. However, it is obvious that the management of many computer-using business firms have not yet learned to plan, organize, and control the operations of their own computers and information services departments. The valuable resource of the computer is not being effectively, efficiently, and economically utilized by business firms. *For example:*

- The computer is not being used *effectively* by companies that use the computer primarily for recordkeeping applications.
- Computers are not being used *efficiently* by information service

FIGURE

20–1 The challenges of the computer

PERFORMANCE CHALLENGE · SOCIETAL CHALLENGE

THE CHALLENGES OF THE COMPUTER

MANAGEMENT CHALLENGE

departments that provide inadequate service to users while failing to properly utilize their computing capacity.

- Many computer systems are also not being used *economically*. Information processing costs have risen faster than other costs in many business firms, even though the cost of processing each unit of data is decreasing due to improvements in hardware and software technology.

Poor computer performance can take many forms, as illustrated by the list of problems in computing gathered from users and management and shown in Figure 20–2. Further, poor computer performance is not limited to small business firms with limited financial and human resources. Many large business firms have openly admitted their failure to manage the computer effectively.

What is the solution to the problem of poor computer performance? Is more hardware, software, and sophisticated computer systems the answer? Or does the solution lie in the emotional reaction of some business computer users who have "pulled the plug" and "disintegrated their integrated information systems" by "decomputerizing"? The solution to poor computer performance does not lie in either extreme position. There are no quick and easy answers to this problem. Such solutions as "better management of computer resources and services" are obvious but much too vague. However, the experiences of successful computer users reveal that the basic ingredient of high-quality computer performance is **extensive and meaningful management and user involvement** in the development and operation of computer-based information systems. This should be the key ingredient in shaping the response of management to the challenge of improving the quality of computer services.

FIGURE

20–2 Performance problems in computing

- Users cannot obtain applications when they want them. There is often a delay of years.
- It is difficult or impossible to obtain changes that managers need in a reasonable amount of time.
- The programs have errors in them or sometimes don't work.
- Systems delivered often do not match the true user requirements.
- Specifications, on which users have to sign off, are difficult to check and are usually full of inconsistencies, omissions, and errors.
- Systems cost much more to develop and to maintain than anticipated.
- Because of the long time required to obtain results, the most important decision-support systems are never implemented. The support is needed more quickly than the time needed to create the programs.

Source: James Martin, *An Information Systems Manifesto*, (Englewood Cliffs, N.J.: Prentice-Hall, 1984), p. 4. Reprinted with permission.

REAL WORLD APPLICATION 20-1

The Rocky MIS Horror Show

Scene I:

What was supposed to be a look at the future of MIS at the annual Society for Management Information Systems (SMIS) conference turned, instead, to be a review of the present. It wasn't pleasant—the picture portrayed by three panelists on a beautiful fall day in Philadelphia.

George Glaser—a long-time McKinsey consultant, professional society leader, and entrepreneur—told a horror story about a friend of his who has inherited a DP shop that features a 370/168 with 600 terminals, 500 of them remote. It provides a response time of 30 seconds. The shop is run by a former systems programmer, who has a staff of eight applications programmers, one systems analyst, and zero systems programmers. Personnel turnover has been running at 60 percent. There are 700 programs, 15 of them major ones, with one assembly language program that has 50 pages of code. There are no useful comments, no more registers available, and the people who wrote the programs are all gone. There is a backlog of 278 change requests going back four years.

Glaser wondered if this installation is atypical, then suggested it is not. He opened his comments with a remark that MIS has "severe maintenance problems, a shortage of people, and the people we have are sinking into a quagmire of undocumented, obsolete systems that are unmaintained and unmaintainable." Makes you feel warm all over?

Scene II:

Who, in the first place, suggested the wonders of MIS to management? Some of the vendors, of course. And justifiably so. The technology was available to produce the results. And vendors sell technology. Accomplishing those advertised results was another thing. And who promised the results would actually happen? Was it not the members of SMIS and their counterparts in systems management? They bought the vendor pitch. They sold management on the expectations of MIS. Management bought the MIS story, put up the dollars, and sat back and awaited the payoff. Is management to blame, or the soothsayers, including consultants who pied pipered management down the primrose path?

We don't share the pessimism of the SMIS panel. For all the horror stories that have emerged from this history of data processing, there are many, many more untold stories involving effective, efficient operations. As we move into the era of information resource management (IRM), the systems profession has a new and challenging opportunity to provide management with the ability to manage information as a major resource. We can benefit from past mistakes. To our mind, most failures in management information systems can be attributed to the following: Too many systems practitioners are limited by a punched-card, data processing mentality; too many management people still think of computer systems as little more than extensions of the accounting department; and all too many top management people and their systems managers are willing to allow vendors to do their systems thinking for them.

- Who is responsible for poor computer performance: Computer professionals? Computer users? Management? Explain.
- How can such situations be improved?
- How can the concept of information resource management help?

Sources: Robert Forest, "The Rocky MIS Horror Show," *Infosystems,* November 1980, p. 91; and Arnold Keller, "MIS: The Pot and the Kettle," *Infosystems,* November 1980, p. 34. Copyright 1980, Hitchcock Publishing Co. Reprinted with permission.

Management Involvement

Proper management involvement requires the knowledgeable and active participation of managers in the planning and control of computer-based information systems resources. Managers must practice **information resource management**: the management of hardware, software, people, data, and information resources. Being an involved manager means knowing the answers to such questions as:

- How do our information system resources contribute to the short- and long-term profitability of this company?
- Have we invested too little or too much in computer resources?
- Do we have realistic long-range plans for information systems development and for acquisition of computer resources that will improve the efficiency of business operations and the quality of management decisions?
- Are information systems development projects and our computer operations being properly managed?
- To sum up, are computer resources being used efficiently, effectively, and economically in every part or activity of this organization?

Without a high degree of management involvement, managers will not know the answer to such questions and thus will not be able to control the quality of computer performance. Management can no longer claim that acquiring knowledge about computer fundamentals and computer use in business is too difficult or time-consuming. (It is hoped this book has shown that this is not the case.) Such knowledge should be sufficient to allow managers to become active participants in the development and management of computer-based information systems. Such participation will provide a form of "on-the-job training," which will further reinforce their ability to manage the computer resource effectively and not be baffled by the "EDP snow job." See Figure 20–3.

FIGURE

20–3 Managers and the EDP snow job

I've seen the ablest and toughest of executives insist on increased productivity by a plant manager, lean on accounting for improved performance, and lay it on purchasing in no uncertain terms to cut its staff. But when these same executives turn to EDP they stumble to an uncertain halt, baffled by the snow job and the blizzard of computer jargon. They accept the presumed sophistication and differences that are said to make EDP activities somehow immune from normal management demands. They are stopped by all this nonsense, uncertain about what's reasonable to expect, what they can insist upon. They become confused and then retreat, muttering about how to get a handle on this blasted situation.

Source: Harry T. Larson, "EDP, a 20-Year Ripoff," *Infosystems,* November 1974, p. 27. Copyright 1974, Hitchcock Publishing Co. Reprinted with permission.

FIGURE

20–4 Levels of management involvement

Several studies have shown that companies successfully using computers view the development and management of computer-based information systems as a responsibility of both top management and operating management. These companies have come to understand the systems analysts cannot design information systems that effectively support the decision needs of management without management involvement in the systems design process. Systems development projects will not "manage themselves." They need the planning and control activities of management personnel. The information services department needs the active support of top management and user management to improve and maintain the quality of computer services. Figure 20–4 illustrates several levels of management involvement, which are indicated below:

- Many business firms use an *executive information services* committee of top management to develop long-range plans and to coordinate the development of information systems. This committee includes the senior management of the major divisions of the firm, as well as the vice-president of the information services organization.

- A *steering committee* of middle managers, operating managers, and management personnel from the information services department may be created to oversee the progress of project teams. The committee meets on a regular basis during the existence of systems projects to review progress made, to settle disputes, and to change priorities, if necessary.

- Development of major strategic information systems requires management involvement through active participation in systems development as members of systems development project teams.

The User Generation

As each succeeding generation of computer systems is developed, it becomes exceedingly difficult for management and computer professionals to pacify computer users with past excuses based on untried applications, inexperienced information services personnel, or inadequate equipment. Most computer users rightly feel that the "experimental" stage has passed and expect high-quality computer services. Both management and computer professionals must realize that we are in a **user generation** of computer usage, which will continue indefinitely into the future.

The attitudes of computer users are accentuated by an increased awareness of the current state-of-the-art of the computer industry. The public news media, computer industry propaganda, and company publications have touted the speed, power, and sophistication of modern computer systems. The microcomputer revolution, with its promise of computer power for every person and product, only adds to the rising expectations of computer users. It is hoped that microcomputers, minicomputers, and the distributed data processing they make possible will do much to meet the increasing expectations of the user generation.

Computer users are demanding economical, efficient, and effective computer-based information systems. They are becoming impatient with the rising costs, the inefficiencies and "downtimes" of computer operations, and the long lead times of information systems development. They want more consistent accuracy, flexibility, and timeliness in the information produced by current information systems. Management users want new information systems to provide information that more effectively supports their planning and decision-making functions. They want these new systems to integrate the information produced by the organization and to disperse it wherever and whenever needed throughout the organization. Computer-using business firms want information systems that allow management and operating personnel without any technical sophistication to easily use an information system in carrying out their assignments. They want flexible, well-planned information systems that can keep pace with the growth in volume and complexity of the business system, without the disruptions of major systems conversions every few years. What the new generation of computer users want is a new generation of *user-oriented information systems*.

User Resistance

The coming of the user generation has intensified the potential for resistance by computer users. Any "new way of doing things" generates some resistance by the people affected. However, computer-based information systems can generate a significant amount of fear and reluctance to change. There are many reasons for this state of affairs, some of which we will explore in a later discussion concerning the impact of computers on society. Whatever the reasons for user resistance, it is the responsibility of business managers and computer professionals to find ways of reducing the conflict and resistance that arises from the use of computers. A brief summary of several reasons for user resistance is outlined in Figure 20–5.

User Involvement

Solving the problems of *user resistance* requires meaningful **user involvement** based on formal methods of (1) *education*, (2) *commu-*

FIGURE

20–5 Reasons for user resistance

Ignorance

Computer users do not have a sufficient knowledge of electronic information processing, while computer professionals do not have a sufficient knowledge of the operations and problems of the business.

Performance

Poor computer performance, resulting in broken promises and inadequate service.

Participation

Users have not been made active participants in systems development and systems maintenance.

Ergonomics

Hardware and software are not designed for ease of use, safety, and comfort of end-users; not "user-friendly."

Communication

Computer users may not understand the technical jargon of computer professionals, and information systems personnel may not understand the unique terminology of each group of computer users.

Personnel Problems

Some computer users resent the influence of computer professionals on their work activities. Information services personnel are viewed as "technical types," with different work assignments, different working conditions, and different promotion and other personnel policies.

Organizational Conflict

The information services department is viewed as trying to gain too much influence and control within the organization, getting involved in too many operations of the company, and receiving a disproportionate share of the financial resources of the company.

---

nication, and (3) *participation*. Like management, user personnel must be educated in the fundamentals of computer technology and its application to business information systems. This basic knowledge should be supplemented by programs of orientation, education, and training concerning specific computer-based information systems.

We have discussed several methods of increasing user participation and communication. We have emphasized, in particular, the necessity of (1) providing resources, such as information centers which allow users to develop their own systems and (2) including user representatives on project teams charged with the development of major information systems. We stressed that direct user participation should provide the type of user involvement required to improve the quality of information services and to reduce the potential for user resistance. Such user involvement helps assure that computer-based information systems are "user-oriented" in their design. Systems that tend to inconvenience or to frustrate their users cannot be effective systems, no matter how efficiently they process data. *Systems must be designed to appear more responsive to the user, rather than appear to force users to be responsive to the system.*

Several methods of user involvement are employed by successful organizations. The manager of the information services department should meet frequently with the heads of user departments on an individual basis to discuss the status of new and existing systems. In addition, some firms have created *user liaison* positions. Computer-user departments are assigned representatives from the information services department, who perform a vital role by "troubleshooting" problems, gathering and communicating information, and coordinating educational efforts. These activities improve communication and coordination between the user and the information services department, because all questions and problems that arise are referred to one individual. This avoids the "runaround" effect that can frustrate computer users and is an important reminder of the user-orientation of the information services department. Finally, the creation of information centers that provide hardware, software, and people resources to users is a major development in user involvement.

THE CHALLENGE TO MANAGEMENT PERFORMANCE

The Impact of Computers on Management

When computers were introduced into business, predictions were made that there would be significant changes in management— because the information processing power and programmed decision-making capability of the computer would cause drastic reductions in employees, including middle management and supervisory personnel. A centralized computer system would process all of the data for the organization, control most of its operations, and make most of its decisions. This has not proven to be the case. Changes in organizational structure and types of personnel have occurred, but they have not been as dramatic as predicted. Naturally, highly automated systems do not require as many people as manual methods. Therefore, there have been significant reductions in the amount of people required to perform certain manual tasks in certain organizations. However, this has been countered to some extent by the need for increased information processing personnel and computer professionals to run the computer-based systems of the organization.

In the previous chapter, we concluded that modern computer systems could support either the *centralization* (with a large central computer) or *decentralization* (with a distributed processing network) of *electronic information processing* within a business firm. The same concept can be applied to the centralization and decentralization of *operations* and *management* within a computer-using organization.

■ **Centralization.** Large central computer systems allow top management to centralize decision making formerly done at lower levels of the organization and reduce the number of branch offices, manufacturing plants, and warehouses needed by the firm.

■ **Decentralization.** Computers and data communication networks allow top management to delegate more responsibility to middle managers and to increase the number of branch offices (or other company units) while still providing top management with the ability to control the organization.

Thus whether the computer encourages centralization or decentralization of business operations and management depends on the philosophy of top management and the nature of the operations of the specific business firm.

The Systems Approach to Management

The challenge of the computer to business management can be considered in a positive sense if the computer is viewed as a "catalyst" for applying the systems concept to business management. Computerizing information systems requires huge commitments of time, money, and personnel. It requires intensive studies of the various operations and information requirements of the business. It puts management "eyeball to eyeball" with the highly sophisticated technology of computer hardware, software, and personnel. It forces painful decisions that change "the way we always used to do things." Faced with these pressures, management can take the easy way out by computerizing information systems in the traditional "piecemeal" approach (i.e., the information requirements of each department in the firm is computerized, one after the other, as resources permit). Instead, management should welcome the computer as a *catalyst* for *the systems approach*. If the firm is a business "system," rather than just a series of departments that perform various functions, the piecemeal approach can be disastrous. Management must use the systems approach when confronted with the need to expand the use of computers in the business firm. Managing a business firm becomes a form of systems development, as illustrated in Figure 20–6.

Enlarging the Job of Management

A major challenge to management arises from the ability of the computer to handle clerical details and simple decisions that can be programmed and, thus, free management from these routine

FIGURE

20–6 A systems approach
to management

Systems Investigation
Survey the subsystems of the business firm and the business environment for problems and opportunities. Separate symptoms from problems. Select the most urgent and most feasible problems to be solved or opportunities to be pursued.

Systems Analysis
Gather and analyze information about the selected problem or opportunity in terms of the systems and subsystems that are involved.

Systems Design
Develop alternative courses of action by designing and testing models of the systems that affect the problem or opportunity.

Programming
Choose a single course of action and develop plans, programs, budgets, policies, and necessary procedures.

Systems Implementation
Put the decision into effect by implementing the plans developed in the programming stage.

Systems Maintenance
Monitor and evaluate the results of the decision, since the subsystems of the business firm and the business environment are subject to continual change. Modify the decision as necessary.

tasks. Many managers can no longer use the excuse that "I'm too tied up with details and paper work" or "I can't get the right information at the right time in the right form in the right place." Management must develop new and creative activities, including the use of the computer to support high-level decisions.

Letting the computer take over routine decisions should not be viewed as a threat by managers but as an opportunity to engage in more activities that are beneficial to the business firm. Many managers have reported that the computer has finally given them the time to "get out of the office and into the field." They can finally spend enough time pursuing their *marketing responsibilities* with customers and salespersons, their *personnel management responsibilities* with subordinates, and their *societal responsibilities* with various public and governmental groups. Managers can spend more time on *planning* activities instead of spending much of their time "putting out fires." Thus, the computer can enable many managers finally to become "managers" rather than "paper shufflers."

Another aspect of the management challenge lies in the ability of the computer to help management make strategic planning and control decisions. The use of the computer must rise above the "paper shuffling" level to a higher level which uses simulation and other mathematical and statistical techniques to analyze the important factors that must be considered in management decisions and

REAL WORLD APPLICATION 20–2

Bergen Brunswig Corporation

Robert E. Martini is president of Bergen Brunswig Corporation one of the nation's largest distributors of pharmaceutical and health-care products. In an interview with Mary Miles, *Computer Decisions*'s New England editor, Martini discussed the Century City, California-based company's innovative use of computers to develop a range of customer services and programs.

Question: Do you see information-resource management as an important part of Bergen Brunswig's future, considering a still "iffy" economy?

Martini: Our business has remained fairly stable throughout the ups and downs of the economy. Our sales and earnings growth over the last five years has been more than 25 percent, compounded annually, much of it coming in gains in market share. Marketing intelligence available through our information resource management has really helped in achieving these results. Good information resource management will always be important to us.

Q: Are you devoting, or do you expect to devote, more personal attention and corporate resources to information technology?

Martini: Our senior management has already devoted a lot of attention to these factors. We have committed human resources to quality assurance and business-systems planning [BSP]. The BSP group coordinates our information center. In addition, Bergen Brunswig is committed to the installation of an IBM 3081, and our operating divisions are now completing installation of IBM's new System/36.

Q: What roles do you see for information technology in your company over the next few years?

Martini: There are two activities in which information technology will play a major part. One is the management of inventory, which rep-

resents about 60 percent of our assets. We are currently installing IBM's *Inforem,* a highly sophisticated inventory-management system. The other is provision of immediate access to financial information.

Q: In some companies, the information explosion has driven a wedge between corporate management and the MIS/dp department. Has this happened at Bergen Brunswig? How have you dealt with the problem?

Martini: About two years ago, we felt we were not managing dp as well as we were managing other aspects of our business. So we developed what we call the "EDP Executive Policy Committee." The idea was, among other things, to establish a much more direct relationship between corporate management and dp. One change we've made to accomplish this has been to classify users' needs in terms of dollars required. Jobs that will cost less than $10,000 are decided on by the operating managers; jobs costing between $10,000 and $50,000 are decided on by the corporate officer in charge; and jobs costing more than $50,000 are decided on by the Executive Policy Committee. All jobs are tracked and reviewed by the committee monthly.

I believe we can now manage dp as well as other parts of the company. Many people—myself included—used to feel that dp, with all its sophisticated buzzwords, was like the tail wagging the dog. But I feel that we have it under control now. And corporate management is very close. The dp vice president reports to both the president and the chairman, and the director of dp operations reports to the dp vice president.

Q: Do you use executive-support systems, such as financial-modeling or decision-support packages?

Martini: We use financial modeling extensively. It's extremely helpful in analyzing acquisitions candidates and in planning new operations.

Q: Do you have a personal computer in your office?

Martini: Not now. But I have one at home—

REAL WORLD APPLICATION 20-2 (*concluded*)

an Apple III. And we have plans at Bergen Brunswig to install an IBM Personal Computer in the office of every manager, director, and officer of the company over the next two years.

Q: How are the executives reacting to this plan?

Martini: It's very interesting. The "new breed" executives we're recruiting almost demanded the use of a personal computer. When they come to interviews with their portfolios under their arms, you can almost imagine them carrying a personal computer instead.

Q: How do the managers who already work at Bergen Brunswig feel?

Martini: The folks who have been around and seen what a personal computer can do for them are very excited at the prospect of using one. Generally, there's a very positive attitude. One reason for this, of course, has been our increased attention to narrowing the gap between DP and corporate management. Another has been our training program. The information center that we established last November uses IBM's ADRS (A Departmental Reporting System). Through this past July, we trained 81 people internally, and will have trained 150 by mid-1984. Each employee in the program receives

20 hours of training; then they create their own programs, access our 3081, and generate reports. So far, those trained have developed 120 programs supporting their own needs.

Q: What accounts for Bergen Brunswig's advanced position in the implementation of information technology?

Martini: We have been willing to take advantage of all the benefits the information-technology explosion can offer us. Top management in any company must have a strong desire to explore technology's possibilities—and it's essential to have outstanding executives directing the dp and MIS efforts. Change is happening, and it's going to continue at a much faster pace.

- How is Bergen Brunswig implementing: information resource management? Management involvement? User involvement?
- What changes in management can you see occurring at Bergen Brunswig because of computers?

Source: Mary Miles, "A View from the Top," *Computer Decisions*, September 15, 1983, pp. 16–18. Reprinted with permission.

to test the possible results of proposed decisions. The computer requires only a few seconds to process business data using many of these techniques. The challenge to management is to become acquainted with such *decision support systems* so that they can intelligently use them in planning and control decisions. See Figure 20–7.

THE SOCIAL CHALLENGE OF THE COMPUTER

We are in the midst of a "computer revolution" that experts expect to continue for many years. There can be no doubt the computer has significantly magnified our ability to analyze, compute, and communicate, thereby greatly improving our ability to plan and control

FIGURE

20–7 Managers and computers

MANAGERS DEPEND ON COMPUTERS TO HELP THEM IN THEIR JOBS. . .

Q. Does computer access have an impact in these areas?

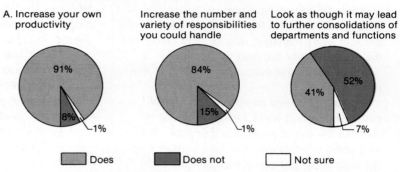

A. Increase your own productivity

Increase the number and variety of responsibilities you could handle

Look as though it may lead to further consolidations of departments and functions

| Does | Does not | Not sure |

. . .BUT NOT MANY HAVE MASTERED OPERATION OF THE MACHINES

Q. Have you taken formal computer training paid for by you or your company?

A. Paid for yourself   Company paid for   Never took computer training

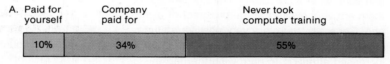

Source: *Business Week,* April 25, 1983, p. 64. Reprinted with permission.

many varieties of human endeavor. However, several social commentators have become alarmed at the "ubiquitous" nature of the computer. They note that computers seem to be present everywhere in all the activities of daily life in our present society. Such commentators worry about our continually increasing dependence on the computer and have identified many adverse social effects of computer usage. What should our attitude be toward the widespread use of the computer in business and society? To answer this question, we shall analyze some of the major social and economic effects of computers and the computer industry.

The Impact of Computers on Society

The impact of computers can be analyzed in terms of social applications and socioeconomic effects. The **social applications** of the computer include its use to solve human and social problems, such as crime and pollution. **Socioeconomic effects** of the computer refer to the impact on society of the use of computers. For example, computerizing a production process may have the *adverse* effect of a decrease in employment opportunities and the *beneficial* effect of providing consumers with products of better quality at lower cost. Business managers must understand the beneficial and adverse effects of computer usage on society. Such an understanding will help them plan and control the development and operation of computer-based information systems within their organizations. We will, therefore, analyze several major aspects of the impact of computers on society. See Figure 20–8.

Impact on Employment and Productivity

The Industrial Revolution of the 18th century saw the development of *mechanization*, in which machines replaced muscle power. The term *automation* began to be used around the middle of this century, and, it refers to the automatic transfer and positioning of work by machines, or to the automatic operation and control of a production process by machines. The assembly line operations of an automobile manufacturer or the petroleum refinery operations

FIGURE 20–8 Major aspects of the computer's impact on society

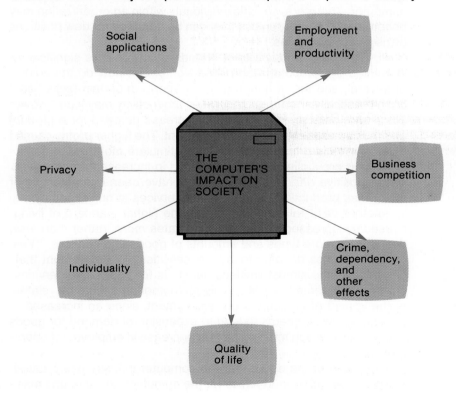

of an oil company are examples of automation. Thus automation is the use of machines to control other machines and physical processes and replaces some of the human brain power and manual dexterity formerly required. The term *cybernation* then came into use to emphasize the automatic control aspect of automation, especially the automatic self-regulating "process control" systems. The increasing use of computers to control automatically all types of production processes, as well as traditional clerical tasks ("office automation"), are major developments of the second half of the 20th century.

The impact of computers on employment and productivity is, therefore, directly related to the use of computers to achieve automation and cybernation. There can be no doubt that the use of computers has created new jobs and increased productivity, while also causing a significant reduction in some types of job opportunities. Computers used for office information processing or for the numerical control of machine tools are accomplishing tasks formerly performed by many clerks and machinists. Also, jobs created by the computer within a computer-using organization require different types of skills and education than do the jobs eliminated by the computer. Therefore, specific individuals within an organization may become unemployed, unless they can be retrained for new positions or new responsibilities.

However, the productivity of an individual worker is significantly increased by computerization. One worker can now do the work of several, and the of time required to perform certain tasks has been drastically shortened. Increased productivity may lead to lower costs and lower prices, which may increase demand for a product and thus generate increased employment. The higher profits caused by increases in productivity may also stimulate more investment to expand productive facilities, resulting in increased employment. These positive effects on employment have been characteristic of the "mass production" of goods and services in our economy.

Another point to remember is that the higher standard of living caused by increased productivity generates *more*, rather than *less*, demand for more types and amounts of goods and services. "Yesterday's luxuries become today's necessities" is a statement that emphasizes the almost limitless demands for goods and services our society seems to exhibit. This phenomenon should be related to the impact of computers on employment, since an increased standard of living seems to lead to expansion of demand for goods and services, which must result in an increase in employment opportunities.

There can be no doubt that the computer industry has created a host of new job opportunities for the manufacture, sale, and maintenance of computer hardware, software, and for other services. Many new jobs, such as systems analysts, computer programmers, and computer operators, have been created in computer-using organizations. Many new jobs have been created in service industries, which provide services to the computer industry and to computer-using firms and to the people that work for them. Additional jobs have been created, because the computer makes possible the production of complex industrial and technical goods and services, which would otherwise be impossible to produce. Thus jobs have been created by activities that are heavily dependent upon the computer in such fields as space exploration, microelectronic technology, and scientific research.

The controversy over the effect of computers on employment will continue as long as activities formerly performed by people are computerized. *Unemployment is more than a statistic*; office and factory workers, whose jobs have been eliminated by computerization, are real people with real employment needs. Such persons will take little comfort in the fact that computers have many beneficial effects upon employment. Business firms and other computer-using organizations, labor unions, and government agencies must continue to provide job opportunities for people displaced by computers. This includes transfers to other positions, relocation to other facilities, or training for new responsibilities. Only if society continues to take positive steps to provide jobs for people displaced by computers can we take pride in the increase in employment caused by computer usage. The effect of computers on employment can be a positive one, if new job opportunities and incentives are provided that offset specific instances of unemployment caused by the computer.

Impact on Competition

The impact of computers on *competition* concerns the effect that computer systems have on the size of business organizations. Computers allow large firms to become more efficient. This can have several anticompetitive effects. Small business firms that could exist because of the inefficiencies of large firms are now driven out of business or absorbed by the larger firms. The efficiency of the larger firms allows them to continue to grow and combine with other business firms and, thus, create the large corporations that exist today. The previously high cost of most computer systems (which only larger firms could afford) accentuated this trend toward bigness.

It is undoubtedly true that computers allow large organizations to grow larger and become more efficient. Organizations grow in terms of people, productive facilities, and such geographic locations as branch offices and plants. Only a computer-based information system is capable of controlling the complex activities and relationships that occur. However, it should be noted that the cost and size of computer systems continues to *decrease*, due to the development of microcomputers and minicomputers, and that the availability of computer services continues to *increase*, due to the activities of computer service bureaus and time-sharing companies. Therefore, even the small firm can take advantage of the productivity and efficiency generated by computer-based systems.

It also should be noted that the computer is changing the *nature* of competition, as well as the size of the competing units. As business firms possess better information on their own internal position and their business environment and, as they use new decision support techniques, the competition between business firms will become very keen and their response to each other's competitive moves will become more accurate and more rapid. Thus only firms with effective computer-based information systems will be able to survive this dynamic competition.

Impact on Individuality

A frequent criticism of computers concerns their negative effect on the *individuality* of people. Computer-based systems are criticized as impersonal systems that dehumanize and depersonalize activities, which have been computerized, since they eliminate the human relationships present in noncomputer systems. Because it is more efficient for an information processing system to deal with an individual as a number than as a name, many people feel a loss of identity that seems inherent in systems where they seem to be "just another number."

Another aspect of the loss of individuality is the regimentation of the individual which seems to be required by some computer-based systems. These systems do not seem to possess any flexibility. They demand strict adherence to detailed procedures, if the system is to work. "Do not fold, spindle, or mutilate" is the statement on punched-card documents that became a popular symbol of the regimentation and inflexibility of computer-based systems. The negative impact of computers on individuality is reinforced by "horror stories," which describe how inflexible and uncaring computer-based systems are when it comes to rectifying their own mistakes. Many of us are familiar with stories of how computerized customer billing and accounting systems have continued to demand payment and send warning notices to a customer whose account has already been paid, despite repeated attempts by the customer to have the error corrected.

Are there any rational arguments against the charges that the computer robs people of their individuality? One major fact that must be considered is summed up by the statement "computers don't make mistakes, people do." That is to say that the errors and inflexibility of computer-based systems are primarily caused by poor systems design or mistakes in computer programming or operations. Thus the computer can be blamed only for occasional hardware malfunctions. Systems analysts, computer programmers, and other information services personnel must accept the responsibility for errors in systems design, computer programming, and data processing operations.

Another point to emphasize is that computer-based systems can be designed to minimize depersonalization and regimentation. "People-oriented" and "user-friendly" information systems can be developed. The computer hardware, software, and systems design capabilities that make such systems possible are increasing rather than decreasing. The use of microcomputers promises to dramatically improve the development of people-oriented information systems (through personal computing and distributed processing) and even of everyday products and services (through microcomputer-powered "smart" products).

The computer is frequently blamed for the "bigness" of business firms and other institutions in which the individual is treated as no more than a statistic. However, it must be remembered that though computers may help make bigness possible, computers alone are not responsible for the growth in size and complexity of our institutions. We live in a society that is attempting to provide *all people*, rather than a small elite, with food, clothing, shelter, employment, education, medical care, and other "necessities" of life while continuing to protect the freedom of the individual. This is an awesome task, accomplished by no previous civilization. Much of the bigness and complexity of modern institutions is caused by our attempt to provide the necessities and amenities of life to vast numbers of people in an efficient and effective manner, rather than reserving them for a small aristocracy. In this regard, the computer is *helping* rather than *hindering* our attempts to provide the "good life" to each individual.

It can also be argued that computers can help promote greater personalization and attention to the individual than would otherwise be possible, given the large size of organizational units, the complexity of individual and organizational relationships, and the volume of individual activities. Computer systems can easily handle large masses of routine transactions, thus allowing *more personal atten-*

tion to important transactions. Computer systems can provide information and analytical techniques that allow individuals a *diversity* of choice so the *individual preferences* of the users of the system can be accommodated in the operation of a system. This is the goal of *people-oriented* and *user-friendly* systems.

Impact on the Quality of Life

The impact of the computer on the quality of life is directly related to its impact upon employment and productivity. For example, computerized business systems increase productivity and allow the production of better-quality goods and services at lower costs. Thus the computer is partially responsible for the high standard of living we enjoy. In addition, the computer has eliminated monotonous or obnoxious tasks in the office and the factory that formerly had to be performed by people. In many instances, this allows people to concentrate on more challenging and interesting assignments, has upgraded the skill level of the work to be performed, and created challenging jobs requiring highly developed skills in the computer industry and within computer-using organizations. Thus computers can be said to upgrade the quality of life because they can upgrade the quality of working conditions and the content of work activities.

Of course, it must be remembered that some jobs created by the computer—data entry, for example—are quite repetitive and routine. Also, to the extent that computers are utilized in some types of automation, they must take some responsibility for the criticism of assembly-line operations that require the continual repetition of elementary tasks, thus forcing a worker to "work like a machine" instead of like a skilled craftsperson. Many automated operations are also criticized for relegating people to a "do nothing" standby role, where workers spend most of their time waiting for infrequent opportunities to "push some buttons." Such effects do have a detrimental effect on the quality of life, but they are more than offset by the less burdensome and more creative jobs created by the computer.

Computers have also contributed to the increased availability of leisure time. The increase in productivity provided by computer usage has helped to allow the average worker to produce more goods and services in less time. We have gone from the six-day week to the five-day week to the four-day week in some industries. The working day has decreased from 12 hours to 8 hours or less. The number of holidays and the length of vacations have increased, as well as the types and length of personal and professional leaves. Young people tend to stay in school longer before seeking permanent employment, while workers can now retire at an earlier age.

Thus, the quality of life is improved because people have more time for recreation, entertainment, education, and creative activities. This development in itself has created more employment, since many new jobs have been created in the "leisure industry" to serve the leisure time activities of people.

Impact on Privacy

Modern computer systems make it technically and economically feasible to collect, store, integrate, interchange, and retrieve data and information quickly and easily. This characteristic has an important beneficial effect on the efficiency and effectiveness of computer-based information systems. However, the power of the computer to store and retrieve information can have a negative effect on *the right to privacy* of every individual. Confidential information on individuals contained in centralized computer data bases by credit bureaus, government agencies, and private business firms could be misused and result in the invasion of privacy and other injustices. Unauthorized use of such information would seriously invade the privacy of individuals, while errors in such data files could seriously hurt the credit standing or reputation of an individual. Such developments were possible before the advent of the computer. However, the speed and power of a large computer with centralized direct-access databases and remote terminals greatly increases the potential for such injustices. The trend towards nationwide integrated information systems with integrated databases by business firms and government agencies substantially increases *the potential* for misuse of computer-stored information. See Figure 20–9.

The Federal Privacy Act strictly regulates the collection and use of personal data by governmental agencies (except for law enforcement investigative files, classified files, and civil service files). The law specifies that individuals have the right to inspect their personal records, make copies, and correct or remove erroneous or misleading information. It also specifies that federal agencies (1) must annually disclose the types of personal data files they maintain, (2) cannot disclose personal information on an individual to any other individual or agency except under certain strict conditions, (3) must inform individuals of the reasons for requesting personal information from them, (4) must retain personal data records only if it is "relevant and necessary to accomplish" an agency's legal purpose, and (5) must "establish appropriate *administrative, technical*, and *physical safeguards* to ensure the security and confidentiality of records." Such legislation should emphasize and accelerate the efforts of systems designers to use hardware, software, and procedural con-

FIGURE

20–9 The scope of U.S. government personal databases

Civil Service

Over 100 million records, mostly dealing with government employes or applicants for government jobs.

Defense Department

Over 400 million records pertaining to service personnel and persons investigated for such things as employment, security, or criminal activity.

Department of Commerce

Over 500 million records, primarily Census Bureau data, but including files on minority businessmen and merchant seamen.

Department of Health and Human Services

Almost two billion personal records, including marital, financial, and health information on recipients of social security, social services, medicaid, medicare, and welfare benefits.

Department of Housing and Urban Development

Almost 50 million records, including data on applicants for housing assistance and federally guaranteed home loans.

Department of Labor

Over 30 million records, many involving people in federally financed work and job-training programs.

Department of Transportation

Over 40 million records, including information on pilots, aircraft, boat owners, and all motorists whose licenses have been withdrawn, suspended, or revoked by any state.

Justice Department

Over 200 million records, including information on criminals and criminal suspects, aliens, persons linked to organized crime, securities-laws violators and "individuals who relate in any manner to official FBI investigations."

Treasury Department

Over one billion records that include files on taxpayers, foreign travelers, persons deemed by the Secret Service to be potentially harmful to the president, and dealers in alcohol, firearms, and explosives.

Veterans Administration

Almost 200 million records, mostly on veterans and dependents now receiving benefits or who got them in the past.

---

trols to maintain the accuracy and confidentiality of computerized databases.

Other Effects

Computer usage creates the *potential* for several other *negative societal effects* that have not been previously mentioned. The potential for fraud and embezzlement by "electronic criminals" has been proven by many widely publicized instances of *computer crime*.

Incriminating personal information in computerized files can be used to blackmail individuals. Fraud or errors in election vote-counting systems can occur. Integrated information systems that allow greater centralization in the control of an organization may give some individuals too much power over other people. In the political sphere, this centralization of power is viewed as a potential threat to democracy if centralized government planning and control robs people of their individual freedoms. Computers can also be misused to distort information about candidates in political campaigns.

Our great and increasing dependence upon computers in the operations of our economy and society is seen as a potential threat by some social observers. Such observers worry about "computers taking over," since we have become so dependent upon their use. They also worry that computer malfunctions might have disastrous consequences if military weapons systems, industrial control systems, and financial information systems are involved. Such potential negative effects pose serious challenges to the *control* aspects of systems design.

Social Applications

Computers can have many direct *beneficial effects* on society when they are used to solve human and social problems through *social applications*, such as medical diagnosis, computer-assisted instruction, governmental program planning, environmental quality control, and law enforcement. Computers can be used to help diagnose an illness, prescribe necessary treatment, and monitor the progress of hospital patients. Computer-assisted instruction (CAI) allows a computer to serve as a "tutor," since it uses conversational computing to tailor instruction to the needs of a particular student. This is a tremendous benefit to students, especially those with learning disabilities.

Computers can be used for crime control through various law enforcement applications that allow police to identify and respond quickly to evidences of criminal activity. Computers have been used to monitor the level of pollution in the air and in bodies of water; to detect the sources of pollution and to issue early warnings when dangerous levels are reached. Computers are also used for the program planning of many government agencies in such areas as urban planning, population density and land use studies, highway planning, and urban transit studies. Computers are being used in job placement systems to help match unemployed persons with available jobs. These and other applications illustrate that the computer can be used to help solve the problems of society.

Systems Design and Social Responsibility

It should be obvious that management must insist that the social and economic effects of computer usage be considered when a computer-based system is being developed. A major management objective should be to develop systems that can be easily and effectively used by people. The objectives of the system must also include the protection of the privacy of the individuals and the defense of the system against fraudulent use. Control hardware, software, and procedures must be included in the systems design. The potential for misuse and malfunction of a proposed system must be analyzed with respect to the impact on computer-using organizations, individuals, and society as a whole.

Many of the potential negative effects of computer usage mentioned previously have or would result from errors in systems design and programming. Increased emphasis on the control capabilities of computer-based systems would protect us from many of these potential effects. Computer-based systems can be designed to prevent their own misuse and remedy their own malfunctions. Computers make it possible for us to monitor the activities of computer-based systems and thus prevent computerized crime and correct systems malfunctions. Management must recognize that the **design and maintenance of system controls** is the key to minimizing the negative effects of computer misuse and malfunction.

However, the elimination of some adverse effects of computer usage may require *government regulation* or *a greater evidence of social responsibility* on the part of the management of computer-using organizations. For example, many business firms have been able to assure their employees that no person would be laid off because of a conversion to computer systems, though some employees have had to accept changes in assignments. Business firms are frequently able to make such a guarantee (and stay in business) because their long-term employment needs have continued to increase due to the growth of the business and the normal attrition of other employees. Such a policy also improves employee morale and productivity and enhances the long-run position of the business firm in society.

It should be obvious that many detrimental effects of the computer on society are caused by improperly designed systems or by individuals and organizations who are not willing to accept the social responsibility for their actions. Like other powerful tools, the computer possesses the potential for great good or evil. Managers, computer users, and computer professionals must accept the responsibility for its proper and beneficial use.

REAL WORLD APPLICATION 20-3

Hacking with the 414s

Put another password in, bomb it out, then try again.   Try to get past logging in, we're hacking, hacking, hacking.   Try his first wife's maiden name, this is more than just a game.   It's real fun, but just the same it's hacking, hacking, hacking." (Hacker's anthem by *"Cheshire Catalyst"*)

Hacking was just a game, they thought. They called themselves the 414s—after the city's telephone area code—as a parody of Milwaukee's tough, inner-city youth gangs that take their names from the city's numbered streets. Like marauding teenagers, they went joyriding along the silent telecommunications highways that link thousands of large, sophisticated computers in banks, universities, corporations, and government installations all across the country. When they found a likely target, they probed for ways to break in, trying one password after another. "We were surprised just how easy it was," says Neal Patrick, a 17-year-old hacker—computer enthusiast—and member of 414s, who were quick to share their triumphs with each other. "It was like climbing a mountain: you have the goal of reaching the top or accessing a computer, and once you reach the peak, you make a map of the way and give it to everybody else." And no one seemed to notice.

The joyride ended abruptly when two FBI agents showed up at Patrick's home in Milwaukee in late July. The 414s are now suspected of having broken into more than 60 business and government computer systems in the United States and Canada, including computers at Los Alamos National Laboratory, Security Pacific National Bank in Los Angeles, and New Yorks Memorial Sloan-Kettering Cancer Center. But as new details of the investigations emerged last week, the Milwaukee capers raised troubling questions about the vulnerability of commercial and government computers. The episode has triggered a massive reappraisal of computer security and brought fresh warnings of more trouble to come. "There are going to be more and more computer crimes," warns David Stein of the Gartner Group, "and they are going to get bigger and more shocking with each revelation."

For all the apparent mystery surround the break-ins, hackers like the 414s were essentially exploiting weaknesses in systems that were designed to be easy to use and were relatively open. "There's this myth that kids can crack secure systems, and that's just not true," says Steve Wozniak, co-founder of Apple Computers. Arpanet—the Defense Advanced Research Projects Agency computer network that links computer-science centers at leading universities, national laboratories, defense contractors, and military installations—is relatively easy to access, but that's because the government designed it that way. Likewise, Telenet, Tymnet, and other networks for computer traffic are so designed that thousands of legitimate users can gain access to the computers quickly and efficiently. Sloan-Kettering, for instance, was linked to Telenet so doctors at more than 80 hospitals around the country could consult Sloan-Kettering's computer to calculate how much radiation to give their patients.

Not surprisingly, the Milwaukee break-ins may mean a bonanza for computer-security firms. No system is entirely impregnable, but there are many security measures that would easily have thwarted the 414s. Several firms now sell dial-back systems to protect against unauthorized entry through networks like Telenet. When a user dials up the computer, he signs on with a name and password; the computer immediately disconnects the line, searches its memory to verify the call, and then dials the preprogrammed number to reconnect the line. "It's so cheap, you wouldn't believe it," says Doug DeVries, computer-security chief at Hewlett-Packard. Another way to secure a computer is to encrypt all data entering and leaving it with a "blackbox" scram-

REAL WORLD APPLICATION 20–3 (*concluded*)

bler. The encryption is so complex that it is virtually impossible to decode without a matching black box.

Such measures may be needed to help protect sensitive computerized information against crimes like embezzlement and industrial espionage, even though the humans running the system represent a threat of a different sort. Most computer crime is committed not by hackers but by insiders who already have access to the systems. Still, law-enforcement officials believe a crackdown on malicious hacking is needed. "This whole area of hacking, or unauthorized entry, should be amenable to deterrence through prosecution," says U.S. Attorney Rudolph Guiliani.

Deterrence is not going to be easy, however, as long as the media glorify hackers like the 414s as the Robin Hoods of the information age. "The media have fallen in love with the kids who do it, perhaps because it shows that we still have control over computers," says computer scientist Jacques Valle. "On a subconscious level, we see the kids break into these big monsters and avenge us for our loss of privacy, individuality, whatever we're afraid of losing to computers." But in avenging that loss of privacy, the hackers may only be demonstrating the vulnerability of privacy in the computer age.

■ Are hackers committing computer crimes or playing games? Explain.
■ Are hackers "demonstrating the vulnerability of privacy in the computer age?" Explain.
■ What steps can be taken for protection against malicious hacking and other computer crimes?

Source: "Beware: Hackers at Play," *Newsweek*, September 5, 1983, pp. 42–48. Reprinted with permission.

SUMMARY

- Poor computer performance in many business firms is well documented and reveals that many computer users and computer professionals have not learned how to manage this vital but expensive business resource. The computer is not being used effectively, efficiently, and economically by many business firms.

- The experiences of successful computer users reveal that the basic ingredient of high-quality computer performance is extensive and meaningful management and user involvement in the development and operation of computer-based information systems. This should be the key ingredient in shaping the response of management to the challenge of improving the quality of computer services. Information resource management, which views information and computer technology as resources that must be managed, is another useful concept for management.

- The challenge of the computer to management performance is based on its role as a catalyst for a systems approach to management. Computer-based information systems challenge management to use systems concepts of decision making and frees them from routine tasks, while allowing them more time for marketing, personnel, and planning activities.

- Computers have had a major impact on society and thus impose serious responsibilities upon the management of computer-using business firms. Computers have had a major effect on employment, productivity, and competition in the business world. Computers have had both beneficial and detrimental effects on individuality, the quality of life, and privacy. Social applications of computers provide a direct beneficial effect to society when they are used to solve human and social problems.

- Business management must accept the responsibility for the proper and beneficial use of computers in business. Management must insist that effective measures be used to ensure that the social and economic effects of computer usage are considered during the development and operation of computer- based information systems.

KEY TERMS AND CONCEPTS

Poor computer performance
Management involvement
The user generation
User resistance

User involvement
Centralization versus
  decentralization
The computer as a catalyst

Systems approach to
management
Management job enlargement
Socioeconomic effects of
computers

Social applications of
computers
Systems design and social
responsibility

REVIEW AND APPLICATION QUESTIONS

1. What is meant by inadequate computer performance? What have been some of the causes of such inadequate performance?
2. How can management involvement in the planning and control of computer-based information systems be implemented? What role does the information resource management concept play in this regard?
3. What is the user generation? What does this new generation of computer users expect?
4. What are some of the causes of user resistance to computerization?
5. How and why does solving the problems of user resistance require meaningful user involvement?
6. Does the computer support the centralization or decentralization of information processing, business operations, and management within a computer-using firm? Explain.
7. How can the computer be a catalyst for the systems approach to management?
8. Why can the computer enlarge and enrich the job of management?
9. What are some of the beneficial and adverse effects of computer usage on society?
10. Do computers create unemployment? Explain.
11. Does the use of computers rob people of their individuality? Explain.
12. What has been the effect of computers on the quality of life?
13. Why is the impact of computers on personal privacy an important issue?
14. What are some of the social applications of the computer that have helped to solve human and social problems?
15. What can managers, computer users, and computer professionals do to ensure the proper and beneficial use of computers?

APPLICATION PROBLEMS

1. If you have not already done so, answer the questions after each Real World Application in this chapter.

2. The information services department at ABC Department Stores was recently studied by a management consulting firm brought in by top management. One of its recommendations was the need for more management involvement in the information systems function. It recommended that this include both corporate management and store managers. Jim Klugman, the VP for MIS, says that he can't see how this will work in practice. Help Jim by outlining several ways this recommendation can be implemented.

3. The management consulting team also recommended more user involvement in systems development and information system operations at ABC Department Stores. The VP for MIS says he won't be able to serve users information needs if they are so involved that they get in the way of his professional MIS staff. Make several recommendations to the VP for MIS on how user involvement could be implemented.

4. ABC Department Stores has learned of an opportunity to build a new store in a proposed shopping center in Houston, Texas. The vice president for planning says she would like to use the systems approach to management in making the decision. Provide one example for each of the stages shown in Figure 20–6 that applies this concept to the decision she must make.

5. Look at Figure 20–8. Can you give one positive and one negative example of the impact of computers on society for each of the seven impact areas shown in that figure? Give it a try.

6. A customer of ABC Department Stores was repeatedly billed for items she had already paid for. The credit department blamed the computer. The MIS department blamed an error in a program. The programmer blamed data entry personnel. Explain how each of these could have caused the error, and how the error could have been avoided.

APPENDIX

Using Popular Software Packages: A Tutorial Introduction

APPENDIX OUTLINE

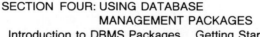

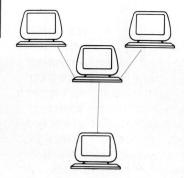

LEARNING OBJECTIVES

The purpose of this appendix is to provide you with a brief, simple, step-by-step introduction to the use of the most popular types of application software packages for microcomputers and many larger computers. They are (1) simple business programs, (2) word processing programs, (3) electronic spreadsheet programs, (4) database management programs, and (5) integrated packages. Reading this appendix and completing its hands-on exercises and assignments should allow you to achieve the *appreciation, knowledge,* and *experience* needed to effectively use such programs.

More specifically, your goal should not be to memorize the commands of WordStar, VisiCalc, dBASE II, or Lotus 1-2-3. These are the specific software packages we will use in this appendix. Instead, you should learn to use such packages to accomplish these basic functions:

- How to load and use simple application packages on a microcomputer.
- How to create, edit, store, and print a document using word processing functions.
- How to build, modify, store, print, and use an electronic spreadsheet.
- How to create and use a database and retrieve, display, and report information
- How to use graphics displays to analyze data and communicate information.

After you attain these objectives, you will still need further knowledge and experience before you can be an advanced business or professional user. You can gain more knowledge by consulting the manuals and tutorials available for most software packages. They provide you with information describing in detail how to use the full capabilities of these packages. With such knowledge and more hands-on experience, you can begin to accomplish many valuable business and professional assignments with these popular software packages.

SECTION ONE: GETTING STARTED WITH SOFTWARE PACKAGES

Conversing with a Computer

The easiest way to get started in computing is to learn how to use a personal computer or computer terminal to carry on a simple conversation with a computer. Such **conversational computing** is a type of *interactive processing*, involving frequent interaction between a person and a computer. A user like yourself can explore and accomplish the solution to a problem with the assistance of a computer system. This usually includes the use of *interactive application software packages*, which are programs specifically designed for conversational computing. No actual *programming* is necessary when such prewritten programs are used, since it has already been accomplished by the system analysts and programmers who developed these programs.

An interactive program is designed to direct the computer system to request and wait for **input** from the user, who must only choose among the alternatives offered by the computer and provide it with **data.** Computer and user "converse" briefly, and simply and a problem is solved for the user. The systems design and programming effort, the complex hardware devices, and the advanced software required are "transparent" to the user. All the user sees are the menus, prompts and responses that appear on the screen as a solution to a problem is accomplished.

Let us use a brief example of conversational computing with a short interactive program to illustrate how simple the use of a computer can be. **No programming is necessary;** only a few simple entries and responses are required. The short program we will use is a business application program called MORTGAGE. It computes (1) monthly mortgage payments and (2) mortgage amortization schedules for prospective homebuyers. We will use this program since it is provided as a demonstration program on the DOS operating system diskette by Microsoft Corporation for the IBM Personal Computer and other similar computers. My comments will assume this type of operating system and computer systems.

Using a Simple Interactive Program

First, you should activate the computer or terminal by such action as inserting a system diskette and turning it on, and/or dialing the telephone number of the time-sharing service or computer center. Once the computer or terminal is activated, it will begin to display or print messages. You respond, using the keyboard of the computer or terminal. Figures showing the displays resulting from an actual session with a microcomputer will follow. They outline the questions, comments, and responses of the computer and the user. My comments explain each figure.

FIGURE A1–1 Getting started: A. Opening display. B. Inserting the DOS disk.
C. The PC keyboard

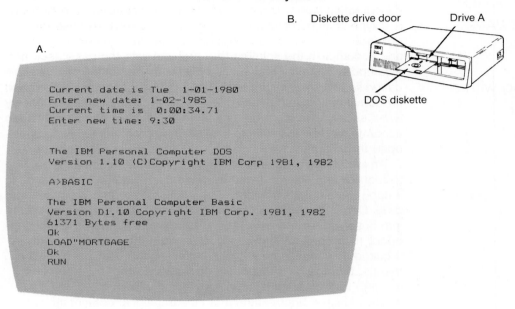

A.

```
Current date is Tue  1-01-1980
Enter new date: 1-02-1985
Current time is  0:00:34.71
Enter new time: 9:30


The IBM Personal Computer DOS
Version 1.10 (C)Copyright IBM Corp 1981, 1982

A>BASIC

The IBM Personal Computer Basic
Version D1.10 Copyright IBM Corp. 1981, 1982
61371 Bytes free
Ok
LOAD"MORTGAGE
Ok
RUN
```

B.   Diskette drive door   Drive A

DOS diskette

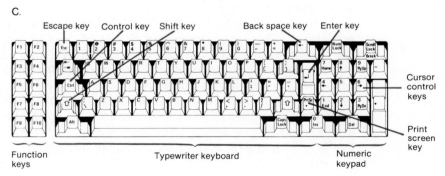

C.

Escape key   Control key   Shift key   Back space key   Enter key

Cursor
control
keys

Print
screen
key

Function
keys

Typewriter keyboard

Numeric
keypad

Figure A1-1.   The procedure for getting started using an IBM
Personal Computer or other similar computer is illustrated above.
The DOS operating system diskette is first inserted in one of the
computer's disk drives. (Usually drive A, the drive on the left.) The
drive door must be opened, the diskette inserted with its label up
and its exposed slot facing the drive, and the door closed. Then
the main computer switch should be turned on, as well as the switch
that turns on the video monitor. The computer first makes date

and time requests and you respond with the current date and time. After the DOS operating system identifies itself with a copyright notice, it displays its operating system prompt: **A**> and a flashing cursor. At this point, you type in the word BASIC because the MORTGAGE program is written in the BASIC programming language. The BASIC interpreter program then identifies itself and displays the BASIC prompt: **OK** and a flashing cursor. You then indicate that you want to use the MORTGAGE program by typing in the command: LOAD "MORTGAGE." The computer responds with an OK, so you ask it to execute the program by typing-in RUN.

Note: Don't forget to press the ENTER (RETURN) key after you type-in each command or response. Also, use the backspace key to "erase" any typing errors you make before you press the ENTER key.

FIGURE

A1–2 Opening menu of the MORTGAGE program

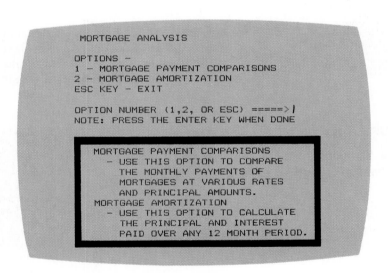

Figure A1–2.   The computer responds with the **menu** display shown above, which explains the options you have when using the MORTGAGE program. It asks you to choose option number 1 or 2 or to use the ESCAPE key to exit from this program. Let's choose option number 1.

FIGURE

A1–3 Mortgage payment comparison prompts and responses

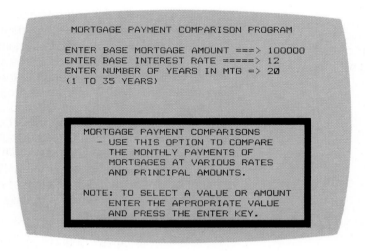

```
MORTGAGE PAYMENT COMPARISON PROGRAM

ENTER BASE MORTGAGE AMOUNT ===> 100000
ENTER BASE INTEREST RATE =====> 12
ENTER NUMBER OF YEARS IN MTG => 20
(1 TO 35 YEARS)


    MORTGAGE PAYMENT COMPARISONS
     - USE THIS OPTION TO COMPARE
    THE MONTHLY PAYMENTS OF
    MORTGAGES AT VARIOUS RATES
    AND PRINCIPAL AMOUNTS.

    NOTE: TO SELECT A VALUE OR AMOUNT
    ENTER THE APPROPRIATE VALUE
    AND PRESS THE ENTER KEY.
```

Figure A1–3.   The computer responds with an explanation of how to use the MORTGAGE payment comparison option and asks you to enter values for the amount of the mortgage, interest rate, and number of years. You respond with the values shown above.

FIGURE

A1–4 Mortgage payment comparison output

```
MONTHLY MORTGAGE PAYMENT COMPARISONS
      20-YEAR MORTGAGE LOAN AMOUNTS
      1      2001     4001     6001
RATES
12.00    0.01    22.03    44.05    66.08
12.25    0.01    22.38    44.75    67.13
12.50    0.01    22.73    45.46    68.18
12.75    0.01    23.09    46.16    69.24
13.00    0.01    23.44    46.87    70.31
13.25    0.01    23.80    47.59    71.38
13.50    0.01    24.16    48.31    72.45
13.75    0.01    24.52    49.03    73.54
14.00    0.01    24.88    49.75    74.62
14.25    0.01    25.25    50.48    75.72
14.50    0.01    25.61    51.21    76.81
14.75    0.01    25.98    51.95    77.91
15.00    0.01    26.35    52.68    79.02
15.25    0.01    26.72    53.43    80.13
15.50    0.01    27.09    54.17    81.25

PRESS SPACE BAR TO CONTINUE
```

Figure A1–4.   The computer responds with the table shown above, which provides comparisons of the monthly mortgage payments at various interest rates and mortgage loan amounts.

FIGURE

A1–5 Mortgage
amortization prompts
and responses

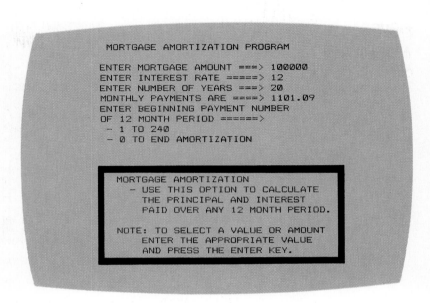

```
MORTGAGE AMORTIZATION PROGRAM

ENTER MORTGAGE AMOUNT ===> 100000
ENTER INTEREST RATE =====> 12
ENTER NUMBER OF YEARS ===> 20
MONTHLY PAYMENTS ARE ====> 1101.09
ENTER BEGINNING PAYMENT NUMBER
OF 12 MONTH PERIOD ======>
- 1 TO 240
- 0 TO END AMORTIZATION


  MORTGAGE AMORTIZATION
    - USE THIS OPTION TO CALCULATE
      THE PRINCIPAL AND INTEREST
      PAID OVER ANY 12 MONTH PERIOD.

  NOTE: TO SELECT A VALUE OR AMOUNT
        ENTER THE APPROPRIATE VALUE
        AND PRESS THE ENTER KEY.
```

Figure A1–5.   If we had chosen option number 2 of the MORTGAGE
program, the computer would respond with the display shown above.
It explains the mortgage amortization option and asks you to enter
values for the amount of the mortgage, interest rate, and number
of years. It then calculates the monthly payment based on the values
you provide. Then it asks you to enter the number of the first month
of a 12-month period for which it will provide a mortgage amortization
analysis (there are 240 monthly payment periods in a 20 year loan).
In this example you choose payment period number 1 to start this
analysis.

FIGURE

A1-6 Mortgage
amortization output

```
        MORTGAGE AMORTIZATION PROGRAM

    ENTER MORTGAGE AMOUNT ===> 100000
    ENTER INTEREST RATE =====> 12
    ENTER NUMBER OF YEARS ===> 20
    MONTHLY PAYMENTS ARE ====> 1101.09


    PYMNT  PRINCIPAL   INTEREST     BALANCE
      1      101.09     1000.00     99898.91
      2      102.10      998.99     99796.81
      3      103.12      997.97     99693.69
      4      104.15      996.94     99589.54
      5      105.19      995.90     99484.35
      6      106.25      994.84     99378.10
      7      107.31      993.78     99270.79
      8      108.38      992.71     99162.41
      9      109.47      991.62     99052.94
     10      110.56      990.53     98942.38
     11      111.67      989.42     98830.71
     12      112.78      988.31     98717.92

    INTEREST FOR 12 PERIODS = 11931.01

    PRESS SPACE BAR TO CONTINUE
```

Figure A1-6. The computer responds with the display shown above, which outlines how each monthly payment you make is divided between repayment of principal, interest payments, the unpaid loan balance, and the amount of interest paid for the 12 periods analyzed.

If your computer system has a printer, and you wish a printed copy of this display or any other, simply press the SHIFT key and the PRTSC (print screen) key at the same time. This will provide you with a printed paper copy of what is displayed on the video monitor.

FIGURE

A1–7 Part of the MORTGAGE program listing

```
Ok
LIST
940 REM The IBM Personal Computer Mortgage
950 REM Version 1.00 (C)Copyright IBM Corp 1981, 1982
960 REM Licensed Material - Program Property of IBM
970 REM Author - Glenn Stuart Dardick
975 DEF SEG: POKE 106,0
980 SAMPLES$="NO"
990 GOTO 1010
1000 SAMPLES$="YES"
1010 KEY OFF:SCREEN 0,1:COLOR 15,0,0:WIDTH 40:CLS:LOCATE 5,19:PRINT "IBM"
1020 LOCATE 7,12,0:PRINT "Personal Computer"
1030 COLOR 10,0:LOCATE 10,9,0:PRINT CHR$(213)+STRING$(21,205)+CHR$(184)
1040 LOCATE 11,9,0:PRINT CHR$(179)+"      MORTGAGE        "+CHR$(179)
1050 LOCATE 12,9,0:PRINT CHR$(179)+STRING$(21,32)+CHR$(179)
1060 LOCATE 13,9,0:PRINT CHR$(179)+"    Version 1.10     "+CHR$(179)
1070 LOCATE 14,9,0:PRINT CHR$(212)+STRING$(21,205)+CHR$(190)
1080 COLOR 15,0:LOCATE 17,4,0:PRINT "(C) Copyright IBM Corp 1981, 1982"
1090 COLOR 14,0:LOCATE 23,7,0:PRINT "Press space bar to continue"
1100 IF INKEY$ <> "" THEN GOTO 1100
^C
Break
Ok
```

Figure A1–7.   You can leave the mortgage amortization part of the program by entering a zero as the beginning payment number. This causes the beginning menu of the MORTGAGE program to be displayed, as was shown in Figure A1–2. If you are finished with the MORTGAGE program, you can press the ESCAPE key as indicated on that menu. This will cause the BASIC prompt: OK to appear, allowing you to enter the name of any other BASIC program you wish to use.

However, you might first like to see a listing of the actual instructions (written in the BASIC programming language) that make up the MORTGAGE program. You can do this by typing the BASIC command: LIST and pressing the ENTER key. The first part of the listing displayed on the video monitor is shown in Figure A1–7. The MORTGAGE program contains almost 200 such instructions. Watch them as they "scroll" by on the screen. (You can stop the scrolling by pressing the CTRL and NUM LOCK keys. Resume the scroll by pressing any other key.) Notice how many of the instructions are concerned with input/output, logical comparisons, and appropriate calculations. Aren't you glad that you did not have to develop this program yourself? Our use of the MORTGAGE program as shown in the previous figures demonstrates that one can learn to **use** a computer without having to learn how to **program** a computer.

FIGURE

A1–8 Directory of program files on the DOS disk

```
A>DIR
COMMAND   COM    4959    5-07-82   12:00p
FORMAT    COM    3816    5-07-82   12:00p
CHKDSK    COM    1720    5-07-82   12:00p
SYS       COM     605    5-07-82   12:00p
DISKCOPY  COM    2019   11-25-83   12:32a
DISKCOMP  COM    1651   11-25-83   12:32a
COMP      COM    1649    5-07-82   12:00p
EXE2BIN   EXE    1280    5-07-82   12:00p
MODE      COM    2509    5-07-82   12:00p
EDLIN     COM    2392    5-07-82   12:00p
DEBUG     COM    5999    5-07-82   12:00p
LINK      EXE   41856    5-07-82   12:00p
BASIC     COM   11392    5-07-82   12:00p
BASICA    COM   16768    5-07-82   12:00p
ART       BAS    1920    5-07-82   12:00p
SAMPLES   BAS    2432    5-07-82   12:00p
MORTGAGE  BAS    6272    5-07-82   12:00p
COLORBAR  BAS    1536    5-07-82   12:00p
CALENDAR  BAS    3840    5-07-82   12:00p
MUSIC     BAS    8704    5-07-82   12:00p
DONKEY    BAS    3584    5-07-82   12:00p
CIRCLE    BAS    1664    5-07-82   12:00p
PIECHART  BAS    2304    5-07-82   12:00p
SPACE     BAS    1920    5-07-82   12:00p
BALL      BAS    2048    5-07-82   12:00p
COMM      BAS    4352    5-07-82   12:00p
       26 File(s)
```

Figure A1–8.   You can end this first exercise by typing and entering the BASIC command: SYSTEM, which returns you to the operating system mode. The DOS operating system prompt: A> will then be displayed. This will allow you to use various system commands and a variety of other programs that are available for use with this operating system. For example, if you enter the system command: DIR the computer will respond with a **directory** of the various programs (files) that are stored on the MS-DOS diskette. This display is shown in Figure A1–8. Notice that there are 26 different programs on the disk, including the MORTGAGE program and two BASIC interpreter programs (BASIC and BASICA), as well as a variety of DOS utility programs and several other demonstration application programs. At this point, if you do not wish to continue, you may remove the DOS diskette from the disk drive and turn off the computer.

HANDS-ON ASSIGNMENTS

Our use of the MORTGAGE program should have demonstrated that **anyone can learn to use a computer** by using a simple prewritten program. Now it's your turn to try a few more without my help. You should use a personal computer or computer terminal and several software packages available for your computer system. Consult the *operations manual* for your computer system if you need more information on operating your computer. Good luck!

A1.1 Use the MORTGAGE package (or a similar program) to find mortgage payment comparisons and a mortgage amortization analysis for a mortgage loan whose amount, interest rate, and number of years are different than that shown in the previous example. For example, you could use a mortgage amount of $75,000 an interest rate of 10 percent, with a fifteen year time period. Print out the results and compare them to those shown in the previous example.

A1.2 Use one of the other programs provided on your computer's operating system diskette, such as those shown in the directory of the MS-DOS diskette shown in Figure A1–8. For example, you could use the program called EDLIN, which is a line editor program on the MS-DOS disk. You could use this program to build a file of data records (such as student names and test scores) and save it on your system diskette. Then you could retrieve this file from the disk, add to, delete, or change (edit) the records in the file, and print out a hard copy.

A1.3 Use any other prewritten programs available for your computer system, whether they involve business applications, statistical analysis, or even computer games!

SECTION TWO: USING WORD PROCESSING PACKAGES

Introduction to Word Processing Packages

The concept of word processing and its impact on the modern office is discussed in Chapter Thirteen: Word Processing and Automated Office Systems. We also discussed how dedicated word processor computers are being replaced by general-purpose computers that can be used for both word processing and data processing jobs. This is especially true in the case of microcomputers. Dozens of word processing packages are now available to turn your microcomputer into a topflight word processing machine. Such word processing programs have become the most popular type of application software package available for use with personal computers.

For our purposes, word processing can be defined as (1) the processing of **text data** (words, phrases, sentences, and paragraphs), for the purpose of (2) the preparation, editing, and printing of **documents** (for example, letters, memos, business forms, reports, and manuscripts). A word processing package allows you to use a microcomputer or other computer to accomplish three primary jobs:

- Create, edit, and format documents.
- Store and retrieve documents.
- Print documents.

Word processing packages are also used to do a fourth major job: the creation and editing of data and program files. Computer users who have word processing packages may use such software to build data files for processing by other application programs, or to write and edit application programs written in a variety of programming languages. We will provide you with a brief example of using a word processing editor to build a data file later in this section.

WordStar is the best known and best selling of all word processing programs for microcomputers. It was designed to provide microcomputer users with all of the features formerly found only on computers dedicated exclusively to word processing. WordStar is a product of MicroPro International Corporation and was first introduced in 1981. Versions of WordStar now exist for many microcomputer systems. Compared to other word processing programs, WordStar may be slightly more awkward to use, but it provides superior control over the format of documents. Its capabilities rival those of many dedicated word processors.

Organization of Word Processing Packages

We can think of word processing packages as having three major levels of organization:

- **Program level**— the types of programs and subprograms that make up the word processing package. For example, a typical package consists of an integrated set of programs, including an editor program, a formatting program, a print program, and optional dictionary and mailing list programs.

FIGURE

A2–1 WordStar menu organization

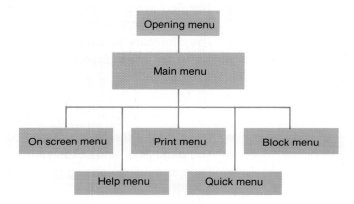

■ **Menu level**— most popular word processing packages provide menus to help the user select commands, or are *menu-driven* (i.e., much of their operation comes from you selecting from a list of choices provided by a series of menus). The menu organization for WordStar is shown in Figure A2–1.

FIGURE

A2–2 WordStar screen organization

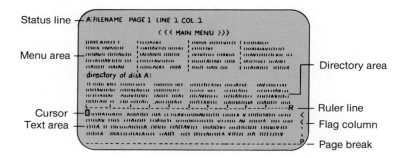

■ **Screen level**— the video screen display of most word processing packages is organized into several specialized areas, including the display of special characters and symbols. The screen organization of WordStar is shown in Figure A2–2. Note that the WordStar screen includes the following:

■ The **status line** indicates whether you are editing or printing and whether certain editing features are in operation.

- The **menu area** displays lists of commands (menus), help screens, messages, or questions (prompts).
- The **cursor,** a small block of light, indicates your place on the screen as you type.
- The **text area,** which can be moved (scrolled) up or down, is where your work appears.
- The **directory** lists the files on your disk.
- The **ruler line** indicates margins and tabs.

Let's describe the functions of the *status line* and the *ruler line* in WordStar in more detail because they provide you with some very useful information. The **status line** shows you the following:

- The name of the file on which you are working.
- The page, line, and column where the cursor is located.
- The current line spacing (single-space, double- space, or other type of spacing).
- Whether the *insert* mode is on or off. Pressing the CTRL and V keys will toggle the insert mode on and off. If it is *off,* anything you type will replace anything previously on the screen. If it is *on,* what you type will cause other material on the screen to move over to make room for what you are typing.

The **ruler line,** which appears just above the screen space available for typing-in text, shows where the margin and tab stops are set. Most word processing packages allow you great flexibility in setting tabs and margins. In WordStar, the location of the margins is marked with an L for the left margin and an R for the right margin. Tab stops are marked with an exclamation point (!) for normal tab stops, or a cross-hatch symbol (#) for a decimal tab stop. A decimal tab stop lines up what you type, based on the location of decimal points in numbers that may be part of your text material. This is helpful when typing reports containing numeric data.

Getting Started

Let's find out how to use a word processing package. We will work through a few simple examples of the use of a microcomputer word processing package to write a simple business letter and build a small data file. The WordStar package will be used, but other packages use many similar commands and functions. Let's use WordStar to do the following tasks:

- Create, edit, store, retrieve, and print a business letter.
- Create, store, retrieve, edit and print a data file.

You begin by inserting your WordStar disk into the disk drive and turning on the computer. (See the beginning of the first section of this appendix if you need additional information on starting a microcomputer and using a floppy disk.) A WordStar disk which also contains the operating system, will load (boot) the operating system first and then display the operating system prompt (such as A>). Or you can insert and load the operating system diskette, remove it from the disk drive, and insert the WordStar disk. In either case, you then load the WordStar program by typing-in WS after the system prompt and pressing the ENTER key. After some initial copyright information is shown, you should then see the OPENING MENU displayed. The choices provided by the most important of these commands are explained in Figure A2–3.

FIGURE

A2–3 Explanation of WordStar opening menu commands

L   *Change the logged disk drive.* This allows you to choose the default disk drive, since you probably loaded your Wordstar disk on drive A but want to save your files on a data disk in drive B.

F   *File directory.* This allows you to show or suppress the file directory on the logged disk. The command is a "toggle." The first time you give the F command, the file directory will disappear from the screen; the next time you give the F command, the directory will reappear.

H   *Set help level.* Wordstar has an on-screen help facility that can be set at four different levels of help. The beginner should normally leave the on-screen help on level 3. When you get a little more familiar with Wordstar, you may want to go to help level 2, which takes most of the help off the screen.

D   *Open a document file.* This command is used for editing a file that is supposed to be fully formatted as a normal word processing document, such as a letter or report.

N   *Open a nondocument file.* This command is used for creating and editing files that are *not* documents. N is typically used for developing data files.

P   *Print a file.* Prints a document or nondocument file.

Underneath the OPENING MENU, a directory of the files on the diskette in disk drive A will also be displayed. If you want to have the documents you prepare stored on a **file disk** in disk drive B, you should insert a formatted diskette in drive B. Then press the L key, type in B:, and press the ENTER key. The computer will then display a directory of any files stored on the disk in drive B which you might have created using WordStar or other software packages. You are now ready to use either the D or N commands, depending on whether you wish to create a document or build some other type of file. Figure A2–4 shows you the OPENING MENU display of WordStar.

FIGURE A2–4 WordStar opening menu

```
            not editing
            < < <  O P E N I N G   M E N U  > > >
    ---Preliminary Commands---  :  --File Commands--  :  -System  Commands-
  L  Change logged disk drive   :                     :   R  Run a program
  F  File directory   now OFF   :  P  PRINT a file     :   X  EXIT to system
  H  Set help level             :                     :
    ---Commands to open a file---  :  E  RENAME a file  :  -WordStar Options-
    D  Open a  document  file    :  O  COPY   a file    :   M  Run MailMerge
    N  Open a non-document file  :  Y  DELETE a file    :   S  Run SpellStar
```

Creating a Document

Let's say you want to write a short business letter. Since this is a document, you need to open a **document file** by using the D command (press the D key). WordStar will then display an explanation of the D command, the rules for naming files, and some of the control characters you can use. It then asks you to name the file you want to edit. Let's call this file: LETTER1 because it is our first letter in WordStar. See Figure A2–5.

A file name in WordStar may contain up to 8 characters, including letters, numbers and some special characters. No distinction is made between uppercase and lowercase letters. If you want your file name to provide additional identifying information, you can add an *extension* to your file name. Simply add a period and three more characters to the end of the file name. For example, you might add .TXT

FIGURE

A2–5 WordStar document file: Creation or editing prompt

```
D            not editing

   Use this command to create a new document file,
   or to initiate alteration of an existing document file.

     A file name is 1-8 letters/digits, a period,
     and an optional 0-3 character type.
     File name may be preceded by disk drive letter A-D
     and colon, otherwise current logged disk is used.

   ^S=delete character    ^Y=delete entry    ^F=File directory
   ^D=restore character   ^R=Restore entry   ^U=cancel command

     NAME OF FILE TO EDIT? LETTER1
```

(for text) or .DOC (for document) to your file names. Thus you could name a report you were writing: REPORT.TXT.

After you enter your file name, a MAIN MENU will be displayed on the screen. You are now using the WordStar editor program. If the WordStar HELP level is set to 3 (as it should be for beginners), the MAIN MENU is really a HELP display. It explains the functions of various control key commands to be used in the creation and editing of your letter. As you can see, this display takes up most of the upper half of the screen. The lower half of the screen is thus available for you to type your letter. You can now create and edit your document by typing it in, using the control keys to help you in the editing process. See Figure A2–6.

Notice that, as you type-in words using an advanced word processing program, the editor constantly reformats and modifies the appearance of the screen. Notice that you do not have to press ENTER at the end of every line; you just keep typing, since the editor does the "carriage-returns" for you. Due to this **word wrap** feature, text material that would extend past the right margin is automatically "wrapped around" to the left margin of the next line. Of course, whenever you want to force the starting of a new line or paragraph, you can do so by pressing the ENTER key.

Creating and editing a simple document requires several fundamental editing operations. For example, you need to move the cursor around the screen and delete or insert text material. Figure A2–7 summarizes the control key combinations you need to press in order to execute some basic editing commands.

All of the WordStar editing commands can be given by pressing the CONTROL key (usually marked CTRL) and holding it down while pressing another key or group of keys. These **control key combinations** are represented on the screen by the caret symbol (^) and the appropriate letter or letters of the keys that need to be pressed. For example, the MAIN MENU tells you that pressing the CTRL

FIGURE A2–6 WordStar main menu

```
      B:LETTER1  PAGE 1 LINE 1 COL Ø1              INSERT ON
                      < < <     M A I N   M E N U     > > >
    --Cursor Movement--   ¦ -Delete- ¦   -Miscellaneous-  ¦  -Other  Menus-
^S char left ^D char right ¦^G  char  ¦ ^I Tab    ^B Reform ¦ (from Main only)
^A word left ^F word right ¦DEL chr lf¦ ^V INSERT ON/OFF    ¦^J Help   ^K Block
^E line  up  ^X line down  ¦^T word rt¦^L Find/Replce again¦^Q Quick ^P Print
      --Scrolling--        ¦^Y  line  ¦RETURN End paragraph¦^O Onscreen
^Z line down ^W line up    ¦          ¦ ^N Insert a RETURN ¦
^C screen up ^R screen down¦          ¦ ^U Stop a command  ¦
L----!----!----!----!----!----!----!----!----!----!--------R
```

FIGURE

A2–7 Fundamental
WordStar editing
commands

Control-Keys	Explanation
	CURSOR MOVEMENT
CTRL-S	Moves cursor one character to the left
CTRL-D	Moves cursor one character to the right
CTRL-A	Moves cursor one word to the left
CTRL-F	Moves cursor one word to the right
CTRL-E	Moves cursor up one line
CTRL-X	Moves cursor down one line
	SCROLLING
CTRL-W	Moves screen view up one line
CTRL-Z	Moves screen view down one line
CTRL-R	Moves up one whole screen
CTRL-C	Moves down one whole screen
	DELETING
CTRL-G	Deletes character to the right of the cursor
DEL	Deletes character to the left of the cursor
CTRL-T	Deletes one word to the right of the cursor
CTRL-Y	Deletes the line the cursor is on
	MISCELLANEOUS
CTRL-I	Moves cursor to next tab mark
CTRL-B	Reformats text to form paragraphs
CTRL-V	Toggles insert mode ON and OFF
RETURN	Starts new paragraph
CTRL-U	Interrupts commands before execution

FIGURE

A2–8 WordStar IBM PC
key equivalents

IBM PC Key	WordStar Command	Explanation
PgUp	CTRL-R	Scroll up 1 screen
PgDn	CTRL-C	Scroll down 1 screen
Home	CTRL-QE	To home position
End	CTRL-QX	To bottom of the screen
Ins		Toggles insert mode
F1	CTRL-JH	Set help level
F2	CTRL-OG	Temporary indent to tab
F3	CTRL-OL	Set left margin at cursor
F4	CTRL-OR	Set right margin at cursor
F5	CTRL-PS	Underline
F6	CTRL-PB	Boldface
F7	CTRL-KB	Mark beginning of block
F8	CTRL-KK	Mark end of block
F9	CTRL-QR	Cursor to beginning of file
F10	CTRL-QC	Cursor to the end of file

and S keys will move the cursor one character to the left (ˆ *S char left*). Thus to move the cursor one character to the left, you should press CTRL, hold it down, and then press S.

If your computer has special **function** keys (such as on the IBM PC and similar computers), a listing of keys and the commands they accomplish may be shown at the bottom of your screen. Figure A2–8 summarizes the WordStar control key commands (version 3.3). Also listed are their equivalents in the IBM PC function keys and other keys. (Refer back to the keyboard in Figure A1–1.)

If your computer has **cursor control** (arrow) keys, you will use them to move the cursor around on your video monitor screen. If your computer does not have such arrow keys, or if you don't like taking your hands off the main part of the keyboard, you can use the control key combinations listed in Figures A2–7 and A2–8.

HANDS-ON EXERCISE A2–1: CREATING AND EDITING A BUSINESS LETTER

Figure A2–9 shows you a simple business letter you should type in your first exercise. Load WordStar, change the logged drive to drive B, and suppress the file directory. Select the D option from the OPENING MENU, and give the file name of LETTER1 to the document file you wish to create. When the MAIN MENU appears, you know you're ready to type and edit your letter using the WordStar editor. Refer to Figures A2–4, A2–5 and A2–6 for displays that will appear on your video screen. Refer to Figures A2–3, A2–7, and A2–8 for the control key combinations you may need to type the letter shown in Figure A2–9. Try to reproduce the spacing and layout of the letter as exactly as possible. For example, set the left margin to column 10, the right margin to column 75, and begin the address in column 55.

Editing and Correcting a Document

Don't worry about any mistakes you make while trying to type the simple letter required in the previous exercise. The beauty of a word processing package is that it makes correcting and revising text material easy to do. Let's briefly review some of the ways you can correct any errors you make while using WordStar. First of all, if you choose the wrong command from the OPENING MENU

FIGURE

A2–9 Sample business
letter: Document File
Letter1

ABC Corporation
123 Aardvark Avenue
Somewhere, XX 12345
January 31, 1985

Mr. Rupert R. Rubout,
456 Zebra Street
Nowhere, XX 12345

Dear Mr. Rubout:

In regard to your letter of January 6, 1985, our Mark IV three-prong, two-slot blivit is available only in the colors magenta, chartreuse, and tangerine. We regret that we cannot accept your order for a grey blivit.

At present, delivery on Mark IV blivits is running about two months from the placement of an order. If we can be of service, please let us know.

Sincerely yours,

Diane D. Delete,
Sales Manager

(such as pressing N to open a nondocument file, when you meant to press D to open a document file), you can immediately get back to that menu by pressing the ESCAPE key. However, if you have responded to prompts within a command function, you will first have to press the CTRL and U keys. The screen will then display the message "interrupted ***Press ESC Key". You should then press the ESCAPE key to get back to the OPENING MENU.

If you open a document or other file and realize it isn't the file you want, you will first have to press the CTRL-KQ key combination to get back to the OPENING MENU. If you have done any typing or made any changes to the file, you will be asked whether you want to abandon the file without saving it. You will have to answer with a Y or N before you can get back to the OPENING MENU. Then you can open another file or perform another function.

Once you begin to type a document, you can use the BACKS-PACE, TAB, and cursor control keys to move around your document on the screen and just type over any mistakes that you make. However, you will also want to use simple editing commands for deleting and inserting characters, words, and lines. These control key combinations simplify corrections and changes, because they minimize having to retype incorrect material. For example, you could use **delete** commands to remove spaces between words or lines, rather than have to retype the material. Or you could use the INSERT mode to insert additional spaces or words in a line without having to retype that line. You will probably want to type your material with the INSERT mode off, and then toggle it on or off depending on whether you wish to insert or replace material that you have typed.

Getting Help

Before we begin to type our first document you should remember that you can get help on a variety of topics by pressing the CTRL and J keys. WordStar was one of the first microcomputer packages to provide **onscreen help** to users. Use this feature whenever you want an explanation of a word processing operation. The CTRL-J command will allow you to select topic areas that you may want explained, or to set the HELP level differently if you wish. The HELP menu is shown in Figure A2–10. It lists the keys you can press to get help on a variety of topics. Notice that you can display and set the help level provided to you by pressing the H key. Figure A2–11 shows you how you can reduce the amount of help menus and explanations that are provided to you. After you become more proficient in WordStar, you should probably reduce the level of help to give yourself more space on the video screen.

Storing and Printing Documents

After you have created and edited a document, you will want to produce a printed copy on your system printer, as well as store a copy of the document on the floppy disk of your computer system. Pressing the CTRL-K-D key combination saves your document to the logged disk and exits from the editor back to the OPENING

FIGURE A2–10 WordStar help menu

```
^J          B:LETTER  PAGE 1 LINE 1 COL 01
                  < < <      H E L P    M E N U     > > >
                               !                   ! --Other  Menus--
   H   Display & set the help level   ! S  Status line   ! (from Main only)
   B   Paragraph reform (CONTROL-B)    ! R  Ruler line    ! ^J  Help  ^K  Block
   F   Flags in right-most column      ! M  Margins & Tabs ! ^Q  Quick ^P  Print
   D   Dot commands, print controls    ! P  Place markers  ! ^O  Onscreen
   I   Index of commands               ! V  Moving text    ! Space Bar returns
                               !                   ! you to Main Menu.
   L----!----!----!----!----!----!----!----!----!----!--------R
```

FIGURE A2–11 WordStar help level selection

```
^JH        B:LETTER  PAGE 1 LINE 1 COL 01

HELP LEVELS
   3  all menus and explanations displayed
   2  main editing menu (1-control-char commands) suppressed
   1  prefix menus (2-character commands) also suppressed
   0  command explanations (including this) also suppressed

CURRENT HELP LEVEL IS 3

ENTER Space OR NEW HELP LEVEL (0, 1, 2, OR 3):

L----!----!----!----!----!----!----!----!----!----!--------R
```

MENU. You can now print your document by using the P option from this menu. After you have pressed the P, you must enter the file name of the document you wish to print (LETTER1, for example). If you press the ENTER key, you will be presented with a list of print options. (See Figure A2–12.) As a beginning user, you can ignore these options by pressing the ENTER key after each option prompt until the actual printing process begins. (*Note*: you can by-pass having to respond to these print options by pressing the ES-CAPE (ESC) key after you type-in the file name of your document.)

Terminating and Restarting

After storing or printing your document, you will return to the OPENING MENU. You can exit completely from WordStar by giving

FIGURE

A2–12 WordStar print options

```
P            not editing




NAME OF FILE TO PRINT? LETTER1
For default press RETURN for each question:
   DISK FILE OUTPUT (Y/N): N
   START AT PAGE NUMBER (RETURN for beginning)?
   STOP AFTER PAGE NUMBER (RETURN for end)?
   USE FORM FEEDS (Y/N): N
   SUPPRESS PAGE FORMATTING (Y/N): N
   PAUSE FOR PAPER CHANGE BETWEEN PAGES (Y/N): N
Ready printer, press RETURN:
```

the X command at this point. After you press the X key, you will be back under the control of the operating system, so the operating system prompt A> or B> will appear.

Note: you should make a habit of continually saving parts of a long document that you are creating. Pressing the CTRL-K-S keys every few minutes allows you to "save as you go" without leaving the display of your document in the MAIN MENU. This action minimizes the amount of your document that you would lose due to an accidental erasure of the contents of main memory.

If you want to return to WordStar, just type in WS after the operating system prompt, as you did to first load the WordStar program. After you are presented with the OPENING MENU, you can retrieve a document you saved previously. Use the D command and enter the name of that document file in response to a file name request. Your document is then retrieved from the disk and displayed on the screen below the MAIN MENU display. You can then begin to work with that document, as you did previously, making additional corrections and revisions as needed.

HANDS-ON EXERCISE A2–2: STORING AND PRINTING DOCUMENTS

Make any additional corrections needed to the letter you typed in the previous exercise. Save this letter on your system disk as the document file: LETTER1. Then have a copy printed on your system printer. Now exit from the WordStar program.

Advanced Word Processing Functions

You have now created, edited, saved, and printed a document. Let's look at some advanced word processing capabilities that we can use to easily make additional changes to a document.

Global Search and Replace

After you have typed a letter, report, or other document, you may wish to find out where and how many times you use a certain word or phrase. You may also wish to replace this word or phrase with alternative text. This is called a **global search and replace** operation. It is a powerful feature of advanced word processing packages. You could use the cursor control and scroll control keys to visually examine the document, but this would be time-consuming and difficult. Instead, you can speed up your search by using commands that help you move around your document more quickly, as well as automatically finding and replacing text material. In WordStar, these commands begin with the use of CTRL-Q keys. Figure A2–13 shows the QUICK MENU, which displays the many CTRL-Q command options. Figure A2–14 briefly explains five commands of greatest interest to beginning users.

Changing the Format of Documents

Word processing packages make it easy to control how a document will look when printed. Several common page-formatting options are provided that allow you to have a choice of several formats and styles for whatever type of document you are using. WordStar

FIGURE A2–13 WordStar quick menu commands

```
^Q        B:LETTER   PAGE 1 LINE 1 COL 01
                    < < <     Q U I C K    M E N U     > > >
     ---Cursor Movement---   : -Delete- :  --Miscellaneous-- : --Other  Menus--
   S left side   D right side  :Y line   rt:F Find text in file : (from Main only)
   E top scrn    X bottom scrn :DEL lin 1f:A Find & Replace   :^J Help  ^K Block
   R top file    C end file               :L Find Misspelling :^Q Quick ^P Print
   B top block   K end block              :Q Repeat command or :^O Onscreen
   0-9 marker    Z down  W up             : key  until  space :Space Bar returns
   P previous    V last Find or Block     : bar or other key :you to Main Menu.
   L----!----!----!----!----!----!----!----!----!----!--------R
```

FIGURE

A2–14 Explanation of QUICK commands

- CTRL-Q followed by E, D, S, or X move you to the top line, (E), right edge (D), left edge (S), or bottom of the screen (X).

- CRTL-Q followed by R or C will move you to the beginning (R) or the end (C) of the whole document.

- CTRL-Q-F will find any "string" of characters (words or phrases, including blanks) in the document. When you give the CONTROL-Q-F command, Wordstar will ask you what you want to find. Just type it in. There are several options; when you are asked for options, enter a question mark (?) and press ENTER. This will get you an explanation of the various options.

- CTRL-Q-A will allow you to make global changes to the text. You can select the word or phrase you want changed, then the word or phrase you want to change it to, and have the changes performed automatically or semiautomatically with pauses for confirmation. The options allowed are the same as for CTRL-Q-F.

- CTRL-L is used after doing a "find" (CTRL-Q-F) or a "replace" (CTRL-Q-A). Pressing CTRL-L will allow you to move directly to the next string to be found or replaced.

provides a group of ONSCREEN commands that allow you to change the format of what appears on the screen, and will eventually be printed. Figure A2-15 shows you the ONSCREEN MENU which displays the options provided for this purpose, all of which begin with CTRL-O. The beginning user does not need to bother with most of these, since WordStar takes care of simple formatting. The ones most likely to be used by you are the commands keys which set margins and tab stops, center lines, and set line spacing.

Changing the format of documents may require you to *reformat* the paragraphs in your document. This is accomplished in WordStar by the use of the CTRL-B editing command. Formatting consists of adjusting the spaces within each line of a document. If you change margins or change the words in a paragraph, the spacing will normally need to be changed, too. Move the cursor in front of the paragraph where you want reformatting to begin, then press CTRL-B. As reformatting proceeds, some words fall at the margin edges. When WordStar encounters one of these, it will pause and ask you if you want to insert a hyphen (-). You can either press the hyphen key to insert the hyphen or press the CTRL-B again to continue reformatting without inserting the hyphen.

Manipulating Document Sections

One of the major capabilities of word processing packages is that they allow you to do "cut-and-paste" operations to your document. This means that you can move sentences, paragraphs, or pages around within the document, rather then having to retype it. The section of your document that is to be manipulated is called a **block**. A block is a section of your document that has been *marked* with special commands. Once a block has been marked, you can move it, delete it, copy it, or write it out to its own file. The **block commands** in WordStar are initiated by using CTRL-K keys. Figure A2-16 shows you the BLOCK MENU, which displays the many docu-

FIGURE A2-15 WordStar onscreen menu commands

```
^O^O^O    B:LETTER   PAGE 1 LINE 1 COL 01
                  < < <  O N S C R E E N   M E N U  > > >
  -Margins & Tabs-  ! -Line  Functions- !  ---More Toggles--  !   -Other  Menus-
  L Set left margin !C Center text       !J Justify    now ON  ! (from Main only)
  R Set right margin!S Set line spacing  !V Vari-Tabs now ON   !^J Help   ^K Block
  X Release margins !                    !H Hyph-help now ON   !^Q Quick  ^P Print
  I Set  N Clear tab!    ---Toggles---   !E Soft hyph now OFF  !^O Onscreen
  G Paragraph tab   !W Wrd wrap now ON   !D Prnt disp now ON   !Space Bar returns
  F Ruler from line !T Rlr line now ON   !P Pge break now ON   !you to Main Menu.
  L----!----!----!----!----!----!----!----!----!----!--------R
```

FIGURE A2–16 WordStar block menu commands

```
^K        B:LETTER1  PAGE 1 LINE 1 COL 01                INSERT ON
                     < < <    B L O C K   M E N U    > > >
   -Saving Files- !  -Block Operations-  ! -File  Operations- !   -Other  Menus-
  S Save & resume ! B  Begin   K  End    ! R  Read  P  Print   !  (from Main only)
  D Save--done    ! H  Hide / Display    ! O  Copy  E  Rename  ! ^J Help   ^K Block
  X Save & exit   ! C  Copy    Y  Delete! J  Delete            ! ^Q Quick  ^P Print
  Q Abandon file  ! V  Move    W  Write  ! -Disk  Operations-  ! ^O Onscreen
  -Place Markers- ! N  Column  now OFF !L Change logged disk! Space Bar returns
  0-9 set/hide 0-9!                      !F Directory now OFF ! you to Main Menu.
  L----!----!----!----!----!----!----!----!----!----!--------R
```

ment manipulating options available. Other CTRL-K options having to do with file management are also shown in the BLOCK MENU. The important block commands for a beginning user are briefly explained in Figure A2–17.

Special Printing Effects

Most word processing packages provide you with special printing effects to emphasize words in your document. Most familiar and useful to the beginning user would be the underlining of words or the printing of words in boldface. In WordStar, such printing effects are options provided by the CTRL-P commands. These are displayed in the PRINT MENU shown in Figure A2–18. In WordStar, these commands do not change the words on the display screen but

FIGURE

A2–17 Manipulating document sections (blocks)

CTRL-K-B	Mark the beginning of a block
CTRL-K-K	Mark the end of a block.
CTRL-D-V	Move the block. The procedure is this: first, you mark the block with CTRL-K-B and CTRL-K-K. Then you move the cursor to the place where you would like to have the block located. Then you give the command CTRL-K-V.
CTRL-K-C	Copy a block. First, mark the block with CTRL-K-B and CTRL-K-K. Then move the cursor to the place where you want the copy and give the command CTRL-K-C. The original block will be untouched, and a duplicate of it will be placed where you want it.
CTRL-K-Y	Delete a block. Mark the block, then give the command. The block will disappear.
CTRL-K-W	Write a block. You can store a marked block by writing it on your disk with this command. Handy if you are creating files of "boiler plate" (i.e., standardized paragraphs).
CTRL-K-R	Read a block. You can insert a file into your document with this command. Handy for the insertion of boiler plate material.

FIGURE   A2-18 WordStar print menu commands

```
^P          B:LETTER1   PAGE 1 LINE 1 COL Ø1              INSERT ON
                        < < <    P R I N T    M E N U    > > >
        ------ Special   Effects --------  ┊ -Printing  Changes-  ┊  -Other   Menus-
    (begin and end) ┊    (one time each)   ┊ A Alternate pitch    ┊ (from Main only)
    B Bold D Double ┊ H Overprint char     ┊ N Standard pitch     ┊^J Help   ^K Block
      S Underscore  ┊ O Non-break space    ┊ C Printing pause     ┊^Q Quick  ^P Print
      X Strikeout   ┊ F Phantom space      ┊ Y Other ribbon color ┊^O Onscreen
      V Subscript   ┊ G Phantom rubout     ┊  --User  Patches--   ┊Space Bar returns
      T Superscript ┊ RET Overprint line   ┊ Q(1) W(2) E(3) R(4)  ┊you to Main Menu.
    L----!----!----!----!----!----!----!----!----!----!----!--------R
```

are inserted as special characters in the text, which cause special print effects during the actual printing process. The two most used CTRL-P commands for a beginning user are the boldface command (CTRL-P-B) and the underline command (CTRL-P-S). (*Note*: beginning users should be reminded that most CTRL-P commands must be applied to both the beginning and end of the word or phrase you wish to affect. If you don't, you may end up with a document that is completely underlined or boldfaced!)

Boldface Printing: CTRL-P-B.   This is usually done by overstriking several times. The way in which you use this command is to place a CTRL-P-B at the beginning and end of what you want in boldface print. The screen display will show the presence of the command as ˆ B. For example, if you want to boldface a word-like **attention,** you would move the cursor to the beginning of the word and type CTRL-P-B. Then move the cursor to the end of the word and type CTRL-P-B again. The word will now look like this: ˆBattentionˆB. The boldface effect will appear when you print the document.

Underlining: CTRL-P-S.   This works the same way as CTRL-P-B. That is, you need a CTRL-P-S at the beginning and end of whatever you want underlined. If you want a word like attention to be underlined, it should look like this when you have used the appropriate CTRL-P-S commands: ˆSattentionˆS.

HANDS-ON EXERCISE A2-3:   ADDITIONAL DOCUMENT REVISION

Retrieve the file containing the letter that you typed and saved in Exercises A2-1 and A2-2 and change it as follows:

1. The letter should inform Mr. Rubout that the color grey is available on special order at an extra cost of $300 per unit.
2. The margins should be reset to 15 on the left and 65 on the right. You will have to rearrange the address of ABC Corporation. Do this by centering it on screen (use CTRL-O-C). Make sure you reformat the letter so the body of the letter fits inside the new margins.
3. Use the replacement command (CTRL-Q-A) to change the spelling of every occurrence of "blivit" to "blivvit".
4. Save and print this revised letter.

Creating and Editing Nondocument Files

At the beginning of this section, we mentioned that word processing packages can be used to create **nondocument files**. Specifically, this capability is used to create data files that will be processed by other application programs, or to create and edit a computer program. Once a data file is created and stored on disk using a word processing package, it can then be processed by a variety of programs. Spreadsheet packages, database management packages, and business application packages (such as payroll or inventory programs) are some examples. Writing a computer program using a WordStar package is done to get the benefits of the editing features of the word processing editor. After such program files are completed, they can then be processed by a *compiler* (language translator program) for such languages as CBASIC, COBOL, or FORTRAN.

After the WordStar program is loaded and the OPENING MENU is displayed, the nondocument file is created by selecting the N command option. You are then provided with a display explaining the creation of a nondocument file and asking you for a file name. See Figure A2–19. Once you have entered a file name, the MAIN MENU is displayed and you are ready to create and edit your nondocument file.

For instance, you may wish to build a **data file** consisting of payroll information (payroll **data records**) for each employee of a company. This might include their names, Social Security numbers, sex, department, rate of pay, and hours worked. Each employee record should fit on one line. Typically, you will press the ENTER key at the end of each line in all data and program files. This makes each line an individual record in the file. All of the editing commands in the MAIN MENU can be used to edit a nondocument file. For example, we can correct errors, and add and delete employee re-

FIGURE

A2–19 WordStar nondocument file creation and editing display

```
    N              not editing

Use this command to create and alter program source files
   and other non-documents.  Word wrap defaults off;
   tabbing defaults to fixed (TAB chars in file; 8-col stops);
   page breaks not shown; hi bit flags not used in file.
For normal word processing uses, use the "D" command instead.

   A file name is 1-8 letters/digits, a period,
   and an optional 0-3 character type.
   File name may be preceded by disk drive letter A-D
   and colon, otherwise current logged disk is used.

NAME OF FILE TO EDIT?
```

cords in the payroll data file we are creating. Figure A2–20 shows the data file (PAYROLL) we will create using the WordStar nondocument file capability. It contains the names, social security numbers, sex, department, hourly pay rate, and hours worked for four employees.

HANDS-ON EXERCISE A2–4: CREATING AND EDITING A NONDOCUMENT FILE

Create the nondocument file PAYROLL shown in Figure A2–20. Use the editing features of WordStar to produce a correct version of this payroll data file. Then save the file and print it out on your system printer.

FIGURE

A2–20 Nondocument file: Payroll data file

Alvarez J.S., 632403718, F, PRODUCTION, 14.00,44.0
Klugman K.L., 435182906, M, FINANCE, 12.00,35.0
OBrien J.A., 576434572, M, INFO SYSTEMS, 12.50,45.0
Porter M.L., 342877915, F, ACCOUNTING, 12.50,40.0

FIGURE A2–21 WordStar command summary

Cursor Controls

^S	Left character
^D	Right character
^E	Up line
^X	Down line
^A	Left word
^F	Right word
^QS	Left end of line
^QD	Right end of line
^QE	Top of screen
^QX	Bottom of screen
^QR	Beginning of file
^QC	End of file
^K 0–9	Set/hide 0 to 9
^Q 0–9	Mark 0 to 9

Scroll

^Z	Scroll down line
^R	Scroll down screen
^W	Scroll up line
^C	Scroll up screen

Delete

^Y	Delete line
^T	Delete right word
^G	Delete character right
[DELETE]	Delete character left
^Q[DELETE]	Delete to left side of line
^QY	Delete to right side of line
^KY	Delete block
^KJ	Delete file

Save

^KD	Done edit
^KS	Save and re-edit
^KX	Save and exit
^KQ	Abandon edit

Print Functions

^PS	Underscore
^PT	Superscript
^PB	Boldface
^PH	Overprint
^PD	Double strike
^PX	Strikeover
^PV	Subscript
^KP	Print

Margins, Tabs

^OL	Set left margin
^OC	Center text
^OF	Set file margin
^OR	Set right margin
^OX	Release margin
^OI	Tab set
^ON	Clear tab
^OG	Paragraph tab

Nonprinting Ruler Line

Position the cursor at the beginning of the line, turn insert on, insert two periods, then type ^P and **RETURN.**

Moving Blocks

^KB	Mark/hide block beginning
^KK	Mark block end
^KV	Move block
^KC	Copy block
^KW	Write block
^KR	Read file
^KH	Hide/display marked
^QB	Cursor block beginning
^QK	Cursor block end

Find

^QF	Find string
^QV	Cursor to starting point
^QA	Find and replace
^L	Find/replace again

Special Functions

^B	Reform paragraph
^QP	Cursor to previous position
^V	Insert off/on
^O	Status
^QQ	Repeat next command
^U	Interrupt
^J	Help menu

Spacing

^OS	Line spacing

Toggles (default bold)

^OW	Word wrap ON/OFF
^OT	Ruler line ON/OFF
^OJ	Justification ON/OFF
^OV	Variable tab ON/OFF
^OH	Hyphen help ON/OFF
^OE	Soft hyphen ON/OFF
^OD	Print display ON/OFF
^OP	Page break ON/OFF
^KN	Block column ON/OFF
^KF	Directory ON/OFF

Dot Commands

Command	Function
.LH	Line height
.CW	Character width
.PL	Paper length
.PO	Page offset
.MT	Margin top
.HM	Heading margin
.HE	Heading
.MB	Margin bottom
.FM	Footing margin
.FO	Footing
.PC	Page number column
.PA	New page
.CP	Conditional page
.OP	Omit page numbers
.PN	Page number
.IG(..)	Comment
.UJ	Microjustification
.BP	Bidirectional print

MailMerge Commands

.DF	Data file
.RV	Read variable
.RP	Repeat
.SV	Set variable
.AV	Ask for variable
.DM	Data message
.CS	Clear screen
.FI	File insert

HANDS-ON ASSIGNMENTS

We have now explained and practiced the creation and editing of a simple letter (a document file) and a data file using the WordStar word processing package. We have also stored, printed, retrieved, and revised these files. This should have given you a good introductory understanding of the capabilities and uses of microcomputer word processing packages. Consult the manual for the word processing package you are using if you need more information. (*Note*: a summary of WordStar commands is shown in Figure A2–21.) Now its time for you to create and edit some documents and data files of your own, using a word processing package like WordStar. Good luck!

A2.1 If you have not already done so, create, edit, and revise the simple business letter as explained in Hands-on Exercises 2–1, 2–2, and 2–3.

A2.2 Retrieve the letter (LETTER1) you modified in Exercise A2–3. Address it to a new person and make appropriate changes in its form and content, using several block, global search and replace, reformatting, and special printing effects commands. Save the letter as LETTER2 and print a copy.

A2.3 Write and edit a short letter or memo. For example, make an announcement to your employees or inquire about a new job opening. Save and print this letter.

A2.4 Retrieve the letter you created in assignment A2–3. Change it so it is addressed to someone else. Change some facts or figures in the letter, using several block, global search and replace and reformatting commands. Save and print this revised letter.

A2.5 Retrieve the PAYROLL data file you created in Exercise A2–4. Make some additional changes to it. For instance, you could delete the record of one employee and replace it with information about a new employee. Also, you should change the rate of pay or hours worked of some of the employees. Finally, save this revised file and print it out on your printer.

A2.6 Create a file of student records made up of student names, social security numbers, and test scores. Save and print this file. Then retrieve it and change it by adding and deleting records and modifying some test scores. Save and print the revised file.

SECTION THREE: USING ELECTRONIC SPREADSHEET PACKAGES

Introduction to Spreadsheet Packages

What is an *electronic spreadsheet?* How does one use such programs? This section will provide answers to these questions and get you started in the use of spreadsheet packages. Let's review what we learned about spreadsheet packages in Chapter Seven: System and Application Software. An **electronic spreadsheet package** is an application program used as a computerized tool for analysis, planning, and modeling. An **electronic spreadsheet** is a worksheet of rows and columns that is stored in the computer's memory and is displayed on its video screen. The computer's keyboard or other devices, such as an electronic mouse or touch screen, is used to enter data and to manipulate the data in the worksheet. Users can build a model by entering the data and relationships (formulas) of a problem into an electronic worksheet, make a variety of changes, and visually evaluate the results of such changes. Figure A3–1 is an example of a simple financial spreadsheet that could be developed with any electronic spreadsheet package. Once an electronic spreadsheet has been developed, it can be stored on a floppy disk or other storage device for later use or be printed out as a paper report on a printer.

Spreadsheet Format and Organization

How are spreadsheets organized? The typical electronic spreadsheet is a matrix or grid of many rows and columns. For example, the spreadsheets of VisiCalc and many other packages have 63

FIGURE

A3–1 Simple financial spreadsheet

```
                    SPREADSHEET EXAMPLE

              ABC COMPANY: FINANCIAL PERFORMANCE

                  1983     1984     1985    TOTAL   AVERAGE
                 ------   ------   ------   ------   ------
   REVENUE        1000     1100     1200     3300     1100

   EXPENSES        600      660      720     1980      660
                 ------   ------   ------   ------   ------
   PROFIT          400      440      480     1320      440

   TAXES           160      176      192      528      176
                 ------   ------   ------   ------   ------
   PROFIT          240      264      288      792      264
   AFTER TAXES
```

columns and 254 rows. Lotus 1-2-3, on the other hand, provides a spreadsheet of 256 columns and 2,048 rows! The spaces formed by the intersection of rows and columns are called **cells**. Thus a VisiCalc spreadsheet contains over 16,000 cells. Cells are identified by their column-row coordinate, (i.e., the number or letter of the column and row in which the cell is located.) In VisiCalc, rows are numbered and columns are specified by letters, with the column of a cell mentioned first, then its row. For example, cell C12 identifies a cell at the intersection of the third column and the twelfth row of the spreadsheet. Thus in VisiCalc, rows are numbered from one to 254, while the 63 columns are specified by the letters A through Z, AA through AZ, and BA through BK. Spreadsheet programs, such as Multiplan, however, use numbers to designate both rows and columns. (Refer back to Figure 7–13 in Chapter Seven for photographs of actual VisiCalc and Multiplan spreadsheet displays.)

Since an electronic spreadsheet is so large, only a section, called a **window**, is displayed on the video screen at any one time. This window can be moved around for you to see and work on any part of the spreadsheet that you wish. For example, the standard window in VisiCalc allows you to view 8 columns and 21 rows anywhere in the spreadsheet. Also, most electronic spreadsheet programs allow you to split the screen into two or more smaller windows. This allows you to view two or more parts of the spreadsheet at the same time, so you can more easily use the spreadsheet. The windows can be displayed horizontally or vertically. They also can be synchronized so they move together around the spreadsheet. Thus the video monitor display of the computer system is a window or group of windows that lets the user look at parts of the much-larger spreadsheet stored in the computer's memory. See Figure A3–2.

A **cursor** (or *cell pointer*) is located at all times in one of the cells of the worksheet. Data are entered into this cell by using the keyboard of the computer. This cursor typically is a *reverse video* rectangle of light, or a *color bar*, that fills one or more spreadsheet cells. The cursor is moved from cell to cell within the spreadsheet by the use of special **cursor control keys** (or combinations of other keys, an electronic mouse, or a touch-screen). The cursor control keys are labeled with either an up, down, left, or right arrow, and move the cursor in those directions. To view other parts of the spreadsheet, you move the cursor across the worksheet with the cursor control key. When the cursor reaches the edge of the current window (top, bottom, left, or right edges), the window begins to shift or **scroll** across the spreadsheet in the direction the cursor is moving. (*Note*: In VisiCalc, the cursor can also be moved to a specific cell on the spreadsheet by typing the > symbol and then

FIGURE

A3–2 The window of an electronic spreadsheet

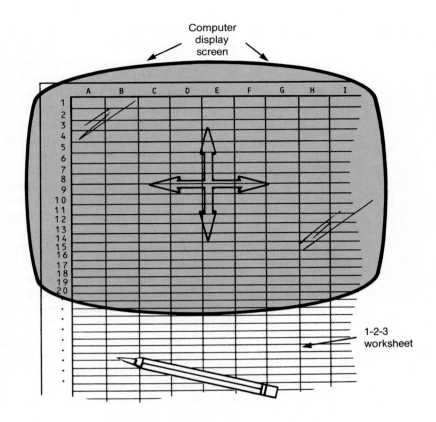

typing the coordinates of the cell to which you want the cursor moved. For example, typing >H21 and pressing the ENTER key would move the cursor to cell H21.)

Each cell in an electronic spreadsheet can be filled with one of three possible types of information: numbers, words, and formulas. More specifically, a cell can contain (1) **alphanumeric data,** such as titles and text material; (2) **numeric data** or numbers; and (3) **mathematical formulas,** which perform standard arithmetic functions (add, subtract, multiply, etc.) as well as **special functions** (sum, average, net present value, etc.) provided by the spreadsheet program.

Most electronic spreadsheet programs display column or row numbers and letters along the top and left-hand margin of the spreadsheet window, as well as additional information at the top or bottom of the screen. Figure A3–3 illustrates a simple electronic spreadsheet as displayed on the video screen of a computer using VisiCalc. You should notice that this display is a **window** that is allowing you to see only 21 rows and 14 columns of the larger

FIGURE A3–3 VisiCalc spreadsheet display

```
C12  (V)  +C8-C10
Move: From...To
C12...D12
         A        B        C        D        E        F        G
  1
  2                        SPREADSHEET  EXAMPLE
  3
  4               ABC  COMPANY:  FINANCIAL  PERFORMANCE
  5
  6                       1983     1984     1985    TOTAL   AVERAGE
  7              -----------------------------------------------
  8  REVENUE              1000     1100     1200    3300     1100
  9
 10  EXPENSES              600      660      720    1980      660
 11              -----------------------------------------------
 12  PROFIT                400      440      480    1320      440
 13
 14  TAXES                 160      176      192     528      176
 15              -----------------------------------------------
 16  PROFIT                240      264      288     792      264
 17  AFTER  TAXES
 18
 19
 20
 21
```

spreadsheet (254 rows and 63 columns) stored in the memory of the computer. Notice that the rectangular cursor is at cell C12 (the profit figure for 1984 of $440 dollars), which is at the intersection of the third column and twelfth row of the spreadsheet. Notice that the spreadsheet contains both words (titles) and numbers. The spreadsheet also contains formulas, but these are not evident on the spreadsheet display itself.

Let's look above the spreadsheet to the three lines of information in the **control panel** at the top of the screen. The first line is called the **entry line** and shows you the column and row location of the cell (C12) where the cursor is located. It also displays the contents of that cell, which in this case is the formula +C8-C10. This formula computes a gross profit figure of $440 at cell C12 by subtracting the contents of cell C10 from the contents of cell C8. (*Note*: (V) before the formula identifies it as a "value" (number or formula.) Text material or "labels" would cause an (L) to be displayed.)

The second line is the **prompt line**. It displays information to help you use VisiCalc *commands* to manipulate the spreadsheet. In this example the MOVE command is being executed, therefore, the prompt line is requesting that you specify the coordinates of the cells involved in a transfer of data. The third line is called the **edit line.** It shows what the user is entering into the spreadsheet. In this case it shows that you wish to move the contents of cell C12 to cell D12.

At the far upper-right corner of the screen is a recalculation order indicator (C), as well as a memory indicator (34). The C indicates that calculations on the worksheet will be done column by column, rather than row by row, which would be indicated by an (R). The 34 indicates the approximate remaining storage positions in main memory. Assuming a 64K main memory, the VisiCalc worksheet and program is using approximately 30K of main memory capacity.

Other spreadsheets have different formats. Figure A3–4 illustrates a simple spreadsheet display using the Multiplan electronic spreadsheet package. Notice that both rows and columns are labeled using numbers. Various commands are listed at the bottom of the screen in a COMMANDS line, which is actually a **menu** that takes up two lines. The third line at the bottom of the screen is a *message line*, which in this case asks you to select the option or type of

FIGURE A3–4 Multiplan spreadsheet display

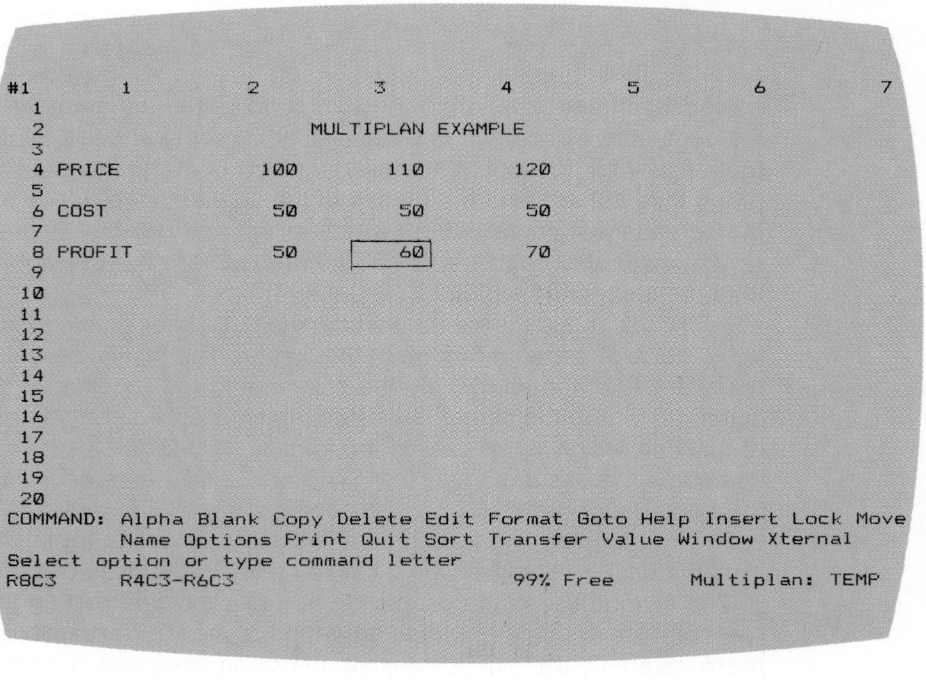

```
#1          1          2          3          4          5          6          7
 1
 2                         MULTIPLAN EXAMPLE
 3
 4  PRICE             100        110        120
 5
 6  COST               50         50         50
 7
 8  PROFIT             50        [60]        70
 9
10
11
12
13
14
15
16
17
18
19
20
COMMAND: Alpha Blank Copy Delete Edit Format Goto Help Insert Lock Move
         Name Options Print Quit Sort Transfer Value Window Xternal
Select option or type command letter
R8C3      R4C3-R6C3                  99% Free        Multiplan: TEMP
```

command you wish to execute. The line at the bottom of the screen is the *status line*. It indicates that the cursor is at row 8, column 3 (R8C3). This cell contains a formula (R4C3-R6C3) which subtracts COST (R6C3) from PRICE (R4C3) which the computer executes to give the PROFIT figure of 60.

Getting Started

At this point you should have a basic idea of what electronic spreadsheet programs are, as well as their many benefits and uses. You should also have a good idea of the format and organization of an electronic spreadsheet, both in memory and as it appears on the video screen. Now it's time to work through a simple example of the use of an electronic spreadsheet package. The basic version of **VisiCalc** will be used, because many other spreadsheet packages are quite similar to this program, which is still the most widely used electronic spreadsheet package. The spreadsheet we will build as we go along will be the ABC Company: Financial Performance spreadsheet example shown in Figures A3–1 and A3–3.

Insert your VisiCalc disk into disk drive A and turn on the computer. (See the beginning of the first section of this appendix if you need additional information on starting a microcomputer and using a floppy disk.) A VisiCalc disk which also contains the operating system, will load (boot) the operating system first and then load the VisiCalc program. Or you can load the operating system from an operating system diskette, remove it from the disk drive, insert the VisiCalc disk, and then type in VC after the system prompt (such as A>). Once the VisiCalc program is loaded from the disk, a blank VisiCalc spreadsheet form will appear on the screen. Notice the entry line, prompt line, and edit line in the control panel at the top of the screen above the spreadsheet. Also notice that the cursor is at the first cell (A1). At this point, you should use the cursor control keys to explore the entire spreadsheet.

HANDS-ON EXERCISE A3–1: VIEWING THE SPREADSHEET

Press the *down-arrow* cursor control key until row number 254 appears in the window on the screen. You now have a window looking at the lower left-hand corner of the spreadsheet in memory. Next, press the *right-arrow* control key until the 63rd column (column BK) appears on the screen. You now have a window through which you can see the lower right-hand corner of the spreadsheet in memory. Now press the *up-arrow* control key until you are back at the first row. You are now viewing the upper right-hand corner of the spreadsheet. Now get back to the upper left-hand corner of the spreadsheet by pressing the HOME key (such as on the IBM PC) or use the *left-arrow* cursor control arrow key. You have now explored the entire 63 column by 254 row spreadsheet provided by VisiCalc. You are now ready to enter data into the cells of the spreadsheet and use various spreadsheet commands.

Using Commands

Electronic spreadsheets use **commands** to manipulate the worksheet and its contents in various ways. For example, you can use the BLANK command to erase the contents of a cell. You could use the REPLICATE command to duplicate the contents of cells, rows, and columns throughout the spreadsheet. Or you can insert or delete a column or row by using the INSERT or DELETE commands.

In VisiCalc and many other spreadsheets, commands are activated by pressing the slash (/) key, which displays a **menu** of *command letters* (the first letter of command words) or the *command words* themselves in the prompt line above the spreadsheet. For example, the prompt line in VisiCalc looks like this:

Command: BCDEFGIMPRSTVW

You then type the appropriate command letter. This usually causes additional prompts to be displayed, which allow you to key in details about the action to be taken. Lotus 1–2–3 and MultiPlan show a menu of command words and prompts at the top or bottom of the screen. (Refer to Figures A3–4 and A5–3.) Also, some packages do not require the use of a slash (/) when entering a command letter. A summary of VisiCalc commands is shown in Figure A3–5.

Entering Data

Data is entered at the cell location where the cursor is placed by simply typing it in and either depressing the ENTER key, or one of the cursor control keys. If you use the ENTER key, the cursor remains at the same cell location. If you use one of the

FIGURE

A3-5 Summary of
selected VisiCalc
commands

Commands	Key	Purpose
Command	/	Call Command Menu
Blank	B	Erase spreadsheet cell at cursor
Clear	C	Erase spreadsheet area
Delete	D	Initiate deletion of row or column
Edit	E	Move entry line to edit line for modification
Format	F	Change format of a cell
Global	G	Call menu of commands that affect entire worksheet
Insert	I	Initiate insertion of row/column
Print	P	Call menu of printing options
Replicate	R	Select replicate option to copy groups of cells from one place to another
Storage	S	Call menu to access disk
Title	T	Initiate or clear title locking
Window	W	Call screen-splitting menu

cursor control keys, the data are entered at the cell location where the cursor was located and the cursor moves to another cell.

It should be noted that you can enter up to 125 characters of data into a cell, but only 8 numbers or 9 letters will be displayed on the screen unless column width is changed. In VisiCalc, the width of all columns can be changed with the /GC command. For example, the command: /GC 20 will make *all* columns 20 characters wide. Other more advanced spreadsheets (such as Multiplan or Lotus 1-2-3) allow the width of individual columns to be changed.

Correcting Errors

If you make a mistake while typing and recognize it before you have pressed the ENTER key, press either the BACKSPACE key or ESCAPE key, then the DELETE key if you wish to erase one character at a time. However, If you wish to erase the entire entry, press the BREAK key. Once you have entered data in a cell, you can correct or change its contents by moving the cursor to that cell. Then enter new data into the cell, or use the BLANK command (/B) to erase the contents of the cell. In any case, you must use the ENTER key or the cursor control keys to complete each of these procedures. Finally, if you want to erase the entire spreadsheet and start over again, press /C and then a Y to confirm your decision.

You can also use the EDIT command (/E) to correct or change part of the contents of a cell without redoing the entire cell. After moving the cursor to that cell, press /E. This displays the cell's contents on the edit line above the spreadsheet. Then use the cursor control keys to move a small cursor in the edit line to the characters you wish to change. Use the BACKSPACE key to erase characters to the left of this cursor. Then key-in your change and press the ENTER key.

Entering Numbers and Text

Electronic spreadsheet programs use simple rules to distinguish between numeric, text, and formula entries, depending on the first character typed. The following rules are common to VisiCalc and many other spreadsheet packages.

- An entry beginning with a letter is assumed to be a text entry (such as a row or column heading) and is identified as a **label.**
- An entry beginning with a number is assumed to be a numeric entry and is identified as a **value.**
- If the first character you enter is a plus (+), minus (−), or an opening parenthesis, it will be treated as a formula entry or as a number. A formula is also identified as a **value.**
- A text entry (a label) can begin with blanks or a number (such as the date 1985) if you first press the double quote key (for example, "1985).

The distinction between numeric and text entries is important, because cells that contain numeric entries can be manipulated by spreadsheet formulas and functions, whereas cells containing text cannot. Also a formula must be differentiated from numeric or text entries, because only the value of the formula, not the formula itself, appears in a cell.

HANDS-ON EXERCISE A3–2:   ENTERING TITLES AND DATA

Enter the titles and headings of the spreadsheet example shown in Figure A3–2. Then enter the data for 1983: revenue of $1000, expenses of $600, etc. See Figure A3–6.

Entering and Using Formulas

Spreadsheet formulas express mathematical relationships between cells, with the cell names acting like algebraic variables in the formula. For example, entering the formula +B5−C2 into cell

FIGURE   A3–6 VisiCalc spreadsheet with titles and 1983 data

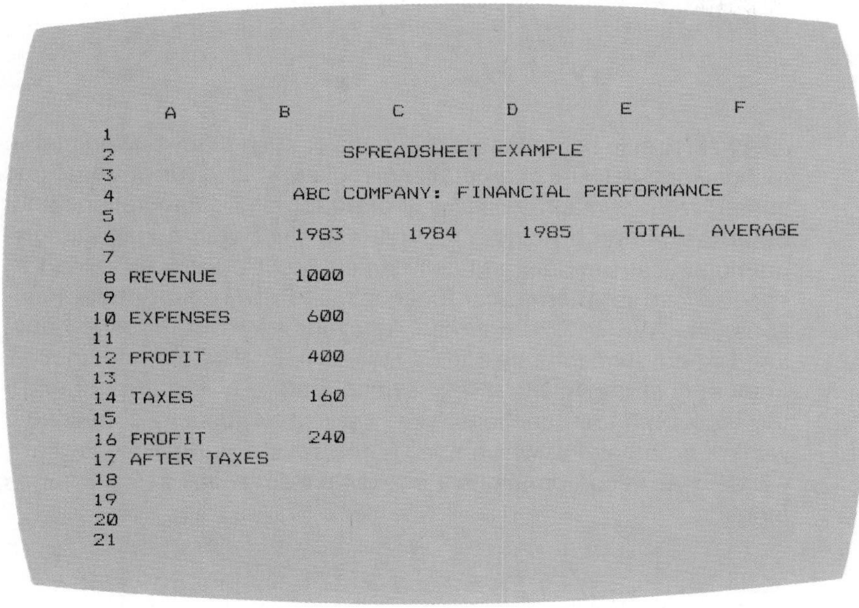

```
              A          B          C          D          E          F
    1
    2                      SPREADSHEET EXAMPLE
    3
    4              ABC COMPANY: FINANCIAL PERFORMANCE
    5
    6                     1983       1984       1985       TOTAL    AVERAGE
    7
    8  REVENUE            1000
    9
   10  EXPENSES            600
   11
   12  PROFIT             400
   13
   14  TAXES              160
   15
   16  PROFIT             240
   17  AFTER TAXES
   18
   19
   20
   21
```

D7 would cause cell D7 to always display the result of subtracting the contents of cell C2 from the contents of cell B5. Spreadsheet formulas use a plus sign (+) for addition, a minus sign (−) for subtraction, an asterisk (∗) for multiplication, a slash (/) for division, and a caret (^) for exponentiation. VisiCalc computes the formula in a strict sequence from left to right, while other spreadsheets use the algebraic practice of doing exponentiation first and then multiplication and division before addition and subtraction. However, as in algebra, parentheses can be used to change the order of arithmetic operations. For example, 1+2∗3 would equal 9 in VisiCalc but have a value of only 7 in a spreadsheet using an algebraic order of operations. However, you could modify the VisiCalc formula with parentheses as follows: +1+(2∗3). This would result in a value of 7.

You should remember that only the result or value of a formula is displayed in a cell on the spreadsheet. However, the formula in any cell is shown on the entry line above the spreadsheet when the cursor is placed over that cell. Thus anytime the value of the cells used in a formula are affected in any way, the value of the cell where the formula itself is stored will be instantly changed. This is the powerful *automatic and instant calculation* feature of all electronic spreadsheet programs. For example, consider the formula, (D7=+B5−C2). Whenever the value of either cell B5 or C2 changes, the value of cell D7 will instantly change to display a new result.

Using Functions

All electronic spreadsheet programs contain many built-in mathematical formulas and computational routines called **functions**. Functions give us a much easier way of performing computations and other tasks than building a formula ourselves with a long string of mathematical symbols and cell names. Most electronic spreadsheets have **mathematical** functions (like SUM), **statistical** functions (like AVERAGE), **financial** functions (like Net Present Value), and **logical** functions (like IF . . . THEN). In VisiCalc, all function entries must begin with the @ symbol before typing the name of the function. Most functions have *arguments* (usually contained within parentheses), which specify the cells or other values that will be used in computations. For example, let's look at the following function:

FIGURE

A3–7 Summary of selected VisiCalc functions

Function	Result
General Computational Functions	
@AVERAGE(list)	Arithmetic mean of the values in a list.
@COUNT(list)	Number of nonblank entries in a list.
@MAX(list)	Largest value in a list.
@MIN(list)	Smallest value in a list.
@SUM(list)	Sum of each value in a list.
@NPV	Calculates the net present value of future cash flows.
@NA	Avoids error messages when cells with labels or blanks are evaluated arithmetically.
Arithmetic Functions	
@ABS(v)	Absolute value of an argument.
@EXP(v)	e (2.71828. . .) to the power specified by an argument.
@INT(v)	Integer portion of an argument.
@LN(v)	Natural log (base e) of an argument.
@LOG10(v)	Logarithm (base 10) of an argument.
@SQRT(v)	Square root of an argument.

@ SUM (A7...A12)

In this example, @ signals that this entry is a function; SUM is the name of the function, and (A7 . . . A12) is the argument. When this function is entered into a cell, it immediately displays the results of adding together the values in cells A7, A8, A9, A10, A11, and A12. A listing of some of the functions in VisiCalc is shown in Figure A3–7.

It should be noted here that the entry of cell coordinates in formulas and functions in VisiCalc and some other electronic spreadsheets can be accomplished in two ways. First, you can type-in the cell coordinates when needed. Or, you can use the cursor movement keys to move the cursor over to a cell. This automatically enters that cell's coordinates into the formula.

HANDS-ON EXERCISE A3–3:   ENTERING AND USING FORMULAS

Enter formulas for 1983 into column B of the spreadsheet you started in Exercise A3–2. No formula is necessary for REVENUE in cell B8; we will assume that it was $1000 in 1983. Enter the following formulas: EXPENSES are (+B8*.6) in cell B10, PROFIT is (+B8−B10) in cell B12, TAXES are (+B12*.4) in cell B14, and PROFIT AFTER TAXES is (+B12−B14) in cell B16. What do these formulas mean? You are using these formulas to specify the following simple mathematical relationships: (1) EXPENSES are 60 percent of REVENUE, (2) PROFIT equals REVENUE minus EXPENSES, (3) TAXES are 40 percent of PROFIT, and (4) PROFIT AFTER TAXES equals PROFIT minus TAXES.

Once you have entered these formulas, you can perform a simple demonstration of the automatic recalculation power of spreadsheet packages, as well as their "what-if" capability. Let's change revenue for 1983 on the spreadsheet. **What** would profit after taxes have been **if** revenue for 1983 had increased to $1500? $1800? $2000? Try it and see, instantly. Figure A3–8 shows what happens when sales were changed to $2000. It also displays the formula that computes net profit after taxes.

FIGURE A3–8 Spreadsheet showing formula display and
recalculated values

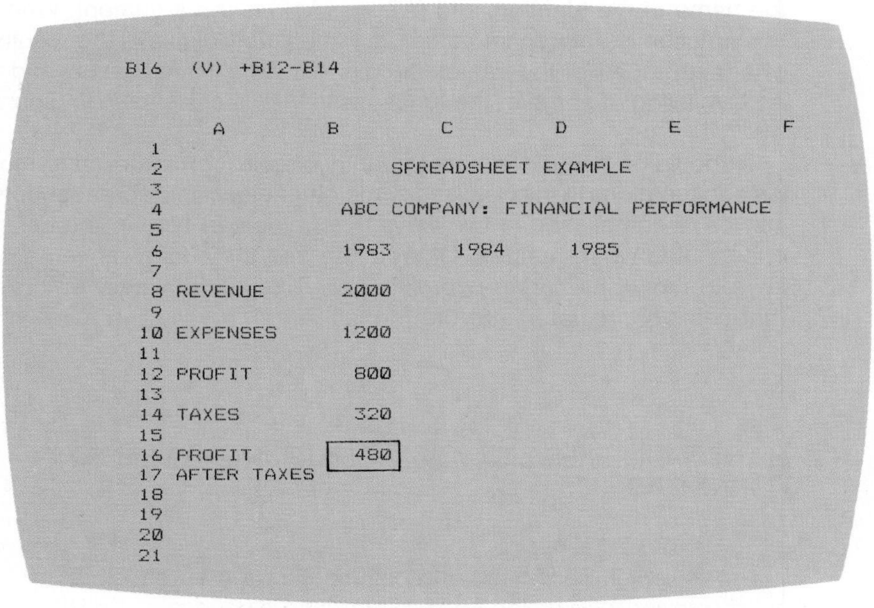

```
B16    (V)   +B12-B14


         A         B         C         D         E         F
   1
   2                    SPREADSHEET  EXAMPLE
   3
   4                ABC  COMPANY:  FINANCIAL  PERFORMANCE
   5
   6                1983      1984      1985
   7
   8  REVENUE       2000
   9
  10  EXPENSES      1200
  11
  12  PROFIT         800
  13
  14  TAXES          320
  15
  16  PROFIT        [ 480 ]
  17  AFTER  TAXES
  18
  19
  20
  21
```

Replicating Spreadsheet Entries

One of the most powerful features of electronic spreadsheet programs is their ability to copy the contents of cells, columns, or rows to any part of the spreadsheet. This eliminates the need to key-in repetitive data, text, formulas, and functions, in column after column, or row after row of the worksheet. This ability obviously saves a lot of time and effort in constructing a spreadsheet.

VisiCalc uses the REPLICATE (/R) command while Multiplan and Lotus 1-2-3 use the COPY command to replicate spreadsheet entries. Let's look at an example of the use of the /R command in VisiCalc. After you type /R the prompt line first asks you to key-in the range, which contains the data to be moved. (This is called the **source range**.) It then asks you to key-in the range to which you want the data copied. (This is called the **target range**.) In VisiCalc, a **range** consists of the coordinates of a cell or part of a row or column. For example, the range of a cell might be A2 . . . A2, the range of a column might be A4 . . . A19, and the range of a row might be A7 . . . H7. As you can see, in entering a range you must first enter the cell name of the beginning of the range followed by a period. (The spreadsheet edit line will display *three* periods.) Then you enter the cell name of the end of the range. The cell names can be typed-in or entered by moving the cursor to the appropriate cells.

The real power of the replication feature of electronic spreadsheets is demonstrated in the replication of formulas. Very frequently, a formula must not only be copied throughout many columns or rows of a spreadsheet but must be so modified that any references to cells contained in the formula are changed each time it is located in a different column or row. Thus when replicating formulas containing cell coordinates, the prompt asks whether each cell reference should be "relative" (R) or "no change" (N). If you type N, the cell coordinates are left unchanged when the formula is copied into another cell. If you type R, the cell coordinate will be changed to reflect the new column and row into which the formula is to be copied. For example, if cell A3 contains the formula +A1—A2, it could be copied into cell B3 either as +A1—A2 (no change) or as +B1—B2 (a relative copy). (*Note*: Multiplan and Lotus 1-2-3 require you to specify the parts of your formula as absolute or relative when you first enter them in the spreadsheet.)

HANDS-ON EXERCISE A3–4: REPLICATING SPREADSHEET ENTRIES

First, you should generate revenue amounts for 1984 and 1985. Rather than entering these amounts directly, let's assume that 1984 revenue will be 10 percent more that 1983, and 1985 revenue will be 20 percent more than 1983. Enter (+B8*1.1) in cell C8, and (+B8*1.2) in cell D8. Notice how the revenue amounts for these years are instantly calculated.

Now you should replicate the formulas in the 1983 cells into the appropriate cells for 1984 and 1985. For example, replicate the formula (+B8*.6) for 1983 EXPENSES in cell B10 into cells C10 and D10 for 1984 and 1985. First press /R. Then respond to the spreadsheet prompts by entering the cell coordinates of the *source range* (B10 . . . .B10) and the *target range* (C10 . . . .D10). Then respond to the prompts asking you whether you want B8 in the formula (+B8*.6) to be copied exactly (N=no change) or changed to reflect the new coordinates for 1984 and 1985 (R=relative). You want the second alternative, so press R, and see what happens. Expense amounts for 1984 and 1985 are instantly calculated and displayed. Move the cursor to cells C10 and B10 and see that the entry line display shows they now contain the formulas (+C8*.6) and (+D8*.6). Now you should repeat the same process to replicate the remaining 1983 formulas into 1984 and 1985. See Figure A3–9.

Storing and Retrieving a Spreadsheet

Spreadsheets can be stored on a floppy disk and retrieved later for additional use. The STORE command /SS is used to store a spreadsheet on the disk. However, the spreadsheet prompt first asks for the name of the "file" in which the spreadsheet will be saved. You must then supply a file name of up to eight characters. For example; BUDGET, CHECK, INCOME, etc. (*Note*: If your computer has only one disk drive, you may wish to remove the VisiCalc program diskette from the disk drive and replace it with a "file disk" of your own on which you can store the spreadsheets and other files that you develop. If your system has two disk drives, the VisiCalc

FIGURE A3–9 Replicating the 1983 formula and calculating values for 1984 and 1985 expenses

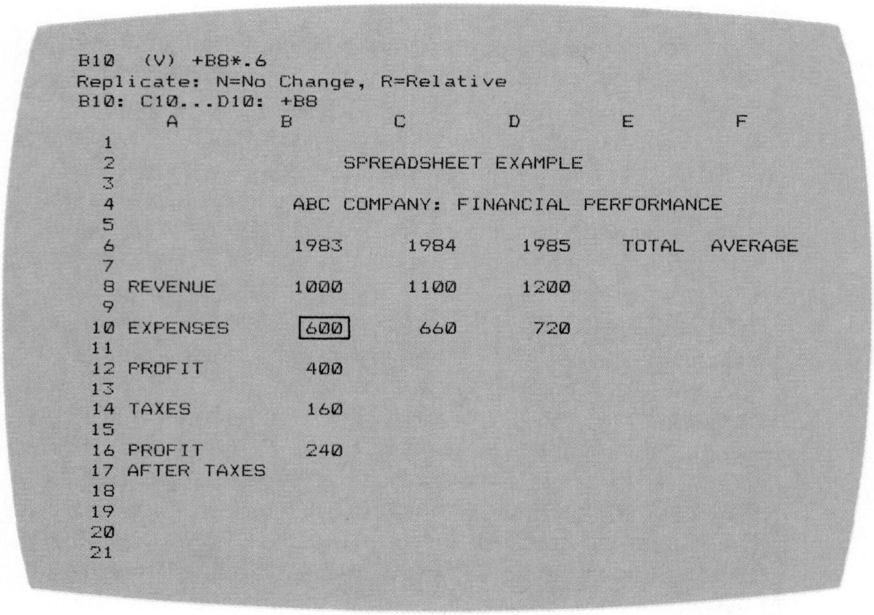

```
B10   (V) +B8*.6
Replicate: N=No Change, R=Relative
B10: C10...D10: +B8
        A            B        C        D        E        F
   1
   2                    SPREADSHEET EXAMPLE
   3
   4            ABC COMPANY: FINANCIAL PERFORMANCE
   5
   6                  1983     1984     1985    TOTAL   AVERAGE
   7
   8 REVENUE         1000     1100     1200
   9
  10 EXPENSES        [600]     660      720
  11
  12 PROFIT          400
  13
  14 TAXES           160
  15
  16 PROFIT          240
  17 AFTER TAXES
  18
  19
  20
  21
```

disk could remain in the first drive and your file disk could be inserted in the second disk drive.)

A spreadsheet stored on a floppy disk can be easily retrieved. In VisiCalc, you should use the command /SL that loads a spreadsheet from the disk into the computer's memory. During the execution of this command, the spreadsheet prompt will ask you for the name of the specific spreadsheet file you wish to load. Once you enter the name that was used to store the file, the spreadsheet is retrieved from the disk, stored in memory, and displayed on the screen.

HANDS-ON EXERCISE A3-5: STORING AND RETRIEVING A SPREADSHEET

Let's first complete our spreadsheet by creating the TOTAL and AVERAGE amount columns. One way to do this is to use formulas containing the SUM and AVERAGE functions to compute total and average REVENUE. Then replicate these formulas into the remaining cells of the appropriate columns. For example, enter the functions @ SUM (B8 . . . D8) into cell E8, and @ AVERAGE(B8 . . . D8) into cell F8. This should result in the instant calculation of the total and average revenue amounts.

Now replicate these formulas to compute total and average expenses, profit, taxes, and profit after taxes. For example, press /R and enter (E8 . . . E8) as the source range, and (E10 . . . E16) as the target range in your TOTAL column. Then press R twice to indicate a relative replication of the formula. The appropriate TOTAL formulas and amounts are instantly inserted and computed. Repeat the same procedure for the AVERAGE column. (*Note*: Zeros and error messages may appear in the blank cells between your spreadsheet values. Remove them using the /B command. Or enter the @ NA function (mentioned in Figure A3-7) in every cell you do not wish affected by calculations.)

Now store the completed spreadsheet by using the /SS command. Give this spreadsheet a file name. (Examples might be ABCPF, EXAMPLE, SHEET1, etc.) If you want to store this file on your second (B) disk drive, the file should be given a name like B:EXAMPLE. Retrieve your spreadsheet using the /SL command, even though it is still on your screen. The screen will go blank and then your spreadsheet will reappear. This proves that you have correctly stored and retrieved your spreadsheet.

Printing Spreadsheets

Once you have completed the spreadsheet and used it to analyze a particular business problem or opportunity, you will probably want to print a paper copy of the spreadsheet on the printer of your computer system. In VisiCalc, the command /P is used to obtain a printout. This will cause the printing of a rectangular area of the worksheet whose upper left corner is the cell in which the cursor was located at the time the /P command was given. The lower right corner of the spreadsheet to be printed must be specified by entering the name of the cell at that corner in response to a spreadsheet prompt.

When you enter the /P command in VisiCalc, the spreadsheet prompt asks whether you wish to send your output to a *printer* or to a *file* on your diskette for later printing. If you enter a P in response to this prompt , you will be asked to enter the cell coordinates at the lower right corner of the spreadsheet you wish to print. As soon as this is done, the computer will begin printing your spreadsheet.

If you want to store a **printfile** of your spreadsheet on your disk for later printing, you must key-in an F after the /P command. The spreadsheet prompt will then ask you to supply a file name for this printfile (which should be different than the file name you used to store the spreadsheet itself). Once you enter the printfile name and the coordinates of the cell at the lower right corner of the spreadsheet, the printfile is stored on your disk.

HANDS-ON EXERCISE A3–6: PRINTING YOUR SPREADSHEET

Print the spreadsheet you completed in Exercise A3–5. First, retrieve it from the disk if you have not done so yet. Be sure the cursor is at the upper left corner of what you want printed. Then use the /PP command. Enter the cell coordinates of the lower right-hand corner of the spreadsheet (such as F17) in response to a spreadsheet prompt. Your spreadsheet will then be printed on your system printer. Notice that this produces a copy of the spreadsheet without the row numbers, column letters, and control panel display that are shown on your screen. (See Figure A3–10.) If you want these to be printed with your spreadsheet, press the SHIFT and the PRINT-SCREEN keys.

Changing a Spreadsheet

Most electronic spreadsheets provide a variety of commands that allow you to change the organization and appearance of the spreadsheet. For example, we have already discussed the VisiCalc command for changing the width of columns with a /GC. Let's discuss just a few more commands that are useful even when developing a simple spreadsheet.

Inserting and Deleting Rows and Columns

Columns and rows can be easily added to or removed from an existing electronic spreadsheet, using the INSERT or DELETE spreadsheet commands. To insert a row, move the cursor to a row above the position where you want a new row to be created and type /IR. All rows below the cursor will be moved down to

FIGURE

A3–10 Printed copy of the completed spreadsheet

```
                    SPREADSHEET EXAMPLE

          ABC COMPANY: FINANCIAL PERFORMANCE

                 1983      1984      1985     TOTAL    AVERAGE
              ---------------------------------------------------
REVENUE          1000      1100      1200      3300      1100
              ---------------------------------------------------
EXPENSES          600       660       720      1980       660
              ---------------------------------------------------
PROFIT            400       440       480      1320       440
              ---------------------------------------------------
TAXES             160       176       192       528       176
              ---------------------------------------------------
PROFIT            240       264       288       792       264
AFTER TAXES
```

make room for the new row. To insert a column, move the cursor to a column to the left of the position where you want a new column to be created and type /IC. The column in which the cursor had been located and all columns to its right will be moved to the right to make room for the new column. All formulas contained in the spreadsheet are automatically adjusted to compensate for the new cell locations that result from these movements.

To delete a row, the cursor is moved somewhere in the row you want to delete, then type /DR. To delete a column, move the cursor somewhere in the column you want to delete, then type /DC. Deleting rows or columns can cause errors in other parts of the spreadsheet that might have referred to a cell in a deleted row or column. Therefore, check your spreadsheet for this possible side-effect after deleting a row or column.

Changing Formats

The format command (/F) allows you to alter the way information is displayed in a cell. Figure A3–11 shows the ways a number entered into a cell could be displayed with variations of the format command. To change the display format of a single cell, move the cursor to that cell, give the command /F and then key-in the letter of the format option you wish to use. The change to this cell can then be used to modify columns or rows by using the replicate (/R) command. However, to change the format of the entire spreadsheet, you must give the global format command /GF whose list of format options is the same as the /F command. (*Note*: one of the most useful format command options is the F$ command, because so many spreadsheets contain financial data expressed as dollars and cents.)

Locking Titles

Most spreadsheets use titles to identify the data in the rows and columns of the spreadsheet. Most electronic spreadsheet packages allow row and title columns to be "locked in place" so the titles can remain on the screen as the cursor moves the screen window to other parts of the spreadsheet stored in memory. This

FIGURE

A3–11 VisiCalc format options

Format Command Option	Cell Value	Displays as:
/FD (default format)	4.5678	4.5678
/FL (left justified format)	4.5678	4.5678
/F$ (dollar and cents format)	4.5678	4.57
/FI (integer format)	4.5678	5
/F* (bargraph format)	4.5678	****

feature also makes it impossible to move the cursor into a title area of the worksheet when using the cursor control key. In VisiCalc, titles are locked using the /T command after moving the cursor to the cell where the lowest row or right-most column of the title is located. The spreadsheet prompt then provides you with several options. You can key-in one of the following:

H   Locks all rows at and above the cursor as horizontal titles.
V   Locks all columns at and to the left of the cursor as vertical titles.
D   Accomplishes the title locking actions of both the H and V options
N   Unlocks all titles.

Multiple Windows

Most electronic spreadsheet programs allow you to subdivide the video screen into two or more windows from which you can view different parts of the spreadsheet stored in memory. For example, VisiCalc allows the creation of two windows, while Multiplan allows up to eight windows. This capability is important because it is frequently impossible to keep the important parts of a spreadsheet that a user wants to see together in one window. Therefore, most spreadsheets have a WINDOW command, which allows you to split the screen into several windows, which can move independently or together around the spreadsheet. The /W command in VisiCalc splits the screen into two windows after you key-in the letter for one of the following five options:

H   Splits the screen horizontally at the cursor.
D   Splits the screen vertically at the cursor.
S   Cancels window synchronization so the windows move separately.
I   Returns you to one window operation.

Note: VisiCalc requires that you use the semicolon (;) key to move the cursor from one window to the other.

HANDS-ON EXERCISE A3–7:   CHANGING THE SPREADSHEET'S APPEARANCE

Change your spreadsheet's appearance by using some of the commands discussed in this section. For example, use the format command option FI to convert all of the cell values in the AVERAGE column to the integer format. This rounds the calculated averages to the closest whole number. Then save and print this final version of the ABC Company's Financial Performance spreadsheet. Use the /T command to lock your titles and headings. Use the /W command to experiment with vertical and horizontal windows for your spreadsheet.

Seeing Your Spreadsheet Program

One way to describe electronic spreadsheet packages is that they allow users to do **visible programming**, using a **visible processor** or **nonprocedural** programming language. However, it is possible to see a "program listing" of the commands used to build any spreadsheet. Figure A3–12 is a listing of the VisiCalc commands used to build our Financial Performance spreadsheet. This listing was produced in the following manner. First exit from VisiCalc back to the operating system prompt. Then press the CTRL and PRTSC (print-screen) keys to activate your printer and enter the MS-DOS command TYPE, followed by the name of the file used to store this spreadsheet. For example:

A> TYPE B:SHEET1.VC

The listing of your VisiCalc "program" is then printed on your printer and displayed on the screen. Do you recognize the cell numbers, headings, formulas, and commands used to build this spread-

FIGURE A3–12 VisiCalc spreadsheet program listing

```
>B17:"XES                  >D12:+D8-D10                >F6:"   AVERAGE
>A17:" AFTER TA            >C12:+C8-C10                >E6:"     TOTAL
>F16:/FI@AVERAGE(B16...D16) >B12:+B8-B10               >D6:"      1985
>E16:@SUM(A16...D16)       >A12:" PROFIT               >C6:"      1984
>D16:+D12-D14             >F11:/FI                     >B6:"      1983
>C16:+C12-C14             >F10:/FI@AVERAGE(B10...D10)  >F4:"NCE
>B16:+B12-B14             >E10:@SUM(A10...D10)         >E4:" PERFORMA
>A16:" PROFIT             >D10:+D8*.6                  >D4:"FINANCIAL
>F15:/FI                  >C10:+C8*.6                  >C4:"COMPANY:
>F14:/FI@AVERAGE(B14...D14) >B10:+B8*.6                >B4:"     ABC
>E14:@SUM(A14...D14)      >A10:" EXPENSES              >E2:"E
>D14:+D12*.4             >F8:/FI@AVERAGE(B8...D8)      >D2:"ET EXAMPL
>C14:+C12*.4             >E8:@SUM(A8...D8)             >C2:"SPREADSHE
>B14:+B12*.4             >D8:+B8*1.2                   /W1
>A14:" TAXES             >C8:+B8*1.1                   /GOC
>F13:/FI                 >B8:1000                      /GRA
>F12:/FI@AVERAGE(B12...D12) >A8:" REVENUE              /GC9
>E12:@SUM(A12...D12)     >B7:"                         /X>A1:>A1:
```

sheet? Do you realize that this entire spreadsheet was built using only one numeric value; the REVENUE figure for 1983? (*Note*: >B8:1000 in the VisiCalc listing.) The rest of the spreadsheet was developed by replicating a few simple formulas and entering appropriate headings.

Spreadsheet listings such as that shown in Figure A3–12 are used primarily to allow spreadsheets and spreadsheet **templates** to be published in books, manuals, and articles. It also demonstrates how VisiCalc stored the Financial Performance spreadsheet on your system disk. Aren't you glad you didn't have to build your spreadsheet by writing this program in the traditional sequential programming way? It would have been a lot harder, wouldn't it? Now you know why we can describe using a spreadsheet package as a **visible programming** experience.

HANDS-ON ASSIGNMENTS

We have now run through a complete example of the creation and manipulation of a simple spreadsheet. This should have helped you tie together the many features of electronic spreadsheets that we have covered in this section. Consult the manual for the spreadsheet package you are using if you need more information. Now it's time for you to create some simple spreadsheets of your own. That is the purpose of the following assignments. Good luck!

A3.1 If you have not already done so, create, manipulate, store, and print the ABC Company Financial Performance spreadsheet as explained in the Hands-on Exercises of this section.

A3.2 Build the simple Checkbook Example spreadsheet shown in Figure A3–13. All values for checks, deposits, and the opening

FIGURE

A3–13 Checkbook example spreadsheet

```
        CHECKBOOK EXAMPLE SPREADSHEET

 DATE   DESCRIPTION   CHECK   DEPOSIT   BALANCE

 9-15                                   1234.56

 9-16   EXXON         20.55             1214.01

 9-17   DEPOSIT                200.25   1414.26

 9-18   K-MART        17.98             1396.28

 9-19   PIZZA HUT     10.43             1385.85
```

balance have to be entered. However, the remaining BAL-ANCE values are computed by formulas you must insert in each cell where a balance in shown. Store and print this spreadsheet.

A3.3 Build the Home Budget Example spreadsheet shown in Figure A3–14. Insert the values for January but use the SUM function to create a formula that computes the total expenses for that month. Then use replicate commands to create the values for February and March. Use the sum and average functions and replicate commands to develop the TOTAL and AVER-AGE columns. Compute the PERCENT column by dividing the total for an expense category by the grand total for three months. For example, the percentage for food is $600 divided by $2190. That could be expressed as a formula like (+E8/E18). Use the format command option F$ to round your percent calculations to two decimal places. Store and print this spreadsheet.

A3.4 Build the Payroll Example spreadsheet shown in Figure A3–15. Key-in employee names, social security numbers, hourly pay rates, total hours worked, and overtime hours worked. However, employee gross pay needs to be calculated by a

FIGURE A3–14 Home budget example spreadsheet

HOME BUDGET EXAMPLE SPREADSHEET

ACCOUNT	JAN	FEB	MAR	TOTAL	PERCENT	AVERAGE
FOOD	200	200	200	600	27.40	200
RENT	300	300	300	900	41.10	300
GAS	100	100	100	300	13.70	100
FUN	80	80	80	240	10.96	80
MISC	50	50	50	150	6.85	50
TOTAL	730	730	730	2190	100	730

FIGURE   A3–15 Payroll example spreadsheet

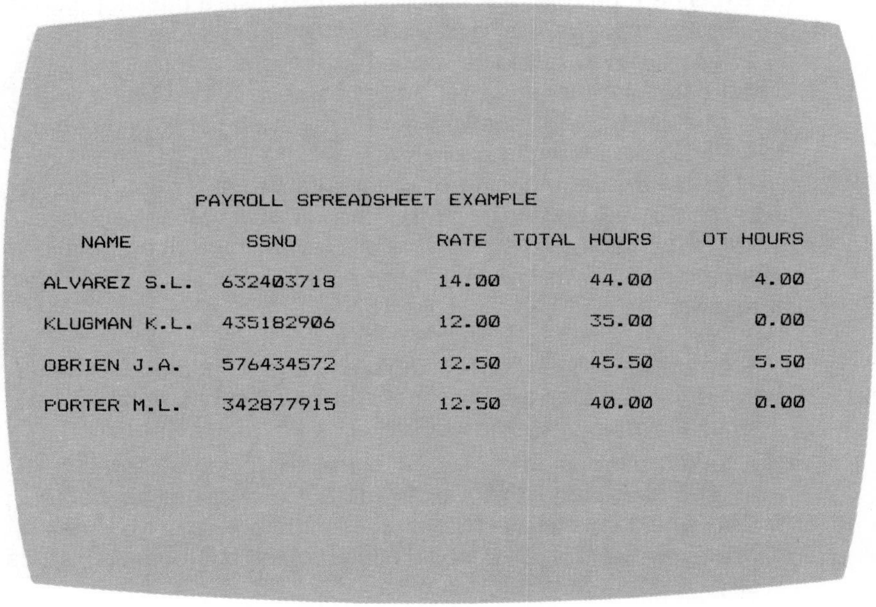

```
              PAYROLL SPREADSHEET EXAMPLE

    NAME           SSNO          RATE  TOTAL HOURS    OT HOURS

 ALVAREZ S.L.   632403718       14.00     44.00         4.00

 KLUGMAN K.L.   435182906       12.00     35.00         0.00

 OBRIEN J.A.    576434572       12.50     45.50         5.50

 PORTER M.L.    342877915       12.50     40.00         0.00
```

formula that should be replicated in the rest of that column. *Hints*: (1) before entering employee Social Security numbers, press the quote key (") so the number is entered as a label, not as a floating point number; (2) if you want to see more of the employees' names on the spreadsheet display, use the /GC command to increase the width of all columns; (3) gross pay should equal hourly rate times hours worked plus overtime pay. Overtime pay should equal 1.5 times the hourly rate times overtime hours worked.

A3.5 Use the spreadsheet you create in these assignments to perform "what-if" analysis. For example, change revenue, expense, or tax values and formulas in the ABC Company's financial spreadsheet. What happens to the company's profits? What might this mean to the company's management? Next, change checks or deposits in the checkbook spreadsheet, expenses values in the home budget spreadsheet, or pay rates in the payroll spreadsheet. Print the results of these changes. Write a short explanation of what happens and its implications for a computer user.

SECTION FOUR: USING DATABASE MANAGEMENT PACKAGES

Introduction to DBMS Packages

In Chapter Eleven, Data Organization and Database Systems, we explained the role of a major system software package called a *database management system* (DBMS). Many types of DBMS packages are now available for use with microcomputer systems. These database management programs have become one of the most popular types of software for use with personal computers. However, before we can explain the use of DBMS packages, we need to review the meaning of several important terms: *character, field, record, file, database,* and *database management system.* (*Note*: Refer back to Chapter Two or Eleven if you need additional explanations of these concepts.) For our purposes let's define them as follows:

- A **character** consists of a single alphabetic, numeric, or other symbol. Examples are the letters of the alphabet, numbers, and special symbols, such as dollar signs and decimal points.
- A **field** is a grouping of characters that represent a characteristic of a person, place, thing, or event. For example, your *name field* would consist of the alphabetic characters of your name, while your *address field* would consist of the numbers and letters of your home address.
- A **record** is a collection of interrelated fields. For example, an employee payroll record might consist of a name field, a social security number field, a department field, a salary field, etc.
- A **file** is a collection of interrelated records. For example, a payroll file might consist of the employee records of a firm.
- A **database** is a collection of interrelated files and records. For example, the database of a business might contain such files as payroll, inventory, customer, etc.
- A **database management system** is a set of computer programs that control the creation, maintenance, and use of a database. For example, we will explain the use of a microcomputer DBMS named dBASE II in this section.

A database management package allows you to set up a database of files and records on your personal computer system. With such computerized files, you can store and retrieve information much faster and efficiently than with a manual filing system using paper files. Most DBMS microcomputer packages allow you to perform three primary jobs:

- Create and maintain (change or update) data files.
- Selectively retrieve and display records from these files to provide you with information you need.

■ Print records from these files in various formats to provide you with printed reports and documents.

Some DBMS microcomputer packages provide a fourth major capability. They contain their own built-in programming language, which allows you to write programs that use the database for more complex jobs. For example, you could develop programs for inventory, payroll, and accounting systems that involve multiple files, menu-driven input, and complex reports. We will not cover this advanced feature because it is beyond the scope of this introductory tutorial.

In this section we will use the **dBASE II** database management package by Ashton-Tate to introduce you to the use of such packages. We will use dBASE II because it is the most popular, widely used, and imitated microcomputer DBMS package. (Other popular microcomputer DBMS packages include dBASE III, R:base 4000, and Condor III.) dBASE II was the first **relational** database management system for microcomputers. Though the relational database structure has its limitations, relational database management systems are easy to understand and use. A relational DBMS allows a user to think of data as arranged in a table, with the records as rows and the fields as columns. This simple tabular structure is a major benefit of the relational database model. (Refer to Chapter Eleven for more information on relational and other types of database structures).

dBASE II is a relational database management system that has a built-in applications development language. Files of data are created, edited, updated, and modified with single English-type commands. You can do relational comparisons, sums, subtotals and totals, sorting, and use indexes for record selection. A limited report generator is built-in, thus providing some ability to customize reports. Its applications development language makes it possible for you to create complex reports and displays. It also allows simultaneous processing of multiple files. Each file in dBASE II can contain up to 65,535 records. Each record can have 32 fields of up to 254 characters, with a maximum of 1,000 characters per record.

Getting Started

Let's find out how to use this important software tool. We will work through simple examples, using the dBASE II database management program. Let's do the following tasks:

■ Create a database.
■ Enter and edit data.

■ Retrieve, display, and report data.
■ Change the database.

Figure A4-1 displays the file we will create and manipulate in this section. It is a simplified payroll file containing information about a few employees of a hypothetical company. Creating and manipulating this file will give you a good introduction to the use of microcomputer DBMS packages.

You begin by inserting your dBASE II disk into the disk drive and turning on the computer. (See the beginning of the first section of this appendix if you need additional information on starting a microcomputer and using a floppy disk.) A dBASE II disk which also contains the operating system, will load (boot) the operating system first and then load the dBASE II program. Or you can load the operating system diskette, remove it from the disk drive, insert the dBASE II disk, and then type-in the word dBASE after the system prompt (such as A>). If you have dual disk drives on your computer system, you may also wish to insert a formatted file disk into the second disk drive. This will allow you to more easily store the files you create for your database on a separate disk. After the dBASE II program is loaded from the disk, it asks you to enter today's date or to press the RETURN key (same as the ENTER key). Then a period (.) and a flashing cursor will appear on the screen. This "dot prompt" means that dBASE II is ready for you to key-in a **command** so it can begin working for you.

DBMS Commands

Many database management packages use commands to carry out their operations. These commands resemble common English verbs, and can be modified to further specify the action desired. A sample of a few commands used in dBASE II is shown in Figure A4-2.

FIGURE A4-1 Employee payroll file example

```
NAME------------ SSNO------ S DEPT----------- RATE- HOUR PAY-----
ALVAREZ J.S.    632403718 F PRODUCTION      14.00 44.0   644.00
KLUGMAN K.L.    435182906 M FINANCE         12.00 35.0   420.00
OBRIEN J.A.     576434572 M INFO SYSTEMS    12.50 45.5   603.12
PORTER M.L.     342877915 F ACCOUNTING      12.50 40.0   500.00
```

FIGURE

A4–2 Sample dBASE II commands

- BROWSE—provides full screen window viewing and editing.
- COPY—makes a copy of an existing database file.
- CREATE—creates new database files.
- DISPLAY—displays records, fields, and expressions.
- EDIT—Alters specific data fields in a database.
- INDEX—creates an index file.
- INSERT—inserts data into a file.
- JOIN—creates a new file from two other files.
- LIST—lists the records in a file.
- LOCATE—finds a record that fits a condition.
- REPORT—formats and displays a report of data.
- SORT—sorts the records in a file on one data field.
- USE—specifies the database file to be used.

Let's look at the general form of a typical dBASE II command to get a better idea how of such commands can be expressed. We will examine the **DISPLAY** command, which allows you to display the contents of files and records on your video screen. The *general form* of the DISPLAY command is shown below. Remember that many other commands used by dBASE II and other DBMS packages use a similar *syntax* or general form.

DISPLAY [scope] [FOR expression] [expression list] [OFF]
Explanation:
   scope: may be ALL, RECORD n, or NEXT n records. (default is the current record)
   expression: is the selection criterion such as AGE >65. (default is all)
   expression list: is a list of the fields to be displayed. (default is all)
   OFF: suppresses the record number of each record.
Examples: DISPLAY 3
            DISPLAY ALL FOR RATE>12.50.AND.DEPT=
            'ACCOUNTING'.OR.DEPT='FINANCE'OFF

As you can see, commands do not have to use their full form. The first example merely displays the contents of the third record in a file. The second example is more complex. It displays all the records of employees who earn more than $12.50 per hour and who belong to either the accounting or finance departments of a firm. All record numbers are to be suppressed.

Notice that periods are used before and after AND and OR, while a single quote mark is used before and after alphanumeric field values. *Note:* the *relational* operators—less than ($<$), greater than ($>$), equal to ($=$), less than or equal to ($<=$), and greater than or equal to ($>=$)—can be used. It should also be noted that dBASE II commands can be abbreviated to their first four letters. For example, DISP instead of DISPLAY. Also, if you make a mistake when typing-in a command, dBASE II gives you the option of re-keying only that part of the command that was incorrect. However, you can always cancel a command by using the ESCAPE key.

Creating a Database

The first thing you do when using a database management package like dBASE II is to create the files you want in your database. What this means is that you are going to specify the characteristics of the fields which make up each record in a particular file. This procedure is also called *defining* the file or database. It is also known as creating the **data dictionary**, since you are defining the characteristics and structure of the records and files in your database, which is the function of a data dictionary. If you're going to create a file, your response to the dBASE II prompt (the period and flashing cursor) is to type the command **CREATE.** (Remember, you must press the ENTER key after you type-in a response.)

Before we create a file, we'd better have a pretty good idea of the *design* or *structure* of the records in that file. Let's agree that we want our database to include a **payroll file** for the employees of our company. This payroll file will contain the records of our employees (i.e., information about each employee that might be needed to properly pay them). For demonstration purposes, let's limit each record to six fields as follows: employee name (NAME), social security number (SSNO), sex (SEX), department (DEPT), hourly rate of pay (RATE), and number of hours worked (HOURS). Figure A4–3 illustrates the dBASE II prompts and the responses you might make in creating the record format for a simple payroll file. Let's take a look at what happens when you create a file.

After you enter the CREATE command, dBASE II asks you to enter the name of the file you want to create. Let's call our file PAY1. (*Note:* file names are limited to 8 characters, to which dBASE II adds a code of .DBF that identifies it as a database file.) We are then asked to specify the structure of each record. This involves specifying the name, type, width, and decimal places of each of the fields that make up the records that will be stored in this file. As we said previously, we are limiting each record in our payroll file to six fields. We give each of these fields a name (up to 10

FIGURE

A4–3 Creating the payroll file

```
. CREATE
ENTER FILENAME: PAY1
ENTER RECORD STRUCTURE AS FOLLOWS:
 FIELD     NAME,TYPE,WIDTH,DECIMAL PLACES
 001       NAME,C,15,
 002       SSNO,C,9,
 003       SEX,C,1,
 004       DEPT,C,14,
 005       RATE,N,5,2
 006       HOURS,N,4,1
 007
INPUT DATA NOW?
```

characters are allowed) and indicate whether they consist of character data (C) or numeric data (N). Also specified is the maximum number of characters each field might contain and the number of decimal places needed for our numeric data fields. (*Note*: a decimal point takes up one character position in a numeric field.)

Each time you key-in information specifying a field, you press the ENTER key and dBASE II responds with a field number for the next field and a flashing cursor. After we finish specifying all six fields, the dBASE II prompt will ask for the specification for a seventh field. At this point we press the ENTER key again to end the file creation process. dBASE II then saves the file structure we have created and immediately asks if we want to enter data into the file. We respond with a Y to indicate that we want to begin the data entry process.

HANDS-ON EXERCISE A4–1:   CREATING A DATABASE

Load a database management package, such as dBASE II. Create the PAY1 file in your database, using the CREATE command. Specify the structure of the records in the file by specifying the name, type, width, and decimal places for each of the six fields in a payroll record: employee name, social security number, sex, department, hourly rate of pay, and number of hours worked.

Entering Data into a Database

Once you have created a file, your next step is to enter data into the file. If you answered with a Y to the dBASE question "input data now?" at the end of the previous file creation process, the screen is erased and you can begin to type-in data. The record number of the first record to be entered into your file is then displayed, along with the name of the first field in that record. Also displayed are two colons, which indicate the width of the field, with a blinking cursor at the first position of that field. You can then begin to type-in data into each field of the record. Figure A4–4 shows what the data entry screen looks like while you are entering data into the fields of a record in the payroll file.

When a field is filled or when you press the ENTER key, the cursor jumps down to the next field. When the last field of the first record is completed, dBASE II automatically displays the record number of the next record and the name of the first field. When you have completed adding records to this file, press the ENTER key when the cursor is at the beginning of the first field of the next record. If you want to stop entering data while in the middle of filling a data field, you must press the control key (CTRL) and the letter Q key simultaneously. In either case, you will leave the data entry mode and once again be presented with the dBASE II dot prompt.

dBASE II is now ready for commands to manipulate the data you have stored in the PAY1 payroll file. However, if you want to stop at this point, you must type the command **QUIT**. This should be typed every time you end your use of dBASE II, since it automatically closes all files. Unless your files are properly closed, they may be automatically erased when dBASE II is terminated.

FIGURE

A4–4 Entering an employee data record into the payroll file

```
RECORD # 00003
NAME      :PORTER M.L.    :
SSNO      :342877915:
SEX       :F:
DEPT      :ACCOUNTING     :
RATE      :12.50:
HOURS     :40.0:
PAY       :  500.00:
```

HANDS-ON EXERCISE A4-2: ENTERING DATA INTO A DATABASE

Enter data into the fields of several employee records in the PAY1 payroll file. Use the same data as shown in Figure A4-1. When you are finished, press the ENTER key instead of filling the fields of another record. This will store the file and return you to the dBASE II dot prompt.

Adding Data to a Database

If you want to add more data records to a previously created file, you must use either the APPEND or INSERT commands. However, whenever you want to work on an established file for any purpose, you must first ask dBASE II to transfer it from the disk into memory. You do this with the **USE** (file name) command. For example:

USE PAY1 or USE B:PAY1 (if the file is on your B drive.)

This *opens* the PAY1 file and *closes* any other file you may have been using. Now you are ready to work on the PAY1 file with other dBASE II commands. If you wish to enter data at the end a file, enter the **APPEND** command. For example:

USE PAY1
APPEND

The structure of the next record that can be added to the file is displayed. This includes field names and widths in the same format as it did when you first entered records into the file after using the CREATE command. You can then begin to add more records to the file.

You can also add more records to the PAY1 file, using the **INSERT** command. The INSERT command allows records to be specified, like the APPEND command, but inserts them into a specific location in a file, rather than being added to the end of the file. The general form of the INSERT command is:

INSERT [BEFORE] [BLANK]

The command INSERT, when used alone, inserts a record just after the "current" record. The *current record* is the last record you worked on in any way, or the last record in a file. Entering INSERT BEFORE will insert a record just before the current record. If INSERT BLANK is used, an empty record is inserted, which can be filled later. For example, if you wanted to insert a record between the second and third records in the PAY1 file, you would give the following sequence of commands:

```
USE PAY1
3
INSERT BEFORE
```

HANDS-ON EXERCISE A4–3:   ADDING DATA TO A DATABASE

Add several records to the PAY1 file. First open the file with the USE command. Then add a record to the end of the file with the APPEND command. Add a record between the second and third records with the INSERT command.

Editing and Correcting Errors

dBASE II and some other database management packages allow *full screen editing* of the data you enter into a file. Errors can be corrected during and after data entry in a variety of ways. During data entry, errors can be corrected by backspacing and writing over them. You can also use the cursor control keys to move the cursor around to make corrections until the last field is completed and the record is stored. If your computer does not have cursor control keys, you can use the control key in combination with several character keys to move the cursor around the screen.

dBASE II makes extensive use of various combinations of the CONTROL key (CTRL key) and alphabetical character keys. This is especially true when entering, correcting, or revising the records in a file. Figure A4–5 summarizes the more important uses of such **control key** combinations. For example, the Ctrl-E, Ctrl-X, Ctrl-S and Ctrl-D can be used in place of the up, down, left, and right cursor control keys, respectively.

If you wish to correct or revise a previously entered record, you can use the **EDIT** command. First you bring the file you want into memory by entering the USE command. Then enter the EDIT command, followed by the number of the record you wish to correct or revise. For example:

```
USE PAY1
EDIT 3
```

FIGURE

A4–5 Editing functions of control key combinations

Ctrl-X	moves cursor down to the next field.
Ctrl-E	moves cursor back to the previous field.
Ctrl-D	moves cursor ahead one character.
Ctrl-S	moves cursor back one character.
Ctrl-V	toggles between overwrite and insert modes.
Ctrl-G	deletes the character above the cursor.
BACKSPACE	deletes the character to the left of the cursor.
Ctrl-C	writes the record to disk and advances to the next record.
Ctrl-R	writes the record to disk and backs up to the previous record.
Ctrl-U	toggles the record deletion mark on and off.
Ctrl-W	saves any changes made and resumes normal dBASE II operation.
Ctrl-Q	quits and returns to normal dBASE II operation without saving any changes made.

When these commands are entered, the third record in the file is displayed just as it was originally entered, including the name and contents of each data field. The cursor control keys can then be used to move the cursor around and make changes.

The **BROWSE** command combines the functions of the DISPLAY and EDIT commands by allowing you to display and edit a screenful of records from a file. BROWSE displays up to 19 records and as many fields as will fit horizontally on the screen. Pressing the CONTROL and B keys allows you to scroll to the right and see any fields that are off the right edge of the screen. Pressing the CONTROL and Z keys allows you to scroll to the left. You can also use cursor control keys and other control-character key combinations (refer back to Figure A4–5) to scroll up and down through the database and to move the cursor around on the screen so you can edit any field of any record in the file. Figure A4–6 shows how the BROWSE command displays the records in the PAY file. *Note:* the fields in each record are aligned under their field names.

Don't forget to use the control key combinations summarized in Figure A4–5 to store any changes you make to a record. For instance, pressing the CONTROL and C keys writes the record

FIGURE

A4–6 BROWSE command display of payroll file

```
. BROWSE
RECORD # :00001
NAME----------- SSNO------ S DEPT----------- RATE- HOUR
ALVAREZ J.S.    632403718 F PRODUCTION      14.00 44.0
KLUGMAN K.L.    435182906 M FINANCE         12.00 35.0
OBRIEN J.A.     576434572 M INFO SYSTEMS    12.50 45.5
PORTER M.L.     342877915 F ACCOUNTING      12.50 40.0
```

the cursor is on to the disk and advances you to the next record. Also remember that pressing the CONTROL and Q keys cancels any changes in the record the cursor is on and returns you to the dBASE II dot prompt. Finally, you can use the ERASE command to clear the screen so you can start a new operation with a blank screen.

HANDS-ON EXERCISE A4–4:   EDITING A DATABASE

Edit several records in the PAY1 file. Use the EDIT command to make changes to one of the records. Use the BROWSE command to make changes to several records. Store the changes on disk with the CONTROL-C command. Return to the dBASE II prompt by using the CONTROL-Q command. For example, change the pay rate or hours worked of several employees. Store the changes and return to the dBASE II prompt by using the CONTROL-W command.

Retrieving Data from a Database

Now that you know how to create, enter, and edit data in a database file, it's time to learn how to retrieve data from your database. Database management packages provide several commands to assist in the retrieval of data. This allows you to be selective in both the format and contents of data you wish to see displayed or printed. In dBASE II, there are five fundamental retrieval commands: LIST, DISPLAY, LOCATE, FIND, and REPORT.

The **LIST** command will display all of the data records in a file, unless it is modified so that it displays only records that meet certain criteria. All of the records in the file will scroll by the screen unless you stop it by pressing the CONTROL and S keys together. The general form of the LIST command is:

LIST [FOR (expression)] [OFF]

If you use the OFF option in this command, the record numbers preceding each record will not be displayed. If you use the FOR option with an expression, only those records for which the expression is *true* will be listed. For example, Figure A4–7 displays the result of asking for (1) a complete listing of records in the PAY1 file, (2) a listing without the record numbers, and (3) a listing of only male employees.

FIGURE A4–7 LIST command examples

```
. LIST
00001   ALVAREZ J.S.      632403718 F PRODUCTION      14.00   44.0
00002   KLUGMAN K.L.      435182906 M FINANCE         12.00   35.0
00003   OBRIEN J.A.       576434572 M INFO SYSTEMS    12.50   45.5
00004   PORTER M.L.       342877915 F ACCOUNTING      12.50   40.0
. LIST OFF
ALVAREZ J.S.        632403718 F PRODUCTION     14.00   44.0
KLUGMAN K.L.        435182906 M FINANCE        12.00   35.0
OBRIEN J.A.         576434572 M INFO SYSTEMS   12.50   45.5
PORTER M.L.         342877915 F ACCOUNTING     12.50   40.0
. LIST FOR SEX = 'M'
00002   KLUGMAN K.L.      435182906 M FINANCE         12.00   35.0
00003   OBRIEN J.A.       576434572 M INFO SYSTEMS    12.50   45.5
```

The **DISPLAY** command is similar to the LIST command, but will not display all of the records in the file unless modified to do so, by adding the modifier ALL. Unlike the LIST command, however, DISPLAY ALL will show you only one screenful of records from a file at a time (about 15 records). Pressing any key displays the next group of records. The general form of the DISPLAY command is:

DISPLAY [scope] [FOR(expression)] [OFF]

Figure A4–8 gives you four examples of the use of the DISPLAY command. Notice that, when DISPLAY is used alone, it will show only the current record. DISPLAY ALL shows all the records in a file but will stop after the screen is full of records. Pressing any key would display the next group of records. The next two variations

FIGURE A4–8 DISPLAY command examples

```
.   DISPLAY
00004   PORTER M.L.       342877915 F ACCOUNTING      12.50   40.0
. DISPLAY ALL
00001   ALVAREZ J.S.      632403718 F PRODUCTION      14.00   44.0
00002   KLUGMAN K.L.      435182906 M FINANCE         12.00   35.0
00003   OBRIEN J.A.       576434572 M INFO SYSTEMS    12.50   45.5
00004   PORTER M.L.       342877915 F ACCOUNTING      12.50   40.0
. DISPLAY RECORD 2
00002   KLUGMAN K.L.      435182906 M FINANCE         12.00   35.0
. DISPLAY NEXT 2
00002   KLUGMAN K.L.      435182906 M FINANCE         12.00   35.0
00003   OBRIEN J.A.       576434572 M INFO SYSTEMS    12.50   45.5
. DISPLAY ALL FOR HOURS > 40.0
00001   ALVAREZ J.S.      632403718 F PRODUCTION      14.00   44.0
00003   OBRIEN J.A.       576434572 M INFO SYSTEMS    12.50   45.5
```

FIGURE A4–9 LOCATE command example

```
   LOCATE FOR RATE = 12.50
RECORD: 00003
. DISPLAY
00003  OBRIEN J.A.       576434572 M INFO SYSTEMS     12.50  45.5
. CONTINUE
RECORD: 00004
. DISPLAY
00004  PORTER M.L.       342877915 F ACCOUNTING       12.50  40.0
```

of the DISPLAY command show how you can selectively display a specific record (record 2), and a group of records (the next two records in a file). Finally, all records that meet a specific condition (employees who worked more then forty hours) are displayed.

Another way to find data in a file is to use the **LOCATE** command. It is much slower then the DISPLAY command. You should use this command when you are looking for records that contain a specific type of data in a file that is not indexed according to that type of data. The general form of the LOCATE command is:

LOCATE [scope] [FOR (expression)]

The LOCATE command will search sequentially through the entire file, starting with the first record in the file, unless you specify that it should begin with the current record that is in use. As soon as a record is found that meets your specifications, its record number is displayed. You then use the DISPLAY command to examine this record. If you want to see whether other records exist that meet your specifications, you must repeatedly type CONTINUE until the entire file is searched. In Figure A4–9, notice how the LOCATE command found the two employees whose hourly rate equaled $12.50.

HANDS-ON EXERCISE A4–5: RETRIEVING DATA FROM A DATABASE

LIST all of the data records in the PAY1 file. DISPLAY the current record. DISPLAY the second record. LIST or DISPLAY only those records that meet specific criteria, such as all female employees. LOCATE the record of the employee that works for the finance department.

Retrieving Other Information

Sometimes you don't want to retrieve the data stored in a file, but instead want to know how many records meet a specific condition, or what the total value of a numeric field is for some of the records in a file. If you want to *count* the number of records that meet a certain condition, you should use the **COUNT** command, whose general form is:

COUNT [scope] [FOR condition] [TO memory variable]

If you want the *total value* of a certain field for all records which meet a specified condition, then you should use the **SUM** command, whose general form is:

SUM field(s) [scope] [FOR condition] [TO memory variable(s)]

Figure A4–10 shows how we have used the COUNT command to count the number of employees who worked over 40 hours, and the SUM command to total the amount of hours worked by male employees.

Besides displaying data selectively from the files in your database, both the LIST and DISPLAY command can be used to provide you with information about the *structure* of a file and the names of the database files stored on the diskette of your computer system. Figure A4–11 shows how LIST was used to find out that there are two database files on disk drive B. It also shows how the DISPLAY STRUCTURE command was used to show some facts about the records stored in the PAY file, including the names and characteristics of the fields in a payroll file record.

FIGURE

A4–10 COUNT and SUM command examples

```
    COUNT FOR HOURS > 40.0
    COUNT = 00002
.   SUM HOURS FOR SEX = 'M'
    80.5
```

FIGURE

A4–11 Displaying
database files and
file structure

```
. LIST FILES ON B

DATABASE FILES      # RCDS     LAST UPDATE
PAY        DBF      00003      01/15/85
SSF        DBF      00002      01/15/80


. USE B:PAY
. DISPLAY STRUCTURE
STRUCTURE FOR FILE:  B:PAY.DBF
NUMBER OF RECORDS:   00003
DATE OF LAST UPDATE: 01/15/85
PRIMARY USE DATABASE
FLD         NAME      TYPE WIDTH      DEC
001         NAME       C    015
002         SSNO       N    009
003         SEX        C    001
004         DEPT       C    014
005         RATE       N    005       002
006         HOURS      N    004       001
** TOTAL **                00049
```

HANDS-ON EXERCISE A4-6:   COUNTING AND SUMMING DATA

Count the number of employees earning $12.50 per hour and
total the amount of hours they have worked. Use the COUNT
and SUM commands.

Printing Reports from a Database

Most database management packages have commands like DIS-
PLAY and LIST for quick database inquiries. Responses can be
displayed on the video screen of your computer or can be printed
on your system printer. (*Note*: on the IBM PC and similar computers,
press the SHIFT and PRINT SCREEN keys to print what is on the
video screen. For continuous printing, toggle the CONTROL and
PRINT SCREEN keys to start and stop printing.)

However if you want output printed in a report format that you
can use repeatedly, with features such as headings and totals, then
you should use commands like the **REPORT** command in dBASE
II. Figure A4–12 shows a dialogue between the user and dBASE
II after the REPORT command is used. As you can see, you are
asked to specify the name, title, and headings of the report, what
fields will be included, and whether subtotals and totals are required.
In this example, we wish to produce a payroll report that gives
information on employees organized into male and female categories. Notice how each column in the report is specified by number
of print positions, the data field used, and a column heading. When
the last column needed for the report is specified, you should press

FIGURE A4–12 Specifying the form of the payroll report

```
. REPORT
ENTER REPORT FORM NAME: PAYR1
ENTER OPTIONS, M=LEFT MARGIN, L=LINES/PAGE, W=PAGE WIDTH
PAGE HEADING? (Y/N) Y
ENTER PAGE HEADING: PAYROLL REPORT #1
DOUBLE SPACE REPORT? (Y/N) N
ARE TOTALS REQUIRED? (Y/N) Y
SUBTOTALS IN REPORT? (Y/N) Y
ENTER SUBTOTALS FIELD: SEX
SUMMARY REPORT ONLY? (Y/N) N
EJECT PAGE AFTER SUBTOTALS? (Y/N) N
ENTER SUBTOTAL HEADING: EMPLOYEES BY SEX
COL     WIDTH,CONTENTS
001     15,NAME
ENTER HEADING: NAME
002     3,SEX
ENTER HEADING: SEX
003     14,DEPT
ENTER HEADING: DEPARTMENT
004     6,HOURS
ENTER HEADING: HOURS
ARE TOTALS REQUIRED? (Y/N) Y
005


    REPORT FORM PAYR1 TO PRINT
```

the ENTER key instead of typing-in the specifications for another column. (Column 005 in this example.) The payroll report will then be displayed on your video monitor. *Note*: If subtotals are used, the records in the file which provides data for the report (the payroll file) must be sorted or indexed according to the subtotal control field (SEX in this example). The SORT and INDEX commands are discussed shortly. See Figure A4–13.

FIGURE

A4–13 The payroll report

```
PAGE NO.  00001
                                     PAYROLL REPORT #1


          NAME        SEX    DEPARTMENT      HOURS

* EMPLOYEES BY SEX M
KLUGMAN K.L.      M     FINANCE           35.0
OBRIEN J.A.       M     INFO SYSTEMS      45.5
** SUBTOTAL **
                                          80.5


* EMPLOYEES BY SEX F
ALVAREZ J.S.      F     PRODUCTION        44.0
PORTER M.L.       F     ACCOUNTING        40.0
** SUBTOTAL **
                                          84.0

** TOTAL **
                                         164.5
```

FIGURE

A4–14 Male employees
payroll report

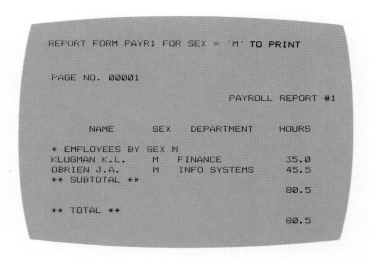

```
REPORT FORM PAYR1 FOR SEX = 'M' TO PRINT


PAGE NO. 00001

                                        PAYROLL REPORT #1


          NAME        SEX   DEPARTMENT      HOURS

  * EMPLOYEES BY SEX M
  KLUGMAN K.L.       M    FINANCE           35.0
  OBRIEN J.A.        M    INFO SYSTEMS      45.5
  ** SUBTOTAL **
                                            80.5

  ** TOTAL **
                                            80.5
```

To print this report on your printer, you must use the **REPORT FORM** command with the **TO PRINT** option. This command also allows you to use a report form repeatedly for full or partial reports. The general form of this command is:

REPORT FORM (form name) [scope] [FOR (expression)]

Figure A4–14 shows how the PAYR1 report form was used to print a payroll report for male employees only.

HANDS-ON EXERCISE A4–7: PRINTING A REPORT

Design and print a report that provides information from the PAY1 file, using the REPORT command. For example, produce a report on the pay rate of employees by male and female categories. Then use the REPORT FORM command to print a report showing similar information for female employees only.

Changing the Database

After you have used your database for awhile, you may decide that some changes are needed. Changing a database usually has one of the four following dimensions:

- Changing the *data* in specific fields for selected records in a file.

- Changing the *structure* (characteristics of selected fields) of the records in a file.
- Changing the *order* of records in a file and deleting unwanted records.
- Generating *new files* that are variations of the files already in the database and deleting unwanted files.

Changing Data

dBASE II allows you to change the data in your files using either the REPLACE or CHANGE commands. If you want to change the contents of one or more fields in many records at one time, you should use the **REPLACE** command. If you want to change the contents of a field, but do it one record at a time, you should use the **CHANGE** command. The general form of these commands are:

REPLACE (scope (field) WITH (data), . . . [FOR (expression)]
CHANGE [scope] FIELD (list) [FOR (expression)]

Examples of these two commands are shown below.

REPLACE ALL RATE WITH RATE *1.1 FOR DEPT =
'ACCOUNTING'
CHANGE ALL FIELD PAY

The REPLACE command example above gives all employees in the accounting department a 10 percent hourly rate increase, while the CHANGE command allows you to change the amount paid to each employee one record at a time.

Sorting Data

Another way that you might want to change your database is to *sort* the records in a file into a different order, or to create a *index* for a file that is organized differently then the file itself. In dBASE II files can be sorted in ascending or descending order with the **SORT** command, whose general form is:

SORT ON (field name) TO (file name) [DESCENDING]

This command asks you to specify the *key* on which the file is to be sorted (field name) and will sort in ascending order unless you supply the descending option. dBASE II will sort for only one key at a time, so multiple sorts are needed if you wish the data sorted on several keys. Figure A4–15 illustrates the use of the SORT command to create a payroll file sorted in social security number

FIGURE A4–15 Sorting the payroll file into social security
number order

```
. USE B:PAY1
. COPY TO TEMP
00004 RECORDS COPIED
. SORT ON SSNO TO TEMP
SORT COMPLETE
. USE TEMP
. LIST
00001    PORTER M.L.         342877915 F ACCOUNTING      12.50   40.0
00002    KLUGMAN K.L.        435182906 M FINANCE         12.00   35.0
00003    OBRIEN J.A.         576434572 M INFO SYSTEMS    12.50   45.5
00004    ALVAREZ J.S.        632403718 F PRODUCTION      14.00   44.0
. COPY TO B:PAY1
00004 RECORDS COPIED
. USE B:PAY1
. LIST
00001    PORTER M.L.         342877915 F ACCOUNTING      12.50   40.0
00002    KLUGMAN K.L.        435182906 M FINANCE         12.00   35.0
00003    OBRIEN J.A.         576434572 M INFO SYSTEMS    12.50   45.5
00004    ALVAREZ J.S.        632403718 F PRODUCTION      14.00   44.0
```

order. It is important to note that we did not sort the payroll file itself, but we created a temporary copy of the payroll file, which we sorted and then copied back to the payroll file. Sorting a file itself without creating a copy could result in the loss of the file.

The LIST command shows that the PAY1 file is now sorted in social security number order. Let's take another look at the **COPY** command that was used in the sorting process. The general form of the COPY command is:

COPY TO (file name) [STRUCTURE] [FIELD list]

In the sorting example, we first copied our PAY1 file to a temporary file named TEMP, with the simplest form of the COPY command; COPY TO TEMP. This copied the file we were using (PAY1) to a temporary file. We then sorted the temporary file in social security number order, using the SSNO field. Notice that we then listed the temporary file to determine if the SORT command had worked properly. Finally, we copied the sorted file back to the PAY1 file. This erases the data previously held in this file and substitutes a newly sorted version of the same data into the file.

HANDS-ON EXERCISE A4-8: SORTING A FILE

Sort the PAY1 file into an ascending numerical order, using employee social security numbers. Don't forget to sort a copy of the file, rather than the PAY1 file itself. Then either copy the new version back to the PAY1 file or keep the new version as a alternative payroll file. (For example, you could call it the PAY2 file.)

Using an Index

Sorting a file can be a slow and involved process if a lot of data has to be sorted using several sorting keys. An alternative is to create and **index** to a file. This index is organized in the order that you wish to access the data in the file. An index is a listing of record numbers and associated field values sorted in ascending order according to the field you specify. For example, an index could consist of record numbers and social security numbers taken from a payroll file. Thus the file itself does not have to be sorted into a numerical order based on to the social security numbers of employees. Instead, the index can be used to quickly find an employee's record given his or her social security number. This greatly accelerates the ability to find a particular record. What might take several minutes using a large file, may take only a few seconds if an index related to the file is used. This occurs since dBASE II does not have to sequentially search through each record in a file, but uses an index instead.

An example of the creation of an index named SSINDEX is shown in Figure A4-16. This index consists of record numbers and social security numbers of records in the PAY1 file and is sorted in ascending order by social security number. This figure also shows how the index is used to find a complete record about an employee using the FIND command. Notice that the file and index to be used must be specified in a USE command. Then simply key-in the FIND

FIGURE A4-16 Creating an index and finding a record

```
. INDEX ON SSNO TO SSINDEX
00004 RECORDS INDEXED
. USE PAY1 INDEX SSINDEX
. FIND   435182906
. DISPLAY
00002  KLUGMAN K.L.      435182906 M FINANCE        12.00  35.0
```

command and specify all or part of the content of a field, such as social security number, name, or department. You must also use the DISPLAY command to display the contents of the record you have found. (*Note*: the FIND command can only be used for a file that has an associated index.)

HANDS-ON EXERCISE A4–9:   CREATING AND USING AN INDEX

Create an index of employee social security numbers and employee record numbers for the PAY1 file. Use this index and the FIND command to display one of the records in the PAY1 file.

Deleting Records and Files

Most database management packages allow you to delete records and files from your database. This is accomplished in dBASE II by the use of the **DELETE** command, whose general form is:

DELETE [scope] [FOR (expression)]

Figure A4–17 shows how the DELETE command is used to delete records by specifying a record number or a specific condition. In this example, the fourth record in the file and the record of the employee belonging to the finance department were deleted. Notice that the DELETE command does not immediately remove the records physically from a file but marks them with an asterisk. dBASE II will ignore these records and not use them in processing. If you change your mind and wish to activate a deleted record, you can do so with the RECALL command. Figure A4–17 shows that record number 4 has been recalled and is no longer deleted. Finally, if you wish to physically erase deleted records from a file, you can do so with the PACK command. Notice how the record for the finance department employee is finally removed from the TEMP file.

The DELETE command can also be used to delete a file. However, once a file is deleted, it is physically erased by the system. The general form of the DELETE FILE command is:

DELETE FILE (drive):(file name)

For example, to delete a file named TEMP1 stored on your file disk in drive B, the command would be:

DELETE FILE B: TEMP1

FIGURE   A4–17 Deleting records from a file

```
. USE TEMP
. LIST
00001   ALVAREZ J.S.      632403718 F PRODUCTION        14.00   44.0
00002   KLUGMAN K.L.      435182906 M FINANCE           12.00   35.0
00003   OBRIEN J.A.       576434572 M INFO SYSTEMS      12.50   45.5
00004   PORTER M.L.       342877915 F ACCOUNTING        12.50   40.0
. DELETE RECORD 4
00001 DELETION(S)
. DELETE ALL FOR DEPT = 'FINANCE'
00001 DELETION(S)
. LIST
00001   ALVAREZ J.S.      632403718 F PRODUCTION        14.00   44.0
00002  *KLUGMAN K.L.      435182906 M FINANCE           12.00   35.0
00003   OBRIEN J.A.       576434572 M INFO SYSTEMS      12.50   45.5
00004  *PORTER M.L.       342877915 F ACCOUNTING        12.50   40.0
. RECALL RECORD 4
00001 RECALL(S)
. PACK
PACK COMPLETE, 00003 RECORDS COPIED
. LIST
00001   ALVAREZ J.S.      632403718 F PRODUCTION        14.00   44.0
00002   OBRIEN J.A.       576434572 M INFO SYSTEMS      12.50   45.5
00003   PORTER M.L.       342877915 F ACCOUNTING        12.50   40.0
```

HANDS-ON EXERCISE A4–10:   DELETING RECORDS

Copy the PAY1 file to a temporary file called TEMP. Delete two records from that file. List the file. Then recall one of the records you marked for deletion and physically remove the other record from the file with the PACK command. List the file again to check on the results of these actions. Finally, delete the TEMP file from the disk.

Changing the Structure of Records

Another important way that you may wish to change your database is to change the *structure* of the records in a file. For example, you may wish to add or delete a field, or change the width of a field in your records. In dBASE II, this accomplished with the **MODIFY STRUCTURE** command. Since this command will destroy the data in a file, it must be used in conjunction with the COPY and APPEND commands. This involves copying the structure of a file into a temporary file and making changes to the fields in that file.

FIGURE

A4–18 Adding the PAY
data field to the employee
record structure

```
. USE PAY1
. COPY TO TEMP
00004 RECORDS COPIED
. USE TEMP
. MODIFY STRUCTURE
MODIFY ERASES ALL DATA RECORDS ... PROCEED? (Y/N) Y
.

           NAME        TYP LEN  DEC
FIELD 01 :NAME          C  015  000  :
FIELD 02 :SSNO          C  009  000  :
FIELD 03 :SEX           C  001  000  :
FIELD 04 :DEPT          C  014  000  :
FIELD 05 :RATE          N  005  002  :
FIELD 06 :HOURS         N  004  001  :
FIELD 07 :PAY           N  008  002  :
FIELD 08 :                             :
FIELD 09 :                             :
FIELD 10 :                             :
```

Once that is accomplished, the original file is converted to the new structure. Figure A4–18 shows how this is accomplished.

Notice how the PAY1 file is copied to a TEMP file. The structure of the TEMP file is then modified by adding a seventh data field, PAY, using the MODIFY STRUCTURE command. PAY is a numeric field that will show an employee's weekly earnings. First, the specifications of this new field are keyed-in and the new structure is saved using the CONTROL-W keys. Then the data from the old file is added to this structure by the use of the APPEND command. See Figure A4–19.

FIGURE A4–19 Adding the new record structure to the payroll file

```
. APPEND FROM PAY1
00004 RECORDS ADDED
. COPY TO PAY1
00004 RECORDS COPIED
. USE PAY1
. LIST
00001  ALVAREZ J.S.    632403718 F PRODUCTION     14.00  44.0      0.00
00002  KLUGMAN K.L.    435182906 M FINANCE        12.00  35.0      0.00
00003  OBRIEN J.A.     576434572 M INFO SYSTEMS   12.50  45.5      0.00
00004  PORTER M.L.     342877915 F ACCOUNTING     12.50  40.0      0.00
```

FIGURE A4–20 Calculating and inserting employee pay amounts

```
. REPLACE ALL PAY WITH RATE*HOURS
00004 REPLACEMENT(S)
. REPLACE ALL PAY WITH RATE*HOURS+RATE*0.5*(HOURS-40.0) FOR HOURS>40.0
00002 REPLACEMENT(S)
. LIST
00001   ALVAREZ J.S.     632403718 F PRODUCTION     14.00  44.0    644.00
00002   KLUGMAN K.L.     435182906 M FINANCE        12.00  35.0    420.00
00003   OBRIEN J.A.      576434572 M INFO SYSTEMS   12.50  45.5    603.12
00004   PORTER M.L.      342877915 F ACCOUNTING     12.50  40.0    500.00
```

We now must copy the temporary file with its new structure back to the original PAY1 file. The LIST command shows us that the change was properly made. Note how the new pay field is in every employee record at a zero value. We then use the REPLACE command to automatically insert the product of multiplying the hours worked by the hourly rate into the PAY field of each record. Also included is a "time-and-a-half" overtime pay calculation for over 40 hours of work by two employees. See Figure A4–20.

HANDS-ON EXERCISE A4–11: ADDING A DATA FIELD

Add a seventh data field (PAY) to the employee records in the PAY1 file. This should be an eight-position numeric data field with two positions after the decimal point. Then automatically insert the result of multiplying the hours worked by the hourly rate into the PAY field of each record. Be sure that all employees working over 40 hours per week receive time-and-a-half overtime pay.

Using Multiple Files

An important capability of a database management system is its ability to easily access the data from several files at the same time. This capability emphasizes that a database is *not* a collection of independent files, and that a DBMS is more than a simple *file management system* (FMS). dBASE II provides the **SELECT** command to allow you to create two active files at the same time. Its general form is:

SELECT [Primary] [Secondary]

Also, dBASE II provides the **JOIN** command to allow you to create a file consisting of data from two active files. The general form of the JOIN command is:

JOIN TO [File] FOR [Expression] FIELD [List]

Thus the JOIN command must specify 1) the name of the new file, 2) a *relational* expression that must be *true* in order to combine records from both *active* files, and 3) a list of fields to be copied to the new file.

Figure A4–21 illustrates the use of two active files, PAY1 (The Primary File) and PERSONNEL (The Secondary File) to create a *new* file, EDUFILE. The JOIN command specifies that a data record is to be created in EDUFILE each time the name of an employee in the name field of the primary file (P.NAME) equals the name field of an employee in the secondary file (S.NAME). You can see that the NAME, SSNO, and SEX fields were contained in both files, while the DEPT field came from the PAY1 file, and the EDUCATION

FIGURE A4–21 Using multiple files

```
. USE PAY1
. LIST
00001   PORTER M.L.      342877915 F ACCOUNTING       12.50   40.0      500.00
00002   KLUGMAN K.L.     435182906 M FINANCE          12.00   35.0      420.00
00003   OBRIEN J.A.      576434572 M INFO SYSTEMS     12.50   45.5      603.12
00004   ALVAREZ J.S.     632403718 F PRODUCTION       14.00   44.0      644.00
. SELECT SECONDARY
. USE PERSONNEL
. LIST
00001   PORTER M.L.      342877915 F CPA       M      2
00002   KLUGMAN K.L.     435182906 M MBA       S      0
00003   OBRIEN J.A.      576434572 M PhD       M      3
00004   ALVAREZ J.S.     632403718 F MBA       S      0
. JOIN TO EDUFILE FOR P.NAME = S.NAME;
   FIELD NAME,SSNO,SEX,DEPT,EDUCATION
. USE EDUFILE
. LIST
00001   PORTER M.L.      342877915 F ACCOUNTING       CPA
00002   KLUGMAN K.L.     435182906 M FINANCE          MBA
00003   OBRIEN J.A.      576434572 M INFO SYSTEMS     PhD
00004   ALVAREZ J.S.     632403718 F PRODUCTION       MBA
.
```

field came from the PERSONNEL file. Note that the PERSONNEL file contained fields for marital status (Single or Married) and number of dependents which were not used. EDUFILE can now be used to provide you with displays and reports containing information formerly stored separately in the PAY1 and PERSONNEL files.

HANDS-ON EXERCISE A4–12:   USING MULTIPLE FILES

Create a new file called PERSONNEL whose records contain fields for employee names, social security numbers, sex, education, marital status, and number of dependents. (You can do this by modifying a copy of the PAY1 file with the COPY, MODIFY STRUCTURE, and APPEND commands.) Then use the SELECT and JOIN commands to create the EDUFILE from the PAY1 and PERSONNEL files as shown in Figure A4–21.

HANDS-ON ASSIGNMENTS

We have now accomplished the creation, editing, and entry of data into a simple database file, as well as the retrieval and reporting of information from that file. We have also modified the file by sorting, copying, and indexing operations, along with the deletion of records and the changing of the file structure. This should have given you a good introductory understanding of the capabilities and use of database management packages for microcomputers. For additional information, consult the user's manual for the DBMS package you are using. Now it's time for you to create and manipulate some database files of your own. Good luck!

A4.1 If you have not already done so, create, interrogate, and manipulate a simple employee payroll file, as explained in the HANDS-ON EXERCISES of this section.

A4.2 Create a Student Exam Scores file, consisting of student records containing student names, social security numbers, sex, and grades on three different exams. Enter data into this file for five students. Store and print this file.

A4.3 Edit the Student Exam Scores file by changing a student's exam score. Add and delete records to this file. Store, display, and print this revised file.

A4.4 Retrieve selected data from the Student Exam Scores file by using the LIST, DISPLAY, LOCATE, and COUNT commands. For example, find and count the records of all female students whose scores on the first exam were greater than 85.

A4.5 Sort the records in your Student Exam Scores file by student names. Also create an index consisting of social security numbers and student record numbers. Use the index and the FIND command to display one of the records in your file.

A4.6 Change the structure of the records in your Student Exam Scores file by adding a new field which totals the three exam scores. (*Hint*: use the MODIFY command to add the new field to the structure of all records. Then use the REPLACE command to automatically insert the sum of all the exams into each student's total point field.) List and print both the new file structure and the newly revised file itself.

A4.7 Design and print a report that provides information from your Student Exam Scores file. For example, produce a report showing the exam scores and total points earned by students segregated into male and female categories. Then use this same report form to print a report showing this type of information only for male students whose total scores exceed 240 points.

SECTION FIVE: USING INTEGRATED PACKAGES

Introduction to Integrated Packages

Let's review what we said about **integrated packages** in Chapter Seven, System and Application Software. Integrated packages combine the ability to do several-general purpose applications in one program. This really benefits you if you wish to perform a variety of information processing jobs using the same files of data. The alternative would be to use separate single-function packages. In that case, you would have to load each program and the same data files into the computer each time you used a different package. To make it worse, many packages will refuse to work with data files created by other programs! Integrated packages have solved the problems caused by the inability of individual programs to communicate and work together with common files of data. However, most integrated packages require more memory capacity and have had to compromise on the speed, power, and flexibility of some of their functions to achieve integration. Therefore, users may prefer single-function packages for those applications that they use heavily.

Integrated packages may combine some of the general-purpose application software functions of **electronic spreadsheets, word processing,** and **graphics** with the system software functions of **database management** and **data communications**. Thus you could process the same file of data with one package, moving from one function to the other by pressing a few keys on your computer keyboard, viewing displays from each on multiple **windows** on your video screen. For example, Figure A5–1 shows how one integrated package (Corporate MBA) allows you to gather and analyze data and present information in a variety of ways without having to use several different software packages.

The most widely used integrated package for microcomputers is 1-2-3 by Lotus Development Corporation. **Lotus 1-2-3** combines electronic spreadsheet, data management, and graphics functions in one program. Other popular integrated packages include *Corporate MBA* by Context Management Systems, *Symphony* by Lotus, and *Framework* by Ashton-Tate, developers of dBASE II and III. These programs combine spreadsheet, data management, graphics, word processing, and data communications functions. Other functions, such as forms generation or executive calendar management, are also provided by these and several other packages.

Some of the advantages of integrated packages can be derived by using an **operating environment** package like TopView, VisiOn, Windows, and DESQ. These packages interconnect several separate application packages so they can communicate and work together and share common data files, as well as allowing the outputs of several programs to be displayed at the same time in multiple windows. These packages should become popular with users who want a way to integrate single-function programs.

FIGURE A5–1 Using an integrated package

. . .Gather information from all the sources you need.

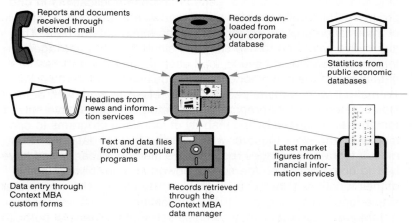

Reports and documents received through electronic mail

Records downloaded from your corporate database

Statistics from public economic databases

Headlines from news and information services

Data entry through Context MBA custom forms

Text and data files from other popular programs

Records retrieved through the Context MBA data manager

Latest market figures from financial information services

. . .Analyze your data the way you choose

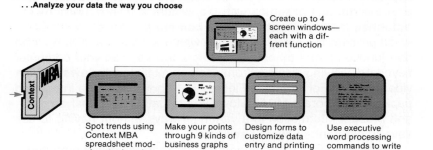

Create up to 4 screen windows— each with a diffrent function

Spot trends using Context MBA spreadsheet models: search and sort records using Context MBA data manager

Make your points through 9 kinds of business graphs

Design forms to customize data entry and printing

Use executive word processing commands to write reports, memos, letters

. . .And present your results exactly the way you want them.

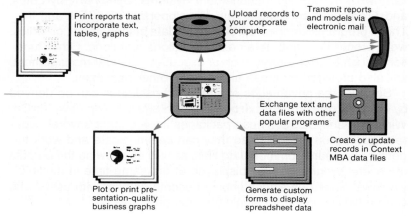

Print reports that incorporate text, tables, graphs

Upload records to your corporate computer

Transmit reports and models via electronic mail

Exchange text and data files with other popular programs

Create or update records in Context MBA data files

Plot or print presentation-quality business graphs

Generate custom forms to display spreadsheet data

If you have used any electronic spreadsheet package, you will not have much trouble understanding and using integrated packages. Many integrated packages use the spreadsheet as the basic structure to organize and accomplish data management, graphics, and word processing, as well as spreadsheet analysis. Thus in this section we will not go into the details of how to accomplish these functions, since we have already covered then in earlier sections of this appendix. You should read these sections and complete the hands-on exercises that lead you through the use of the word processing, electronic spreadsheet, and database management packages they describe.

Our objective in this section is to highlight the major similarities and differences between such single-function packages and integrated packages. We will use Lotus 1-2-3, since it has become the acknowledged standard in microcomputer integrated packages and is so widely used for business applications. Also, even the newest integrated packages have not proven themselves to be as fast, memory-efficient, and flexible as 1-2-3, even though they offer word processing and communications functions. It appears that much work needs to be done before integrated packages are developed that integrate many basic functions without sacrificing some speed, power, and flexibility. Thus in this section you will be shown how to use an integrated package to:

- Build and use an electronic spreadsheet.
- Create and use data files to store and retrieve information.
- Graph selected information from electronic spreadsheets and data files.

Getting Started

Like most integrated packages, the Lotus 1-2-3 package contains several diskettes and an extensive user's manual. The diskettes include the main 1-2-3 program diskette (the 1-2-3 *system disk*), a backup copy of the system disk, an extensive tutorial disk, a utilities disk, and a PrintGraph disk used to print graphs. If you have a new 1-2-3 package, you should read the section in the user's manual ("Getting Started"), which tells you how to customize your version of 1-2-3 to fit your particular computer and operating system. A properly prepared 1-2-3 systems disk is all you will need to carry out most 1-2-3 functions.

Insert your 1-2-3 system disk in Drive A and turn on the computer. (See the beginning of the first section of this appendix if you need additional information on starting a microcomputer and using floppy disks.) If your computer is already on and in the operating system mode, type in the word LOTUS after the operating system prompt. In either case, the LOTUS ACCESS SYSTEM menu will be displayed. (See Figure A5–2.) It gives you a choice of using the main 1-2-3 program, or several other programs such as:

- **File-Manager**— Allows you to store, catalog, copy, erase, and rename files.
- **Disk-Manager**— Allows you to copy, compare, and check your disks.
- **PrintGraph**— Sets up for the use of the PrintGraph disk.
- **Translate**— Allows use of files from other packages, such as VisiCalc and dBASE II.

You should select the 1-2-3 option by moving the **cursor** (Lotus calls it a **cell pointer**) to the 1-2-3 entry on the access menu and

FIGURE A5–2 The primary menus of Lotus 1-2-3

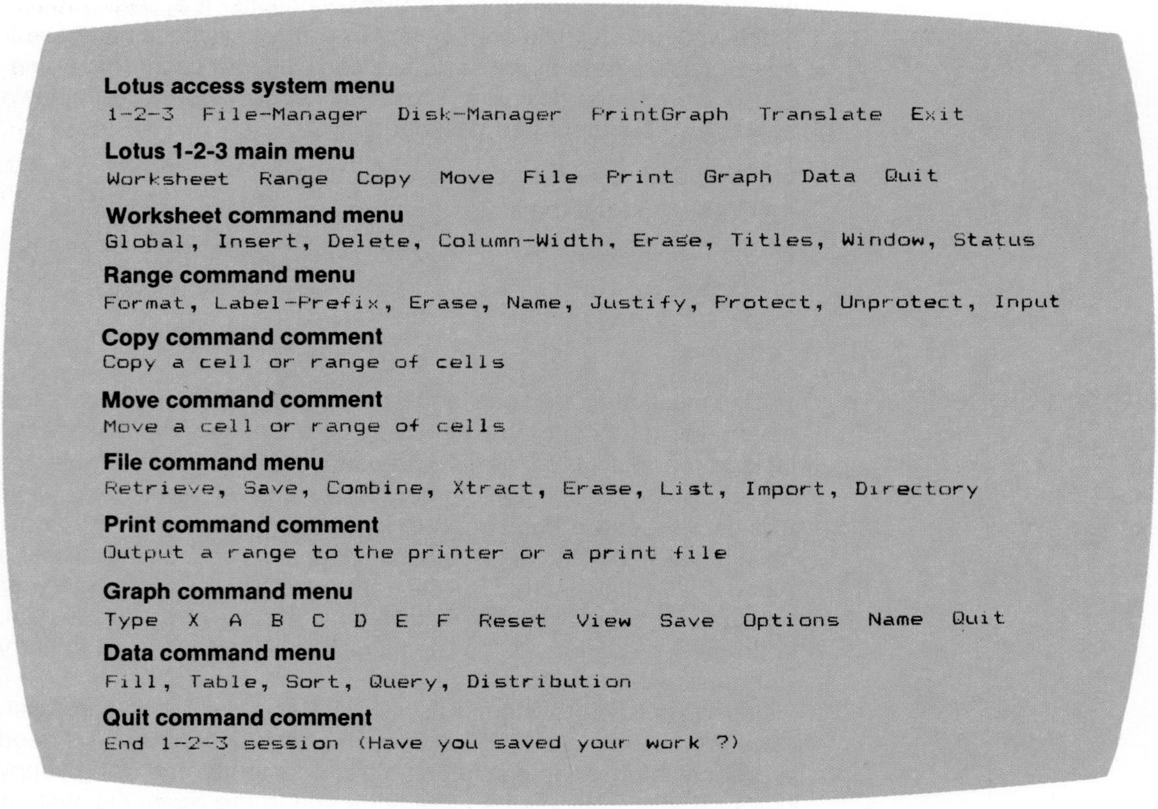

Lotus access system menu
1-2-3 File-Manager Disk-Manager PrintGraph Translate Exit

Lotus 1-2-3 main menu
Worksheet Range Copy Move File Print Graph Data Quit

Worksheet command menu
Global, Insert, Delete, Column-Width, Erase, Titles, Window, Status

Range command menu
Format, Label-Prefix, Erase, Name, Justify, Protect, Unprotect, Input

Copy command comment
Copy a cell or range of cells

Move command comment
Move a cell or range of cells

File command menu
Retrieve, Save, Combine, Xtract, Erase, List, Import, Directory

Print command comment
Output a range to the printer or a print file

Graph command menu
Type X A B C D E F Reset View Save Options Name Quit

Data command menu
Fill, Table, Sort, Query, Distribution

Quit command comment
End 1-2-3 session (Have you saved your work ?)

pressing the ENTER key, or by typing a 1 and then pressing the ENTER key. This should emphasize one of the important features of 1-2-3. You can select an option or command from a menu by moving the cursor to it (using the cursor control keys, an electronic mouse, or a touch-screen) and pressing the ENTER key. Or you can use the keyboard to enter the first character of a command displayed on the menu. Thus the 1-2-3 package is a well-designed **menu-driven** program.

Erase the Lotus 1-2-3 copyright information that is displayed on the screen by pressing any key. The 1-2-3 spreadsheet display (Lotus calls it a **worksheet**) then appears on the screen. It looks like the VisiCalc spreadsheet display, which should reassure users who have learned to use VisiCalc or other similar spreadsheets. You could begin to enter data, labels, and formulas into the spreadsheet right now, just as you did using VisiCalc. However, let's first take a look at the basic command menus of 1-2-3.

Pressing the slash key (**/**), as in VisiCalc, provides you with a menu of commands. This is the **main menu** of 1-2-3. Selecting any of these main menu commands will provide you with a **command menu** or comment that specifies the options available to accomplish that command. Selecting an option from a command menu will provide you with a comment, prompt, or **submenu** of additional options! Thus several levels of menus are provided by 1-2-3 to accomplish its major functions. Figure A5–2 displays the options or comments provided by the main menus and primary command menus of 1-2-3.

Just as in VisiCalc and other spreadsheet packages, 1-2-3 displays a **control panel** above its worksheet. It consists of three lines of information. See Figure A5–3.

FIGURE

A5–3 The 1-2-3 display screen format

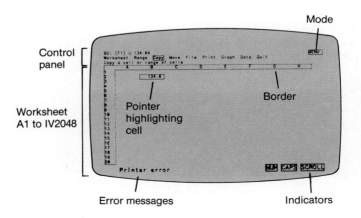

- **First line.** Shows the cell address where the cursor or cell pointer is presently located on the worksheet, the display format, protection status, and the actual contents of the cell in which the cursor is located.

- **Second line.** Shows a menu of command options or of the characters being entered or edited along with appropriate prompts or comments.

- **Third line.** Shows a submenu of command options or short comments explaining what menu item the cursor is highlighting.

One other feature of 1-2-3 should be mentioned at this time. Like other integrated packages, 1-2-3 makes extensive use of the **function keys** found on many professional-quality microcomputers. Figure A5–4 outlines how you can use the ten function keys on the IBM PC keyboard. (The 1-2-3 package supplies you with a plastic template to lay next to the function keys to remind you of their uses.)

Correcting Errors and Getting Help

You are now ready to select a specific 1-2-3 command or to enter items in the worksheet and perform various functions on the data it contains. But what if you make a mistake or need help? Here's what you do.

- If you make a mistake while typing and recognize it before you press the ENTER key, press the BACKSPACE key to erase one character at a time, or the ESCAPE key to erase all of the characters at once.

- Once you have entered something into a cell, you can change its contents by moving the cursor to that cell. Then enter new data into that cell, or type /RE to erase the contents of that cell. In

FIGURE A5–4 What the function keys do in 1-2-3

```
F1: Help      Display Help screen
F2: Edit      Switch to/from Edit mode for current entry
F3: Name      Display menu of range names
F4: Abs       Make/Unmake cell address "absolute"
F5: GoTo      Move cell pointer to a particular cell
F6: Window    Move cell pointer to other window
F7: Query     Repeat most recent Data Query operation
F8: Table     Repeat most recent Data Table operation
F9: Calc      Ready mode: Recalculate all formulas
              Value and Edit modes: Convert formula to its value
F10: Graph    Draw graph using current graph settings
```

either case, you must use the ENTER key to complete each of these procedures.

■ Sometimes 1-2-3 will give you a "beep" and display the word EDIT on the mode indicator after you make an entry. This means you have made an error and have been placed into the "edit mode." (You can also get into this mode voluntarily by pressing the F2 (EDIT) function key.) The edit mode allows you to change selected characters in a cell entry by using several keys to move the cursor and add or delete characters. Use the right and left cursor control keys to move the cursor one character to the right or left, the HOME key to move to the first character, and the END key to move the cursor to the last character of the entry you are editing. The DELETE key (DEL) will delete the character at the cursor; the BACKSPACE key will delete the character to the left of the cursor. Then insert a new character by simply typing it in.

■ If you have selected a command and don't want to complete it, just keep pressing the ESCAPE key until you return to a menu or submenu you prefer, or to the 1-2-3 worksheet and its READY mode indicator.

■ If you want to erase the entire spreadsheet and start over again, press /WE and then a Y to confirm this serious decision!

■ One of the best features of 1-2-3 is its extensive (over 200) **HELP screens.** If you need help at any time, press the F1 function key (the HELP key). This will cause the display of a HELP screen that contains explanations of the command or function that you were working on just before you pressed the HELP key. (This is called a *context-sensitive* HELP facility.) You can select additional levels of HELP by moving the cursor to a specific topic on the HELP screen and pressing the ENTER key. When you are done with the HELP screen, press the ESCAPE key. This will return the program to where you were before you asked for help. See Figure A5–5.

Spreadsheet Format and Organization

If you have used an electronic spreadsheet package before, you won't have much trouble using the spreadsheet feature of 1-2-3 and other integrated packages. Whether this is your first time or not, you will be asked to refer occasionally to Section Three: Using Electronic Spreadsheet Packages. You should try to build a simple spreadsheet like the ABC Company-Financial Performance spreadsheet developed in that section. Figure A5–6 shows the same spreadsheet built using the spreadsheet function of 1-2-3. To help you accomplish this, we will point out any major differences between

FIGURE A5–5

A. The 1-2-3 HELP index screen

```
Help Index               Select one of these topics for additional Help

How to use The Help Facility      How to Start Over
"Beep!" -- Errors and Messages    How to End a 1-2-3 Session

Special Keys                      Moving the Cell Pointer
The Control Panel                 Cell Entries
Modes and Indicators              Erasing Cell Entries

Formulas                          Operators
"@" Functions

Cell Formats -- Number vs. Label  Column Widths

1-2-3 Commands                    Keyboard Macros
Command Menus                     Function Keys

Ranges                            Menus for File, Range, and Graph Names
Pointing to Ranges                Filenames
Range-Editing Keys
```

B A HELP screen example: Special keys

```
                                                    18-20
Special Keys


Function Keys invoke a variety of 1-2-3 operations.

The [Alt] key is a special kind of Shift key. You use it in combination with
letter keys to invoke keyboard macros.

The Home key moves "to the beginning" in a variety of contexts.

The End key moves "to the end" in a variety of contexts.

The [Esc] key undoes your current action, one step at a time.
```

VisiCalc and 1-2-3 spreadsheet operations. For example, Figure A5–7 summarizes the similarities and differences in the basic commands of VisiCalc and 1-2-3.

Lotus 1-2-3 can create a large spreadsheet in memory—256 columns by 2,048 rows, or over 520,000 **cells**! The 1-2-3 program adjusts the size of the spreadsheet to fit the amount of memory

FIGURE

A5–6 Example
spreadsheet built with
Lotus 1-2-3

```
                    SPREADSHEET EXAMPLE

          ABC COMPANY: FINANCIAL PERFORMANCE

          1983      1984      1985    TOTAL   AVERAGE

REVENUE   1000      1100      1200    3300     1100
          -------------------------------------------
EXPENSES   600       660       720    1980      660
          -------------------------------------------
PROFIT     400       440       480    1320      440
          -------------------------------------------
TAXES      160       176       192     528      176
          -------------------------------------------
PROFIT     240       264       288     792      264
AFTER TAXES
```

FIGURE   A5–7 Comparison of VisiCalc and Lotus 1-2-3 commands

VC Command	VC Meaning	1-2-3 Command	1-2-3 Meaning
/B	Blank (cell)	/RE	Erase a cell or range of cells
/C	Clear (worksheet)	/WE	Erase worksheet
/D	Delete row/column	/WD	Delete rows or columns
/E	Edit entry	F2 [Edit]	Edit entry
/GF	Format (global)	/WGF	Formats the worksheet (global)
/F	Format a cell	/RF	Formats a cell or range
/G	Global	/WG	Sets global worksheet parameters
/I	Insert row/column	/WI	Insert rows or columns
/M	Move	/M	Moves a cell or range of cells (not directly equivalent)
/P	Print	/P	Prints contents of worksheet to printer or file
/R	Replicate	/C	Copies a cell or range of cells to a target cell or range of cells. Absolute cell references are specified before copying.
/S	Storage	/F	File commands
/T	Titles	/WT	Titles
/V	Version	none	Displayed at startup
/W	Window	/WW	Window
/	Repeating label	none	Use label prefix "\"

your computer has. For example, if you have 128K of RAM, it will assign 30K to the spreadsheet; if you have 256K of RAM, it will assign 160K to the spreadsheet. Refer back to Figure A5–3. It shows you the details of the 1-2-3 spreadsheet display screen. Notice that, like VisiCalc, letters are used to designate columns and numbers are used to designate rows. Thus cell B3 is the address of the cell in the second column of the third row.

Remember, the display screen is just a **window** that lets you see a portion of the larger worksheet in memory. Lotus calls the section of the spreadsheet you can see through a window a **page**. Each page is initially eight columns wide and 20 rows long, unless you change the width of the columns or split the screen into two windows. Lotus 1-2-3 allows you to split the screen into two horizontal or vertical windows (just like VisiCalc) using the **/ Worksheet Window** sequence of commands. However, like Multiplan, it allows you to change the width of individual columns, as well as changing the width of all columns equally, as VisiCalc does. This is accomplished with the **/ Worksheet Column-Width** command sequence. Lotus 1-2-3 also allows you to make changes to the format of the entire spreadsheet, insert or delete columns or rows, and "lock" titles and headings so they stay on the screen even when you are moving around the spreadsheet. Figure A5–8 outlines these and other command sequences that change the format or appearance of the worksheet.

Other commands that modify parts of the worksheet format are included in the **Range** sequence of commands. Several of these commands are summarized in Figure A5–8. Thus if you want to change the way numbers are displayed in part of the spreadsheet you would use the **/ Range Format** command sequence. (The **/**

FIGURE

A5–8 Commands that modify the 1-2-3 worksheet format

Enter / **Worksheet** and one of the following commands:

Global   Establish formats for the entire worksheet.

Insert   Insert blank columns or rows.

Delete   Delete columns or rows.

Column-Width   Change the width of individual columns.

Erase   Erase the worksheet in memory.

Titles   Lock horizontal and vertical titles.

Window   Split the screen into horizontal or vertical windows.

Enter / **Range** and one of the following commands:

Format   Alter the display format of a cell or range.

Label-Prefix   Align labels in a cell or range.

Name   Assign a name to a cell or range.

Protect   Protect the contents of a cell or range from alteration.

Worksheet Global Format command sequence would affect the entire spreadsheet.) For example, you might want all of the money values in a column to display a dollar sign and two decimal places. This command sequence allows you to select from several format options and to choose to have up to fifteen decimal places displayed. Thus if you wanted two decimal places shown, a number like 12.30 could appear as:

Format Option	Cell Display
General	12.3
Fixed	12.30
Currency	$12.30
Percent	1230.00%
Scientific	1.23E + 01

Note: in 1-2-3, a **range** is a cell, column, row, or a rectangular grouping of cells, columns, and/or rows. A range is identified by the cells in two of its diagonally opposite corners. Thus a range can have an address of B5 to F12 or F12 to B5, etc.

Like Multiplan, 1-2-3 allows you to name a cell or range in your spreadsheet with a name up to 15 characters long by using the **Range Name** command sequence. Thus you could give the name SALES to the group of cells in row B, columns three through twelve (B3 through B12) by selecting the following sequence:

/ Range Name Create
Enter Name: SALES
Enter Range: B3..B12

Now any time you wish to use the values in this range you could refer to it as SALES, instead of B3..B12. For example, you could add all the values in these cells together by using the function @ SUM (SALES). Or you could COPY or PRINT just the values in the range of cells called SALES. If you give individual cells a name, you could even use names in formulas. Thus if B3 is named REVENUE and C3 is named EXPENSES, you could use a formula like (REVENUE − EXPENSES) instead of (B3 − C3).

One final worksheet format feature of 1-2-3 that should be mentioned is its **cell protection** capability. You can protect the contents of any cell or range of cells from alteration. When you first use 1-2-3, all cells can be altered. However, all cells can be protected if you use the **/ Worksheet Global Protection** command sequence. Then you can remove this protection or install it back again to any cell or range of cells with the **/ Range Unprotect** or **/ Range Protect** command sequences. This capability is a good safety feature that protects important parts of a worksheet from accidental alteration.

HANDS-ON EXERCISE A5–1: Viewing the Spreadsheet

Before we continue, you should become familiar with the 1-2-3 spreadsheet by using the cursor control keys (or electronic mouse) to move the screen window around the entire spreadsheet in memory. (This is called "scrolling" the window.) See how many columns and rows there are by looking at the column letters and row numbers as they scroll by. Then use the PAGE UP and PAGE DOWN keys (Pg Up and Pg Dn), to move up or down a page at a time. Then use the TAB key to move a page at a time to the right of the spreadsheet. To move a page at a time to the left, press the SHIFT key as well as the TAB key. If you want to go directly to a certain cell in the worksheet, press the F5 function key (the GOTO key) and enter its cell address (such as H23) in response to the GoTo prompt. Finally, use the HOME key to return you to the first cell (A1) of the spreadsheet.

HANDS-ON EXERCISE A5–2: Changing the Spreadsheet Format

Explore the worksheet commands shown in Figure A5–8 to modify the appearance and format of the spreadsheet. Select each command. Then move the control panel cursor to each of the options in its submenu, noticing each explanation given. Notice the wealth of alternatives you have to change the format and appearance of the spreadsheet. We don't have room to explain most of them in this appendix. You will have to explore them on your own with the help of the 1-2-3 user's manual and HELP menus. But you should try a few of them. (*Remember*: use the ESCAPE key to get yourself out of any command sequence you don't want to continue with.) For example, you should try changing column widths individually or for the entire spreadsheet (a global change); insert and delete rows or columns; lock titles and split the screen into two windows and then clear it back to a single window. Try formatting a column so numeric entries display a dollar sign, or protect it so its values can't be changed.

Making Spreadsheet Entries

Data is entered into the cell location where the cursor rests by typing it and pressing the ENTER key or one of the cursor control keys. As with other spreadsheet programs, 1-2-3 expects any entry you make into a spreadsheet cell to be either a number, a formula, or text (a **label**). If you start an entry with a number, 1-2-3 assumes it is a number; start with a letter, 1-2-3 assumes it is a label; start with either + − (@ # $ and 1-2-3 assumes either a formula or a number. If you mix numbers, letters, and special characters improperly, 1-2-3 will refuse to accept your entry. It will give you a "beep" and put you into the EDIT mode so you can erase (press the ESCAPE key) or correct your entry! An apostrophe (') appears automatically in front of a label entry beginning with a letter. If you want a label to start with a number or special character, you have to start the entry with an apostrophe. Labels are automatically left-justified in their cells; numbers and formulas are automatically right-justified. (*Note*: numbers are not allowed to use the last position at the right of a cell. It is reserved for a decimal point, even if there is none.) If you want to change this automatic justification, start your entries as follows:

' Will left justify your cell entry.
" Will right justify your cell entry.
∧ Will center your cell entry.
\ Will repeat your next character in the rest of the cell.

Remember that the distinction between numeric and label entries is important, because cells containing numeric entries can be manipulated by formulas and functions, whereas cells containing text material cannot (with a few exceptions). Lotus (unlike VisiCalc) also allows labels to go beyond the boundaries of a cell (helpful for titles and other text material), whereas numeric data and formulas cannot. Also, a formula must be differentiated from numeric and text entries, because only the value of the formula, not the formula itself, is usually displayed in a cell. You should read the section on *Entering Numbers and Text, Entering and Using Formulas*, and *Using Functions* in Section Three of this appendix for important information on how VisiCalc, 1-2-3, and many spreadsheet packages handle these activities.

With a few exceptions, VisiCalc and 1-2-3 have identical built-in spreadsheet **functions**. Therefore, the VisiCalc functions summarized in Figure A3–6 of Section Three can be used in 1-2-3 spreadsheet formulas. (One exception is the function to compute an arithmetic mean, which is AVG in 1-2-3 and AVERAGE in VisiCalc.) However, 1-2-3 has many more functions than VisiCalc. For example, instead of just having a net present value NPV function like Visicalc, 1-2-3 also has IRR internal rate of return, FV future value, and PV present value functions. See the 1-2-3 user's manual for a listing and explanation of the extensive built-in functions of 1-2-3.

HANDS-ON EXERCISE A5–3: Starting and Using a Simple Spreadsheet

Enter the titles and headings of the spreadsheet example, shown in Figure A5–6, and data for REVENUE in 1983 of $1000. Then enter the formulas for EXPENSES (B8*0.6), PROFIT (B8—B10), TAXES (B12*0.4), and PROFIT AFTER TAXES (B12—B14). What happens as you enter each formula? Notice that the formula for a cell is shown only on the first line of the control panel. The cell itself displays the *value* or *result* of the computation of the formula. Do you realize that the entire example spreadsheet shown in Figure A5-6 is based on the entry of only one numeric data element: 1983 sales of $1,000? All other numbers in the spreadsheet are generated by formulas!

But let's get back to the simple spreadsheet you have just built as displayed in Figure A5–9. What do the formulas you have entered mean? Nothing very complicated. You have just told 1-2-3 that (1) EXPENSES are 60 percent of REVENUE, (2) PROFIT equals REVENUE minus EXPENSES, (3) TAXES are 40 percent of PROFIT, and (4) PROFIT AFTER TAXES equals PROFIT minus TAXES. Now let's see a simple demonstration of the powerful automatic recalculation and "what-if" capability of the electronic spreadsheet function of 1-2-3. **What** would profit after taxes have been **if** revenue for 1983 had increased to $1,500? $1,800? $2,000? Try it and see, instantly.

Copying Spreadsheet Entries

Do you want to key-in repetitive data, text, formulas, and functions, in column after column, row after row of a worksheet? Of course not. Like the electronic spreadsheet packages, 1-2-3 saves you a lot of time and effort in constructing a worksheet by its ability to copy the contents of any part of a spreadsheet to any other part of the spreadsheet. Thus cells, columns, rows, and other ranges can be copied or *replicated*.

One feature of 1-2-3 that is very helpful in the copying process

FIGURE

A5–9 Starting an electronic spreadsheet

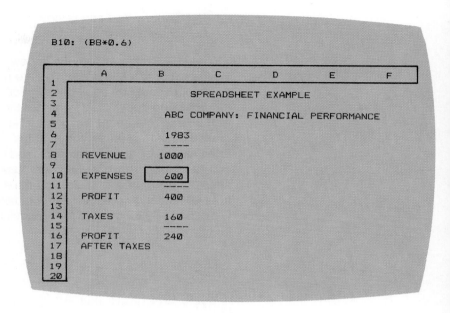

(as well as in many other commands) is its **expanding cursor**. You are usually prompted to supply the coordinates of a range during the execution of many 1-2-3 commands. For example, during the execution of the **/ Copy** command you are asked to:

- Enter range to copy from:
- Enter range to copy to:

You can, of course, just key-in the column and row coordinates of the ranges involved. (VisiCalc calls them the *source* and *target* ranges.) Or you could use the expanding cursor to "paint a picture" of the parts of the worksheet involved. This involves the following process:

- Move the cursor to a corner of the range you want to copy.
- Enter **/Copy.**
- Use the cursor keys (or electronic mouse or touch- screen) to indicate the range you want to copy. Notice how the cursor expands to "paint" the range in reverse video. Then press the **Enter** key.
- Move the cursor to a corner of the range you want to copy material into. Then **anchor** the cursor to this corner by pressing the **period** (.) key. Now use the cursor control keys to expand the cursor until it highlights the entire range. Then press the

ENTER key. You can remove an anchored cursor by pressing the ESCAPE key.

There is a major difference in how 1-2-3 copies formulas. Unlike VisiCalc (but like Multiplan), you are not asked to specify whether a formula should be copied (1) without changing its cell references (an **absolute** copy) or (2) whether the formula should be copied with its cell references changed to indicate its new column and row address (a **relative** copy). Lotus 1-2-3 assumes that the **absolute** value of labels and numbers, and the **relative** value of formulas and functions are what you want copied. If you want to copy the absolute value of a formula, you must place a dollar sign ($) in front of its cell references. For example, if you copied the formula (B8*0.5 + B20) from its present cell to cell G2, it would be copied as (+ G8*0.5 + B20) into cell G2.

HANDS-ON EXERCISE A5–4:   Completing a Spreadsheet

Finish the spreadsheet shown in Figure A5–7. You don't have to key-in all of the numbers and formulas. instead, do the following:

■ Key-in the column headings for 1984 (in C6) and 1985 (in D6), TOTAL (in E6) and AVERAGE (in F6). Key-in or copy the dotted line below these figures if you want to.

■ Key-in formulas for the revenues for 1984 and 1985, assuming that 1984 revenues will be 10 percent of 1983 (+B8*1.1 in cell C8) and that 1985 revenue will be 20 percent of 1983 (+B8*1.2 in cell D8). Notice how the revenue amounts for those years are instantly calculated and displayed.

■ Now copy the range that includes the formulas for 1983 EXPENSES, PROFIT, and PROFIT AFTER TAXES (B10..B16) to the range that will include those same figures for 1984 and 1985 (C10 to D16). Again notice how the appropriate amounts are instantly calculated and displayed. (Even the dotted lines between amounts have been copied!) Move the cursor to the cells with number values and see for yourself, from the control panel display, that they now contain formulas adjusted to reflect their new cell addresses.

■ Enter the formulas for TOTAL REVENUE and AVERAGE REVENUE. But use the SUM and AVERAGE functions to save yourself some work. Thus enter SUM (B8..D8) into cell E8, and AVG (B8 . . . D8) into cell F8. Now copy the formulas in these two cells into the remaining cells of columns E and F of your spreadsheet. Thus, copy range E8..F8 to range E10..F16. Then erase any zeros or error messages appearing between your spreadsheet values, using the **/ RANGE ERASE** command. (Use the backward slash (\) and the minus key to enter dotted lines in your spreadsheet if you wish.) Now your spreadsheet should look just like Figure A5–6. Congratulations!

Storing and Printing Spreadsheets

Once you have completed a spreadsheet, you will want to save it for later use as a file on a magnetic disk. The next time you want to use that particular spreadsheet you can easily retrieve it from your disk and display it on your video screen. You will also want to print a paper copy of a completed spreadsheet from time to time on the printer of your computer system. These actions are accomplished very easily by 1-2-3.

HANDS-ON EXERCISE A5–5:   Storing, Retrieving, Printing, and Using a Spreadsheet

■ Use the **/ File Save** command sequence to save your spreadsheet. This includes giving your spreadsheet a name (of up to eight characters). How about EXAMPLE1?

■ Use the **/ File Retrieve** command sequence to retrieve the EXAMPLE1 spreadsheet, even though it is still displayed on your screen. The screen will go blank and then your spreadsheet will reappear. This proves that you have correctly stored and retrieved your spreadsheet.

■ Use the **/ Print Printer Range** command sequence to print your spreadsheet. You must enter the range coordinates of the entire spreadsheet (A1..F17) if you want all of it printed. Then use the **Go** command to start printing and the **Quit** command to complete this command sequence. (If you wanted to save your spreadsheet as a **printfile** for printing at a later time, you would use the **/ Printfile** command sequence.)

■ You have now built your first spreadsheet. It wasn't too difficult, was it? Now you can use it as a decision-support tool by playing "what-if games" as you did earlier. For example, retrieve the spreadsheet from the diskette and change revenue figures or change the tax rate and see what happens to your "bottom line." Save or print any of these spreadsheet variations, if you wish. However, this is not necessary. The original EXAMPLE1 spreadsheet is stored safely on your disk.

Using Data Management Capabilities

Most integrated packages have limited data management capabilities. They are not true database management systems (DBMS), like dBASE II and III or R:base 4000. Instead they have limited **file management** capabilities. They use an electronic spreadsheet as a simple relational data **file**, where columns are data **fields** and rows are data **records**. They then add the ability to manipulate and interrogate the file to extract information about the records in the file. That's it. Doesn't sound very impressive, does it? But it is, because integrated packages allow you to use the speed and power of your computer to manage your business and personal records without having to change to a specialized DBMS package and learn a lot of new command sequences. Thus integrated packages provide the file management capabilities many users need.

Lotus 1-2-3 can be used for a variety of data management operations, but let's use its three most important file management capabilities. You should learn to use 1-2-3 to do the following:

■ Create a data file.
■ Sort a data file.
■ Interrogate a data file.

Creating Data Files

You don't have to use special commands (like the CREATE command in dBASE II) to create a data file when you use 1-2-3. The main requirement is that the first row of your spreadsheet file consists of labels that are **field names**. For example, the cells in the first row of an employee payroll file might contain field names describing **attributes**, such as *name, social security number, sex, de-*

partment, etc. Each succeeding row can then consist of an individual employee payroll record. The cells of each row would contain data fields describing the attributes of each employee.

The only other major file creation requirement is that the widths of each column be adjusted to reflect the number of positions in each field of the data records. For example, the employee name field might consist of fifteen positions, while the social security number field might be nine positions wide. So you would adjust the widths of the columns containing these fields by using the **Worksheet Column-Width** command sequence. (*Note*: don't forget to add one space to a numeric field since 1-2-3 saves one additional space on the right of such fields for a decimal point.)

HANDS-ON EXERCISE A5–6:   Creating a Data File

Create the employee payroll file shown in Figure A5-10. Yes, it's the same file you created in Section Four, using dBASE II. Enter the field names in the first row of your spreadsheet and adjust the widths of each column. You can use the same field widths (plus one position for numeric fields) you used before: NAME = 15, SSNO = 10, SEX =2, DEPT =14, RATE = 6, and HOURS = 5 positions. Then enter the data records for the four employees into your spreadsheet file. Easy, isn't it?

Before you move on, you had better save your payroll file on disk so you won't lose it accidentally. Then make a printed copy of it. Use the **/ File Save** command sequence. Give your file a name like PAY1. Then print a copy of the file using the **/ Print Printer** command sequence. Both of these activities are handled just like you did when saving and printing your example spreadsheet.

FIGURE

A5–10 The employee payroll file

```
EMPLOYEE PAYROLL FILE
NAME            SS#         SEX DEPARTMENT        RATE    HOURS
ALVAREZ J.S.    632403718  F   PRODUCTION        14.00   44.00
KLUGMAN K.L.    435182906  M   FINANCE           12.00   35.00
OBRIEN J.A.     576434572  M   INFO SYSTEMS      12.50   45.50
PORTER M.L.     342877915  F   ACCOUNTING        12.50   40.00
```

Sorting a Data File

We frequently want to sort the records in a file in various ways to make it easier to extract, display, and print information in a variety of formats. For example, the employee records in our payroll file could be so sorted that they could be arranged sequentially by name, social security number, sex, department, etc. The **/ Data Sort** command sequence of 1-2-3 even allows you to sort data in ascending or descending order, using one or two fields as sorting *keys*. For example, you could sort employee records in an ascending order, using the name field as your **primary key** and social security number as your **secondary key.** Thus records would be arranged in alphabetical order by employee names. If two employees had the same name, the record of the employee with the lowest social security number would be placed first.

HANDS-ON EXERCISE A5-7: Sorting the Payroll File

Sort the records in the payroll file you created in the previous exercise by social security number. After entering **/ Data Sort,** do the following:

■ Enter **/ Data Range** to indicate the range of the worksheet that you want sorted. In response to the prompt: **Enter Data Range:,** you should enter the range coordinates (A2..F5) of the spreadsheet file, excluding the first row of field names. (Use the expanding cursor to indicate this, then press ENTER.)

■ Now choose the **Primary-Key** option from the command submenu. Move the cursor anywhere in column B and press the ENTER key to indicate that you want to sort the records by social security number. Then choose an ascending order for sorting, by entering an **A** in response to a prompt.

■ We could now choose the **Secondary-Key** option and go through the same operations for sorting on a secondary key field, such as employee names. But it really isn't necessary, if we assume that all social security numbers are unique. So enter the **Go** option from the submenu and your payroll records will be instantly sorted by social security number! See Figure A5-11.

FIGURE

A5–11 Payroll file sorted by social security number

```
EMPLOYEE PAYROLL FILE
NAME           SS#          SEX DEPARTMENT         RATE     HOURS
PORTER M.L.    342877915 F     ACCOUNTING         12.50    40.00
KLUGMAN K.L.   435182906 M     FINANCE            12.00    35.00
OBRIEN J.A.    576434572 M     INFO SYSTEMS       12.50    45.50
ALVAREZ J.S.   632403718 F     PRODUCTION         14.00    44.00
```

Interrogating a Data File

Now that you have created, saved, printed, and sorted a file, it's time to learn how to extract information from it. Lotus 1-2-3 doesn't provide you with all of the data interrogation and reporting capabilities of a DBMS package. It does, however, provide the **/ Data Query** command sequence, which allows you to find the records in a file that meet certain criteria. Such records can be highlighted on your display screen with the **Find** option or copied to another part of the spreadsheet using the **Extract** option. The **Duplicate** option is similar to the Extract option, except duplicate records are eliminated. Finally, the **Delete** option deletes records meeting certain criteria from a file.

HANDS-ON EXERCISE A5–8: Interrogating the Payroll File

■ Use the **/ Data Query** command sequence and the **Find** option to highlight the records of all female employees in the payroll file. First, select the **Input** option and specify the range coordinates of the data file, using the expanding cursor. This is called the **Input Range**. In this case, its coordinates are A2 to F6. (The field name row (the first row of the file) must be included in a range when using the / Data Query command sequence.) Press the ENTER key to establish this range.

■ Next select the **Criterion** option. You must now indicate a **criterion range.** In most cases, you must build a criterion range in some other part of the spreadsheet before you use the / Data Query command. For example, you could set up a criterion range in cells C9 and C10. First you would enter the field name (SEX) in cell C9 and the code for a female (F) in cell C10. Then use the command sequence mentioned earlier and specify C9..C10 as your criterion range.

■ Now select the **Find** option. The record of J. S. Alvarez is immediately highlighted by the cursor, because she is the first female employee in the file. Press the down-arrow cursor control key and the cursor instantly highlights the record of M. L. Porter, the next (and last) female employee. Use the down-arrow and up-arrow keys to highlight records that meet your criteria.

■ Use the F7 function key (the **Query** key) at any time to repeat your most recent file query. You won't have to reenter any of the range coordinates or criteria. The 1-2-3 program keeps those specifications in memory.

HANDS-ON EXERCISE A5–9: Extracting and Printing Information from a File

■ Let's use the **Extract** option to pull information out of a file so it can be displayed and printed. For example, extract the names and hours of employees who have worked more than forty hours from the payroll file. First, build a **Criterion Range** consisting of the HOURS field name in cell B9, and the formula (+F3>40) in cell B10. That formula means that you want 1-2-3 to search column F beginning with Cell F3 and identify all records where hours worked are greater than 40. (Use the Text option of the / Range Format command to format the criterion range if you want the formula to be displayed in its cell.)

■ Now build an **Output Range** in some other part of the spreadsheet. You should specify at least the field names of the fields you want extracted from the file. For example, you could build an output range consisting of employee names and hours worked by entering NAME in cell A14 and HOURS in cell B14.

■ Now use the **/ Data Query** command sequence. First, select the Input option and specify the **Input Range** as the entire file (A2 . . . F6). Then select the Output option and specify the **Output Range** as A14 . . . B14. Then select the Criterion Option and specify the **Criterion Range** as B9 . . B10. Now select the **Extract** option. The names and hours of the two employees who worked more than 40 hours should be instantly displayed in the output range. See Figure A5–12.

■ Before you use the **/ Print** command to print the output range on your computer printer you could place an appropriate heading above the output range. For example, enter the heading OVERTIME EMPLOYEES in row thirteen above the output range. Then use the **/ Print Printer** command sequence to print the range (A13 . . . B16) that includes this heading as well as the output range. This simple example demonstrates that 1-2-3 has a limited report generation capability.

Note: you can link criterion ranges in *and/or* relationships. For example, you can combine the female employee and overtime employee criterion ranges into a single range. Entering multiple criteria in the same row of a range establishes an "and" relationship (for example, female *and* overtime employees). Placing criteria in differ-

FIGURE A5–12 File extraction report example

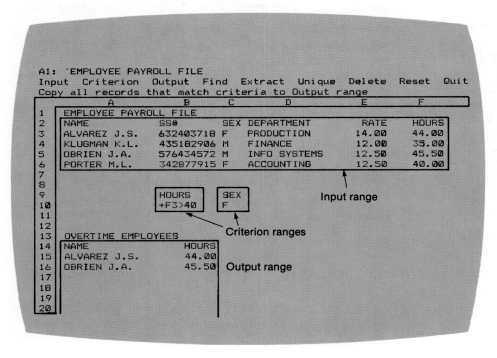

ent rows of a range establishes an "or" relationship (for example, female *or* overtime employees).

Using Graphics Displays

One of the outstanding features of integrated packages is their ability to graph parts of your spreadsheets or files easily and immediately. No separate graphics package is necessary. Once you enter a simple command sequence, your results are displayed instantly. For example, 1-2-3 provides you with the very simple **/ Graph** command sequence. Graphics displays thus become just another method of manipulating and displaying parts of your spreadsheets or files.

HANDS-ON EXERCISE A5–10: Graphing Your Spreadsheets and Files

Let's close our introductory tutorial on integrated packages by graphing parts of the ABC Financial Performance spreadsheet and the Employee Payroll File. It will give you a taste of how easy graphics becomes when using a microcomputer and a package with graphics capabilities.

■ First, let's graph part of the Financial Performance spreadsheet. Retrieve that file from your disk. Now enter the **/ Graphics** command. Select the **Type** option from the Graphics command. Now you must choose one of the following types of graphs from the Type option submenu:

Line   Bar   XY   Stacked-Bar   Pie

■ After you enter your choice, select the **X** option from the graphics command menu. You are then prompted to enter the X-axis range coordinates. Let's decide right now to graph PROFITS AFTER TAXES from 1983, 1984, and 1985. Therefore, enter the range coordinates (B6 . . . D6) in which the headings for each year are displayed on the spreadsheet.

■ Now select the **A** option from the graphics command menu. You are asked to enter the coordinates of the first data range. Enter B16 . . . D16, which are the coordinates of the range that includes the PROFIT AFTER TAXES for each year.

■ Now enter the **View** command and your graph appears instantly on the screen. See Figure A5–13. Which type of graph did you display? Do you want to try another? Its easy. Just press the ESCAPE key, select the **Type** option, choose another type of graph, and enter the **View** command. Presto! you have another type of graphic display. Do you want to add a few sub-titles to your graph to explain what it illustrates? Select the **/ Graph Options Titles** command sequence and key-in graph and axis titles.

■ How about using graphics to help you answer "what-if" questions? It's easy. Press the ESCAPE key until you are back in the READY mode. Change the example spreadsheet any way you want. For example, **what-if** EXPENSES were 70 percent of REVENUE? Change the formula in cell B10 and see how this affects your *bottom line* (PROFIT AFTER TAXES). However, instead of just looking at numbers on a spreadsheet, why not see the change graphically? Just press the **F10** function key (the **Graph** key). Instantly, a graph of the new bottom line appears. Thus, 1-2-3 makes it easy to use graphics to support repetitive "what-if" analysis.

■ Now let's graph part of the Employee Payroll File. Erase the screen and retrieve that file. Use the **/ Graph** command sequence to graph the hours worked by each employee.

FIGURE

A5–13 Bar graph of annual profits after taxes

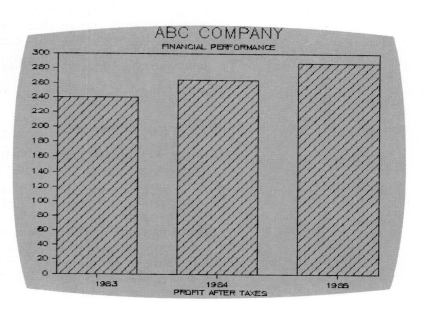

FIGURE

A5–14 Bar graph of hours worked by employees

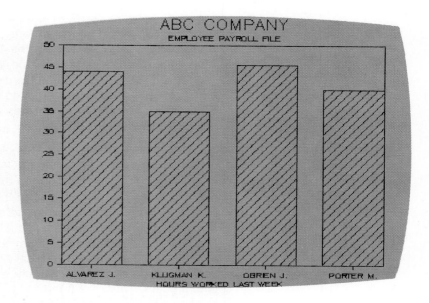

Choose a different type of graph than the ones you used previously. Figure A5–14 shows a bar graph of these results.

■ If you want to save your spreadsheet and file with their current graphics settings, use the **/ File Save** command sequence. However, if you want to prepare a printed copy of your graphs, use the **/ Graph Save** command sequence. You will need to use the special PrintGraph diskette to print a copy of your graphs on a printer that has graphics capabilities.

HANDS-ON ASSIGNMENTS

We have now completed several basic examples of the major functions of an integrated package, using Lotus 1-2-3. We have shown you how this package can be used for spreadsheet analysis, file management, and graphics. There's a lot more to what 1-2-3 and any integrated package can do for you. However, you should feel confident that, with additional practice and use of the user's manual, you will be able to accomplish more advanced applications. Now it's time for you to develop some simple spreadsheets, data files, and graphics displays on your own. That is the purpose of the assignments that follow. Good luck!

A5.1 If you have not already done so, complete the spreadsheet, file management, and graphics exercises as explained in the Hands-On Exercises of this section.

A5.2 Build the Home Budget Example spreadsheet shown in Figure A3–14 of Section Three. Insert the values for January but use the SUM function to create a formula that computes the total expenses from that month. Then use copy commands to create the values for February and March. Use the sum and average functions and copy commands to develop the TOTAL and AVERAGE columns. Compute the PERCENT column by dividing the total for an expense category by the grand total for three months. For example, the percentage for food is $600 divided by $2,190. That could be expressed as a formula like (+E8/E18). Use the / Range Format command and the percent option to round your percent calculations to two decimal places. Store and print this spreadsheet.

A5.3 Build the Payroll Example Spreadsheet shown in Figure A3–15 of Section Three. Key-in employee names, social security numbers, hourly pay rates, total hours worked, and overtime hours worked. However, employee gross pay needs to be calculated by a formula that should be replicated in the rest of that column. *Hint*: (1) before entering employee social security numbers, press the quote key (') so the number is entered as a label, not as a floating point number; (2) if you want to see more of the employee' names on the spreadsheet display, use the /GC command to increase the width of all columns; (3) gross pay should equal hourly rate times hours worked plus overtime pay; (4) overtime pay should equal 1.5 times hourly rate times overtime hours worked.

A5.4 Treat the spreadsheet you developed in A5.3 as a data file. Use the / Data Query, Find, and Extract command sequences to highlight and to print the names of all employees who worked overtime.

A5.5 Create graphics displays of parts of the spreadsheets and data files you developed in previous assignments. For example, develop a pie chart of home budget expense items or a bar graph of employee gross pay. Make changes to entries in these spreadsheets and use graphics to help you perform what-if analysis.

Glossary for Computer Users

The following extensive glossary includes terms which are fundamental to effective understanding and communication between *business computer users* and *computer specialists.* Most definitions used are consistent with those published by several official sources. However, the form of such definitions is *not* designed to express exact standards for computer professionals but to assist the beginning computer user in business.

Two major glossaries are:

- Charles J. and Roger J. Sippl, *Computer Dictionary,* 3d ed. (Indianapolis, Howard W. Sams & Co., 1980).

- Martin H. Weik, *Standard Dictionary of Computers and Information Processing,* 3d ed. (Rochelle Park, N.J.: Hayden Book Co., 1983).

Absolute Address. An address that is permanently assigned by the computer designer to a particular physical storage location.

Access Method. A technique for moving data between primary storage and input/output and secondary storage devices.

Access Time. The time interval between the instant that the CPU requests a transfer of data to or from a storage device and the instant such an operation is completed.

Accumulator. A register in which the results of arithmetic or logic operations are formed.

Acoustic Coupler. A modem which converts digital data into a sequence of tones which are transmitted by a conventional telephone hand set to a receiving modem which transforms the data back to digital form.

Ada. A programming language named after Augusta Ada Byron, considered the world's first computer programmer. Developed in 1980 for the U.S. Department of Defense as a standard high-order language. It resembles an extension of Pascal.

Address. A name, number, or code that identifies a particular location in storage or any other data source or destination.

Address Modification. The process of altering the address portion of a machine instruction.

ADP: Automatic Data Processing. Data processing performed by electronic or electrical machines with a minimum of human assistance or intervention. The term is applied to both electromechanical punched card data processing and electronic data processing.

ALGOL: ALGOrithmic Language. An international procedure-oriented language that is widely used in Europe. Like FORTRAN it was designed primarily for scientific-mathematical applications.

Algorithm. A set of well-defined rules or processes for the solution of a problem in a finite number of steps.

Alphanumeric. Pertaining to a character set that contains letters of the alphabet, numeric digits, and special characters such as punctuation marks. Also called alphameric.

Analog Computer. A computer that operates on data by measuring changes in continuous physical variables, such as voltage, resistance, and rotation. Contrast with Digital Computer.

APL: A Programming Language. A mathematically oriented language originated by Kenneth E. Iverson of IBM. Real-time and interactive versions of APL are being utilized in many time-sharing systems.

Application Development System. A system of computer programs that provides interactive assistance to programmers in the development of application programs.

Application Generator. A software package that supports the development of an application through an interactive terminal dialogue, where the programmer/analyst defines screens, reports, computations, and data structures using a high level language.

Application Software. Programs which specify the information processing activities required for the completion of specific tasks of computer users. Examples are electronic spreadsheet and word processing programs or inventory or payroll programs.

Arithmetic-Logic Unit (ALU). The unit of a computing system containing the circuits that perform arithmetic and logical operations.

Array. An arrangement of elements in one or more dimensions.

Artificial Intelligence (AI). An area of computer science attempting to develop computers that can hear, walk, talk, feel and think. A major thrust is the development of computer functions normally associated with human intelligence, such as reasoning, inference, learning, and problem solving.

ASCII: American Standard Code for Information Interchange. A standard code used for information interchange among data processing systems, communication systems, and associated equipment. The coded character set consists of seven-bit coded characters (eight-bits including a parity check bit.)

Assemble. To translate a symbolic language program into a machine language program by substituting absolute operation codes for symbolic operation codes and absolute or relocatable addresses for symbolic addresses.

Assembler. A computer program that assembles.

Assembler Language. A programming language that utilizes symbols to represent operation codes and storage locations. Also called a symbolic language.

Associative Storage. A storage device in which storage locations are identified by their contents, not by names or positions.

Asynchronous. Involving a sequence of operations without a regular or predictable time relationship. Thus, operations do not happen at regular timed intervals, but an operation will begin only after a previous operation is completed. In data transmission, involves the use of start and stop bits with each character to indicate the beginning and end of the character being transmitted.

Audio-Response Unit. An output device of a computer system whose output consists of the spoken word. Also called a voice synthesizer.

Audit Trail. The presence of data processing media and procedures which allow a transaction to be traced through all stages of data processing, beginning with its appearance on a source document and ending with its transformation into information on a final output document.

Automated Office Systems. Automated systems which combine word processing, data processing, telecommunications, and information systems technologies which automate much office activity. Also called electronic office or office-of-the-future systems.

Automatic Teller Machine (ATM). A special purpose intelligent terminal used to provide remote banking services.

Automation. The automatic transfer and positioning of work by machines or the automatic operation and control of a work process by machines, i.e., without significant human intervention or operation.

Auxiliary Operation. An offline operation performed by equipment not under control of the central processing unit.

Auxiliary Storage. Storage that supplements the primary storage of the computer. Same as Secondary Storage.

Backend Processor. Typically a smaller general-purpose computer that is dedicated to database processing using a database management system (DBMS). Also called a database machine.

Background Processing. The automatic execution of lower-priority computer programs when higher-priority programs are not using the resources of the computer system. Contrast with Foreground Processing.

Backup. Standby equipment or procedures for use in the event of failure, damage, or overloading of normally used equipment and facilities.

Bar Codes. Vertical marks or bars placed on merchandise, tags, or packaging which can be sensed and read by optical character reading devices. The width and combination of vertical lines are used to represent data.

Base Address. A given address from which an absolute address is derived by combination with a relative address.

BASIC: Beginners All-Purpose Symbolic Instruction Code. A programming language developed at Dartmouth College which is widely utilized by time-sharing systems.

Batch Processing. A category of data processing in which data is accumulated into "batches" and processed periodically. Contrast with Realtime Processing.

Baud. A unit of measurement used to specify data transmission speeds. It is a unit of signaling speed equal to the number of discrete conditions or signal events per second. In many data communications applications it represents one bit per second.

Binary. Pertaining to a characteristic or property involving a selection, choice, or condition in which there are two possibilities, or pertaining to the number system which utilizes a base of two.

Bit. A contraction of "binary digit" which can have the value of either 0 or 1.

Block. A grouping of contiguous data records or other data elements which are handled as a unit.

Blocking. Combining several data records or other data elements into blocks in order to increase the efficiency of input, output, or storage operations.

Bootstrap. A technique in which the first few instructions of a program are sufficient to bring the rest of itself into the computer from an input device. Contrast with Initial Program Loader (IPL).

Branch. A transfer of control from one instruction to another in a computer program that is not part of the normal sequential execution of the instructions of the program.

Bubble Memory. See Magnetic Bubble Memory.

Buffer. Temporary storage used to compensate for a difference in rate of flow of data or time of occurrence of events when transmitting data from one device to another.

Bug. A mistake or malfunction.

Bundling. The inclusion of software, maintenance, training, and other EDP products or services in the price of a computer system.

Bus. A set of conducting paths for movement of data and instructions which interconnects the various components of the CPU. It may take the form of a cable containing many wires or of microscopic conducting lines on a microcomputer chip.

Business Data Processing. Use of automatic data processing in accounting or management.

Business Information System. Information systems within a business organization that support one of the traditional "functions of business," such as marketing, finance, or production. Business information systems can be either operational or management information systems.

Byte. A sequence of adjacent binary digits operated upon as a unit and usually shorter than a computer word. In many computer systems, a byte is a grouping of eight bits which can represent one alphabetic or special character or be "packed" with two decimal digits.

C. A low-level structured language developed by AT&T-Bell Laboratories as part of the UNIX operating system. It resembles a machine-independent assembler language and is presently popular for system software programming.

Cache Memory. A high-speed temporary storage area in the CPU for storing parts of a program or data during processing.

CAD: Computer-Assisted Design. The use of computers and advanced graphics hardware and software to provide interactive design assistance for engineering and architectural design.

Calculator. A data processing device suitable for performing arithmetical operations which requires frequent intervention by a human operator.

Call. To transfer control to a subroutine.

CAM: Computer-Aided Manufacturing. The use of minicomputers and other computers to automate the operational systems of a manufacturing plant.

Cathode Ray Tube (CRT). An electronic vacuum tube (television screen) which displays the output of a computer system.

Central Processing Unit (CPU). The unit of a computer system that includes the circuits which control the interpretation and execution of instructions. In many computer systems, the CPU includes the arithmetic-logic unit, the control unit, and primary storage unit. The CPU is also known as the central processor or the mainframe.

Cellular Radio. A radio communications technology which divides a metropolitan area into a honeycomb of cells to greatly increase the number of frequencies and thus the users that can take advantage of mobile phone service.

Chain. A list of data records which are linked by means of pointers. Though the data records may be physically dispersed, each record contains an identifier by which the next record can be located.

Chaining. The use of a pointer in a record to indicate the address of another record that is logically related to the first.

Channel. A path along which signals can be sent. More specifically, a small special-purpose processor that controls the movement of data between the CPU and input/output devices.

Character Printers. Slow-speed printers that print serially (one character at a time) as typewriters do.

Charge-Coupled Device (CCD). A slower serial access form of semiconductor memory, which uses a silicone crystal's own structure to store data.

Check Bit. A binary check digit; for example, a parity bit.

Check Digit. A digit in a data field which is utilized to check for errors or loss of characters in the data field as a result of data transfer operations.

Check Point. A place in a program where a check or a recording of data for restart purposes is performed.

Clock. (1) A device that generates periodic signals

utilized to control the timing of a synchronous computer. (2) A register whose content changes at regular intervals in such a way as to measure time.

COBOL: COmmon Business Oriented Language. A business data processing language.

CODASYL: COnference on DAta SYstems Languages. The group of representatives of users and computer manufacturers who developed and maintain the COBOL language.

Coding. Developing the programming language instructions which direct a computer to perform a data processing assignment.

Collate. To combine items from two or more ordered sets into one set having a specified order not necessarily the same as any of the original sets.

Communications Carrier. An organization that supplies communications services to other organizations and to the public as authorized by government agencies.

Communications Channel. The part of a communications system that connects the message source with the message receiver. It includes the physical equipment used to connect one location to another for the purpose of transmitting and receiving information. Frequently used as a synonym for communications link or communications line.

Communications Control Program. A computer program that controls and supports the communications between the computers and terminals in a data communications network.

Communications Controller. A data communications interface device (frequently a special-purpose mini or microcomputer) which can control a data communications network containing many terminals.

Communications Monitors. Computer programs which control and support the communications between the computers and terminals in a data communications network.

Communications Processors. Multiplexers, concentrators, communications controllers, and cluster controllers that allow a communications channel to carry simultaneous data transmissions from many terminals and also may perform error monitoring, diagnostics, and correction, modulation-demodulation, data compression, data coding and decoding, message switching, port contention, buffer storage, and serving as an interface to satellite and other advanced communications networks.

Communications Satellite. Earth satellites placed in stationary orbits above the equator which serve as relay stations for communications signals transmitted from earth stations.

Compile. To translate a high-level programming language into a machine-language program.

Compiler. A program that compiles.

Computer. (1) A data processing device that can perform substantial computation, including numerous arithmetic or logic operations without intervention by a human operator during the processing. (2) An electronic device that has the ability to accept data, internally store, and execute a program of instructions, perform mathematical, logical, and manipulative operations on data, and report the results.

Computer-Aided Design (CAD). The use of computers and advanced graphics hardware and software to provide interactive design assistance for engineering and architectural design.

Computer-Aided Manufacturing (CAM). The use of minicomputers and other computers to automate the operational systems of a manufacturing plant.

Computer Application. The use of a computer to solve a specific problem or to accomplish a particular job for a computer user. For example, common business computer applications include sales order processing, inventory control, and payroll.

Computer-Assisted Data Entry. Methods and devices that use the computer itself to assist a user or data entry operator while performing the data input function.

Computer-Assisted Instruction (CAI). The use of computers to provide drills, practice exercises, and tutorial sequences to students.

Computer-Assisted Programming. A computer user or programmer can design and code the processing logic of a computer program with substantial realtime assistance from a computer system. This involves using a microcomputer or computer terminal to code, translate, test, debug, and develop alternatives for a new program in a realtime interactive process.

Computer-Based Information System. A system which uses the computer hardware, software people, and data resources of electronic information processing systems to collect, transform and transmit information in an organization.

Computer Industry. The industry composed of firms which supply computer hardware, software, and EDP services.

Computer Program. A series of instructions or statements, in a form acceptable to a computer, prepared in order to achieve a certain result.

Computer Specialist. A person whose occupation is related to the providing of computer services in computer-using organizations or in the computer industry, for example, a systems analyst, programmer, or computer operator.

Computer System. Computer hardware and software as a system of input, processing, output, storage, and control components. Thus, a computer system consists of input and output devices, primary and secondary storage devices, the central processing unit, and the control units within the CPU and other peripheral devices. Computer software can also be considered as a system of programs concerned with input/output, storage, processing, and control.

Computer User. Anyone who uses a computer system or its output. Same as end user.

Concentrator. A special-purpose mini or microcomputer that accepts information from many terminals using slow-speed lines and transmits data to a main computer system over a high-speed line.

Conditional Transfer. A transfer of control in the execution of a computer program that occurs if specified criteria are met.

Console. That part of a computer used for communication between the operator and the computer.

Control. (1) The systems component that evaluates "feedback" to determine whether the system is moving toward the achievement of its goal and then makes any necessary adjustments to the input and processing components of the system to ensure that proper output is produced. (2) Sometimes synonymous with feedback-control. (3) A management function that involves observing and measuring organizational performance and environmental activities and modifying the plans and activities of the organization when necessary.

Control Card. A punched card that contains input data required for a specific application of a general routine. For example, "job control cards" are a series of cards coded in "job control language" (JCL), which directs an operating system to load and begin execution of a particular program.

Control Program. A program that assists in controlling the operations and managing the resources of a computer system. It is usually part of an operating system.

Control Unit. A subunit of the central processing unit that controls and directs the operations of the entire computer system. The control unit retrieves computer instructions in proper sequence, interprets each instruction, and then directs the other parts of the computer system in the implementation of a computer program.

Conversational Computing. A type of real-time processing involving frequent man-machine interaction. A dialogue occurs between a computer and a user, in which the computer directs questions and comments to the user in response to the questions, comments, and other input supplied by the user.

Counter. A device such as a register or storage location used to represent the number of occurrences of an event.

Cryogenics. The study and use of devices utilizing the properties of materials near absolute zero in temperature. The superconductive nature of such materials provide ultrahigh-speed computer logic and memory circuits.

Cursor. A movable point of light displayed on most video display screens to assist the user in the input of data. The cursor may look like a dot, short underline, or other shape that indicates the position of data to be entered or changed.

Cybernetic System. A system that uses feedback and control components to achieve a self-monitoring and self-regulating capability.

Cylinder. An imaginary vertical cylinder consisting of the vertical alignment of data tracks on each surface of magnetic disks, which are accessed simultaneously by the read/write heads of a disk storage device.

Data. A representation of facts, concepts, or instructions in a formalized manner suitable for communication, interpretation, or processing by humans or machines.

Data Bank. (1) A comprehensive collection of libraries of data utilized by an organization. (2) A centralized common database that supports several major information systems of an organization.

Database. A nonredundant collection of logically related records or files. A database consolidates many records previously stored in separate files so that a common pool of data records serves as a single central file or data bank for many data processing applications.

Database Management System (DBMS). A generalized set of computer programs that controls the creation, maintenance, and utilization of the databases and data files of an organization.

Database Processing System. An electronic data processing system that uses a common database for both the storage and processing of data.

Data Communications. Pertaining to the transmitting of data over electronic communication links between a computer system and a number of terminals at some physical distance away from the computer.

Data Communications System. An electronic data processing system that combines the capabilities of the computer with high-speed electrical and electronic communications.

Data Entry. The process of converting data into a form suitable for entry into a computer system. Also called data capture or input preparation.

Data Management. Control program functions that provide access to data sets, enforce data storage conventions, and regulate the use of input/output devices.

Data Medium. The material in or on which a specific physical variable may represent data.

Data Processing. The execution of a systematic sequence of operations performed upon data.

Data Processing System. A system that accepts data as input and processes it into information as output.

Debug. To detect, locate, and remove errors from a program or malfunctions from a computer.

Decision Support System (DSS). An information system that utilizes decision rules, decision models, a comprehensive data base, and a decision maker's own insights in an interactive computer-based process, leading to a specific decision by a specific decision maker.

Decision Table. A table of all contingencies that are to be considered in the description of a problem, together with the actions to be taken.

Dedicated Computer. Typically, a general-purpose computer that has been "dedicated," or committed, to a particular data processing task or application.

Diagnostics. Messages transmitted by a computer during language translation or program execution that pertain to the diagnosis or identification of errors in a program or malfunctions in equipment.

Digital Computer. A computer that operates on digital data by performing arithmetic and logical operations on the data. Contrast with Analog Computer.

Digitizer. A device that is used to convert drawings and other graphic images on paper or other materials into digital data which is entered into a computer system.

Direct Access. A method of storage where each storage position has a unique address and can be individually accessed in approximately the same period of time without having to search through other storage positions.

Direct Access Storage Device (DASD). A storage device that can directly access data to be stored or retrieved, for example, a magnetic disk unit.

Direct Address. An address that specifies the storage location of an operand.

Direct Input/Output. Devices such as terminals that allow data to be input into a computer system or output from the computer system without the use of machine-readable media.

Direct Memory Access (DMA). A type of computer architecture in which intelligent components other than the CPU (such as a channel) can directly access data in main memory.

Disk Pack. A removable unit containing several magnetic disks which can be mounted on a magnetic disk storage unit.

Display. A visual presentation of data.

Distributed Databases. The concept of distributing databases or portions of a database at remote sites where the data is most frequently referenced. Sharing of data is made possible through a network which interconnects the distributed databases.

Distributed Processing. Also called distributed data processing (DDP). A major form of decentralization of information processing made possible by a network of computers dispersed throughout an organization. Processing of user applications is accomplished by several computers interconnected by a data communication network rather than relying on one large centralized computer facility or on the decentralized operation of several completely independent computers.

Distributed Processing Network. A network of computers and intelligent terminals distributed throughout an organization. Basic network structures include the *star network,* in which end user computers are tied to a large central computer, and the *ring network,* where local computers are tied together on a more equal basis.

Document. A medium on which data has been recorded for human use, such as a report or invoice.

Documentation. A collection of documents or information which describes a computer program, information system, or required data processing operations.

Double Precision. Pertaining to the use of two computer words to represent a number.

Down Time. The time interval during which a device is malfunctioning or inoperative.

Dump. To copy the contents of all or part of a storage device, usually from an internal device onto an external storage device.

Duplex. In communications, pertaining to a simultaneous two-way independent transmission in both directions.

Duplicate. To copy so that the result remains in the same physical form as the source. For example, to make a new punched card with the same pattern of holes as an original punched card.

Dynamic Relocation. The movement of part or all of an active computer program and data from one part or type of storage to another without interrupting the proper execution of the program.

EBCDIC: Extended Binary Coded Decimal Interchange Code. An eight-bit code that is widely used by current computers.

Echo Check. A method of checking the accuracy of transmission of data in which the received data are returned to the sending device for comparison with the original data.

Edit. To modify the form or format of data, for example, to insert or delete characters such as page numbers or decimal points.

Effective Address. The address that is derived by applying indexing or indirect addressing rules to a specified address to form an address that is actually used to identify the current operand.

EFT: Electronic Funds Transfer. The development of banking and payment systems that transfer funds electronically instead of using cash or paper documents such as checks.

Electromechanical Data Processing. The use of electromechanical devices such as typewriters and calculators to process data into information.

Electronic Data Processing (EDP). The use of electronic computers to process data automatically.

Electronic Information Processing. Also widely known as electronic data processing or EDP. The use of electronic computers to process information automatically. Human intervention in the processing cycle is not necessary since an electronic computer can automatically execute a stored program of processing instructions.

Electronic Mail. The transmission, storage, and distribution of text material in electronic form over communications networks.

Electronic Mouse. A small device which is electronically connected to a computer and which is moved by hand on a flat surface in order to move the cursor on a video screen in the same direction. Buttons on the mouse allow users to issue commands and make responses or selections.

Electronic Spreadsheet Package. An application program used as a computerized tool for analysis, planning, and modeling which allows users to enter and manipulate data into an electronic worksheet of rows and columns.

Emulation. To imitate one system with another so that the imitating system accepts the same data, executes the same programs, and achieves the same results as the imitated system. Contrast with Simulation.

Encription. To scramble data or convert it, prior to transmission, to a secret code that masks the meaning of the data to unauthorized recipients. Similar to enciphering.

End User. See Computer User.

Enterprise System. An integrated system that merges electronic data processing, word processing, automated office systems, telecommunication systems, management information systems, and other computer-based information systems that support the modern organization or enterprise.

Ergonomics. The science and technology emphasizing the safety, comfort, and ease of use of human-operated machines, such as computers. The goal of ergonomics is to produce systems that are user friendly, i.e., safe, comfortable, and easy to use. Ergonomics is frequently called human factors engineering.

Executive Routine. A routine that controls the execution of other routines. Synonymous with supervisory routine.

Expert System. A computer-based information system which uses its knowledge about a specific complex application area to act as an expert consultant to users. The system consists of a knowledge base and software modules that perform inferences on the knowledge and communicate answers to a user's questions.

Facilities Management. The use of an external service organization to operate and manage the electronic data processing facilities of an organization.

Facsimile. The transmission of images and their reconstruction and duplication on some form of paper at a receiving station.

Feedback. (1) Information concerning the components and operations of a system. (2) The use of part of the output of a system as input to the system.

Feasibility Study. Part of the process of systems development which determines the information needs of prospective users and the objectives, constraints, basic resource requirements, cost/benefits, and feasibility of proposed projects.

Feedback-Control. A systems characteristic that combines the functions of feedback and control. Information concerning the components and operations of a system (feedback) is evaluated to determine whether the system is moving toward the achievement of its goal, with any necessary adjustments being made to the system to ensure that proper output is produced (control).

Fiber Optics. The technology that uses cables consisting of very thin filaments of glass fibers that can conduct the light generated by lasers at transmission frequencies that approach the speed of light.

Field. A subdivision of a data record that consists of a grouping of characters which describe a particular category of data, for example, a "name field" or a "sales amount field." Sometimes also called an item or word.

Fifth-Generation Computer. A new type of computer that would be able to see, hear, talk, and think. This would depend on major advances in computer processing speed and flexibility, user input/output methods, and artificial intelligence.

File. A collection of related data records treated as a unit. Sometimes called a data set.

File Label. A unique name or code that identifies a file.

File Maintenance. The activity of keeping a file up-to-date by adding, changing, or deleting data.

File Processing. Utilizing a file for data processing activities such as file maintenance, information retrieval, or report generation.

Firmware. The use of microprogrammed read-only memory modules in place of "hardwired" logic circuitry. See also Microprogramming.

Fixed-Length Record. A data record that always contains the same number of characters or fields. Contrast with Variable-Length Record.

Fixed-Point. Pertaining to a positional representation in which each number is represented by a single set of digits, the position of the radix point being fixed with respect to one end of the set, according to some convention. Contrast with Floating-Point.

Fixed Word-Length. Pertaining to a computer word or operand that always has the same number of bits or characters. Contrast with Variable Word-Length.

Flag. Any of various types of indicators used for identification.

Flip-Flop. A circuit or device containing active elements, capable of assuming either one or two states at a given time. Synonymous with toggle.

Floating-Point. Pertaining to a number representation system in which each number is represented by two sets of digits. One set represents the significant digits or fixed-point "base" of the number, while the other set of digits represents the "exponent," which indicates the precision of the radix point.

Floppy Disk. A small plastic disk coated with iron oxide which resembles a small phonograph record enclosed in a protective envelope. It is a widely used form of magnetic disk media which provides a direct access storage capability for microcomputer and minicomputer systems.

Flowchart. A graphical representation in which symbols are used to represent operations, data, flow, logic, equipment, etc. A "program flowchart" illustrates the structure and sequence of operations of a program, while a "system flowchart" illustrates the components and flows of data processing or information systems.

Foreground Processing. The automatic execution of the computer programs that have been designed to preempt the use of the computing facilities. Contrast with Background Processing.

Format. The arrangement of data.

FORTRAN: FORmula TRANslator. A high-level procedure-oriented programming language widely utilized to develop computer programs that perform mathematical computations for scientific, engineering, and selected business applications.

Fourth Generation Languages (4GL). Programming languages that are easier to use than high-level languages like BASIC, COBOL, or FORTRAN. They are also known as nonprocedural, natural or very high level languages.

Front-End Processor. Typically a smaller general-purpose computer that is dedicated to handling data communications control functions in a communications network, thus relieving the host computer of these functions.

Function. A specific purpose of an entity or its characteristic action.

General-Purpose Application Programs. Programs which can perform common information processing jobs for users from all application areas. For example, word processing programs, electronic spreadsheet programs, and graphics programs can be used by individuals for home, education, business, scientific and many other purposes.

General-Purpose Computer. A computer that is designed to handle a wide variety of problems. Contrast with Special-Purpose Computer.

Generate. To produce a machine-language program by selecting from among various alternative subsets of coding the subset that embodies the most suitable methods for performing a specific data processing task based upon parameters supplied by a programmer or user.

Generator. A computer program that performs a generating function.

Gigabyte. One billion bytes. More accurately, 2 to the 30th power, or 1,073,741,824 in decimal notation.

GIGO. A contraction of "Garbage In, Garbage Out," which emphasizes that data processing systems will produce erroneous and invalid output when provided with erroneous and invalid input data or instructions.

Graphics. Pertaining to symbolic input or output from a computer system, such as lines, curves, and geometric shapes, using video display units or graphic plotters and printers.

Handshaking. Exchange of predetermined signals when a connection is established between two communications terminals.

Hard Copy. A data medium or data record that has a degree of permanence and that can be read by man or machine. Similar to Document.

Hardware. Physical equipment, as opposed to the computer program or method of use, such as mechanical, magnetic, electrical, or electronic devices. Contrast with Software.

Hash Total. The sum of the numbers in a data field which is not normally added, such as account numbers or other identification numbers. It is utilized as a "control total," especially during input/output operations of batch processing systems.

Header Card. A card that contains information related to the data in cards that follow.

Header Label. A machine-readable record at the beginning of a file containing data for file identification and control.

Heuristic. Pertaining to exploratory methods of problem solving in which solutions are discovered by evaluation of the progress made toward the final result. It is an exploratory trial-and-error approach guided by rules of thumb. Contrast with Algorithmic.

Hexadecimal. Pertaining to the number system with a radix of 16. Synonymous with sexadecimal.

High-Level Language. A programming language that utilizes macro instructions and statements that closely resemble human language or mathematical notation to describe the problem to be solved or the procedure to be used. Also called a compiler language.

HIPO Chart (Hierarchy + Input/Processing/Output). Also known as an IPO Chart. A design and documentation tool of structured programming utilized to record input/processing/output details of the hierarchical program modules.

Hollerith. Pertaining to a particular type of code or punched card utilizing 12 rows per column and usually 80 columns per card. Named after Herman Hollerith, who originated punched card data processing.

Host Computer. Typically a larger central computer that performs the major data processing tasks in a computer network.

Hybrid Computer. A computer for data processing which utilizes both analog and digital representation of data.

Icon. A small figure on a video display that looks like a familiar office or other device, such as a file folder (for storing a file), a wastebasket (for deleting a file), or a calculator (for switching to a calculator mode).

Impact Printers. Printers that form images on paper through the pressing of a printing element and an inked ribbon or roller against the face of a sheet of paper.

Index. An ordered reference list of the contents of a file or document together with keys or reference notations for identification or location of those contents.

Index Register. A register whose contents may be added to or subtracted from the operand address prior to or during the execution of a computer instruction.

Index Sequential. A method of data organization in which records are organized in sequential order and also referenced by an index. When utilized with direct access file devices, it is known as index sequential access method or ISAM.

Indexing. The use of index registers for address modification in stored-program computers.

Information. (1) Data that has been transformed into a meaningful and useful form for specific human beings. (2) The meaning that a human assigns to data by means of the known conventions used in their representation.

Information Center. A support facility for the computer users of an organization. It allows users to develop their own application programs and to accomplish their own information processing tasks. The users are provided with hardware support, software support (in the form of 4GL), and people support (trained user consultants).

Information Processing. A concept that covers both the traditional concept of processing numeric and alphabetic data, and the processing of text, images, and voices. It emphasizes that the production of information products for users should be the focus of processing activities.

Information Processing System. A system of input, processing, output, storage, and control functions that transform data resources into information products using hardware, software, and people as resources.

Information Resource Management (IRM). A management concept that views data, information, and computer resources (computer hardware, software, and personnel) as valuable organizational resources which should be efficiently, economically, and effectively managed for the benefit of the entire organization.

Information Retrieval. The methods and procedures for recovering specific information from stored data.

Information System. A system which uses personnel, operating procedures, and data processing subsystems to collect and process data and disseminate information in an organization.

Information Theory. The branch of learning concerned with the likelihood of accurate transmission or communication of messages subject to transmission failure, distortion, and noise.

Initialize. To set counters, switches, addresses, and variables to zero or other starting values at the beginning of or at prescribed points in a computer program.

Input. Pertaining to a device, process, or channel involved in the insertion of data into a data processing system. Opposite of output.

Input/Output (I/O). Pertaining to either input or output, or both.

Input/Output Control System (IOCS). Programs which control the flow of data into and out of the computer system.

Input/Output Interface Hardware. Devices such as I/O ports, I/O busses, buffers, channels, and input/output control units, which assist the CPU in its input/output assignments. These devices make it possible for modern computer systems to perform input, output, and processing functions simultaneously.

Inquiry. A request for information from a computer system.

Installation. (1) The process of installing new computer hardware or software. (2) A data processing facility such as a computer installation.

Instruction. A grouping of characters that specifies the computer operation to be performed and the values or locations of its operands.

Instruction Cycle. The phase in the execution of a computer instruction during which the instruction is called from storage and the required circuitry to perform the instruction is readied.

Integer. A whole number as opposed to a real number which has fractional parts.

Integrated Circuit. A complex microelectronic circuit consisting of interconnected circuit elements that cannot be disassembled because they are placed on or within a "continuous substrate" such as a silicon chip.

Integrated Packages. Software that combines the ability to do several general-purpose applications (such as word processing, electronic spreadsheet, and graphics) into one program.

Intelligent Terminal. A terminal with the capabilities of a microcomputer or minicomputer, which can thus perform many data processing and other functions without accessing a larger computer.

Interactive Processing. A type of realtime processing in which users at online terminals can interact with the computer on a realtime basis. This may take the form of inquiry/response, conversational computing, online data entry, or interactive programming.

Interactive Program. A computer program that permits data to be entered or the flow of the program to be changed during its execution.

Interactive Programming. Designing and coding the processing logic of a computer program with substantial realtime assistance from a computer system. Interactive programming has become feasible through the use of software tools, such as application development systems, that provide interactive assistance to programmers in their development of application programs.

Interface. A shared boundary, such as the boundary between two systems, for example, the boundary between a computer and its peripheral devices.

Interpreter. A computer program that translates and executes each source language statement before translating and executing the next one.

Interrupt. A condition that causes an interruption in a data processing operation during which another data processing task is performed. At the conclusion of this new data processing assignment, control may be transferred back to the point where the original data processing operation was interrupted or to other tasks with a higher priority.

Inverted File. A method of data organization in which a data element identifies a record in a file instead of the original identifier or key.

Iterative. Pertaining to the repeated execution of a series of steps.

Job. A specified group of tasks prescribed as a unit of work for a computer.

Job Control Cards. See Control Card.

Job Control Language (JCL). A language for communicating with the operating system of a computer to identify a job and describe its requirements.

Justify. (1) To adjust the printing positions of characters toward the left- or right-hand margins of a data field or page. (2) To shift the contents of a storage position so that the most or the least significant digit is at some specified position.

K. An abbreviation for the prefix "kilo," which is 1,000 in decimal notation. When referring to storage capacity it is equivalent to 2 to the 10th power, or 1,024 in decimal notation.

Key. One or more characters within an item of data that are used to identify it or control its use.

Keyboarding. Using the keyboard of a typewriter, word processor, or computer terminal.

Keypunch. (1) A keyboard-actuated device that punches holes in a card to represent data. Also called a card-punch. (2) The act of using a keypunch to record data in a punched card.

Key-to-Disk. Data entry using a keyboard device to record data directly onto a magnetic disk.

Key-to-Tape. Data entry using a keyboard device to record data directly onto magnetic tape.

Label. One or more characters used to identify a statement or an item of data in a computer program or the contents of the data file.

Language. A set of representations, conventions, and rules used to convey information.

Language Translator Program. A program that can convert the programming-language instructions of computer programs into machine-language instructions. Also called language processors. Major types include assemblers, compilers, and interpreters.

Large-Scale Integration (LSI). A method of constructing electronic circuits in which thousands of circuits can be placed on a single semiconductor chip.

Library. A collection of related files or programs.

Library Routine. A proven routine that is maintained in a program library.

Light Pen. A photoelectronic device that allows data to be entered or altered on the face of a video display terminal.

Line Printer. A device that prints all characters of a line as a unit. Contrast with Character Printer.

Linear Programming. In operations research, a procedure for locating the maximum or minimum of a linear function of variables that are subject to linear constraints.

Linkage. In programming, the coding that connects two separately coded routines.

Liquid Crystal Displays (LCDs). Electronic visual displays that form characters by applying an electrical charge to selected silicon crystals.

List. (1) An ordered set of items. (2) A method of data organization that uses indexes and pointers to allow for nonsequential retrieval.

List Processing. A method of processing data in the form of lists.

Load. In programming, to enter data into storage or working registers.

Local. Connected to a computer by regular electrical wires. In close proximity to a computer. Contrast to remote access.

Local Area Network (LAN). A communications network which typically uses coaxial cable to connect computers, word processors, terminals, and electronic copying machines and dictation systems within a limited physical area such as an office building, manufacturing plant, or other worksite.

Location. Any place in which data may be stored.

Log. A record of the operations of a data processing system.

Logical Data Elements. Data elements that are independent of the physical data media on which they are recorded.

LOGO. An interactive graphical language used as a tool for learning a variety of concepts (color, direction, letters, words, sounds, etc.) as well as learning to program and use the computer. Forms and figures are used (sprites and turtles) which a child learns to move around on the screen to accomplish tasks.

Loop. A sequence of instructions in a computer program that is executed repeatedly until a terminal condition prevails.

Machine Cycle. The timing of a basic CPU operation as determined by a fixed number of electrical pulses emitted by the CPU's timing circuitry or internal clock.

Machine Instruction. An instruction that a computer can recognize and execute.

Machine Language. A programming language where instructions are expressed in the binary code of the computer.

Macro Instruction. An instruction in a source language that is equivalent to a specified sequence of machine instructions.

Mag Stripe Card. A plastic wallet-size card with a strip of magnetic tape on one surface; widely used for bank credit cards.

Magnetic Bubble. An electromagnetic storage device that stores and moves data magnetically as tiny magnetic spots, which look like bubbles under a microscope as they float on the surface of a special type of semiconductor chip.

Magnetic Card. A card with a magnetic surface on which data can be stored.

Magnetic Core. Tiny rings composed of iron oxide and other materials strung on wires that provide electrical current that magnetizes the cores. Data is represented by the direction of the magnetic field of groups of cores. Widely used as the primary storage media in second- and third-generation computer systems.

Magnetic Disk. A flat circular plate with a magnetic surface on which data can be stored by selective magnetization of portions of the flat surface.

Magnetic Drum. A circular cylinder with a magnetic surface on which data can be stored by selective magnetization of portions of the curved surface.

Magnetic Ink. An ink that contains particles of iron oxide which can be magnetized and detected by magnetic sensors.

Magnetic Ink Character Recognition (MICR). The machine recognition of characters printed with magnetic ink. Contrast with Optical Character Recognition.

Magnetic Tape. A tape with a magnetic surface on which data can be stored by selective magnetization of portions of the surface.

Mainframe. (1) Same as central processing unit. (2) A larger size computer system, typically with a separate central processing unit, as distinguished from microcomputer and minicomputer systems.

Management Information System (MIS). An information system that provides the information needed to support management functions.

Manual Data Processing. (1) Data processing requiring continual human operation and intervention, which utilizes simple data processing tools, such as paper forms, pencils, and filing cabinets. (2) All data processing that is not automatic, even if it utilizes machines, such as typewriters, adding machines, and calculators.

Mark-Sensing. The electrical sensing of manually recorded conductive marks on a nonconductive surface.

Mass Storage. (1) Devices having a large storage capacity, such as magnetic disks or drums. (2) Secondary storage devices with extra large storage capacities (in the hundreds of millions of bytes) such as magnetic strip and card units.

Master File. A data file containing relatively permanent information, which is utilized as an authoritative reference and is usually updated periodically. Contrast with Transaction File.

Mathematical Model. A mathematical representation of a process, device, or concept.

Matrix. A two-dimensional rectangular array of quantities.

Megabyte. One million bytes. More accurately, 2 to the 20th power, or 1,048,576 in decimal notation.

Memory. Same as Storage.

Menu. A displayed list of items (usually the names of data processing jobs) from which a video terminal operator makes a selection.

Menu Driven. A characteristic of most interactive processing systems which provide menu displays and operator prompting which assist a video terminal operator in performing a particular job.

Merge. To combine items from two or more similarly ordered sets into one set that is arranged in the same order.

Message. An arbitrary amount of information whose beginning and end are defined or implied.

Microcomputer. A very small computer, ranging in size from a "computer on a chip" to a small typewriter-size unit.

Micrographics. The use of microfilm, microfiche, and other microforms to record data in greatly reduced form. The use of computers in the field of micrographics involves computer output microfilm, or COM, in which microfilm is used as a computer output medium; computer input microfilm, or CIM, where microfilm is used as an input medium; or computer-assisted retrieval or CAR, in which special-purpose computer terminals or minicomputers are used as micrographics terminals to locate and retrieve a document stored on microfilm.

Microprocessor (MPU). A microcomputer central processing unit (CPU) on a chip and without input/output or primary storage capabilities in most types.

Microprogram. A small set of elementary control instructions called microinstructions or microcodes.

Microprogramming. The use of special software (microprograms) to perform the functions of special hardware (electronic control circuitry). Microprograms stored in a read-only storage module of the control unit interpret the machine-language instructions of a computer program and decode them into elementary microinstructions, which are then executed.

Minicomputer. A small (for example, desktop size) electronic, digital, stored-program, general purpose computer.

Mnemonic. The use of symbols which are chosen to assist the human memory, which are typically abbreviations or contractions, such as "MPY" for multiply.

Modem: MOdulator-DEModulator. A device converts the digital signals from input/output devices into appropriate frequencies at a transmission terminal and converts them back into digital signals at a receiving terminal.

Module. A unit of hardware or software that is discrete and identifiable and designed for use with other units.

Monitor. Software or hardware that observes, supervises, controls, or verifies the operations of a system.

Multiplex. To interleave or simultaneously transmit two or more messages on a single channel.

Multiplexor. An electronic device that allows a single communications channel to carry simultaneous data transmission from many terminals by dividing a higher-speed channel into multiple slow-speed channels.

Multiprocessing. Pertaining to the simultaneous execution of two or more instructions by a computer or computer network.

Multiprocessor Computer System. Computer systems that use a multiprocessor architecture in the design of their central processing units. Instead of having one CPU with a single control unit, arithmetic-logic unit, and primary storage unit (called a uniprocessor design), the CPU of a multiprocessor computer contains several types of processing units, such as support microprocessors or multiple arithmetic-logic and control units.

Multiprogramming. Pertaining to the concurrent execution of two or more programs by a computer by interleaving their execution.

Multitasking. The concurrent use of the same computer to accomplish several different information processing tasks. Each task may require the use of a different program, or the concurrent use of the same copy of a program by several users.

Nanosecond. One billionth of a second.

Natural Language. A programming language that is very close to human language. Also called very high-level language.

Nest. To embed subroutines or data in other subroutines or data at a different hierarchical level such that the different levels of routines or data can be executed or accessed recursively.

Network. An interconnection of computers, terminals, and communications channels and devices.

Network Architecture. A master plan designed to promote an open, simple, flexible, and efficient data communications environment through the use of standard protocols, standard communications hardware and software interfaces, and the design of a standard multilevel data communications interface between end users and computer systems.

Node. A terminal point in a communications network.

Noise. (1) Random variations of one or more characteristics of any entity such as voltage, current, or data. (2) A random signal of known statistical properties of amplitude, distribution, and special density. (3) Any disturbance tending to interfere with the normal operation of a device or system.

Nonimpact Printers. Printers that use specially treated paper which forms characters by laser, thermal (heat), electrostatic, or electrochemical processes.

Nonprocedural Languages. Programming languages that allow users and professional programmers to specify the results they want without specifying how to solve the problem.

Numeral. A discrete representation of a number.

Numeric. Pertaining to numerals or to representation by means of numerals. Synonymous with numerical.

Numerical Control. Automatic control of a process performed by a device that makes use of all or part of numerical data, generally introduced as the operation is in process.

Object Program. A compiled or assembled program composed of executable machine instructions. Contrast with Source Program.

Octal. Pertaining to the number representation system with a radix of eight.

OEM: Original Equipment Manufacturer A firm that manufactures and sells computers by assembling components produced by other hardware manufacturers.

Offline. Pertaining to equipment or devices not under control of the central processing unit.

Online. Pertaining to equipment or devices under control of the central processing unit.

Operand. That which is operated upon. That part of a computer instruction which is identified by the address part of the instruction.

Operating System. Software that controls the execution of computer programs and that may provide scheduling, debugging, input/output control, accounting, compilation, storage assignment, data management, and related services.

Operation. A defined action, namely, the act of obtaining a result from one or more operands in accordance with rules that specify the result for any permissible combination of operands.

Operation Code. A code that represents specific operations. Synonymous with instruction code.

Operational Information System. An information system that collects, processes, and stores data generated by the operational systems of an organization and produces data and information for input into a management information system or for the control of an operational system.

Operational System. A basic subsystem of the business firm as a system which constitutes its input, processing, and output components. Also called a physical system.

Operations Research (OR). The use of the scientific method to provide criteria for decisions concerning the actions of people, machines, and other resources in a system.

Optical Character Recognition (OCR). The machine identification of printed characters through the use of light-sensitive devices.

Optical Disks A mass storage medium using technology similar to that used for video disks (laser beams used to burn pits on a plastic disk). The disks are currently capable of storing billions of bits.

Optical Scanner. A device that optically scans printed or written data and generates their digital representations.

Output. Pertaining to a device, process, or channel involved with the transfer of data or information out of a data processing system.

Overflow. That portion of the result of an operation that exceeds the capacity of the intended unit of storage.

Overlapped Processing. Pertaining to the ability of a computer system to increase the utilization of its central processing unit by overlapping input/output and processing operations.

Overlay. The technique of repeatedly using the same blocks of internal storage during different stages of a program. When one routine is no longer needed in storage, another routine can replace all or part of it.

Pack. To compress data in a storage medium by taking advantage of known characteristics of the data in such a way that the original data can be recovered.

Packet. A group of data and control information in a specified format that is transferred as an entity.

Packet Switching. A data transmission process that transmits addressed packets such that a channel is occupied only for the duration of transmission of the packet.

Page. A segment of a program or data, usually of fixed length, that has a fixed virtual address but can in fact reside in any region of the internal storage of the computer.

Paging. A process that automatically and continually transfers pages of programs and data between primary storage and direct access storage devices. It provides computers with advanced multiprogramming and virtual memory capabilities.

Parallel. Pertaining to the concurrent or simultaneous occurrence of two or more related activities in multiple devices or channels.

Parity Bit. A check bit appended to an array of binary digits to make the sum of all the binary digits, including the check bit, always odd or always even.

Parity Check. A check that tests whether the number of ones or zeros in an array of binary digits is odd or even.

Pascal. A high-level, general-purpose, structured programming language named after Blaise Pascal. It was developed by Niklaus Wirth of Zurich in 1968.

Pass. One cycle of processing a body of data.

Patch. To modify a routine in a rough or expedient way.

Pattern Recognition. The identification of shapes, forms, or configurations by automatic means.

PCM: Plug Compatible Manufacturer A firm that manufactures computer equipment that can be plugged into existing computer systems without requiring additional hardware or software interfaces.

Peripheral Equipment. In a data processing system, any unit of equipment, distinct from the central processing unit, that may provide the system with outside communication.

Personal Computing. The use of microcomputers by individuals for educational, recreational, home management, and other personal applications.

PERT: Program Evaluation and Review Technique A network analysis technique utilized to find the most efficient scheduling of time and resources when developing a complex project or product.

Physical Data Element. The physical data medium which contains one or more logical data elements. For example, a punched card is a single physical record which may contain several logical records.

Picosecond. One trillionth of a second.

PILOT: Programmed Inquiry, Learning Or Teaching. A special-purpose language designed to develop CAI (computer-aided instruction) programs.

It is a simple interactive language which enables a person with minimal computer experience to develop and test interactive CAI programs.

PL/1: Programming Language 1. A procedure-oriented, high-level, general-purpose programming language designed to combine the features of COBOL, FORTRAN, ALGOL, etc.

Plasma Display. Output devices that generate a visual display with electrically charged particles of gas trapped between glass plates.

Plot. To map or diagram by connecting coordinate values.

Plotter. A hard-copy output device that produces drawings and graphical displays on paper or other materials.

Point-of-Sale (POS) Terminal. A computer terminal used in retail stores that serves the function of a cash register as well as collecting sales data and performing other data processing functions.

Pointer. A data item associated with an index, a record, or other set of data that contains the address of a related record.

Port. (1) Electronic circuitry that provides a connection point between the CPU and input/output devices. (2) A connection point for a communications line on a CPU or other front-end device.

Position. In a string, each location that may be occupied by a character or binary digit and may be identified by a serial number.

Precision. The degree of discrimination with which a quantity is stated.

Private Branch Exchange (PBX). A switching device that serves as an interface between the many telephone lines within a work area and the local telephone company's main telephone lines or trunks. Computerized PBXs can handle the switching of both voice and data in the local area networks that are needed in such locations.

Privileged Instruction. A computer instruction whose use is restricted to the operating system of the computer and is not available for use in ordinary programs.

Problem-Oriented Language. A programming language designed for the convenient expression of a given class of problems.

Procedures. Sets of instructions used by people to complete a task.

Procedure-Oriented Language. A programming language designed for the convenient expression of procedures used in the solution of a wide class of problems.

Process. A systematic sequence of operations to produce a specified result.

Process Control. The use of a computer to control an ongoing physical process, such as industrial production.

Processor. A hardware device or software system capable of performing operations upon data.

Program. (1) A series of actions proposed in order to achieve a certain result. (2) An ordered set of computer instructions that cause a computer to perform a particular process. (3) The act of developing a program.

Program Library. A collection of available computer programs and routines.

Programmed Decision. A decision that can be automated by basing it on a decision rule that outlines the steps to take when confronted with the need for a specific decision.

Programmer. A person mainly involved in designing, writing, and testing computer programs.

Programming. The design, writing, and testing of a program.

Programming Language. A language used to prepare computer programs.

Prompt. Messages that assist the operator in performing a particular job. This would include error messages, correction suggestions, questions, and other messages that guide an operator through the work in a series of structured steps.

Protocol. A set of rules and procedures for the control of communications in a communications network.

Prototyping. A ''quick and dirty'' type of systems development where an actual working model (a prototype) of the information system needed by a user is quickly developed using an application generator and an interactive process between a systems analyst and a user.

Pseudocode. An informal design language of structured programming, which expresses the processing logic of a program module in ordinary English-language phrases.

Punched Card. A card punched with a pattern of holes to represent data.

Punched Tape. A tape on which a pattern of holes or cuts is used to represent data.

Query. A request for specific data or information.

Query Language. A high-level, English-like language provided by a database management system, which enables users to easily extract data and information from a database.

Queue. (1) A waiting line formed by items in a system waiting for service. (2) To arrange in or form a queue.

Random Access. Same as Direct Access.

Random Access Memory (RAM). One of the basic types of semiconductor memory used for temporary storage of data or programs during processing. Each memory position can be directly sensed (read) or changed (write) in the same length of time, irrespective of its location on the storage medium.

Random Data Organization. A method of data organization in which logical data elements are distributed randomly on or within the physical data medium. For example, logical data records distributed randomly on the surfaces of a magnetic disk file.

Read. To acquire or interpret data from a storage device, a data medium, or any other source.

Read Only Memory (ROM). A basic type of semiconductor memory used for permanent storage. Can only be read, not ''written,'' i.e., changed. Variations are Programmable Read Only Memory (PROM) and Erasable Programmable Read Only Memory (EPROM).

Realtime. Pertaining to the performance of data processing during the actual time a process transpires in order that results of the data processing can be used in guiding the process.

Realtime Processing. Data processing in which data is processed immediately rather than periodically. Contrast with Batch Processing.

Record. A collection of related items or fields of data treated as a unit.

Register. A device capable of storing a specified amount of data such as one word.

Relative Address. The number that specifies the

difference between the absolute address and the base address.

Remote Access. Pertaining to communication with the data processing facility by one or more stations that are distant from that facility.

Reproduce. To prepare a duplicate of stored data or information.

Remote Job Entry (RJE). Entering jobs into a batch processing system from a remote facility.

Robotics. The technology of building machines (robots) with computer intelligence and human-like physical capabilities.

Rounding. The process of deleting the least significant digits of a numeric value and adjusting the part that remains according to some rule.

Routine. An ordered set of instructions that may have some general or frequent use.

RPG: Report Program Generator. A problem-oriented language which utilizes a generator to construct programs that produce reports and perform other data processing tasks.

Run. A single continuous performance of a computer program or routine.

Scan. To examine sequentially, part by part.

Schema. An overall conceptual or logical view of the relationships between the data in a database.

Secondary Storage. Storage that supplements the primary storage of a computer. Synonymous with auxiliary storage.

Sector. A subdivision of a track on a magnetic disk surface.

Segment. (1) To divide a computer program into parts such that the program can be executed without the entire program being in internal storage at any one time. (2) Such a part of a computer program.

Semiconductor Secondary Storage (RAM Disk). A method which uses software and control circuitry to make the main processor and the operating system program treat part of the computer's semiconductor storage (RAM) as if it were another disk drive. This offers the advantages of being faster and less expensive than magnetic disk units but has smaller storage capacities and is a volatile storage medium.

Semiconductor Storage. Devices which consist of microelectronic integrated circuit chips. They are the most widely used primary storage devices in modern computers. Frequently called RAM—random access memory.

Sequence. An arrangement of items according to a specified set of rules.

Sequential Access. A sequential method of storing and retrieving data from a file. Contrast with Random Access.

Sequential Data Organization. Organizing logical data elements according to a prescribed sequence.

Serial. Pertaining to the sequential or consecutive occurrence of two or more related activities in a single device or channel.

Serial Access. Pertaining to the process of obtaining data from or placing data into storage, where the access time is dependent upon the location of the data most recently obtained or placed in storage. Contrast with Direct Access.

Service Bureau. A firm offering computer and data processing services. Also called a computer service center.

Service Program. A program that provides general support for the operation of a computer system, such as input/output, diagnostic, and other "utility" routines.

Set. (1) A collection. (2) To place a storage device into a specified state, usually other than that denoting zero or space character.

Set up. To arrange and make ready the data or devices needed to solve a particular problem.

Setup Time. The time required to set up the devices, materials, and procedures required for a particular data processing application.

Sign Position. A position, normally located at one end of a numeral, that contains an indication of the algebraic sign of the number.

Signal. A time-dependent value attached to a physical phenomenon that conveys data.

Significant Digit. A digit that is needed for a certain purpose, particularly one that must be kept to preserve a specific accuracy or precision.

Simplex. Pertaining to a communications link that

is capable of transmitting data in only one direction. Contrast with Duplex.

Simulation. The representation of certain features of the behavior of a physical or abstract system by the behavior of another system. Contrast with Emulation.

Skeletal Coding. Sets of instructions in which some addresses and other parts remain undetermined. These addresses and other parts are usually determined by routines that are designed to modify them in accordance with given parameters.

Small Business Computer. A small computer used primarily for business applications.

Smart Products. Industrial and consumer products with "intelligence" provided by built-in microcomputers or microprocessors, which significantly improve the performance and capabilities of such products.

Software. A set of computer programs, procedures, and possibly associated documentation concerned with the operation of a data processing system. Contrast with Hardware.

Software Package. A computer program supplied by computer manufacturers, independent software companies, or other computer users. Also known as canned programs, proprietary software, or packaged programs.

Solid State. Pertaining to devices whose operation depends on the control of electric or magnetic phenomenon in solids, such as transistors and diodes.

Sort. To segregate items into groups according to some definite rules.

Source Data Automation. The use of automated methods of data entry which attempt to reduce or eliminate many of the activities, people, and data media required by traditional data entry methods. The objective is to reduce the error rate of data entry and provide the data in a machine-readable form as soon as possible.

Source Document. The original written record of an activity, such as a purchase order or sales invoice.

Source Program. A computer program written in a language that is an input to a translation process. Contrast with Object Program.

Special Character. A graphic character that is neither a letter, a digit, nor a space character.

Special-Purpose Computer. A computer that is designed to handle a restricted class of problems. Contrast with General-Purpose Computer.

Spooling. Simultaneous peripheral operation online. Storing input data from low-speed devices temporarily on high-speed secondary storage units, which can be quickly accessed by the CPU. Also, writing output data at high speeds onto magnetic tape or disk units from which it can be transferred to slow-speed devices, such as a card punch or printer.

Statement. In computer programming, a meaningful expression or generalized instruction in a source program, particularly in high-level programming languages.

Storage. Pertaining to a device into which data can be entered, in which they can be held, and from which they can be retrieved at a later time.

Storage Allocation. The assignment of blocks of data to specified blocks of storage.

Storage Protection. An arrangement for preventing access to storage for either reading or writing or both.

Store. To enter or retain data in a storage device. Sometimes synonymous with storage device.

Stored Program Computer. A computer controlled by internally stored instructions, which can synthesize, store, and in some cases alter instructions as though they were data, and which can subsequently execute these instructions.

String. A linear sequence of entities such as characters or physical elements.

Structure Chart. A design and documentation technique used in structured programming to show the purpose and relationships of the various modules in a program.

Structured Programming. A programming methodology that uses a "top-down" program design and a limited number of control structures in a program to create highly structured "modules" of program code.

Structured Walk-Throughs. A structured programming methodology that requires a peer review by other programmers of the program design and coding to minimize and reveal errors in the early stages of programming.

Subroutine. A routine that can be part of another routine.

Subschema. A subset or transformation of the logical view of the database schema that is required by a particular user application program.

Subsystem. A system that is a component of a larger system.

Supercomputer. A category of the largest, fastest, and most powerful computers available.

Supervisor. The main control program of an operating system.

Switch. (1) A device or programming technique for making a selection. (2) A computer that controls message switching among the computers and terminals in a data communications network.

Symbol. A representation of something by reason of relationship, association, or convention.

Symbolic Address. An address expressed in symbols convenient to the computer programmer.

Symbolic Coding. Coding that uses machine instructions with symbolic addresses.

Synchronous. A characteristic in which each event, or the performance of any basic operation, is constrained to start on, and usually to keep in step with, signals from a timing clock. Contrast with Asynchronous.

Synergism. A system characteristic where the whole of the system is equal to more than the sum of its component parts.

System. (1) A group of interrelated or interacting elements. (2) A group of interrelated components that seeks the attainment of a common goal by accepting inputs and producing outputs in an organized process. (3) An assembly of methods, procedures, or techniques united by regulated interaction to form an organized whole. (4) An organized collection of people, machines, and methods required to accomplish a set of specific functions.

Systems Analysis. (1) Analyzing in detail the components and requirements of a system. (2) Analyzing in detail the information needs of an organization, the characteristics and components of presently utilized information systems, and the requirements of proposed information systems.

Systems Development. (1) Conceiving, designing, and implementing a system. (2) Developing infor-

mation systems by a process of investigation, analysis, design, programming, implementation, and maintenance.

Systems Development Generator. A software tool that allows analysts to define the inputs, outputs, processing, storage, and control requirements of an information system in a high-level, structured-type language. The requirements are analyzed by the system which will generate specifications for programs and hardware necessary to meet the requirements of the system.

System Software. Programs that control and support operations of a computer system. System software includes a variety of programs, such as operating systems, database management systems, communications control programs, service and utility programs, and programming language translators.

Table. A collection of data in which each item is uniquely identified by a label, by its position relative to the other items, or by some other means.

Tabulate. To form data into a table or to print totals.

Telecommunications. Pertaining to the transmission of signals over long distances, including not only data communications but also the transmission of images and voices using radio, television, and other communications technologies.

Teleconferencing. The use of video communications to allow business conferences to be held with participants who are scattered across a country, continent, or the world.

Teleprocessing. See Data Communications.

Terabyte. One trillion bytes. More accurately, 2 to the 40th power, or 1,009,511,627,776 in decimal notation.

Terminal. A point in a system or communication network at which data can either enter or leave. Also, an input/output device at such a point in a system.

Throughput. The total amount of useful work performed by a data processing system during a given period of time.

Time-Sharing. Providing computer services to many users simultaneously while providing rapid responses to each.

Top-Down Design. A methodology of structured

programming in which a program is organized into "functional modules," with the programmer designing the main module first and then the lower-level modules.

Touch-Sensitive Screen. An input device that accepts data input by the placement of a finger on or close to the CRT screen.

Track. The portion of a moving storage medium, such as a drum, tape, or disk, that is accessible to a given reading head position.

Transaction File. A data file containing relatively transient data to be processed in combination with a master file. Synonymous with detail file.

Transaction Terminal. Terminals used in banks, retail stores, factories, and other worksites that are used to capture transaction data at its point-of-origin. Examples are point-of-sale (POS) terminals, and automated teller machines (ATMs).

Transducer. A device for converting energy from one form to another.

Transform Algorithm. Performing an arithmetic computation on a record key and using the result of the calculation as an address for that record. Also known as key transformation.

Translator. A device or computer program that transforms statements from one language to another, such as a compiler or assembler.

Transmit. To send data from one location and to receive the data at another location.

Truncate. (1) To terminate a computational process in accordance with certain rules. (2) To remove characters from the beginning or ending of a data element, especially digits at the beginning or ending of a numeric quantity. Contrast with Rounding.

Turnaround Document. Output of a computer system that is normally printed in a special font (such as utility and telephone bills) and returned to the organization as machine-readable input.

Turnaround Time. The elapsed time between submission of a job to a computing center and the return of the results.

Turnkey Systems. Computer systems where all of the hardware, software, and systems development needed by a user are provided.

Unbundling. The separate pricing of hardware, software, and other related services.

Unconditional Transfer. Pertaining to an unconditional departure from the normal sequence of execution of instructions in a computer program.

Unit Record. Pertaining to a single physical record that contains a single logical record.

Universal Product Code (UPC). A standard identification code using bar coding, printed on products which can be read by the optical supermarket scanners of the grocery industry.

Update. To incorporate into a master file the changes required to reflect the most current status of the records in the file.

User-Friendly. A characteristic of human-operated equipment and systems which makes them safe, comfortable, and easy to use.

Utility Program. A standard set of routines that assists in the operation of a computer system by performing some frequently required process such as sorting or merging.

Variable. A quantity that can assume any of a given set of values.

Variable-Length Record. Pertaining to data records that contain a variable number of characters or fields.

Variable Word Length. Pertaining to a machine word or operand that may consist of a variable number of bits or characters. Contrast with Fixed Word Length.

Verify. To determine whether a transcription of data or other operation has been accomplished accurately.

Videotex. An interactive information service provided over phone lines or cable TV channels. Users can select specific video displays of data and information (such as electronic Yellow Pages or their own personal bank checking account register).

Virtual Machine. Pertaining to the simulation of one type of computer system by another computer system.

Virtual Memory. The use of secondary storage devices as an extension of the primary storage of the computer, thus giving the "virtual" appearance of a larger "virtually unlimited" main memory than actually exists.

Voice Mail. A variation of electronic mail where digitized voice messages rather than electronic text are accepted, stored, and transmitted.

Voice Recognition. Direct conversion of spoken data into electronic form suitable for entry into a computer system. Also called voice data entry.

Volatile Memory. Memory (such as electronic semiconductor memory) that loses its contents when electrical power is turned off.

Wand. A handheld optical character-recognition device used for data entry by many transaction terminals.

Word. (1) A character string or bit string considered as an entity. (2) An ordered set of characters handled as a unit by the computer.

Word Processing. The automation of the transformation of ideas and information into the readable form of communication. It typically involves the use of computers to manipulate characters, words, sentences, and paragraphs in order to produce office communications in the forms of letters, memos, messages, documents, and reports.

Word Processing Systems. Information processing systems that rely on automated and computerized typing, dictation, copying, filing, and telecommunication systems used in modern offices.

Write. To record data on a data medium.

Zero Suppression. The elimination of nonsignificant zeros in a numeral.

Illustration Credits

Chapter 1	The Computer Revolution (from left to right)	Figure 4–3	Courtesy IBM Corporation
	Courtesy Intel Corporation	Figure 4–4	Courtesy Apple Computer, Inc.
	Courtesy Intel Corporation	Figure 4–5	A. Courtesy IBM Corporation
	Courtesy IBM Corporation		B. Courtesy Apple Computer, Inc.
	Courtesy Texas Instruments	Figure 4–6	Courtesy Duncan-Atwell Computerized
Figure 1–1	Courtesy Sperry Corporation		Technologies, Inc.
	Courtesy Wang Laboratories	Figure 4–7	Courtesy Hewlett-Packard Co.
	Courtesy Hewlett-Packard Co.	Figure 4–9	Courtesy Texas Instruments
	Courtesy Apple Computer, Inc.	Figure 4–12	A. Courtesy of Digital Equipment Corpora-
Figure 1–3	Courtesy IBM Corporation		tion
Figure 1–5	Courtesy IBM Corporation		B. Courtesy of Prime Computer Corporation
Figure 1–6	Courtesy IBM Corporation	Figure 4–13	A. Courtesy Sperry Corporation
Figure 1–8	Courtesy IBM Corporation		B. Courtesy IBM Corporation
Figure 1–9	Culver Pictures, Inc.	Figure 4–14	Courtesy Cray Research Inc.
Figure 1–10	Courtesy UNIVAC Division of the Sperry	Figure 4–15	Courtesy IBM Corporation
	Corporation	Figure 4–16	Courtesy IBM Corporation
Figure 1–11	Courtesy Sperry-Univac	Figure 4–17	Courtesy Tandem Computers
Figure 1–12	Courtesy Burroughs Corporation and AT&T		
	Bell Laboratories	Chapter 5	Storage Concepts and Hardward (from left
Figure 1–16	A. Courtesy Hewlett-Packard Co.		to right)
	B. Courtesy IBM Corporation		Courtesy IBM Corporation
Figure 1–18	Courtesy IBM Corporation		Courtesy of BASF Corporation
			Courtesy of BASF Corporation
Chapter 2	Introduction to Information Processing		Courtesy Intel Corporation
	(from left to right)	Figure 5–6	A. Courtesy IBM Corporation
	Courtesy Mohawk Data Sciences		B. Courtesy IBM Corporation
	Courtesy Radio Shack, a Division of Tandy	Figure 5–7	Courtesy Intel Corporation
	Corporation	Figure 5–8	Courtesy IBM Corporation
	Courtesy Apple Computer, Inc.	Figure 5–11	A. Courtesy of Sigma Designs, Inc.
	Courtesy AT&T Bell Laboratories		B. Courtesy of Dysan Corporation
		Figure 5–12	A. Courtesy Vertex Peripherals
Chapter 3	Introduction to Computers (from left to		B. Courtesy Sperry Corporation
	right)	Figure 5–14	Courtesy IBM Corporation
	Courtesy of Exxon Office Systems	Figure 5–17	Courtesy IBM Corporation
	Courtesy Cray Research Inc.	Figure 5–18	Courtesy Sperry Corporation
	Courtesy IBM Corporation	Figure 5–19	Courtesy IBM Corporation
	Courtesy AT&T Bell Laboratories	Figure 5–20	Courtesy Intel Corporation
Figure 3–2	A. Courtesy Sperry Corporation	Figure 5–21	Courtesy Quadram Corporation
	B. Courtesy IBM Corporation	Figure 5–22	Courtesy 3-M Company
Figure 3–6	Courtesy IBM Corporation		
Figure 3–12	A. Courtesy Intel Corporation	Chapter 6	Input/Output Concepts and Hardware
	B. Courtesy Motorola Inc.		(from left to right)
			Courtesy Calcomp Inc.
Chapter 4	Microcomputers and Other Computer		Courtesy IBM Corporation
	Systems (from left to right)		Courtesy IBM Corporation
	Courtesy Sperry Corporation		Courtesy Hewlett-Packard Co.
	Courtesy of Televideo Corporation	Figure 6–6	Courtesy IBM Corporation
	Courtesy of Racal-Milgo	Figure 6–7	Courtesy Visual Technology, Inc.
	Courtesy Sperry Corporation	Figure 6–8	Courtesy Management Science America,
Figure 4–1	A. Courtesy IBM Corporation		Inc., (MSA)
	B. Courtesy Apple Computer, Inc.	Figure 6–9	Courtesy Apple Computer, Inc.
	C. Courtesy Hewlett-Packard Co.	Figure 6–11	Courtesy ISSCO Corporation
	D. Courtesy AT&T Information Systems		

Chapter 12   Data Communications Systems (from left to right)
Courtesy Martin Marietta Data Systems
Courtesy Harris Corporation
Courtesy of Racal-Milgo
Courtesy of Racal-Milgo
Figure 12–4   Courtesy Quadram Corporation
Figure 12–5   A. Courtesy of Racal-Milgo
B. Courtesy IBM Corporation
Figure 12–6   Courtesy Rolm Corporation
Figure 12–9   Courtesy Martin Marietta Data Systems
Figure 12–10   A. Courtesy of American Satellite Company
Figure 12–11   Courtesy Motorola
Figure 12–12   Courtesy Satellite Business Systems
Figure 12–13   Courtesy Harris Corporation
Figure 12–14   Courtesy CompuServe
Figure 12–16   Courtesy AT&T
Figure 12–18   Courtesy of Formation, Inc.
Figure 12–19   Courtesy Hewlett-Packard Co.
Figure 12–20   Courtesy Hewlett-Packard Co.
Figure S12–1   Courtesy IBM Corporation
Figure S12–6   Courtesy of Digital Equipment Corporation

Chapter 13   Word Processing and Office Communications (from left to right)
Courtesy IBM Corporation
Courtesy Tektronix Inc.
Courtesy of Televideo
Courtesy of MSA
Figure 13–2   Courtesy of Data General Corporation
Figure 13–4   Courtesy IBM Corporation
Figure 13–5   Courtesy IBM Corporation
Figure 13–6   Courtesy IBM Corporation
Figure 13–7   Courtesy IBM Corporation
Figure 13–8   Courtesy Select Information Systems
Figure 13–10   A. Courtesy of Software Products International
B. Courtesy of Software Products International
Figure 13–11   Courtesy MCI
Figure 13–12   Courtesy Martin Marietta Data Systems
Figure 13–13   Courtesy Context Management Systems
Figure 13–15   Courtesy of Digital Equipment Corporation

Chapter 14   Management Information and Decision Support Systems (from left to right)
Courtesy of MSA
Courtesy Sperry Corporation
Courtesy of Exxon Office Systems
Courtesy of Grid
Figure 14–13   Courtesy of Execucom Systems Corporation

Figure 14–14   Courtesy of Information Builders, Inc.

Chapter 15   Computer-Based Information Systems: Marketing, Production/Operations, and Personnel (from left to right)
Courtesy of Exxon Office Systems
Courtesy of MSA
Courtesy Martin Marietta Data Systems
Courtesy of Televideo
Figure 15–7   Courtesy IBM Corporation
Figure 15–8   Courtesy IBM Corporation
Figure 15–9   Courtesy NCR Corporation
Figure 15–11   A. Courtesy Hewlett-Packard Co.
B. Courtesy Hewlett-Packard Co.
Figure 15–15   A. Courtesy Cincinnati Milacron
B. Courtesy Cincinnati Milacron
Figure 15–17   Courtesy IBM Corporation
Figure 15–18   Courtesy IBM Corporation
Figure 15–20   Courtesy IBM Corporation

Chapter 16   Computer-Based Information Systems: Accounting and Finance (from left to right)
Courtesy of Hayes Corporation
Milton & Joan Mann/Cameramann International
Courtesy of Data Graphics
Courtesy NCR Corporation
Figure 16–5   Courtesy IBM Corporation
Figure 16–7   Courtesy IBM Corporation
Figure 16–9   Courtesy IBM Corporation
Figure 16–10   Courtesy IBM Corporation
Figure 16–12   Courtesy IBM Corporation
Figure 16–13   Courtesy IBM Corporation
Figure 16–15   Courtesy IBM Corporation
Figure 16–17   Courtesy IBM Corporation
Figure 16–18   Courtesy IBM Corporation
Figure 16–20   Courtesy IBM Corporation
Figure 16–21   Courtesy IBM Corporation
Figure 16–22   Courtesy IBM Corporation
Figure 16–25   Courtesy NCR Corporation
Figure 16–27   A. Courtesy of Dow Jones & Company
B. Courtesy of Dow Jones & Company
Figure 16–28   Courtesy IBM Corporation

Chapter 17   Information Systems Development (from left to right)
Courtesy of Exxon Office Systems
Courtesy of Exxon Office Systems
Courtesy Sperry Corporation
Courtesy of MSA
Figure 17–4   (left) Courtesy M. Bryce & Associates, Inc.
(right) Courtesy High Technology Systems, Inc.

Chapter 18   Acquiring Information Systems Resources
              (from left to right)
              Courtesy Tektronix, Inc.
              Courtesy of Printronix
              Courtesy Sperry Corporation
              Courtesy Sperry Corporation

Chapter 19   Managing Information Resources (from left
              to right)
              Courtesy Sperry Corporation
              Courtesy of Racal-Milgo
              Courtesy IBM Corporation
              Courtesy Hewlett-Packard Co.
Figure 19–15 Courtesy Johnson Systems Inc.
Figure 19–19 Courtesy Cullinet Corporation

Chapter 20   Computers, Management, and Society
              (from left to right)
              Courtesy Apple Computer, Inc.
              Courtesy of Racal-Milgo
              Courtesy Apple Computer, Inc.
              Courtesy of Exxon Office Systems

Appendix (from left to right)
              Courtesy Apple Computer, Inc.
              Courtesy AT&T Bell Laboratories
              Courtesy AT&T Bell Laboratories
              Courtesy AT&T Bell Laboratories
Figure A2–1   Courtesy MicroPro International Corpora-
              tion
Figure A2–2   Courtesy MicroPro International Corpora-
              tion
Figure A2–21 Courtesy MicroPro Corporation
Figure A3–2   Courtesy Lotus Development Corporation
Figure A5–1   Courtesy Context Management Systems
Figure A5–3   Courtesy Lotus Development Corporation
Figure A5–7   Courtesy Lotus Development Corporation

Index

This book has been set CAP in 10 and 9 point Spectra, leaded 2 points. Part numbers are 27 point Avant Garde Book and part titles are 18 point Avant Garde Book. Chapter numbers and titles are 18 point Avant Garde Extra Light. The size of the type page is 36½ by 49 picas.